THE
PASSPORT
BOOK

*The Complete Guide
to Offshore Residence,
Dual Citizenship
and
Second Passports*

ROBERT E. BAUMAN JD

THE PASSPORT BOOK

*The Complete Guide
to Offshore Residence,
Dual Citizenship
and
Second Passports*

Eleventh Edition

ROBERT E. BAUMAN JD

THE SOVEREIGN SOCIETY

THE SOVEREIGN SOCIETY
55 NE 5th Avenue, Suite 200
Delray Beach, FL 33483
Tel.: (866) 584-4096
Email: www.sovereignsociety.com/contact-us
Web: http://www.sovereignsociety.com

ISBN: 978-0-692-25859-0

Notice: This publication is designed to provide accurate and authoritative information in regard to the subject matter covered. It is sold and distributed with the understanding that the authors, publisher and seller are not engaged in rendering legal, accounting or other professional advice or services. If legal or other expert assistance is required, the services of a competent professional advisor should be sought.

The information and recommendations contained in this brochure have been compiled from sources considered reliable. Employees, officers and directors of The Sovereign Society do not receive fees or commissions for any recommendations of services or products in this publication. Investment and other recommendations carry inherent risks. As no investment recommendation can be guaranteed, The Society takes no responsibility for any loss or inconvenience if one chooses to accept them.

The Sovereign Society advocates full compliance with applicable tax and financial reporting laws. U.S. law requires income taxes to be paid on all worldwide income wherever a U.S. person (citizen or resident alien) may live or have a residence. Each U.S. person who has a financial interest in, or signature authority over bank, securities, or other financial accounts in a foreign country that exceeds $10,000 in aggregate value, must report that fact on his or her federal income tax return. An additional report must be filed by June 30th of each year on an information return (Form TDF 90 22.1) with the U.S. Treasury. Willful noncompliance may result in criminal prosecution. You should consult a qualified attorney or accountant to ensure that you know, understand and comply with these and any other reporting requirements.

About the Author

Robert E. Bauman JD

Bob Bauman, legal counsel to The Sovereign Society, served as a member of the U.S. House of Representatives from 1973 to 1981. He is an author and lecturer on many aspects of wealth protection and offshore citizenship and residence. A member of the District of Columbia Bar, he received his Juris Doctor degree from the Law Center of Georgetown University in 1964. He has a B.S. degree in International Relations from the Georgetown University School of Foreign Service (1959) and was honored with GU's Distinguished Alumni Award. He is the author of *The Gentleman from Maryland* (Hearst Book Publishing, NY 1985); and the following books, all published by The Sovereign Society: *The Complete Guide to Offshore Residence, Dual Citizenship and Second Passports* (2001- 2011); *The Offshore Money Manual* (2000); editor of *Forbidden Knowledge* (2009); *Panama Money Secrets* (2005); *Where to Stash Your Cash: Tax Havens of the World* (2013) *Swiss Money Secrets* (2008); *How to Lawyer-Proof Your Life* (2009); His writings have appeared in *The Wall Street Journal, The New York Times, National Review*, and many other publications.

Notes From the Author

In this eleventh edition of *The Passport Book: The Complete Guide to Offshore Residence, Dual Citizenship and Second Passports,* I have included much beyond basic residence and passport information. That includes greatly expanded sections on each country's current economic, political and social situations. This is supplemented by the excellent travel opinions of *Lonely Planet* and that travel service's impressive website: http://www.lonelyplanet.com.

Throughout this text, I provide Internet websites for American and foreign embassies and selected other Internet websites. These websites contain extensive information about both U.S. and foreign nations and issues related to citizenship, residence, visas, and passports in each country. The websites of many of the foreign and U.S. embassies and consulates also indicate availability of links to Facebook, Twitter, Flickr and YouTube videos. In addition, we recommend the following Internet sources:

- **U.S. State Department Background Notes —**
  http://www.state.gov/r/pa/ei/bgn

These web pages include facts about the land, people, history, government, political conditions, economy, and foreign relations of independent states, some dependencies, and areas of special sovereignty. The Background Notes are updated and revised by the Office of Electronic Information and Publications of the Bureau of Public Affairs as they are received from the Department's regional bureaus and are added to the database of the Department of State's website.

- **U.S. State Department Travel Warnings —**
  http://travel.state.gov/travel/travel_1744.html

This website provides up-to-date Consular Information Sheets for every country of the world with information on such matters as the health conditions, crime, unusual currency or entry requirements, any areas of instability, and the location of the nearest U.S. Embassy or Consulate in the subject country.

- **United Kingdom Current Travel Advice by Country —**
  https://www.gov.uk/foreign-travel-advice

This website provides travel advice for all tourists and visitors of the United Kingdom.

- **U.S. Library of Congress Law Guides —**
  http://www.loc.gov/law/help/guide/nations.php

This website provides access to the constitution and basic laws of every country in this book, as well as all other countries.

- **Chiefs of State and Cabinet Members of Foreign Governments — https://www.cia.gov/library/publications/world-leaders-1/index.html**

This list of government officials also includes the heads of the central banks, Ambassadors to the United States and Permanent Representatives to the United Nations.

- **The Doing Business project —**
  http://www.doingbusiness.org

A project of the World Bank and the International Finance Corporation, this website provides objective measures of government regulations for local firms doing business in 183 economies and selected cities.

- **Foreign Account Tax Compliance Act (FATCA)** — http://www.pwc.com/us/en/financial services/publications/fatca-publications/intergovernmental-agreements-monitor.jhtml

  An updated list of countries that have signed FATCA agreements with the U.S. government.

Smart Traveler App

For a U.S. traveler going abroad this app provides easy access to frequently updated official country information, travel alerts, travel warnings, maps, U.S. Embassy locations, and more that appear on the http://travel.state.gov site. Travelers can also set up e-itineraries to keep track of arrival and departure dates and make notes about upcoming trips. The app is compatible with iPhone, iPod touch, and iPad.

On-Line Smart Traveler Enrollment Program (STEP)

The U.S. State Department offers an online Smart Traveler Enrollment Program (STEP) website which allows U.S. citizens to record foreign trip and residence information that the Department can use to communicate with you and assist you in case of an emergency. U.S. citizens who travel or reside abroad can access this site at https://travelregistration.state.gov

ACKNOWLEDGEMENTS

Many people assisted in the production of this Eleventh Edition of *The Passport Book*, a text that was first suggested by the late Bob Kephart, the founder of The Sovereign Society in 1997.

My sincere appreciation goes to my editors Latasha Williams and Jennifer Somerville; to Bruce Borich who, for the fourth time, labored with the layout and design; to Erika Nolan who has long tolerated the author's idiosyncrasies; to our business manager, Brian O'Connor and to the many readers who made valuable suggestions that improved the text over past editions.

Special appreciation goes to Helvi Cranfield of *Lonely Planet* publications head office in Melbourne, Australia, who made arrangements for our use of interesting and colorful excerpts from the *Lonely Planet Travel Guides* reproduced with permission from the *Lonely Planet* website www.lonelyplanet.com © 2007 Lonely Planet.

I owe special thanks, acknowledged in the relevant chapters with their contact information, to the following ladies and gentlemen: Australia – Terence M. Dwyer CTA; Austria – Mark Nestmann LLM; Belize – Carlo Mason, Esq.; Cayman Islands – Hon. Timothy Ridley OBE; Denmark – Thomas Fischer, Esq.; The Netherlands – Hon. Trey Wyatt; Panama – Rainelda Mata-Kelly, Esq.; U.S. Virgin Islands – Marjorie Rawls Roberts, Esq.; Uruguay – Juan Federico Fischer, Esq.; Switzerland – Robert Vrijhof, Esq. and Marc Sola, Esq.; South Africa – Edward C. Baumann, Esq.

Bob Bauman JD
Delray Beach, Florida

TABLE OF CONTENTS

+Indicates new countries added in this edition

PART I

PART II

Part III

*Overseas territories of the United Kingdom

FOREWORD

THOUGHTS ON SECOND CITIZENSHIP FOR U.S. CITIZENS

Benjamin Franklin — one of the most astute and beloved of America's Founding Fathers — once observed: *"Where liberty dwells, there is my country."*

Well known for his broad-minded views and liberality, with that utterance, Franklin may have been expanding on another famous statement he made shortly after signing the U.S. Constitution on September 17, 1787. Leaving Independence Hall in Philadelphia, he was asked by a citizen: *"What have you given us?"*

Franklin replied: *"A republic — if you can keep it."*

Whether we have remained true to the intent of America's Founding Fathers is certainly open to question in our day and time ... especially since the terror attacks on September 11, 2001, the PATRIOT Act, massive government surveillance, the continuing economic weakness, massive budget deficits and debt and the flood of restrictive and questionable laws imposed on Americans.

That question of freedom is certainly raised by the size, scope and power of government at all levels ... especially as manifested in oppressive and complex taxation laws, debt and spending policies ... and more recently with the federal government's intrusion into all Americans lives, by National Security Agency (NSA) and FBI spying.

So acute has the tax issue become for the middle class, and for people of even modest wealth, many are seeking or have already acquired a new home in another nation — more hospitable places where taxes are low or non-existent — and where many of America's original ideals are still alive and honored.

Disrespect and disillusionment with government today is stronger than ever before. Never have people been more polarized in their views. The last time the United States suffered under such weak and ineffective national leadership was during the unfortunate administration of the hapless James Buchanan (1857–1861) which helped usher in the Civil War.

Today's disillusionment, even fear, is seen in a lack of confidence in the financial markets and growing anger over current political and economic gamesmanship. Individual confidence is now at its lowest point in years. A poll in April 2014 showed that only 33% of likely U.S. voters thought that America's best days were in the future, while a plurality, 48%, believed the nation's best days were in the past.

But the United States is certainly not alone in this disillusionment with oppressive government and exorbitant taxes and controls.

The politicians in the United Kingdom, Germany, France, and many other countries confiscate well over half of a citizen's annual income to finance the insatiable demands of ever-growing welfare states and their dependent citizenry.

For these reasons, citizens of many countries should, and indeed, have a right to consider the possibility of acquiring a second citizenship … particularly in a country where taxes are more reasonable.

Beyond that, there exists the possibility of making a new home in a new country — even the possibility of eventually leaving your native citizenship behind for new adventures.

It may seem a radical idea to those who were born, raised and lived in only one country, but almost anyone with the financial means and determination can become an international citizen. This is accomplished by acquiring a legal second citizenship in another country and, with that enhanced status, an official second passport.

The new passport can expand your legal rights; for an American, allowing freer world travel with fewer problems from curious border guards or nosey customs and tax officials. It can open doors that otherwise would remain closed to you. Best of all, a second citizenship/passport can serve as the key to reducing your taxes and protecting your assets — or even saving your life.

In this eleventh edition of *The Passport Book: The Complete Guide to Offshore Residence, Dual Citizenship and Second Passports*, you will discover how and where this second citizenship and second passport "magic" can work for you.

Bob Bauman

Robert E. Bauman JD
Delray Beach, Florida

Part I

Passport History

The natural human tendency is to live life in the present and to forget much of the past. Most people don't realize how often that history does repeat itself, offering valuable warnings of what may come again.

On many occasions, history has proven the many flexible uses and powers of that official personal document known as a passport and having a second passport can double those powers.

From serving as a life insurance policy that protects you from political violence at home and abroad ... to guaranteeing a greater degree of liberty and security in the age of greedy governments and rising tax rates ... a second passport has become an indispensable fact of life for millions of free individuals the world over. (An estimated 40 million American citizens currently may be eligible for a second passport.)

But it hasn't always been that way ...

Foreign travel in the modern world means having to deal with all the inconveniences imposed by national sovereignty — international borders, customs officials, passports, visas, and identity documents. (Add to that the nuisances of rude security inspections, X-ray machines, sniffing dogs and luggage searches.) It means having to suffer officious customs and immigration agents, secret government "no fly" lists, bribe-seeking border guards and unreasonable, unexplained delays.

One of the most significant benefits of the European Union, for example, is that it comprises a common geographic area of 28 countries inside of which all such cross border difficulties are greatly reduced for those who hold an EU country passport.

Few realize that this modern liberal EU travel policy actually harkens back to earlier times before passports became the rule.

Until shortly before the First World War (1914–1918), most countries did not require their citizens to have official passports.

In those slower, less traveled times, document-free international travel was the general rule. Before the last century, passports were usually rare special travel documents used to protect official emissaries of nation states at war with each other, allowing safe conduct for surrender or peace negotiations.

The first modern travel document, known as the "Nansen Passport," was issued to White Russian faction refugees in the prolonged civil war that followed the 1918 anti-Tsarist Russian Revolution led by the Communist Bolsheviks.

That document took its name from Fridtjof Nansen, a Norwegian explorer (later a delegate to the ill-fated League of Nations in Geneva), who first proposed the passport concept.

That passport, administered by the League of Nations, successfully served hundreds of thousands of refugees as a travel and identity document until the outbreak of World War II in September 1939. The International Refugee Organization (IRO) replaced the defunct League's Nansen Passport Office from 1930 to 1945, but had no authority to issue refugee documents.

In a 1951 treaty, the "Convention on the Status of Refugees" (CSR), the United Nations (U.N.) attempted to define the rights of international refugees. Effective in 1960, after the required 35 countries ratified it, the U.N. CSR authorized signatory countries to issue travel documents for those they determined eligible for refugee status, applying the Convention's criteria.

But each nation interpreted the CSR in its own fashion, so the world soon became cluttered with hundreds of thousands of refugees fleeing from wars, ethnic conflicts, famine, and pestilence. These unfortunates were admitted by some countries, rejected by others, and the result was misery on a grand scale in places as diverse as the Balkans, Israel and Palestine, Iraq, Hong Kong, Vietnam, Cambodia, Rwanda, Somalia, Syria and numerous other countries.

On the subject of the right of persons to travel freely, the United Nations Universal Declaration of Human Rights states:

Article 13 — Everyone has the right to freedom of movement and residence within the borders of each state. Everyone has the right to leave any country, including his own, and to return to his country.

Article 15 — Everyone has the right to a nationality. No one shall be arbitrarily deprived of his nationality nor denied the right to change his nationality.

It goes without saying that these so-called "rights" of free movement, travel and residence have been, and are, systematically violated by almost every nation, including both dictatorships and democracies.

The United States and the United Kingdom are among the worst violators when it suits the political convenience of the government in power at the moment.

Since World War II, domestic politics has dominated the history of world refugee problems.

In 1956, the U.S. government, under President Dwight Eisenhower, welcomed thousands of refugees from the failed Hungarian popular revolt against Russian-backed Communists, who at the time dominated Hungary. The revolt failed in part because President Eisenhower chose not to help the Hungarians militarily and to avoid confrontation with Soviet Russia.

During more than four decades of the Castro brothers' regime in Cuba, the U.S. has repeatedly admitted tens of thousands of Cuban refugees, who — with their offspring — now constitute a large part of the Latino majority of U.S. citizens in South Florida.

In contrast, in what has been called a racist policy, the U.S. has turned away thousands of Haitian "boat people" trying to escape dictatorship and poverty in the last decade. In a shameful act, the British refused to give citizens of Hong Kong full U.K. citizenship rights when Communist China took over the colonial government in 1997, mainly because of a feared U.K. voter backlash against admitting more immigrants "of color." Before and during World War II (1939–1945), the U.S. government, under President Franklin D. Roosevelt, refused to admit thousands of European Jewish refugees — trying to escape Hitler and Nazi persecution — into America, which resulted in many of them being killed in the Holocaust.

Tribal wars in Africa and wars in the Balkans involving Serbia, Bosnia, Albania, and Kosovo, have produced hundreds of thousands of refugees whose fate seemed the least concern of many world leaders. More recently, these scenes of refugee horror have been repeated in Syria and its neighbors, Turkey, Lebanon and Iraq.

The English political philosopher and politician, Edmund Burke (1729–1797), observed in another time: *Early and provident fear is the mother of safety.*

That is still good advice for any potential world traveler.

Being "politically correct," or "PC" as they say, isn't a nuisance when it comes to travel; it's a wise precaution. (One that often means travel using a national passport that keeps the bearer as far away as possible from international controversy.)

It may be a fact of your political life that your home nation's passport may provide you little or no safety margin, but another nation's passport will.

Some countries are more popular and accepted in the world than others, as most Americans well know. Some countries are respected in some parts of the world, despised in others. Some countries are universally condemned and ostracized. Whichever categories your nation happens to fall into at the moment is likely to reflect on your personal fate when you present your passport bearing the official stamp of your government.

As I noted, travel in many parts of the world using a U.S. passport can make you an instant target for criminal or terrorist groups. If your government is out of world favor at the moment, your passport could be confiscated, revoked or suspended at will.

It's a fact of international political life that citizens of certain countries, the U.S. among them, at times find travel abroad more difficult.

For many reasons, some countries impose strict visa requirements each time a foreign national wants to enter their country. It's their way of keeping out troublemakers and other supposed "undesirables."

In the wake of the 9/11 terror attacks, the United States has greatly increased visa requirements for visitors from nations previously free to come to America without first obtaining a visa. Other nations have adopted similar post-9/11 visa restrictions where none existed before.

Indeed, it is now a requirement that any U.S. citizen who leaves the country must have a U.S. passport (or an equivalent document) in order to return. That applies even for Americans visiting Canada and Mexico and vice versa.

Until 2009, it was illegal for U.S. citizens to visit Cuba because of the official U.S. embargo aimed at toppling the Castro brothers' Communist dictatorship. Some Americans who violated this travel ban were prosecuted, fined and jailed. Under the Obama administration, travel restrictions for U.S. persons with relatives in Cuba were eased significantly.

Even a citizen whose passport usually allows easy international access can find a visa denied due to temporary travel restrictions during trade sanctions or political disturbances. And even if you finally do obtain a desired visa, it can take weeks of procedural delays. When my daughter-in-law wished to accompany her husband (my son) on a U.S. visit, it took over three months for her to obtain a visa, even though she was married to a U.S. citizen.

Holding second citizenship and a passport issued by a peaceful, non-controversial country, such as Canada or Sweden, can save your life when traveling in times of political unrest, civil war, and in other delicate situations abroad. For good reasons, countless thousands of international businessmen, wealthy individuals, and others worldwide consider having an alternative passport as an added form of life insurance.

In an unsettled, ever-changing world, acquiring a second citizenship can be a wise decision, an investment in your future. Your second citizenship is a choice for life, which can act as a protective shield extended to your spouse and your children.

Moreover, there is usually no need to surrender or change your present nationality while you enjoy the benefits of your second passport. Most countries allow what is known as "dual nationality."

But by far the most valuable aspect of the second passport is safety.

Certainly, the events of September 11, 2001 ("9/11") demonstrated the mass horror that fanatical terrorism can produce. But in recent years, there have been many individual acts of terrorism in all parts of the world — acts which have killed and maimed thousands of people.

Depending on your age, you may remember the terse United Press International news dispatch on June 17, 1985, datelined Algiers: "A body identified by a freed TWA flight attendant as Robert Stethem was hurled off the Boeing 727 onto the airport tarmac on Friday night. The body was later taken to a U.S. airbase for identification."

The dead American was U.S. Navy Petty Officer Stethem, a victim of the terrorist hijacking over Greece of Trans World Airlines Flight 847, carrying 153 people as it flew from Athens to Rome. The young sailor was returning from an assignment in Nea Makri, Greece.

Over several days, the terrorists, later identified as Iranian Shiite Muslims based in Syria, forced the Boeing 727 to Beirut, then to Algiers, back to Beirut, and again to Algiers. Groups of passengers were released during the initial stops. The dozen terrorists threatened to blow up the airplane if anyone approached it parked on the tarmac.

The terrorists systematically forced all passengers to show their passports, targeting U.S. and Israeli citizens for special, unwanted attention. During a violent rampage, they brutally beat and tortured Robert Stethem. Although in civilian clothes, Petty Officer Stethem was singled out from the passengers as a U.S. Navy sailor and American citizen and ultimately killed when terrorist demands were not met.

On June 30, 1985, the hostages were allowed to go free.

And more than 25 years later, some of those believed to be responsible are thought to be in Lebanon, Libya or Iran. One is in

prison in Germany. At the time, a U.S. State Department spokes-
man claimed the Iranian Embassy in Syria was "the mastermind"
behind this and other Lebanese Shiite airline hijackings.

No doubt you have lost count, as have I, of the many similar,
brutal terrorist attacks that have occurred since that fateful June
day in 1985. The horrendous events of September 11, 2001, have
eclipsed scores of other attacks in recent years.

Not all of these events involved airplane hijackings, but many resulted in random death and injury to persons unlucky enough to
be in the wrong place at the wrong time. In the 1980s alone, 17
American citizens were kidnapped and held by Arab terrorists, the
entire U.S. Embassy staff in Tehran, Iran, was held hostage for more
than a year in 1979 to 1980. In the mid-1980s, the U.S. Embassy
in Beirut was destroyed, along with the lives of many U.S. Marines.
More recently, U.S. Embassies in east African cities of Dar es Salaam,
Tanzania and Nairobi, Kenya, were bombed with great loss of life.

Among the terrorist events that are etched in memory are the brutal
suicide hijackings of four U.S. airliners on September 11, 2001, followed by the carnage and destruction of the Twin Towers of the World
Trade Center in New York City, the crash into the Pentagon just outside of Washington, D.C., and the fourth plane, United Airlines Flight
93, which was also heading to Washington D.C., but crashed into a
field in Pennsylvania after its passengers decided to try to overcome the
hijackers. Since then, the world has seen more attacks in Israel, Kenya, Bali, Madrid, London, Mumbai, Pakistan, Iraq and elsewhere. In
many of these terror attacks, such as in Mumbai, those who held U.S.
and U.K. passports were singled out for death.

Would Robert Stethem's young life have been spared had he
been able to produce a different passport, say from a more neutral,
less targeted nation such as Canada? Of course, we will never know.

The point is that the acquisition and use of a second passport should not be viewed as sinister evidence of international criminal intent or illegal tax evasion, but as an intelligent means of defending oneself in the highly dangerous and volatile age in which we now live.

A second passport could save your life — and the lives of those you love.

There is another highly disturbing trend that makes a second, foreign passport of great value to you.

Depending on your nation's policies, your government may use your passport to restrict your basic human right to travel, rather than to guarantee that right.

Use of a passport could be made contingent on payment of taxes and on reporting of worldwide income and assets. This sort of passport control allows government to restrict, monitor, and record your travels. As frequent U.S. travelers know, your every exit and entrance from the United States is recorded in real time by immigration computers as you come and go.

In various ways, governments increasingly use issuance of a passport as a means of coercion over their own citizens. In America, for example, your passport is the property of the U.S. government, and you must surrender it to the government upon demand. The circumstances under which the government has the power to refuse or renew your passport can vary from a pending federal arrest warrant to owing more than $2,500 in delinquent child support payments.

When the U.S. State Department revokes your passport, you lose all privileges associated with it. Without the right to travel or live in a foreign country — if you're traveling or living abroad — suddenly you're an illegal alien subject to possible immediate deportation to the United States.

Indeed, even applying for a U.S. passport gives you an alarming indication of how far the U.S. government has gone in using that document as a basis for possible investigation leading to a conviction for multiple crimes. Go to this website and read the U.S. Passport Application:

http://www.state.gov/documents/organization/212239.pdf

Government control of passport issuance and revocation undoubtedly will expand in the future. Already the U.S. Internal Revenue Service (IRS) is considering a nefarious way to use the tax system to limit our freedom of movement.

A 2011 report by the Government Accountability Office (GAO) claimed the IRS could collect billions in owed taxes by blocking delinquent Americans from acquiring or renewing U.S. passports until they settle their alleged tax debts.

And as yet another sign than a quasi-police state has taken shape in America, in 2011 the U.S. State Department proposed an extensive "Biographical Questionnaire" (Form DS-5513) that applicants might have been required to complete in order to receive or renew a passport. The questions ask for everything from the details of your mother's prenatal and postnatal medical care, if any, to the name and telephone number of every supervisor you've had at every job in your life, including as a temporary worker.

It turns out the U.S. State Department has used a version of this form in "special cases" illegally for years. Some passport applicants receive a "Supplemental Worksheet" that includes many of the same questions. The Supplemental Worksheet must be completed "in its entirety" and stated true under penalty of perjury.

But the U.S. State Department never bothered to obtain the required Office of Management and Budget (OMB) "control number" for the Supplemental Questionnaire. And that means you can't be forced to complete it. But if you don't, you may not receive a passport.

Since 1986, the U.S. State Department has been informing the IRS of all persons who renew their U.S. passports using a foreign address. Since passport renewals require an applicant's Social Security number, this is also used by the IRS to see if applicants have filed income tax returns.

Ten years ago an IRS official speaking at a conference in Zurich said a special effort was being made by the agency to track all U.S. citizens who renewed U.S. passports while living in Switzerland, for reasons we can surely guess.

And there is a growing tendency in major countries to follow the dictatorial lead of the United States in taxing their non-resident citizens.

Alternative citizenship becomes, therefore, increasingly important as a powerful tool you can employ for truly international tax planning. As a national of two different countries, you also may be able to enjoy extra privacy in your banking and investment activities. Since the enactment of the 2001 PATRIOT Act financial privacy in America is dead. Some other countries have far better privacy laws that are enforced in favor of the individual.

Now you probably are beginning to see why a second passport may be highly useful. Your qualification for a second nation's passport — one that comes with no restrictive strings attached — can serve as your passport to greater freedom. It can be your key to a whole new world of free movement, expanded international investment, greater flexibility, and even adventure.

In addition, it can mean safe passage as compared to delay ... or even worse.

Terrorism is defined, for purposes of the 2001 PATRIOT Act, as actions that "appear to be intended ... to intimidate or coerce a civilian population." Title 18 of the U.S. Code, section 2331, defines terrorism as "premeditated, politically motivated violence" against "noncombatant targets by sub-national groups," usually with the goal to influence an audience.

This definition in 2001 was new to American law and first appeared in Section 802 of the PATRIOT Act. That section defined "domestic terrorism" as activities that: (a) involve acts dangerous to human life that are a violation of the criminal laws of the United States or of any State; (b) appear to be intended: (i) to intimidate or coerce a civilian population; (ii) to influence the policy of a government by intimidation or coercion; or (iii) to affect the conduct of a government by mass destruction, assassination or kidnapping; and (c) occur primarily within the territorial jurisdiction of the United States.

Section 802 has received a lot of media attention and has been opposed by conservative American groups, such as the Eagle Forum, as well as fundamentalist Christian groups. That's because this section creates a new crime that could be used by government to prosecute pro-life, anti-abortion protesters or, for that matter, demonstrators opposing or advocating all sorts of political causes, left or right, that the government may wish to silence.

Therein is a grave threat to individual freedom and personal liberty.

Doubtless, you don't fit the profile of an Al-Qaeda jihadist bent on terror. But if faceless government bureaucrats suspect you of terrorism or treason, they can confiscate your passport and, in some limited cases, even strip you of your citizenship.

From the government's viewpoint, this strategy can be useful. You lose your passport and any diplomatic protections your country extends to its citizens. If you are abroad when this happens you must also apply for a visa to re-enter your own country.

The United Kingdom is the undisputed champion of this strategy. Since 2006, the U.K. has stripped 42 people of their citizenship, including at least five born in the U.K.

From the government's perspective, being able to revoke the citizenship of an "enemy of the state" is a rather useful power. A century ago, during World War 1, a jingoistic U.S. government used this power to strip the U.S. citizenship of German immigrants living in America, whom it considered disloyal. In a 1958 decision, the U.S. Supreme Court declared that deprivation of citizenship could not be used as a punishment by the government.

If you were born in the U.S., the government legally cannot revoke your citizenship unless you intend to lose it.

If you're a naturalized citizen, you can lose your citizenship only if you obtained it under false pretenses, or if you; (a) refuse to testify before Congress (during 10 years after naturalization); (b) join a subversive organization (during five years after naturalization); (c) are dishonorably discharged from the military, if military service was the means by which you acquired citizenship.

In 2010, a highly questionable bill was proposed in the U.S. Congress that would have revoked the citizenship of individuals, including native-born Americans, deemed to be "engaging in, or purposefully or materially supporting, hostilities" against the United States. Hundreds of dual nationals traveling outside the U.S. have been stripped of their U.S. passports and their ability to re-enter the U.S.

It is difficult for most of us to conceive of engaging in "hostilities" against the U.S. government. But go back and read the PATRIOT Act definition of "terrorism." On the surface, this definition looks like what most of us would perceive to be terrorism.

But "terrorism" now has a very broad definition in America.

A mother disciplining her two children on a Frontier Airlines flight was confronted by a flight attendant, which led to an altercation and ultimately the mother's arrest and conviction for a federal felony defined as "an act of terrorism" under the PATRIOT Act. She was one of more than 200 flight passengers who have been convicted under the Act. In most cases, there was no evidence the passengers had attempted to hijack an airplane or physically attack flight crew members. Many have simply involved raised voices, foul language, mental problems or drunken behavior.

Once the government classifies you as a terrorist, it can seize and use forfeiture laws to take everything you own, whether or not those assets are connected to terrorism. It can detain you indefinitely, without ever charging you with a crime.

Occupy Wall Street hoodlums and Tea Party activists should be worried. If you become "hostile" in your opposition to the ruling party, you just might find yourself involuntarily expatriated or in permanent military detention.

The global trend is clear. Governments are using passport revocation and the loss of nationality as a weapon against their political enemies. Given this reality, it only makes sense to obtain a second nationality and passport, "just in case."

But before going further, let's examine the elements of citizenship and the meaning of the document known as a passport.

Citizenship can be loosely defined as the legal relationship between a person and the sovereign nation in which he or she lives, a status that is defined by the laws of that nation, conferring or limiting a person's duties and rights. Only through the formal process of citizenship acquisition, called naturalization, can one legally acquire the right to a second passport.

In an essay entitled *Citizenship in a Globalized World*, Greta Gilbertson of Fordham University summed up the meaning of citizenship: "Citizenship is a multidimensional concept that means membership in a specific nation-state and the formal rights and obligations that this membership entails. Citizenship can also be understood as a status and an identity. The principle premise of citizenship is that nation-states can set and control the parameters of membership."

Citizenship and territory considered together define the nation-state. Territory determines the geographical limits of national sovereignty; citizenship determines who the country's people are. Beyond these geographic boundaries and those human limits lie foreign lands, foreign sovereignty and foreigners.

Drawing the boundary within which some human beings are included and others excluded as foreigners, permitting some of them to acquire citizenship with certain conditions and others to lose citizenship, all are powers of the country exercised on behalf of citizens by their governments.

A passport plays an important part in the nation-states as a personal identification and travel document for international use issued by a sovereign nation, usually to its own citizens, but to others as well.

Most familiar are government-issued passports based on a person's national citizenship.

However "official" they may appear, certain fraudulent passports sold or "issued" by commercial sellers are illegal and, therefore, useless. I will say more about that later. Many governments designate attorneys and others to act as their official agents on second-citizenship matters, but only the government itself can issue official passports.

There are special travel documents, such as "diplomatic passports"

and other temporary travel documents issued by international organizations or individual countries. Diplomatic passports are only legal
if issued by the proper authorities of the nation or international organization the person represents, and then only if the passport holder is
properly accredited as a diplomat in the receiving nation.

Because those with diplomatic passports get special, expedited
treatment, offering bogus, high-priced "diplomatic passports" is
a favorite Internet tactic of fraudsters aimed at the ignorant and
the gullible.

As you read this book, keep in mind two major legal principles
of citizenship law that are used to determine a person's citizenship
status:

> **Place of birth**, or the principle of *jus soli* (Latin for "right
> of soil"), meaning that being born within the geograph-
> ic territory over which a country maintains sovereignty
> usually automatically makes the newborn child a citizen
> of that country.

> **Bloodline**, or the principle of *jus sanguinis* (Latin for
> "right of blood"), which describes citizenship resulting
> from the nationality of one parent or the other, or from
> earlier ancestors, usually parents and grandparents.

There is little doubt that government bureaucrats and tax collectors see dual nationality (being an official citizen in more than one
nation at the same time) as a serious threat to their control over the
citizenry they profess to serve.

As more U.S. citizens acquire dual nationality, the debate has intensified. Whether they're eager to work or retire abroad, free of red
tape and restrictions … or to strengthen ties with their ancestral
lands, record numbers of people are obtaining a second, foreign
passport, including many Americans.

Advocates see dual citizenship as a ticket to unimpeded labor mobility and a check on the power of nationalism. "I can understand why the dilution of national identity is lamented, but it's irreversible," says Peter Spiro, a professor of international law at Temple University. Dual citizenship, he says, has spread at "an explosive pace" because governments are "playing it as a mechanism for keeping an economic hook" on their citizens who move to another country.

To some social conservatives, dual citizenship is seen as inconsistent with patriotism. Stanley Renshon, a political scientist at New York's City University and author of the book, *The 50% American*, called it "the civic equivalent of a one-night stand."

In an ever-more globally connected world, dual citizenship is becoming commonplace. In 1996, for example, only seven of 17 Latin American countries allowed some form of dual nationality; by 2014, all 17 did. In 2006, India changed its policy to allow a modified form of dual citizenship for Indians living outside their home country. That means every major country whose nationals migrate to the U.S. in large numbers now allows dual citizenship, except for China, South Korea and Cuba.

Dual nationality simply means that a person is legally a citizen of two countries at the same time, qualified as such under each nation's law.

This status may result automatically, as when the 14th Amendment to the U.S. Constitution guarantees that a child born in the U.S. is a U.S. citizen; or when a child born in a foreign country to a U.S. citizen parent becomes both a U.S. citizen and a citizen of the country where he or she is born. In the latter instance, the child must usually formally confirm acceptance of that second birth citizenship before their 18th birthday.

Or it may result from an operation of law, as when a U.S. citizen acquires foreign citizenship by marriage to a spouse from another nation, or a foreign person naturalized as a new U.S. citizen retains the citizenship of their country of birth.

If you are a U.S. citizen or a U.S. permanent resident alien ("green card holder"), keep in mind one very important point as you read this book ... under U.S. law, having a second passport does not jeopardize American citizenship. It is fully legal for a U.S. person to hold two or even more citizenships based on U.S. Supreme Court holdings.

However, U.S. citizens, including dual nationals, must, by law use their U.S. passport when entering or leaving the United States. Dual nationals may also be required by their other, foreign country to use that country's passport to enter and leave its territory.

But the point to remember is that acquiring and using a foreign passport does not endanger U.S. citizenship.

Some countries do not permit their citizens to hold dual citizenship or a passport from another nation. This was the case in America until 1967, when the U.S. Supreme Court upheld the right of U.S. citizens to hold a second, foreign passport. Before that time, the official rule was that a person acquiring second nationality automatically lost U.S. citizenship even though the rule was loosely enforced.

Today, in fact, renunciation of U.S. citizenship requires an explicit signed declaration filed with a U.S. Embassy or consulate abroad; otherwise, it is almost impossible to end or lose citizenship status.

Since the 1967 U.S. Supreme Court case, the official policy of the U.S. government is to presume a U.S. citizen does not wish to surrender their citizenship, even if they engage in certain activities that might in the past have indicated otherwise.

Proof of their intention is required before expatriation is officially recognized. The burden of proof is on the government to show intentional abandonment of U.S. citizenship. This presumption is set forth in a U.S. Department of State publication, *Advice About Possible Loss of U.S. Citizenship and Dual Nationality,* (1990). See http://travel.state.gov/content/travel/english/legal-considerations/us-citizenship-laws-policies.html.

A U.S. citizen by birth or naturalization or a U.S. noncitizen national will lose U.S. nationality ("expatriate") her or himself by committing a statutory act of expatriation only if the act is performed (1) voluntarily and (2) with the intention of relinquishing U.S. citizenship. The U.S. Supreme Court has spoken (*Afroyim v. Rusk,* 387 U.S. 253 (1967) and *Vance v. Terrazas,* 444 U.S. 252 (1980)): an American citizen cannot lose U.S. nationality unless he or she voluntarily relinquishes that status.

As a matter of policy, the U.S. government recognizes dual nationality, but does not encourage it because of what the bureaucrats view as problems and conflicts that may result. Indeed, the U.S. Department of State website still fails to make clear that dual nationality is legal for Americans.

Foreign people who became naturalized U.S. citizens until recently had to swear to renounce "fidelity to any foreign prince, potentate, state or sovereignty." But that outdated oath has been changed, and the U.S. never did make any attempt to enforce that part of the oath.

People born in the U.S. can enjoy second citizenship if they qualify for citizenship in another country. While it's impossible to know exactly how many Americans have acquired another passport, Professor Stanley Renshon of City University of New York puts the number of U.S. citizens who either hold, or are entitled to hold, a second passport at upward of 40 million, many of them Americans of Mexican origin.

On the basis of blood ancestry several countries — notably Ireland, Italy, Poland and Israel (as I will explain later) — positively encourage qualified Americans and others to sign up for their citizenship. But the U.S. doesn't expect or require information concerning American citizens that become dual nationals.

No doubt, legal tax avoidance is near the top of the U.S. government's list of major "problems" it sees resulting from Americans who enjoy dual nationality.

Other Countries

The law of many countries holds that the exercise and acquisition of dual citizenship need not affect a person's original national legal status. Many people are automatically entitled to dual citizenship under various nations' laws, such as American children and grandchildren of Irish parents and grandparents.

In addition, several countries now grant "economic citizenship" based on investments made by a foreign national in the issuing country. This may confer a limited or full citizenship status on the recipient, but it does not usually affect that person's original citizenship.

In the final analysis, it is the law of the nation that is seeking to impose its control over a dual national that determines whether expatriation, or loss of citizenship, occurs. Dual nationals owe allegiance and obedience to the laws of both countries of which they are citizens. Either country has the right to enforce its laws, especially when the person is located physically within that country.

Some countries do demand that a foreign national seeking citizenship formally renounce his or her original national allegiance. That, in theory, as I just noted, used to be the U.S. rule before 1967.

All newly naturalized U.S. citizens must take an Oath of Allegiance, but they do not have to renounce their other nationality or surrender their second passport. However, in varying degrees, the renunciation rule of other nationalities is followed to some extent in Italy, France, Spain, and Portugal.

A few other countries, notably Japan and the People's Republic of China, automatically exclude from citizenship any child born from the matrimonial union of one of their citizens and a parent from a foreign nation.

Brave New World

The trend toward multiple nationalities has the potential to overturn traditional notions of how people think of themselves, their careers and their communities.

It's drawn attention from scholars, many of whom believe nationalities are artificial and, thus, interchangeable. "Most academics are happy to declare the end of the nation-state," says T. Alexander Aleinikoff, who studied international migration trends for the Carnegie Endowment for International Peace. Aleinikoff continues, "Dual citizenship is seen as a part of that."

Some critics worry that the trend has dangerous implications for a unified common society. "If people can become dual citizens, why not have allegiances to three, four or even eight countries?" asks Mark Krikorian, director of the Center for Immigration Studies, a think tank in Washington, D.C. Mr. Krikorian worries that native-born Americans will be harmed by a loosening of the traditional notion of "us" and "them." Leftist opponents of Krikorian have accused him of having "racist" views, which he denies.

Fueling the soul searching over identity and nationality is the fast spread of capital and culture around the world — "globalization." Rapid transportation and instant communication links make it possible for many people literally to call "home" anywhere they can plug in a modem, or get enough bars on their cell phone.

"Whether you're a migrant or a high-tech worker, you can move around the globe and you're not boxed in to any one single notion of belonging or identity," said Noah Pickus, a professor of public policy at Duke University, who edited a book forecasting migration and citizenship in the 21st Century. Pickus predicts that, "This is an emotional issue that has far-reaching implications we can only begin to imagine at this point."

In recent years, for example, Americans with dual nationality have served as officials in the governments of Yugoslavia, Armenia and Estonia. A retired U.S. government employee, Valdas Adamkus, was elected president of his native Lithuania, while a former New York City attorney, still a U.S. citizen, Leonel Antonio Fernández Reyna, served two non-consecutive terms as president of the Dominican Republic.

In recent years, Colombia, Ecuador, Brazil, and the Dominican Republic, have allowed their citizens to hold a second passport. South Korea and the Philippines are considering it. And, in a move that substantially boosted the number of the world's dual citizens, Mexico, in 1998, began allowing its dual nationals to hold a U.S. passport. Naturalized Mexican Americans are allowed to reclaim their Mexican passport, and a constitutional amendment now allows them to vote in Mexican elections.

Scholars say that increasing numbers of U.S. immigrants are maintaining ties to their homelands, just as native-born Americans are reconnecting to roots overseas. "The old model of nationality is outmoded in this globalizing world," says Aihwa Ong, an anthropologist at the University of California at Berkeley. Ms. Ong, who wrote a book on the trend (*Flexible Citizenship: The Cultural Logics of Transnationality*), calls the new way of living "flexible citizen-ship." Other scholars prefer the term "trans-nationals."

In fact, no one knows just how many citizens worldwide claim a second nationality.

A possible 40 million Americans are eligible to become dual citizens based on their family ties to foreign lands that allow dual citizenship. (See the chapters on Ireland, Italy, Mexico, Poland and Germany.) The requirement for gaining citizenship in many countries is being born there, or the birth there, of a parent or grandparent.

Relying on U.S. Census data, some estimates say that the pool of eligible American dual nationals grows by at least 500,000 each year, based on the number of U.S. children born to foreign-born American parents.

In supporting dual citizenship, some foreign governments have an economic incentive to maintain, or even strengthen, ties with emigrants who settled in the U.S. or other wealthy countries. An estimated 30% of all Latino immigrants to the U.S. send billions of dollars annually back to their native countries, and govern-ments fear these remittances may decline over time.

The worldwide recession in 2008 to 2010 decreased these "remittances" considerably, just as high unemployment in the U.S. slowed down the flow of illegal immigration from Mexico and Central American countries. Reports in 2014 said this flow picked up again, especially among illegal migrants from Central American countries.

What some have called "immigrant dual citizenship" permits im-migrants to maintain their origin citizenship while becoming a cit-izen of their new country. An increasing number of migrant-send-ing states — Colombia, the Dominican Republic, Ecuador, Italy,

Mexico, and Turkey — have changed their policies to allow dual citizenship. These policies are beneficial to sending states, especially in light of the growing importance of remittances and investment from nationals living abroad.

Do Americans Need a Second Passport?

People of even modest wealth who live in places where civil war or political and economic turmoil is a possible threat — such as Argentina, the Balkans, (home to the shattered pieces of the former Yugoslavia), or Ukraine ... or people facing continued political uncertainty, such as Hong Kong since the 1997 handover to Communist Beijing, or Thailand with its many coups — obviously can use a safe refuge for their escape. If besieged people enjoy the legal status afforded by a second nationality, their chance of safety is far more certain.

In a time when threats turn into physical menace, threatened people simply head to their "other" country.

But what about American citizens?

The "good old U.S.A." has been the favorite destination of millions of refugees throughout its history, and remains so. The Statue of Liberty in New York Harbor still welcomes those "huddled masses" and "wretched refuse" from other shores who want to become Americans.

So why would any U.S. citizen need to acquire a second nationality, and the additional passport that goes with that expanded political status?

One very good reason I have already explained: increasingly, the U.S. government imposes highly burdensome restrictions on the freedoms that the nation's Founding Fathers set down in the U.S. Constitution.

For people of even moderate wealth, in particular, there is now an extensive webcast to catch persons "the government" decides may be committing a wrongful act. And the current definition of "wrong" is so expansive as to be all-inclusive in the bureaucratic mind. Then, too, almost every other American politician constantly demands ever higher taxes on the so-called "rich" who already pay most of the taxes.

For example, the very fact that one has an offshore bank account, creates an offshore trust, or owns shares in an international business corporation — any and all of these innocent financial choices can suggest potential tax evasion in the jaundiced eyes of the IRS.

Schengen Area

The personal advantages of having an extra passport can be substantial, as in the case of the European Union Visa Waiver Program — commonly referred to as the "Schengen Area." Schengen takes its name from a small village in Luxembourg where the agreement was signed in 1985.

The Schengen Area encompasses today almost all EU States and a few associated non-EU countries. These 28 countries have abolished passport and other border controls on their common national borders. This area functions as a single unit for international travel purposes, with a common visa policy. At the same time, Schengen states have strengthened external border controls with non-Schengen states.

Twenty-two of the 28 European Union (EU) member states and all four European Free Trade Association (EFTA) member states participate in the Schengen Area. Of the six EU members that do not form part of the Schengen Area, four— Bulgaria, Croatia, Cyprus and Romania, are legally obliged to join the area, while the other two, Ireland and the United Kingdom, have opted out.

Four non-members of the EU, but members of EFTA, Iceland, Liechtenstein, Norway, and Switzerland, participate in the Schengen Area while three European microstates, Monaco, San Marino, and the Vatican, can be considered as de facto parts of the Schengen Area as they do not have border controls with the Schengen countries that surround them. The Schengen area currently covers a population of over 400 million people and an area of approximately 1.7 million square miles.

As a separate matter, under basic EU law, anyone with an EU passport, for example, can live and work permanently in any of 28 European countries without having to fight through the usual immigration barriers.

What some call "supranational rights" have developed over the past half century in Europe as demonstrated by EU citizenship. British Commonwealth citizenship is another example of a supranational membership or citizenship system that predates modern regional and political associations such as the EU.

The EU embodies the idea of a common citizenship across all 28 EU member states and eventually might serve as the basis for a unified European identity. EU citizenship transforms the notion and practices associated with state sovereignty, a key principle underlying citizenship. But freedom of movement, the most widely known right of EU citizenship, still restrains the ability of individual countries to exclude foreigners, thereby weakening national sovereignty.

Second Passports for the British

The same threats to individual liberty hold true of the official attitude of the United Kingdom and its immigration bureaucrats.

It is estimated that in recent years, 600,000 or more U.K. citizens have been driven into exile because of extremely high taxes. Once domiciled abroad in places such as Italy, Spain, Portugal, Singapore, or Bermuda, many Brits used to return home like migratory birds spending six months annually "vacationing" in the U.K. Stay one day more than six months and, under the old law, they would be liable to pay U.K. income taxes for the entire year.

Realizing this, the tax collector, Her Majesty's Revenue and Customs, adopted rules making long stays by Brits living abroad more difficult. Today, if a Brit maintains a home or apartment within the U.K., even a single day's visit results in full income taxes on all worldwide income. Without a U.K. home, the allowable non-taxable visit is 90 days per year, but only after an initial three-year continuous absence.

Until 2009, former U.K. residents could enter and leave the U.K. using a legitimate, non-British passport, thus entry and departure records produced no tax demands. The person came and went free from Revenue and Customs' counting of days. But the U.K. law that allowed unrestricted dual citizenship has been changed and now requires the use of a U.K. passport for exit and entry even if the person has dual citizen status.

A similar "days-in, days-out" rule applies in the U.S.

A foreigner who establishes residence in the U.S. for more than 122 days annually, and engages in what can be called "business activity," can be held liable for U.S. income taxes on all worldwide income. The IRS may decide if he/she is a "U.S. person" (as this legal status is described for tax purposes). He/she may have to submit to an unpleasant interrogation to get tax clearance before being permitted to leave. Any legal resident alien in the U.S. is also counted as a "U.S. person" for tax purposes by the IRS.

At this writing the IRS has been pushing for several years for the adoption of a broad rule that would require all U.S banks and businesses to report to foreign tax collectors U.S. accounts held in the names of foreign residents living in the U.S. Such reporting never before has been required and experts say it could cost the U.S. billions in foreign investments at a time when America needs every foreign investor it can get. Opponents revealing such financial information on foreigners' American holdings contend that current U.S. law forbids such revelations.

Multinational Corporations Do It

There is an apt analogy between multinational corporations doing business around the world and individuals that legally hold dual or multiple citizenship, using their passports for world travel and business.

By registering and qualifying under local laws in more than one political jurisdiction, a corporation has the right to do business in each country where they qualify. Or a corporation in one nation may choose to set up a subsidiary company in a foreign nation where they conduct business. The subsidiary company may be owned by a parent company in a foreign land, but the local government treats it as one of their own domestic corporations (i.e., as a local citizen).

In fact, to induce a foreign company to set up shop, many governments offer special incentives, such as tax holidays, discounts on energy and raw materials, free land, subsidized local labor, cash grants, and other attractions.

Why? Because ruling powers want to stay in office and that's easier to do when the local populace is employed and prosperous.

The major impetus to form multinational businesses, however, did not arise because of extravagant foreign inducements. This international movement didn't grow primarily to exploit profitable local opportunities in foreign lands. Instead, explosive growth of the multinationals came about, in part, to evade excessive business restrictions and high taxes in the company's home nation, especially in the United States and the United Kingdom.

Now, the same pressures are also forcing individual citizens to look elsewhere for protection from high taxes and excessive government control.

Until relatively recently, many countries did not permit their citizens to have foreign bank accounts, own foreign currencies or hold foreign investments. Those that did allow these financial activities abroad still imposed strict reporting requirements, currency controls, costly exit permits, and special transactions taxes.

But, "dual nationals," as dual citizens are also known, like multinational corporations, can move about the world in such a way as to minimize or avoid currency and other controls.

Dual nationality is not without its inherent contradictions.

Members of Mick Jagger's famous Rolling Stones rock group moved to France in 1972 in order to escape high British income taxes. Yet, many wealthy (and not so wealthy) Frenchmen have moved to the U.K. in order to avoid high French taxes. This anomaly exists because most high tax countries often exempt from local taxes foreigners who reside within their borders less than six months a year.

A foreign citizen who winters in California for four months, travels or lives outside the U.S. for three months, then spends the remaining five months in his own country, may be able to avoid paying taxes anywhere! More importantly, this roaming individual can escape many of the currency controls, investment restrictions, and the burdensome paperwork that comes with a permanent attachment to one geographic place on the world map.

In order to enter a foreign country and live there for six months as a tourist, one generally needs a passport. As I have said, some countries also require foreign tourists to obtain a "visa," a prior written permission to enter that country, which is attached to your passport.

And in order to remain longer, to work or to purchase a home, a "residence permit" is needed. "Non-work residence permits" are typically granted to entrepreneurs and others who do not compete in the local job market.

Fortress America

As noted earlier, on the subject of the right of all persons to travel freely, the United Nations "Universal Declaration of Human Rights" Article 13 states: *"Everyone has the right to freedom of movement and residence within the borders of each state. Everyone has the right to leave any country, including his own, and to return to his country."*

But what happens when the government makes it difficult, if not nearly impossible, for foreigners to enter the United States, even for legitimate purposes?

That very serious question has to be raised about the entry policies of the government governing who, when, and how foreigners now may come to the United States. Since the terrorist attacks of September 11, 2001, U.S. entry restrictions have become so severe, many say unreasonable, that hundreds of thousands of foreigners have been excluded or have just given up trying.

This has resulted in major economic losses, as smart foreign business people refuse to suffer the less-than-friendly treatment at U.S. airports and reroute their travel to avoid changing planes in American cities.

Thousands of foreign students have stopped applying for admission to American colleges and universities because of the time and red tape required to be admitted to the country, thus losing a chance to train a friendly and much-needed group of future leaders whose knowledge of America will be limited.

Reasonable Restrictions

There is certainly justification for increased scrutiny at American borders, but it appears the bureaucrats at the U.S. Department of Homeland Security prefer to make travel to the U.S. unpleasant for millions of foreigners in the faint hope of perhaps deterring or detecting a few terrorists. Meanwhile, every day hundreds of illegal entries occur on our southern border.

The U.S. is already one of the most restrictive countries in the world when it comes to allowing visitors into the country. But, as I have explained, the U.S. Visa Waiver Program (VWP) does allow the citizens of 27 selected countries to enter the U.S. for stays of up to three months without a visa. See http://travel.state.gov/content/visas/english/visit/visa-waiver-program.html.

These countries are mainly western European countries, plus Australia, New Zealand, and a few others such as Japan and, oddly enough, Brunei. Nevertheless, persons entering from these and other countries have been subjected to being fingerprinted and photographed at U.S. entry points, sometimes repeatedly.

Speaking of Visas

The United States is not the only country, however, that can play visa games.

For American travelers headed overseas, getting a visa, when required, can be the worst part of the trip. It requires contacting a foreign embassy or consulate in the U.S., filling out forms, surrendering your passport for days or a week and paying a high fee, sometimes only with cash or a money order.

For a multi-country trip, just getting all your visas approved can take a month. It was that way decades ago, and even with the rise in global travel and online tools, the same primitive system pretty much exists today. When I visited China a few years ago, it took me two weeks to get the visa, and I had to pay a visa expediting company to do it for me.

Using an expediter can be expensive, often costing $150 to $400. But the system is reliable and fast, usually producing a visa overnight or in a few days. There are about a hundred passport and visa agencies nationwide. The two biggest are CIBT, based in McLean, VA (http://www.us.cibt.com) and Travisa, in Washington, D.C. (http://www.travisa.com).

SECOND PASSPORTS: IMPORTANT CONSIDERATIONS

Legality

The single most important consideration when evaluating the usefulness of a proposed alternative citizenship and the validity of a second passport is whether both are fully legal in every respect.

That fact may seem obvious, but the proliferation of fly-by-night passport fraud operations — especially on the Internet — requires not only this reminder, but strict adherence to it when you make second passport plans and decisions.

If you plan to spend a considerable sum of money to acquire a second citizenship and then use a second passport as your basis of personal international movement, you should demand that these documents and your new status be in strict accord with the constitution and laws of the issuing nation.

A few countries actually do have provisions in their law that give the head of government, or other government ministers, discretion regarding the granting of citizenship to foreign nationals in rare, exceptional cases. Even then, if criminal bribery is involved, the person acquiring the passport may face revocation of this previously granted citizenship after a subsequent political change in the issuing government.

Persons with such questionable documents frequently are subject to blackmail by being forced to pay further "fees" later on. That is why it is imperative that second citizenship be firmly based upon clear proven provisions in the existing law of the issuing nation.

In the United States, passport fraud is a federal crime punishable by up to 10 years in prison and a fine of $250,000. Other countries have similar laws. Ronald Noble, Secretary General of Interpol, the global police network, has been especially critical of the inability of governments to authenticate documentation, stating that forged and illegal passports are increasingly easy to obtain. That means government immigration and air safety agents are on increased lookout for questionable passports.

In 2012, the Canadian government notified about 1,800 of its "citizens" that they were suspected of fraudulently obtaining Canadian passports and citizenship and would be stripped of both upon conviction.

The prospective second passport client most at risk is one lured into an "instant" or "immediate" passport deal that promises to waive residence requirements and grant quick citizenship.

Immediate passports are a favorite lure for attracting unsuspecting and ill-informed would-be buyers who need and want a quick passport, but haven't done sufficient investigative groundwork.

As you will learn in a moment, the only two nations that in the past issued immediate citizenship — the Commonwealth of Dominica and Saint Kitts and Nevis — have been joined by a growing group of countries offering "passports for sale."

Even legal passport programs can come and go swiftly, so a passport candidate must always determine what actually is current.

Ireland had an immediate citizenship program for wealthy investors, which ended in 1996, but Ireland has now established a new and comparable program. A similar Cape Verde economic citizenship program ended in 1997. The same year, the Seychelles canceled their program in the face of European Union complaints about its questionable operation. Belize ended a similar program in 2001, as did Grenada, but the latter is back at it again now. Rumors always float in the offshore community that one or another of these former programs may be revived, usually by operators who claim inside information.

A recent Internet search using the terms "second passport" and "economic citizenship program" produced thousands of websites offering allegedly "instant" passports from Argentina, Brazil, Chile, the Dominican Republic, Greece, Guatemala, Honduras, Panama, Paraguay, Peru, Tonga, Vanuatu, Venezuela, and Western Samoa.

None of these countries has such an official program. The reasonable implication is that what these sites offer is both fraudulent and illegal.

All of this may also reflect a little known fact; that there is an expansive, lucrative underground black market in forged and faked passports.

Even legal passports can go astray. A few years ago the Western Samoan government announced 150 of its official passports simply had been "lost." Since then, thousands of official passports have been stolen or lost in France, Australia, Finland, and Belgium. In 2009, the United Kingdom admitted that in the prior year over 15,000 of their passports had been lost, stolen or disappeared.

U.S. government security agencies uncovered a criminal ring in Thailand that produced counterfeit passports and other travel documents, including hundreds of fake U.S. passports sold on the black market. In addition to U.S. counterfeit passports, investigators found French, Spanish, Belgian and Maltese counterfeit documents that police said were sold to a group of Thai and Burmese collaborators. The passports were then sold to gangs linked to prostitution, terrorism and smuggling. Other fake passports found included Malaysian, Singapore and Japanese travel documents.

Passport Fraud

A few years ago, had you read the classified advertisements in such respectable journals as the *International Herald Tribune* or *The Economist*, you would have seen an advertisement that promised to provide a "European Union passport, fully registered and renewable" for only US$19,500. A contact telephone number in Ireland was listed.

When we made inquiries of this advertiser, the person who answered the telephone said that, for a price, his company could arrange "official citizenship" in the Netherlands and/or Switzerland. When we asked for citations to specific Dutch and Swiss laws authorizing the sale of such passports, the spokesperson gave several answers: (a) the company had a special deal with senior Dutch and Swiss officials; (b) they had arranged an accelerated naturalization process; and (c) their legal counsel, who could explain more fully how all this worked, was away at the moment.

Consular officers at both the Swiss and Dutch embassies were astonished when told about the company and their claims. The officials confirmed what we already knew. Neither nation has ever had an economic citizenship/passport program at any price. They assured us that their national police authorities would be immediately alerted about this passport fraud and actions taken to end it.

We cite this example only because it is typical of the passport frauds that abound in offshore publication ads, even in well-respected publications like these. As we said, the Internet is loaded with hundreds of passport fraud websites masquerading as legitimate passport services, many claiming to have official sanction from the countries whose "passports" they hawk.

Throughout this report, you will find numerous references to true passport frauds involving counterfeit documents. We also tell you about passport frauds resulting from corrupt and dishonest officials in some countries, now and in the past, such as Belize, Panama and the Dominican Republic, where there may be legitimate second passport programs.

Unlike the fraudulent passport huckster and their false claims, what you read here you can believe and rely upon. We're not selling passports. We're speaking the truth.

International Recognition

Before you acquire a second passport, be certain that the passport you are considering commands widespread acceptance and prestige in the international community. If it's not likely to be recognized by all other countries, it is worthless from the start.

In this age of instant communications, it takes only hours, certainly no more than a few days, before customs and immigration officials worldwide know when an individual passport is called into question.

In recent times this happened with official, but illegally issued Dominican Republic passports, mentioned above and with passports issued by Panama. In the latter case, a high passport official resigned alleging she had been pressured into issuing passports to various foreign business associates of the outgoing president, later indicted for this and other alleged crimes.

Of course, if you intend to become a citizen of another nation, and possibly spend time there, your consideration should include geographic location, language, stability of the political and legal system, the banking and business environment, visa-free travel possibilities, and, of course, total initial and future costs.

Do You Need a Lawyer?

There is something to be said for dealing directly with the officials of the nation from which you seek a second citizenship. This can be done at the appropriate embassy in your nation's capital city or at a local consulate. Information and applications can be obtained by telephone or fax but also by government and embassy websites, most of which have much information concerning residence, immigration and citizenship. (At the end of each country chapter in this book you will find embassy websites and other contact information.)

But that assumes you have the time, expertise and patience to navigate the often tedious foreign bureaucratic route that can take months or even years. Working directly with diplomatic and consular officials eliminates the middleman and probably lessens the chance of fraud or mistakes.

Nevertheless, it is better to employ an experienced attorney based in your own nation or intended country, who is an established, reputable professional specializing in immigration and passport matters. These experts usually know the legitimate shortcuts and have personal acquaintances with the involved foreign nation officials. That can speed up your application and approval process considerably.

Caution may dictate using an escrow agent; a trustworthy third party that holds your citizenship and passport fees until the transaction is complete. A bank, law firm, solicitor, or other escrow agent can serve this purpose. The agent will hold your money, usually in the form of a certified check payable to the agent, will receive your passport of other documents, permitting you to inspect them before a final payment is made.

If you are satisfied after a genuine passport or other documents have been delivered, the escrow agent makes payment and delivers the passport to you. An agent's fee for services will range from 1-10% of the transaction value. In most second passport cases, "advanced fees" should be avoided. If you are willing to place cash in escrow, expense advances seldom should be required.

Recommended Service Providers

Henley & Partners are the world's leading specialists in international residence and citizenship planning. They also provide multi-jurisdictional real-estate advice, tax planning and fiduciary services for private clients. All services and contacts are completely confidential. Inquiries can be directed to any of the Henley & Partners offices listed in the individual country pages of this book.

Christian H. Kalin, Partner
Klosbachstrasse 110, CH-8024
Zurich, Switzerland
Tel.: +41 44 266 22 22
Email: christian.kalin@henleyglobal.com
Web: https://www.henleyglobal.com

A senior member of The Sovereign Society's Council of Experts, Christian Kalin is a qualified professional who assists those interested in acquiring residence and citizenship in many countries.

Mark Nestmann LLM, President
2303 N. 44th Street #14-1025
Phoenix, AZ 85008
Tel.: (602) 688-7552
Email: service@nestmann.com
Web: http://www.nestmann.com

Since 1963, the *Travel Information Manual* (TIM) has supplied the air travel industry with reliable and comprehensive up-to-date country information on entry and health requirements as well as visa, customs and currency regulations. The TIM booklet, issued monthly, offers a complete package to help travelers save time, and avoid fines and delays. For contact information, visit: https://www.iata.org/publications/Pages/tim.aspx. Also, visit their website for services at https://www.iata.org/services/Pages/index.aspx.

Henley & Partners continuously analyze visa regulations of almost all countries and territories in the world. They publish and regularly revise a visa guide you will find useful. See http://www.henleyglobal.com/citizenship/visa-restrictions/. The Henley & Partners *Visa Restrictions Index 2013* can be found on the same web page.

PART II

Economic Citizenship Programs

Citizenship for Sale

Because "citizenship" is a legal relationship between a person and his/her national government, each government is by law empowered to define the criteria for its citizenship.

Residence — not to be confused with full citizenship — is the right to live in a particular place.

It is granted by most countries to wealthy foreign investors and other select individuals the government considers desirable. Residence status is the first step toward eventual citizenship and a second passport.

Only a few countries have enacted explicit laws that grant citizenship to foreign nationals based purely on economic considerations — and without imposing actual prior physical residence requirements.

This system is referred to as "economic citizenship programs" and it offers an opportunity to acquire a new nationality quickly and simply, without major difficulties — if you are willing to pay the high price. In addition, once accepted, these programs can give you special rights and privileges in the United Kingdom, visa-free travel to over 100 countries and/or a front-row local seat at some of the world's best offshore financial centers.

Until recently, only two nations belonged to this exclusive economic citizenship club — the Commonwealth of Dominica and Saint Christopher and Nevis (known as Saint Kitts and Nevis to the locals), both in the Eastern Caribbean Sea. A third country,

Austria, offers a highly exclusive and very expensive economic passport in exchange for a payment of US$1 million.

Now numerous countries have jumped aboard the "passports for sale" bandwagon, their debt-ridden governments seeking immediate cash and investments from wealthy foreigners who qualify.

At this writing, Malta is one of the most recent to adopt such a direct "citizenship for sale" program, but others include Cyprus, and Antigua and Barbuda. Several other countries recently have begun offering immediate residence leading to citizenship based on various investment amounts with strings attached. In this group are Hungary, Romania, Bulgaria and Grenada. (For more information, see the sections on the countries named.)

Before considering the economic citizenship programs that do exist, here is a necessary reality check.

The pages of the *International Herald Tribune, The Economist* and other publications run adverts offering "official passports" from a long list of countries. You are told in these advertisements that all you need to do is pay the price asked. The implication always is that the passports offered are somehow "official," yet buying from the advertised seller allows you to avoid going through official channels to obtain the prized passport. For a price they will do it all *for* you. More likely, they will do it *to* you.

The fact is that in almost every country it may be possible to make direct payments or bribes to dishonest government officials in return for passports and citizenship documents. The list of governments involved in such scandals, in recent years, is long, including the United States.

But if these documents are not issued under a currently authorized, legitimate government program then they are "black market" items and buying them constitutes a crime. Those fooled into acquiring "passports" in this back-door way run the serious risks of exposure, arrest and deportation.

However, there are indeed legal, valid and official economic citizenship programs available to those willing to pay the price.

Australia, Canada, Portugal, Switzerland, the United Kingdom, and the United States are all examples of countries that offer varying degrees of residence and/or citizenship to wealthy individuals and investors.

But only two countries offer relatively fast, immediate, *quid pro quo*, citizenship in return for investments; the Commonwealth of Dominica and Saint Kitts and Nevis.

Many other nations offer what amounts to immediate economic *residence*, but not immediate full *citizenship*.

As I mentioned above, a third country, Austria, also grants citizenship if a foreign person invests substantially in that country, but the process for obtaining this is difficult and limited to special circumstances.

The Dominican Republic also offers quick citizenship after a minimum residence period of only six months if you invest in a local business or real estate. However, the Dominican Republic has suffered passport issuance scandals in recent years, and this weighs against the nation as a choice for obtaining a reputable second passport.

Uruguay offers a stepped up citizenship for retirees and families. (See the sections on Austria, Dominican Republic and Uruguay for details.)

Each of these programs grants eventual citizenship, evidenced by an official naturalization certificate, or certificate of registration, identifying the named person as entitled to citizenship rights, some with qualifications. The official passport is granted after the naturalization process which can require several years of residence. In each of these countries, the initial residence permit process usually takes about 90 days, but citizenship takes much longer.

Commonwealth of Dominica & Saint Kitts and Nevis

In the sections on the Commonwealth of Dominica and Saint Kitts and Nevis that follow, I give more information about the current conditions in each country than I have for most other countries in this book. I assume that if you are interested in becoming a citizen of either country, at a considerable price, you will want to know as much as possible about your new country as any loyal citizen should.

Both countries are member states in the Organization of Eastern Caribbean States (OECS), which includes Antigua and Barbuda, Dominica, Grenada, Saint Kitts and Nevis, Saint Lucia, and Saint Vincent and the Grenadines. These countries, following the example set by the European Union (EU), allow all OECS citizens to enter their territories and remain for an indefinite period in order to work, establish businesses, provide services, or take up residence.

Under the United Kingdom West Indies Act of 1967, both countries adhere to a judicial appeals system in which the Eastern Caribbean Supreme Court (ECSC) acts a final court of appeal for the area. The Court consists of two divisions: a Court of Appeal and a High Court of Justice. The Court of Appeal is itinerant, traveling to each member state and territory, where it sits at various times during the year to hear appeals from the decisions of the High Court and Magistrates Courts in member states in both civil and criminal matters.

The Registry of the Court of Appeal is located at the headquarters of the ECSC in Castries, Saint Lucia. Member states include

Antigua, Anguilla, Dominica, Grenada, Saint Vincent, Saint Kitts and Nevis, and Saint Lucia. Both countries are also members of the 15-nation Caribbean trade bloc known as CARICOM which also has five associate member states.

It is worth noting that, in addition to seasonal hurricanes, earthquakes are a regular occurrence in the Eastern Caribbean region but most do not exceed magnitude 3–4.

Commonwealth of Dominica

Government:	Parliamentary Democracy
Capital:	Roseau
National Day:	Independence Day: November 3, 1978 (from the U.K.)
Population:	73,449 (July 2014 est.)
Area:	291 sq. miles / 754 sq. kilometers
Ethnic groups:	Black, mixed black and European, Syrian, Carib, Amerindian
Languages:	English (official), French Patois
Religion:	Roman Catholic 61.4%, Seventh Day Adventist 6%, Pentecostal 5.6%, Baptist 4.1%, Methodist 3.7%, Church of God 1.2%, Jehovah's Witnesses 1.2%, other Christian 7.7%, Rastafarian 1.3%, other or unspecified 1.6%, none 6.1%
Life Expectancy:	76.59
Currency:	East Caribbean dollar (XCD)
GDP:	US$1.015 billion (2013 est.)
GDP per capita:	US$14,300 (2013 est.)

Whether you're into trekking high into the mountaintops or exploring the watery world below, Dominica is the place to go for those who prefer hiking boots over high heels and are content with a night life where the only music is the murmur of the jungle. Dominica has surprisingly long drives for such a small island, so it's better to pick a spot or two and explore instead of bouncing around. Don't miss the ancient forests of the Morne Trois Pitons National Park, home to the otherworldly Boiling Lake and the spectacular Trafalgar Falls.

There are a few sandy beaches, but most require a little gumption to find and there are usually only a few lodging choices nearby, at most. There are no direct international flights and the island-hopping it takes to get here has kept the package tours at bay. The locals are so friendly that it's almost fun to get lost just to have an excuse to approach people on their front porches.

Whereas some of the bigger Caribbean cities are decidedly scary, in the capital city of Roseau the locals often stop visitors just to wish them a good visit. Rasta culture is strong, and those offended by the sight of Rastafarians taking their sacrament might have to cover their eyes. — Lonely Planet

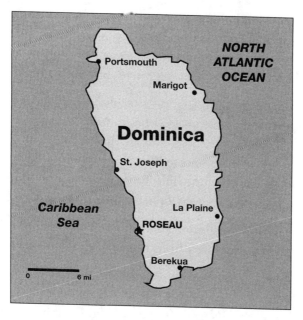

History and Overview

Dominica is located at the Northern end of the Windward Chain of the Lesser Antilles in the Caribbean Sea, between the

French islands of Guadeloupe and Marie-Galante to the north, and Martinique to the south.

Dominica was the last of the Caribbean islands to be colonized by Europeans due to the fierce resistance of the native Caribs. France ceded possession to Great Britain in 1763, which made the island a colony in 1805. In 1980, two years after independence, Dominica's fortunes improved when a corrupt and tyrannical administration was replaced by that of the late Mary Eugenia Charles, the first female prime minister in the Caribbean, who remained in office for 15 years. Some 3,000 Carib Indians still living on Dominica are the only pre-Columbian population remaining in the eastern Caribbean.

A volcanic island plunging steeply into the sea on all sides, Dominica lacks substantial beaches. Thus, it was overlooked in the Caribbean tourism boom of the past quarter century, which saw massive hotel and resort development elsewhere throughout the region.

It has, nonetheless, undergone a steady increase in the affections of eco-tourists and nature lovers, who flock to Dominica for its largely unspoiled landscapes, romantic in their grandeur: "Too much blue, too much purple, and too much green. The flowers too red, the mountains too high, the hills too near," as Jean Rhys, a native of Dominica, has a character say in her novel, *Wide Sargasso Sea*.

Nature treks and reef diving are common topics in travel writing about Dominica, but apart from reggae festivals, nightlife is not.

Christopher Columbus visited the island in 1493. As he landed on a Sunday, he called the island Dominica (Sunday Island). Known also as the "Nature Island" of the Caribbean, Dominica boasts a wide range of unique nature attractions, including unspoiled rain forests, an abundance of spectacular waterfalls in its 365 rivers, the second-largest volcanic boiling lake (190° F) in the world, and world-class hiking in many nature reserves. The island is also a birdwatcher's paradise and offers fabulous scuba diving in the coral reefs with 30-meter underwater visibility.

While not exactly cut off from the world — the island is readily accessible by air from Antigua, Barbados and Puerto Rico — people settling in Dominica may find themselves a little bit away from the beaten track, as air connections to mainland destinations are not as frequent as elsewhere in the Caribbean. There are plans for a new international airport. (The island should not be confused with the Spanish-speaking Dominican Republic to which it has no ties.)

With a perfect Caribbean climate, the island covers an area of almost 300 square miles and supports a population of about 74,000 citizens, including some 3,000 descendants of the original Carib native peoples. Dominicans are some of the friendliest of all Caribbean islands. English is the official language, but early French rule is evident in a local Creole dialect.

Independent since 1978 and a full member of the British Commonwealth, Dominica enjoys a Westminster-style unicameral parliamentary government, free elections, and has had several peaceful transfers of political power. The East Caribbean dollar is the strong local currency and there is little crime. Prime Minister Roosevelt Skerrit has been in office since 2004. The next elections are scheduled in 2018.

Economy

The economy depends on agriculture and is highly vulnerable to climatic conditions, notably tropical storms. Agriculture, primarily bananas, accounts for 20% of GDP and employs 40% of the labor force. Tourism has become a major growth sector offering good investment opportunities, but it is not yet well developed because of the rugged coastline, lack of beaches, and the lack of an international airport. Hurricanes in the past devastated the country's banana crops but the economy recovered, fueled by increases in construction, soap production, and tourism

The nation is relatively poor, and the Dominica government is adopting a structured approach to economic development through a number of programs, including promotion of Dominica as an eventual offshore banking and company formation center, and with its attractive economic citizenship program. Dominica is a member of the nine-member Organization of Eastern Caribbean States (OECS).

The country's economy has been affected by a number of factors including the world recession which has reduced tourism receipts and investment in the islands, but also by World Trade Organization (WTO) decisions relating to the banana trade.

Added to these problems the national debt-to-GDP ratio led Prime Minister Roosevelt Skerrit's Labor Party government, which was re-elected in 2011, to bite the bullet and pursue an International Monetary Fund program of austerity.

Caribbean Development Bank figures show that in 2007, Dominica's national debt was 111.17% of GDP. Although public debt levels continue to exceed pre-recession levels, the debt burden declined from 78% of GDP in 2011 to approximately 70% in 2012, one of the lowest levels in the Eastern Caribbean.

Other possible investment benefits offered to foreigners include business tax holidays of up to 15 years, unrestricted repatriation of profits, economical hydroelectricity, and the possibility of tax-free entry of produced goods into the U.S. market — a proposal suggested by the U.S. government, but not yet adopted.

Economic Citizenship Program

Dominica's program that allows foreign persons to acquire citizenship in exchange for a direct financial contribution to the country's economic development has operated successfully in its present form since 1991, but not without problems. With its important banana export industry struggling, Dominica began offering economic citizenships to foreign nationals who invested in local development projects, mainly in the tourism industry.

The economic citizenship program is a considerable source of government income, but it has been politically controversial with opponents denouncing "selling citizenship" to foreigners. The program has been an issue in several national elections since its adoption and has been suspended in the past as political party control changed hands. The current Labor Party government supports the program.

In spite of these problems, more than a thousand foreign persons have been granted economic citizenship in return for private investments. More recently, the economic citizenship program has broadened, placing new emphasis on capital investments directed by the government itself.

The Dominica program is specifically authorized by the nation's constitution (section 101). The government has set a limited quota of applications as authorized in section 8 of the Citizenship Act (Chapter 1) and associated policy guidelines.

The new Dominica citizen has the right to live and work there at any time. Equally important, as a citizen of a British Commonwealth nation, the new citizen enjoys special rights and privileges within the United Kingdom. In addition, they can travel on their Dominica passport without a visa to more than 100 countries and territories, including the U.K. and Hong Kong.

Dominica passports are valid for 10 years and are renewable. Those who receive such passports are not liable for any taxes in Dominica on income earned outside the nation, unless they choose to become a tax resident of the country.

Dominica is generally considered a safe destination in the Caribbean, but a rise in the murder rate in recent years has led to some calls for the death penalty to be reinstated.

Payment/Investment Options

Over the years, there have been several sanctioned investment routes to acquire economic citizenship, including investment in long-term and low-yield government bonds, direct cash contribution to the government, or investments in particular designated projects.

The current Labor government position is that money contributed to acquire citizenship should go to specific projects only. The present guidelines for economic citizenship name school construction, renovation of the hospital, construction of a national sports stadium, and promoting the offshore sector as targets for these cash inputs.

For now, and in the foreseeable future, there are two options to acquire citizenship:

1. Direct Family Cash Option: (family of four, investor, spouse, two children under 18 years)

   Required contribution: US$300,000.

   Children between 18 and 21 years: US$25,000 per child (up to two children).

   Additional children under the age of 18 years, US$50,000 per child.

2. Direct Cash Single Option: Required contribution — US$250,000.

For both options, the cash contribution is due only after the application has been provisionally approved by the Government.

Other government fees include: application fee US$1,000 per application (non-refundable); processing fee US$200 per applicant (non-refundable); naturalization fee US$550 per applicant; and Stamp Fee US$15 per applicant.

Depending on what an attorney or other professional may charge, usual legal fees can cost US$35,000 for single applicant or applicant and spouse; US$45,000 for applicant, spouse, and up to two children; US$5,000 for each additional dependent child. 50% of the legal fee is refunded if a primary applicant is not approved. There is also a $500 escrow fee. Due diligence fees vary, US$4,000 to US$8,000.

The government guarantees the return of all investment funds if an application is rejected for any reason or withdrawn, but US$2,200 in processing fees is non-refundable.

Since granting citizenship is at the sole discretion of the government, there is no guarantee that applications will be approved. The government also has introduced more onerous due diligence requirements.

Application Procedure

A group application for Dominica citizenship for one family (including the main applicant, spouse and two unmarried dependent children under the age of 18) must be accompanied by copies of passports, birth and marriage certificates, and police clearances (see below). The applicant must also contribute to the nation's economy using one of the options described above.

Approval normally requires from six to 12 weeks. Usually, the main family applicant must visit the country to be interviewed by the Minister of Legal Affairs or his representative. All applicants are required to visit Dominica to attend an interview before becoming citizens.

It is required that new citizens take an Oath of Citizenship before senior government officials on the island. Citizens of Dominica are allowed to hold dual citizenship, and the acquisition of citizenship is not reported to other countries.

Required Documents

The following documents must accompany an application. Documents not in English must be translated and certified by a professional translation service on the firm's letterhead bearing its signature and stamp. Certified document copies in the original language must also be provided.

Document:	For:
Application form	Each person, including children
Personal information form	Each person, including children
Business background information	Each working adult
Birth certificate (certified copy)	Each person, including children
Marriage certificate (certified copy)	Married couples
Divorce certificate (certified copy)	Divorced persons
Medical certificate, including HIV test (original)	Each person, including children
Certificate of no criminal record	Each person (16 years and over) (original)
Two personal references (originals)	Main applicant
Bank reference (original)	Main applicant
Copy of passport or ID document	Each person, including children (certified copy)
Twelve color passport photos	Each person, including children

Contacts

Embassy of the Commonwealth of Dominica

3216 New Mexico Avenue NW, Washington, DC 20016
Tel.: (202) 364-6781
Email: Embdomdc@aol.com

Dominica Consulate General/UN Mission

Suite 900, 820 Second Avenue
New York, NY 10017
Tel.: (212) 599-8478
Email: domum@onecommonwealth.org

There is no American Embassy in Dominica. The nearest U.S. Embassy is located in Barbados.

United States Embassy, Barbados

Wildey Business Park
Wildey St. Michael, Barbados
Tel.: (246) 227-4399
Email: BridgetownACS@state.gov
Web: http://barbados.usembassy.gov

Residence & Immigration Professionals:

The Minister of Finance of Dominica appoints official foreign agents to administer the application process on behalf of the government. One of these appointed official agents is Mark Nestmann, a senior member of The Sovereign Society Council of Experts. Mark is a qualified professional who assists those interested in acquiring residence and citizenship in Dominica, St. Kitts Nevis and other countries. Henley & Partners Ltd. also is an official agent.

Mark Nestmann LLM, President

The Nestmann Group, Ltd.
2303 N. 44th Street #14-1025

Phoenix, AZ 85008
Tel.: (602) 688-7552
Email: service@nestmann.com
Web: http://www.nestmann.com

Henley & Partners Ltd.
Christopher Willis, Managing Partner
Henley & Partners Caribbean Ltd
Sugar Bay Club, Zenway Boulevard
Frigate Bay, St Kitts, West Indies
Tel.: +869 662 6262
Email: christopher.willis@henleyglobal.com
Web: https://www.henleyglobal.com/citizenship-dominica-citizenship

Saint Kitts and Nevis

Government:	Parliamentary Democracy
Capital:	Basseterre
National Day:	Independence Day: September 19, 1983 (from the U.K.)
Population:	51,538 (July 2014 est.)
Area:	101 sq. miles / 261 sq. kilometers
Ethnic groups:	Predominantly black; some British, Portuguese, Lebanese
Language:	English
Religion:	Anglican, other Protestant, Roman Catholic
Life Expectancy:	75.29 years
Currency:	East Caribbean dollar (XCD)
GDP:	US$952 million (2013 est.)
GDP per capita:	US$16,300 (2013 est.)

Near-perfect packages — that's how you might think of St Kitts and Nevis after a visit.

The two-island nation combines beaches with the beauty of the mountains, plenty of activities to engage your body and some rich history to engage your mind. The legacies of the sugar industry have been recycled into pleasant plantation estates good for lunch or just a stay. And the local culture is almost a Caribbean cliché: mellow, friendly, familiar and with a pulsing soca beat.

But if the pair offers much that's similar, they also differ in the details. St Kitts is the larger and feels that way, from the hustle of intriguing Basseterre to the resort enclave of Frigate Bay. You could spend a few days exploring all of its beaches, with their cool bars, water activities and pure vacation vibe. Circling the main part of the island, there's plenty to see: the languid charms of the plantations and the astonishing bulk of Brimstone Fortress.

Nevis is a neater package. It has one volcanic mountain rather than a range, and its one main road is a circle that takes you around the island in under two hours. There's a handful of beaches with the usual fun, and Charleston, the charming main town, can be walked end to end in 15 minutes.

History here centers on the big names of Horatio Nelson and Alexander Hamilton. Nature walks take you into the verdant upper reaches of the peak. Even if you just stay on one island, frequent ferry service means that you can easily enjoy both. — Lonely Planet

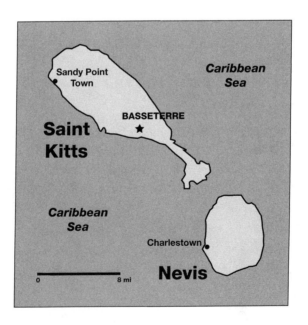

History and Overview

If there is one offshore haven country that has all the things needed for smooth offshore financial operations, it is the two-island Federation of St. Kitts and Nevis, (pronounced KNEE-vis), although the financial center is on the island of Nevis.

Tucked away in the Leeward Islands of the eastern Caribbean, (formerly the British West Indies), located 225 miles east of Puerto Rico and about 1,200 miles south of Miami, you will find St. Kitts and Nevis.

Each tropical island is a volcanic mountain rising over 3,000 feet from the sea, with about 75% of the total population living on St. Kitts.

The islands' balmy, virtually unchanging weather, splendid beaches and accommodations have made them popular vacation spots, offering a wide range of recreational amenities. Visitors to St. Kitts and Nevis tend to find the islands' pace to be more leisurely even than that of other Caribbean holiday spots.

This small, two-island country's greatest assets are its considerable natural beauty and the financial center located on Nevis. To encourage potential tourism, the government has agreements with foreign-owned hotel and condominium developers. St. Kitts is a popular tourist destination, with white sand beaches, deep sea fishing, golf, tennis, and casino gambling.

Since 1994, the federation has been part of the Association of Caribbean States (ACS) trading bloc of over 60 million people. AOL Travel, a travel website, named St. Kitts and Nevis the fourth top travel destination, highlighting the islands' lush rainforests, rich history, and exquisite renovated plantations.

Nevis Tourism describes the island of Nevis as "…a tiny jewel just eight miles long and six miles wide. The Spanish explorers called Nevis, 'Nuestra Senora de las Nieves' (Our Lady of the Snows) as a religious tribute to the white clouds surrounding the island's central volcanic peak.

Nevis, the smaller of the two islands, has gained international fame for two well-known historical figures. It was the birthplace of American patriot Alexander Hamilton, the first Secretary of the U.S. Treasury. It was also the setting in 1787 of the wedding to an island woman, Frances "Fanny" Nisbet, of Captain Horatio Nelson (1758–1805), the celebrated and much wounded British Royal Navy officer who led numerous victories at sea during the Napoleonic Wars, the most notable of which was the Battle of Trafalgar in which he died. You may have seen his impressive monument in Trafalgar Square, site of London's annual New Year's Eve celebration.

Economy

The economy of St. Kitts and Nevis depends on tourism. Since the 1970s, tourism has replaced sugar as the traditional mainstay of the economy. Following the 2005 harvest called "Crop", the government closed the sugar industry, after undergoing several decades of losses. To compensate for lost jobs, the government has embarked on a program to diversify the agricultural sector and to stimulate other sectors of the economy, such as export-oriented manufacturing and offshore banking.

Roughly 200,000 tourists visited the islands in 2009, but reduced tourism arrivals and foreign investment led to an economic contraction in 2009 to 2012, and the economy returned to growth only in 2013. Like other tourist destinations in the Caribbean, St. Kitts and Nevis is vulnerable to damage from natural disasters and shifts in tourism demand. Caribbean Development Bank figures show that in 2007 the public debt of St. Kitts and Nevis was 182.92%, almost twice that of its entire GDP. The government has made notable progress on reducing its public debt — from 154%

of GDP in 2011 to 83% in 2013 — although it still faces one of the highest levels in the world, largely attributable to public enterprise losses.

St. Kitts and Nevis is one of the few Caribbean nations that maintain diplomatic relations with the Republic of China (Taiwan) rather than with the mainland People's Republic of China controlled by the Communists. That it does so, is in part, evidence of the difficult economic situation in the islands. Taiwan has provided the islands with extensive development loans at low rates, and in 2011, even provided 5,000 laptops for the school system.

Until a few years ago, sugar cane production was a large part of the economy, but it ended when that industry could not compete with other countries, costing a loss of several thousand jobs.

Crime also has been a serious problem. An increase in the number of homicides in the islands produced special legislation aimed at curbing gang violence in 2011. Most of the deaths of 42 persons killed over the 20 months were connected to some form of gang activity. Because of this spike in murders and gang crime, the legislature urged Prime Minister Denzil Douglas to declare a national state of emergency. Douglas has served as prime minister since 1995, with elections scheduled in 2015.

Secession

The British first settled the islands in 1623, but control was disputed with the French until 1783, when the British prevailed. Independence was achieved on September 19, 1983, and the two-island federation is a member of the British Commonwealth. It is a parliamentary democracy based on the Westminster model, but the constitution of St. Kitts and Nevis allows either island to secede upon a referendum vote.

In 1998, defying international pleas, residents of the seven-mile-long island of Nevis voted on whether to secede from St. Kitts and become the smallest nation in the Western Hemisphere. Approval of two-thirds of the island's voters was required for secession. The vote was 2,427 for secession (62%) and 1,418 against, falling just short of the two-thirds required.

The vote was the culmination of a struggle that began with Britain's colonization in 1628. In 1882, Britain stripped Nevis of its legislature and wed it to St. Kitts. When the islands became independent in 1983, Nevis reluctantly joined in a federation with neighboring St. Kitts, but Nevisians insisted on a constitutional clause allowing them to break away.

After years of complaining that they are treated like second-class citizens by the federal government, the seat of which is located on St. Kitts, they invoked that right with the failed 1998 referendum. Nevis retains the right to secede, and proponents vowed that they would try again, but, in the years since the vote, the issue has faded.

Offshore Financial Center

Nevis, the "tax haven" half of the federation, has its own Island Assembly and a no-nonsense strict banking and business privacy law. Its pro-offshore laws have existed for almost 30 years — so there is plenty of experience and precedent in the local courts — and the legislative assembly keeps the applicable laws current. There are well-established offshore financial service companies that can do what you want, and some have convenient U.S. branch offices.

Nevis owes much of its success to its deserved reputation as the business-friendly "Delaware of the Caribbean." Over the last 25 years the Nevis parliament has adopted and constantly updated excellent offshore corporation, trust and limited liability company laws, augmented by strong financial privacy.

There are no exchange controls and until recently there were no tax information exchange treaties with other countries. However, the country has signed 18 TIEAs including those with Canada and the United Kingdom, but none with the United States as yet.

Unsuccessful moves by the St. Kitts-based government to take over the Nevis financial sector have played a major role in spurring continuing calls for secession.

Asset Protection Trusts

Building on their reputation for statutory corporate cordiality, in 1994, the Island Assembly adopted the Nevis International Trust Ordinance, a comprehensive, clear and flexible asset protection trust (APT) law. This law is comparable — and in some ways superior — to that of the Cook Islands in the South Pacific, already well known as an APT world center.

The Nevis law incorporates the best features of the Cook Islands law, but is even more flexible. The basic aim of the law is to permit foreign citizens to obtain asset protection by transferring property titles to an APT established in Charlestown, Nevis.

Nevis simply is taking advantage of the worldwide growth in medical, legal and professional malpractice lawsuits. Legislative and judicial imposition of no-fault personal liability on corporate officers and directors has become a nasty fact of business life. A Nevis trust places personal assets beyond the reach of foreign governments, litigious plaintiffs, creditors, and contingency fee lawyers.

Under the 1994 law, the Nevis judiciary does not recognize any non-domestic court orders regarding its domestic APTs. This forces a foreign judgment creditor to start all over again, retrying a case in a Nevis court with Nevis lawyers. A plaintiff who sues an APT must first post a US$25,000 bond with the government to cover court and others costs before a suit will be accepted for filing. In addition, the statute of limitations for filing legal challenges to a Nevis APT runs out two years from the date of the trust creation. In cases of alleged fraudulent intent, the law places the burden of proof on the foreign claimant.

Fast Citizenship for Sale

The St. Kitts and Nevis passport is well-regarded internationally and the program has been carefully managed with very few passports issued. St. Kitts and Nevis citizens enjoy a passport with an excellent reputation and very good visa-free travel to many nations. For visa-free travel throughout Europe, a St. Kitts and Nevis passport can be combined with a residence permit in a European Union country.

To view and download the Citizenship-by-Investment information leaflet of the Government of St. Kitts and Nevis, visit https://www.henleyglobal.com/citizenship-saint-kitts-nevis-citizenship.

Citizens of St. Kitts and Nevis are allowed to hold dual citizenship, and the acquisition of citizenship is not reported to other countries.

The Citizenship-by-Investment Program was established in 1984 and requires applicants to make an economic contribution to the country. In exchange, they and their families are granted full citizenship.

Under their current citizenship-by-investment rules, to qualify for St. Kitts and Nevis citizenship, an investment of at least US$400,000 in designated real estate, plus additional government and due diligence fees are required.

Alternatively, a cash contribution can be made to the Sugar Industry Diversification Foundation in the amount of US$250,000 (for a single applicant).

Using the charitable contribution is an easier route for most applicants because it provides a set cost and avoids further expenses associated with owning real estate in a foreign country. Plus, you don't have to live in St. Kitts and Nevis to secure your second citizenship, so buying real estate could just be an additional burden if you're not interested in spending time there.

Sugar Industry Diversification Foundation Option

OPTION # 1: Make a contribution to the Sugar Industry Diversification Foundation (SIDF, a public charity) starting from US$250,000 (for a single applicant). However, this includes all government fees.

Required contributions:

- (SIDF, a public charity) starting from US$250,000 (for a single applicant). However, this includes all government fees.

- Single applicant: US$250,000 non-refundable contribution, due diligence fee of US$7,500.

- Applicants with up to three dependents (spouse and two children below the age of 18): US$300,000 contribution.

- Applicant with up to five dependents (i.e. one spouse and four children): US$350,000.

- Applicant with up to seven dependents: US$450,000.

- Additional contribution for each dependent above seven: US$50,000, due diligence fees of US$4,000 per dependent age 16 or older.

- Each dependent child 18 to 25 years old and enrolled full-time as university undergraduate: US$35,000.

- Each dependent parent 62 years or older living with and supported by head of household: US$35,000.

Registration, application, due diligence, and processing fees: application fee: US$250 per applicant plus 17% VAT; consulting fee, US$1,200 per application.

Investment in Designated Real Estate Option

OPTION # 2: Make an investment of at least US$400,000 in one of the approved real-estate developments in addition to paying government fees, other fees and taxes.

Required investment:

Minimum US$400,000, plus approximately 7% in taxes, duties, and fees; Alien land owner's tax, 10% to 12% of purchase price, may apply; title insurance cost varies depending on the cost of the property.

Application fee:

- US$250 per applicant plus 17% VAT.

- Security fee, US$3,500 per applicant.

- Processing fee, US$250 per applicant.

- Court fees, no additional charge.

- Consulting fee, $1,200 per application.

Registration fee (after grant of approval):

- Head of household: US$35,000.

- Spouse and each child under the age of 18 years: US$15,000.

- Each dependent child 18 to 25 years enrolled full-time as university undergraduate: US$35,000.

- Each dependent parent 62 years or older living with and supported by head of household: US$35,000.

Depending on what an attorney or other professionals may charge, usual legal fees can cost US$20,000 for single applicant or applicant and spouse; US$25,000 for applicant, spouse, and up to two children; US$5,000 for each additional dependent child. Also, 50% of the legal fee is refunded if primary applicant is not approved. There is also a $500 escrow fee. Due diligence fees are from US$4,000 to US$8,000.

The real estate option requires the purchase of a condominium or villa from an approved list of developers with a minimum investment of US$400,000. Transaction costs add 10% to the purchase price (i.e., at least US$35,000, and likely US$50,000 or more) as real estate prices are now at a relatively high level in St. Kitts and Nevis.

A current list of approved real estate projects for investment is at: http://www.ciu.gov.kn/?q=approved-real-estate

Processing time for charitable contribution applications takes up to three months and dual citizenship is permitted, with no residence requirement. Using the real estate option lengthens the average processing time from four to 12 months or longer. The real estate cannot be re-sold until at least five years after purchase.

Documents required include:

- Application for citizenship completed.

- Birth and marriage certificates.

- Police certificate or affidavit showing no criminal record.

- Evidence of financial assets.

- Medical certificate showing a negative HIV test result.

A valid passport or birth certificate and photo ID that contains both name and date of birth and a return or onward ticket are re-

quired of U.S. citizens entering St. Kitts and Nevis, Stays up to one
month are granted and anyone requiring an extension must apply
to the Ministry of National Security. There is an airport departure
tax and an environmental levy.

Contacts

Embassy of St. Kitts and Nevis
OECS Building
3216 New Mexico Avenue NW, Washington, DC 20016
Tel.: (202) 686-2636
Email: stkittsnevis@embassy.gov.kn
Web: http://www.embassy.gov.kn

Consulate Generale of St. Kitts and Nevis
412-414 East 75th Street, 5th Floor
New York, NY 10021
Tel.: (212) 535-1234, (212) 535-5555
Email: sknconsulgeneral@aol.com
Web: http://www.stkittsnevis.org/contactus.html
Official government website: http://www.stkittsnevis.org

Recommended Residence & Immigration Consultants:

Mark Nestmann, a senior member of The Sovereign Society
Council of Experts, is a qualified professional who assists those
interested in acquiring foreign residence and citizenship and
works with agents of the government. Henley & Partners Ltd.
also are recommended official agents.

Mark Nestmann LLM, President
The Nestmann Group
2303 N. 44th Street #14-1025
Phoenix, AZ 85008
Tel.: (602) 688-7552

Web: http://www.nestmann.com

Henley & Partners Ltd.
Corner New & Central Streets, P.O. Box 630
Basseterre, St. Kitts, West Indies
Tel.: +1 869 465 00 50
Web: www.henleyglobal.com/stkittsnevis
Contact: Mr. Wendell E. Lawrence
Email: wendell.lawrence@henleyglobal.com

PART III

COUNTRIES BY REGION

SECTION 1

NORTH AMERICA

Canada

Government:	Confederation with Parliamentary Democracy
Capital:	Ottawa
National Day:	Independence Day: 1 July (1867 from the U.K.)
Population:	34,834,841 (July 2014 est.)
Total Area:	3,855,103 sq. miles / 9,984,670 sq. kilometers
Languages:	English 59.3% (official), French 23.2% (official), other 17.5%
Ethnic groups:	British Isles origin 28%; mixed 26%; French origin 23%; other European 15%; other Asian, African, Arab 6%; Amerindian 2%
Religion:	Roman Catholic 46%, Protestant 36%, other 18%
Life Expectancy:	81.67 years
Currency:	Canadian dollar (CAD)
GDP:	US$1.518 trillion (2013 est.)
GDP per capita:	US$43,100 (2013 est.)

The globe's second-biggest country has an endless variety of landscapes. Spiky mountains, glinting glaciers, spectral rainforests, wheat-waving prairies — they're all here, spread across six time zones. Expect wave-bashed beaches, too. With the Pacific, Arctic and Atlantic Oceans gnashing on three sides, Canada has a coastline that'd reach halfway to the moon, if stretched out.

It's the backdrop for plenty of 'ah'-inspiring moments — and the playground for a big provincial menagerie. We mean big as in polar bears, grizzly bears, whales and everyone's favorite, the ballerina-legged moose. You're pretty much guar-

anteed to see one of these behemoths when you leave the city behind.

Winter or summer, grand adventures lurk throughout Canada. Whether it's snowboarding Whistler's mountains, surfing Nova Scotia's swell, hiking Newfoundland's Appalachian Trail or kayaking the Northwest Territories' white-frothed South Nahanni River, outfitters will help you gear up for it. Gentler adventures abound, too, like strolling Vancouver's Stanley Park seawall, swimming off Prince Edward Island's (PEI) pink-sand beaches, or ice skating Ottawa's Rideau Canal. Before you know it, you'll be zipping up the fleece and heeding the call to action (and maybe having a go at dog-sledding, walleye fishing, snow-kiting…).

Canada takes in the world's largest per capita annual immigration numbers — around 250,000 people a year, of whom 43% go to Toronto. While this is cool in multicultural terms — allowing you to shop for Buddha trinkets in Vancouver's Chinatown, chow on curry in Toronto's Little India, or sip a Vietnamese café au lait in Montreal — it also causes growing pains. Mainly, it's becoming difficult for Canada to maintain its high-caliber social and physical infrastructures in the face of such relentless population growth. — Lonely Planet

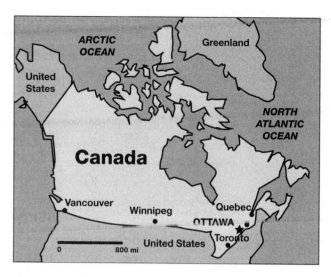

Why Canada?

Canada and the United States long have been staunch, if uneasy, allies. These friendly neighbors share the largest undefended border in the world. Until post-September 11, 2001, ("9/11") a day-trip between the two countries required only a short discussion with an unarmed customs official. International incidents occasionally arise, but, for the most part, are resolved before tempers flare.

In all, the two countries do more than merely coexist; in the past, they have shared an amicable relationship unprecedented in world history. The need for greater anti-terrorist border security has pushed both nations to greater cooperation on systems of identifying international travelers and information sharing. More and more Americans are beginning to take advantage of these close ties.

Every day, thousands choose Canada as an excellent place to visit, do business, even live — and with good reason.

A 2014 survey of quality of life — conducted by the U.S.

human resources consulting firm Mercer — found Vancouver, Ottawa, Toronto, and Montreal (in that order), among the top 30 cities in the world. Montreal, the lowest Canadian city in the grouping, had a score better than the top-ranked U.S. city, San Francisco.

Leading economists at the United Nations in New York City researched the best countries in which to live and work. They judged Canada to be number one. Japan came in second, the United States only sixth, and the United Kingdom tenth. The factors the U.N. officials used in making their choice include Canada's high standard of living, minimal social class divisions, low crime rate, clean environment, beautiful scenery, economic opportunities, government support services, extensive infrastructure, comprehensive shopping and sports facilities, affordable housing, and the generous hospitality of the Canadian people.

Despite long, harsh winters, a continuing bilingual English-French problem, and long-standing separatist sentiments in the province of Quebec, overall, the U.N. officials found Canada to be the most attractive nation in the world.

And what's more, most Canadians are nice people.

Canada is not without its problems. Twelve years ago, the Canadian dollar hit an all-time low, with the "loonie" — so-called for the bird on the face of the dollar coin — at about C$1.50 to the US$1.00. By 2008, a much stronger loonie was at par with the U.S. dollar. In early 2014, it dropped back to C$1.10 to the American dollar.

Canadian Economic "Miracle"

Whether it's the housing market, long-term unemployment or the enormously high national debt, the U.S. economy is a mess. When Americans look north they see a very different picture.

Though Canada and the United States are often viewed as very similar, the bigger, chillier neighbor of the U.S. has better weathered recent economic storms which brought banks, auto companies and other American businesses to their knees when the financial crisis struck in 2008.

Not only has it outshined the U.S., but Canada came through the recession better overall than most other Western economies. That's been great for Canadian workers. Canadian wages in the last 20 years have increased 17% more than in the U.S.

Whereas the U.S. unemployment rate in the past six years soared to nearly 12% (with an effective real rate of as much as 16%), at the worst point Canada's was only 7.6%. Canadians also enjoy less income inequality, meaning there's less disparity between rich and poor. In addition, Canada has a foreign trade balance surplus with the U.S. compared to overall U.S. monthly trade deficits of over US$40 billion.

Much of this success flows from natural factors, but also from a Conservative Party government that has cut taxes and regulations, reduced deficit spending and avoided the senseless trillion dollar bailouts of companies and banks — because none were needed. Banks in Canada are among North America's leaders, both profitable and outperforming their American counterparts because of their conservative lending policies and tighter government restrictions on lending capital requirements.

Immigrants: A Conditional Welcome

The virtues of Canada as a place to live are known around the world. Recent immigration figures attest to the fact. In recent years, for example, Canada's population of 34 million has increased annually by about 250,000 immigrants.

A modern nation built by European settlers, Canada's top

sources of immigrants have been from the United States, India, Vietnam, Poland, the United Kingdom, the Philippines, Guyana, and El Salvador. The increasing numbers have also included many wealthy Asians, especially residents of Hong Kong, although some of these persons have returned home as dual nationals.

Canada now has the highest per capita immigration rate of any nation in the world; an influx that has caused wide spread public demand for limitations. Some polls show that as many as three out of five Canadians favor a moratorium on all new immigration. Some immigrants are more welcome than others for a variety of reasons. As you will learn in a moment, you may be just the type of new citizen Canada welcomes with open arms.

By mid-2014, Canada had welcomed more than 75,900 new citizens. Comparatively, in the first three months of 2013, Canada welcomed 35,320 new Canadians. In 2013, 128,936 people were granted Canadian citizenship — an average of 10,745 each month. Canada granted citizenship to an average of 160,000 people a year until 2012, after Ottawa raised the language requirement and introduced a new knowledge test.

About one in six Canadians is foreign born, double the ratio in the United States. Canada admits aunts, uncles, nieces, nephews, and fiancés. Common law spouses and same-sex partners are recognized under Canadian law but not for immigration purposes. On arrival, so-called "landed immigrants" — those given residence status — immediately are entitled to the same menu of health care, welfare and university benefits as lifelong Canadian citizens.

An increasingly popular practice is to apply for refugee status in Canada, then disappear during the one-year review period. Most are presumed to have sneaked or been smuggled across the border into the United States. In an age of increased anti-terrorism vigilance, the U.S. government has been critical of Canadian refugee laxness.

2014 Immigration Law

In 2014, more stringent residence and citizenship requirements were imposed by a new law, the "Strengthening Canadian Citizenship Act." Critics of the Act including Amnesty International and the Canadian Association of Refugee Lawyers contended it was too restrictive. Among other powers, the Act allows the government power to revoke the citizenship of Canadians who have dual citizenship and are found guilty in terrorism or treason cases.

The Act also terminated the existing Canadian Federal Immigration Investors Programs (FIIP), and over 25,000 pending applications were returned, the majority originating from China.

Canada's liberal immigration policies may have been abused. In arguing in support of the Act, Immigration Minister Chris Alexander said it would reinforce the value of citizenship by cracking down on fraud. He cited pending citizenship fraud investigations that identified more than 3,000 citizens and 5,000 permanent residents. Most of the targeted individuals did not live in the country and paid large fees for assistance to questionable immigration consultants to concoct fake proof of residence in Canada looking toward eventual citizenship.

The Conservative government said another aim of the Act is to ensure that new citizens are prepared for full participation and integration into Canadian society. Applicants are now required to show English and French language proficiency and to pass a "knowledge about Canada" test. Those aged 16 to 64 are required to take the tests.

The Act requires that permanent residents be physically present in the country for longer periods than before in order to gain citizenship. Under former rules, permanent residents had to be living in Canada for three out of four years. Now, they must be physically present for at least 183 days during four out of six years before their citizenship application. In addition, permanent residents seeking citizenship must intend to continue to live in Canada. The new law means that the residence requirement does in fact require actual physical presence in Canada.

Individuals who have strong family or other ties to Canada are favored for residence. Canadian Consulates will provide a personal history information form to be completed and submitted with copies of relevant birth records to the Registrar of Canadian Citizenship in the capital city of Ottawa. A "Certificate of Canadian Citizenship" automatically is issued to anyone who qualifies for citizenship by family descent. If you are lucky enough to qualify, this is the least complicated basis on which to establish a new legal residence in Canada.

In 2014, the government also began promoting a "Start-up Visa" program designed to attract entrepreneurs from around the world with ideas for new business ventures. It links immigrant entrepreneurs with experienced private-sector organizations who are experts in working with start-ups. For more information see http://www.cic.gc.ca/english/immigrate/business/start-up/index.asp

Quebec Immigrant Investor Program

Even though the Canadian FIIP has been terminated, the French-speaking Province of Quebec for the time being is offering a similar program, but with a limited annual applicant quota of 1,750, of which no one country can have more than 1,250 of the total.

Quebec immigration authorities allocate quotas to authorized financial intermediaries who will screen and accept the applicants with the highest chance of success. This program is available to individuals with entrepreneurial, investor, or self-employed experience. Each category has its own requirements and selection process.

Applicants must show that they can become economically established in Canada and have the intention of settling in Quebec. Upon provincial approval, candidates will receive a *Certificat de sélection du Québec* (CSQ — Québec selection certificate) and thereafter a Canadian Immigration Permanent Resident Visa. For information see http://www.immigration-quebec.gouv.qc.ca/en/informations/rules-procedures.html

About Canadian Taxes

Before we get to the good news — a possible big tax break for new immigrants — you should know that the Canadian tax system is tough and comprehensive. Combined Canadian federal and provincial personal income taxes range from 48% to 54%, depending on the province. And the Canadian tax burden has been a direct cause of capital flight, which is relatively unrestricted, as you shall see below.

The combined federal-provincial top marginal Canadian tax rate is 39% in Alberta, while in Ontario it is 46.41% compared to an average federal rate of 39.6% in the U.S. Quebec has the highest combined tax at 53%.

However, there is one very attractive feature of Canadian tax policies; unlike the United States, Canada does not tax the worldwide income or foreign assets of its *non-resident* citizens. Canada taxes only the worldwide income of its resident citizens and resident aliens who live in Canada at any time during the calendar year. "Residents," by law, include individuals, corporations and trusts located in Canada.

Enjoying Life Tax-Free

Although tough Canadian taxes may be for the average native-born citizen living within the Canadian border, there is a huge loophole available.

A qualified immigrant accepted for eventual Canadian citizenship is eligible for zero taxes on the source of your income income if it is from an offshore, non-canadian "inbound" trust. Such a trust can be created before you move to Canada and become a citizen. But an 'inbound trust must not have any assets contributed by a Canadian tax resident. The assets must come from sources other than those of the Canadian tax resident beneficiary. Previously 'immigrant trusts' created with the new immigrant assets were allowed but were abolished in 2014.

Canadian citizens and resident aliens employed by certain "international financial centers" are also forgiven 50% of all income taxes.

The federal estate tax was abolished in 1971, but the provinces do impose death duties and these fees can be considerable.

The heirs of a wealthy American with an estate of US$5.3 million or more could pay a marginal rate as high as 40% as of 2014. Worse still, state estate taxes and probate fees are added to these hefty federal sums. In sharp contrast, Canadians pay no federal estate taxes.

After living five years in Canada as a new citizen, you can move your residence to another country, and you then pay taxes only on income earned or paid from within Canada. You pay no taxes on your worldwide income.

Americans living abroad do not enjoy this distinct tax advantage, although some may qualify for the US$99,200 (2014 amount) annual "foreign earned income exclusion" under U.S. law, if they are employed and actually live abroad.

With a view to deterring tax exiles, Canada imposes a "departure" tax on individuals or corporate entities seeking to change residence to another country. Individuals who have been a resident in Canada for less than five years are exempt from departure tax. Under the departure tax, all the individual's capital assets are deemed sold at a fair market value on which capital gains tax is payable.

A Scenario

Let us suppose you, as an American citizen, wish to sell an established business, or convert fixed assets into liquid cash for investment or other purposes.

Depending on how long you have held the property and how the liquidation deal is structured, you may face U.S. capital gains taxes. While short-term gains are taxed as ordinary income, the taxes on long-term gains (for assets held more than one year) can range from 5% to 28%. Depending on your tax bracket, income taxes can be 40% or more.

In either case, a major part of the cash proceeds from the sale or conversion will be devoured by the U.S. Internal Revenue Service and state tax authorities — before you ever see a thin dime.

How can you avoid this enormous tax burden?

What if the title of the U.S. business is transferred to a foreign trust, conveniently located in a low or no-tax offshore jurisdiction? Moreover, what if that trust is structured to qualify as a Canadian inbound trust?

Once you are a Canadian, that previously created inbound trust can pay you benefits and income for five years, tax-free, if you carefully follow the regulations that govern this incredible tax break. You can be a free spirit with little or no income or capital gains tax liability in either the U.S. or Canada.

Testing the Waters

Maybe you would like to test the northern waters before making any major decision about a future in Canada …

Fortunately, Americans thinking about emigrating can explore working life north of the border for an extended period. The North American Free Trade Agreement (NAFTA) allows reciprocal were extended for periods of up to one year, but the U.S. Citizenship and Immigration Services (USCIS) has increased the period of stay granted to nonimmigrant professional workers from Canada or Mexico from one to three years, the same as the initial period of admission given to H-1B professional workers. Eligible nonimmigrants may now be allowed to receive extensions of stay in increments of up to three years. The prior maximum period of stay was only one year.

Those welcome to work in Canada include those Americans who do research and designing, purchasing, sales and contract negotiation, customs brokering, financial services, public relations, advertising, tourism, and market research. It also includes professionals, so long as they are paid by a U.S. source.

Canadian Immigration Process

The immigration process begins with a visit to the Canadian Embassy. It is located at Fourth Street and Pennsylvania Avenue NW, Washington, D.C. You can also try a Canadian Consulate, located in New York and other major U.S. cities.

There you receive an "Immigration Questionnaire" requiring basic personal information about you, your spouse and family. Within a few weeks, a more detailed questionnaire will be presented if the applicant is initially found acceptable. After this second document is reviewed, a personal interview and medical examinations are needed.

If all goes well, you will shortly receive a visa for entry into Canada as a landed immigrant: "Welcome, *bienvenue au Canada.*"

A distinct advantage that comes with this new citizenship is the international official acceptance of the Canadian passport, one of the most respected in the world. Moreover, as citizens of a member nation of the British Commonwealth, Canadians are allowed to enter Britain without obtaining a prior visa, as well as almost 100 other countries.

It is worth noting that Canada recognizes the principle of dual nationality. They allow successful applicants for citizenship to retain their nationality of origin. For reasons that will become obvious in a moment, that choice is not a viable option for an ex-American expatriating to Canada.

Canada for Expatriation

Canada is a leading nation for exercising perhaps the most effective wealth protection strategy for U.S. persons — expatriation. However, for a U.S. citizen (and many others), expatriation means voluntarily ending their native citizenship and becoming a Canadian citizen.

Wealthy persons who remain American citizens stand to lose millions of dollars to the IRS. Consider this — at death, the U.S. government could take up to 40% of the assets you leave to your children and heirs — and that is after having paid on average up to more than 40% of your earnings in federal and state income taxes every year. For those with estates worth millions, the prospect of having their money enrich the coffers of the IRS and spent by profligate U.S. politicians should be enough to suggest drastic, but legal, tax avoidance measures.

One of the options wealthy Americans are increasingly turning to is expatriation. Perhaps surprising to some, many of them choose Canada as their new home.

Expatriation is a drastic measure, but it may be the only escape from U.S. taxes for the wealthiest of Americans. This strategy definitely is not for everyone, but it may make sense for you.

There are certain trade-offs involved, and each must be researched and considered carefully. Most importantly, you must do it correctly to make it work. Here I will explain the intricacies of expatriation, and why Canada might be the right place to go.

A Big Change — U.S. Expatriation

Almost 3,000 Americans officially renounced their U.S. citizenship in 2013, according to U.S. Treasury Department records, a 221% increase over 2012. In the first quarter of 2014, 1,001 U.S. citizens formally renounced their U.S. citizenship, a number higher than in any full year before Barack Obama assumed office. At this current rate, the total number of formal renunciations in 2014 will exceed 4,000, which would exceed by a thousand the previous record year of 2013.

For years, formal expatriation was a rarity in America. As recently as the early 1990s, only a few hundred citizens took this step each year. Now the numbers are almost 10 times higher.

One major reason for this increase is the onerous 2009 Foreign Account Tax Compliance Act (FATCA), under which offshore financial institutions — banks, investment houses, insurers, and the like — are required, under penalty of exclusion from the U.S. banking system, to report most U.S. citizen accounts held overseas.

Thousands of people, who have U.S. citizenship by birth, but who live in and are citizens of the country of their parent's origin, discovered that they were also liable to report under this insane U.S. law. Canadians, in particular, felt the bite of FATCA. Any Canadians whose parents might have lived near the U.S. border and were born in a nearby American hospital were trapped in a bureaucratic U.S. tax nightmare because by place of birth they were U.S. citizens. Their local Canadian banks now have to report on their accounts to the U.S. IRS, even though these people have no other connection to the U.S.

It required more than a year of official Canadian protests and negotiations with Washington to produce a procedure that eases the worst of FATCA for Canadians caught in its web. Required U.S. reports now are filed by Canadian banks with Canadian tax authorities and then transmitted to Washington.

The potential American immigrant to Canada leaving the U.S. behind eventually will have to surrender U.S. citizenship, formally renouncing his or her U.S. status, which Americans have a legal right to do.

But for some wealthy Americans, soak-the-rich politicians have determined to make leaving America as painful and as costly as possible.

U.S. Exit Tax

On June 17, 2008, President George Bush signed "anti-expatriation" legislation, Public Law No: 110-245, unanimously passed by Congress. This law dramatically changed the former income tax regime applicable to both U.S. citizens who expatriate (end U.S. citizenship) and long-term U.S. residents (e.g., "green card holders") who decide to end their U.S. residence. (The Act applies to both groups and calls them collectively "covered individuals.")

This 2008 expat tax, amounts to an "exit tax" and had been a political goal of left wing Democrats for a decade or more. It was adopted in the U.S. Congress as a legislative rider on an Iraq war veterans' benefits bill. It is worth noting historically that the only other three countries that imposed a punitive tax on exiting citizens were Nazi Germany, Soviet Russia and apartheid South Africa.

Under the law, a person who is a "covered individual" falls within the clutches of the expatriation provisions if, on the date of expatriation or termination of U.S. residence, (1) the individual's average annual net U.S. income tax liability for the five-year period preceding that date was US$155,000 or more (adjusted for inflation); or, (2) the individual's net worth as of that date is US$2 million or more; or (3) the individual fails to certify under penalties of perjury that he or she has complied with all U.S. federal tax obligations for the preceding five years.

Of course, if you do not fit within the above definitions (really a "means test" of sorts), this law may offer an opportunity to escape U.S. taxes now, before you become more prosperous in the future.

But under the law "covered individuals" are taxed enormously under IR Code section 877A. This tax is imposed on all assets as if the person's worldwide assets had been sold for their fair market value on the day before expatriation or residence termination. The Act allows in 2014 exclusion of the first US$663,000 of net gain (as adjusted for inflation annually).

This phantom gain will presumably be taxed as ordinary income (at 2014 rates as high as 39.6% or more) or as capital gains (at either a 15%, 25%, or 28% rate), under whatever the then-current tax law may be. As of 2014, the CGT is 15%. In addition, any assets held by any trust or portion of a trust that the covered individual was treated as owning for U.S. income tax purposes (i.e., a grantor trust) are also subject to this tax.

Of course, if you are lucky and don't come within these definitions, the law may offer a very real opportunity to escape U.S. taxes, especially if you have a good prospect of becoming more prosperous in the future. You can leave now and escape the tax.

Do It the Right Way

Here is how to expatriate from the U.S. and avoid pitfalls along the way:

It is crucial to obtain proper legal and tax advice on expatriation in order to be effective in surrendering citizenship. The worst outcome is to wind up with an ambiguous dual nationality status. In that case, you go through an extended period retaining not only U.S. citizenship, but citizenship in another country as well. You may then find yourself within the potential grasp of two government taxing authorities.

Generally, an ex-American who properly surrenders citizenship is treated by U.S. law just as any other non-resident foreigner. That means being taxed at a flat 30% rate on certain types of passive income derived from U.S. sources, and on net profits from the sale of a U.S. trade or business at regular graduated rates. Expatriates can safely be present in the U.S. only about 122 days a year. Stay any longer and they expose themselves to IRS claims for full U.S. taxation based on alien residence.

Another strict caution: you must be certain to obtain valid foreign citizenship before you surrender your U.S. citizenship — if you fail to do so, you could become a "stateless" person, the proverbial "man without a country."

A person without a passport and a nationality is legally lost in this world of national borders and bureaucratic customs officials, and is not entitled to the legal protection of any government.

U.S. Expatriation Process

Valid surrender must be an unequivocal act in which a person manifests an unqualified intention to relinquish U.S. citizenship.

In order for the surrender to be effective, all of the conditions of the statute requirements must be met; the person must appear in person and sign an oath before a U.S. consular or diplomatic officer at a U.S. Embassy or Consulate outside the United States. Surrender of citizenship not in the form prescribed by the U.S. Secretary of State has no legal effect.

Because of the way in which the law is written and interpreted, Americans cannot effectively renounce their citizenship by mail, through an agent or while physically within the United States. Keep in mind that in recent years there have been long waiting periods for U.S. persons seeking expatriation appointments at U.S. embassies and consulates, many months is some case in Europe and elsewhere.

Once surrender is accomplished in the presence of an American diplomatic or consular officer abroad, all documents are referred to the U.S. Department of State. The Office of Overseas Citizens Services reviews them to ensure that all criteria under the law are met, but the State Department has no discretion to refuse a proper surrender of citizenship. The courts have held this personal right to be absolute.

Long before such a drastic final step is taken toward ending U.S. citizenship, the new Canadian immigrant should have his or her official Canadian citizenship in order, papers in hand, and an es-tablished residence in their new homeland.

This will most likely be in the metropolitan areas of Montreal, Toron-to or Vancouver, where the vast majority of immigrants decide to live.

As a general rule, a Canadian resident is deemed non-resident from the date of his departure if he can show he "severed all residential ties with his country." As previously mentioned, Canada imposes a departure tax on individuals or corporate entities seeking to change residence to another county. The departure capital gains tax rate is tied to the individual's personal income tax rate. Some exceptions apply, such as selling one's primary residence which may be exempt from taxation.

If you become a non-resident of Canada for tax purposes, you must file a final departure tax return, which is due April 30 after the year in which you sever your residential ties with Canada. It is important that you seek professional advice to ensure that all of your departure tax issues are taken into consideration in your final tax return, and that you take the steps necessary to properly sever your residence from a tax perspective.

Visiting Canada

Since the terror attacks of September 11, 2001, entry into Canada has tightened and now is solely determined by Canadian Border Services Agency (CBSA) officials in accordance with Canadian law, see http://www.cbsa.gc.ca for details.

Canadian law requires that all persons entering Canada must carry both proof of citizenship and identity. A valid U.S. passport or NEXUS card satisfies these requirements for U.S. citizens. The NEXUS program allows pre-screened travelers expedited processing by U.S. and Canadian officials at dedicated processing lanes at designated northern border ports of entry, at NEXUS kiosks at Canadian preclearance airports, and at marine reporting locations. (More on NEXUS cards later.)

If U.S. citizen travelers to Canada do not have a passport or approved alternate document such as a NEXUS card, they must show a government-issued photo ID (driver's license) and proof of U.S. citizenship such as a U.S. birth certificate, naturalization certificate, or expired U.S. passport. Children under 16 need only present proof of U.S. citizenship.

U.S. citizens entering Canada from a third country must have a valid U.S. passport. A visa is not required for U.S. citizens to visit Canada for up to 180 days. Anyone seeking to enter Canada for any purpose besides a visit (to work, study or immigrate) must qualify for the appropriate entry status, and should contact the Canadian Embassy or nearest consulate and see the Canadian immigration website at: http://www.cic.gc.ca/english/index.asp.

Anyone with a criminal record, including even misdemeanors or driving while impaired (DWI), may be barred from entering Canada and must qualify for a special waiver well in advance of any planned travel for further processing, which may take some time.

The U.S. and Canada now share criminal history data, so Canadian border agents can view records from the F.B.I.'s database, and Canada shares its criminal records with the U.S. Travelers may be denied entry to Canada if they have committed any one of a wide range of crimes, including theft, assault, dangerous driving, driving while under the influence of drugs or alcohol, and possession of a controlled substance. The Canadian border enforcement is also strict about requiring prior work permits if you intend to work in Canada, even in some cases when "work" consists of only a single instance of paid employment. Agents have been known to confiscate and examine cell phones and laptops seeking evidence of false statements.

For information on entry requirements, contact the Canadian Embassy:

501 Pennsylvania Avenue NW
Washington, DC 20001
Tel.: (202) 682-1740

Canadian consulates are in Atlanta, Boston, Buffalo, Chicago, Dallas, Detroit, Los Angeles, Miami, Minneapolis, New York, San Juan or Seattle.

The Canadian Embassy website is http://www.canadianembassy. org.

Contacts

Embassy of Canada
501 Pennsylvania Avenue NW
Washington, DC 20001
Tel.: (202) 682-1740
Email: Washington-im-enquiry@international.gc.ca
Web: http://www.canadianembassy.org/

The Government of Canada has 16 (one embassy, 12 consulates general and three trade) offices in the U.S. to provide services and resources to Canadians and Americans.

For a list of U.S. offices, see http://can-am.gc.ca/offices-bureaux/index.aspx?lang=eng

For information on immigration consult Citizenship and Immigration Canada: http://www.cic.gc.ca/english/immigrate/index.asp

For visa information, see http://www.cic.gc.ca/english/visit/visas.asp

United States Embassy
490 Sussex Drive
K1N-1G8 Ottawa, Ontario
Tel.: + (613) 238-5335
Web: http://www.usembassycanada.gov/

Recommended Residence & Immigration Consultants:

Henley & Partners Canada Ltd
2020 University, Suite 1920
Montreal, Quebec H3A 2A5 Canada
Tel.: +1 (514) 288-1997
Email: canada@henleyglobal.com
Web: www.henleyglobal.com/canada

HSBC Building, Suite: 1030
885 West Georgia Street
Vancouver, BC V6C 3E8
Tel.: +1 (604) 689-8871

Toronto, Ontario
Tel.: +1 (647) 427-4408

Republic of Mexico

Government:	Federal Republic
Capital:	Mexico (Federal District)
National Day:	Independence Day: 16 September (1810 from Spain)
Population:	120,286,655 (July 2014 est.)
Total Area:	761, 606 sq. miles / 1,972,550 sq. kilometers
Languages:	Spanish, Mayan, Nahuatl, regional languages
Ethnic groups:	Mestizo (Amerindian-Spanish) 60%, Amerindian 30%, white 9%, other 1%
Religion:	Roman Catholic 89%, Protestant 6%, other 5%
Life Expectancy:	75.43 years
Currency:	Mexican peso (MXN)
GDP:	US$1.845 trillion (2013 est.)
GDP per capita:	US$15,600 (2013 est.)

Jungles, deserts; teeming cities, one-street pueblos; fiesta fireworks, Frida's angst: Mexico conjures up so many contradictory images. One thing's for sure: no preconceptions will ever live up to the reality.

From the southern jungles to the smoking, snow-capped volcanoes and the cactus-dotted northern deserts, all surrounded by 10,000km of coast strung with sandy beaches and wildlife-rich lagoons, Mexico is an endless adventure for the senses. A climate that ranges from temperate to hot almost everywhere makes for a life spent largely in the open air. Take it easy by lying on a beach, dining alfresco or strolling the streets of some pretty town, or get out and snorkel warm Caribbean reefs, hike mountain cloud forests or take a boat in search of dolphins or whales.

Mexico is packed with history and culture. Its pre-Hispanic civilizations built some of the world's great archaeological monuments, from Teotihuacán's towering pyramids to the exquisitely decorated temples of the Maya. The Spanish colonial era left beautiful towns full of gorgeous, tree-shaded plazas and elaborately carved stone churches and mansions. Modern Mexico has seen a surge of great art from the likes of Diego Rivera and Frida Kahlo. Top-class museums and galleries around the country document Mexico's long and fascinating history and its endless creative verve. Popular culture is just as vibrant, from the underground dance clubs of Mexico City to the sentimental crooning of ranchera singers.

Travel in Mexico is what you make it and the country caters to all types of voyager. Try renting a car: Mexico has some excellent roads, and outside the cities traffic is mostly light.

At the heart of your Mexican experience will be the Mexican people. A super-diverse crew from city hipsters to shy indigenous villagers, they're justly renowned for their love of color and frequent fiestas but are also philosophical folk, to whom timetables (while worthy of respect) are less important than simpatía (empathy). You will rarely find Mexicans less than courteous; they're often positively charming, and they know how to please their guests. They may despair of ever being well governed, but they are fiercely proud of Mexico, their one-of-a-kind homeland with all its variety, tight-knit family networks, beautiful-ugly cities, deep-rooted traditions, unique agave-based liquors and sensationally tasty, chili-laden food. It doesn't take long to understand why. — Lonely Planet

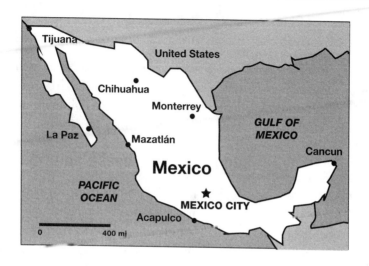

History and Overview

Mexico, the southern part of the North American continent, dwarfs Central America to the south by its sheer size. The United States forms its northern border, while Guatemala and Belize lie to the south. Its eastern seaboard is the Gulf of Mexico and to the west is the Pacific Ocean.

Some 50% of the country has a hot and dry climate with many arid desert regions, while 25% of the land in the south is tropical rain forest. Mountainous, with several peaks over 16,000 feet, the climate varies considerably across the country and at various altitudes.

In the 10th century, Mexico had one of the most highly developed civilizations in the world. Mexico was the site of several advanced Amerindian civilizations — including the Olmec, Toltec, Teotihuacan, Zapotec, Maya, and Aztec. Under dominance of the Aztecs, it built an empire of over 15 million people. Spanish Conquistadors arrived in 1519 and, within two years, the Aztecs were defeated and Spanish control consolidated. Administered as the

Viceroyalty of New Spain for three centuries, it achieved its independence early in the 19th century.

With silver deposits and other mineral wealth, New Spain, as it was then called, became an important part of the Spanish Empire. Remnants of Mexico's pre-Colombian and colonial past are abundant throughout the country, constituting a major asset in the world's cultural heritage.

As Spain's European influence waned, agitation for Mexican independence grew. In 1824, a federal Republic was formed and, in 1836, Spain formally recognized Mexico's independence. That same year, Texas, colonized by the U.S., separated from Mexico. The Mexican-American War in the mid-1840s, fought over territorial issues, was settled with Mexico ceding almost half its claimed territory to the U.S.

For the next 70 years, Mexico suffered endless revolutions and internal power struggles. That included an ill-fated attempt (1861-1866) by Emperor Napoleon III of France to install Hapsburg royalty, Maximillian and Carlotta, as emperor and empress of Mexico. Backed by Mexican conservatives and the Catholic Church, and for a time, the French army and navy, this produced five years of internal war and Maximillian's death by firing squad ordered by Mexico's president, Benito Juarez.

For most of the last century, one political party, the Institutional Revolutionary Party (or PRI) dominated the government, entrenching its power and corruption. The elections held in 2000 marked the first time in 90 years since the 1910 Mexican Revolution that an opposition candidate, Vicente Fox of the National Action Party (PAN), defeated the long-time party in government, the PRI. He was succeeded in 2006 by another PAN candidate, Felipe Calderón. The 2012 election returned the PRI to power with the election as president of Enrique Peña Nieto.

Economy

By the 1980s, Mexico's socialist economics and deficit spending produced a deepening financial crisis, repeated peso devaluations, and continuing social unrest. In 1995, a severe economic crisis followed the announcement of a huge international trade deficit. An estimated US$11 billion fled the country as nervous investors pulled out. Severe austerity measures and a multi-billion dollar bailout by the United States kept Mexico afloat but another peso devaluation devastated middleclass wage earners. By the year 2000, Mexico was in economic recovery and able to repay U.S. loans.

The global financial crisis beginning in late 2008 caused a massive economic downturn the following year, although growth returned in 2010. Ongoing economic and social concerns include low real wages, underemployment for a large segment of the population, inequitable income distribution, and few advancement opportunities for the largely indigenous population in the impoverished southern states.

Mexico now has a free market economy in the trillion dollar class. It contains a mixture of modern and outmoded industry and agriculture, increasingly dominated by the private sector. Recent administrations have expanded competition in seaports, railroads, telecommunications, electricity generation, natural gas distribution, and airports. Per capita income is roughly one-third that of the US; income distribution remains highly unequal.

The number of state-owned enterprises has fallen from more than 1,000 in 1982 to fewer than 200 currently, but some of these are major industries such as oil and natural gas. The government is slowly privatizing and expanding competition in sea ports, railroads, telecommunications, electricity, natural gas distribution, and airports. At this writing, President Nieto is pushing for partial privatization of Mexico's state owned gas and oil monopoly, Pemex.

Proximity to the United States and economic stability make Mexico an attractive location for foreign direct investment. From 2000 through 2012, U.S. foreign direct investment in Mexico totaled US$291.7 billion (51.4%), concentrated largely in the manufacturing (43%) and financial sectors (20%).

In Mexico, a maquiladora is a manufacturing operation in a free trade zone where factories import material and equipment from abroad on a duty-free and tariff-free basis for assembly, processing, or manufacturing and then export the assembled, processed and/or manufactured products, sometimes back to the raw materials' country of origin. Currently, about 1.3 million Mexicans are employed in one or more of approximately 3,000 maquiladoras, most associated with U.S. companies. These arrangements offer significant cost cutting to foreign companies because of the lower labor costs, even considering transport and providing needed employment.

Drug Wars

Mexico can be said to be a "high crime" nation, especially in Mexico City, but in rural areas as well. Robbery, carjacking, kidnapping for ransom, and street crime are rampant, often with the complicity of local police. Criminals posing as taxi drivers are a special threat. Extreme caution is advised at all times, especially when traveling anywhere by car. Since 2007, Mexico's powerful drug-trafficking organizations have engaged in bloody feuding, resulting in tens of thousands of drug-related homicides. You should also be very wary of interaction with Mexican police who too often stop foreigners and demand bribes under threat of arrest and jail.

Violent drug gang wars along the U.S.-Mexican border have killed hundreds there, many thousand elsewhere and raised the issue of rampant police and government corruption. The level of drug-related violence throughout Mexico is a major problem, with the states of Chihuahua, Sinaloa, Durango and northern Baja California the worst affected.

Tourists are not specifically targeted, but any travelers visiting these areas, and in particular the cities of Ciudad Juárez, Nogales and Tijuana should exercise extreme caution. The U.S. Department of State warns U.S. citizens about the risk of traveling in Mexico due to threats to safety and security posed by criminal organizations in the country. U.S. citizens have been the target of violent crimes, such as kidnapping, carjacking, and robbery in various Mexican states.

For information on security conditions in specific regions of Mexico, which can vary, travelers should reference the state-by-state assessments.

For current U.S. government warnings see: http://travel.state.gov/content/passports/english/alertswarnings/mexico-travel-warning.html

Thanks to the American demand for, and consumption of, drugs, Mexico is a major drug-producing and drug transit nation.

It is the world's second largest opium poppy cultivator yielding a potential production of 50 metric tons of pure heroin, or 125 metric tons of "black tar" heroin, the dominant form of Mexican heroin in the western United States. The government conducts the largest independent illicit-crop eradication program in the world. Mexico continues as the primary transshipment country for U.S.-bound cocaine from South America, with an estimated 95% of annual cocaine movements toward the U.S. stopping in Mexico. Major drug syndicates control the majority of drug trafficking throughout the country. They are also producers and distributors of ecstasy and a major supplier of heroin and the largest foreign supplier of marijuana and methamphetamine to the U.S. market.

Related to this drug activity, Mexico has become a significant money-laundering center, producing recent criminal convictions of Mexican banks, including HSBC.

Americans in Mexico

Diversity of possible lifestyles in Mexico has made the country a major magnet for expatriates and retirees from developed countries across the entire Northern Hemisphere. One can live either very inexpensively or, for those on less limited budgets, quite luxuriously there. Colonies of expatriates have been established throughout the country, particularly in highland areas with temperate climates. The popularity of these localities is somewhat subject to fashion.

For example, Lake Chapala, not far from Guadalajara, has been a "hot" destination. Other towns with large immigrant populations include Cuernavaca, Puebla, San Miguel de Allende, and Mexico City.

According to the official 2010 Census of Mexico, there were 738,103 Americans living in the Mexican Republic at that time. The U.S. State Department estimates that more than one million Americans live there now. Mexico has become the most popular foreign country for migrant U.S. citizens. In the year 2000, there were 343,591 Americans living in Mexico and in 1990 only 194,619. No doubt a large number are U.S. retirees who have moved there to enjoy a lower cost of living and warmer weather. More than 150,000 people cross the border every day for study, tourism or business.

Given the continuing U.S. economic recession, some experts think that as many as five million Americans may migrate to Mexico, Panama and other Latin American countries during the next 10 to 15 years. If you are planning such a move south, be very careful to study and understand Mexico's immigration and property laws before you make a final decision.

One of many U.S. State Department travel warnings noted that since 2006, in the Mexican government's anti-drug war, over 35,000 people were killed in narcotics-related violence. Most of those killed were members of rival criminal groups but many innocent persons died including Mexican law enforcement, military personnel and some U.S. citizens and U.S. government personnel. As noted above, you should review the U.S. State Department's Mexico Security Update.

Dual Nationality

Since 1998 the Mexican Constitution has allowed the principle of dual nationality to apply to all former Mexican citizens who have obtained citizenship from another nation. All such persons can apply for reinstatement of their original Mexican citizenship, the largest group being the million or more Mexican-Americans who have become U.S. citizens.

Since the U.S. also recognizes dual nationality, this presents no problem for naturalized U.S. Mexican-Americans. Those who have their Mexican citizenship reinstated are given all privileges that status confers, except voting rights in Mexican elections. Dual nationals are not, however, subject to compulsory military service. If they formally re-establish a residence in Mexico, they can vote as well.

Mexican law recognizes dual nationality for Mexicans by birth, meaning those born in Mexico or born abroad to Mexican parents. U.S. citizens located in Mexico who are also Mexican nationals are considered Mexican by local authorities.

Travelers possessing both U.S. and Mexican nationalities must carry with them proof of their citizenship of both countries. Under

Mexican law, dual nationals entering or departing Mexico must identify themselves as Mexican.

Residence and Citizenship

FMT Tourist Permit

The first time you go to Mexico, you'll probably use a Tourist Permit, known as an FMT (Forma Migratoria Para Tourista). You will be given one on your flight into the country or at the border when you cross by car. FMTs can also be obtained for US$20 at any Mexican Consulate, although there is no reason to do this in advance.

Your FMT tourist card allows you to remain in Mexico up to six months (180 days) without working. Border officials do not automatically offer the 180-day visa, especially if you are traveling by plane. More commonly, you will receive a 90-day visa, so be sure to ask for the full 180 days. Your FMT is easily renewed, if you leave Mexico within the allotted 180-day period and re-enter the country. Some people never bother obtaining any other type of visa. However, if you are going to make Mexico your permanent home, and purchase property there, you should obtain a more permanent visa.

On an FMT, you can bring in a reasonable amount of personal effects. This varies according to the customs inspector. Yes, there is an official list, but it is seldom followed.

You can bring in personal communications equipment, cameras and a laptop computer, for instance. You may have to pay a duty (15% to 20% on a desktop PC, for instance) but if the items are for your use, you likely can convince the customs inspector that they are for personal use and not for resale, and you will be waved through without any duty owed. Resort airport destination custom officials usually do not bother obvious short-term tourists.

Mexico has by statute created a variety of residence, visa and immigration plans in an effort to attract foreign nationals for varying reasons. Some are aimed at wealthy U.S. persons across the border. Others are geared to attract immigrants who possess needed skills or those who can demonstrate that they are of independent means.

Visitante Rentista

One residence category is known, in Spanish, as Visitante Rentista. It is directed toward nationals from western countries such as the U.S., Canada, Australia, and those in Europe. Mexican Consulates in those countries will issue a visa valid for one year, renewable in Mexico, to those who can demonstrate proof of a minimum monthly income of US$1,156 for the head of family, plus US$578 for each dependant.

Inmigrante Rentista

The Inmigrante Rentista visa program works in much the same way, except that it is granted directly by the Mexican government and is valid for a period of five years. The basic requirement is proof of a monthly income of at least US$1,800 for head of household and US$900 for each dependent. This is the path to eventual Mexican citizenship.

Unlike the less strict Visitante Rentista program, the applicant must also submit a medical health certificate and a police clearance certificate. Also, unlike the lesser plan, after five years of residence in Inmigrante Rentista status, the visa holder qualifies for permanent residence and may eventually seek nationality and a passport.

Citizenship is generally available after five years official residence, but at least six months each year must be spent within the country.

Foreign nationals wishing to invest in Mexico are also eligible for special residence visas upon government approval of the proposed investment, which must be in an amount not less than 40,000 times the minimum daily wage, currently MXN$1,800,000

(US$138,000). The Investor visa applicant must also submit a health certificate and police clearance and other documentation.

Various other Mexican one-year temporary entry permits are available for students, technical personnel and business visitors. These do not grant official residence status and do not lead to a passport or permanent residence in five years.

Full details on all these programs can be obtained from any Mexican Consulate or the Embassy. See a list at: http://www.mex-online.com/consulate.htm

Real Estate Laws

Mexico is a civil law country, as compared to the U.S. and the Commonwealth of Nations that have a common law system.

Mexican laws and practices regarding purchase and rental of real estate, including time-shares, are markedly different from and far more complicated than those in the United States. U.S. citizens should be cautious of the inherent risks involved and of the absolute need to obtain authoritative information and legal guidance prior to any real estate investment.

Foreigners may be granted the right to own real property only under very specific conditions and, in some areas, such as along the coasts, foreign ownership is forbidden by law.

The use of competent local legal assistance for any real estate or business purchase is a must. A list of local attorneys can be obtained from the U.S. Embassy or nearest Consulate in Mexico.

Potential purchasers of real estate should obtain title insurance prior to investing in real property. Information on title insurance companies and investing in property, in general, can be obtained from the State Tourism Offices in Mexico.

Travel to Mexico

Travelers to and from Mexico will be required to have a passport or other secure, accepted documents such as U.S. Passport Card or citizenship documents (certified copy of a U.S. birth certificate, naturalization certificate, consular report of birth abroad, or a certificate of citizenship) to enter or re-enter the United States. A change from prior travel requirements, it means that all United States citizens re-entering the U.S. from countries within the Western Hemisphere must now possess U.S. valid passports or equivalent Passport Cards. See http://travel.state.gov/content/passports/english/passports/information/card.html

U.S. citizens traveling as tourists or entering Mexico by air must pay a fee to obtain a tourist card, also known as an FMT, available from Mexican Consulates, Mexican border crossing points, Mexican tourism offices, airports within the border zone, and most airlines serving Mexico. The fee for the tourist card is usually included in the price of a plane ticket for travelers arriving by air, and may be refundable in certain cases.

Tourist cards are only valid for three months for single entry up to 180 days, cost about US$20, and require proof of U.S. citizenship, photo ID, and proof of sufficient funds. A departure tax of varying amounts is paid at the airport when not included in the cost of the airline ticket and these can range from US$28 to US$45 per person, depending on the port of departure.

Minors require notarized consent from parents if traveling alone, with one parent or in someone else's custody. Mexican regulations limit the value of goods brought into Mexico by U.S. citizens arriving by air or sea to US$300 per person and by land to US$50 per person. Amounts exceeding the duty-free limit are subject to a 32.8% tax. Upon arrival in Mexico, business travelers must complete a form authorizing the conduct of business, but not employment, for a 30-day period.

Citizens of Canada, the U.K, Ireland, Australia, New Zealand, and much of Western Europe need no visa to enter Mexico as tourists for less than 180 days. Every visitor does need a valid passport and a tourist card.

A Mexican tourist card is not strictly necessary for anyone who only intends to visit the northern border towns and stay less than three days, though you still need a U.S. passport and photo ID.

For further information, contact the Embassy of Mexico at: 1911 Pennsylvania Avenue NW, Washington, D.C. 20006 Tel.: (202) 736-1000 Web: embamex.sre.gob.mx/eua/ or a Mexican Consulate in 19 U.S. cities.

U.S. citizens planning to work or live in Mexico should apply for the appropriate Mexican visa (FM-2 or -3). Tourists should avoid demonstrations and other activities that may be deemed political by Mexican authorities.

U.S. driver's licenses are valid in Mexico. Mexican auto insurance is required for all vehicles, including rental vehicles in Mexico. Travelers should obtain full-coverage insurance when renting vehicles in Mexico. Travelers arriving in their own vehicle can easily obtain Mexican insurance on the U.S. side of the land border and should do so.

If a traveler is involved in a vehicular accident resulting in damages or injuries to another party, the driver can be arrested and detained by Mexican authorities until a settlement is arranged with the injured party, and/or, depending upon the extent of damages or injuries to the other party, the traveler may face charges filed by the Mexican judicial authorities.

For information concerning Mexican driver's permits, vehicle inspection, road tax, or mandatory insurance, contact the Mexico Tourism Board: Web: http://www.visitmexico.com/en/ Viaducto

Miguel Alemán 105 Col. Escandón Mexico City, C.P. 11800. Tel.: +52 55 5278 4200

Health Care

In general, health care in Mexico is very good and in many places excellent. Most doctors and dentists receive at least part of their training in the U.S., and many U.S. doctors have trained in Mexico, notably in Guadalajara. Every mid-size to large city in Mexico has at least one first-rate hospital. A big plus is that the cost of health care in Mexico is generally one-half or less what you might pay in the United States. Prescription drugs manufactured in Mexico cost about 50% less than the same drugs in the U.S.

One additional type of insurance coverage you may want to consider is medical evacuation insurance. While many hospitals and clinics in Mexico's largest cities offer excellent, up-to-date care and facilities, you may feel better knowing you can be evacuated to your own physicians in the U.S. in the case of an emergency.

Illegal Immigration

Even a casual observer of current events knows that "illegal immigration" is a hot political topic in both Mexico and the United States.

In the U.S. attempts by the State of Arizona to defend its borders against a flood of illegal immigrants from Mexico and Central America has met with local majority approval, but also charges that such laws are bigoted and unjust.

These charges have been especially strong from Mexico, with former Mexican president, Felipe Calderon, accusing the State of Arizona of indulging in "racism." President Obama and his U.S. Department of Justice took the unprecedented political move of suing the State of Arizona in an attempt to prevent the state from enforcing U.S. immigration laws and questioning persons about their citizenship status.

The U.S. Department of Homeland Security reported in 2010 that the illegal immigrant population in 2009 was 10.8 million, 60% of them Mexicans. A more generally accepted figure is at least 12 million illegal immigrants in the U.S. in 2014. At this writing, the U.S. Congress continues to debate "immigration reform" legislation with sharp divisions making any new action doubtful.

In this context, it is worth considering some facts about strict Mexican immigration laws that have received scant attention in the U.S.

The Mexican constitution strictly defines the rights of citizens — and the denial of many fundamental rights to non-citizens, legal and illegal. Under the constitution, the Ley General de Población, or General Law on Population, spells out specifically the country's immigration policy.

It is an interesting law and one that should cause Americans to ask why their southern neighbor is pushing to weaken U.S. immigration laws and policies, when Mexico's own immigration restrictions until recently were among the toughest on the North American continent.

A felony is a crime punishable by more than one year in prison, and Mexican law made it a felony to be an illegal alien in Mexico.

Perhaps attempting to persuade its powerful neighbor to the North to do the same, in 2011 Mexico's immigration laws were revised. The law has now become more "humane" and immigrant friendly, its authors claim.

Among the current law's provisions:

1. Illegal entry into Mexican territory is decriminalized. It is no

longer a criminal offense to enter Mexico illegally; violators will merely be sent back to where they last came from. Previously, illegal immigration was a felony, punishable by up to two years in prison. Immigrants who were deported and attempted to re-enter Mexico could be imprisoned for 10 years. Visa violators could be sentenced to six-year terms. Mexicans who helped illegal immigrants were also subject to criminal prosecution.

2. Illegal migrants are not jailed. They are taken to a facility run by the Instituto Nacional de Migración (INM) where they are fed, clothed, given medical care and the ability to contact their families in their country of origin.

3. Illegal migrants have the right to seek political asylum or refuge in Mexico and have a right to a hearing before a judge.

4. Local police, the military, customs and even the Policia Federal do not have the authority to question any foreigner's migratory status. They do not have authority to arrest or detain any person suspected of being in the country illegally. Only officials from the INM can do this.

5. Illegal migrants can be given the opportunity to regularize their status and obtain a work/residence permit.

6. Controls are loosened for citizens/nationals of neighboring Belize, who find employment in certain Mexican states (i.e. Quintana Roo, where Cancun is located) to ease the process of a work/residence permit.

The 2011, law expedites the permanent resident application process for retirees and other foreigners. For granting permanent residence, the law uses a point system based on factors such as level of education, employment experience, and scientific and technological knowledge.

Those of us who have had first-hand experience with bribe-seeking Mexican police must wonder whether immigration enforcement is quite as gentle as these provisions suggest.

Mexican law requires legal foreign visitors and immigrants in the country to have the means to sustain themselves economically; that they are not burdens on society but are of economic and social benefit to society. They must be of good character and have no criminal records and must be contributors to the general well-being of the nation.

The law also ensures that immigration authorities have a record of each foreign visitor and that foreign visitors do not violate their visa status. Foreign visitors are banned from interfering in the country's internal politics; those who enter under false pretenses are imprisoned or deported. Foreign visitors violating the terms of their entry are imprisoned or deported and those who aid in illegal immigration can be sent to prison.

Contacts

Embassy of Mexico
1911 Pennsylvania Avenue NW
Washington, DC 20006
Tel.: (202) 728-1600.
Email: http://embamex.sre.gob.mx/eua/index.php/en/contact-us
Web: embamex.sre.gob.mx/eua/

Consular Office
2827 16th Street NW
Washington, DC 20009
Tel.: (202) 736-1000

United States Embassy
Paseo de la Reforma 305
Colonia Cuauhtemoc, 06500 Mexico, DF

From Mexico:
Tel.: (01-55) 5080-2000

From the U.S.
Tel.: 011-52-55-5080-2000
General email: Emb.eua.mex@state.gov
Email for US citizens: acsmexicocity@state.gov
Web: http://mexico.usembassy.gov/

There are nine official U.S. consulates and 10 consulate agents in Mexican cities including resorts. See http://travel.state.gov/content/passports/english/country/mexico.html

United States of America

Government:	Republic
Capital:	Washington, District of Columbia
National Day:	Independence Day: 4 July (1776)
Population:	318,892,103 (July 2014 est.)
Total Area:	3,718,711 sq. miles / 9,631,417 sq. kilometers (50 states + Washington, D.C.; excludes territories)
Languages:	English 82.1%, Spanish 10.7%, other Indo-European 3.8%, Asian and Pacific island 2.7%, other 0.7% (2000 census). US has no official national language; English has official status in 28 of the 50 states; Hawaiian is an official language in Hawaii.
Ethnic groups:	White 79.96%, Hispanic 15.1%, black 12.85%, Asian 4.43%, Amerindian and Alaska native 0.97%, native Hawaiian and other Pacific islander 0.18%, two or more races 1.61% (2007 estimate). The US Census Bureau considers as "Hispanic" persons in the U.S. of Spanish/Hispanic/Latino origin including Mexican, Cuban, Puerto Rican, Dominican Republic, Spanish, and Central or South American origin who may be of any race or ethnic group (white, black, Asian).
Religion:	Protestant 51.3%, Roman Catholic 23.9%, Mormon 1.7%, other Christian 1.6%, Jewish 1.7%, Buddhist 0.7%, Muslim 0.6%, other or unspecified 2.5%, unaffiliated 12.1%, none 4% (2007 est.)
Life expectancy:	79.56 years
Currency:	U.S. dollar (USD)
GDP:	US$16.72 trillion (2013 est.)
GDP per capita:	US$52,800 (2013 est.)

> *Passport highlights: U.S. immigration law is arguably the most complex in the world, with over 50 different types of non-immigrant visas and a number of ways of gaining coveted permanent residence (the "Green Card"). There is a visa program for investors willing to invest US$1 million to create at least ten new jobs. In certain rural areas with high unemployment, the investment level can be as little as US$500,000. It is frequently better to obtain one of the non-immigrant visas and later apply for an adjustment of status to "lawful permanent residence."*
>
> *Naturalization is available after five years of residence in the U.S.*

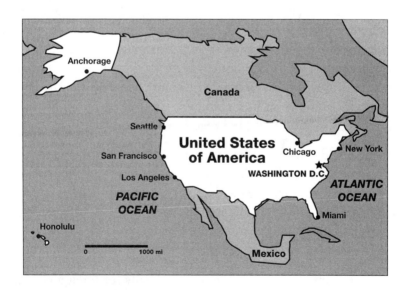

World's Most Costly Passport

The United States is indeed a "nation of immigrants," as the late U.S. President Franklin D. Roosevelt once observed.

The U.S. has been the goal of millions of immigrants for nearly 250 years. Originally 13 British colonies, its founding dates to 1620 when immigrant "Pilgrims," escaping religious oppression in England, landed on Plymouth Rock in what was to become the Massachusetts Bay Colony.

As a country of every race and language, the U.S. continues to be a desired destination for the homeless, oppressed and persecuted as well as for successful individuals who want to invest or live in this "bastion of capitalism."

The immigrant's theory has always been that, in America, anyone with ambition, drive, and creativity can become wealthy. The U.S. is said to be the most economically free country in the world and, with fewer restrictions on free enterprise it's an easy place for an entrepreneur to succeed. The economy functions best with the least amount of government control, and during the presidency of Ronald Reagan (1981-89), privatization and deregulation became government policy. With the election of President Obama in 2008, those policies are being reversed as government intervenes in many areas of the economy in what critics have denounced as socialism and even fascism.

Wages and prices are free of most controls. Until the global recession beginning in 2008, in most cases, supply and demand and free market forces operated with relative freedom. In 2009 to 2010 banking, finance, auto manufacturing and other areas that received trillions of dollars in taxpayer bailout funds were essentially taking orders from the federal government.

U.S. tax laws are highly complex, especially for foreign citizens (known as "resident aliens") living full or part-time in the U.S. There are special profitable tax breaks denied by law to U.S. citizens, but freely given to foreign citizens who invest in the U.S., but to qualify, they cannot live in the United States. They must live elsewhere. Some legal domestic tax shelters exist, but a good lawyer or accountant is needed to understand how they work. A wealthy American without careful tax planning can pay half or more of his/her income in federal and state income and other taxes. It is this group on which President Obama has made clear he wants to impose new and higher taxes.

As still the leading world power, no one has to be told that the U.S. is diplomatically and militarily active worldwide maintaining foreign aid programs and waging war or conducting "military actions" and lethal drone strikes in far-flung places such as Iraq, Afghanistan and Libya. Internal opposition to these wars and their costs has grown.

Even though the election of President Obama would change foreign attitudes toward America, U.S. policies are now even more unpopular abroad, so if you are traveling on a U.S. passport, you may encounter hostility, and even violence in some places.

American laws classify more acts as criminal than the statutes of anywhere else in the world. The U.S. now has the highest percentage of its population in prison, surpassing even South Africa under apartheid and the former Soviet Union at its oppressive zenith. Two-thirds of these prisoners are serving drug-related sentences. This horrifying reality, which most Americans never seem to consider, dramatically conflicts with the personal freedom and liberty upon which the country was founded.

Economically, things are still comparatively better in the U.S. than in most other countries, but the global recession in 2008 hurt America as well as the world.

This world economic downturn, the sub-prime mortgage crisis, investment bank failures, falling home prices, and tight credit pushed the United States into a recession by mid-2008 and by 2011 unemployment reached nearly 10%.

The U.S. standard of living is still near the top per capita and the possibility of making your fortune still exists, but U.S. GDP growth slipped in 2009 into negative territory and by 2011 was still anemic. By 2014, full recovery still had not occurred, making this period the longest recovery in U.S. history.

Nevertheless, the U.S. remains attractive to many foreign-born people as a possible part-time residence, a place of financial opportunity and perhaps even citizenship, although for many that would mean paying much higher taxes.

The U.S. has the most powerful, diverse and technologically advanced economy in the world, with an estimated 2013 per capita income of US$52,800.

Until recently, private individuals and business firms made most of the decisions in this market-oriented economy. The government buys needed goods and services predominantly in the private marketplace. U.S. firms are at or near the forefront in technologic advances, especially in computers, medical, aerospace, and military equipment, although that advantage has narrowed in recent years.

U.S. business firms enjoy considerably greater flexibility than their counterparts in Western Europe and Japan in decisions to expand capital plants, lay off surplus workers and develop new products. At the same time, they face higher barriers to entry in their rivals' home markets than their rivals face in coming to U.S. markets. They also labor under the second highest corporate tax rate in the world at 35%.

Until the 2008 to 2011 recession, prior years witnessed solid increases in real output, low inflation and an unemployment rate below 5%. Long-term problems now include shoring up the banking and financial sectors, inadequate investment in economic infrastructure, curbing rapidly rising medical costs of an aging population, sizable trade deficits, a huge national budget deficit, a US$17 trillion dollar national debt, income inequality and stagnation of family income in the lower economic groups.

Immigration: Continuing Debate

As the Cato Institute notes "… one of King George III's many 'injuries and usurpations' listed in the Declaration of Independence was 'obstructing the Laws for Naturalization of Foreigners' and 'refusing to pass others to encourage their migration.'"

The first U.S. Congress adopted the Naturalization Act of 1790 which contained no restrictions on immigration. That law restricted citizenship to white residents, excluding indentured servants, slaves, and former slaves, but everyone had the right to come the new United States and work.

Article I, Section 8, Clause 4 of the United States Constitution expressly gives the United States Congress the power to establish a uniform rule of naturalization. Subsequent laws such as the Immigration and Naturalization Act set forth the legal requirements for the acquiring and terminating U.S. citizenship.

The requirements became more explicit in 1868 with the ratification of the Fourteenth Amendment to the Constitution. Amendment XIV, Section 1, Clause 1 states: "All persons born or naturalized in the United States, and subject to the jurisdiction thereof, are citizens of the United States and of the State wherein they reside."

This citizenship clause (also known as the naturalization clause) provides a broad definition of citizenship and its adoption represented a reversal by Congress of that portion of the *Dred Scott v. Sanford* (1857) decision in which a majority of the U.S. Supreme Court declared that African Americans were not citizens but were property and therefore they could not become

U.S. citizens nor could they enjoy the privileges and immunities of citizenship.

The Civil Rights Act of 1866 already had granted U.S. citizenship to all people born in the United States; the framers of the Fourteenth Amendment enshrined this principle in the Constitution in order to stop the Supreme Court from ruling the 1866 law unconstitutional for want of congressional authority to pass such a law, or a future Congress from altering it by a bare majority vote. Exercising their legislative powers during more than two centuries, the Congress has many times addressed immigration issues, almost always with much national debate and controversy.

In 1898 the Supreme Court ruled, in the case of *United States v. Wong Kim Ark*, that all children of immigrants born under U.S. jurisdiction were citizens regardless of race. The Page Act in 1875 barred the immigration of contracted laborers, prostitutes, and former convicts in their country of origin. The 1882 Chinese Exclusion Act halted Chinese immigration and an agreement with Japan halted Japanese immigration in 1907.

Thousands of immigrants from Eastern and Southern Europe came to America in the early 20th century, prompting wide spread support for numerical quotas on immigrants and enactment of the Emergency Quota Act of 1921, which imposed numerical limits for the first time.

As of 2014, President Obama and a politically divided U.S. Congress have made no progress toward immigration reforms that would give legal status to the estimated 12 million illegal immigrants. Past efforts at reform also have failed dismally.

The United States receives more immigrants than any other country. But its system for dealing with them is a model of dysfunction, with over 12 million illegally present in 2014, up 48%

since 2000. In the last century, U.S. immigration restrictions have created a complicated system that makes legal immigration very difficult for most would-be immigrants.

Deportation Policy

In 2011, the Obama administration announced that it was suspending deportation proceedings against many illegal immigrants, especially young people, who they decide pose no threat to national security or public safety.

The claim was that this would help thousands of illegal immigrants who came to the United States as young children, graduated from high school and want to go on to college or serve in the armed forces. It also helped Obama's 2012 re-election campaign with Hispanic American voters.

Officials said that they were not granting relief to a whole class of people, but would review cases one by one, using new standards meant to distinguish low- and high-priority cases. They said they would exercise "prosecutorial discretion" to focus enforcement efforts on cases involving criminals and those who have flagrantly violated immigration laws.

The decision would, through administrative action, help many intended young illegal immigrant beneficiaries of legislation, the so-called "Dream Act," that has failed to pass in Congress for a decade.

This more lenient policy was in sharp contrast with previous tough Obama deportation policies, as well as those since. The U.S. Immigration and Customs Enforcement (ICE) recorded a record number of deportations of illegal immigrants in recent years according to an analysis of government statistics, with the spike driven primarily by increased deportations of people stopped for drunk driving and other traffic violations.

A 2014 New York Times analysis of internal government records showed that since President Obama took office, two-thirds of the nearly two million deportation cases involve people who had committed minor infractions, including traffic violations, or had no criminal record at all. Twenty percent, or about 394,000, of the cases involved people convicted of serious crimes, including drug-related offenses, the records show.

Those cases more than quadrupled from 43,000 during the last five years of President George W. Bush's administration to 193,000 during the five years President Obama has been in office. In that same period, removals related to convictions for entering or re-entering the country illegally tripled under President Obama to more than 188,000.

Recently, the Obama administration announced consideration of policies that could shield from deportation tens of thousands of immigrants now removed each year solely because they committed repeat immigration violations, such as re-entering the country illegally after having been deported, failing to comply with a deportation order or missing an immigration court date.

Such a policy would fall short of the sweeping changes sought by activists. They want Obama to expand the two-year-old program that grants work permits to certain immigrants brought here illegally as children to include other groups, such as all parents of any children born in the U.S.

Resident Aliens

Legal U.S. "resident aliens," foreign citizens legally in residence in the U.S., may apply for citizenship after five years of residence.

During this time, the U.S. person is subject to all applicable taxes paid by U.S. citizens. Investigation of citizenship applications used to be lax. A decade ago, tens of thousands of immigrants were admitted with few background checks, many with criminal records, but stricter checks are now in place.

Since the terror attacks of September 11, 2001, ("9/11") immigration laws are far more strictly enforced. There are severe penalties for misrepresentation, use of fake IDs and stolen Social Security numbers, with the penalties including deportation, and possible incarceration prior to being deported.

Under U.S. law, certain groups have been excluded in the past from entering the country as "undesirables, including homosexuals, drug users, HIV-infected persons, unpopular political activists as well as controversial artists, musicians, writers, and scholars. Tax expatriates (ex-U.S. citizens who surrender citizenship to avoid taxes) were added to this ignominious list in 1997 and in 2008 future ex-U.S. persons were also subjected to an onerous exit tax.

The U.S. Citizenship and Immigration Service (USCIS), formerly the U.S. Immigration and Naturalization Service (INS), is now a bureau of the U.S. Department of Homeland Security. It has the dubious honor of being notoriously arbitrary, offensive and high-handed in its actions. It is also one of the most inefficient and poorly run agencies, according to official reports from the U.S. General Accounting Office. There was serious discussion of abolishing the agency in 2002, but it was folded into the newly created Homeland Security instead.

Immigration regulations are subject to arbitrary interpretations by ill-trained hearing officers and a decision may depend on prejudices of the bureaucrat involved. Corruption on the part of immigration officials is not unknown, but historically, it is the exception and not the rule.

A prospective new U.S. citizen is well advised to hire an American attorney who specializes in immigration matters. The cost can be US$20,000 or more. Beware of "expert" immigration lawyers who make big promises, demand advance fees, then fail to produce.

Not having a lawyer can prejudice your case, so check references and get a good one. Aliens do not have the same or as many rights as U.S. citizens and may not have a right to judicial review of a negative USCIS administrative decision.

For official U.S. State Department web links concerning citizenship, see http://www.uscis.gov/us-citizenship

Immigration Process

U.S. citizenship may be acquired by:

1. Birth within the United States or its territories;

2. Birth outside the U.S. to one or both U.S. parents;

3. The formal naturalization process.

After five years of legal residence, it is possible for qualified persons to apply for and acquire U.S. citizenship. Because of extreme complexity of the law, each immigration case requires individual assessment to find the best legal path and especially to plan for all possible tax implications in advance.

U.S. immigration law does offer distinct possibilities for foreign persons willing to invest in America, and using this route may produce relatively quick permanent resident status.

Nevertheless, when the exact potential impact of U.S. taxes is calculated, "green card" status may be worth avoiding for an individual foreigner.

Military Enlistees Program

It is worth noting that non-U.S. citizens and permanent residents (green card holders) now are permitted to enlist in the American military. Under a 2009 program intended to increase the number of highly skilled soldiers, the American military now allows some temporary immigrants to enlist.

The program is open to foreigners who have lived legally in the U.S. for at least two years on temporary visas, including high-skilled employment visas and student visas. As an enticement, the government offers an expedited path to citizenship and will waive naturalization fees.

The naturalization process for most foreigners on temporary visas can often take more than a decade. But people in the new program will be able to become citizens within six months. To maintain their citizenship, the military enlistees must honorably complete their service, which ranges from two to four years of active duty, plus reserve duty, depending on their specialty.

U.S. Tax Status

For tax purposes, the Internal Revenue Code defines a "U.S. person" as any individual who is a U.S. citizen, a U.S. resident alien deemed to be a permanent resident or a U.S. domiciled corporation, partnership, estate, or trust.

Unlike almost every other country the U.S. imposes taxes on all worldwide income of its citizens and of those non-citizens with permanent U.S. resident ("green card") status, regardless of where they actually live in the world. (Most countries have a much fairer "territorial" tax system that exempts their citizens from some or all taxes if they live abroad.)

U.S. Internal Revenue Code (IRC) Sec. 61 states: "Except as otherwise provided ... gross income means all income from whatever source derived." The IRS and courts interpret this to include income of every nature and wherever it may be earned in the world, including offshore income.

For a wealthy foreign national, a so-called "high net worth individual" (HNWI), obtaining U.S. permanent resident status definitely may not be the best possible step because of U.S. taxes, especially income taxes.

Many beneficial investment and tax advantages under U.S. law can be obtained by a foreign national who does not live in the U.S. full-time, thus, he/she has no need for a green card.

There is an existing entry program for foreign investors willing to commit US$1 million to create at least 10 new jobs. In certain rural areas or those with high unemployment, the investment level can be as little as US$500,000.

This program has been accused of being abused and has been investigated for fraud and USCIS corruption. Until recently this program was not widely used.

The holder of a green card is entitled to work and reside in the United States on a permanent basis. However, green card status may be better avoided because, once granted, the U.S. views the cardholder as a "U.S. person" for taxation purposes.

A green card is a strong indication of having acquired a U.S. domicile. That also means being subjected to U.S. estate and gift taxes on all worldwide income. Estate taxes were raised in 2013, but not as much as President Obama wanted. He wanted to tax estates valued at more than US$3.5 million at 45%, higher than the 2012 level of 35% on estates over US$5 million. The final law raised the tax to 40%, but kept the exemption at US$5 million, (US$10 million for married couples) indexed for inflation. State death taxes must also be added to the above.

Punitive U.S. Expatriate "Exit Tax"

Persons considering acquiring U.S. citizenship should know that a person that remains a U.S. resident alien for eight years or more, and then leaves the U.S. may be subject to punitive U.S. tax expatriation laws at the time of departure. These punitive tax penalties are imposed based on a net worth formula without regard to a determination that the long-term residence was ended to avoid U.S. taxes. See http://www.irs.gov/Individuals/International-Taxpayers/Expatriation-Tax

U.S. expatriation tax rules have been toughened considerably. The anti-expat rules are aimed at U.S. persons who relinquish their U.S. status for tax avoidance purposes. This includes both U.S. citizens as well as permanent resident aliens who have lived in the U.S. for eight of the 15 immediately preceding tax years.

Under a 2008 law, a person who is a "covered individual" falls within the clutches of the expatriation provisions if, on the date of expatriation or termination of U.S. residence, (1) the individual's average annual net U.S. income tax liability for the five-year period preceding that date was US$155,000 or more (adjusted for inflation); or, (2) the individual's net worth as of that date is US$2 million or more; or (3) the individual fails to certify under penalties of perjury that he or she has complied with all U.S. federal tax obligations for the preceding five years.

Of course, if you do not now fit within the above definitions (really a "means test" of sorts), this law may offer an opportunity to escape U.S. taxes now, before you become more prosperous in the future.

But under the law "covered individuals" are taxed enormously under IR Code section 877A. This tax is imposed on all assets as if the person's worldwide assets had been sold for their fair market value on the day before expatriation or residence termination. The Act allows — in 2014 — an exclusion for only the first US$663,000 of net gain (as adjusted for inflation annually).

This phantom gain will presumably be taxed as ordinary income (at 2014 rates as high as 39.6% or more) or as capital gains (at either a 15%, 25%, or 28% rate), under whatever the then current tax law may be. In 2014 the CGT was 15%. In addition, any assets held by any trust or portion of a trust that the covered individual was treated as owning for U.S. income tax purposes (i.e., a grantor trust) are also subject to this tax.

Undoubtedly, many people caught by this tax would have to sell their assets to pay the tax, possibly leaving little or nothing.

Still More Taxes

Equally as bad, the stay-at-home U.S. relatives of wealthy former American citizens or resident aliens could find themselves owing tax if they receive gifts of money or property from their expatriate offshore relatives.

The 2008 "exit tax" law also imposes an additional tax of potentially far-reaching scope: gifts and bequests to U.S. persons from covered individuals (beyond the annual gift tax exclusion of US$14,000 per person) are now subject to a U.S. "transfer tax" imposed on the U.S. transferee at the highest federal transfer tax rates then in effect (39.6% in 2014).

Talk about highway robbery! Not only is wealth taxed away from a generous expatriate who gives a gift, the American recipient of the gift is punished with a 35% tax on that gift.

So think very carefully about becoming a U.S. resident alien or citizen, because once you come within those categories, the only way out is expatriation and the possibility of a major tax bill when you leave.

Immigration Law Complexities

In comparison to the contentious immigration reform debate since President Obama's election in 2008, prior to that date there were dramatic reforms in national immigration laws. Few of these changes affected non-immigrant visitors or travelers, but if they are a green card holder, the changes are major. However, for those seeking residence and caught on long U.S. waiting lists, new possibilities and priorities are available.

Some great opportunities now exist if you want a "non-immigrant" visa in order to do business in the U.S., but you don't want to become a U.S. citizen.

The period spent in the U.S. as a holder of an immigrant visa — a resident alien with a green card — counts toward the five-year requirement for citizenship. Time spent in the U.S. on a non-immigrant visa does not count.

A green card holder must pay U.S. taxes on all worldwide income, but a non-immigrant visa holder may avoid most U.S. taxes, even on some income earned within the U.S. In most categories of non-immigrant visas, the length of stay is at the discretion of the reviewing immigration officer at the place of entry. The applicant must not intend to abandon his home country residence, nor should the person's foreign passport have an expiration date that occurs while they will be in the United States.

A visa applicant must be certifiably free from mental or physical disability, alcoholism or drug addiction. They must be literate and not associated with an organization seeking to overthrow the government of the United States.

Congress now caps visas for foreign workers, a clunky system that does not match supply too precisely with demand. Business has long bemoaned the limits on skilled immigrants in particular, who have founded 52% of all Silicon Valley start-ups.

The U.S. government requires most foreigners to obtain a travel visa if they wish to travel to America, purportedly to prevent unauthorized immigrants, terrorists, and other foreign-originated security threats from coming into the country disguised as tourists. But a 2013 report by the Cato Institute argued that, by making it unnecessarily costly and difficult for foreigners to visit the country, the United States is impeding economic growth that would occur under a more sensible visa policy.

Non-Immigrant Visa Categories

Type A-1, -2, -3: Diplomats, accredited foreign officials, and their immediate families.

Type B-1: Business visitors for less than a three-month stay, but can be extended up to one year.

Type B-2: Visitors for pleasure. Tourists are admitted for six months, may not take jobs and must leave at the end of their stay. A six-month extension is routinely granted upon filing a written request giving reasons.

Type C-1, -2, -3: Transit visas for immediate and continuous transit through the U.S., including to the United Nations headquarters.

Type D: For the crew of ships and aircraft, who will leave on another ship or aircraft after a short stay.

Type E-1, -2: Business persons and investors who will manage or work in a business with substantial trade between the U.S. and their foreign country. This visa class is permitted under bilateral U.S. trade treaties.

A spouse and unmarried children under 21 also are entitled to this visa and to work in the U.S. The E-1 "treaty trader visa is for an employee of a business in which there is "substantial trade" between the U.S. and the foreign national's home country, or for a U.S. business in which there has been substantial investment (US$50,000 or more) by a businessman from that country.

These are the only nonimmigrant visas that allow for indefinite extensions. This usually means at least 50% of the trade must be between the U.S. company and the foreign nation with which there is a relevant international trade agreement with the U.S.

Type F-1, -2: A student visa, issued for the length of a recognized course of study, with a spouse and unmarried children. Under limited circumstances, the visa holder may be employed, usually by the educational institution attended. The student must have been accepted by an educational institution and show availability of funds to cover the educational costs.

To obtain a student visa, your place of study has to be confirmed, approved in advance, and no change of school is allowed without USCIS approval. You are only permitted employment if it is considered necessary training in the chosen career field; such as a medical student completing a required hospital internship. F-1 visa holders are also allowed to work on campus without permission from the USCIS. Your spouse or children may not hold jobs.

Type G-1, -2, -3, -4, -5: Another diplomatic visa for a "designated principal resident representative" of a recognized foreign government or international organization, including staff.

Type H-1A, -1B, -2A, -2B, -3, -4: The principal visas available for those wishing to work in the U.S. with certain desirable skills such as nurses, specialty occupations, temporary agricultural worker, temporary non-agricultural workers, trainees, and their families.

Politics and H-1B Visas

The H-1B visa for a "specialty occupation as a "specialist knowledge worker" usually is granted to a graduate or graduate equivalent, and allows entry for up to six years to work for a U.S. company. The question of "graduate equivalent" is often misunderstood and many foreign non-graduates with proper documentation may be able to enter the U.S. on this basis.

However, H-1B visas have long been an internal U.S. political issue, with labor unions claiming Americans should be hired over foreigners.

Until recently private individuals and business firms made most of the decisions in this market-oriented economy. Those who advocate free trade say it is in the nation's interest to hire highly skilled foreigners who are educated in the U.S. rather than have foreign companies benefit from their American training.

The U.S. demand for professionally trained nurses and physical therapists is evidenced by a special H-1A visa for health care personnel. This requires a license (or equivalent) to practice and certification that the applicant is fully qualified to engage in the intended employment.

HB-1 visas are highly prized and proposals have been made to increase available slots. In 2014 the USCIS received about 172,500 H-1B petitions, including petitions filed for the advanced degree exemption. This was many more than the 65,000 general-category cap and 20,000 cap under the advanced degree exemption. Winners are determined by a computer-generated random selection process, or lottery, to select enough petitions.

The H-2B visa allows entry for both skilled and unskilled workers. The main requirement is for a "labor certification" from the prospective employer stating there are no unemployed but qualified U.S. citizens or permanent residents who can fill the vacancy. Holders of this visa usually cannot apply for permanent residence.

The H-3 visa is for training in the U.S. of a type to augment present experience and qualifications for future foreign employment, especially if this is for a U.S. employer. The H-2A visa is for agricultural workers.

Type I: For accredited representatives of foreign newspapers and broadcasting organizations.

Type J-1, -2: For a student or academic on a short-term educational exchange or training program and family. This visa is used in a program to bring exchange visitors to the U.S. to acquire skills that can be used in their home country.

The United States Information Agency designates which programs are available. For those who want to work in the U.S. for a short period, this is usually the easiest visa to obtain.

Type K-1, -2: For a person engaged to be married to a U.S. citizen or resident alien who seeks entry solely to marry. Minor children may also qualify for entry under this category. The marriage must occur within 90 days of arrival and the couple must show they met within the last two years. After marriage, the foreign party may apply for "conditional permanent residence" in the U.S., which is valid for two years. Thereafter, the person may apply for permanent residence based on the marriage. Marriage to a U.S. citizen does not guarantee permanent residence status and marriages of this type are investigated with suspicion by the USCIS.

If a visa is granted, the residence period for the spouse applying for U.S. nationality is reduced from five to three years.

Type L: A visa for personnel transferred to the U.S. by an international company for five to seven years. If a U.S. company has an affiliate or subsidiary in either country, the L-1 "intra-company transferee visa" is used, mainly for a manager, executive or an employee with specialized knowledge.

It does not allow a spouse or children to work without first obtaining visas of their own. Under some circumstances, owners, stockholders or partners in an international company may be able to qualify for this visa.

Type M-1, -2: An alien coming to the U.S. for vocational study at an educational institution approved by the USCIS. Immediate family members may also qualify.

Type N: For a former employee of an international organization who has resided in the U.S. for long periods of time in the G-4 non-immigrant category. (Granted only in very special situations.)

Type O-1, -2: For persons with extraordinary personal abilities in the sciences, arts, education, business, or athletics, together with their family.

Type P-1, -2, -3: For entertainers or athletes who cannot qualify under the extraordinary ability standard for the O category, but who are part of a group or team.

Type Q: Persons coming to the U.S. for participation in an international cultural exchange program designated by the U.S. Attorney General.

Type R-1, -2: A temporary visit by a religious worker, including family.

Visas other than C, D or K categories may be extended if you apply to stay before the visa expires. When you make a visa application, you will be told of any additional documents needed, usually proof of intent to return to your home country, such as proof of property ownership. You can apply for Type B visas by letter or at a U.S. Embassy or Consulate. Visa Types A, G, H-2, and H-3, as well as most I and L visas, are applied for by a U.S. employer.

With H-1 visas, you or your employer must prove your case. If you go to the U.S. on an L visa and want to change jobs or are self-employed, and not eligible for an E visa, you may need an immigrant visa.

Admission to the U.S. for non-immigrants chiefly depends on the decision of the immigration officer at the place of entry. If you have a return ticket for transportation back to your home country and sufficient assets — though you need not have an American bank account — a stay for three or six months is usually automatic.

The U.S., unlike many other countries, allows you to change visa status after entering. This permits you to change your non-immigrant visa when you have established contacts to obtain an immigrant visa. If you want to immigrate and do not qualify immediately for an immigrant visa, a brief stay in the U.S. on a non-immigrant visa, say as a student enrolled in a one-year program, gives you "a foot in the door."

A major problem with the USCIS visa programs is the inordinate time it requires to obtain any type of visa, even those for visitors or tourists.

As part of the "war on terror," since September 11, 2001, ("9/11") the government has used immigration, passport and visa laws to exclude anyone who might be suspect in the slightest degree. Since that time, the wait for a visa of any kind can require many months and repeated visits to a U.S. embassy or consulate abroad. These delays have become so onerous that many foreign governments have lodged official protests with the U.S. State Department, so far to no avail.

Visa Waiver Program

Over 10 million people have visited the U.S. using the "Visa Waiver Program" (VWP), a program for visitors from countries that allow reciprocal visa free visits by Americans. This program grants admission to the U.S. for up to 90 days as a B-1 or B-2 status visitor. Usually no extensions of stay are permitted.

To use the VWP, the applicant must: 1) complete U.S. CIS Form I-94W, provided by the airline on which you arrive; 2) produce a home nation, machine-readable passport valid for at least six months beyond the end of the U.S. visit; 3) possess a round-trip ticket; and 4) prove means of financial support while in the U.S.

The 37 countries currently (in 2014) designated as VWP countries are: Andorra, Australia, Austria, Belgium, Brunei, Chile, Czech Republic, Denmark, Estonia, Finland, France, Germany, Hungary, Iceland, Ireland, Italy, Japan, Latvia, Liechtenstein, Lithuania, Luxembourg, Malta, Monaco, the Netherlands, New Zealand, Norway, Portugal, Republic of Korea, San Marino, Singapore, Slovak Republic, Slovenia, Spain, Sweden, Switzerland, Taiwan and the United Kingdom.

Other countries may be added in the future.

As a VWP visitor, you are not allowed to change status to another non-immigrant classification without first leaving the U.S. If you are using the waiver program and wish to apply for a green card, you must do so only at a U.S. Embassy or Consulate abroad. Any evidence that you intend to seek employment, such as resumes or letters of recommendation, should be sent ahead and not brought with you personally, lest they create the wrong impression if your papers are searched upon entry.

The Visa Waiver Program is really meant as a tourist option, so avoid it if you can. If you are from a qualifying VWP country, you can just as well get a standard visitor's visa, with much more flexibility. The VWP is useful for a short holiday visit of 90 days or less and precludes extensions or changes that might be necessary.

ESTA Registration Mandatory

All Visa Waiver Program (VWP) travelers are required to pay a fee and obtain travel authorization through the Electronic System for Travel Authorization (ESTA) prior to boarding a carrier to travel by air or sea to the United States. (Land ports from Canada and Mexico are exempt.)

Citizens of countries in the U.S. Visa Waiver Program (VMP) do not need a visa for short (three month's) visit but they must be ready upon entry to the U.S. to answer a series of electronic questions such as: "Do you have a communicable disease; physical or mental disorder; or are you a drug abuser or addict?"

The entry questionnaire is a required part of the ESTA system and answers determine whether a foreign traveler is admitted and given permission to visit the U.S. One question asks arriving visitors whether they ever have been arrested or convicted of a violation related to a controlled substance or an offense involving "moral turpitude," a broad legal term including fraud, larceny and "the intent to harm persons or things."

The New York Times summed up the current situation: "As immigration policies tighten and the security and technology to enforce them increase, travelers can find themselves caught in a web of suspicion that prevents them from visiting some countries. A past arrest or conviction, even a public admission of illegal activity, can be grounds for inadmissibility. So can political activism or the impression that a traveler is visiting on business without obtaining a work visa. While governments have long aspired to be more vigilant about their borders, databases and the digital tracks people leave have made it easier for agents to investigate and deny entry to some travelers."

The U.S. Customs and Border Protection (CPB) agency says that having ESTA approval or a visa does not guarantee admission to the United States and that border officers make final admissibility decisions on the spot. To date, a daily average of nearly 400 people were refused entry. Agents at entry ports must enforce immigration and customs laws, as well as more than 400 laws for other agencies, so mistakes are likely.

ESTA is yet another automated security system used to verify the eligibility of visitors to travel to the U.S. under the VWP. VWP allows citizens and nationals of selected countries, including Australia, Japan, Singapore and most Western European countries, to travel to the U.S. for business or tourism for a period of up to 90 days without the need for a visa.

ESTA authorizations generally are valid for two years and enable multiple entries into the U.S. While an ESTA authorization is not a guarantee of admission to the U.S., it serves to prevent some VWP applicants from being refused admission and returned to their home country following inspection by U.S. Customs and Border Patrol (CBP) after arriving in the U.S. on an international flight. ESTA is accessible online at https://esta.cbp.dhs.gov

CBP strongly recommends that VWP travelers apply for authorization at least three days prior to departing for the U.S. If an application for travel authorization is denied, the VWP traveler will be required to apply for a visa at a U.S. Embassy or Consulate before traveling to the U.S. Visitors who have a visa in their passport such as a B-1 or B-2; other nonimmigrant visa holders such as F-1 students or H, L, and O temporary workers, as well as permanent residents (green card holders) do not have to obtain prior ESTA authorization.

Machine-Readable Passport Requirements

The U.S. Department of Homeland Security requires that all persons traveling under the auspices of the Visa Waiver Program

(VWP) must present a machine-readable passport (MRP) to travel to the United States without a visa.

Machine-readable passports include two optical characters, typeface lines at the bottom of the biographic page of the passport that, when read, deters fraud and helps confirm the passport holder's identity quickly.

VWP travelers who possess an older non-machine readable passport may also apply for a non-immigrant visa at a U.S. Embassy or Consulate abroad if seeking entry for business or tourist visits to the United States. Information on the Visa Waiver Program and how to apply for a U.S. visa is available at http://www.travel.state. gov/content/visas/english.html

The machine-readable passport requirements do not affect the separate deadline requiring VWP country passports issued on or after October 26, 2005, to contain biometrics in order to be used for visa-free travel to the United States.

Note: U.S. immigration officials at entry points may now fingerprint and photograph all arriving foreigners traveling to the U.S. The reason given is to keep track of visitors, particularly those who overstay their allotted visa time limits. This is justified as one of many anti-terrorism measures.

US-VISIT Program

US-VISIT is an electronic check-in system for foreign travelers to the United States, including many who have status that allows them to remain in the U.S.

Upon arrival, travelers subject to this system are fingerprinted and photographed, and their travel documents are scanned. Each traveler's information is checked against immigration and law enforcement databases to determine whether the individual is eligible to enter the U.S. or should be prohibited from entering because of risks such as past visa or criminal violations or national security concerns.

US-VISIT is operational at 115 U.S. airports, 15 seaports, 154 land border ports of entry, and at selected pre-flight inspection stations abroad. It applies to groups of foreign nationals who are required to go through finger scans, photographs or other biometric data upon entry to the United States through the US-VISIT program that includes:

1. U.S. lawful permanent residents;

2. Canadian citizens, other than those entering the U.S. for business or pleasure or transiting through the U.S.;

3. Immigrant visa holders;

4. Foreign nationals paroled into the U.S. and;

5. Foreign nationals entering under the Guam Visa Waiver Program.

Nonimmigrant visa holders (students and temporary workers) and foreign nationals traveling to the U.S. under the Visa Waiver Program (VWP) are required to comply with US-VISIT on arrival. Several groups of foreign nationals are exempt from US-VISIT, including foreign nationals under the age of 14 or over the age of 79, foreign nationals holding certain diplomatic and official visas and foreign nationals registered in the National Security Entry-Exit Registration System (NSEERS).

See http://www.dhs.gov/us-visit-traveler-information

Immigrant Visas

The U.S. has an annual worldwide maximum quota of 675,000 permanent immigrant admissions. Applicants are considered on a first-come, first-served basis.

The two major exceptions to these numerical limits are refugees and asylum seekers. An annual political asylum quota is set by Congress, depending on disturbances in various parts of the world. In recent years the annual quota has been 48,000. Since World War II, more refugees have found homes in the U.S. than any other nation and more than two million refugees have arrived in the U.S. since 1980. The refugee category can be as high as 200,000 visas annually, but availability is for applicants from countries suffering political crisis that the U.S. Congress formally recognizes.

Family Sponsored Immigrants

The U.S. allows a maximum of 226,000 persons admitted annually for the purposes of family reunification divided into four categories, here in the order of preference:

1. Unmarried sons, daughters of U.S. citizens and their children (23,400 annual total);

2. Spouses, children, unmarried sons and daughters of lawful permanent resident aliens. At least 70% must go to spouses and children, the remainder to unmarried sons and daughters (114,200);

3. Married sons, daughters of U.S. citizens and their spouses and children (23,400); and

4. Brothers, sisters of U.S. citizens and their spouses and children, provided the U.S. citizens are under 21 years old (65,000).

If there are insufficient applicants in any class, those numbers become available to immigrants in other family classes. Visa availability in the family sponsored visa preference categories varies widely depending on your country of origin. Natives of the Philippines, Mexico, India, and the Dominican Republic typically face the longest delays, sometime 10 years or more.

If you qualify for employment-based immigration and are from one of these countries, you should pursue that route rather than the family option.

1990 Immigration Law

The 1990 immigration reform law and subsequent restrictions, such as tightened qualifications for welfare assistance to immigrants, result from a continuing U.S. national debate about whether further immigration should be restricted, or even ended.

Labor unions and isolationists have formed an unusual alliance on this issue.

The unions charge that immigration causes massive job losses for Americans, although others claim they create new jobs and pay taxes. Some conservatives say the American way of life is threatened by non-English speakers who are changing the nation's culture. Both groups seem to forget President Franklin Roosevelt's truism that the only natives in America are Indians; everyone else is descended from immigrants.

Most businesses, especially agriculture, strongly favor liberal immigration because they need qualified people and want cheap labor willing to take the low-paying jobs that most Americans reject. What this means to a prospective immigrant is that great opportunities do exist if the person has desirable skills.

The 1990 reform law tripled the number of employment based visas, making available 140,000 slots for this category divided into five preference groups, as follows:

1. Priority Workers: extraordinary ability in the sciences, arts, education, business, or athletics. Outstanding professors and researchers and certain multinational executives and managers are also included (28.6%);

2. Members of Professions: holding advanced degrees and people of exceptional ability in the sciences, arts and business (28.6%);

3. Professional Skilled and Unskilled Workers: those holding baccalaureate degrees, skilled workers with at least two years' experience and other workers whose skills are in short supply in the U.S. (28.6%, but unskilled workers are subject to a sub-limit of 10,000);

4. Special Immigrants: religious workers and ministers of religion, international organization employees and immediate family members, and specially qualified current and former U.S. government employees (7.1%); and

5. Investors: people who create jobs for at least 10 unrelated people by investing capital in a new commercial enterprise. Minimum capital required between US$500,000 and US$1 million, depending on unemployment rate in the geographic area (see below for "Investor Immigration") (7.1%).

How to Obtain Employment Visas

All employment preference categories described above require filing a first petition with the USCIS seeking classification within the specific visa preference sought. If granted, a second application for the visa needs to be filed at a U.S. Consulate.

Before filing for a visa under either the second or third preference described above the applicant's prospective employer must apply for and obtain an approved "alien employment certification" application from the U.S. Department of Labor. (A DOL certification is not required for the first, fourth and fifth preferences.)

The DOL certification states your employer's finding that there is no U.S. worker available and qualified for the position, and that the proposed wages and working conditions offered are on par with that of other similar U.S. workers.

The employer must conduct a recruitment campaign for the job at issue, advertising the position in newspapers and at its work site. With some artistic skill, the job description is usually tailored to fit these requirements.

The second step is filing the visa petition with the USCIS in the state where employment is to occur. Usually, an employer does this, but in cases where an applicant has "extraordinary ability," they can file their own petition.

USCIS acceptance of the preference petition means you are qualified for that preference category. This decision allows the filing with a U.S. Consulate of the second application; this one seeking an immigrant visa. But this filing is also contingent on a determination by the U.S. Department of State that an immigrant visa is immediately available, based on the total numbers remaining in the annual quota.

Each month, the Department of State publishes a "Visa Office Bulletin" listing the latest priority dates available for immigrant visas in each preference and countries that are oversubscribed for annually allotted visas. Sometimes a visa number is available immediately, but demand backlogs develop frequently.

Under the former system, five-year waits were common, but since the 1990 law, major delays for employment based-visas have not improved. In one recent year it was reported that the applications of over 300,000 immigrant workers trying to stay in the U.S. were caught up in the USCIS bureaucratic maze with some cases going as far back as 1998.

If you already legally are in the U.S. at the time an immigrant visa becomes available, you may apply to adjust status to permanent residence. This is useful if you entered on a business visa, found a job and want to accept it without the expense of leaving the country and then applying for a visa at a consulate. It is not possible to adjust status from an expired visa or if there is a pending complaint that you have violated your visa, such as by working on a visitor's visa.

Immigration Based on Investment

The fifth employment-based preference (EB-5 visa) granted to immigrant investors has drawn the most attention, probably because it is a blatant "buying your way" into U.S. citizenship that only the wealthy can afford. Immigration lawyers and promotional groups specializing in this aspect of the law are making big fees from thousands of wealthy foreigners willing to pay them and the U.S. government to gain quick citizenship.

The U.S. limits the number of investor EB-5 immigrant visas to 10,000 each year. In 2012, the latest year for which data is available, 7,641 were granted; 80% went to Chinese investors. In 2013 a total of 6,434 foreign investors applied for visas under the program, up from 6,040 in 2012. The 5% rate of growth in the program in 2013 was lower than in recent years, when the number of applications increased by 58%, in 2012, and 94% in 2011.

The program started in 1990 and recently has been plagued by allegations of fraud and charges of mismanagement by immigration officials. This has led to increased scrutiny of the program which has caused delays in the application process, immigration lawyers say. To date, the agency estimated the program raised $8.6 billion and created at least 57,300 jobs since 1990.

Before I explain this process, carefully consider whether you want to subject your business and financial life to the scrutiny attached to citizenship under this investment program.

It means being taxed by the U.S. on all your worldwide income, totally opening your books to the U.S. Internal Revenue Service (IRS) and paying taxes far above those imposed by many other low tax countries. In addition, failure to comply with U.S. laws can mean huge fines, penalties, interest, and even prison. Consider, too, that your citizenship is contingent on the investment being a success. If it fails, or if you don't comply with all the rules, your citizenship status is revoked.

Having considered all of that, here is how the investor citizenship program works:

If you invest at least US$500,000 in a designated U.S. "high unemployment targeted employment area," then citizenship can be yours. Your investment must benefit the U.S. economy and create full-time employment for at least 10 direct or indirect qualified employees, who cannot be you as the investor, or your family or any non-immigrant visa holders; and it must be a true profit-making business.

You cannot set up a corporation to own a personal residence, which employs a staff of 10. The assets of the business may not be used to finance it, meaning an actual advance cash investment is required. You must also be prepared to document the legitimate sources of the money to be used. Multiple investors in the same enterprise are allowed provided each investment meets the minimum requirements and creates 10 direct or indirect jobs, meaning 10 people would have to open a US$10 million business employing 100 people.

The purchase of an existing business is only permitted as part of a restructuring that increases the overall capital and employment of that existing business.

"It is a win-win-win," said Steve Yale-Loehr, an EB-5 visa expert who teaches immigration law at Cornell University, "the business gets capital, residents get jobs and the investor gets a green card."

The program has not always been popular. In the 1990s, what was then the Immigration and Naturalization Service (INS) had a hard time keeping tabs on whether EB-5 investments were creating jobs. "There were fears that the program was not achieving its intended purpose," Mr. Yale-Loehr said.

But the agency, now renamed Citizenship and Immigration Services (CIS), has since found a way to streamline the process by permitting entities outside the federal government, called "regional centers," to screen investors and monitor job creation. As a result, Mr. Yale-Loehr said, "the EB-5 program has risen from the ashes."

Of the 10,000 EB-5 visas available each year, 5,000 are set aside for investors in 17 regional centers. As might be expected, the specific details of the program are quite extensive and require a lawyer to interpret. Among the many drawbacks to this program is that approval in this category, unlike the other permanent residence visa categories, results in a conditional visa for the first two years. Continued involvement with the business and proof of its success are necessary to have your visa renewed after two years.

If your business fails during the first two years, regardless of the reason, your visa will be revoked. There are no exceptions. Proof of having made your best effort will be ignored.

As you might expect, this program has been charged with being used for political purposes. In several instances EB-5 "regional centers" have been created in favored in geographic areas, such as New York City, where political influence appeared to make the determination.

Refugees

After six years of major declines across the Southwest, illegal border crossings again soared in South Texas. The U.S. Border Patrol made more than 90,700 apprehensions in the Rio Grande Valley in the first six months of 2014, a 69% increase over 2013.

These migrants were no longer primarily Mexican laborers. Instead they were Central Americans, including many families with small children and youngsters without their parents, who risk a dangerous journey across Mexico. The increasing numbers of migrants caught here ask for asylum, causing lengthy legal procedures to determine whether they qualify.

There may be circumstances in which you can gain U.S. residence as a political refugee or asylum seeker. However, if you fit better into another visa category, you should do so. Refugee and asylum seeker status is politically controversial in the U.S. and is actively opposed by immigration authorities. So-called "economic refugees" are generally rejected.

To qualify as a "political" refugee, a person must demonstrate that they are fleeing from their home country because of past persecution or have a well-founded fear of future persecution.

Legal efforts have been pushed to redefine "persecution" in broader terms, including homosexuality and genital mutilation of African females. Under the Obama administration both of these groups have been given more liberal consideration. Refugees must make application from outside the U.S. and must have a financial sponsor in the United States.

Even before independence in 1776 and to the 20th century, America was the world's safe haven for religious refugees. In 1921 the U.S. Congress imposed the nation's first immigration quotas, (the Emergency Quota Act) thwarting the hope for millions of people seeking to flee dictatorship, war, and genocide. Such restrictions were used by the U.S. government under President Franklin Roosevelt who shamefully turned away ships full of German Jews fleeing Nazi Germany.

In recent years a marked increase in asylum seekers has produced concerns that many of these claims are fraudulent, as well as demands for reforms. Those seeking U.S. asylum who claimed a reasonable fear of returning to their home countries grew from 5,369 in 2009 to 36,035 in 2013, a six-fold increase in four years. In 2013, 76% of these claims were made by unauthorized immigrants apprehended while crossing the border, which explains most of the increase in claims since 2009.

Making such a claim starts a long legal process allowing many unauthorized immigrants claiming asylum to work legally in the U.S. for years on a de facto work permit. This loophole is growing in popularity.

Retired Foreign Persons

A major attraction for foreigners looking at America is lower cost U.S. real estate. A non-immigrant B-2 visa allowing a stay of up to six months is not difficult to obtain. However, realize that a U.S. stay in excess of 122 nights makes a foreign visitor liable for U.S. income taxes.

A foreign person who wants to retire permanently to the U.S. might be better to obtain a non-immigrant H-2 visa and open a small business. That will not bring U.S. citizenship, but it can assure continued permanent residence.

Illegal Immigrants

There are 318 million people in the United States, and it is estimated that more than 20 million are illegal aliens, mainly from Mexico, Central and South America.

Until recent years, U.S. land borders have been largely unguarded and unfortified. Coastal surveillance by air has been more vigilant because of the failed "war on drugs" but illegal entry from Mexico, Cuba, Haiti, or Central America has been a common occurrence.

Increased U.S. citizen concern about international terrorism and drug smuggling has produced massive new government spending on border patrols and fences. Much greater surveillance of the land border with Mexico and coastal waters is in place. New walls and fences have been erected.

Inspections at border crossings with Mexico and Canada have been stepped up often causing long traffic backups. The number of Citizenship and Immigration Services (CIS) and Customs officers has increased and, for the first time, U.S. military forces patrol some border areas. Vigilante squads of volunteers augment official patrols, although they are not welcomed by professional border officers who see them as an added problem.

In the last years of the Bush administration, CIS conducted numerous unannounced raids on companies that employed illegal aliens, especially those engaged in agricultural and food processing. Thousands of illegal aliens were arrested and deported, often braking up families in which children or one parent was a U.S. citizen. The Obama administration announced that it would end such raids, but in fact over a million people were deported, a far greater number than ever before.

One of the glaring contradictions in U.S. law is that although in theory illegal aliens are subject to arrest and instant deportation, many welfare and social services agencies cannot legally withhold benefits from them while they are otherwise illegally in the country. Typically, one government agency fails or refuses to communicate with another, thereby creating this paradox.

In some more politically liberal jurisdictions, such as San Francisco, elected officials have forbidden police to inquire about or report the immigration status of arrested persons, regardless of how serious the alleged crime may be. In other places, such as Arizona, police are allowed to ask immigration status only as part of a lawful investigation.

As a result, many illegal aliens openly receive welfare benefits for months or years without the CIS knowing about them. This, plus assistance from organized church groups, makes the U.S. a very attractive destination for Mexicans, Haitians and Central Americans, who seek education, medical benefits and subsistence until they find a job or start a business.

As former president, George W. Bush proposed a "guest worker" program but many in Congress were opposed, seeing this as an "amnesty" for millions of illegal immigrants who should instead be deported. President Obama has made a similar proposal but not really pushed for it.

It should be noted that thousands of illegal aliens were arrested and deported soon after the September 11, 2001 terrorist attacks in the U.S. Many were Muslims and/or from countries in the Middle or Far East. Although suspected of terrorist involvement, most were picked up and deported because their only crime was being in the U.S. on an expired visa or with no visa — and looking suspicious.

Under current law, even a legal immigrant with U.S. citizenship or green card status can be deported if convicted of a felony. This has resulted in some long-time U.S. residents being deported, even as their spouse or family remains in the U.S.

The law notwithstanding, a U.S. Senate review of 2013 ICE data revealed that less than 0.2% of the 12 million illegal immigrants and visa overstays who were not convicted of a serious criminal offense were placed In removal proceedings. Further, merely 0.08% of the 12 million who were not convicted of a serious crime or a repeat immigration offender were placed in removal proceedings. Thus, 99.92% of illegal immigrants and visa overstays without serious crime convictions or repeat immigration offenses did not face deportation.

The Senate report noted two 2013 local news reports, one from Arizona, the other from Texas, about ICE simply releasing illegal immigrant workers "because they did not have known outstanding warrants or criminal convictions" and was therefore considered low priority.

It seems that under the Obama administration almost none of the 12 million illegals are in danger of being deported.

Immediate Passports

Only U.S. citizens or key alien employees of the U.S. government can obtain instant U.S. passports legally, and then only with proper proof and documentation.

The most important requirement is a certified copy of a birth certificate issued by the state of birth. This must show a file or reference number, the date of birth and the official certification of the issuing office. Passport offices rarely check authenticity with birth certificate issuing offices, but they might check if a passport application looks suspicious.

Hospital birth certificates will not suffice for a U.S. passport application. Notification of Birth Registration forms filed with U.S. Consulates abroad may be accepted without birth certificates on a case-by-case basis, but the original birth certificate plus a translation certified by a U.S. Consulate abroad is usually required.

When applying for a passport, a U.S. citizen born abroad, with at least one parent who was a U.S. citizen, and who has been a recent U.S. resident, must submit a certified copy of a "Consular Report of Birth" or Certification of Birth. Naturalized U.S. citizens must submit either a Certificate of Naturalization or Certificate of Citizenship.

To prove identity, a passport applicant must show a valid U.S. current photo ID, such as an expired U.S. passport, a driver's license, or any government-issue photo ID card. Alternatively, a business card or school/college ID with a photograph and name on it can be accepted at the discretion of a passport officer.

The U.S. requires a passport application to be accompanied by two identical pictures, in color, taken within the previous six months. Photo size is 2 x 2 inches, full front view, with plain white or off-white background. Image size between 1 and 1 3/8 inches measured from top of the head — including hair and bottom of chin. Dark glasses that hide eyes are not acceptable, hats or other headgear must not be worn and photos from coin-operated booths are not acceptable.

Any passport applicant 13 years or older must appear in person and sign the application in the presence of a U.S. passport agent or consular official. Parents can sign for younger children.

Previous U.S. passport holders can renew by mail using standard Form DSP-82. The official fee for a passport for a person 16 years or older is US$165, but expedited delivery adds to the cost. See http://travel.state.gov/content/passports/english/passports/information/costs.html

Tip: As a former member of the U.S. House of Representatives myself, I advise anyone who needs a new passport or a renewal in a true emergency to call the office of their Member of Congress or U.S. Senators. Congressional inquiries made to the Passport Office get speedy and immediate action, often within 48 hours or less.

Passports for U.S. Border Crossings

Since the September 11, 2001 ("9/11") terrorist attacks, the U.S. government has required that all people entering the country, Mexicans, Canadians and Americans included, must carry an official passport or an equivalent travel document.

At this writing, Canadian and Mexican citizens can cross the U.S. border using passports or other photo or official identity documents.

Currently, all persons traveling by air outside of the United States are required to present a U.S. passport or other valid travel document to enter or re-enter the United States.

American citizens and resident aliens (green card holders) must show a valid U.S. passport or NEXUS card or other special travel document approved by the U.S. Department of Homeland Security when entering the country by land or sea from Canada, Mexico, the Caribbean and Bermuda.

Caribbean destinations include Anguilla, Aruba, The Bahamas, Barbuda, British Virgin Islands, Cayman Islands, Dominica, Dominican Republic, Grenada, Jamaica, Montserrat, Netherlands Antilles, St. Kitts & Nevis, St. Lucia, St. Vincent and the Grenadines, and the Turks and Caicos.

You can download a passport application from the U.S. State Department website at http://travel.state.gov/content/passports/english/passports/apply.html and take the completed (but not signed) form and the required documents and fees with you to the nearest passport issuing office, listed in the blue pages of the telephone directory under "U.S. Government."

A routine application will take about four weeks to process.

Electronic Passports

The Department of State now issues only Electronic Passports (e-passports). They claim that this is to better facilitate international travel for U.S. citizens and to enhance border security.

The passport combines face recognition and radio frequency ID (RFID) chip technology. The chip, embedded in the cover of the passport, holds the same information that is printed in the passport: name, date of birth, gender, place of birth, dates of passport issuance and expiration, passport number, and photo image of the bearer. Previously issued passports without electronic chips will remain valid until their expiration dates.

The e-passport integrates the latest concepts in electronic document protection and readability, but many claim it also violates personal privacy. That is because the RFID chips can be read at a distance by anyone with an electronic reader. To address privacy concerns, the Department of State says it has incorporated an anti-skimming device in the passport front cover.

The Department of State began issuing the first U.S. e-passports to the American public in 2006. For more information about the Electronic Passport, see http://travel.state.gov/content/passports/english/passports/FAQs.html#ePassport

The U.S. Passport Card can be used to enter the United States from Canada, Mexico, the Caribbean, and Bermuda at land border crossings or sea ports-of-entry and is more convenient and less expensive than a passport book.

The Passport Card cannot be used for international travel by air. See http://travel.state.gov/passport/ppt_card/ppt_card_3926.html

Global Entry Program

Global Entry is a voluntary U.S. Customs and Border Protection program that allows quick, expedited clearance for pre-approved, low-risk travelers upon arrival in the United States.

Though intended for frequent international travelers, there is no minimum number of trips necessary to qualify. When entering the U.S. participants use automated kiosks located at select airports instead of waiting in long lines for individual passport clearance.

At airports, participants go to Global Entry electronic kiosks, present their machine-readable passport or U.S. permanent resident card, place their fingertips on the scanner for fingerprint verification, and answer questions on a touch-screen computer for a customs declaration. They do not have to fill out the paper Customs Declaration Form 6059B. The kiosk issues the traveler a printed transaction receipt and directs the traveler to baggage claim and the exit.

Travelers must be pre-approved for the Global Entry program. All applicants undergo a rigorous background check and personal interview before enrollment that must be supported by a birth certificate and other documents. See http://www.cbp.gov/travel/trusted-traveler-programs/global-entry

NEXUS is a similar quick entry program for travel between the U.S. and Canada and for travel into the U.S. from Mexico via land, SENTRI. See http://www.cbp.gov/travel/trusted-traveler-programs

Aliens seeking to lawfully enter into the U.S. must establish their admissibility to the satisfaction of the CBP officer. This is done as part of the inspection process. See http://www.cbp.gov/travel/international-visitors

Passport Fraud

In Part I of this book I warned against the possibility of passport fraud when a person is acquiring a foreign citizenship and with it, a second passport. But passport fraud can occur in another instance: when a foreign person is seeking a U.S. passport.

In 2011, in the San Francisco area alone, 15 people were charged with passport fraud in one three-month period, part of a four-year-old "zero tolerance" program. The U.S. State Department "Operation Death Match" initiative, begun in 2005, tracks down fraud by cross-referencing death certificates, especially those of young children, with passport applications, searching for those who steal the identities of the recently deceased.

In addition to using others' identities, offenses can include using false identification, making false statements when applying for a passport, or counterfeiting government identification documents. Cases of U.S. passport fraud are almost always prosecuted.

Summary

For reasonable peace of mind and maximum security, probably the most useful U.S. status for foreign nationals is that of non-immigrant visitor, or legal residence under one of the several business visa categories. Anyone seriously contemplating permanent residence, leading to U.S. citizenship, should first retain skilled U.S. tax advisors and an expert immigration attorney.

Contacts and Information on the Web

U.S. Citizenship and Immigration Service. Web: http://www.uscis.gov/

USCIS Forms On-Line — Visas and Applications. Web: http://www.uscis.gov/forms

USCIS services available include: citizenship, asylum, lawful permanent residence, employment authorization, refugee status, inter-country adoptions, replacement immigration documents, family and employment-related immigration, and foreign student authorization. Web: http://www.uscis.gov/portal/site/uscis — Click on "Services"

Downloadable file of the official *U.S. Guide to Naturalization*. Web: http://www.uscis.gov/natzguide

Passport Renewal. Web: http://travel.state.gov/content/passports/english/passports/renew.html

U.S. citizens can apply for passport renewal by mail if they already have a passport, it is their most recent one, it was issued within the past 12 years, and if the person was over age 16 when it was issued. U.S. citizens who are residents abroad should renew their passports at the nearest U.S. Embassy or Consulate. Passports renewed by mail can only be forwarded to U.S. addresses. If your passport has been mutilated, altered or damaged, you cannot apply for renewal by mail. You must apply in person using Form DSP-11, present evidence of U.S. citizenship and have acceptable identification.

Obtain a Form DSP-82, "Application For Passport By Mail". Follow instructions and fee schedule and submit. See http://www.passportsandvisas.com/forms/dsp82.html

If your name changed since your previous passport was issued, enclose a certified copy of the court order, adoption decree, marriage certificate, or divorce decree specifying another name for you to use. (Photocopies are not acceptable.) If your name has changed by other means, you must apply in person. Mail (if possible, in a padded envelope) the completed DSP-82 application and attachments to:

National Passport Center
P.O. Box 371971
Pittsburgh, PA 15250-7971
Web: http://travel.state.gov/content/passports/english/about-us.html

Your previous passport will be returned to you with your new passport. If you wish to use an overnight delivery service, include the appropriate fee for overnight return delivery of your passport. Please note that overnight service will not speed up processing time unless payment for expedited service is also included. If the service of your choice will not deliver to a post office box, send it to:

Passport Services
Lockbox, Attn: Passport Supervisor 371971
500 Ross Street, Room 154-0670
Pittsburgh, PA 15262-0001

SECTION 2
CENTRAL AMERICA
AND THE CARIBBEAN

Commonwealth of The Bahamas

Government:	Parliamentary democracy
Capital:	Nassau, New Providence Island
National Day:	Independence Day: 10 July (1973)
Population:	319,031 (July 2013 est.)
Total Area:	5,382 sq. miles / 13,940 sq. kilometers
Language:	English (official), Creole (among Haitian immigrants)
Ethnic groups:	African 85%, European 12%, Asian & Hispanic 3%
Religion:	Baptist 35.4%, other Christian 15.2%, Anglican 15.1%, Roman Catholic 13.5%, Pentecostals 8.1%, Church of God 4.8%, Methodist 4.2%, unspecified 2.9%, other 0.8%
Life expectancy:	71.69 years
Currency:	Bahamian dollar (BSD)
GDP:	US$11.04 billion (2012 est.)
GDP per capita:	US$31,300 (2012 est.)

Scattered like dabs of possibility on an adventurer's palette, The Bahamas are ready-made for exploration. Just ask Christopher Columbus, he bumped against these limestone landscapes in 1492 and changed the course of history. But adventure didn't end with the Nina, the Pinta and the Santa Maria. From pirates to blockade dodgers to rum smugglers, wily go-getters have converged and caroused on the country's 700 islands and 2400 cays for centuries.

So what's in it for travelers? There's sailing to Abacos; diving Andros' blue holes; kayaking the countless cays around Exumas; lounging on Eleuthera's beaches; pondering pirates in Nassau. In-

deed, there's a Bahamian island to match most every water-and
sand-based compulsion; each of them framed by a backdrop of
gorgeous, mesmerizing blue ocean. — Lonely Planet

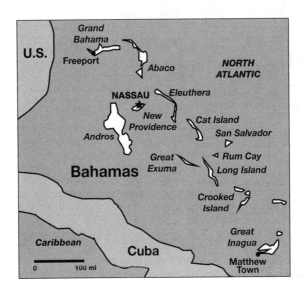

History and Overview

The Bahamas is the financial haven country nearest to the U.S.,
just minutes from Miami by airplane or a few hours by boat, 744
air miles from New York City. Bahamas has successfully promoted
itself as a destination for U.S. jet setters, and unfortunately a lot
of these islands are Americanized. Yet, there are still opportunities
among its 700 islands and 2,400 cays to disappear into a mangrove
forest, explore a coral reef and escape the high-rise hotels and pack-
age-tour madness.

The nation consists of over 700 islands, only 22 inhabited.
The main islands are Grand Bahama, Andros, Eleuthera, Abaco,
and New Providence Island, site of the capital, Nassau. The second-largest city is Freeport, on Grand Bahama. Eighty-five percent

of the Bahamian population is of African heritage. About two-thirds of the population resides on New Providence Island. Many Bahamians' ancestors arrived on these islands when they served as a staging area for the slave trade in the early 1800s. Others accompanied thousands of British loyalists who fled the American colonies during the Revolutionary War.

Arakawa Indians inhabited these islands when Christopher Columbus arrived in 1492, but they remained largely unexplored by Europeans until 1717, when they came under control of the British Crown. Because of the American Revolution, in 1776, the islands were briefly in American hands, followed by Spanish control in 1781. In 1783, they again became British territory, remaining so until independence was declared on July 10, 1973.

The Bahamas is a member of the British Commonwealth and a parliamentary democracy based on the Westminster model. Since independence, the nation has acquired a deserved reputation for official corruption and government venality, although this has lessened in recent years.

Low-lying limestone or coral islets with sandy beaches, the Bahamian archipelago provides year-round recreational opportunities on land and in the water. The variety of its marine habitats assures a broad range of prospects for enthusiasts of deep-sea and reef fishing, diving, and sailing.

Some of the islands' regattas and powerboat races draw participants and spectators from around the globe. The subtropical climate, warmed by the Gulf Stream, allows dry land activity around the calendar as well, including golf, polo, cricket, and tennis.

Over 300,000 people live in this archipelago, the oldest offshore money haven in the Americas. An independent nation since 1973, its origins as an offshore financial center date to 1908 when the Royal Bank of Canada opened a branch in Nassau. Today, tourism, hotel, resort, and convention industries are doing well and the islands are a retirement haven for the very wealthy, many of them prominent U.S. and European expatriates.

Economy

The Bahamas is one of the wealthiest Caribbean countries with an economy heavily dependent on tourism and offshore banking. Tourism together with tourism-driven construction and manufacturing accounts for approximately 60% of GDP and directly or indirectly employs half of the archipelago's labor force. Steady growth in tourism receipts and a boom in construction of new hotels, resorts, and residences had led to solid GDP growth in recent years. Tourism, in turn, depends on growth in the U.S., the source of more than 80% of the visitors.

Financial services constitute the second-most important sector of the Bahamian economy and, when combined with business services, account for about 36% of GDP. However, since 2000, when the government enacted new stricter regulations on the financial sector, many international businesses and banks have left The Bahamas. Manufacturing and agriculture combined contribute approximately a tenth of GDP and show little growth, despite government incentives aimed at those sectors. Overall growth prospects in the short-run rest heavily on the fortunes of the tourism sector.

The economy of The Bahamas shrank at an average pace of 0.8% annually from 2007 to 2012. Tourism, financial services, and construction, mainstays of the national economy remained weak. These challenges, coupled with a growing public debt, increases in government expenditures, a narrow revenue base, and heavy dependence on customs and property taxes have limited prospects for growth in The Bahamas.

Being close to the U.S. has its advantages, but also it can cause problems for offshore business and banking, especially if privacy is a major concern. The U.S. and Bahamian dollars are equal in value. Since 2000, 200 of 223 private banks in The Bahamas have closed and 30,000 "brass plate" international business companies were stricken from the official register. Bahamian banks find it difficult to avoid U.S. government pressures when Washington wants information. And since 2003, there has been a Tax Information Exchange Agreement between Washington and Nassau. The government announced that it would sign a FATCA enforcement treaty with Washington in 2014.

Keeping Money Clean

Anti-money laundering laws are tough and make violations punishable by a possible sentence of 20 years in jail and/or a US$100,000 fine for each instance. A "Currency Declaration Act" requires reporting of all cash or investment transfers, in or out of the islands, in excess of US$10,000. Offshore financial trustees and attorneys are required to maintain records of beneficial owners of offshore trusts and international business corporations. Previously, professional attorney-client privilege rules prevented revealing such information.

Following the U.S. model, the Banks and Trust Companies Act authorizes government bank inspections and requires reports of "suspicious activities." New account applicants must show a valid passport and other official identification as well as business references, and banks have a legal duty to identify "beneficial owners" of accounts.

The Drug Trafficking Act of 1986 outlaws money laundering and makes it an extraditable offense. The U.S.-Bahamian "Mutual Legal Assistance Treaty" (MLAT) requires cooperation between Washington and Nassau in all financial investigations. The Bahamas has similar treaties with Canada and the U.K. The Bahamas levies no taxes on capital gains, corporate earnings, personal income, sales, inheritance, or dividends.

Tax freedom is available to all resident corporations, partnerships, individuals, and trusts. The International Business Companies Act of 1990 permits cheap, fast incorporation. Incorporation costs include registered agent, nominee directors and nominee officers, which can total up to US$1,500-$2,400. (Keep in mind that the U.S. and Bahamian dollar are equal in value.)

The government and the local financial community are pushing hard to re-establish the islands as an international securities trading center with emphasis on emerging countries' investments. Locals want closed-end funds to be listed and traded on the Bahamian Stock Exchange, but at far less cost and with greater privacy guarantees than are available in the U.S.

Residence and Citizenship

Although what is called a Bahamian "resident alien passport" is available, full citizenship usually is allowed only after marriage to a Bahamian national. In most cases, it's best not to be a citizen of the place in which you actually live most of the time. Full citizenship gives your home place government more control over you than you want or need.

Thus, becoming a Bahamian national could spoil a potentially beautiful home base for your international operations. Under an amended 2011 immigration law, it is possible to establish residence in The Bahamas, and the government has set these specific guidelines for individual foreigners to establish permanent residence: All applicants are required to invest a minimum of US$500,000 in the country which may be in the form of the purchase of a property with a minimum value of US$500,000.

With investment of US$1.5 million residence the government

promises that applications will be reviewed within 21 days under an accelerated procedure. Foreigners who spend less than US$1.5 million are still eligible to apply for permanent residence status but observers who know how the government operates say that process could take years. Permanent residence falls into two categories, one for those wishing to work in the islands, and the other for those who do not wish to work.

Non-Bahamians who own property can apply to the Director of Immigration for an annual home owner's residence card. This card is renewable annually and entitles the owner and minor children in the family to enter and remain in the country with minimal entry and exit formalities.

The 2011 "New Investment Policy" Act increased the investment required for accelerated consideration of economic permanent residence from B$500,000 to B$1.5 million. The Act also increased the minimum capital investment on foreign-owned investment projects from B$250,000 to B$500,000. (One Bahamian dollar = USD$1.00).

Wealthy foreigners can obtain permanent residence in one of three categories:

Category I: Individual Investor: This status is available for those who have a proven personal net worth of at least US$2 million, reside in The Bahamas, and make a minimum investment of at least US$1.5 million, which cannot be repatriated from the country for at least 10 years. The principal applicant must invest a minimum of US$500,000, either in securities or in government approved business, with an additional required US$500,000 capital expenditure to purchase or build a business place. This achieves permanent residence, but not Bahamian citizenship. A non-citizenship travel document is issued.

Category II: Group Investor: This status is easiest to obtain, requiring a minimum US$500,000 investment in a government-approved project, a plan similar to Canada's investor citizenship law. The exact amount depends on the individual project, usually a tourist-related development, such as rental town houses or vacation resorts.

Category III: Entrepreneur: This requires an agreed-upon investment in a government-approved program for a period of at least 10 years.

Agency/attorney fees for help in qualifying for any of these categories averages US$20,000.

For foreigners, application and approval for citizenship is a lengthy and tedious process. The law favors long-term permanent residents and spouses of Bahamians. Under citizenship laws:

a) Anyone born in the former colony of The Bahamas islands prior to July 10, 1973, and who was a then citizen of the United Kingdom, became a citizen of The Bahamas on that Independence Day.

b) Anyone born outside of The Bahamas, and who was a citizen of the United Kingdom, and whose father became a Bahamian citizen (under the above law) also became a citizen.

c) Any woman who was married to someone who became a Bahamian citizen (under the above law) was also entitled to become a citizen of the Bahamas.

If none of the above immigration laws apply these may apply:

If your goal is to reside in The Bahamas on an annual basis, you can do so if;

1. Your spouse or dependent is a Bahamian citizen.

2. Your spouse or dependent is a resident permit holder.

3. You are an independent economic resident.

4. You are a resident homeowner, or a seasonal resident home-owner.

If you seek Bahamian immigration on a permanent basis, you must;

1. Be able to prove "good character" with no criminal record.

2. Show evidence of financial support.

Employment

Permanent residence falls into two categories, one for those wishing to work in the islands and the other for those who do not want to work. No foreign immigrant may be offered a job that a skilled Bahamian is "qualified" to do but that word can have many meanings. Usually, any job that does not require a higher education degree is off limits to foreigners (such as a waiter, bartender, maid or housekeeper). Jobs which most Bahamians don't want are available; which is why many farm workers and gardeners are Haitian immigrants.

Any Bahamian employer with job vacancies must first advertise locally. If no local worker is found the employer must apply to the Department of Immigration for permission to recruit outside of The Bahamas. A prospective foreign employee must provide documentation to prove qualifications such as a college or other degree.

Each employer granted a work permit is required to place a bond to repatriate the foreign employee and his dependents and to pay any public charges, including medical expenses, incurred by the employee. Fees for work permits run from US$250 for a farm worker to US$7,500 for professionals and executives.

Visas

Holders of a Bahamian passport are entitled to visa free travel to 136 countries, many of them fellow members of the British Commonwealth.

Visas are not required for U.S. citizens for stays in The Bahamas for up to eight months. All U.S. citizens traveling by air or by sea to and from the Caribbean, Bermuda, The Bahamas, Panama, Mexico, and Canada are required to have a valid passport or other documents to enter or re-enter the United States.

U.S. Citizenship and Immigration Services immigration and customs agents are located in Bahamian airports for processing returning U.S. persons, which removes the need for arrival processing in Miami, New York or other U.S. destinations. There is an airport departure tax of US$15 for travelers age six years or older and of US$18 for those leaving Freeport.

Contacts

Embassy of The Bahamas
2220 Massachusetts Avenue NW
Washington, DC 20008
Tel.: (202) 319-2660
Email: bahemb@aol.com

Consulates General
231 East 46th Street
New York, NY 10017
Tel.: (212) 421-6420
Email: consulate@bahamasny.com

Suite 818, Ingraham Building
25 SE Second Avenue
Miami, FL 33131
Tel.: (305) 373-6295

Email: bcgmia@bellsouth.net

2970 Clairmont Road, Suite 690
Atlanta, GA 30329
Tel.: 404-214-0492
Email: bahamasconsulatega@bahconga.com

United States Embassy
42 Queen Street
Nassau, The Bahamas
Tel.: + (242) 322-1181
Email: embnas@state.gov
Web: http://nassau.usembassy.gov/

Barbados

Government:	Parliamentary democracy
Capital:	Bridgetown
National Day:	Independence Day: 30 November (1966)
Population:	288,725 (July 2013 est.)
Total Area:	66 sq. miles / 431 sq. kilometers
Language:	English
Ethnic groups:	Black 93%, white 3.2%, mixed 2.6%, East Indian 1%, other 0.2%
Religion:	Protestant 63.4% (Anglican 28.3%, Pentecostal 18.7%, Methodist 5.1%, other 11.3%), Roman Catholic 4.2%, other Christian 7%, other 4.8%, none or unspecified 20.6% (2008 est.)
Life expectancy:	4.75 years
Currency:	Barbadian dollar (BBD) = US$0.50
GDP:	US$6.961 billion (2012 est.)
GDP per capita:	US$25,000 (2012 est.)

Many Caribbean islands have beaches, but where Barbados differs is what lies behind the surf and sand. No matter your budget or style, you can find a place to stay that suits you, whether cheap, funky, restful or posh. All the comforts of home are close at hand if you want them as Barbados is one of the most developed islands in the region. The literacy rate approaches 98% and the capital Bridgetown and its surrounds are booming.

Away from the luxury resorts of the west coast and the well-developed south coast, however, is where you'll find what makes the island special. Central Barbados has a rolling ter-

rain of limestone hills and amid this lush scenery are fascinating survivors of the colonial past. Vast plantation homes show the wealth of these settlers and face up to the brutality of the slave trade. Museums document this engrossing history while several botanic gardens exploit the beauty possible from the perfect growing conditions. — *Lonely Planet*

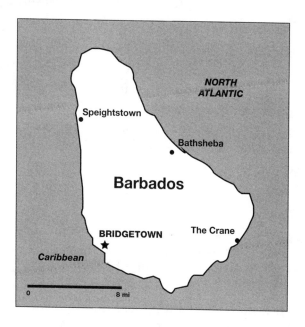

History and Overview

Barbados is the easternmost island in the Caribbean area in the North Atlantic Ocean, northeast of Venezuela. Barbados sits almost a hundred miles east of its closest neighbor, so when the Spaniards, Danes, French, and others were busy fighting over the rest of the Caribbean, Barbados sat back and remained solidly British. Barbados is the "Little England" of the Caribbean. Home to the national sport of cricket, Barbados hosted the final matches of the Cricket World Cup in 2007.

"Bajans" as the islanders call themselves, are as West Indian as any of their Caribbean neighbors, but have tended to borrow selectively rather than assume English customs. The island was uninhabited when first settled by the British in 1627. Slaves worked the sugar plantations established on the island until 1834 when slavery was abolished in the U.K. The economy remained heavily dependent on sugar, rum and molasses production through most of the 20th century.

The gradual introduction of social and political reforms led to complete independence from the U.K. in 1966 under a Westminster parliamentary form of government. In the 1990s, tourism and manufacturing surpassed the sugar industry in economic importance. Historically, the Barbadian economy had been dependent on sugarcane cultivation and related activities, but production in recent years has diversified into light industry and tourism.

Economy

Barbados is the wealthiest and most developed country in the Eastern Caribbean and enjoys one of the highest per capita incomes in Latin America. Historically, the economy was dependent on sugarcane cultivation and related activities but in recent years has diversified into light industry and tourism with about four-fifths of GDP and exports being attributed to services.

Offshore finance and information services are important foreign exchange earners and thrive from having the same time zone as eastern U.S. and Canadian financial centers and a relatively highly educated workforce. Tourism, financial services, and construction industries were hard hit by the global economic crisis in 2008 causing the economy to contract and grow below 1% annually since 2010. The government continues its efforts to reduce unemployment, to encourage direct foreign investment and to privatize remaining state-owned enterprises.

In early 2014, the government was having a difficult time combatting deficits under fiscal management requirements imposed by the International Monetary Fund (IMF) as a condition for loans. In 2013, debt reached 94% of GDP and the government planned to lay off 3,000 employees.

Canadian Presence

Government officials have stepped up efforts to attract Canadian investors. Direct foreign capital investment, a major part of its economy dropped by nearly 5% largely because British and U.S.-based companies cut back on expansion overseas.

Investment by Canadian companies looking to avoid paying Canadian tax on income derived from foreign earnings has grown from US$500-million in 1987 to US$51.7-billion in 2012. Nearly 9% of Canadian direct investment offshore is done in Barbados. Canadian subsidiaries, which include a large number of mining, oil and gas and financial services companies, account for one-third of the 3,750 corporate structures registered here in 2011, Barbados is promoting its expanding network of bilateral double taxation treaties and appealing to Canadian companies to invest, in order to take advantage of them.

Of the 50 international banks; 78% are Canadian; of the 144 mining companies 41% are Canadian and of the 230 oil and gas companies, 30% are Canadian. Barbados 2.5% corporate tax rate has attracted Canadian investors since Canada signed its own double taxation treaty with the country in 1987. Under the treaty, Canadian companies can set up a subsidiary in Barbados to conduct international business. If the company has five employees in Barbados and maintains a management presence there, it can repatriate profits to Canada without paying Canadian tax.

Barbados' stable business environment, well-educated population and sophisticated business infrastructure have been key draws for Canadian and other foreign companies. Barbados' other major industries are tourism and sugar production. Corporate taxes earned from offshore investments in the country make up 5% of the GDP. Offshore companies employ about 4% of the work force, most of them professionals such as accountants, lawyers and business school graduates.

The government and private sector both work as part of the Caribbean Community (CARICOM) Single Market and Economy (CSME), the EU-style single market in the Caribbean area.

Residence and Citizenship

The Constitution of Barbados defines citizens as those born on the island before 1966 who were citizens of the United Kingdom and U.K. colonies at the time of the 1966 independence, or those born overseas as children of fathers who were or would have been citizens of Barbados but for their death.

The constitution also allows for acquisition of citizenship through registration for British Commonwealth citizens after seven years of ordinary and lawful residence. Citizenship can also be acquired through marriage. According to the constitution, there is no requirement of residence or duration of marriage although foreign female spouses must take an oath of allegiance. Barbados recognizes the principle of dual citizenship.

The Barbadian Constitution provides citizenship by:

1. birth: of a child born within the territory of Barbados, regardless of the nationality of the parents.

2. descent: a) of a child born abroad, in wedlock, whose father is a citizen of Barbados. The child must be registered with the

nearest Barbadian diplomatic representative; b) of a child born abroad, out of wedlock, whose mother is a citizen of Barbados. The child must be registered with the nearest Barbadian diplomatic representative.

3. registration: foreign women who marry a citizen of Barbados may apply for citizenship through registration.

4. naturalization: a person may acquire Barbadian citizenship after having a residence of at least five years.

U.S. citizens must enter Barbados using a valid U.S. passport. No visa is needed to enter for stays up to 28 days. There is a departure tax for travelers over the age of 12.

Contacts

Embassy of Barbados
2144 Wyoming Avenue NW
Washington, DC 20008
Tel.: (202) 939-9200
Web: http://barbadosembassy.org/
Email: washington@foreign.gov.bb

Consulate General
800 2nd Avenue, 18th Floor
New York, NY 10017
Tel.: (212) 867-8435

Consulate General
150 Alhambra Circle, Suite 1270
Coral Gables, FL 33134
Tel.: (305) 442-1994

United States Embassy
Wildey Business Park
Wildey St. Michael, Barbados

Tel.: (246) 227-4399
Email: BridgetownACS@state.gov
Web: http://barbados.usembassy.gov

Belize

Government:	Parliamentary democracy
Capital:	Belmopan
National Day:	Independence Day: 21 September (1981)
Population:	334,297 (July 2013 est.)
Total Area:	8,867 sq. miles / 22,966 sq. kilometers
Languages:	English (official), Spanish, Mayan, Garifuna (Carib), Creole
Ethnic groups:	Mestizo 48.7%, Creole 24.9%, Maya 10.6%, other 9.7%, Garifuna 6.1%
Religion:	Roman Catholic 49.6%, Protestant 27% (Pentecostal 7.4%, Anglican 5.3%, Seventh Day Adventist 5.2%, Mennonite 4.1%, Methodist 3.5%, Jehovah's Witnesses 1.5%), other 14%, none 9.4%
Life expectancy:	68.4 years
Currency:	Belize dollar (BZD) fixed at BZD2 = US$1.00
GDP:	US$2.967 billion (2012 est.)
GDP per capita:	US$8,700 (2012 est.)

With one foot planted in the Central American jungles and the other dipped in the Caribbean Sea, Belize blends the best of both worlds. Offshore, kayakers glide from one sandy, palm-dotted islet to another, while snorkelers swim through translucent seas, gazing at a kaleidoscope of coral, fish, dolphins and turtles. Inland, explorers investigate ruins of ancient civilizations, and birders aim their binoculars at some 570 species.

Between national parks, wildlife sanctuaries and marine reserves, more than 40% of the country's area is protected in one

*form or another, creating a haven for countless creatures of land,
sea and sky. Belize is a very diverse little nation, and because it's
so small, you can escape from the heat of the beach, up to the
cooler highlands in no time. From its Caribbean shores to its
jungle interior, this country has great natural beauty; blue water
and deserted beaches, inland retreats where jaguar and scarlet
macaw still live in their natural habitat. — Lonely Planet*

History and Overview

Belize is the only officially English-speaking country in Central
America, although Spanish is rapidly becoming the majority language
due to immigration. It borders the Caribbean Sea, east of Guatemala
and south and east of Mexico. Its mixed population includes descendants of native Mayans, Chinese, East Indians, and Caucasians. An
influx of Central American immigrants, mainly Guatemalans, Salvadorans, and Hondurans, has changed Belize's ethnic composition.

Independent since 1981, its language came from its colonial days when it was called British Honduras. Belize has the largest barrier reef in the Western Hemisphere and great deep-sea diving. Inland, visitors and residents enjoy ecotourism in lush tropical rain forests and exploration of countless Mayan architectural sites and sacred caves, with many yet to be discovered. To the east in the Caribbean, there's a sprinkle of tropical islands included within the nation's borders, providing access to sport fishing in the lagoons and open sea.

A member of the British Commonwealth, Belize retains many of the colonial customs and features familiar in places like the Cayman Islands and Bermuda. The first settlers were probably British woodcutters, who in 1638, found the valuable commodity known as "Honduran mahogany."

Economy

Bananas, sugarcane and citrus fruit are the principal crops. Like many small countries dependent on primary commodities, Belize recognized the benefits of introducing tax haven services to boost its income.

Migration continues to transform Belize's population. There are about 16% of Belizeans who live abroad, while immigrants constitute approximately 15% of the population. Belizeans seeking job and educational opportunities have preferred the United States rather than former colonizer Great Britain because the U.S. is closer and has strong trade ties with Belize. Mestizos have become the largest ethnic group, and Belize now has more native Spanish speakers than English or Creole speakers, despite English being the official language. In addition, Central American immigrants are establishing new communities in rural areas. Recently, Chinese, European, and North American immigrants have become more frequent.

Tourism is the number one foreign exchange earner, followed by exports of marine products, citrus, cane sugar, bananas, and garments. Government deficit spending policies, initiated in 1998 led to GDP growth averaging nearly 4% in 1999 to 2007. Oil discoveries in 2006 bolstered this growth. Growth has been about 2% per year during 2010 to 2012, as a result of the global slowdown, natural disasters, and a temporary drop in the price of oil, according to International Living "Economy in Belize."

With weak economic growth and a large public debt burden, spending is now tight. In 2012 and 2013, the government restructured its US$544 million commercial external debt. A key government objective remains the reduction of poverty and inequality with the help of international donors. Although Belize has the second highest per capita income in Central America, this masks a huge income disparity between rich and poor.

Offshore Financial Center

In 1992, the Belize National Assembly enacted major legislation, which they continue to modernize, with the goal of making the country a competitive offshore financial center. Drafters combed tax haven laws worldwide and came up with a series of minimal corporate and tax requirements, which could well fit your offshore business needs.

The laws include the Trust Act, which allows a high level of asset protection, great freedom of action by the trustee, and no taxes on income earned outside Belize. There is also a statute allowing the creation of international business companies. These corporations can be formed in less than a day for about US$1,000. You only need one shareholder and/or director, whose name can be shielded from public view.

Since 1990, when the International Business Companies Act

became law, foreigners have registered about 5,000 IBCs. That's a relatively small number compared to a place like the Cayman Islands, but the number is growing. There are no local income taxes, personal or corporate and no currency exchange controls. Locals pay a 25% corporate tax.

Belize City, the main center for business, has also seen major growth in the shipping registry business encouraged by a maritime registry law. Other laws favor offshore insurance companies, limited liability partnerships and banking.

There is an anti-money laundering law that is enforced. Under pressure from leading nations and the Organization for Economic and Community Development (OECD), Belize has compromised what used to be very strict banking secrecy. With the aim of being removed from the OECD "grey" list, Belize has signed tax information exchange agreements with the United Kingdom, Australia, the Netherlands, Ireland, France, Finland, Norway, Sweden, Iceland, Greenland, Denmark, the Faro Islands, Portugal, Mexico and Poland, but not with the U.S.

So far, the Belize banking sector is tiny and those with firsthand experience complain that the local banks are less than competent and careless with account information. Indeed, Belize is most definitely a third-world country. Visa credit cards are issued by Belize Bank International, Ltd., owned by BHI Corporation, a holding company with banking and financial services in Belize. BHI also has major stakes in many local Belizean businesses and industries. Belize Bank is the largest commercial banking operation and is a correspondent of the Bank of America.

Belize's investment policy is codified in the Belize Investment Guide, which sets out the development priorities for the country. A country "Commercial Guide for Belize" is available at: http://belize.usembassy.gov/country_commercial_guide.html.

A major problem has been the Belize government's inability to live within its means. Budget deficits, spending cuts and attempts to raise taxes resulted in major street protests in 2005, disrupting business and normal life for weeks. Oil discoveries starting in 2006 bolstered economic growth and exploration efforts continue. Major concerns continue to be the sizable trade deficit and unsustainable foreign debt. A key objective remains the reduction of considerable poverty with the help of international donors.

If you're a shopper and move to Belize, you'll experience withdrawal. There's little opportunity for non-essential shopping in Belize, and there are no big chain stores — no Wal-Mart, Costco, or Sam's Club. This is a small country where life is simple. You'll find everything you need but often not everything you might want. In most respects, Belize remains very much a Third World country.

A more serious concern living in Belize can be health care. Again, this is a small country, and its health care resources are limited. When you consider that the entire country is home to fewer than 340,000 residents, it's not surprising that you don't find the breadth of health care facilities you might be used to elsewhere.

You will, on the other hand, find competent, dedicated general practitioners and some highly qualified specialists. However, if you have a sensitive medical condition, you'll likely want to head to Mexico or the United States for care.

Passport Problems

Two decades ago, it was easy to obtain a genuine Belize passport by fraudulent means. This was done by paying a few hundred American dollars to local police, a government official or a lawyer with connections. They, in turn, would certify to passport authorities that the "applicant" was known to them as having been a Belize resident for at least five years. Poor or non-existent official record keeping also lent itself to the widespread use of fake Belize birth certificates to obtain passports.

The nation's cabinet officially ended the Belize economic citizenship program in 2002. A constitutional reform commission had urged the change, but pressure from the U.S. and Canadian governments undoubtedly was also a factor. Even after the law was repealed, it appeared that some of the economic citizenship passports were still being sold under the table. Periodic rumors circulate claiming the economic citizenship program might be revived.

With this past history the Belize passport is not well regarded internationally and it offers only limited visa-free travel to about 25 countries, including the United Kingdom and neighboring Mexico but not to the United States.

Qualified Retired Persons Program

In 1998, the Retired Persons Incentives Act was enacted with hopes of making Belize a retirement haven for foreign citizens and also bringing needed foreign currency into the country. The Act establishes a residence program for "qualified retired persons" (known as QRPs), offering them significant tax incentives to become permanent residents (but not citizens) of Belize. The program is aimed primarily at residents of the United States, Canada and the United Kingdom, but is open to all.

A qualified retired person is exempted from all taxes on income from sources outside Belize. QRPs can own and operate their own international business based in Belize, also exempt from local taxes. Local income is taxed at a graduated rate of 15 to 45% and QRPs need a work permit in order to earn local income.

For the QRP, import duties of up to a maximum of US$15,000 are waived for personal effects, household goods and for a motor vehicle or other transport, such as an airplane or boat. There is no minimum time that must be spent in Belize and QRPs can maintain that status, so long as they maintain a permanent local residence.

To qualify for the QRP program, the applicant must be 45 years of age or older and prove personal financial ability to support oneself and any dependents. A spouse and dependents (18 years and younger) qualify along with the head of household. Initial fees for the program are US$700 for the qualified retiree and US$350 for each dependent, plus US$100 for an ID card upon application approval. Application fees for QRP residence vary by nationality, ranging from US$250 to US$5,000. For U.S. nationals the fee is US$1,000 per person. Time for approval of a permanent residence application varies greatly because of the Belize bureaucracy.

Minimum financial requirements include an annual income of at least US$24,000 (or equivalent) from a pension, annuity or from other sources outside Belize. By the 15th of each month, at least US$2,000 must be deposited in the QRP's Belize account, or by April 1 annually US$24,000 must be placed in deposit.

For information and application forms, contact:

Immigration and Nationality Department
Ministry of National Security and Immigration
Belmopan City, Belize
Tel.: 011-501-222-4620
Web: http://www.belize.gov.bz/

Belize Tourism Board
P.O. Box 325, 64 Regent Street
Belize City, Belize
Tel.: 011-501-227-2420
Toll free from US: 1-800-624-0686

Email: info@travelbelize.org
Web: http://www.travelbelize.org

See also: http://www.belizeretirement.org/

Contacts

Embassy of Belize
2535 Massachusetts Avenue NW
Washington, DC 20008
Tel.: (202) 332-9636
Email: ebwreception@aol.com
Web: http://www.embassyofbelize.org

Belize Travel Information Office
New York City
Tel.: (800) 624-0686.

United States Embassy
Floral Park Street
Belmopan, Cayo Belize
Tel.: + (501) 822-4011
Email: embbelize@state.gov
Web: http://belize.usembassy.gov/

Bermuda

Government:	British Crown colony, parliamentary self-governing U.K. territory
Capital:	Hamilton
National Day:	Bermuda Day: 24 May
Population:	69,467 (July 2013 est.)
Total Area:	20.6 sq. miles / 53.3 sq. kilometers
Languages:	English (official), Portuguese
Ethnic groups:	Black 54.8%, white 34.1%, mixed 6.4%, other 4.3%, unspecified 0.4%
Religion:	Anglican 23%, other Protestant 18%, Roman Catholic 15%, none 14%, other 12%, African Methodist Episcopal 11%, unaffiliated 6%, unspecified 1%
Life expectancy:	80.93 years
Currency:	Bermudian dollar (BMD) 1 BMD = US$1.00
GDP:	US$5.6 billion (2011 est.)
GDP per capita:	US$86,000 (2011 est.)

Think Bermuda and images of tidy pastel cottages, professional gents in ties and shorts, pink sand beaches, and quintessential British traditions like cricket matches and afternoon tea spring to mind. For once, the stereotype matches the reality. And don't forget the billions in tax haven Bermuda's banks.

"You go to heaven if you want — I'd rather stay here in Bermuda." So gushed Mark Twain in the 19th century, and Bermuda's promise of sun and sea still lures vacationers to its shores. These days celebs like Michael Douglas and Catherine Zeta-Jones and New York City mayor Michael Bloomberg call

Bermuda home, and millionaire executives pop over from the U.S. for a little R&R. The island makes for a delightful get-away vacation. If you're looking for peace and quiet, Bermuda has pampering resorts to soothe your soul.

Romantics will find atmospheric inns with four-poster beds and candlelight dining. Or perhaps you want to really let loose. Jump on a motor scooter and let the wind whip through your hair. — Lonely Planet

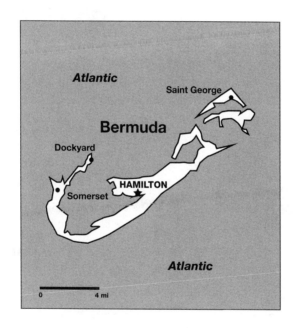

History and Overview

Bermuda is the largest remaining colonial possession of Great Britain in land area, a self-governing overseas territory of the U.K., 750 miles southeast of New York City and 3,445 miles from London, off the U.S. coast of South Carolina. Although it is self-governing, it is ultimately under British law and often under policy pressure from London.

Bermuda was first settled in 1609 by shipwrecked English colonists headed for Virginia. Vacationing to the island to escape North American winters first developed in Victorian times. Tourism continues to be important to the island's economy, although its role as a highly successful international offshore business center has overtaken it now. A referendum on independence from the U.K. was soundly defeated in 1995.

Economy

Based on a remote archipelago that makes up a land mass of only 21 square miles, Bermuda has one of the world's most unusual and enviable economies. Bermuda enjoys the third highest per capita income in the world, more than 50% higher than that of the U.S.; the average cost of a house by the late 2000s exceeded US$1 million. Gross domestic product exceeds US$5.85 billion, growth is running at about 4% and inflation hovers around 2%.

The territory has a healthy balance of payments surplus, employment levels are high among the population of nearly 69,000 and the average wage is more than US$660 per week. Of course, the global recession has had an impact here as elsewhere.

Renowned for its pink, sandy beaches and moderate climate warmed by the Gulf Stream, Bermuda has long been a favored playground of affluent tourists from both sides of the Atlantic. At least three publicly managed golf courses and more than a dozen private courses crowd the islands' scanty land area. Aquatic activities of all kinds are another major attraction of Bermuda. Renowned yacht races both in the archipelago and with Bermuda as a goal draw thousands of sailors and boaters annually. Snorkeling, whale watching and other kinds of ecotourism are among pleasures awaiting visitors and residents.

"Despite four years of recession and a public debt of US$1.4 billion, Bermuda enjoys the fourth highest per capita income in the world, about 70% higher than that of the U.S. The average cost of a single-family home is about US$1.1 million. Its economy is primarily based on international business and the provision of financial services to that sector, and to a lesser extent tourism. A number of reinsurance companies relocated to the island following the September 11, 2001 attacks on the U.S. and again after Hurricanes Katrina, Rita, and Wilma in 2005, contributing to the expansion of an already robust international insurance and re-insurance sector. Bermuda's tourism industry, which derives over 80% of its visitors from the U.S., continues to struggle although it is still important as a job creator. Bermuda must import almost everything. Agriculture is limited due to the small size of the island and Bermuda's industrial sector is small," according to *The World Factbook*.

International business contributes over 60% of Bermuda's economic output and about 41% of Bermuda's GDP. It has a long history as a re-insurance, captive insurance, tax and banking haven. This is a world-class financial outpost that is now a major competitor of London itself, not to mention a very pleasant place to visit or live in any season.

Bermuda's historic role as an offshore financial center for the U.K. was diminished by numerous restrictions imposed by the British government under the Labor Party which was ousted in the 2010 U.K. election. The attitude of the Conservative/Liberal U.K. coalition government that replaced Labor has not been much better. A number of leading international corporations moved their global headquarters away from Bermuda to Switzerland where they have more legal protection and guaranteed lower taxes. A similar exodus of U.K. corporations to Switzerland for the same reasons continues.

In 2010, a total of 15,078 international companies were registered in Bermuda, many U.S.-owned. They are an important source of foreign exchange for the island, and spent an estimated $2 billion in Bermuda in 2009. They are drawn by the island's friendly, tax-neutral environment, established business integrity, and minimal regulation.

During the year 2013, Bermuda became the first offshore financial center to be granted "conditional qualified jurisdiction" status by the U.S. National Association of Insurance Commissioners (NAIC), joining an exclusive group that includes Germany, Switzerland and the United Kingdom.

Over 60% of these companies operate in a tax "exempted" status meaning their business is conducted outside Bermuda (except for the minimal contacts needed to sustain an office on the island). Bermuda imposes no corporate income, gift, capital gains, or sales taxes but there is a real estate tax. The income tax is extremely low, just 11% on income earned from employment in Bermuda.

Residence

The "Jewel of the Atlantic" is also a great place to live, but a word about real estate restrictions. Demand is high and supply short. And you have to be quite wealthy. In general, non-Bermudians are permitted to own only one local property. Acquisition is allowed only after careful background checks (at least one bank reference and two or more personal references). Purchase licenses are issued by the Department of Immigration and take six months or more for approval. A real estate tax based on the total purchase price is payable at settlement: 22% for detached homes, 15% for condominiums.

Out of 20,000 residential units on the island, only 256 detached homes and 480 condominiums qualify for non-Bermudian purchasers based on government set values. The price for a single home starts at US$1.5 million, US$375,000 for condominiums. In a recent year, over US$40 million was spent by non-Bermudians for the few available properties. The reported average cost of a house in 2013 was US$1.5 million.

The buyers tend to be rich and famous. Aging rock star David Bowie owns property on the island, while former Italian Prime Minister Silvio Berlusconi and Texan Ross Perot, the one-time U.S. presidential candidate, are neighbors. International celebrities such as former New York Mayor Michael Bloomberg, a local land owner, can pass almost unnoticed on the island, a luxury unavailable on the streets of Manhattan or London.

Canadians currently have a special interest in buying on the island because Canadian tax laws make living abroad particularly attractive. (See the chapter on Canada). The Immigration Department reports that citizens of more than 80 different countries work on the island, with the U.K. providing the most, followed by Canada, Portugal, the U.S., the Philippines, and workers from the Caribbean.

There are about 8,000 work permit holders on the island, a large number out of so small a population. Employers must apply to the Department of Immigration when they want to hire a non-Bermudian, showing proof that no suitably qualified islander is available. An estimated 8,000 registered U.S. citizens live in Bermuda, many of them employed in the international business community.

In recent years, friction has grown between native Bermudians and expatriates who come here for employment in the financial sector, the argument mainly based on disparities between wages. This has led to restrictions on the total number of expatriates allowed and their length of stay, and it is a continuing local political issue.

Solid Banks

Such extensive worldwide finance and insurance activity requires a highly sophisticated banking system. Bermuda provides this with up-to-date services and fiber optic connections to the outside world. The three local banks clear over US$3 billion daily.

Bermuda's three banks follow very conservative, risk averse policies. They hold an average of 85% of customer liabilities in cash and cash equivalents. The Bank of Bermuda, founded in 1889, has assets exceeding US$5 billion and offices in George Town, the Cayman Islands, Guernsey, Hong Kong, the Isle of Man, Luxembourg, and an affiliate in New York City. The Bank of Bermuda is owned by HSBC. Butterfield Bank (founded in 1859) also has offices in all of those tax havens, except the Caymans. The Bermuda dollar circulates on par with the U.S. dollar. U.S. currency is accepted everywhere in the islands.

There are no exchange controls on foreigners or on exempt companies, which operate freely in any currency except the Bermuda dollar.

Unlike the Cayman Islands or The Bahamas, Bermuda has no bank secrecy laws officially protecting privacy, but bank and government policy and court decisions make it difficult to obtain information in most cases. To do so requires a lengthy judicial process. Bermuda has tax information exchange agreements (TIEAs) with the United States, France, Germany, the U.K. and 18 other countries.

In 2013, Bermuda signed an intergovernmental agreement (IGA) with the U.S. to implement FATCA. Internationally outside of FATCA as a British overseas territory, Bermuda also has signed an IGA with the U.K. version of its FATCA-like law and has committed to wider exchange of information with the U.K., Germany, France, Italy and Spain.

A 1988 mutual legal assistance treaty with the U.S. allows for governmental exchange of information in certain criminal cases. Bermuda has strict anti-drug and money laundering laws. On a comparative 1-to-10 international financial and bank privacy scale, Bermuda ranks about a five.

Entry/Exit Requirements

Of interest to U.S. expatriates, Bermuda residents have visa-free entry into the United States.

U.S. citizens entering Bermuda must present a U.S. passport or a certified U.S. birth certificate, and photo identification. All U.S. citizens traveling by air or by sea to and from Bermuda are required to have a valid passport or other documents to enter or re-enter the United States. U.S. CIS immigration and customs agents are located in Hamilton, Bermuda airport for processing returning U.S. persons, which removes the need for arrival processing in Miami, New York or other U.S. destinations.

For additional information on entry requirements, travelers may contact the British Consulate, 845 Third Avenue, New York, NY 10022, Tel.: (212) 745-0200, or the Bermuda Department of Immigration, Web: http://www.immigration.gov.bm/portal/server. pt/ For additional entry requirements, contact:

Bermuda Department of Tourism
675 3rd Avenue
New York, NY 10017
Tel.: (212) 818-9800

20 Church Street, Hamilton HM11, Bermuda
Tel.: +1 (441) 296-9200
Email: contact@bermudatourism.com
Web: http://www.bermudatourism.com

Contacts
Embassy of the United Kingdom
3100 Massachusetts Avenue NW

Washington, DC 20008
Tel.: (202) 588-6500
Email: britishembassyenquiries@gmail.com
Web: https://www.gov.uk/government/world/organisations/
british-embassy-washington

U.S. Consulate General
Crown Hill, 16 Middle Road
Devonshire DV0, Bermuda
Tel.: + (441) 295-1342
Email: HmlAmConGen@state.gov
Web: http://hamilton.usconsulate.gov/

British Virgin Islands

Government:	Overseas territory of the U.K., self-governing
Capital:	Road Town
National Day:	Territory Day: 1 July
Population:	31,912 (July 2013 est.)
Total Area:	59 sq. miles / 153 sq. kilometers
Language:	English
Ethnic groups:	Black 82%, white 6.8%, other 11.2% (includes Indian and mixed)
Religion:	Protestant 86% (Methodist 33%, Anglican 17% Church of God 9%, Seventh-Day Adventist 6%, Baptist 4%, Jehovah's Witnesses 2%, other 15%), Roman Catholic 10%, other 2%, none 2%
Life expectancy:	78.12 years
Currency:	U.S. dollar (USD)
GDP:	US$853.4 million (2010 est.)
GDP per capita:	US$42,300 (2010 est.)

What happens when steady trade winds meet an is-land-flecked channel with tame currents and hundreds of protected, salt-rimmed bays? Every mariner worth his sea salt sails there — which is how the British Virgin Islands (BVIs) became a sailing fantasyland. More than 40 islands bob in the group, welcoming visitors with an absurd amount of beach. British Virgin Islands are so beautiful you'd happily marry the closest iguana just so you could stay there forever. Think dra-matic green hills, blue skies, tripped-out sunsets and beaches where the loudest noise is the 'donk' of a coconut dropping on sand as soft as a baby's bottom. — Lonely Planet

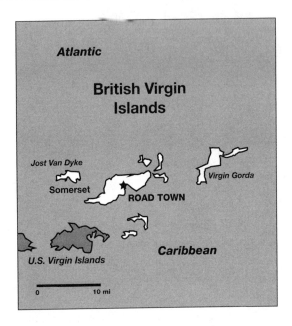

History and Overview

The British Virgin Islands (BVI) are a British overseas territory, part of the British West Indies, lying about 60 miles east of Puerto Rico. There are about 50 islands in the BVI, many of them uninhabited. Tortola is the main island; other islands include Virgin Gorda, Jost Van Dyke and Anegada.

First inhabited by Arawak and later by Carib Indians, the Virgin Islands were settled by the Dutch in 1648 and then annexed by the English in 1672. The islands were part of the British colony of the Leeward Islands from 1872 to 1960 and were granted autonomy in 1967. The economy is closely tied to the larger and more populous U.S. Virgin Islands to the west.

Economy

The economy, one of the most stable and prosperous in the Caribbean, is highly dependent on tourism generating an estimated

45% of the national income. In recent years more than 350,000 tourists annually, mainly from the U.S., visited the islands. The economy, one of the most stable and prosperous in the Caribbean, is highly dependent on tourism, generating an estimated 45% of the national income.

International financial services produce 50% of the GDP. In the mid-1980s, the government began offering offshore registration to companies wishing to incorporate in the islands, and incorporation fees now generate substantial revenues. Over 500,000 companies are on the offshore registry, second in number only to Hong Kong and greater than in Panama. That figures out to be more than 17 companies for every one of the BVI's 31,000 people.

The only corporation documents on public record are the Memorandum and Articles of Association of each company. Names of directors are not public, much like the incorporation privacy laws of the State of Delaware.

In 2014, bank records stolen by investigative journalists revealed that two BVI companies had 21,000 clients from mainland China and Hong Kong who were using the BVI as a tax haven, many of them relatives of, or members of, the Communist Chinese ruling elite. In response, the BVI proposed a new law whereas a person who publishes in any media unauthorized information on BVI companies may be fined up to US$1 million or jailed for up to 20 years.

In 2013, the BVI received $92 billion in foreign direct investment, the fourth largest world amount, more than that which Brazil and India received combined. That was up 40% compared to 2012, continuing a trend that began after the 2008 economic crisis. Unlike most countries where foreign direct investment is used by companies on new acquisitions and projects, most of the BVI money was transferred quickly in and out of the country or moved through the treasury accounts of large firms incorporated there.

The adoption of a comprehensive insurance law in 1994, which provides a blanket of confidentiality with regulated statutory process for investigation of criminal offenses, made the BVI even more attractive to international business. Livestock raising is the most important agricultural activity; poor soils limit the islands' ability to meet domestic food requirements. Because of traditionally close links with the U.S. Virgin Islands, the BVI has used the US dollar as its currency since 1959.

Ultimately, the financial industry here is under indirect control of the British government in London. The Labor Party during its control that ended in 2010 forced changes relaxing financial privacy and permitting international exchange of tax information. The islands now have in place a Tax Information Exchange Treaty (TIEA) with the United States. In 2013, the BVI Premier announced the decision to negotiate an IGA with the U. S. to implement FATCA.

Residence and Citizenship

The 2002 British Overseas Territories Act granted British citizenship to the islanders, who can hold British passports and may work in the U.K. and the European Union. The territory has tightened immigration regulations because illegal immigrants have used the islands as a springboard to the U.S.

U.S. citizens need a valid U.S. passport, onward or return tickets, and sufficient funds for their stay. Visitors wishing to stay longer will need to apply for an extension from the Immigration Department in Road Town, Tortola, or at the Government Administration Building in Virgin Gorda. At the end of 60 days, visitors must report to the Department's main office in Road Town for an extension. Extensions of up to 90 days are issued at the discretion of the immigration officer subsequent to an interview.

If you plan to exit and then re-enter the British Virgin Islands during a sailing vacation, you must be certain to follow the proper procedures for clearing your yacht and crew with both BVI Customs and Immigration. Keep in mind that Americans traveling by air or sea outside of the United States are required to present a passport or other valid travel document to enter or re-enter the United States.

Contacts

BVI's interests in the U.S. are represented by:

Embassy of the United Kingdom
3100 Massachusetts Avenue NW
Washington, DC 20008
Tel.: (202) 588-6500
Email: britishembassyenquiries@gmail.com
Web: https://www.gov.uk/government/world/organisations/british-embassy-washington

The U.S. has no embassy in the BVI. The nearest is:

United States Embassy
Wildey Business Park
Wildey, St. Michael BB 14006
Barbados, West Indies
Tel.: + (246) 227-4000
Web: http://barbados.usembassy.gov

A U.S. Consular Agent resident in Antigua is closer to the BVI and assists U.S. citizens, available by appointment only.

U.S. Consulate Office
Jasmine Court, Suite #2
Friars Hill Road, St. John's, Antigua
Tel.: 268-463-6531, cell 268-726-6531
Email: ANUWndrGyal@aol.com

Cayman Islands

Government:	British Crown colony, self-governing territory of the U.K.
Capital:	George Town (on Grand Cayman)
National Day:	Constitution Day: first Monday in July
Population:	53,737 (July 2013 est.)
Total Area:	101 sq. miles / 262 sq. kilometers
Language:	English (official) 95%, Spanish 3.2%, other 1.8%
Ethnic groups:	Mixed 40%, white 20%, black 20%, expatriates 20%
Religion:	Church of God 25.5%, Roman Catholic 12.6%, Presbyterian/United Church 9.2%, Seventh Day Adventist 8.4%, Baptist 8.3%, Pentecostal 6.7%, Anglican 3.9%, other religions 4%, non-denominational 5.7%, other 6.5%, none 6.1%, unspecified 3.2%
Life expectancy:	80.91 years
Currency:	Caymanian dollar (KYD) 1 = US$1.27
GDP:	US$2.577 billion (2009 est)
GDP per capita:	US$46,516 (2009 est)

Three tiny islands make up the British Overseas Territory of the Cayman Islands, balanced precariously on one side of the enormous Cayman Trench, the deepest part of the Caribbean. While synonymous worldwide with banking, tax havens and beach holidays, there's much more to this tiny, proud nation, even if you do need to look quite hard to find it.

What's so surprising about the Caymans at first is how un-British they are — it would be hard to design a more

Americanized place than Grand Cayman, where the ubiquitous SUVs jostle for space in the parking lots of large malls and US dollars change hands as if they were the national currency.

Cayman Islands are crawling with a fun-loving mix of deal-cutting bankers with briefcases and cell phones, scuba divers in neon-hued wetsuits and English folk checking the cricket scores over a tipple. The islands vibrate with color: coral reefs, bright orange frogfish, sociable stingrays and reggae beats on the street. Thanks to a thriving tourism and cruise ship industry, resorts and condos have sprung up all over, and you can count on every convenience, from air conditioning and cold beer to swanky shopping and ESPN. But if you want to get away from it all, it's easy to escape satellite dishes and slickness, not the least of them underwater. — Lonely Planet

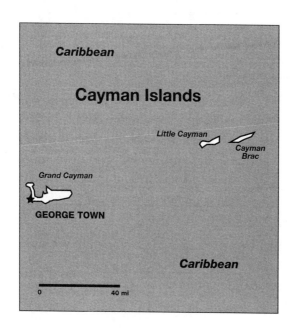

History and Overview

Located in the Caribbean, the three-island group (Grand Cayman, Cayman Brac and Little Cayman) lies south of Cuba and northwest of Jamaica. The Cayman Islands remained largely uninhabited until the 17th century. A variety of people settled on the islands, including pirates, refugees from the Spanish Inquisition, shipwrecked sailors, deserters from Oliver Cromwell's army in Jamaica, and slaves. The majority of Caymanians are of African and British descent, with considerable interracial mixing. Great Britain took formal control of the Caymans, along with Jamaica, under the Treaty of Madrid in 1670.

Following several unsuccessful attempts, permanent settlement of the islands began in the 1730s. The Cayman Islands were colonized from Jamaica by the British during the 18th and 19th centuries, and were administered by Jamaica after 1863. In 1959, the islands became a territory within the Federation of the West Indies, but when the Federation dissolved in 1962, the Cayman Islands chose to remain a British dependency.

The Cayman Islands are located just south of Miami and Cuba. In total land mass, the Cayman Islands aren't very impressive: just three specks in a 100-square-mile area south of Cuba, home to 53,737 souls. These three tiny islands are balanced precariously on the edge of the enormous Cayman Trench, the deepest part of the Caribbean Sea, in what historically was known as the British West Indies.

Grand Cayman, (the largest at 76 square miles), is home to the capitol in George Town, and to most of its people. It's in the same U.S. Eastern Standard Time Zone, convenient for daily business hours, although the Islands don't use Daylight Savings Time.

In American politics, the Caymans have become a classic political football, kicked around by hypocritical candidates. President Barack Obama denounced offshore havens, specifically the Cayman Islands, in both of his presidential campaigns, calling the islands a hotbed of tax evasion.

Yet, many of his own chosen appointees and political friends used the Cayman Islands for investment and banking including former president Bill Clinton, John Kerry, 2004 Democratic presidential candidate and current U.S. Secretary of State, Jack Lew, U.S. Secretary of the Treasury and, of course, Mitt Romney, 2012 Republican presidential candidate, who was attacked repeatedly by Obama for having offshore bank, investment and retirement accounts.

Thanks to these hypocritical politicians and their news media allies, few places in the world have gotten a worse rap in popular perception than the Cayman Islands. Its good name has been tarnished precisely because it is the center for great riches — and for no taxes. The truth about the Cayman Islands is drastically different.

World Class Financial Center

With no direct taxation, the islands are a thriving offshore financial center. Many thousands of offshore companies are registered here, including hundreds of banks and trust companies. In March 2013, its 222 licensed banks held total assets of US$1.725 trillion. Over 80% of all the world's investment funds are believed to be registered in the Cayman Islands. As at January 2012, there were 9,138 investment funds registered with the Cayman Islands Monetary Authority (CIMA) and this does not include the numerous closed-ended or private equity funds which are not required to register. The net asset value of these funds was US$1.8 trillion.

Cayman is a tax neutral jurisdiction. There are no corporate, capital gains, income, profit, withholding or inheritance taxes. Cayman investment fund structures, companies, limited partnerships and trusts are all tax exempt for periods ranging from 20 years (corporations) to 50 years (partnerships and trusts). The government imposes no restrictions on investment policies and there is also no requirement to have directors, administrators or custodians who are resident in the Cayman Islands.

There are no personal taxes on income, capital gains or sales of real estate, nor are there any death duties, inheritance or gift taxes. The Cayman Islands levy no taxes on corporate income. An annual fee is levied on all companies and banks based on shared capital. Duties on imported goods average 22%, with certain items duty free.

Cayman has highly qualified professional service providers including attorneys, accountants, banks and administrators. The "Big Four" accounting firms are represented and 40 of the world's top 50 banks have offices on the island.

Cayman's legal system is based on English common law and local legislation. Laws constantly are reviewed and updated to meet requirements of the financial services industry. The court system is highly developed and there is a dedicated Financial Services Division. Cayman's final court of appeal remains the Privy Council of the United Kingdom in London.

Banking confidentiality is strong in the Caymans because its legal system is based on British common law, the 1995 Banks and Trust Companies Law and the 1995 Confidential Relationships Preservation Law. Banking staff and government officials face civil and criminal sanctions if information is disclosed without authorization. Several laws permit the enforcement of foreign judgments or the disclosure of information in response to a court order, but usually only based on probable cause of criminal activity or drug use or dealing.

Ultimately, the government and the financial industry here is under indirect control of the British government in London. Under Labor Party rule that ended in 2010, the islands were forced to relax what had been very strict financial privacy laws and expand exchange of tax information.

For 15 years, the Paris-based Organization for Economic Co-operation and Development (OECD) has led the international anti-money laundering campaign. The OECD Financial Action Task Force (FATF) sets standards and judges individual jurisdictions. In April 2013, the Cayman Islands received the FATF seal of approval, giving the islands high marks for transparency and fighting tax evasion.

In 2013, the islands signed an agreement with the U.S. to enforce FATCA. In 2014, the government of the islands established tax information exchange agreements with 33 countries and jurisdictions including the United States, the United Kingdom, France, Italy, Singapore and Switzerland.

The Cayman Islands have tough anti-money laundering laws exceeding those in many countries. Since 1990, it has had a mutual legal assistance treaty (MLAT) with the U.S. that has been used nearly 200 times to thwart criminals. Since 2009, it has had a coveted place on the OECD's "White List" of international good guys.

Tourism is a mainstay, accounting for about 70% of GDP and 75% of foreign currency earnings. The tourist industry is aimed at the luxury market and caters mainly to visitors from North America. Total tourist arrivals exceeded 1.9 million in 2008, with about half from the U.S. The Islands' estimated GDP was nearly US$3 billion in 2013, with a per capita GDP of about US$46,000, the 19th highest of any jurisdiction, behind the U.S. but well ahead of the United Kingdom, Germany, France, Canada and Japan.

About 90% of the islands' food and consumer goods must be imported. Caymanians enjoy one of the highest outputs per capita and one of the highest standards of living in the world, comparable to that in Switzerland.

Belonger Status

"Belonger" status is a legal classification of persons who are born or live in British overseas territories. It refers to people who have close ties to a specific territory, normally by birth and/or ancestry. The requirements for belonger status, and the rights that it confers, vary in each territory.

The rights associated with belonger status usually include the right to vote, to hold elective office, to own real property without the need for a license, to reside in the territory without immigration restrictions, and to accept employment without the requirement of a work permit.

In general, to be born with belonger status a person must be born in a territory to a parent who holds belonger status. There are ways to pass belonger status to a child born outside the territory, but these are limited to minimize the number of belongers who do not live in the territory.

In independent countries these rights would-be incidents of the nation's citizenship or nationality. Since British Overseas Territories are not independent countries, they cannot confer full citizenship in the usual sense. Instead, people with close ties to Britain's Overseas Territories all hold the same nationality, known as "British Overseas Territories Citizen" (BOTC). The status of BOTC is defined by the British Nationality Act 1981 and subsequent amendments.

Keep the belonger status in mind as you consider other British Overseas Territories, other than the Cayman Islands, including Bermuda, the Turks and Caicos Islands, Gibraltar, and the British Virgin Islands.

Persons born in a British Overseas Territory after May 21, 2002, automatically acquire British citizenship (even if they do not acquire citizenship in one of the territories) so long as one parent is a British citizen, settled in the U.K., or settled in an Overseas Territory. There are various procedural means by which the U.K. citizenship can be formally claimed.

Residence and Citizenship

Citizenship is difficult to obtain because that status is tied to British overseas territory immigration law, but permanent residence is easy; invest US$400,000 in a new home and show US$150,000 in annual income and you're in. (One Cayman dollar (1.00 KYD) = US$1.22, and the U.S. dollar is accepted everywhere.)

While many people come to the Cayman Islands to visit or invest, thousands of others come to work. With a booming tourist industry and a financial services sector that ranks around fifth in the world, Cayman attracts migrant workers with a diversity of talents. As of January 2014, there were more than 26,400 work permit holders, around three quarters of the entire workforce, and from 125 countries.

Holders of Cayman Islands passports were able to apply for British citizen passports from May 2002, after the British Overseas Territories Act became law. This meant that all Caymanians acquired dual citizenship and a passport if the individual chose to be recognized as a United Kingdom citizen by applying for a British passport.

In recent years, there has been domestic controversy concerning the granting of citizenship to foreigners. This can be done either by the Immigration Board or by the Cabinet. A few years ago the Cayman Islands Cabinet approved Cayman citizenship for large numbers of foreign residents who were in the Caymanian "belonger" status, granting special dispensation.

There have been complaints that it is too difficult to acquire citizenship here. A foreign resident must have lived on the island for 10 years before they can apply for permanent residence, the first step to citizenship. Applications are handled by the Caymanian Status & Permanent Residency Board and are judged on a point system. The applicant is expected to have particular skills or professional expertise, have invested in property or a business, made a significant contribution to the community and to have close connections to the islands through relationships and family. Applications can be denied at the discretion of the board. Once an applicant is awarded permanent residence, they can apply for citizenship.

Two laws aimed at financial services sector employees allow them to obtain more easily immediate residence permits of 3 to 5 years duration. The law names every conceivable banking business and service position and sets fees based in salaries, with those earning US$150,000 paying US$12,500 for citizenship status.

For details and application forms visit the Cayman Islands Immigration website: http://www.immigration.gov.ky

Visas

Keep in mind that Americans traveling by air or sea outside of the United States are required to present a passport or other valid travel document to enter or re-enter the United States.

U.S. and Canadian citizens don't need visas but the best proof of citizenship is a valid passport. Citizens of the EU, the U.K. or the Commonwealth, Israel, Japan need passports but not visas. Visa-free travel is available to citizens of 91 countries. Travelers from elsewhere may need visas as well as passports.

U.S. citizens traveling to the Cayman Islands for work must obtain a temporary work permit from the Department of Immigration of the Cayman Islands; Tel.: + (345) 949-8344. There is a departure tax for travelers age 12 and older included in the airfare.

Contacts

The Cayman Island interests in the U.S. are represented by:

Embassy of the United Kingdom
3100 Massachusetts Avenue NW
Washington, DC 20008
Tel.: (202) 588-6500
Email: britishembassyenquiries@gmail.com
Web: https://www.gov.uk/government/world/organisations/
british-embassy-washington

The U.S. has no diplomatic offices in the Cayman Islands; relations are conducted through the U.S. Embassy in London and the British Embassy in Washington, D.C. The Cayman Islands are part of the consular district administered by the U.S. Embassy in Kingston, Jamaica.

United States Embassy
142 Old Hope Road
Kingston 6, Jamaica
Tel.: + (876) 702-6000
Email: kingstonacs@state.gov
Web: http://kingston.usembassy.gov/

U.S. Consular Agency
150 Smith Road
Smith Road Center, Unit 202B
George Town, KY1-1010
Grand Cayman, Cayman Islands
Tel.: (345) 945-8173

Email: CaymanACS@state.gov
Web: http://kingston.usembassy.gov/service/consular-agents.
html

Cayman Department of Tourism
Tel.: Miami at (305) 599-9033, New York (212) 889-9009,
Houston (713) 461-1317, and Chicago (630) 705-0650.
Web: http://www.caymanislands.ky

Cayman Immigration Department
94A Elgin Avenue
George Town, Grand Cayman
Tel.: + (345) 949-8344
Web: http://www.immigration.gov.ky/

Republic of Costa Rica

Government:	Democratic republic
Capital:	San Jose
National Day:	Independence Day: 15 September (1821)
Population:	4,695,942 (July 2013 est.)
Total Area:	19,730 sq. miles / 51,100 sq. kilometers
Languages:	Spanish (official), English
Ethnic groups:	White (including mestizo) 94%, black 3%, Amerindian 1%, Chinese 1%, other 1%
Religion:	Roman Catholic 76.3%, Evangelical 13.7%, Jehovah's Witnesses 1.3%, other Protestant 0.7%, other 4.8%, none 3.2%
Life expectancy:	78.60 years
Currency:	Costa Rican colon (CRC)
GDP:	US$58.55 billion (2012 est.)
GDP per capita:	US$12,500 (2012 est.)

Mention Costa Rica and people think paradise. The country's Disney-like cast of creatures, ranging from howler monkeys to toucans — are populous and relatively easy to spot. The waves are prime; the beauty is staggering and the sluggish pace seductive. A peaceful oasis in a tumultuous region, this tiny nation draws 1.5 million visitors every year.

What's on tap? The question is what isn't? Active travelers can surf, hike, snorkel and spot wildlife for starters. The incredibly varied topography means you can cruise the cloud forest one day, visit an active volcano the next, and finish relaxing on a hot sandy beach. Adrenaline junkies have a myriad ways to make mothers worry — among them zipping through can-

opy lines hundreds of meters long and riding the rough surf of the Pacific. Choice and variety name the game.

Of course, the frenzy to snatch up a piece of Shangri-la has its consequences. Since the boom, tourism is more chic and less cheap. Classic destinations are now crowded destinations and local culture is often lost or cast aside. Lucky for Costa Rica that its do-gooder fans, ranging from ecologists to proud "Ticos" (Costa Ricans), are vocal and vigilant. Nature here suffers its blows, like everywhere, but at least it is taken seriously. —Lonely Planet

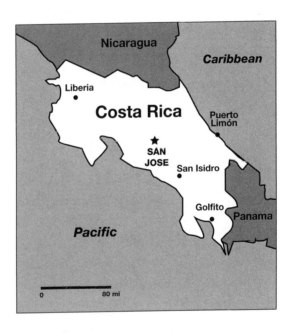

History and Overview

Located between Nicaragua to the north and Panama to the south, Costa Rica straddles Central America, bordered by the Caribbean Sea on the east and the Pacific Ocean on the west.

It has been called "The Switzerland of the Americas" for two reasons, because of its impressive terrain marked by a rugged, mountainous interior, and because the country fancied itself to be a leading offshore tax haven. The mountains remain, but this is no tax haven and its reputation as a financial center is not the best.

The highest peak in the region is Chirripó Grande, rising to nearly 12,500 feet. Not far north of the equator, the nation enjoys a lush, tropical climate, low cost of living, low taxes, high-quality medical care, educated citizens, as well as highly developed agricultural and tourist industries. In 1502, Columbus made a landfall in this area and gave it the name "Costa Rica," which means "rich coast."

Perhaps nowhere in the Western Hemisphere is the tension between conservation of natural assets and the drive for development so readily apparent as in Costa Rica. The "Ticos," as the inhabitants call themselves, take great pride in the extensive marine and beach environments, lowland and highland forests, and cultural attractions their country offers. Acutely conscious of the stress that tourists, retirees and industrialists put on Costa Rica's delicate natural and human resources, the government has instituted guidelines for "sustainable tourism" aimed at minimizing visitors' impact on the country's parks and resort areas.

The World Factbook states: "Although explored by the Spanish early in the 16th century, attempts at colonizing were unsuccessful for many reasons including disease from mosquito-infested swamps, brutal heat, resistance by natives, and pirate raids. It was not until 1563 that a permanent settlement of Cartago was established in the cooler, fertile central highlands. The area remained a Spanish colony for 250 years. In 1821, Costa Rica became one of several Central American provinces that jointly declared their independence from Spain. Two years later it joined the United Provinces of Central America, a federation that disintegrated in 1838, when Costa Rica proclaimed its sovereignty and independence."

The nation has a strong democratic tradition. After a turbulent beginning, it inaugurated an era of peaceful democracy in 1889, interrupted only twice, by a dictatorial interlude in 1917 to 1919 and an armed uprising in 1948. In April 2014, historian and former diplomat Luis Guillermo Solis, the candidate of the moderate Citizen Action Party, was elected president in a race in which he faced no opposition. The incumbent National Liberation Party (PLN) candidate withdrew after this party lost support because of alleged corruption and economic crisis under outgoing President Laura Chinchilla.

In 1949, Costa Rica dissolved its armed forces. Costa Rica is considered one of the relatively more stable democracies in Latin America. It has a high literacy rate (95%) and a good health care system. The cost of living is reasonably low and with about US$2,000 a month, an individual could live an expatriate lifestyle in a modern studio apartment, complete with a swimming pool.

Economy

Although it still maintains a large agricultural sector, Costa Rica has expanded its economy to include strong technology and tourism industries. The standard of living is relatively high. Land ownership is widespread.

After experiencing positive growth, the Costa Rican economy shrank slightly in 2009 due to the global economic crisis. The services sector, about 68% of GDP, was the most affected, with tourism falling by 8%. The economy experienced a rebound in 2010. Costa Rica enjoys the region's highest standard of living, with a per capita income of about US$12,500, and an unemployment rate of 6.7%.

Foreign investors remain attracted by the country's political stability and relatively high education levels, as well as the fiscal incentives offered in the free-trade zones. Costa Rica has attracted one of the highest levels of foreign direct investment per capita in Latin America. However, many business impediments, such as many levels of bureaucracy, difficulty of enforcing contracts in the courts, and weak investor protection, remain.

The government sustained social spending, almost 20% of GDP annually, and has provided universal access to education, health care, clean water, sanitation, and electricity. Since the 1970s, expansion of these services has led to a decline in infant mortality, an increase in life expectancy at birth, and a sharp decrease in the birth rate.

However, poverty has remained around 20% for nearly 20 years and the strong social safety net — put in place by the government — has eroded due to increased financial constraints on expenditures. Immigration from Nicaragua has increasingly become a costly concern for the government.

Problems

According to the U.S. Department of State, "Upwards of 20,000 private American citizens, including many retirees, reside in the country and more than 600,000 American citizens visit Costa Rica annually. There have been some vexing issues in the U.S.-Costa Rican relationship, principal among them longstanding expropriation and other U.S. citizen investment disputes, which have hurt Costa Rica's investment climate and produced tensions.

Land invasions from organized squatter groups who target foreign landowners also have occurred, and some have turned violent. The U.S. government has made clear to Costa Rica its concern that Costa Rican inattention to these issues has left U.S. citizens vulnerable to harm and loss of their property."

Unlike many of their Central American neighbors, present-day

Costa Ricans are largely of European rather than of mestizo descent; Spain was the primary country of origin. However, an estimated 10% to 15% of the population now is Nicaraguan, of fairly recent arrival and primarily of mestizo origin. Descendants of 19th-century Jamaican immigrant workers constitute an English-speaking minority and, at 3% of the population, number about 119,000. Few of the native Indians survived European contact; the indigenous population today numbers about 29,000 or less than 1% of the population.

Costa Rica is a popular regional immigration destination because of its job opportunities and social programs. Almost 9% of the population is foreign-born, with Nicaraguans comprising nearly three-quarters of that foreign population. Many Nicaraguans who perform unskilled seasonal labor enter Costa Rica illegally or overstay their visas, a continuing source of tension.

The estimated 300,000 to 500,000 Nicaraguans in Costa Rica — legally and illegally — are an important source of mostly unskilled labor, but also place heavy demands on the social welfare system.

The U.S.-Central American Free Trade Agreement (CAFTA) entered into force in 2009, after significant delays within the Costa Rican legislature. Nevertheless, economic growth slowed as the 2008 to 2011 global downturn reduced export demand and investment inflows.

Crime Problems

In late 2013, the U.S. State Department warned that crimes are a significant concern and the U.S. Embassy reports a steady increase in crime. Foreign visitors are potential targets for criminals who usually operate in small groups, but also operate alone. The most common crime against tourists is theft, with thieves primarily looking for cash, jewelry, credit cards, electronic items and passports. Serious crimes do occur and have been committed against Americans; at least seven U.S. citizens have been murdered in Costa Rica since January 2012. Daytime robberies in public places occur, and thieves are often armed and violent.

Since January 2012, 21 U.S. citizens who were sexually assaulted have reported to the Embassy, with at least six victims reporting that they were given date rape drugs. While the Costa Rican police claim to investigate all reported cases of rape, there have been no convictions in sexual assault cases of U.S. citizens. Carjackings have occurred, with motorists confronted at gunpoint while stopped at traffic lights or upon arrival at their homes.

Incidents of crime commonly occur in downtown San Jose, at beaches, the airport, and at national parks and other tourist attractions. There have been assaults on tourist buses in recent years. Travelers who stay in a group, keep valuables out of sight, do not wear jewelry, and travel during daylight hours lessen their risk. Local law enforcement agencies have limited capabilities. People offering money exchange on the street pass off counterfeit U.S. dollars and local currency. Credit card fraud is also growing.

Passport Problems

Over the years, Costa Rica has been plagued with scandals involving "honorary" consular and diplomatic appointments. Authorities also broke up a criminal group, including a former director of Immigration and Security that was selling visas. It was also discovered that "humanitarian and cultural visas" were granted to expatriate Cubans in return for cash payments of US$5,000 to US$7,000. The illegal sale of passports appears to be a continuing problem. For these reasons, carrying a Costa Rican passport can subject a person to close scrutiny at border points, resulting in delays and questioning.

I have assisted in several Instances where obviously illegal Costa Rican "official passports" were being offered by questionable law firms in both San Jose and in Panama.

Residence and Citizenship

Citizenship is conferred in the following ways:

1. by birth: on a child born within the territory of Costa Rica, regardless of the nationality of the parents.

2. by descent: on a child born abroad, at least one of whose parents is a citizen of Costa Rica.

3. by naturalization: The following categories of people are eligible to be naturalized:

   a) Central Americans, Spaniards and Latin Americans (all categories by birth) who have resided in the country for at least five years;

   b) Central Americans, Spaniards and Latin Americans, other than by birth, as well as other foreign nationals, who have resided in the country for at least seven years; and

   c) a foreign woman who has married a citizen of Costa Rica and either has lost her own citizenship or applies for Costa Rican citizenship.

Local attorneys complain that the immigration process takes far too long and is getting worse.

Costa Rica has a checkered history of official programs for foreign persons wishing to become citizens. A since repealed 1971 law offered citizenship for non-nationals who purchased both a home in Costa Rica and a US$30,000 government bond. After five years, a permanent resident could qualify for citizenship and a passport that was renewable and allowed visa-free travel to most countries.

Because the nation then had few extradition treaties, several wealthy U.S. criminal fugitives took advantage of the program, became permanent residents and lived openly in the country. Perhaps the most notorious of these was Robert Lee Vesco (1935-2007) who was called "the undisputed king of the fugitive U.S. financiers." Accused by the SEC of securities fraud in 1973, Vesco fled to Costa Rica. With a US$2.1 million donation to a project of the then president of Costa Rica, José Figueres, he was able to have a special law adopted that protected him from extradition. Under U.S. pressure, the program was eventually closed down.

Now, another residence program is in place that requires no upfront investment. Instead, the foreign applicant must guarantee to bring a certain amount of hard currency into the country each month to be exchanged for the Environmental Citizenship.

The program recognizes two categories, *pensionados* (retired persons) and *rentistas* (recipients of passive income). *Pensionados* must import at least US$600 per month from an established pension source for a term of at least five years. *Rentistas* must get at least US$1,000 per month for five years, generally, from a guaranteed source such as certificates of deposit at a recognized bank. All applicants must stay in the country for at least four months, or 120 days annually, but this need not be continuous.

All applicants receive the same rights and privileges. They can reside in Costa Rica and are not taxed on foreign source income. They are not allowed to work in the country, but can conduct business there for the purpose of receiving dividends rather than a salary. Local income is subject to a 17% flat tax. Imported motor vehicles are hit with a whopping duty of 100%, with household goods subject to duties from 25% to 100%.

A spouse and dependents can be included on a single application, and after seven years residence, they qualify for nationality.

The Costa Rican Association of *Pensionados* and *Rentistas* says that two people who own a house can live quite comfortably here on US$1,000 a month.

In the past, Costa Rica did not allow dual nationality and required surrender of other passports upon naturalization. The right to hold dual nationality now is recognized in law.

Environmental Citizenship

The nation has an unusual residence program for foreigners willing to invest in reforestation projects qualified under Costa Rica's environmental law No. 7575. Individuals who invest in Forestales Alegria, S.A. (Melina Farm) can qualify for Investor Residency Status, similar to a U.S. green card, which allows permanent residence and most rights and privileges of citizenship. Investors receive registered title to a designated parcel of land, a return on investment and tax-free income. This program stems from the government's strong environmental policies that have made the nation a leader in forestry conservation. Over 90% of remaining forests are protected and the nation has the world's largest percentage of land dedicated to national parks.

Land Investment Cautions

Notwithstanding this program, foreign investors should exercise extreme caution before investing in real estate. Costa Rica has a long history of investment and real estate scams and frauds perpetrated against foreign visitors. U.S.-style land title insurance is generally unavailable and there have been numerous instances of duly registered properties reverting to previously unknown owners who possess clear title and parallel registration. Due to irregular enforcement of property rights, existence of unresolved expropriation claims, and squatter invasions, property protections are uncertain, particularly in rural areas.

Some U.S. citizen landowners have had long expropriation disputes with the government of Costa Rica. Claims from the 1970s to the present day remain unresolved, with the landowners uncompensated. Existing unenforced government expropriation decrees cloud land titles even when owners remain in possession.

Real estate throughout the country has been invaded by organized squatter groups against which the government has been reluctant to act. These groups, often supported by politicians and their political organizations, take advantage of legal reforms allowing people without land to claim title to unused agricultural property. This is common in rural areas, where local courts show considerable sympathy for squatters. The squatters regularly resort to threats and actual violence and often are able to block U.S. citizen landowners from entering their property.

For entry into Costa Rica, U.S. citizens must present valid passports that will not expire for at least thirty days after arrival, and an outbound ticket. Passports should be in good condition; Costa Rican immigration will deny entry if the passport is damaged in any way.

Costa Rican authorities generally permit U.S. citizens to stay up to ninety days; to stay beyond the period granted, travelers must submit an application for an extension to the Office of Temporary Permits in the Costa Rican Department of Immigration. Border officials can be difficult. It required two hours to return after I made the mistake of crossing the border from Panama for lunch at a village café in Costa Rica. No doubt a cash bribe would have speeded up the process.

Tourist visas are usually not extended except under special circumstances, and extension requests are evaluated on a case-by-case basis. There is a departure tax for short-term visitors. Tourists who stay over 90 days may experience a delay at the airport when departing. Persons who overstayed previously may be denied re-entry to Costa Rica.

Contacts

Embassy of Costa Rica
2112 S Street NW
Washington, DC 2008
Tel.: (202) 499-2991
Email: concr-us-wa@rree.go.cr
Web: http://www.costarica-embassy.org/

United States Embassy
Calle 98 Vía 104, Pavas
San Jose, Costa Rica
Tel.: + (506) 2519-2000
Email: irc@usembassy.or.cr
Web: http://sanjose.usembassy.gov/

Dominican Republic

Government:	Representative democracy
Capital:	Santo Domingo
National Day:	Independence Day: 27 February (1844)
Population:	10,219,630 (July 2013 est.)
Total Area:	18,815 sq. miles / 48,730 sq. kilometers
Language:	Spanish
Ethnic groups:	Mixed 73%, white 16%, black 11%
Religion:	Roman Catholic 95%, other 5%
Life expectancy:	77.62 years
Currency:	Dominican peso (DOP)
GDP:	US$97.68 billion (2012 est.)
GDP per capita:	US$9,500 (2012 est.)

The Dominican Republic (DR) is a land of contrasts — - the physical kind, like the highest peak and the lowest point in the Caribbean, and the more metaphorical kind, like that between the urban street life of Santo Domingo and the rural villages only a short drive away. Santo Domingo, or "La Capital" as it's typically called, is to Dominicans what New York is to Americans, a collage of cultures; or what Havana is to Cubans, a vibrant beating heart that fuels the entire country. It's also a living museum, offering the sight of New World firsts scattered around the charming cobblestone streets of the Zona Colonial.

The DR is also famous for the large all-inclusive resorts that dominate much of the country's prime beachfront real estate. However, the result is less like the high-rise congestion of Cancun or Miami and more like low slung retirement communi-

ties, albeit ones populated by families, couples and singles of all
ages looking for a hassle-free holiday. — *Lonely Planet*

History and People

The Dominican Republic is the second largest nation in the Caribbean, with a population of over 10 million descended from Spanish settlers and their African slaves. Two million live in the greater Santo Domingo capital area. There are an estimated one million expatriate Dominicans in the U.S., with which the DR has close economic ties and trade.

The DR's tropical latitude gives it a moderate year-round climate and its extensive beaches make it a popular tourist destination. Santo Domingo is accessible by air from New York (three hours), Miami (two hours) and San Juan (45 minutes). The terrain is varied and includes Lake Enriquillo, the lowest point in the Caribbean, and Pico Duarte, the highest. Watershed areas contain many rivers and streams, and the economy traditionally has been agricultural. Mining of silver, gold, nickel, and bauxite is also significant.

The Dominican Republic on the island of Hispaniola shares that island, somewhat uneasily, with Haiti. The people on opposite sides of this island have faced each other across this divided body of land for nearly four centuries. Their two cultures are studies in contrast. Haiti was colonized by the French; the Dominicans were colonized by the Spanish. In Haiti, people speak Creole; in the Dominican Republic, they speak Spanish. In Haiti, the national sport is soccer; in the Dominican Republic, the national sport is baseball. In Haiti, the national religion is voodoo and Roman Catholicism; in the Dominican Republic, it is Roman Catholicism. On the Haitian side of the Massacre River, which divides the two countries, when it is 7 a.m., it's 8 a.m. on the Dominican side.

Hispaniola is an island divided by two peoples who, to some extent, have shaped their identities in opposition to each other. In fact, the Dominican Republic is the only country in the New World that celebrates its independence from another American country, because for Dominicans, the separation from Haiti in 1844 is their Independence Day. Between 1822 and 1844, Haiti occupied the Dominican end of the island.

Historically, the Dominican Republic, the eastern two thirds of the island of Hispaniola, was the seat of the original capital of the Spanish New World. The French ruled Haiti as a colony on the western third of the island, where a successful slave revolt in 1804 brought independence.

Control of the island was divided between Haitians and the Spanish until 1916, when U.S. troops occupied it for eight years to ensure debts were paid to U.S. and European banks. In 1930, a dictator, Rafael Trujillo, gained power, ruling until his assassination in 1961. In 1965, U.S. President Lyndon Johnson sent in the U.S.

Marines to end civil war and democracy was introduced. Quadrennial elections produced repeated re-election of the corrupt, aging Joaquín Balaguer until 1996. The former reform president, Leonel Fernández Reyna, first elected in 1996, and later to two more non-consecutive terms, is a dual DR-U.S. citizen, American-educated attorney and a former resident of New York City. The current president is Danilo Medina Sánchez.

The 1966 Constitution guarantees free enterprise and individual freedoms. The legal system is much like that of Napoleonic Code civil law countries and Dominican Republic courts apply French judicial precedents.

Economy

The Dominican Republic economy underwent significant reform in the 1990s. Tourism and business-free zones are bright spots. There are 1.5 million foreign visitors annually occupying 32,000 (and growing) hotel rooms, leading all Caribbean countries. Tourism accounts for 17% of the GNP and provides 50% of the DR's hard currency.

Industrial-free zones allow duty-free passage of raw materials and finished products, employing over 164,000. These free zones are for exports, mostly to the U.S., and over 250 companies now operate in free zone industrial parks, with major textile and electronics segments. The special free zones allow owners to operate a business free from corporate income tax for up to 20 years. Offshore business based here is also tax-free for its foreign earnings.

Transportation and communication infrastructure is extensive, with two major international airports and a good domestic highway system. Telecommunications are good and the DR is part of the U.S. direct-dialing phone network. The phone company is owned by Verizon and service is excellent. The greatest handicap to economic activity has been the serious shortfall in electricity generation.

The Dominican Republic has long been viewed primarily as an exporter of sugar, coffee, and tobacco, but in recent years the service sector has overtaken agriculture as the economy's largest employer, due to growth in telecommunications, tourism, and free trade zones. The economy is highly dependent upon the U.S., the destination for more than half of exports. Remittances from the US amount to about one-tenth of GDP, equivalent to almost half of exports and three-quarters of tourism receipts.

The country suffers from marked income inequality; the poorest half of the population receives less than one-fifth of GDP, while the richest 10% enjoys nearly 40% of GDP. High unemployment and underemployment remains an important long-term challenge. The Central America-Dominican Republic Free Trade Agreement (CAFTA-DR) came into force in March 2007, boosting investment and exports and reducing losses to the Asian garment industry.

The growth of the Dominican Republic's economy rebounded from the global recession in 2010 to 2012 and remains one of the fastest growing in the region although its fiscal situation is weak; the fiscal deficit climbed from 2.6% in 2011 to approximately 8% in 2012.

The country also serves as a transfer point for transatlantic cocaine shipments to Europe and Africa. During the year 2011, Italian authorities seized within a two-week period one ton of Columbian cocaine shipped from the Dominican Republic. There were rumors that drug kingpins had ordered several attacks that occurred on DR government officials and judges dealing with drug cases.

Illegal Immigrants

In 2011, the government began applying a law that denies citizenship to children of illegal immigrants. They also began to deport people who had been born and lived in the U.S. for years, advocacy groups contend. The deportations were taken as a sign of impatience with the poor recovery in Haiti. Several countries, including the DR, granted a grace period on Haitian migrants and refugees after the massive Haitian earthquake on January 12, 2010. To date, the catastrophic event has left many Haitians displaced and an estimated 500,000 remain in the DR.

In September 2013, the DR's Constitutional Court issued a ruling that effectively "denationalized" hundreds of thousands of the DR's own people. The ruling retroactively denied Dominican citizenship to anyone born in the country after 1929 that did not have at least one parent of Dominican blood. Anyone not meeting this test was deemed "illegal" in the country.

Officials said the ruling was irreversible but in May 2014 the legislature adopted a law that said children born to foreign parents could be citizens, provided they have Dominican government identification documents and are in the civil registry.

Those without documents could apply for legal residence and eventually citizenship if they can prove they were born in the Dominican Republic, something human rights groups said could be difficult for many people who lacked the awareness to seek or keep birth certificates or other records.

Advocates for Haitian migrants and their children said the law change was an important, if imperfect, step. While it may clear up and validate the legal status of thousands of people, many others, including some of the poorest who lack documents, may remain in limbo or be forced to register as foreigners regardless of how long they had been there.

A 2013 immigrant census estimated 245,000 Dominican-born, first generation children of immigrants living in the country, with the vast majority, some 210,000, being of Haitian descent.

Dating back to 1929, the 2013 court ruling covered several generations. Human rights experts estimate that the number of affected people was over 450,000. Critics contended the ruling revealed an ugly racial policy.

Word of Caution

Up front you need to know that when it comes to acquiring second passports, the problem with the Dominican Republic is its bad reputation.

The respected Henley & Partners of Zurich, one of The Sovereign Society's preferred providers for residence and citizenship says about the DR: "There is a constant practice of illegal sales of passport and citizenship documents by corrupt government officials, and therefore passports from the Dominican Republic have a bad reputation."

Unless you make it your residence and live there, we do not recommend that anyone acquire Dominican Republic citizenship, not even legally. In 1999, a Russian national was arrested at London's Heathrow International Airport with a suitcase full of official Dominican Republic passports.

In recent years, there have been several similar scandals in which quantities of DR passports were apparently sold by people with government connections. Although the stolen passports involved were official, the fact that they were being sold on the black market called into question everyone traveling on DR passports. The customs and immigration services of every major nation know this and act accordingly, much to the chagrin of the legal DR passport holders.

By some estimates, in recent years almost 10,000 passports were sold illegally, for as little as US$5,000 and for as much as US$18,000. The sellers claimed that the passports were valid for six years with automatic renewal at any Dominican Republic Consulate. Needless to say, they were not renewed.

At the present time, there is no "instant" DR passport program available, regardless of what you may be told. Yet, one continues to see numerous advertisements in international publications promising quick "official" DR passports, always at inflated prices.

There are too many legitimate second passport possibilities without having to chance it with a DR passport. Stay away unless you make your second home or business there.

Special Naturalization

Having said that, although "instant" DR passports are supposedly no longer a legal possibility, a form of "legal" citizenship is available on the grounds listed below in as little as six months. The following conditions leave a great deal of room for negotiation and suggest a possible mutual understanding of a pecuniary nature with officials using influential DR attorneys.

To qualify for "special" naturalization, one of the following conditions must be satisfied:

- Authorization from the Chief Executive to establish and maintain a DR domicile for not less than six months;

- Continuous DR residence for at least two years;

- Continuous DR residence for at least six months and either having founded/currently operating a DR business or owning real estate;

- Continuous residence for at least six months and marriage to a Dominican at the time application is submitted;

- Authorization from the Chief Executive to establish domicile, and, within three months, owning at least 30 hectares of land under cultivation, or;

- Continuous residence for six months, having performed technical or special services for the armed forces.

Residence and Citizenship

Dominican Republic visas are of several kinds: diplomatic, official, courtesy, business, tourist, residence, or student. Applications for business or tourist visas can be made at any Dominican Republic Consulate.

Most tourists can enter without a visa for a period of up to 90 days if they have a valid passport. Consular fees are charged on business, dependent, tourism, residence, and student visas. The Ministry of Foreign Affairs can revoke visas without prior notice. Residence visas require a great deal more documentation and must be submitted at the Dominican Republic Consulate nearest the applicant's actual residence.

If a residence visa is granted, the recipient must arrive in the DR within 60 days, then apply to the Immigration Department for a provisional residence card, which is valid for one year and renewable annually.

The official DR passport allows visa-free travel to very few countries, probably a reflection of the poor international attitude held by other countries toward anyone with a DR passport.

Fast Track Retirement

In the past, one of the Dominican Republic requirements for residence was that applicants prove they had assets or investments in the country equal to 500,000 DR pesos, about US$11,600 under 2014 exchange rates. This could be established by a U.S. dollar denominated Certificate of Deposit with a local DR bank.

Following the example of Panama and Belize, the Dominican Republic enacted a law aimed at attracting foreign residence with a fast track residence system, especially aimed at foreign retirees.

With the approval of Law 171-07 on Foreign Retirees, the Dominican Republic bills itself as "a paradise for people wanting to retire to an idyllic setting."

The 2007 law provides a fast-tracked residence program with simplified paperwork, all within 45 days. It also allows the import of duty-free household goods and a host of tax breaks. These tax breaks include reductions on motor vehicle taxes, exemption on transfer taxes for the first purchase of local real estate, a 50% reduction on taxes on mortgages, a 50% reduction on the annual property tax, exemption on taxes on dividends and interest, and a 50% reduction on capital gains taxes.

The minimum monthly income required under the new law is US$1,500 for retirees with a government or private pension and US$2,000 in verified income from all others. For information contact: Secretary of State for Foreign Relations, Independence Ave. #752 , Santo Domingo, Dominican Republic. Tel.: 1 + (809) 535-6280.

All DR residents are subject to income tax on global income and residents' estates, excluding real estate located abroad, which is not subject to DR inheritance tax. Above US$4,800, the income tax rate is applied progressively.

Those with a net income in excess of US$12,000 are taxed at a rate of 25%. For corporations, foreign or domestic, and for dividends, a single rate of 30% is taken for income tax.

Citizenship

Under the law, in addition to those methods described above, citizenship is conferred in the following ways:

1. by birth: on a child born in the territory of the Dominican Republic, regardless of the nationality of the parents with two exceptions: a) when the child's parent is an illegal immigrant; b) when a child is born to a diplomatic representative.

2. by descent: on a child born abroad, at least one of whose parents is a citizen.

3. by naturalization: citizenship may be acquired by a person who has legally resided in the country for at least two years and has renounced former citizenship.

The normal naturalization process takes between 12 and 18 months to complete. Once the process is complete, dual citizenship is permitted. A spouse need not fulfill residence requirements for naturalization if applications are made jointly. Children over the age of 18 may obtain citizenship after one year of residence if the application is made jointly with the mother.

Contacts

Embassy of the Dominican Republic
1715 22nd Street NW
Washington, DC 20008
Tel.: (202) 332-6280
Email: embassy@us.serex.gov.do
Web: http://www.domrep.org

United States Embassy
Calle Cesar Nicolas Penson Esq. & Calle Leopoldo Navarro
Santo Domingo, Dominican Republic
Tel.: + (809) 221-2171

Email: reference@usemb.gov.do
Web: http://santodomingo.usembassy.gov/

Dominican Republic Ministry of Tourism
Web: http://www.godominicanrepublic.com/rd/

Republic of El Salvador

Government:	Republic
Capital:	San Salvador
National Day:	Independence Day: 15 September (1821)
Population:	6,108,590 (July 2013 est.)
Total Area:	8,124 sq. miles / 21,040 sq. kilometers
Languages:	Spanish, Nahua (among some Amerindians)
Ethnic groups:	Mestizo 90%, white 9%, Amerindian 1%
Religion:	Roman Catholic 57.1%, Protestant 21.2%, Jehovah's Witnesses 1.9%, Mormon 0.7%, other religions 2.3%, none 16.8%
Life expectancy:	73.93 years
Currency:	U.S. dollar (US$)
GDP:	US$46.09 billion (2012 est.)
GDP per capita:	US$7,300 (2012 est.)

El Salvador sneaks up on you: in lefty lounge bars in San Salvador, at sobering museums and war memorials, and along lush cloud-forest trails; it's a place of remarkable warmth and intelligence, made all the more appealing for being so unexpected. Travelers tend to skip El Salvador, wooed by marquee destinations such as Guatemala and Costa Rica, and unnerved by stories of civil war and gang violence.

But the war ended almost 20 years ago, and crime, while serious, is almost exclusively played out between rival gangs; tourists are virtually never involved. And though El Salvador has fewer protected areas than its neighbors, you get them practically to yourself — including pristine forests, active volcanoes and sparkling lakes. — Lonely Planet

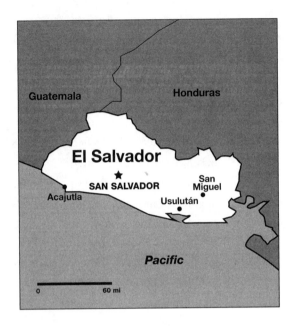

History and Overview

El Salvador is located in Central America, bordering the North Pacific Ocean, between Guatemala and Honduras. El Salvador is the smallest and most densely populated country in Central America.

El Salvador achieved independence from Spain in 1821 and from the Central American Federation in 1839. A 12-year civil war, which cost nearly 75,000 lives, ended in 1992 when the government and leftist rebels signed a treaty that provided for military and political reforms.

Salvadorans fled during the 1979 to 1992 civil war and migrated to the United States and Canada, they also fled to neighboring Mexico, Guatemala, Honduras, Nicaragua, and Costa Rica. Emigration to the U.S. increased again in the 1990s and 2000s as a result of deteriorating economic conditions, natural disasters (Hurricane Mitch in 1998 and earthquakes in 2001), and family reunification. To date, at least 20% of El Salvador's population lives abroad.

In 2009, El Salvador made electoral history when the leftist Farabundo Martí National Liberation Front (FMLN) party won the presidential elections, defeating the ruling Nationalist Republican Alliance by 51.2% to 48.7% of the vote. Since its independence from Spain in 1821, El Salvador always has been ruled by conservative rightist governments, often military dictatorships, until the early 1990s.

In the 2014 presidential election, Salvador Sánchez Cerén the vice president was elected as president. He has admitted that as a FMLN guerrilla commander in the 1980s he participated in brutal slayings during the civil war that claimed 70,000 lives. Cerén immediately faced a difficult problem. More than 20 years after its brutal civil war ended, El Salvador remains a violent country convulsed by a culture of gang violence. A controversial 2012 truce between the gangs dramatically lowered the national homicide rate. However, since Cerén took office, that pact is about to disintegrate.

Economy

The smallest country in Central America, El Salvador has the third largest economy, but growth has been minimal in recent years. Economic growth decelerated in 2009 due to the global slowdown and to El Salvador's dependence on exports to the U.S. and remittances from the U.S. El Salvador leads the region in remittances per capita with inflows equivalent to nearly all export income, some US$4 billion annually. The remittances account for close to 20% of GDP, are the second largest source of external income after exports, and have helped reduce poverty and reduce the trade deficit.

Hoping to stimulate the sluggish economy, the government is striving to open new export markets, encourage foreign investment, and modernize the tax and health care systems. Implementation, in 2006, of the Central America-Dominican Republic Free Trade Agreement, which El Salvador was the first to ratify, is viewed as a key policy to help achieve these objectives. With the adoption of the U.S. dollar as its currency in 2001, El Salvador has lost control over monetary policy and must concentrate on maintaining a disciplined fiscal policy.

Salvadorans have been subject to social and migration policies tailored for them by the United States government with the support of the Salvadoran government. The Nicaraguan Adjustment and Central American Relief Act (NACARA), a 1997 U.S. law allowed Salvadorans (along with Nicaraguans, and Guatemalans) in the U.S. to receive immigrant benefits and relief from deportation. As many as 146,000 Salvadorans were able to secure legal U.S. residence status.

U.S. ties to El Salvador are dynamic and growing. More than 19,000 American citizens live and work full-time in El Salvador. Most are private business people and their families, but a small number of American citizen retirees have been drawn to El Salvador by favorable tax conditions.

Taxes levied by the government include a value added tax (VAT) of 13%, income tax of 20%, excise taxes on alcohol and cigarettes, and import duties. The VAT accounted for about 49.7% of total tax revenues in 2010. El Salvador's public external debt in January 2010 was about $11.2 billion, 53% of GDP.

Residence and Citizenship

Citizenship law is based on the Constitution and provides for citizenship:

1. by birth: for a child born in El Salvador, regardless of the citizenship of the mother or father.

2. by descent: for a child born abroad of a Salvadoran mother or father.

3. by naturalization: after fulfillment of the following conditions:

    a) Persons of any origin must have maintained residence in El Salvador for at least five years. Spaniards and native Hispano-Americans need only reside for one year. Foreign spouses of Salvadoran citizens need to reside at least 2 years after the marriage.

    b) Persons can obtain citizenship from the legislative branch for noteworthy services rendered to the republic.

El Salvador recognizes a special citizenship designation for natives of other states that constituted the Federal Republic of Central America, who, having domicile in El Salvador, declare before a competent authority their desire to be Salvadoran.

Salvadorans, by birth, have the right to enjoy dual or multiple citizenships. This right is not extended to those whose citizenship is acquired through naturalization.

To enter the country, U.S. citizens must present a current U.S. passport and either a Salvadoran visa or a one-entry tourist card. The tourist card may be obtained from immigration officials for a US$10 fee upon arrival in the country. U.S. travelers who plan to remain in El Salvador for more than 30 days can apply in advance for a multiple-entry visa, issued free of charge, from the Embassy of El Salvador in Washington, D.C.

El Salvador is a party to the "Central America-4 (CA-4) Border Control Agreement" with Guatemala, Honduras and Nicaragua. Under its terms, citizens of the four countries may travel freely across land borders from one of the countries to any of the others without completing entry and exit formalities at immigration checkpoints. U.S. citizens and other eligible foreign nationals, who legally enter any of the four countries, may similarly travel among the four without obtaining additional visas or tourist entry permits for the other three countries.

Warning

The U.S. Embassy considers El Salvador a critical crime threat country with rampant street gang activity. El Salvador has one of the highest homicide rates in the world. Both violent and petty crimes are prevalent throughout El Salvador, and U.S. citizens have been among the victims. The Embassy is aware of at least nine American citizens who were murdered in El Salvador during 2010 to 2011 and more recently.

Extortion is on the rise and U.S. citizens and their family members have been victims in various incidents. Violent, organized gangs are a major factor in the crime situation and are often behind extortion attempts. Some areas of El Salvador are effectively controlled by gangs. Many gangs have access to military-style hardware, including automatic weapons and hand grenades.

Travelers should remain in groups and avoid remote or isolated locations in order to minimize their vulnerability. Travelers should also avoid displaying or carrying valuables in public places.

Contacts

Embassy of El Salvador
1400 16th Street NW, Suite 100
Washington, DC 20036
Tel.: (202) 595-7500
Email: correo@elsalvador.org
Web: http://www.elsalvador.org

United States Embassy
Boulevard Santa Elena

Antiguo Cuscatlan
La Libertad, El Salvador
Tel.: + (503) 2501-2999
Email: congensansal@state.gov
Web: http://sansalvador.usembassy.gov

Republic of Guatemala

Government:	Republic
Capital:	Guatemala City
National Day:	Independence Day: 15 September (1821)
Population:	14,373,472 (July 2013 est.)
Total Area:	42,043 sq. miles / 108,890 sq. kilometers
Languages:	Spanish 60%, Amerindian 40% (23 Amerindian dialects)
Ethnic groups:	Mestizo (mixed Amerindian-Spanish — in local Spanish called Ladino) and European 59.4%, K'iche 9.1%, Kaqchikel 8.4%, Mam 7.9%, Q'eqchi 6.3%, other Mayan 8.6%, indigenous non-Mayan 0.2%, other 0.1%
Religion:	Roman Catholic, Protestant, traditional Mayan
Life expectancy:	71.46 years
Currency:	Quetzal (GTQ)
GDP:	US$77.84 billion (2012 est.)
GDP per capita:	US$5,200 (2012 est.)

Despite its turmoil, travelers flock to Guatemala because it offers Central America in concentrated form: its volcanoes are the highest and most active, its Mayan ruins the most impressive, its earthquakes the most devastating, and its history decidedly intense. Guatemala is a magical place. If you're into the Maya, the mountains, the markets or a million other things, you're bound to be captivated.

People come and they stay. Or they leave and return. There's almost too much going on here, and even the shortest trip takes you completely different places, with new challenges and surpris-

es. Students of Spanish flock to Antigua, a gorgeous town nestled between three volcanoes, while those travelers seeking more off-the-beaten-track destinations might head to lesser known places like Lago de Izabal or Nebaj, a Maya village hidden in a remote fold of the Cuchumatanes Mountains. And sooner or later, just about everyone ends up in the Highlands — Lago de Atitlan being an irresistible drawing card. — Lonely Planet

History and Overview

Guatemala is one of the Central American Republics with two coastlines, on the west, the Pacific Ocean, and on the east, the Caribbean Sea. Its northern border is with Mexico and to the east is Belize. Honduras and El Salvador border it to the south.

There are indications that ancient peoples existed here as long ago as 1500 BC. But, by 1520 AD, and the arrival of the Spanish, these civilizations had largely disappeared and Guatemala became the center of Spanish rule in Central America. In 1821, Guatemala achieved independence from Spain. After suffering under dictators for a century, Guatemala became a democracy in 1944. Its history since then, marked by civil war, Communist and leftist guerilla insurgency, has been turbulent, to say the least.

During the second half of the 20th century, it experienced a variety of military and civilian governments, as well as a 36-year guerrilla war. In 1996, the government signed a peace agreement formally ending the conflict, which had left more than 100,000 people dead and had created, by some estimates, some one million refugees.

Economy

Guatemala is the most populous country in Central America with a GDP per capita roughly one-half that of the average for Latin America and the Caribbean. The agricultural sector accounts for nearly 15% of GDP and half of the labor force; key agricultural exports include coffee, sugar and bananas.

Still rebuilding from the last episode of civil strife, Guatemala is dangerous for those traveling outside the major urban or resort areas. Lush tropical forests, mountain lakes and major Mayan ruins attract visitors from around the world. However, infrastructure is poor throughout most of the country, and crime against foreigners is a major problem in most rural areas.

The 2006 Central American Free Trade Agreement (CAFTA) has spurred increased investment in the export sector, but concerns over security, the lack of skilled workers and poor infrastructure continued to hamper foreign participation.

The distribution of income remains highly unequal with more than half of the population below the national poverty line. The agricultural sector accounts for one-fourth of GDP and two-thirds of exports, employing more than half of the labor force. Coffee, sugar and bananas are the main products. Manufacturing and construction account for one-fifth of the GDP.

Since 1996, the government implemented a program of economic liberalization and political modernization. The signing of the peace accords in 1996, which ended 36 years of civil war, removed a major obstacle to foreign investment.

Guatemalans have a history of emigrating legally and illegally to Mexico, the United States, and Canada because of a lack of economic opportunity, political instability, and natural disasters. Emigration, primarily to the U.S., escalated during the 1960 to 1996 civil wars and after a peace agreement. Thousands of Guatemalans who fled to Mexico returned after the war, but labor migration to southern Mexico continues.

From the time a civil war began in Guatemala in the early 1960s until the 1996 Peace Accords, more than a million Guatemalans fled their country, the majority to the United States. Tens of thousands gained legal residence under general amnesty legislation in 1986. In 1997, the U.S. Congress passed the Nicaraguan Adjustment and Central American Relief Act, which allowed Guatemalans protected under the settlement to apply for U.S. residence.

Given Guatemala's large expatriate community in the United States, it is the top remittance recipient in Central America, with inflows serving as a primary source of foreign income equivalent to nearly two-thirds of exports.

Warning

Guatemala is not a very safe country. There are just too many armed robberies, rapes and murders of tourists. The two most frequently reported types of incidents involving tourists are highway robbery, when a vehicle is stopped and its occupants relieved of their belongings, and robberies on walking trails. Criminal activity is a problem in many parts of Guatemala. In 2011, the government advised against visiting the northern region of Petén (this includes Tikal) following murders in the area.

The U.S. Embassy website in 2014 warns: "Guatemala has one of the highest violent crime rates in Latin America. While most of the tourists visiting Guatemala are able to safely complete their tours, it is important that visitors observe basic precautions in order to avoid becoming a victim of crime." According to official figures, an average of 15 people are murdered in Guatemala each day, making the country one of the most violent in Latin America on a per capita basis. Homicides rose slightly in 2013 from 2012, to 6,072.

Residence and Citizenship

Citizenship is conferred in the following ways:

1. by birth: on a child born within the territory of Guatemala, regardless of the nationality of the parents, including birth on any Guatemalan ship or aircraft.

2. by descent: on a child born abroad, at least one of whose parents is a citizen of Guatemala.

3. by naturalization: upon fulfillment of the following conditions:

    a) the person must renounce previous citizenship;

    b) the person must have legally resided in the country for one of the following time periods:

       i) Five years collectively without being out of the country

       for more than one year;

       ii) periods of time that total 10 years;

       iii) two years continuously.

Other persons who may be eligible for citizenship include:

a) a person who has rendered service to Guatemala;

b) a person who has lived in another Central American country;

c) a person who is stateless;

d) a person who is accomplished in science, art or philanthropic efforts.

Dual citizenship is not recognized, except in the case of certain countries of Central and South America that provide for such under treaties.

A valid U.S. passport is required for all U.S. citizens, regardless of age, to enter Guatemala and to depart Guatemala for return to the U.S.

Contributors Welcome

Guatemala does not officially market and sell citizenship, but the government is willing to receive immigrants as new citizens if they "contribute to the country." For those interested, this requires a personal visit to Guatemala and obtaining two responsible local sponsors to vouch for an applicant's character and good standing.

Naturalization can be obtained by those who establish a two-year residence in Guatemala. With the right local connections, this waiting period can be reduced or waived. As in many Latin American nations, the sale of official passports is certainly not unknown in Guatemala, so be careful.

Warning: proceed with caution if you choose to follow this option. Some lawyers in Guatemala and other Central American countries, including Panama, make it a specialty "to arrange" for these special Guatemalan passports, at great cost to clients and profits for themselves. Be sure those with whom you are dealing in this situation are legitimate, both as attorneys and as government representatives, whether in Guatemala or elsewhere.

A Guatemalan passport is good for travel to most countries in Europe without a visa, and dual citizenship here is common. Most upper-class Guatemalans hold U.S. and Spanish passports. Spain gives special consideration to Guatemalans, who, by treaty, need only two years of residence in Spain to acquire Spanish citizenship or vice-versa. (See the chapter on Spain for details.)

Upon a grant of citizenship, a person receives a passport valid for five years, a national ID card, a driver's license, and a naturalization certificate. Name changes to make a foreign name sound more like that of a Guatemalan national are not uncommon. Guatemala does not inform a new citizen's home country about the naturalization event.

Guatemala is a member of the "Central America-4 (CA-4) Border Control Agreement" with El Salvador, Honduras and Nicaragua. Under the terms of the agreement, citizens of the four countries may travel freely across land borders from one of the countries to any of the others without completing entry and exit formalities at immigration checkpoints.

U.S. citizens and other eligible foreign nationals, who legally enter any of the four countries, may similarly travel among the four without obtaining additional visas or tourist entry permits for the other three countries. Immigration officials at the first port of entry determine the length of stay, up to a maximum period of 90 days.

Contacts
Embassy of Guatemala
2220 R Street NW
Washington, DC 20008

Tel.: (202) 745-4952
Email: info@guatemala-embassy.org
Web: http://www.guatemala-embassy.org/

United States Embassy
Avenida Reforma 7-01, Zone 10
Guatemala Ciudad, Guatemala
Tel.: + (502) 2326-4000
Email: AmCitsGuatemala@state.gov
Web: http://guatemala.usembassy.gov/

Republic of Honduras

Government:	Democratic constitutional republic
Capital:	Tegucigalpa
National Day:	Independence Day: 15 September (1821)
Population:	8,448,465 (July 2013 est.)
Total Area:	43,278 sq. miles / 112,090 sq. kilometers
Languages:	Spanish, Amerindian dialects
Ethnic groups:	Mestizo (mixed Amerindian-European) 90%, Amerindian 7%, black 2%, white 1%
Religion:	Roman Catholic 97%, Protestant 3%
Life expectancy:	70.81 years
Currency:	Lempira (HNL)
GDP:	US$37.64 billion (2012 est.)
GDP per capita:	US$4,700 (2012 est.)

Like its neighbors, Honduras is experiencing tremendous changes: an expanding tourist economy, a maturing political scene, and the whole globalization thing, including maquilas, free trade agreements —even implementing Daylight Savings Time. Honduras remains deeply entrenched in a two-front war against gangs and HIV/AIDS. Illegal logging is emerging as another major concern and a key issue among Honduras' growing environmental community.

Honduras today is a place of change, too fast for those who'd like the country to remain "undiscovered, too slow for those frustrated by persistent remnants of the "Banana Republic" days, whether in undue foreign influence or lax enforcement of environmental laws. Hondurans themselves take it all in their stride, and travelers with an open mind and a bit of Spanish will find many fascinating conversations in store. — *Lonely Planet*

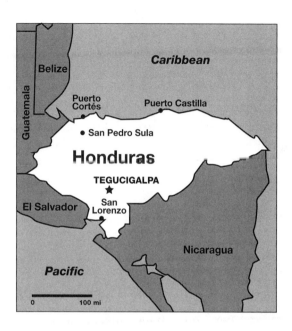

History and Overview

Honduras is in Central America, bordering the Caribbean Sea, between Guatemala and Nicaragua and bordering the Gulf of Fonseca (North Pacific Ocean), between El Salvador and Nicaragua.

On July 30, 1502, Christopher Columbus first saw Honduran soil and he claimed the territory in the name of his sovereigns, Ferdinand of Aragon and Isabella of Castile. Once part of Spain's vast empire in the New World, Honduras became an independent nation in 1821. After two and a half decades of mostly military rule, a freely elected civilian government came to power in 1982. During the 1980s, Honduras proved a haven for anti-Sandinista contras fighting the Marxist Nicaraguan government and an ally to Salvadoran government forces fighting leftist guerrillas. The country was devastated by Hurricane Mitch in 1998, which killed nearly 5,600 people and caused US$2 billion in damage.

Economy

Honduras, the second poorest country in Central America, suffers from extraordinarily unequal distribution of income, as well as high underemployment. While historically dependent on the export of bananas and coffee, Honduras has diversified its export base to include apparel and automobile wire harnessing. Nearly half of Honduras's economic activity is directly tied to the U.S., with exports to the U.S. accounting for 30% of GDP and remittances for another 20%.

About 65% of the population lives in poverty and per capita income is one of the lowest in the region. Poverty rates are higher among rural and indigenous people and in the south, west, and along the eastern border than in the north and central areas where most of Honduras' industries and infrastructure are concentrated.

Honduras seeks expanded trade under the U.S.-Central America Free Trade Agreement (CAFTA) and gets debt relief under the Heavily Indebted Poor Countries (HIPC) initiative. Growth remains dependent on the economy of the U.S., its largest trading partner, on continued exports of non-traditional agricultural products (such as melons, chilies, tilapia, and shrimp), and on reduction of the high crime rate.

Economic growth declined in the 2008-2011 recession as a result of reduction in export demand and tightening global credit markets. Remittances represent over a quarter of GDP or nearly three-quarters of exports. The 2006 CAFTA has helped foster investment. Despite improvements in tax collections, the government's fiscal deficit is growing due to increases in current expenditures and financial losses from the state energy and telephone companies.

In 1997, the U.S. Congress passed the Nicaraguan Adjustment and Central American Relief Act, which among other things allowed Hondurans in the U.S. to apply for U.S. residence and eventual citizenship. In 2007, the Bush administration extended the "temporary" status of 230,000 Salvadorans, 78,000 Hondurans and 4,000 Nicaraguans in the United States. Salvadorans had this temporary status for six years, and the Hondurans and Nicaraguans for eight years.

Honduras has the world's highest number of homicides per capita with an average of 19 murders each day in 2013, down from 20 a day in 2012. Putting an end to Honduras' vicious cycle of violence was the main theme in the 2013 election, won by the National Party's Juan Hernandez who vowed to restore order, adopting a militarized approach to curbing warring gangs.

Residence and Citizenship

Citizenship laws are based upon the Honduran Constitution. Citizenship is conferred in the following ways:

1. by birth: for any child born within the territory of Honduras, regardless of the nationality of the parents. Children of diplomats are excluded. A child born on a Honduran vessel or aircraft or on a merchant vessel located in Honduran territorial waters also obtains citizenship regardless of the nationality of the parents.

2. by descent: to a child born abroad when at least one parent is a citizen of Honduran birth.

3. by naturalization:

   a) for any citizen of a Central American country by birth who has resided one year in Honduras;

   b) for Spaniards and Spanish-Americans by birth who have resided two years in Honduras;

c) for any person who has resided in Honduras for at least three years;

d) for a person who is married to a Honduran citizen by birth;

e) to a person granted citizenship by the Honduran National Congress;

f) to a person admitted to Honduras for economic reasons, who has resided in Honduras for at least one year.

Dual citizenship is permitted for the following persons:

a) a child of Honduran citizens born abroad;

b) a Honduran who acquires foreign citizenship by marriage;

c) a person granted citizenship by act of the National Congress;

d) citizens of countries with which Honduras has dual nationality treaties;

e) Hondurans seeking citizenship of countries with which Honduras has a dual nationality treaty.

The citizenship of those whose citizenship was acquired through marriage, and that of their children, is not revoked upon dissolution of the marriage. A person may voluntarily surrender citizenship by submitting letters of renunciation to a Honduran Embassy.

A U.S. passport valid for at least three months from the date of entry is required to enter Honduras. Though not required by law, some travelers have reported difficulty departing Honduras using a passport with less than three months of validity from the date of departure. A visa is not required, but tourists must provide evidence of return or onward travel.

Honduras is a member of the "Central America-4 (CA-4) Border Control Agreement" with Guatemala, El Salvador and Nicaragua. Under the terms of the agreement, citizens of the four countries may travel freely across land borders from one of the countries to any of the others without completing entry and exit formalities at immigration checkpoints. U.S. citizens and other eligible foreign nationals, who legally enter any of the four countries, may similarly travel among the four without obtaining additional visas or tourist entry permits for the other three countries. Immigration officials at the first port of entry determine the length of stay, up to a maximum period of 90 days. In 2014, the government suspended 10 consular officials in the U.S. for selling false identification papers.

Contacts

Embassy of Honduras
3007 Tilden Street NW
Washington, DC 20008
Tel.: (202) 966-7702
Web: http://www.hondurasemb.org/
Email: embassy@hondurasemb.org

Honduras Institute of Tourism
Tel.: 1-800-410-9608 (in the U.S.)
Web: http://www.hondurastips.honduras.com

United States Embassy
Avenida La Paz
Tegucigalpa M.D.C., Honduras
Tel.: + (504) 2236-9320, 2238-5114
Email: usahonduras@state.gov
Web: http://honduras.usembassy.gov/

Republic of Nicaragua

Government:	Republic
Capital:	Managua
National Day:	Independence Day: 15 September (1821)
Population:	5,788,531 (July 2013 est.)
Total Area:	49,998 sq. miles / 129,494 sq. kilometers
Languages:	Spanish 97.5% (official), Miskito 1.7%, other 0.8%, English and indigenous languages on the Atlantic coast
Ethnic groups:	Mestizo (mixed Amerindian and white) 69%, white 17%, black 9%, Amerindian 5%
Religion:	Roman Catholic 58.5%, Evangelical 21.6%, Moravian 1.6%, Jehovah's Witnesses 0.9%, other 1.7%, none 15.7%
Life expectancy:	72.45 years
Currency:	Nicaraguan córdoba (NIO)
GDP:	US$26.38 billion (2012 est.)
GDP per capita:	US$4,400 (2012 est.)

For visitors of a certain age, just the name Nicaragua — taken from a tribal chief of such wisdom and power that he may never fade from this nation's collective memory — evokes grainy film footage of camouflage clad guerrillas, punctuated by gunfire and a 1980s soundtrack. Despite having ended more than 15 years ago, leaving Nicaragua one of the safest countries in the Americas, the Contra War is too often our collective memory of the land of Nicarao.
— Lonely Planet

History and Overview

Nicaragua is located in Central America, bordering both the Caribbean Sea and the North Pacific Ocean, between Costa Rica and Honduras.

The Pacific coast of Nicaragua was settled as a Spanish colony from Panama in the early 16th century. Independence from Spain was declared in 1821 and the country became an independent republic in 1838. Britain occupied the Caribbean Coast in the first half of the 19th century, but gradually ceded control of the region. Violent opposition to government manipulation and corruption by the ruling Somoza family spread by 1978 and resulted in a short-lived civil war that brought the Marxist Sandinista guerrillas to power in 1979.

Nicaraguan aid to leftist rebels in El Salvador caused the U.S. government to sponsor anti-Sandinista contra guerrillas through much of the 1980s. Free elections in 1990, 1996 and 2001, saw the leftists Sandinistas defeated, but a rigged voting system in 2006 allowed the return of former Sandinista President José Daniel Ortega Saavedra with only 35% of the votes. Ortega immediately pledged his solidarity with Cuba's Communist leader, Fidel Castro and Venezuela's far left firebrand, the late Hugo Chávez.

Nicaragua is the second-poorest country in the Western Hemisphere. In 2010, the economy grew by 4.5%, according to official government sources, largely due to an increase in demand for Nicaraguan exports abroad and increased consumer spending at home. There is widespread underemployment and a heavy external debt burden. Distribution of income is one of the most unequal on the globe.

While the country has progressed toward macroeconomic stability in the past few years, GDP annual growth has been far too low to meet the country's needs, forcing the country to rely on international economic assistance to meet fiscal and debt financing obligations.

Nicaragua ratified the U.S.-Central America Free Trade Agreement (CAFTA), which provides an opportunity for the country to attract investment, create jobs and expand economic development. Nicaragua signed a three-year Poverty Reduction and Growth Facility (PRGF) with the International Monetary Fund (IMF) in October 2007. The continuity of a relationship with the IMF helps support foreign donor confidence, despite private sector concerns surrounding Ortega and his radical leftist politics, which has scared away needed investment. Remittances, mainly from the U.S., account for almost 15% of GDP.

Purchasing Property

U.S. citizens should be aware of the risks of purchasing real estate in Nicaragua and should exercise caution before committing to invest there. The 1979 to 1990 Sandinista government expropriated some 30,000 properties, many of which are still involved in disputes or claims. Land title remains unclear in many cases. Although the government has resolved several thousand claims by U.S. citizens for compensation or return of properties, there remain hundreds of unresolved claims registered with the U.S. Embassy. Potential investors should engage competent local legal representation and investigate their purchases thoroughly in order to reduce the possibility of property disputes.

The judicial system offers little relief when the purchase of a property winds up in court. The U.S. Embassy is aware of numerous cases in which buyers purchase property supported by what appears to be legal titles, only to find themselves subsequently embroiled in legal battles when the titles are contested by an affected or otherwise interested third party.

Once a property dispute enters the judicial arena, the outcome may be subject to corruption, political pressure and influence peddling. Many coastal properties have been tied up in courts, leaving the buyer unable to proceed with the intended development pending lengthy and uncertain litigation. In other cases, squatters have simply invaded the land while the police or judicial authorities are unable (or unwilling) to remove the trespassers. The U.S. Embassy advises that those interested in purchasing Nicaraguan property exercise extreme caution.

Residence and Citizenship

Temporary and permanent residence permits are available.

Under the law, citizenship is conferred:

1. by birth: to a child born within the territory of Nicaragua, regardless of the nationality of the parents. The only exception is a child of foreign officials serving international organizations or

their countries, unless the parents choose to solicit citizenship for the child.

2. by birth: to a child born to unknown parents, found within the territory, until parentage becomes known.

3. by descent to:

> a) a child born abroad, one of whose parents is a citizen of Nicaragua.
>
> b) a child born abroad, whose mother or father was formerly Nicaraguan, if the child applies for citizenship after reaching the age of majority.

4. by naturalization:

> a) for a child of foreign parents, born on a Nicaraguan boat or airplane, if the parents apply for naturalization of the child.
>
> b) for a child born abroad, whose mother or father was formerly Nicaraguan.
>
> c) for a person who has lived legally as a resident in Nicaragua for at least three years.

A valid U.S. passport is required to enter Nicaragua. U.S. citizens must have an onward or return ticket and evidence of sufficient funds to support themselves during their stay.

A visa is not required for U.S. citizens; however, a tourist card must be purchased upon arrival. Tourist cards are typically issued for 30 to 90 days.

Nicaragua is a party to the "Central America-4 (CA-4) Border Control Agreement" with Guatemala, Honduras and El Salvador. Under the terms of the agreement, citizens of the four countries may travel freely across land borders from one of the countries to any of the others without completing entry and exit formalities at immigration checkpoints.

U.S. citizens and other eligible foreign nationals, who legally enter any of the four countries, may similarly travel among the four without obtaining additional visas or tourist entry permits for the other three countries. Immigration officials at the first port of entry determine the length of stay, up to a maximum period of 90 days.

Safety and Security http://travel.state.gov/content/passports/english/country/nicaragua.html

Contacts

Embassy of Nicaragua
1627 New Hampshire Avenue NW
Washington, DC 20009
Tel.: (202) 939-6570
Email: nicaraguan.embassy@embanic.org

United States Embassy
Kilometro 5 1/2 (5.5, Carretera Sur)
Managua, Nicaragua
Tel.: + (505) 2252-7100
Email: consularmanagua@state.gov
Web: http://nicaragua.usembassy.gov

Republic of Panama

Government:	Constitutional democracy
Capital:	Panama City
National Day:	Independence Day: 3 November (1903)
Population:	3,559,408 (July 2013 est.)
Total Area:	30,193 sq. miles / 78,200 sq. kilometers
Languages:	Spanish (official), English 14%; many Panamanians are bilingual
Ethnic groups:	Mestizo 70%, Amerindian and mixed (West Indian) 14%, white 10%, Amerindian 6%
Religion:	Roman Catholic 85%, Protestant 15%
Life expectancy:	78.13 years
Currencies:	U.S. dollar (USD); balboa (PAB)
GDP:	US$35.76 billion (2012 est.)
GDP per capita:	US$15,400 (2012 est.)

Unfettered by tourist crowds, Panama's natural gifts shine. Although most visitors to Central America set their sights on tourist-clogged Costa Rica and Guatemala, it's hard to shake the feeling in Panama that you're in on a secret the rest of the traveling world has yet to discover.

Although the "gringo trail" has already swung south to Panama's Caribbean archipelago of Bocas del Toro, the careless overdevelopment plaguing most Costa Rican beach towns is still refreshingly absent here. In fact, Panama's highlights are still very much off-the-beaten-path destinations, though it's likely that this will change in the years to come. Until its anticipated tourism boom explodes, however, Panama remains accessible on a budget, and there's no

shortage of beaches, mountains and rain forests to explore.
— Lonely Planet

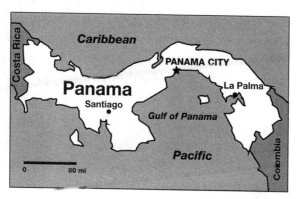

Preface: The Sovereign Society recommends Panama as one of the world's best offshore financial centers, as well as an excellent asset protection and residential haven. Only hours by air from the United States, Panama offers a variety of lifestyles and geographic areas with a century-long history of working closely with Americans. Panama's real estate is no longer a bargain, but the current multi-billion dollar expansion of the Panama Canal contributes to the country's continued growth, the fastest in Latin America. Notwithstanding the easing in bank secrecy laws, in many ways Panama still has it all as an offshore leader.

History and Overview

When you think of Panama, you think of one of the great technical wonders of the world — the Panama Canal.

Located in southeastern Central America, Panama is bordered by both the Caribbean Sea and the Pacific Ocean, situated with Colombia to the south and Costa Rica to the north. It enjoys a major world strategic position encompassing the isthmus that forms the land bridge connecting North and South America, including the location of the Panama Canal linking the Atlantic Ocean via the Caribbean Sea with the Pacific Ocean.

Important in the days of the Spanish conquest, Panama gained independence from Spain in 1821 and joined a union of Colombia, Ecuador, and Venezuela; Simon Bolivar's ill-fated Republic of Gran Colombia. When the latter dissolved in 1830, Panama remained an isolated province of Colombia.

In 1903, with the active "gun boat" encouragement of U.S. President Theodore Roosevelt, Panama declared its independence from Colombia and immediately gave the U.S. a concession to build what became the Panama Canal. Completed in 1915, this wonderful canal became the focal point of a U.S.-Panama love-hate relationship for the rest of the century — and its construction gave a major boost to America's new standing as a power in the world.

Along with the old millennium, 96 years of official United States presence in Panama officially ended at midnight, December 31, 1999. Panama finally had what its nationalistic politicians had demanded — full control and sovereignty over its famous Canal.

In the years since, the Panamanians have managed the canal and its intricate operations very well, but many problems do persist in one of the richest per capita of all Latin American countries.

World Financial Center

Panama is not so well known for what it has become in the last 25 years. After Miami, it is Latin America's second largest international banking and business center, with ties to Asia, Europe and a special relationship with the United States that continues.

Panama was one of the fastest growing economies in the world in 2007 with real growth rising to 11.2%. The GDP slowed to 8%

and lower during the recession of 2008 to 2011. Panama's GDP rate dropped in 2013 from the 2011 to 2012 double digit levels of 10% or more as numerous public works neared completion. The country still had a 2013 growth of 8.4% and GDP grew by 8% on average for the last six years. The Panamanian economy dodged the 2008 global crisis and has expanded due to public and private projects, including the Panama Canal expansion.

Buoyed by a strong, sophisticated services industry and a maritime and logistical transportation hub, Panama has taken advantage of global trade flows and has reduced the national poverty level to about 30% of the population. From 2006 to 2012 poverty was reduced by 10% points, while unemployment dropped from 12% to near zero in 2013. However, Panama has the second most unequal income distribution in Latin America.

The government has implemented tax and social security reforms, and backs regional trade agreements and development of tourism. Not a CAFTA signatory, Panama in 2006 independently negotiated a free trade agreement with the U.S. which was opposed by American labor unions and their Democrat allies in the U.S. Senate who blocked the trade treaty for almost five years. The U.S.-Panama Trade Promotion Agreement finally was approved by the U.S. Congress and signed into law in October 2011, and entered into force one year later.

Between 1955 and 2004, inflation averaged 2.4%, and, for the decade of the 1990s, barely exceeded 1% per year. Annual inflation has averaged 1.7% for the past 30 years, lower than in the U.S.

Panama's dollarized economy rests primarily on a well-developed service sector that accounts for 75% of GDP. Services include operating the Panama Canal, banking and other offshore financial services, the Colon Free Zone, insurance, container ports, flagship registry, and tourism.

Canal Expansion

Then, there is the wealth represented by the Panama Canal, gen erating nearly US$1 billion in annual tolls (not all of which must be plowed back into constant maintenance), and the thousands of acres of land from former U.S. military installations, prized real estate with an estimated value of US$4 billion. The government and the people in a 2006 national referendum made an historic decision to launch a multi-billion dollar canal expansion project to keep the waterway competitive.

Economic growth has been bolstered by the Panama Canal expansion project that was scheduled to be completed by 2014 at a supposed cost of US$5.3 billion — about 25% of Panama's GDP. The expansion project will more than double the Canal's capacity, enabling it to accommodate ships that are now too large to transverse the Canal, and has helped to reduce the high unemployment rate to near zero. Southern and east coast U.S. ports now are deepening harbors and channels to take advantage of the larger vessels this will permit.

In late 2013, work on the canal expansion halted in an acrimonious battle between Panama and the Spanish-led contract builders over US$1.6 billion in cost overruns. In 2007, I predicted this would happen: "The hallmark of Panama's finances for years to come will be the proposed expansion of the canal, expected to cost at least US$5.25 billion, (my guess is that it will cost much more), with construction expected to be completed in 2014."

I never believed that the Canal expansion could be achieved for the announced price of the European consortium bid — a price designed to undercut the U.S. bidder, Bechtel, by US$1 billion. The so-called *Grupos Unidos por el Canal*, the Spanish-Dutch consortium that won the contract to design and construct the locks portion of the project in July 2009, did so with a bid US$36 million below the Panama Canal Authority's own cost estimate. From all reports the construction has been unusually free from the corruption that has marked many projects in Panama, so that does not appear to be the reason for the cost overruns.

This consortium was so inept (or unqualified) for the work that it started building with inferior grade concrete that had to be replaced. You would think that if the U.S. Army Corps of Engineers and U.S. companies could build the existing and lasting Canal as they did in 1904 to 1914, this consortium could at least figure out what grade of concrete to use. With trillions of dollars' worth of world trade and international port development at issue, there is no question that the expansion will be completed, even if delayed.

Miami South

A first-time American visitor to Panama City will marvel at the modern skyscrapers, first-class hotels and restaurants, excellent internet and other communications, and the thoroughly, perhaps too American ambiance. Downtown Panama City, the balmy, tropical capital on the southern, Pacific end of the Canal, suggests Los Angeles or Miami, except arguably more locals speak English here than in some parts of South Florida.

The main drag on the Pacific waterfront, Avenida Balboa, has been transformed into the modern, eight-lane *Cinta Costera* (Coastal Beltway) that runs from the downtown *Paitilla* neighborhood to the *Casco Viejo*, the old original part of Panama City.

Panama is a growing but as yet not so well known tourist destination, with attractions ranging from the Canal to natural parks in many different topographic zones offering some of the most fascinating "ecotourism" in the Western Hemisphere.

The country offers a wide variety of prospective places to settle or retire in, each seemingly more attractive than the next. From island chains on both the Caribbean and Pacific coasts to lush, temperate highland regions, the country offers a broad range of options as to scenery, climate, and level of development.

Yes, Panama also has a long history of government corruption that continues. This hasn't seemed to affect the loosely regulated banking sector, but bribery, cronyism, nepotism, and kickbacks in government dealings regularly make headlines here.

All this changed somewhat for the better in 2009 when millionaire free market businessman, Ricardo Martinelli, was elected president for a five-year term with an unprecedented majority of all voters. Fighting corruption was one of the president's major promises, but Panama is not about to change overnight and some questions remain whether the president fulfilled his promise based on appointments of relatives and friends

In the May 2014 elections, the winner of a five-year term was Juan Carlos Varela, vice president under Martinelli, although the outgoing president did not support him. Varela, a 50-year-old engineer, is the scion of one of Panama's wealthiest old families and part owner of a namesake rum distillery. He is a leader in the right of center Panamenista Party and likely will build on Martinelli's success and continue close ties with the United States.

Big Banking

In many ways, the Republic of Panama is ideally suited for the offshore investor who wants strong financial privacy and no local taxes, corporate or personal. South of Miami, Panama is the leading banking and financial center in Latin America with over 80 banks, and many local branches of global banks such as Barclays and Dresdner.

Its proximity to the growing Latin market makes it a natural as a base for world business operations and, in spite of its history it isn't directly under the thumb of either the U.S., or, like Bermuda or the Cayman Islands, subject to the dictates of U.K. politics.

The major players here are the foreign-owned multinational banks representing some 30 countries from Andorra to Hong Kong. Nearly every major global bank has a full-service branch office in Panama. They hold 72% of a reported total US$89.78 billion in January 2013 assets, a 10% increase over 2012. Banking alone accounts for about 7.5% of the nation's GDP. In 2014, Bancolombia based in Medellin, Colombia, paid US$2.1 billion to acquire HSBC Panama, which had been the banking chain with the most local offices.

With no central bank, no Federal Reserve and no government lender of last resort, Panama's banks have been encouraged to, and have stayed highly liquid. In 2013, a 58% loan to holdings ratio put the banks in a strong position, compared to major U.S. banks that had to resort to billions in federal bailouts to stay afloat. Total bank assets amount to about 215% of GDP.

Historic Change

Ever since Panama created itself as a an offshore banking and financial center 60 years ago, successive governments had vowed to resist international demands for information about assets held by foreign citizens in the country. Students of financial history realize that, along with Luxembourg and Liechtenstein, Panama adopted specific tax haven legislation as far back as the 1920s and the country has modernized its laws regularly.

Until the global financial crisis struck in 2008, Panama faced little pressure to release such data, because other jurisdictions like Switzerland and the Cayman Islands were more popular with tax evaders. Once the OECD began its decade long anti-tax haven campaign and convinced many of the biggest havens to change, Panama stood out as a major strict privacy hold out.

In 2010, under great international pressure, especially from the U.

S. government, Panama abandoned its long tradition of bank secrecy and tight financial privacy after years of denying it would ever do so.

The law of Panama still contains statutory guarantees of financial privacy and confidentiality. Violators can suffer civil and criminal penalties for unauthorized disclosure. But under the old law, there was no requirement to reveal beneficial trust or corporate ownership to Panamanian authorities unless a court ordered it. A 2010 law requires all banks and financial and legal professionals to ascertain beneficial ownership and keep non-public records that are open to official government inspection. Law 33, 2010 repealed the then-existing right to have bearer shares. Now all stock certificates must be in the name of the beneficial owners.

These changes were a prelude to an official reversal of Panama's traditional policy of not having any double taxation agreements and no tax information exchange agreements (TIEA) with other countries. The government logically argued that it didn't need TIEAs because it does not tax foreign earnings under its territorial tax system, only earnings from within Panama are taxed.

These modifications undoubtedly were a response to blacklist threats by the Organization for Economic and Community Development (OECD) with the backing of the Obama government and other major high-tax nations.

Their demand had been that Panama (and all so-called "tax havens"), ease their privacy laws and provide automatic exchange of tax information. Unspecified international sanctions were threatened. On November 30, 2010 the Martinelli government signed the country's first-ever tax information exchange treaty (TIEA). The pact, signed with the United States, allows each country to request and receive a full report on the holdings in the other country of any of its citizens suspected of tax evasion tax fraud on a showing of probable cause.

High Panama government officials — whom I met — said that under the TIEA, persons subject to a U.S. investigation request would be notified of that fact but no appeal to the courts would be allowed at that point. I was also told that the U.S IRS would be required to submit specific names, particular bank accounts and bank identification and that no "fishing expeditions" would be allowed.

Since Panama only taxes economic activity within its territory, meaning that no American assets are subject to its levies, the deal represented a clear surrender to American demands that had been made repeatedly over many years.

Offshore banking and IBCs were major revenue sources in the past. The economic health of Panama depends on financial activities with safeguards sufficient to ensure legal compliance. However, to claim Panama has cleaned up its dirty money act would be too optimistic.

In U.S. government circles, a bank account in Panama raises immediate suspicion about the account holder. But that's also true of accounts in Bermuda, the Cayman Islands, Nevis, the Channel Islands, and anywhere else in the world the IRS can't readily stick its official nose into private financial activity.

While "dollarization" is debated as a novel concept elsewhere in Latin America, since 1904, the U.S. dollar has been Panama's official paper currency. (The local equivalent is the "balboa" and there are Panamanian coins that circulate along with U.S. coins.)

Service by many international airlines, excellent communications, telephone, mail, and telex all make travel and living here first rate. Local laws and customs encourage free trade and there are minimal import or export duties, especially if the Colon Free Trade Zone is used. Ship registration is cheap and consequently, the growing Panamanian merchant marine of registered commercial ships is now second only to that of Liberia.

However suspect it may have been in the past, Panama has become one of the major financial crossroads of the world.

Base your business there and you're connected everywhere.

Residence and Citizenship

There are many and varied programs in Panama for foreigners who wish to make it their home. All resident visa applications must be made through a Panamanian attorney.

There is no minimum or maximum age requirement, except that those younger than 18 years old, the legal age of emancipation in Panama, qualify as dependents of their parents.

None of these visas automatically grant the right to work. Work permits must be applied for and obtained separately.

In recent decades, Panama deliberately has positioned itself as a first-class retirement haven, with some of the most appealing programs of special benefits for foreign residents and retirees anywhere in the world.

Panama also offers a variety of visas for investors, persons of high net worth, wealthy retirees, business and agricultural business investors and entrepreneurs, and those who simply want to immigrate and become Panamanian citizens.

Compare Panama's hospitable offer to resident and passport programs elsewhere in the world, places where legal costs alone can amount to more than US$10,000 — and that doesn't include the capital investment required to qualify in these nations.

Programs offered in the Caribbean require up to, and beyond, a quarter of a million dollars. Examples: economic citizenship status from the Commonwealth of Dominica or St. Kitts & Nevis, the last two nations still offering fast track citizenship, each can cost upward of US$250,000.

Entry Requirements

U.S. citizens traveling by air to and from Panama must present a valid passport when entering or re-entering the United States. Sea travelers must have a valid U.S. passport (or other original proof of U.S. citizenship, such as a certified U.S. birth certificate with a government-issued photo ID).

In 2011, the Martinelli government abolished a longstanding and irritating law that required travelers to purchase a tourist card at the U.S. airport of departure or in Panama before clearing customs. U.S. tourists are allowed to stay in Panama for 180 days (although you may only drive with a foreign driver license for 90 days, which is the official tourist visa term).

2008 Immigration Law

A liberal immigration law that offered many inducements has in the past been one of the most attractive features for foreigners considering retirement or a second home in Panama.

In 2008, a revised general immigration law, Public Law No. 3 of 2008, came into effect. Generally, fees for all services were increased, some substantially. Under the 2008 law:

• Foreigners who already had their legal residence in Panama were "grandfathered in" and retained their existing status, although the requirements became more expensive. The cost of visas, permits and fees for filing various documents also was raised.

• The so-called *pensinado* program that has been so popular with foreigners (see below) remained in place, but whereas an applicant in the past only had to prove an established pension income of $500 per month (or $750 per couple), that was increased to $1,000 a month. However, those pensioners who own Panama property worth at least $100,000 only need to prove a pension of $750 per month. A *pensionado* with dependents must now show pensions of $250 for each dependent in addition to the basic $1,000 pension (or can open an account in Panama and deposit $2,000 per dependent).

- Investors visas now are more expensive. Example: it requires an investment of $60,000 to get a visa as an agricultural or reforestation investor *(inversionista forestal)*, rather than the previous $40,000.

Every foreigner must register with a central registry and update their status with a change in address, change in economic or marital status. Once the permanent residence is approved, all foreigners are issued an identity card *(cédula)* which is the former practice.

How It's Done

You must travel to Panama in order to obtain any of the available long-term visas and be present for the application filing and again when your visa is issued to you. The Pensioner Visa *(pensionado)* requires about four to six months to be issued and others about five to six months on average.

If you obtain a visa to reside in Panama, but wish to live overseas, it is recommended that you visit Panama at least once a year, although legally you may stay out of the country for up to two years.

Once you file an application for any of these Panamanian visas — and while it is being approved — you are required to obtain a "multiple-entry permit" should it be necessary for you to travel out of the country during this time. The permit for multiple-entry is valid for one year and is different to that offered by Panamanian Consulates overseas.

Panama truly does offer probably the best residence deal in the world today. For this comparatively small price, the benefits are incomparable. And living in Panama offers an extraordinary financial opportunity. Property prices are continuing to climb — but at a much slower pace and you still have a chance to buy at comparatively low prices.

Pensionado Program *(Turista Pensionado)*

Perhaps the best known of the resident visas is the so-called *pensionado* or pensioner visa. Panama law stipulates that anyone entering the country as a qualified *pensionado* is guaranteed to retain that legal status so long as they choose to stay in the country.

That is a very important point. The law states that, if the requirements for this visa are changed at a later date (as they were in 2008), the changes will not affect anyone who already has *pensionado* status, so long as the person maintains the required minimum level of income. The law is written so that the promise to today's retirees will be kept and they will be protected tomorrow.

The visa application process for Panama's basic *pensionado* program is simple; a onetime application and no renewals or additional fees. Getting your permit takes about four to six months.

It's fast, affordable and easy.

As we explain below, other, more complicated Panama residence programs do require that you file for renewal each year and some require substantial investments. But the *pensionado* costs no more than a few thousand dollars for legal fees and processing — then you receive Panamanian resident status for life.

What follows are detailed descriptions of the *pensionado* program and other visa programs that you may also find useful. The Sovereign Society stands ready to help you in meeting these program requirements and we can recommend reliable professionals in Panama who can assist you.

Under the famous *pensionado* program, the applicant must show proof of personal entitlement to a monthly income from an official foreign program (Social Security, disability, military retirement, government pension), or a private corporate pension plan, in the amount of at least US$1,000, plus an additional US$250 each for a spouse and other dependents. A letter of certification of the retirement income and amounts from the appropriate authorities are required.

For private pensions, other documents will be required, including bank statements showing past retirement deposits.

When the visa petition is filed with the Immigration and Naturalization Directorate by the applicant's attorney, a one-year interim card visa for residence status is granted within a few days. The *pensionado* status can be granted for life and entitles the holder to a one-time exemption of up to US$10,000 on duties on imported household goods, plus a reduction every two years of duties on an imported automobile. It also entitles the person, as a matter of right, to the many discounted prices for goods and services.

Living as a resident of Panama with the *pensionado* visa does not count for the five years of residence needed to qualify for an application for full Panamanian citizenship.

Private Income Retiree Visa: *(Rentista Retirado)*

A variation on the *pensionado* visa, this is for retired persons who don't have a guaranteed monthly pension or may no longer be employed, but who have received a retirement lump sum or have other wealth.

The law grants a special travel document (not a passport) and immediate residence (not immediate citizenship) to those applicants that establish a five-year certificate of deposit (CD) at the National Bank of Panama, provided that the CD produces a minimum of

US$850 per month in interest income which is not taxed. (At recent rates, the CD would have to be in the amount of US$340,000 or more.) This visa program admits an applicant, a spouse and children under 18 years old.

This visa (and the CD) is renewable every five years on the same date. The visa includes a Panamanian travel document (for the principal applicant only) that is not an official passport, and it does not grant citizenship.

Keep this point in mind — many Panama sources try to sell this particular visa, charging high fees, falsely representing it as an official passport, which it is not. It is only a travel document.

This visa does give a one-time exemption of up to US$10,000 on duties on imported household goods, plus a reduction every two years from duties on the importation or purchase locally of a motor vehicle.

To open a time deposit account at the National Bank of Panama, an applicant must submit:

- three letters of commercial references, at least two from banks, duly authenticated;

- three letters of personal reference, duly authenticated;

- two photocopies of the applicant's passport, duly authenticated;

- **Form for Opening of Account** with complete formation, available at any National Bank of Panama branch;

- **Form for Verification of References** provided by the Panamanian Association of Credit (APC); and profile of the applicant.

The two forms (four and five) should be completed by the applicant in the presence of a National Bank official, unless the

applicant confers a special power of attorney on a peisoinal rep
resentative to act on their behalf, which is usually the applicant's
Panama attorney.

Immigrant Visas

The immigrant visa is provisionally granted for two years. At the
end of two years, a petition for permanent residence must be filed.
Once this is approved, a permanent residence permit and a Panamanian identification card (cédula) will be issued. Five years after
obtaining a permanent visa, the holder is eligible to apply for and
receive full Panamanian citizenship.

Person of Means Visa *(Solvencia Económica Propia)*

This visa is for wealthy folks who wish to live in Panama without
being employed or starting a business, and who have the financial
means to do so.

The person must, either:

1. have a three-year fixed term deposit in any bank located in
   Panama in a minimum of US$300,000, or;

2. invest in real estate worth US$300,000 in Panama which must
   be fully paid up and titled in the name of the applicant or
   under a Private Interest Foundation, of which the applicant
   is founder and beneficiaries are the founder and/or his dependents, or;

3. have created a combination of the above with a minimum value of US$300,000.

Investor Visa *(Inversionista)*

This visa is issued to those who want to invest in an allowed
business in Panama. (Certain retail businesses and some professions are reserved to Panamanians only.) There must be a mini-

mum investment of US$160,000 and minimum of five permanent Panamanian employees hired.

A similar visa is available for those who intend to invest in agricultural projects and farming.

Permanent Resident Visa for Nationals of Specific Countries (Visas de Residencia Permanente para Nacionales de Paises Específicos)

In 2012, President Martinelli signed an order creating a new category of "Immediate Permanent Resident" for foreign nationals. Executive Order 343, later replaced by Executive Order 416, aimed this new category for foreigners from 48 listed countries "that maintain friendly, professional, economic, and investment relationships with the Republic of Panama" which included the United States. This change was seen as confirmation of Panama's need for qualified talent to continue growth both foreign direct investment and skilled international professionals.

To qualify, you must have a bank account in Panama with at least US$5,000 and either a Panamanian corporation, real estate or employment offer.

Under this new immigration category, with some categories excepted, qualified applicants will be able to engage in professional and economic activities, establish businesses and have the right to work in Panama, permissions that in the past have been difficult to obtain. After five years they will be eligible to apply for full citizenship.

The law grants residence in one application and a cédula, not only to qualified foreign individuals, but also to dependent spouses, children under 18, family members with disabilities and dependent parents. Children aged from 18 to 25 can be included if they are students.

Applications must be made to the National Immigration Service (NIS) through an attorney and a one-year interim card will be issued at that time. Approval time for the permanent residence is two to six months. The work permit must be applied for after the permanent residence is approved before the Ministry of Labor. Experience shows you will need to be represented by a qualified Panamanian attorney. Rainelda Mata-Kelly JD, (see below) can assist applicants who qualify with this quick-residence category.

Citizenship

Citizenship regulations are outlined in the Panamanian Constitution. The following are the ways in which citizenship is acquired:

1. by birth: to a child born within the territory of the Republic of Panama, regardless of the nationality of the parents.

2. by descent: from a Panamanian who has established legal residence in Panama:

    a) for a child born abroad, one of whose parents is a Panamanian by birth, or;

    b) for a child born abroad, one of whose parents is a Panamanian by naturalization. The child must declare their intention to elect Panamanian nationality no later than one year after reaching age 18.

3. by naturalization: Citizenship may be acquired upon fulfillment of the following conditions:

    a) a person has lived in Panama for at least five years, has a command of the Spanish language, is knowledgeable of Panamanian history, and has renounced their previous citizenship, or;

    b) a child under age seven, born abroad and adopted by Panamanian nationals, does not need a naturalization certification. The child, however, must declare their intention to elect Panamanian nationality not more than one year after reaching age 18.

Spanish citizens and citizens of certain other Latin American nations may become citizens of Panama under different requirements. In such cases, the petitioner is obligated to fulfill the same conditions that would apply to a Panamanian national wishing to seek citizenship in the petitioner's country of origin.

Dual Citizenship

Only Panamanian citizens by birth have the right to hold dual citizenship. To apply for citizenship, you must sign an affidavit stating that you will renounce your existing citizenship. However, when a foreign citizen is naturalized as a Panamanian citizen, government officials do not ask that the person surrender their non-Panama passport nor do they notify the person's home government.

This is much like the U.S. situation where newly naturalized U.S. citizens swear an oath to "renounce" any existing citizenship, but the U.S. government does not require any formal renunciation and does not take their existing passports, since the U.S. Supreme Court has upheld the right to dual citizenship.

Contacts

Embassy of Panama
2862 McGill Terrace NW
Washington, DC 20009
Tel.: (202) 483-1407
Email: info@embassyofpanama.org
Web: www.embassyofpanama.org/

Consulates:
New York (212) 840-2450, Philadelphia (215) 574-2994,
Atlanta (404) 525-2772, Chicago, Houston (713) 622-4451,
Los Angeles (562) 612-4677, Miami (305) 447-3700, New
Orleans (504) 525-3458, and Tampa (813) 886-1427.

United States Embassy
Building 783, Demetrio Basilio Lakas Avenue
Clayton, Republic of Panama
Tel.: +507-207-7000
Email: Panamaweb@state.gov
Web: http://panama.usembassy.gov/

Rainelda Mata-Kelly, Esq.
Suite 406-407, Tower B
Torres de las Americas, Punta Pacifica
Panama City, Republic of Panama
Tel.: + (507) 380-0606
Email: rmk@mata-kelly.com
Web: http://www.mata-kelly.com

Ms. Mata-Kelly specializes in Panamanian immigration, administrative, commercial and maritime law and assists clients with real estate, contracts, incorporation, and other legal issues. She is a senior member of The Sovereign Society Council of Experts.

United States Embassy
Building 783, Demetrio Basilio Lakas Avenue
Clayton, Republic of Panama
Tel.: +507-207-7000
Email: Panamaweb@state.gov
Web: http://panama.usembassy.gov/

Republic of Trinidad and Tobago

Government:	Parliamentary democracy
Capital:	Port of Spain
National Day:	Independence Day: 31 August (1962)
Population:	1,225,225 (July 2013 est.)
Total Area:	1,980 sq. miles / 5,128 sq. kilometers
Languages:	English (official), Hindi, French, Spanish, Chinese Ethnic groups: Indian (South Asian) 40%, African 37.5%, mixed 20.5%, other 1.2%, unspecified 0.8%
Religion:	Roman Catholic 26%, Hindu 22.5%, other 10.8%, Anglican 7.8%, Baptist 7.2%, Pentecostal 6.8%, other Christian 5.8%, Muslim 5.8%, Seventh Day Adventist 4%, none 1.9%, unspecified 1.4%
Life expectancy:	71.96 years
Currency:	Trinidad and Tobago dollar (TTD)
GDP:	US$26.35 billion (2012 est.)
GDP per capita:	US$19,800 (2012 est.)

It's Carnival in Port of Spain. Soca music throbs in the streets, and a woman furrows her brow, shaking and gyrating as the beads on her bikini seem close to flying off. She is Trinidad and Tobago. An East Indian couple serves pungent curried doubles at lightning speed on the street corner, fishermen plunk their catch on splintering docks as the new morning spreads over an azure ocean, an oil-industry businessman walks from crumbling streets into a modern air-conditioned building where he navigates the global economy for his nation, and a crazy-haired steel-pan player lays into an oil drum reaching a seventh-level of ecstasy — they are all Trinidad and Tobago.

National pride, a sordid history of slavery and indenture, and the love of music and limin' unite the myriad colors, ethnicities and cultures that make up the dual-island nation of Trinidad and Tobago. Dive in. Be prepared to experience beaches so mesmerizing you'll forget your name, first-class diving through coral wonderlands, a Carnival to end all Carnivals, and luxuriant rainforests prime for bird-watching, hiking, and cycling. Of the two islands, Tobago is the laidback pleasure center, while hard-working Trinidad has less of a tourist infrastructure...but plenty of natural and nocturnal attractions.

But don't expect anyone to hold your hand. The oil and gas industry leaves tourism low down on the priority list. Upscale resorts and hotels are out there, and more so on Tobago, but generally you jump in the mix and accept the services that facilitate a sun-drenched ball, whether it be peaceful, sand-filled, rollicking, or all of the above. — Lonely Planet

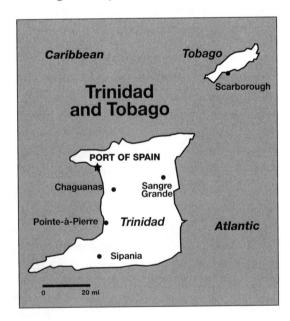

History and Overview

Columbus landed on Trinidad in 1498, and the island was settled by the Spanish a century later. Original inhabitants, Arawak and Carib Indians, were largely wiped out by the Spanish colonizers and their imported diseases, and survivors were gradually assimilated. Although it attracted French, free black and other non-Spanish settlers, Trinidad remained under Spanish rule until the British captured it in 1797.

During the colonial period, Trinidad's economy relied on large sugar and cocoa plantations. Tobago's development was similar to other plantation islands in the Lesser Antilles and quite different from Trinidad's. During the colonial period, French, Dutch and British forces fought over possession of Tobago.

The islands' sugar industry was hurt by the emancipation of the slaves in 1834. Manpower was replaced with the importation of contract laborers from India between 1845 and 1917, which boosted sugar production as well as the cocoa industry. The discovery of oil on Trinidad, in 1910, added another important export. Independence was attained in 1962. The country is one of the most prosperous in the Caribbean thanks largely to petroleum and natural gas production and processing. Tourism, mostly in Tobago, is targeted for expansion and is growing.

A parliamentary democracy of the Westminster style, Trinidad and Tobago has earned a reputation as an excellent investment site for international businesses and has one of the higher growth rates and per capita incomes in Latin America. The economy benefits from low inflation and a growing trade surplus. The government is coping with a rise in violent crime.

The twin-island nation is in its 16th consecutive year of real GDP growth as a result of economic reforms adopted in the early 1990s, tight monetary policy and, until recently, buoyant markets for its export commodities. Growth has been fueled by investments in liquefied natural gas (LNG), petrochemicals, and steel. Additional petrochemical, aluminum, and plastics projects are in various stages of planning. Trinidad and Tobago is the leading Caribbean producer of oil and gas, and its economy is heavily dependent upon these resources but it also supplies manufactured goods, notably food products and beverages, as well as cement to the Caribbean region. Oil and gas account for about 40% of GDP and 80% of exports, but only 5% of employment.

The country is also a regional financial center, and tourism is a growing sector, although it is not as important domestically as it is in many other Caribbean islands. The U.S. is the country's leading trade partner. The economy benefits from a growing trade surplus with the U.S. Crime and bureaucratic hurdles continue to be the biggest deterrents for attracting more foreign direct investment and business.

Residence and Citizenship

Citizenship is conferred in the following ways:

1. by birth: of a child born in Trinidad and Tobago, regardless of the nationality of the parents. The exception is a child born to foreign diplomatic personnel, neither of whom is a citizen of Trinidad and Tobago.

2. by descent: to a child born abroad, either of whose parents are citizens of Trinidad and Tobago.

3. by registration: the following are eligible for citizenship by registration:

    a) Commonwealth citizens, citizens of Ireland, British Protected Persons (BPP), and foreign husbands of Trinidad and Tobago wives who are of good character, speak English, have resided in the country for five years, and have renounced previous citizenship.

b) A foreign woman currently married to a citizen of Trinidad and Tobago.

4. by naturalization: may be acquired if the person is of good character, knows English, has resided for eight years in the country, plans to continue there and has renounced former citizenship. This applies to foreign husbands of Trinidad and Tobago wives not eligible for citizenship by registration.

Citizens by birth or descent are permitted to hold dual citizenship but dual citizenship is not recognized in the case of naturalized or registered citizens.

A passport is required of U.S. citizens for entry to Trinidad and Tobago and for return to the United States. U.S. citizens do not need a visa for tourism or business-related visits of 90 days or less. Work permits are required for compensated and some non-compensated employment, including missionary work. Visas may be required for travel for purposes other than business or tourism.

Contacts

Embassy of the Republic of Trinidad and Tobago
1708 Massachusetts Avenue NW
Washington, DC 20036
Tel.: (202) 467-6490
Web: http://www.ttembassy.org/

United States Embassy
15 Queen's Park West
Port of Spain, Trinidad and Tobago

Tel.: + (868) 622-6371
Email: info@ttembwash.com
Web: http://www.ttembassy.org

Turks and Caicos Islands

Government:	Overseas territory of the U.K.
Capital:	Grand Turk (Cockburn Town)
National Day:	Constitution Day: 30 August (1976)
Population:	47,754 (July 2013 est.)
Total Area:	166 sq. miles / 430 sq. kilometers
Language:	English
Ethnic groups:	Black 87.6%, white 7.9%, mixed 2.5%, East Indian 1.3%, other 0.7%
Religion:	Baptist 35.8%, Church of God 11.7%, Roman Catholic 11.4%, Anglican 10%, Methodist 9.3%, Seventh Day Adventist 6%, Jehovah's Witnesses 1.8%, other 14%
Life expectancy:	79.4 years
Currency:	U.S. dollar (USD)
GDP:	US$558.9 million (2013 est.)
GDP per capita:	US$29,100 (2007 est.)

The Turks and where? That's the reaction most people have when you mention these tropical isles. Like all great Shangri-Las, this one is hidden just under the radar. Be glad that it is, as this tropical dream is the deserted Caribbean destination you've been looking for. And the best part — it's only 90 minutes by plane from Miami; this slice of paradise is just around the corner.

So why would you want to go there? How about white-sand beaches, clear blue water and a climate that defines divine. Secluded bays and islands where you'll see more wild donkeys than other traveler; historic towns and villages that look like some-

thing out of a pirate movie, where life creeps along at a sedate pace. While development is on the rise, all one has to do is dig a bit deeper, catch a boat to the next island over and the solace of solitude returns: islands like Grand Turk (part of the Turks Islands) are set in a time long past, with dilapidated buildings, salt ponds and narrow lanes, and contrast with the ever-expanding Providenciales, tourist gateway to the Caicos Islands.

Divers and beach aficionados will rejoice at the quality of the sea here. Clear warm waters teem with sea life, yet are devoid of crashing waves. Even the most ardent land lubber can't help but be mesmerized by the azure water and golden sand. — Lonely Planet

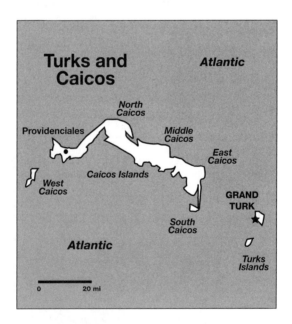

History and Overview

The Turks and Caicos Islands (TCI) are an archipelago of eight major, inhabited islands and numerous uninhabited cays. They lie in the Atlantic Ocean east of Cuba nearest to the larger island to the south of Hispaniola (shared by Haiti and the Dominican Republic).

The Turks and Caicos Islands are 575 miles southeast of Miami at the southern end of The Bahamas chain. The Turks and Caicos are called the "Isles of Perpetual June" because they enjoy a year-round comfortable climate cooled by trade winds, but with abundant sunshine.

The islands are graced with 230 miles of sandy beaches, and have become a major stopover for eco-tourists, divers who have begun to discover some of the finest coral reefs and walls in the world. From the walls of Grand Turk, West Caicos and Providenciales' Northwest Point to the historic wrecks south of Salt Cay, a dozen world-class coral walls have become a magnet for serious scuba enthusiasts. In 2014, the travel review site TripAdvisor.com chose Providenciales as No. 2 among the 10 best islands in the world for tourism.

From late December through April, the Atlantic herd of about 2,500 humpback whales swim past on their annual migration to the Mouchoir Bank, some 20 to 30 miles southeast of the islands. During this period, divers can listen to an underwater concert of whales' songs. In summer, divers can swim among manta rays that cruise the faces of the seawalls. Encounters with dolphins are not uncommon.

In 1512, Europeans first visited these uninhabited islands but no settlement resulted. In the late 17th century, British settlers from Bermuda came in search of salt. Gradually, over many years, the area also was settled by some U.S. planters and their slaves. With the local abolition of slavery in 1838, these planters left. Until 1848, the Turks and Caicos were under the jurisdiction of The Bahamas. In 1873, they became a dependency of Jamaica and remained so until 1959. In 1962, Jamaica gained independence and the Turks and Caicos became a British Crown colony. Since 1976, it has had local autonomy. Although independence was agreed upon for 1982, the policy was reversed and the islands remain a British overseas territory.

In ensuing years, there has been a continuing political struggle between the islanders on the one hand and the colonial governors and the Foreign Office in London on the other. This was partially due to a strong pro-independence movement, but also because of alleged drug smuggling in the TCI. A low-keyed but persistent movement has been afoot for some years seeking to have Canada annex the Turks and Caicos. Despite having adherents in both jurisdictions, this idea has not gained any serious momentum.

The legal system is based on English common law and the law of Wales, with some laws from Jamaica and The Bahamas.

Economy

The Turks and Caicos Islands are an English-speaking British overseas territory that combines tax-free status, an idyllic climate and close proximity to the United States. They enjoy freedom from income, corporate and estate taxes. There are no exchange controls and the U.S. dollar is the country's legal tender. There is a wide range of financial and other professional services readily available.

The local economy is based on tourism, fishing and offshore financial services. Most capital goods and food for domestic consumption are imported. The U.S. has been the leading source of tourists, accounting for more than half of the 87,000 visitors in a recent year. The tourism sector accounted for 42.8% of GDP in 2012. Most tourist facilities are located on Providenciales (Provo) and Grand Turk Islands. Major sources of government revenue include fees from offshore financial activities and customs receipts.

In 2014, the economy had stabilized significantly and there was a return to economic growth. Public finances and business confidence improved. Tourism and resort developers returned and several large-scale tourism-related construction projects were planned.

If maximum financial privacy is important to you, keep in mind that the TCI are a British Overseas Territory and, ultimately, under the police and political control of the government of the United Kingdom. (See above.) That means, under current U.K. policies, automatic exchange of tax information with foreign governments upon request.

Political Turmoil

Despite pressing fiscal challenges, the premier, Rufus Ewing, enjoys an extended honeymoon period in the wake of an unpopular intervention by London which saw U.K. direct rule imposed on the overseas territory for several years. The U.K. remains heavily involved in local administration as protection of its interests as guarantor for a US$260 million rescue loan agreed in 2011. Tax reforms remain a priority.

During the year 2008, the royal Governor created a Commission of Inquiry to examine corruption on the part of members of the House of Assembly including the Prime Minister. In 2009, based on the Commission's findings of systemic corruption, the British parliament in London suspended the island's constitution and removed its elected parliament. In 2012, the U.K. Foreign Minister determined that sufficient progress had been made to reinstate local government under a new constitution that came into effect in October. In November 2012, a new House of Assembly was elected and Rufus Ewing became Prime Minister under a new constitution.

The 2008 investigation covered allegations of corruption in

public land sales, distribution of government contracts and development deals and the granting of voting rights, and the misuse of public funds. Published findings pointed to a "high probability of systemic corruption or other serious dishonesty" among the ruling elite, including the removed Prime Minister, Dr. Michael Eugene Misick LLB. Legal action resulted in the recovery to public ownership of thousands of acres of land sold during Misick's administration.

Residence

There are a few categories of residence in TCI which arise in different ways, namely:

1. **Temporary Residence Permits:** 30-day permits granted to tourists on arrival that can be extended on application for a further 30 days.

2. **Residence Permits:** entitle individuals to reside in the islands for a period of one year from the date of issuance for a government fee of US$1000.00 per annum. This residence permit is called a "Temporary Residence Certificate." The TRC must be renewed annually for a fee of about US$1,000.00 plus US$150.00 for a spouse and US$50.00 for each child. Holders of the permit are not allowed to work while in the Islands, must be in good health and must be able to support oneself and family.

3. **Permanent Residence Permits (PRC):** These are for the duration of the life of the holder and extend to the holder's spouse and dependents until the age of majority when they can apply for their own PRC. PRC's are issued to applicants who have made the requisite investment in TCI and come either with the right to work (individuals who have held work permits for five years) and without the right to work (in the retirement investment category). The investment prerequisite for PRC's in the

retirement category varies depending on the location in which the investor acquires property.

4. **Work Permits:** This permit is required for non-Turks and Caicos Islanders who desire to work in the Islands. Conditions of work permits vary. The majority of permits are issued on a year to year basis but it is possible for employed persons to obtain permits for three years and self-employed persons for five years.

5. **Citizenship/Belongership:** entitle individuals to vote in general elections and to be considered for public offices. This status is restricted to individuals who have made significant contributions to the Islands (if they are not born to TCI citizens).

Under several programs, investors in the Turks and Caicos are entitled to apply for and receive a Permanent Residence certificate, which costs US$50,000 for self-employed persons, US$30,000 for skilled workers, US$15,000 for retired persons, and US$8,000 for unskilled workers.

Qualifying investments vary according to the status of the applicant and the location of the investment in the islands, but US$250,000 is the usual capital input required for start-ups or acquisitions on the main island of Providenciales; US$125,000 for investments in the other inhabited "out" islands of Grand Turk, Salt Cay, South Caicos, Middle Caicos, or North Caicos.

In return, the investor is granted a "Permanent Residence Certificate." Certain other foreign individuals may qualify by investing at least US$50,000 in government-authorized investments.

The government provides import and export incentives for establishing new enterprises or expanding existing ones that benefit employment and the TCI's economy. There is also relief from duties and fees, mainly on the import of materials for construction projects, but also on exports. The incentives are not restricted to

TCI-owned enterprises. The level of fiscal concessions available to a foreign investor is greater for businesses based outside the main island of Providenciales.

To apply for citizenship, one must have held a Permanent Residence Certificate for at least 12 months and have been resident in the TCI for at least five years. Such status is not granted to large numbers of persons primarily because of the very real concerns of the indigenous population that they may become a minority in their own country.

The following documents must be submitted with an application for TCI permanent residence: 1) four passport-style photographs of you and any dependents; 2) a medical certificate for each applicant and each dependent, dated no more than one month prior containing a negative HIV test; 3) a birth certificate for each person; 4) marriage and divorce certificates, where appropriate; 5) a copy of passports; 6) a bank reference showing good financial standing; 7) a certificate of no criminal convictions; 8) a character reference from an attorney/solicitor or other professional; 9) a letter declaring the investor has sufficient means to support him/herself and any dependents and has obtained a local residence; and 10) the formal application for a permanent residence certificate. Other information may also be required.

A permanent residence certificate can be revoked but only in certain limited circumstances, such as conviction of serious crimes or an act of disloyalty to the British Crown.

Citizenship

The description "British Dependent Territories" originated in the British Nationality Act of 1981. The British Dependent Territories individually were left to determine what link there should be between citizenship and immigration control. The immigration laws in each dependent territory determine who has a "right of abode" in the particular U.K. "overseas territory," the phrase now used by London.

Because the Turks and Caicos is an overseas territory of the United Kingdom and not an independent country, the government cannot confer citizenship. Persons resident in Britain's overseas territories, hold British citizenship. In 2002, the British Overseas Territories Act restored full British citizenship status to all inhabitants of the U.K. overseas territories, including the Turks and Caicos. As in the Cayman Islands, rights normally associated with citizenship derive from what is called "belonger" status and island natives or descendants from natives are said to be "belongers," the term locals use.

As I explained in the Cayman Islands section, the "belonger" status does not refer to nationality. Belonger status gives all the rights which normally come with citizenship, including voting, however there is one difference; it does not give nationality. People who have lived in Turks and Caicos for many years, made a considerable contribution and have shown good character may be granted "belongership status" which is usually reserved only for the native people, sometimes called "Turks Islanders."

For tourist stays up to 30 days, U.S. citizens need a passport, onward or return tickets, and sufficient funds for their stay. U.S. citizens do not need visas to enter as tourists, however if they remain for more than 24 hours each person must fill out an immigration form. A departure tax is required of all persons 12 years of age and older. In order to arrange for longer stays or obtain work permits, travelers should contact the Turks and Caicos Immigration Department at + (649) 946-2939, web: http://www.immigration.tc/

Contacts

For information on the Turks and Caicos, a British Overseas Territory, contact:

Embassy of the United Kingdom
3100 Massachusetts Avenue NW
Washington, DC 20008
Tel.: (202) 588-6500
Email: britishembassyenquiries@gmail.com
Web: https://www.gov.uk/government/world/organisations/british-embassy-washington

Turks and Caicos Tourism Office
80 Broad Street, Suite 3302
New York, NY 10004
Tel.: (646) 375-8830
Toll Free: (800) 241-0824
Email: info@turksandcaicostourism.com
Web: http://www.turksandcaicostourism.com/contactus.html

There is no U.S. Embassy or Consular Agency in the Turks and Caicos. The U.S. Embassy in Nassau, The Bahamas, has responsibilities over the territory.

United States Embassy
42 Queen Street
Nassau, The Bahamas
Tel.: + (242) 322-1181
Email: embnas@state.gov
Web: http://nassau.usembassy.gov/

United States Virgin Islands

Government:	United States unincorporated territory
Capital:	Charlotte Amalie, St. Thomas
National Day:	Transfer Day: 31 March (1917)
Population:	106,405 (2010 census)
Total Area:	136 sq. miles / 352 sq. kilometers
Languages:	English 74.7% (official), Spanish or Spanish Creole 16.8%, French or French Creole 6.6%, other 1.9%
Ethnic groups:	Black 76.2%, white 13.1%, other 6.1%, mixed 3.5%, Asian 1.1%
Religion:	Baptist 42%, Roman Catholic 34%, Episcopalian 17%, other 7%
Life Expectancy:	79.61 years
Currency:	U.S. dollar (USD)
GDP:	US$422.3 million (2013 est.)
GDP per capita:	US$18,800 (2009 est.)

St John is the greenest island, literally and figuratively. It cloaks two thirds of its area in parkland and sublime beaches, ripe for hiking and snorkeling. It also leads the way in environmental preservation, with limited development and several low-impact tent-resorts for lodging. Dizzying cruise-ship traffic and big resorts nibbling its edges make St Thomas the most commercialized island. St Croix is the odd-island-out located far from its siblings and offering a mix of rainforest, sugar plantations, old forts and great scuba diving. Its economy is not based on tourism, which makes it feel even more off-the-beaten path.

While the islands are American territories (and a favorite of American tourists since they don't require a passport), West Indian culture remains their strongest influence. Calypso and reggae rhythms swirl through the air, and curried meats, callaloo soup and mango-sweetened microbrews fill the tables. — Lonely Planet

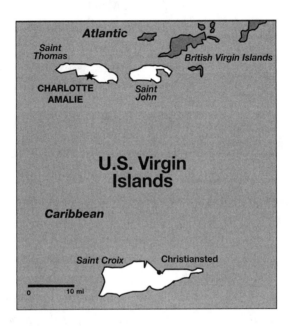

History and Overview

The Virgin Islands of the United States, as the islands are officially styled, constitutionally are "an unincorporated territory" of the U.S. With the Caribbean Sea to the south and the Atlantic Ocean to the north, the U.S. Virgin Islands ("USVI") offers a variety of deep sea and coastal fishing. Their tropical climate and minimal industrial development assure an abundance of unspoiled reefs for divers and snorkelers, with sandy beaches ringing deep coves. The large number of isolated, secure anchorages in the USVI and the

British Virgins just to the east have made the chain a center for yachting. A thriving charter-boat industry in the USVI draws tens of thousands of visitors annually for crewed sailing adventures.

The islands — St. Croix, St. John, St. Thomas, and Water Island — have a strategic value for the United States since they command the Anegada Passage from the Atlantic Ocean into the Caribbean Sea as well as the approach to the Panama Canal. U.S. citizenship status was conferred on USVI inhabitants in 1927. Although they do not vote in U.S. presidential elections, residents are represented by a non-voting Delegate in the U.S. House of Representatives and also send voting delegates to the Democratic and Republican Conventions.

U.S. Low Tax Paradise

The USVI lies 1100 miles southeast of Miami, Florida — and it's one of the most impoverished jurisdictions under the American flag. But most visiting mainland Americans only know the islands as a vacation venue with beautiful resort hotels, white sandy beaches and blue lagoons.

According to *The World Factbook*: "Tourism, trade, and other services are the primary economic activities, accounting for about 57% of GDP and about half of total civilian employment. Goods-producing industries account for 23% of GDP and government represents 20%. The islands hosted nearly 2.74 million visitors — 2.2 million cruise ship and 536,000 air passengers in 2011. The manufacturing sector consists primarily of rum distilling, electronics, boats, and watch assembly. The agriculture sector is small, with most food being imported although there is a growing focus on supporting local agriculture and farmers markets occur regularly. The islands are vulnerable to damage from storms."

Those on the four principal islands — St. Croix, St. John, St.

Thomas, and Water Island — have a per capita income in the territory of only US$18,800. That is less than half the average in the continental United States and US$10,000 less than in Mississippi, the poorest American state.

In addition to poverty, the USVI has another unusual distinction.

The USVI has several development tax credits designed to incentivize businesses to relocate to (or start in) the USVI. These tax credits apply against USVI source and effectively connected income, and are effectively "blessed" by the U.S. Congress which specifically permits the USVI to reduce taxes on such income. The low-tax hating OECD denounced the USVI as the U.S. version of "unfair tax competition." What specifically upset the OECD were the territory's tax exempt companies since they cannot be owned more than 10 percent by U.S. or USVI persons, although this "ring fencing" was specifically created by the U.S. Congress in 1986 in the U.S. Internal Revenue Code. (The USVI was removed from the OECD "unfair tax" black list in 2002.)

The islands have been territorial possessions of the United States since they were purchased from Denmark in 1917. The territorial government operates according the 1954 Revised Organic Act. The U.S. Department of the Interior oversees the large national park within the territory, and the U.S. Coast Guard oversees the ocean surrounding the islands. The U.S. Customs and Border Patrol oversees the various ports of entry into the USVI. Most internal functions of government, such as the local police and business licensing, are overseen by the territory government. The U.S. federal courts and territory courts operate in conjunction with each other, in a similar fashion to U.S federal relations with a U.S. State. The USVI elects one non-voting member to the House of Representatives, and has a unicameral legislature, consisting of 15 senators, that enacts local laws, and a governor who functions as the chief executive of the territory. Seven of the senators in the legislature are from St. Croix, seven are from St. Thomas/Water Island, and one represents St. John, but is elected territory-wide.

The Naval Services Appropriation Act of 1922 (Title 48 U.S.C. § 1397) provides in part: "The income tax laws in force in the United States of America…shall be held to be likewise in force in the Virgin Islands of the United States, except that the proceeds of such taxes shall be paid to the treasuries of said islands." Accordingly, USVI residents and corporations pay their federal taxes on their worldwide income to the Virgin Islands Bureau of Internal Revenue (the "BIR"), and not to the U.S. IRS. Persons who are born in the USVI or those who become naturalized U.S. citizens in the USVI, for purposes of U.S. federal gift and estate taxes, are treated as nonresidents of the United States as long as they are domiciled in the USVI (or another U.S. possession). Since the USVI has no estate or gift taxes, this means that upon death, the estates of such persons owe zero U.S. or territorial estate or gift taxes as long as they are domiciled in the USVI at the time of death or at the time of making a gift and have no U.S. assets. (As with any other nonresidents of the United States, for gift and estate tax purposes, assets located in the U.S. mainland are subject to federal estate and gift tax.)

Investment Tax Incentives

The U.S. Congress allows the USVI to incentivize businesses to relocate to the USVI to promote the economic self-sufficiency of the territory. The USVI administers tax incentives through various programs within the territory. One major incentive is the Economic Development Program, administered by the USVI Economic Development Authority. The USVI Economic Development Authority approves companies to be eligible for the Economic Development Credit, which is a 90% tax credit against eligible income.

This tax incentive, currently offered for periods of 10 to 30 years, depends on the business location within the USVI (with possible five-year extensions), and is available to corporations, partnerships and limited liability companies that are formed in or register to do business in the USVI (although from a U.S. tax standpoint it would not make sense to have a U.S. corporation as a beneficiary). The tax credit applies to income from USVI sources and to income that is effectively connected with a USVI trade or business, such as fees for services performed in the USVI, and certain related income, such as sales of inventory and dividends and interest from non-U.S. sources received by approved companies based in the USVI. (Legislation currently before the USVI Legislature would provide increase the minimum benefit period to 20 years and the extension period to 10 years.)

For many years, a few U.S. investors with business activities ranging from petroleum production, aluminum processing, hotel and other tourism activities, to transportation, shopping centers, and financial services, took advantage of the Economic Development Program and enjoyed income with a relatively low tax rate on eligible income. As a result of an expansion of the type of company that could be eligible for the Economic Development Credit to include various service based companies, about 100 companies qualified for the program in the early 2000s, employing nearly 3,100 people.

The tax benefit program began paying dividends immediately after hedge fund managers, investment managers, consultants, and other businesses serving clients outside the USVI first started moving to the USVI in 1995. The islands' tax revenue doubled from US$400 million to US$800 million in a five-year period ending in 2005. The increase effectively erased a US$287.6 million deficit for the territory. The Economic Development Program was worth about US$100 million annually to the local economy and was crucial in lifting the territory from a financial crisis to a fiscal year surplus in excess of US$50 million.

Paradise Lost

Prior to 2005 the IRS had not issued guidance regarding what constitutes a "bona fide" resident of the USVI. The test to determine residence within the USVI prior to 2005 was based on an analysis focused on the intent of the individual with few objective criteria to determine residence. The IRS issued a notice in 2004 that specifically stated that it believed that large partnerships that were beneficiaries of the Economic Development Program and that were also aggressively promoting membership within the partnership were economic shams not entitled to recognition by the IRS. Subsequent U.S. Tax Court and Circuit Court decisions have, however, favored the USVI and its taxpayers.

In 2003, the IRS raided a financial services firm in St. Croix, accusing the firm of sheltering income for dozens of partners who were not actually bona fide residents of the USVI. Six years later all the parties charged as a result of the raid were acquitted on all counts by a federal jury in St. Croix.

Six Month Residence Requirement

U.S. legislation adopted in 1986 provided that the territory's tax benefits applied to income from sources within the USVI and to income "effectively connected" with a USVI trade or business, but directed the Treasury Department to issue special regulations to define the terms "source" and "effectively connected" income for this purpose. But the diligent Treasury Department in Washington went 18 years without issuing any regulations on the matter.

As part of the American Jobs Creation Act of 2004, Congress enacted a law that defined a "bona fide" resident of an American territory as a person who spends 183 days or more within that territory, has a tax home within the territory, and does not have a closer connection to the U.S. or a foreign country. Additionally, this statute specifically defined income that is sourced, or "effectively connected" to a U.S. territory, to not include income that Is U.S. sourced, or "effectively connected" to a U.S. trade or business.

U.S. Senator Charles Grassley (R-Iowa) slipped these changes into this major tax bill without any hearings, and with no notice to the USVI Delegate to the U.S. Congress, the islands' governor, or the U.S. Interior Department, all of whom were stunned to learn what had happened. This major change was imposed without any testimony, territorial input, and certainly without any consideration or understanding of the critical importance of the territory's Economic Development Program to its impoverished economy.

The Congressional Joint Committee on Taxation estimated in a wild guess that Grassley's legislative rider would increase federal revenue by US$400 million over a 10-year period, which never happened.

Treasury Department Rules

In what locals call "a reign of tax terror" that began after 2004, the IRS opened several hundred audits on individuals who filed as USVI residents and on businesses that were beneficiaries of the Economic Development Program. Many of the individual audits were of persons who had no economic development credits and made no tax exemption claims on their income tax returns. (Many of the audits have subsequently been closed with no change to the tax returns as filed.)

The former chief executive officer of the USVI Economic Development Authority has said: "In the States, they definitely see that they are losing taxes when some of their taxpayers move elsewhere. All of the people everywhere are competing for the same business. What's wrong with the Virgin Islands attracting some of those people?"

After the 2004 Grassley law was adopted, about 50 hedge funds and other financial services companies halted activities temporarily, left the islands, or decided not to start already-approved businesses in the territory. Americans seeking legal tax breaks sought find them in more secure (and non-U.S.) tax jurisdictions such as Panama, Uruguay, the Channel Islands, Singapore or Hong Kong. The islands' financial boom withered, crushed by the IRS and Grassley with a combination punch of the changed law and subsequent Treasury Department rules that govern income eligible for USVI tax credits. However, in recent years applications to the Economic Development Program have increased in light of the IRS guidance that was finalized in 2008 and the improved U.S economy.

Residence

As a territory of the United States, the USVI is subject to the same restrictive immigration laws as mainland America. Nonetheless, those already possessing U.S. permanent residence or citizenship may move freely to the USVI and benefit from the exemption from income and, where applicable estate and gift taxes for residents, as well as a tax holiday program for businesses established there if they qualify.

The old, pre-Grassley rules required a person to be a bona fide USVI resident on the last day of the tax year, "looking to all the facts and circumstances," similar to the "domicile" IRS test for estate and gift tax purposes. There was no "number of days present" test and no requirement that a person be a resident for all or most of the year to file as a tax resident for that year.

The rules now require a resident to be present physically in the USVI at least 183 days, or roughly six months, every year. The IRS set up four alternative ways to meet the "physical presence test" residence requirement. Only one of the five tests need be met in a given year, and different tests can be met in different years. The individual must:

1. be present no more than 90 days in the United States mainland during a taxable year;

2. be present in the USVI more days than in the U.S. mainland and not have more than US$3,000 in earned income from mainland U.S. sources;

3. be present an average 183 days annually in the USVI over a rolling three-year period, or;

4. meet an IRS "no significant connection" test.

This last test means no house (other than a rental property), no spouse, no minor kids, and no voting registration in the mainland United States — and no days counting requirement.

The residence rules also require a "bona fide resident" to have a "closer connection" to the USVI than anywhere else which is measured by where you are registered to vote, what mailing address you use, where most of your clothes hang, where you have homes, where you bank, and where your family actually lives.

The IRS also drafted a form for island residents that it claimed the agency needed to prove valid residence. IRS Form 8898 requires those who stop filing tax returns with the IRS, in order to file them in the USVI, to list where their immediate family lives, where their cars are registered and where they hold driver's licenses. Several of the questions on the Form 8898 do not deal with "closer connection" criteria enumerated in the Treasury regulations such as where a taxpayer's cars are registered and where a taxpayer keeps financial information, and therefore it is unclear how this form would help the IRS determine residence.

Something for Everyone

Notwithstanding all of the above, tax breaks can still be yours — but to qualify it is an absolute necessity that you actually live and make your main residence in the USVI.

The USVI offers several types of benefit programs that are either fully or partially exempt from both USVI taxes and U.S. federal income and corporate taxes as well.

One type is a USVI corporation (or partnership or LLC) that qualifies for the benefits of the Economic Development Program for its USVI business activities. Most beneficiaries of this program are in one of three areas — hotels, manufacturing, and service businesses serving clients outside the USVI. But benefits are also available for businesses engaged in transportation, marinas, large retail complexes, medical facilities, e-commerce and recreation businesses. Most of the service businesses that have obtained benefits are engaged in fund management, general management, and financial services activities.

The beneficiaries that do qualify are fully exempt from most local taxes, including the gross receipts tax (otherwise 5%), property taxes (otherwise 0.75%) and excise taxes on raw materials and building materials. Beneficiaries also get a 90% credit against their USVI income taxes (although for C corporations the credit is equal to 89% of taxes). Beneficiaries also enjoy a special customs duty rate of one percent on raw materials that would otherwise be taxed at 6 percent. They are exempt from U.S. federal income taxes on their USVI personal and business operations. The 90% credit also applies to dividends or allocations to a beneficiary's USVI bona fide resident owners — which is why it is so critical to meet the residence requirements.

To qualify for these generous benefits, a business must employ at least 5 persons full-time (a minimum of 32 hours a week), for a financial business, and 10 persons full-time for any other type of business, and must make an initial capital investment of US$100,000 or more. Corporate beneficiaries must also provide health and life insurance and a retirement plan to employees and must purchase goods and services locally if possible. In addition, beneficiaries must make certain contributions to scholarships and public education, and provide a plan for civic participation. Beneficiaries must also implement a management training program for their employees.

Applicants under the Economic Development Program are required to provide a substantial amount of information, including detailed formation and good standing documents for the applicant and affiliate entities, a detailed business plan, employee job descriptions and salaries, and detailed financial information, including a five-year projection, income tax returns, verification of business financing, and bank reference letters. Each beneficial owner of the applicant company must be identified with ownership, contact, and biographical information. Background questions must also be answered for each beneficial owner.

Following submission of an application for benefits, the application is presented at a public hearing before a seven-member Economic Development Commission, and upon receipt of a favorable recommendation, the application is forwarded to the USVI Governor for final review. The Governor statutorily has 60 days to approve or disapprove the application. Upon approval, the beneficiary must select the date or dates it would like to commence economic development benefits. Once commencement dates have been chosen, the beneficiary will receive a certificate — which is a contract between the USVI Government and the beneficiary — setting out the various tax credits, exemptions, and the time period of the beneficiary's benefits.

Businesses can also qualify for tax benefits under the University of the Virgin Islands Research and Technology Park ("RTPark"), which is an instrument of the USVI Government that was created to foster the development and expansion of a technology sector in the USVI. Benefits under the RTPark are similar to those under the Economic Development Program.

RTPark applicants must qualify as "Knowledge-Based Businesses," which includes "e-Commerce Businesses." A "Knowledge-Based Business" is statutorily defined to include any business that uses highly skilled or highly educated personnel and a high level of research and development to create intellectual assets and property." An "e-Commerce Business" is defined to mean any business involving electronically based data transactions for digitally based commerce.

The RTPark beneficiary, or "Protected Cell," must provide the RTPark with an equity interest in the Protected Cell entity, and negotiate an initial fee to the RTPark and an ongoing payment that can be a set amount or a percentage of gross income. Protected Cells work closely with the University of the Virgin Islands to develop opportunities for students and faculty.

Applications (including extensive due diligence) are reviewed by the RTPark Board and, upon receipt of a favorable recommendation, by the USVI Governor. Benefits are available for a 15-year period regardless of where the Protected Cell operates within the USVI and may be renewed for periods of 10, then five, years.

Finally, an overseas investor can obtain U.S. flag protection for non-U.S. investments by using a USVI exempt company ("EC"). An EC offers many of the benefits of tax-free corporations established in traditional tax-free jurisdictions with special advantages only available to a corporation established in a U.S. flag jurisdiction. ECs are exempt from all taxes on income from business activities outside the USVI and the United States, and on USVI source income such as interest and dividends. An EC is covered by the United States' extensive network of treaties of friendship, commerce and navigation and bilateral investment treaties. ECs also give foreign investors access to the U.S. court system for dispute resolution. Further an EC can be used to own an aircraft for which an "N" registration number is desired from the U.S. Federal Aviation Administration. An "N" registration number indicates that the aircraft is maintained to high U.S. standards. U.S. or USVI persons must own less than 10% of the stock of an EC, but it can be owned by individuals or companies from any other country. A company must elect to be an EC at the time of incorporation by affirmatively electing EC status in its Articles of Incorporation.

Come on Down

Moving your residence to the USVI is no more difficult than moving from one U.S. state to another. The USVI has a well-developed infrastructure. The legal system is subject to the U.S. Constitution and is part of the U.S. Third Circuit Court of Appeals. The U.S. court system, postal service, currency, and customs and immigration agencies serve the islands. There is no restriction against maintaining a second home elsewhere inside or outside of the United States, as long as you maintain your principal residence in the USVI and meet the described tests.

The tax incentives in the USVI have limits, but certainly are worth considering for any high net worth foreign person thinking about U.S. naturalization, or any current U.S. citizen willing to relocate to a warmer climate to legally avoid burdensome taxes.

The benefits are particularly strong for businesses with a global, rather than a U.S., focus because certain foreign source (but not U.S.) dividends and interest are treated as effectively connected USVI income for tax credit purposes and owners of such a business do not have to spend 183 days in the USVI as long as they are in the United States for no more than 90 days and have a closer connection to the USVI and a USVI tax home.

Obviously, the USVI tax exemptions are unique in that they require a foreign or U.S. person to reorder their personal, travel and business lives in a major physical way. It means moving to and establishing a personal residence and/or business headquarters in the USVI. However, this may be a comparatively small price to pay compared to the substantial tax savings that can result from such a move — and since the United States is almost unique in taxing its citizens regardless of where they reside, the USVI (and other territories) are the only place where U.S. citizens can live and get permanent reductions on their taxable income.

Contacts

Hon. Donna M. Christensen
Delegate to the U.S. House of Representatives
1510 Longworth House Office Bldg.
Washington, DC 20515
Tel.: 202-225-1790
Email: https://donnachristensen.house.gov/contact-me/email-me
Web: http://donnachristensen.house.gov/

USVI Information: http://www.usvi.net/usvi/

USVI Economic Development Authority: http://www.usvieda.org

V.I. Bureau of Internal Revenue
6115 Estate Smith Bay, Suite 225
St. Thomas, V.I. 00802
Tel.: (340) 715-1040
Web: http://www.viirb.com/

Recommended Attorney:

Marjorie Rawls Roberts, PC, LLB, JD, AB
5093 Dronningens Gade, Ste. 1
St. Thomas, VI 00802
Mail: P.O. Box 6347, St. Thomas, VI 00804

Tel.: + (340) 776-7235
Email: jorie@marjorierobertspc.com
Web: http://www.marjorierobertspc.com/

SECTION 3
LATIN AMERICA

Antigua and Barbuda

Government:	Constitutional parliamentary democracy
Capital:	Saint John's (Antigua)
National Day:	Independence Day: 1 November (1981)
Population:	87,884 (July 2011 est.)
Total Area:	171 sq. miles / 443 sq. kilometers in two islands
Language:	English
Ethnic:	Most of African origin, British, Portuguese, Lebanese, Syrian.
Religion:	Anglican 25.7%, Seventh Day Adventist 12.3%, Pentecostal 10.6%, Moravian 10.5%, Roman Catholic 10.4%, Methodist 7.9%, Baptist 4.9%, Church of God 4.5%, other Christian 5.4%, other 2%, none or unspecified 5.8% (2001 census)
Life expectancy:	75.48 years
Currency:	East Caribbean dollar (XCD)
GDP:	US$1.425 billion (2010 est.)
GDP per capita:	US$16,400 (2010 est.)

On Antigua, life is a beach. It may seem like a cliché, but this improbably shaped splotch of land is ringed with beaches of the finest white sand, made all the more dramatic by the azure waters, which are so clear they'll bring a tear to your eye or a giggle to your holiday-hungry throat. And if life on Antigua is a beach, its isolated neighbor Barbuda is a beach. The pair couldn't be any more different. While the first looks like something nasty under a microscope, the latter is just one smooth, sandy low-rise amidst the reef-filled waters. Birds, especially the huffing and puffing frigates, greatly outnumber people.

On Antigua, there are lots of people, many famous. Gui-tar-picker Eric Clapton, rag-trader Giorgio Armani, huckster, scribe Ken Follett and taste-maker for the masses, Oprah, all have winter homes here. Some of the Caribbean's most exclusive resorts shelter in the myriad bays and inlets. But mere mortals thrive here as well. Visitors of every budget will find a beach they can almost call their own. — Lonely Planet

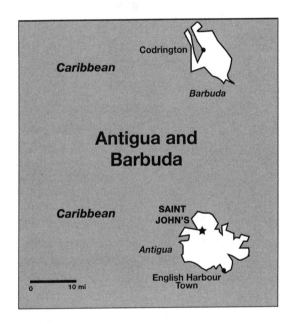

History and Overview

Antigua and Barbuda is a twin-island nation situated in the Leeward Islands, between the Caribbean Sea and the North Atlantic Ocean, east-southeast of Puerto Rico.

Antigua was first inhabited by the Siboney ("stone people"), whose settlements date at least to 2400 BC. The Arawaks, who originated in Venezuela and gradually migrated up the chain of islands now called the Lesser Antilles, succeeded the Siboney. The warlike Carib people drove the Arawaks from neighboring islands but apparently did not settle on either Antigua or Barbuda. Christopher Columbus landed on the islands in 1493, naming the larger one "Santa Maria de la Antigua," the literal Spanish translation of which is "Saint Mary of the Old." The English colonized the islands in 1632. Sir Christopher Codrington established the first large sugar estate in Antigua in 1674, and leased Barbuda to raise provisions for his plantations. Barbuda's only town is named after him. He and others brought slaves from Africa's west coast to work the sugar plantations until slavery was abolished in 1834. The islands became an independent state within the British Commonwealth of Nations in 1981.

Economy

Tourism continues to dominate the economy, accounting for more than half of GDP. Weak tourist arrival numbers in the last two decades have slowed the economy, however, and pressed the government into a tight fiscal corner. The dual-island nation's agricultural production is focused on the domestic market and constrained by a limited water supply and a labor shortage stemming from the lure of higher wages in tourism and construction. Manufacturing comprises enclave-type assembly for export with major products being bedding, handicrafts and electronic components. Prospects for economic growth will continue to depend on income growth in the industrialized world, especially in the U.S., which accounts for slightly more than one-third of tourist arrivals.

But changes are pending and the islands' government is waiting before deciding to buy into this deal; after nine years, a lawsuit over property rights and eminent domain will go to the U.K. Privy Council. National elections are to be held in 2014. A major issue is the government's culpability for its role in promoting the islands as an offshore financial center.

Unfortunately, the government needs cash because its finances are a mess. Several years ago Antigua and Barbuda promoted itself as an offshore financial center. However, the leading player was one Robert Allen Stanford of Houston, Texas, now serving a 110-year U.S. prison sentence after conviction of a massive Ponzi scheme and bank fraud of US$7 billion, all based in Antigua and Barbuda. Stanford was allowed to take virtual control of the country's banking system and invested heavily in numerous projects, with official approval.

It is impossible to believe that government officials were oblivious to Stanford's wrongdoings. He arrived on the island in 1990, after British regulators ousted him from Montserrat following a banking scandal. Within a few years, he became the biggest employer on the island and became a confidant of the Birds, perhaps the most powerful family in Antigua.

Following the crash of Stanford's empire the government made a desperate plea for help to the International Monetary Fund (IMF), as the Antigua Barbuda Investment Bank also collapsed. The government is in debt to the Communist Chinese government for outstanding interest-free loans granted between 1988 and 1992. They have become "expert at re-scheduling rather than paying debts, and has "compulsorily acquired" (rather than "expropriate") private property of international investors, without compensation."

In 2009, the U.S. Securities and Exchange Commission accused Leroy King, the head of Antigua's Financial Services Regulatory Commission, of accepting tens of thousands of dollars in bribes from Stanford to ignore his Ponzi scheme. In 2012, federal prosecutors in Miami revealed a criminal investigation into alleged fraud, corruption, extortion, and money laundering by former Prime Minister Lester Bird and his associates, much of it funded by Stanford.

Despite the scandal and corruption, none of this has had much effect in Antigua. Lester Bird is no longer prime minister, but he is still a major power in the opposition Antigua Labor Party. And, five years after Stanford's fall from grace, the Antigua courts have charged no one with any misconduct or lack of oversight in relation to Stanford's activities.

In my opinion new foreign investors would do well to steer clear of these islands.

This scandal gave the island nation a black eye at a time when international pressure already was being stepped up on all offshore tax havens. Following the collapse of Stanford's empire the government made a desperate plea for help to the International Monetary Fund (IMF), and recently the Antigua Barbuda Investment Bank collapsed. Extending their influence in Latin America, Communist Chinese officials agreed that Antigua and Barbuda could delay payment of their outstanding loans.

Passports for Sale

Antigua and Barbuda was first discovered by Christopher Columbus in 1493, but its current government is not the first to discover selling passports and citizenship as a source of needed cash. Since 2012 such sales have been actively promoted.

The two-island country is selling citizenship for an investment of at least US$400,000 in new real estate projects; a non-refundable contribution to the government of US$250,000 (for a single applicant) or for investments from US$1.5 to US$5 million in an eligible business, plus processing fees of US$50,000 for an individual and US$200,000 for a family of four.

There is another reason to avoid these deals. Along with only the United States and the African country of Eritrea, Antigua and Barbuda is one of the few nations in the world that tax their non-resident citizens on their worldwide income. The top tax rate is 25%. A legislative attempt to exempt non-resident citizens from paying income tax was defeated in 2013.

For all the reasons mentioned above, including worldwide income taxation, there are better options available.

Residence and Citizenship

Citizenship occurs by birth within the territory of Antigua and Barbuda, regardless of the nationality of the parents. (Exceptions are children born to diplomatic personnel.) Citizenship by descent is conferred on a child born abroad, at least one of whose parents is a citizen.

The following are eligible to obtain citizenship through registration:

1. a person married to a citizen at least three years in an existing marriage where the spouses are not living apart;

2. a Commonwealth citizen who has been a resident or domiciled for a period of seven years in Antigua and Barbuda;

3. a person who has been a resident or domiciled for a period of seven years in Antigua and Barbuda is entitled to acquire citizenship by naturalization.

Dual citizenship is recognized, and no person can be deprived of citizenship solely on the grounds they plan to become a citizen of another country, nor can they be required to renounce citizenship of another country.

A passport, or a certified birth certificate and picture ID (e.g., a driver's license) are required for U.S. citizens to enter Antigua and Barbuda. Immigration officials are strict about getting exact information about where visitors are staying, and will often request to see a return ticket or ticket for onward travel. There is a departure tax payable when leaving the country.

Contacts

Embassy of Antigua and Barbuda

3216 New Mexico Avenue NW
Washington, DC 20016
Tel.: (202) 362-5122
Email: embantbar@aol.com

Additional information:

Antigua and Barbuda Department of Tourism
Web: http://www.antigua-barbuda.org/

The United States maintains a limited official presence in Antigua. The Ambassador and embassy officers are resident in Barbados and travel to Antigua frequently.

United States Embassy

Wildey Business Park
Wildey, St. Michael
Barbados, West Indies
Tel.: (246) 227-4000
Web: http://barbados.usembassy.gov

A U.S. Consular Agent resident in Antigua assists U.S. citizens available by appointment only.

U.S. Consular Agent

Jasmine Court, Suite #2
Friars Hill Road
St. John's, Antigua
Tel.: 268-463-6531, cell: 268-726-6531
Email: ANUWndrGyal@aol.com

Immigration consultant:

Henley & Partners
11 Old Parham Road
St. John's
Tel.: +1 268 460 7750
Email: antigua@henleyglobal.com

Argentine Republic

Government:	Republic
Capital:	Buenos Aires
National Day:	Revolution Day: 25 May (1810)
Population:	42,610,981 (July 2013 est.)
Total Area:	1,068,302 sq. miles / 2,766,890 sq. kilometers
Languages:	Spanish (official), English, Italian, German, French
Ethnic groups:	White (mostly Spanish and Italian) 97%; Mestizo, Amerindian, and other non-white groups 3%
Religion:	Roman Catholic 92%, other 4%, Protestant 2%, Jewish 2%
Life expectancy:	77.32 years
Currency:	Argentine peso (ARS)
GDP:	US$735.1 billion (2012 est.)
GDP per capita:	US$17,900 (2012 est.)

The secret is out: with its gorgeous landscapes, cosmopolitan cities and lively culture, Argentina is a traveler's paradise. It stretches almost 2200 miles from Bolivia to the tip of South America, encompasses a wide array of geography and climates, and is almost the size of India. Nature lovers can traverse the Patagonian steppe, climb South America's highest peak, walk among thousands of penguins and witness the world's most amazing waterfalls. Hikers can sample the stunning scenery of the lush Lake District with its glorious lakes and white-tipped mountains and revel in Patagonia's glacier-carved landscapes and painted Andean deserts.

City slickers will adore fabulous Buenos Aires, full of opportunities to learn Spanish, watch futbol (soccer), dance the sexy tango and interact with dynamic and beautiful portenos (Buenos Aires locals). You'll be out shopping for designer clothes at affordable prices and eating the world's best steaks every day while partying at nightclubs all night long. — Lonely Planet

History and Overview

The Argentine Republic is the second largest country in Latin America and occupies most of the southern part of the continent. Five countries form its borders; Chile to the east, Bolivia and Paraguay to the north, Brazil and Uruguay to the northeast. The Rio Colorado flows east and divides the country in two. Argentina is home to a wide variety of terrain, including jungle, pampas, infertile plain, and South America's highest mountain, Mount Aconcagua.

Like most South American countries, Argentina is a former Spanish colony. Argentina celebrated its bicentennial in 2010, rejoicing in 200 years of independence from Spain. May 25 is the date celebrated as the Dia de la Revolucion de Mayo, "May Revolution Day." Buenos Aires famous Plaza de Mayo, more recently known for protests by family members of those who "disappeared" during Argentina's military regime (1976 to 1983), is named for this turbulent week in 1810. The country formally declared its independence from Spain in 1816 and became a republic in 1852. After Bolivia, Paraguay, and Uruguay went their separate ways to become independent countries, the area that remained became Argentina. The country's population and culture were heavily shaped by immigrants from throughout Europe, with Italy and Spain providing the largest percentage of newcomers from 1860 to 1930.

During the 20th century, the nation's political course has veered from military dictatorship to fledgling democracy, with many periods of internal political conflict between conservatives and leftists and between civilian and military factions.

In 1918, Argentina was a prosperous, debt-free nation thriving with exports for the reconstruction of Europe after World War I. Now years of corruption, debt, and economic centralization have ruined the country and its economy. The people have lost their freedom and lives have been destroyed by government controls on prices, capital, the media and every aspect of life. Dictatorial leaders have nationalized private pensions, confiscated private assets, jailed the opposition, caused recurrent currency crises and corrupted public institutions.

Peronista Populism

Thanks to rich natural resources and foreign investment, a modern agriculture and a diversified industry were gradually developed. After World War II, a long period of dictatorship under Juan Perón and his Peronista Party was followed by military junta rule. Since 1983, Argentina in name has had a democratically elected president as head of government. But provincial politics and its caudillo system have dominated the nation. That explains in part Argentina's widespread populism and its history of odd political alliances.

Argentine populism is not a synonym for Leftism; it is closer to fascist corporatism than to socialism, involving strong leaders such as Juan Perón. Unlike Chile or Uruguay, Argentina never developed a stable two or three-party system of conservatives and liberals or social democrats. Instead, Argentina has two populist movements: Radicalism and Peronism. Both were lukewarm about capitalism, and both boosted public employment and spending.

Perón's support was built on an unstable coalition of corporatist trade unions and the conservative local provincial caudillos. The result has been what one political scientist calls "a state-dominated society" with rampant corruption and family political dynasties, especially in rural areas. The same power elite have been running the country for decades. Workers, business and other interest groups make deals with the government rather than seeking real political change. This system has discouraged democratic opposition, and bred military intervention and political violence.

Nevertheless, Argentina is a cosmopolitan country with a population of about 42 million, many of Spanish, German, Italian, and English descent. Buenos Aires, the capital, is one of the largest cities in the world with a population of over 11 million. Its elegant architecture and broad avenues justify its local nickname, the "Paris of the New World." Fun-loving and generous, the *Porteños* — the capital's residents — describe themselves as "Italians who speak Spanish and pretend to live like English lords."

The dramatic, sensuous tango developed among Buenos Aires' working classes and has come to symbolize city's life, alternately vibrant and tragic. Elsewhere in Argentina, visitors enjoy excellent hunting and fishing, pleasant beaches, outstanding ski resorts, huge ranches where the old Gaucho traditions linger, and ecotourism in the Paraná-Iguazú Falls region, the Andes, Patagonia, and Tierra del Fuego.

Argentina received some much-needed good news in late 2013 with the election of Cardinal Jorge Mario Bergoglio, Archbishop of Buenos Aires, as Pope Francis, the 266th Pope of the Catholic Church, the first ever pontiff from the Americas.

Economy

In early 2014 *The Wall Street Journal* commented: "In Buenos Aires these days, a sobering theory is making the rounds ... Argentina is destined to experience an economic meltdown about once per decade, and there isn't much anyone here can do about it."

The Journal added: "In the 1940s, President Juan Perón closed the Argentine economy to trade with the rest of the world. In the 1960s, the country endured stagnation, inflation and military coups. In 1975, 1981 and 1989, failed economic plans led the currency to plunge. The last crisis hit in 2001, when Argentina defaulted on about $100 billion in sovereign bonds. The default — the largest ever at the time — brought down Argentina›s banks, currency and government."

Argentina is one of the more highly-developed countries in the Western Hemisphere. Its people are among the most educated in South America, with a literacy rate of 90%. Its economy has gradually shifted from an exclusive dependence on large-scale livestock and agriculture production to one in which service and industrial sectors are dominant.

Since the 1950s, it has been one of the 20 largest trading countries in the world. However, until recently, economic growth has been hampered by excessive inflation caused by government deficit spending and anti-free market policies.

The nation had one of the highest Latin American standards of living, at the turn of the century, and is anxious to regain its past glory. Although one of the world's wealthiest countries 100 years ago, Argentina suffered during most of the 20th century from recurring economic crises, persistent fiscal and current account deficits, high inflation, mounting external debt, and capital flight.

Argentina was once the eighth-largest economy in the world, but it steadily declined through the 20th century thanks to decades of repressive dictatorships and inconsistent government economic experiments. This ended ignominiously in 2001, when it defaulted on US$81 billion in sovereign debt, plunging 60% of its 35 million people into poverty as the peso lost much of its value.

The severe depression, public and external indebtedness, and a bank run culminated in 2001 in the most serious economic, social, and political crisis in the country's turbulent history, including a run on banks. The interim president declared a default on Argentina's foreign and International Monetary Fund debts, as well as on private debts, the largest in history. The economy bottomed out in 2002, with real GDP 18% smaller than in 1998 and almost 60% of Argentines falling below the poverty line. There were violent public protests and the resignation of several interim presidents in 2001 to 2002.

The peso's decade-long one-to-one peg to the U.S. dollar also ended in 2002, with the devalued peso, high unemployment causing sporadic civil disorders. At the same time, kidnapping, robbery, and other crimes against persons and property have surged dramatically, requiring travelers there to exercise caution.

The World Factbook added: "Real GDP rebounded to grow by an average 8.5% annually over the next six years, taking advantage of previously idled industrial capacity and labor, an audacious debt restructuring and reduced debt burden, excellent international financial conditions, and expansionary monetary and fiscal policies." Inflation also increased, however, during the administration of President Néstor Kirchner, which responded with price controls on businesses, as well as export taxes and restraints, and beginning in 2007, using phony understated inflation data.

Cristina Fernández de Kirchner succeeded her deceased husband as president in 2007, and rapid economic growth began to slow sharply as her government policies harmed exports and the world economy fell into recession. Massive farmer protests stymied her efforts to hike export taxes still further but her government nationalized all private pension funds in 2008, which bolstered government coffers, but failed to assuage investors' concerns about the direction of economic policy.

The economy rebounded strongly but slowed in 2011 even as government continued deficit spending and stimulus which kept inflation in double digits. The government expanded state intervention in the economy and the Congress nationalized the oil company YPF owned by Spain's Repsol.

The government consistently has spent more, and, with little ability to borrow abroad, it turned to other sources. In 2008, Kirchner nationalized private pension funds worth some US$30 billion, and has nationalized an airline and a major oil company. The government printed money to finance itself falsifying the inflation rate it claimed to be 11%, but which independent analysts put at about 28%.

Onerous formal and informal restrictions imports were imposed including pre-registration and pre-approval of all imports. The government also tightened controls over opposition political parties and curbed press freedoms. Repression and the import and export taxes scared away some foreign investment.

There are acute problems with the way in which Argentina is managed: corruption, government secrecy, authoritarian tendencies, confiscatory taxes, repression of free expression and official lying about unpleasant inflation statistics.

President de Kirchner far out polled her rivals in 2011 and easily won re-election easily. Mrs. Kirchner, who leads a center-left faction of the Peronista Party, rebuilt her support after a four-month tax revolt in 2008 by farmers, a major force in the country, pushed her popularity rating below 30%. Strong economic growth since then has helped to create jobs, raise wages and allow the government to extend welfare programs. She also adopted numerous subsidies and vote buying spending programs aimed at farmers and other organized groups, especially in rural areas.

In 2014, investors pulled out of Argentina's currency and bonds as its financial situation deteriorated. After a good year in 2013, the government bonds fell sharply as a deep drop in the value of the peso and dwindling foreign-exchange reserves raised questions about the country's ability to pay future debts. Spooked investors recalled the economic and social turbulence of Argentina's infamous 2001 debt default.

Argentines endured price rises of nearly 30% in 2013. In 2014, inflation was predicted to hit 45% approaching the annual rate of 56% in Venezuela, a regional ally experiencing social unrest.

Spanish Connection

Argentina is among the Latin American countries whose citizens are given preferential treatment when applying for Spanish citizenship. Argentineans also qualify for a reduced, two-year residence period in Spain when seeking Spanish nationality.

In 2008, Spain adopted a law that grants citizenship to the descendants (children and grandchildren) of persons exiled from

Spain during the Spanish Civil War (1936 to 1939) and during the subsequent rule of the late General Francisco Franco. When the law took effect hundreds lined up at the Spanish Consulate in Buenos Aires to apply for Spanish citizenship.

Residence and Citizenship

Citizenship is conferred in the following ways:

1. by birth:

    a) to a child born in Argentina, except to accredited ministers of foreign powers;

    b) to a child born in Argentine legations or on Argentine warships, or;

    c) to a child born in neutral waters on ships flying the Argentine flag.

2. by descent to a child born abroad, both of whose parents are Argentine citizens.

3. by naturalization:

    a) for a qualified person (see below) who must have resided within the Republic for at least two years.

    b) to a person who must have married an Argentine citizen. Marriage does not automatically confer citizenship and a spouse must fulfill the two-year residence requirement.

Dual citizenship is recognized for children, 18 and younger, born abroad, who acquire citizenship of their birth country. Upon reaching maturity at age 18, a declaration of allegiance must be made to only one country. Citizens of Spain can hold dual citizenship under a treaty with Argentina.

Argentina accepts up to 100,000 immigrants a year, with particular interest in trained professionals.

Residence can be arranged by submission of a birth certificate, police certificate of good conduct or lack of criminal record, and a marriage certificate, if applicable. Proof of adequate education and/or work experience is required. People of independent means or the self-employed are favored, and those with firm business proposals may receive a reduced residence requirement.

Exact guidelines applicable to foreign nationals seeking residence are unclear, which is not unusual in Latin America, and decisions are made on a case-by-case basis. Two years of bona fide residence is required for naturalization, but not all that time need be in the country. An Argentinean passport is valid for five years.

Argentineans also qualify for a reduced residence period in Spain when seeking Spanish nationality. (See this book's section on Spain.)

Argentinean law recognizes dual nationality. Dual citizens, who are also considered to be citizens of Argentina, and who remain in Argentina for more than 60 days, are required to use an Argentine passport to depart the country.

Argentineans who use a second passport experience no problems with the nation's customs service. If you have dual nationality, when entering the country, a customs official may stamp "Argentino" on the entry page of your other passport, as recognition of dual nationality status. The 1995 Mercosur Agreement allows individuals holding Argentinean passports to have free access to other Latin American member states.

For Americans a U.S. passport is required for entry. U.S. citizens do not need a visa for visits up to 90 days for tourism and business.

But there is a catch. The government of Argentina charges

U.S. citizens visiting for business or tourism an "entry fee" of US$131.00, for Canadians US$70.00 for single entry and Australians US$100.00. This fee is collected only at Buenos Aires Ezeiza International Airport. Once paid, the fee permits multiple entries into Argentina for 10 years. For all other entry points you should pay the entry fee before you arrive online at https://virtual.provinciapagos.com.ar/ArgentineTaxes/

U.S. citizens who arrive in Argentina with an expired or damaged passport may be refused entry and returned to the United States at their own expense. An airport tax is collected upon departure, payable in dollars or Argentine pesos.

An Argentine passport allows visa-free travel to 133 countries, including most of Europe and nearly all of South and Central America. It's also the first passport in South America that entitles its holder to visa-free entry into the U.S., although some post-9/11 restrictions now apply.

Contacts

Argentine Embassy
1600 New Hampshire Avenue NW
Washington, DC 20009
Tel.: (202) 238-6400
Email: embassyofargentina.us
Web: http://embassyofargentina.us/embassyofargentina.us/en/home.htm

United States Embassy
Avenida Colombia 4300
(C1425GMN) Buenos Aires, Argentina
Tel.: + (54) 11-5777-4533
Email: BuenosAires-ACS@state.gov
Web: http://buenosaires.usembassy.gov/

Republic of Bolivia

Government:	Republic
Capital:	La Paz
National Day:	Independence Day: 6 August (1825)
Population:	10,461,053 (July 2013 est.)
Total Area:	424,164 sq. miles / 1,098,580 sq. kilometers
Languages:	Spanish, Quechua, Aymara (all official)
Ethnic groups:	Quechua 30%, Mestizo (mixed white-Amerindian) 30%, Aymara 25%, white 15%
Religion:	Roman Catholic 95%, Protestant (Evangelical Methodist) 5%
Life expectancy:	68.22 years
Currency:	Boliviano (BOB)
GDP:	US$47.88 billion (2010 est.)
GDP per capita:	US$4,800 (2010 est.)

Simply superlative — this is Bolivia. It's the hemisphere's highest, most isolated and most rugged nation. It's among the earth's coldest, warmest, windiest and steamiest spots. It boasts among the driest, saltiest and swampiest natural landscapes in the world. Although the poorest country in South America (and boy do Bolivians get tired of hearing that), it's also one of the richest in terms of natural resources.

It's also South America's most indigenous country, with over 60% of the population claiming Indigenous heritage, including Aymará, Quechua, Guaraní and over 30 other ethnic groups. Bolivia has it all...except, that is, for beaches. Bolivia's social and political fronts have been in flux since the appointment of the country's first indigenous president.

Optimism is generally high, especially among the indigenous majority, although many changes are afoot. Protests, marches and demonstrations are a perpetual part of the country's mind-boggling landscape. This is a truly extraordinary place. Put on your high-altitude goggles, take a deep breath (or three) and live superlatively. — Lonely Planet

History and Overview

Bolivia, named after the famed Latin American independence fighter, Simon Bolivar, broke away from Spanish rule in 1825. Much of its subsequent political history has consisted of a series of nearly 200 coups and countercoups. Democratic civilian rule was established in 1982, but the country suffers from difficult problems of deep-seated poverty, social unrest and illegal drug production. Bolivia's income inequality is the highest in Latin America and one of the highest in the world. Public education is of poor quality, and educational opportunities are among the most unevenly distributed in Latin America.

In 2005, Bolivians elected the leader of the "Movement Toward Socialism" party, Evo Morales as president, by the widest margin of any leader since the restoration of civilian rule in 1982. He was re-elected in 2009. He ran on a promise to challenge the country's traditional political ruling class and empower the nation's poor majority.

Since taking office, his controversial ultra-leftist strategies have increased racial and economic tensions between the Amerindian populations of the Andean west and the nonindigenous communities of the eastern lowlands. He has threatened to expropriate and redistribute privately owned lands and businesses, and has allied himself with the radical late leftist president of Venezuela, Hugo Chávez.

A major factor that makes Bolivia less attractive as a place to live is continuing civil unrest. Much of this unrest occurs among native Amerindian tribes and Mestizos, who feel the government has ignored their needs. In 2003 to 2005, the national presidency changed hands three times in response to street riots demanding changes in national policies before Morales, himself a Mestizo, won election.

Putting politics aside Bolivia's advocates alert the potential immigrant that this landlocked country, cascading down the eastern slopes of the Andes through rain forests and onto a high plain, is not likely to satisfy cravings for modern conveniences and exciting urban experiences.

The country's only golf club, more than 13,000 feet above sea level in La Paz, is the highest in the world. Lake Titicaca is the world's highest navigable body of water. Anacondas and jaguars feature more prominently in travelogues about Bolivia than spas and nightclubs.

Because of the climatic and topographical diversity of its regions and the high proportion of its Spanish colonial architecture still extant, Bolivia can indeed be endlessly rewarding for ecological explorers, anthropological tourists and those seeking its rich cultural heritage.

For centuries, until a 2009 referendum, Bolivia had a system of citizenship rooted in Spanish colonialism under which the nation›s 36 different indigenous peoples were not legally considered to be full citizens. Quechua and Aymara Indians make up about 55% of Bolivia's population.

An article in *CounterPunch* commented: "The government of President Evo Morales came to power in 2006 with bold plans to change all this. Its main promise to its indigenous and impoverished base of support was to reform the constitution to assure the indigenous majority the full exercise of its citizenship, and to redistribute national wealth in favor of the poor."

Morales, himself an Aymara Indian, won a 2009 referendum on a new constitution granting special privileges to Bolivia's indigenous people. The electorate split along racial lines, with the country's elite white and mixed-race minorities largely opposing the measure. In 2009, President Morales easily won re-election, and his party took control of the legislative branch of the government, which has allowed him to continue and expand his leftist policies. He is up for a predicted re-election in 2014.

Economy

With its long history of semi-feudal social controls, dependence on mineral exports and bouts of hyperinflation, Bolivia has remained one of the poorest and least developed Latin American countries. However, it has experienced generally improving economic conditions since the 1980s, when market-oriented policies reduced inflation from 11,700% in 1985 to about 20% in 1988.

Bolivia has entered into a free-trade agreement with Mexico and the southern Latin American common market (Mercosur). Before the election of President Morales, the government was privatizing numerous state-owned businesses, airlines, telephone companies, railroads, electric power and oil companies. Morales reversed these trends with a vengeance. He nationalized the oil and gas sector and expropriated more than 20 private companies in a variety of industries.

Bolivia, long one of the poorest and least developed Latin American countries, reformed its economy after suffering a disastrous economic crisis in the early 1980s. The reforms spurred real GDP growth, which averaged 4% in the 1990s, and poverty rates fell. Economic growth, however, lagged again beginning in 1999 because of a global slowdown and homegrown factors such as political turmoil, civil unrest, and soaring fiscal deficits, all of which hurt investor confidence.

In 2003, violent protests against the pro-foreign investment economic policies of the former president led to his resignation and the cancellation of plans to export Bolivia's newly discovered natural gas reserves to large Northern Hemisphere markets.

In 2005, the government passed a controversial natural gas law that imposes on the oil and gas firms significantly higher taxes as well as new contracts that give the state control of their operations. Meanwhile, foreign investors have stopped investing and have taken the first legal steps to secure their investments. Real GDP growth in 2003 to 2005, helped by increased demand for natural gas in neighboring Brazil, was positive, but still below the levels seen during the 1990s.

Private investment as a share of GDP, however, remains among the lowest in Latin America, and inflation remained at double-digit levels in 2008. The decline in commodity prices in late 2008, the lack of foreign investment in the mining and hydrocarbon sectors, and the suspension of trade benefits with the United States posed challenges for the Bolivian economy. Bolivia has less than half the rate of private investment of most other countries in South America.

In 2013, Bolivia saw definite improvement, much of that based on exports of natural gas. The economy grew an estimated 6.5% among the highest rates in the region. Inflation is low, the budget is balanced, and government debt has been cut. The country has a large US$14 billion "rainy-day" fund of foreign reserves equal to more than half of its GDP, or 17 months of imports. Also, in 2013, growth was the strongest in 30 years continuing a several-year trend. The number of people living in extreme poverty fell to 24% in 2011, down from 38% in 2005, the year before Morales took office.

Political unrest has occurred in the so-called "Media Luna" departments of Santa Cruz, Tarija, Beni, and Pando, Bolivia's four eastern departments voted in favor of increasing regional autonomy, and the other five provinces opposed the measure.

A powerful positive consequence of Bolivia's early stage of development is its extremely low cost of living. A comfortable existence can be maintained for less than US$20,000 per year, with housing costs at a small fraction of the figures for equivalent lodging in the developed world.

On the other hand, underdevelopment means that infrastructure and amenities lag considerably behind those expected in industrialized countries.

Citizenship and Residence

Almost 7% of Bolivia's population lives abroad, primarily working in Argentina, Brazil, Spain, and the United States. In recent years, more restrictive immigration policies in Europe and the U.S. have increased the flow of Bolivian emigrants to neighboring Argentina and Brazil.

Citizenship is conferred in the following ways:

1. by birth within the territory of Bolivia, regardless of the nationality of the parents. The only exception is a child born in Bolivia to parents in the service of a foreign government, such as a diplomat and spouse.

2. by descent when a child is born abroad to either a Bolivian mother or father; either by returning to live in Bolivia, or by being registered at a Bolivian consulate in the nation where the child is born.

3. by naturalization when the person fulfills the following conditions:

   a) a person with no ties to Bolivia may obtain citizenship after residing in the country for at least two years;

   b) a foreign woman, married to a Bolivian citizen acquires her husband's citizenship as long as she lives in the country and agrees to accept citizenship. Nationality is not lost through widowhood or divorce. Persons who have Bolivian spouses or have had children born in Bolivia need only to reside in the country for one year before being eligible for citizenship.

Dual citizenship is not recognized except for children (18 and under) born abroad who acquire citizenship of their birth country. Upon reaching maturity at age 18, a declaration of allegiance must be made to only one country.

Permanent residence is available in Bolivia for foreigners and their dependents that own property or invest in the country, and to retirees and their families showing adequate means of support, from whatever source.

Residence visas must be renewed every two years. Absence from Bolivia for more than three months without authorization of the Foreign Ministry is grounds for revocation of a residence visa.

Permanent residents are eligible for naturalization after five years in Bolivia. Ownership of real estate or investment in Bolivia entitles a person to a residence visa, with naturalization authorized after five years of residence

Persons making grants to certain public or semi-public development projects may qualify for immediate Bolivian citizenship. Radical political upheaval and restrictive laws has made residence and investment here far less attractive.

Investor Citizenship

Bolivia has a loose program under which quasi-government corporations seek private grants from foreign nationals of approximately US$25,000. Donors are recognized as a "benefactor to Bolivia" and this serves as the basis for conferral of citizenship. Some variations on this program have quoted prices as low as US$10,000.

The US$25,000 package includes a cédula or identity card, a driver's license, and certificate of citizenship. The single contribution includes the main applicant, spouse and dependent children under 18. No visit to Bolivia is necessary.

Bolivian passports, although valid for five years, are renewable every two years while in the country. The passports allow travel to most European countries without visas, although this passport is causing concern. As you can imagine, this arrangement has led to the illegal sale of official passports, which appears to continue, making foreign nations wary.

Civil marriage in Bolivia of a resident foreign national to a Bolivian requires certain documentary evidence. A Bolivian potential spouse should check with the Office of the Civil Registry in La Paz at + (591) 2-316-226 to determine what documents are required.

A U.S. passport is required to enter and depart Bolivia. The Bolivian government now requires U.S. citizens to obtain visas to visit Bolivia: more information about visa procedures can be found at http://bolivia.usembassy.gov/

Tourist cards are issued upon arrival in Bolivia. A "Defined Purpose Visa" for adoptions, business or other travel requires one application form, one photo, and an US$85 fee. Business travelers must include a letter from their company explaining the purpose of their trip. An exit tax must be paid at the airport when departing Bolivia.

Prior to visiting high-altitude locations over 10,000 feet above sea level, such as La Paz, travelers may wish to discuss the trip with their personal physician and request advice concerning medication and activity at high altitudes.

Contacts

Embassy of Bolivia
3014 Massachusetts Avenue NW
Washington, DC 20008
Tel.: (202) 483-4410
Web: http://www.bolivia-usa.org
Consulates: Los Angeles, San Francisco, Miami, New Orleans, and New York.

United States Embassy
2780 Avenida Arce
Casilla 425, La Paz, Bolivia
Tel.: + (591) 2-216-8000
Email: lpzwebmail@state.gov
Web: http://lapaz.usembassy.gov

Federative Republic of Brazil

Government:	Federative Republic
Capital:	Brasília
National Day:	Independence Day: 7 September (1822)
Population:	201,009,622 (July 2013 est.)
Total Area:	3,286,488 sq. miles / 8,511,965 sq. kilometers
Languages:	Portuguese (official), Spanish, English, French
Ethnic groups:	White 53.7%, mulatto 38.5%, black 6.2%, other (includes Japanese, Arab, Amerindian) 0.9%, unspecified 0.7%
Religion:	Roman Catholic (nominal) 73.6%, Protestant 15.4%, none 7.4%, other 1.8%, Spiritualist 1.3%, Bantu/voodoo 0.3%, unspecified 0.2%
Life expectancy:	73.02 years
Currency:	Real (BRL)
GDP:	US$2.33 trillion (2012 est.)
GDP per capita:	US$11,700 (2012 est.)

Sprawling across half of South America, Brazil has captivated travelers for at least 500 years. Powdery white-sand beaches, lined with palm trees and fronting a deep-blue Atlantic, stretch for more than 7000km. Dotting this coastline are tropical islands, music-filled metropolises and enchanting colonial towns. Inland, Brazil offers dazzling sights of a different flavor: majestic waterfalls, red-rock canyons, and crystal-clear rivers — all just a small part of the natural beauty. Its larger and more famous attractions are the Amazon and the Pantanal, the pair hosting some of the greatest biodiversity on the planet.

Wildlife-watching is simply astounding here, as is the opportunity for adventure — though you needn't go to the jungle to find it. Kayaking, rafting, trekking, snorkeling and surfing are just a few ways to spend a sun-drenched afternoon in nearly any region in Brazil. Some of the world's most exciting cities lie inside of Brazil's borders, and travelers need not come to Carnaval to experience the music, dance and revelry that pack so many calendar nights. Given the country's innumerable charms, the only drawback to traveling in Brazil is a logistical (and financial) one: you simply won't want to leave. — Lonely Planet

History and Overview

It can be big, brassy, bawdy, and balmy, as in Rio or São Paulo. It can be the deepest, darkest jungle, as in the Amazon. But with all its attractions, Brazil, one of the world's most diverse and potentially rich countries, is often overlooked as an offshore home for expatriates. It is also one of the most "high crime" nations in Latin America, especially in the major cities.

The nation of Brazil will unquestionably play a major role in the 21st century. It is rich in natural resources and produces a vast array of sophisticated goods, including jet aircraft and computers. Brazil is actually the fifth largest country in the world and has the seventh largest economy. It has a population of nearly over 200 million, 60% of which is under the age of 18 and the proud Brasileros have snagged the 2016 summer Olympic Games, a first for any Latin American country.

Brazil could be a perfect second home. It is very democratic, without all the rules and regulations most industrialized countries insist upon. With nearly 3,000 miles of ocean beaches, you can while away time and enjoy an average annual temperature of 75° F (24°). Many wealthy Americans and Europeans move to Brazil to get away from the cold weather, high taxes, government controls and regulations, lawsuits, divorces, and even prosecution.

Brazilians are a friendly and fun-loving people who possess a refreshing "live and let live" attitude to life. They enjoy soccer, good food and, of course, a good carnival!

Some figures which might surprise you: 75% of all Brazilians are home owners, whether it be a mansion or a more simple affair, with 78% owning their furniture and household appliances. Ninety percent of all automobiles are paid for and 87% of these run on alcohol, helping to reduce the level of pollution, maintain the environment, and, thus, increase the standard of living available in the country.

The national language is Portuguese, but German, English, Japanese, Korean, and African communities are already well established in this cosmopolitan South American country.

Following three centuries under the rule of the Kingdom of Portugal, Brazil became an independent nation in 1822. It became a republic in 1889. Brazilian coffee exporters politically dominated the country until populist leader Getúlio Vargas came to power in 1930.

By far, the largest and most populous country in South America, Brazil overcame more than a half-century of military intervention in the government in 1985 when the military peacefully ceded power to civilian rulers.

Luiz Inácio da Silva, commonly known as "Lula," was elected president in 2002, after his fourth campaign for the office. He was re-elected in 2006 for a second four-year term. Lula, an ex-union leader, was Brazil's first working-class president. In office, he followed a prudent fiscal path warning that social reforms would take years and that Brazil had no alternative but to maintain tight fiscal austerity policies.

In 2010 the term-limited Lula's hand-picked successor, Dilma Rousseff, was elected as Brazil's first female president, pledging to continue Lila's policies. Her years in office have been marked by the resignation of cabinet members and other officials for corruption and influence peddling on government contracts.

In 2013 it was revealed that the U.S. National Security Agency (NSA) had been listening to President Rousseff's cell phone calls and widely employing secret surveillance on many Brazilians. A wave of protest swept the country and Rousseff took the unusual step of canceling a scheduled state visit to Washington, in spite of an apology from President Obama. The government is developing its own domestic Internet system in an effort to thwart official American spying.

Economy

Possessing large and well-developed agricultural, mining, manufacturing, and service sectors, Brazil's economy outweighs that of all other South American countries and is expanding its presence in world markets. Prior to the institution of a major stabilization plan, Plano Real (Real Plan) in mid-1994, stratospheric inflation rates had disrupted economic activity and discouraged foreign investment.

Since then, tight monetary policy has brought inflation somewhat under control. Brazil continues to pursue industrial and agricultural growth and development of its interior. Exploiting vast natural resources and a large labor pool, it is, today, South America's leading economic power and a regional leader. Highly unequal income distribution remains a pressing problem.

After the global financial crisis began in 2007, both Brazil's currency and its stock market lost value. After record growth in 2007 to 2008, the onset of the global financial crisis caused two quarters of recession as global demand for Brazil's commodity-based exports dwindled and external credit dried up.

However, Brazil was one of the first emerging markets to begin a recovery. Consumer and investor confidence revived and GDP growth returned to positive in 2010, boosted by an export recovery. Brazil's strong growth and high interest rates make it an attractive destination for foreign investors.

The World Factbook reports: "In 2010, consumer and investor confidence revived and GDP growth reached 7.5%, the highest growth rate in the past 25 years. Rising inflation led to measures to cool the economy; this and the deteriorating international economic situation slowed growth to 1.3% in 2012. Brazil's historically high interest rates have made it an attractive destination for foreign investors. Large capital inflows over the past several years have contributed to the appreciation of the currency, hurting the competitiveness of Brazilian manufacturing and leading the government to intervene in foreign exchange markets and raise taxes on some foreign capital inflows."

Well-funded public pensions have nearly wiped out poverty among the elderly, but limited social spending on children has restricted investment in education, a primary means of escaping poverty. Brazil's poverty and income inequality levels remain high despite improvements in the 2000s and continue to affect mainly the Northeast, North, and Center-West, women, and black, mixed race, and indigenous populations. Lack of opportunity has contributed to Brazil's high crime rate, particularly violent crime in cities and favelas. In recent years there have been numerous large street demonstrations, some bordering on riots, many protesting government corruption as well as high spending in preparation for the 2014 World Cup competition and the 2016 Olympics, both in Brazil.

Anti-Tax Haven Policy

Traditionally, Brazilian government policy makers have opposed offshore tax havens because they believe low or no-tax jurisdictions have been abused by Brazilians, who illegally avoid taxes and reporting requirements and hide their identity as beneficial owners of assets.

Brazilian law defines a "tax haven" as any country that imposes no income tax or levies a tax of 20% or less on income. Brazilian citizens who live offshore in a tax haven are subjected to a withholding tax of from 15% to 25% on all remittances, payments of interest, royalties or service fees paid to them from Brazilian sources. More than 40 countries are listed by Brazil as tax havens, including the U.S. Virgin Islands.

A person who obtains permanent residence is considered to be a tax resident from the date of entry into the country or the date of issuance of a permanent residence visa. Taxes are levied on worldwide income from that date until 12 months after you depart the country and file a certificate of departure. Obtaining citizenship confirms the same tax result. If a person has no permanent resident visa, they may be considered a tax-resident after more than 183 days per year in the country, although there are various ways this time period is determined, including an average over a three-year period. Because Brazil has no double taxation agreement with the U.S. Americans resident in Brazil can owe taxes in both countries on the same income.

Investment Residence Program

Brazil has an official economic investment permanent residence program. Those investing at least US$50,000 in Brazil's economy are eligible for registration in this program. Investments must be to establish commercial or industrial activities that create new jobs.

Brazil, not surprisingly, is an attractive place for would-be immigrants with wealth. If you move the money out of Brazil once the residence process is complete, you still retain your permanent residence visa for yourself and your family.

Many use the US$50,000 to start companies to convince authorities that they plan to reside in Brazil. Permanent residence may also be obtained through normal immigration channels, a relatively easy task if procedures are followed properly. Naturalization is then available after four years.

Permanent Residence Visa

North Americans and Europeans can normally obtain permanent residence in 60 to 90 days if they use a reputable Brazilian immigration firm that knows how to cut through red tape. Without qualified professional help, the process can be prolonged.

Since 2011, many thousands of Americans, British and European moved to Brazil to fill an acknowledged shortage of well-educated professionals of types, including engineers, business managers as well as entrepreneurs taking advantage of the expanding economy.

An application for residence is submitted to government officials in the capital, Brasília, for approval. Once an application is approved, the Brazilian Consulate nearest to where the applicant currently resides will be notified and, in turn, notify them.

The applicant then takes the notification and his/her existing passport to the Brazilian Consulate and a permanent visa will be stamped into your home country passport. The approved applicant then has 60 to 90 days to enter Brazil and apply for a Brazilian national ID card (also known as the green card), and a national banking number.

Once this procedure is complete, you are free to live, work, or invest in Brazil, or alternatively, you can return to your country of origin. If you want your visa to remain valid, however, you must enter Brazil every two years or it will be rescinded. The administrative fees for this whole procedure are usually in the area of US$31,000 for a single applicant or US$36,500 for a family consisting of husband, spouse and all children less than 18 years of age.

Once permanent residence visas are obtained the holder is free to exercise all rights of a Brazilian national except voting, running for public office or purchasing land in certain restricted areas adjacent to military bases and international border areas.

Permanent residence visas can also be obtained through employment if the potential resident has a local employer submit the necessary paperwork on his behalf to the Ministry of Labor.

Naturalization

In the Western Hemisphere, Brazil has been a leader in admitting immigrants, along with the United States, Argentina and Canada. Since the 1980s, the government has offered amnesty to illegal immigrants benefiting tens of thousands of foreigners living in Brazil. The latest amnesty in 2009 admitted about 45,000 foreigners.

Permanent residents in Brazil become eligible for naturalization and the Brazilian passport after four years. One need not live in Brazil during this interim period. As long as you enter Brazil at least once every two years in order to keep your permanent visa valid, you can spend the remainder of the time wherever you wish.

Naturalization can be achieved in one year from the date of issue of a resident permit should you marry a Brazilian or father a Brazilian child. Your name must appear on the birth certificate for you to qualify, but fathering a child need not mean marriage. A child born outside of wedlock still qualifies you for naturalization within a year. It is also possible to achieve naturalization after one year through marriage to a Brazilian.

Naturalization brings with it the all-important Brazilian passport. This travel document permits visa-free travel to all Western European countries and over 130 other countries worldwide. Brazilians do still have to obtain a B-1 or B-2 visa for travel into the U.S.; similar visa restrictions apply to Canada and Mexico.

The South American Mercosur agreement, in force since 1995, allows those with a Brazilian passport free entry into Argentina, Paraguay, Uruguay, and Chile. This free transit was instituted to increase trade opportunities and cross border business ventures.

Brazilian citizen status can also provide a faster back door into the European Union. If a Brazilian applies for and receives permanent residence in Portugal, he/she will only have to wait three years, half the usual time, before being granted Portuguese citizenship and the rights of an EU citizen. This unique situation prevails because Brazil is a former Portuguese colony. More Portuguese nationals live in Brazil than those who live in their home country of Portugal.

Dual nationality is allowed in Brazil due to a revision of the constitution in 1994. As long as you profess loyalty to Brazil, you are entitled to hold on to any other nationality you possess.

A 2007 constitutional amendment granted nationality to children born to a Brazilian parent living abroad. Previously such children risked ending up stateless, and it is estimated that up to 200,000 children may have benefitted from this development.

Brazilian authorities generally respect personal privacy and freedom of action. They do not inform authorities in a foreign national's home country about naturalization.

During the naturalization process, the applicant is offered the option of changing his/her name to make it sound more Portuguese. Applicants for naturalization must be able to speak some Portuguese. A naturalization judge may ask questions related to the impending action. Don't let the language requirement daunt you. Brazil has been a popular destination for Americans since the U.S. Civil War (1861 to 1865) when many thousands, mostly from the defeated Confederacy, sought refuge there. We would rate Brazil as a top place for a passport as well as a great place to live.

A passport and a Brazilian visa are required for U.S. citizens traveling to Brazil for any purpose. Brazilian visas must be obtained in advance from the Brazilian Embassy or Consulate nearest to the traveler's place of residence. There are no "airport visas," and immigration authorities will refuse entry to Brazil to anyone not possessing a valid visa. All Brazilian visas, regardless of the length of validity, must initially be used within 90 days of the issuance date or will no longer be valid, Immigration authorities will not allow entry into Brazil without a valid visa. The U.S. government cannot assist travelers who arrive in Brazil without proper documentation.

On a related note, the U.S. census Bureau estimated that there were 351,914 Brazilian Americans living in the United States in 2008, but other sources clam the number to be as high as one million or more, with 300,000 living in Florida alone.

Contacts
Embassy of Brazil
3006 Massachusetts Avenue NW
Washington, DC 20008
Tel.: (202) 238-2700
Web: http://washington.itamaraty.gov.br/en-us/
Consulates: New York, Chicago, Los Angeles, Miami, Houston, Boston, and San Francisco.

United States Embassy
SES Avenida das Nações
Quadra 801, Lote 3, 70403-900
Brasília, Distrito Federal
Tel.: + (55) 61-3312-7000
Email: pergunte-ao-consul@state.gov
Web: http://brasilia.usembassy.gov/

U.S. Consulate General Rio de Janeiro
Av. Presidente Wilson, 147 - Castelo
20030-020 - Rio de Janeiro, RJ
Tel.: + (55-21) 3823-2000
Web: http://www.consuladodoseua-rio.org.br/

U.S. Consulate General São Paulo
Rua Henri Dunant, 500
Chacara Santo Antonio,
São Paulo- SP, 04709-110
Tel.: + (55-11) 5186-7000
Web: http://saopaulo.usconsulate.gov/

U.S. Consulate Recife
Rua Gonçalves Maia, 163 - Boa Vista
50070-060 - Recife, PE
Tel.: + (55-81) 3416-3050
Web: http://portuguese.recife.usconsulate.gov

Republic of Chile

Government:	Republic
Capital:	Santiago
National Day:	Independence Day: 18 September (1810)
Population:	17,216,945 (July 2013 est.)
Total Area:	292,260 sq. miles / 756,950 sq. kilometers
Language:	Spanish (official), Mapudungun, German, English
Ethnic groups:	White and white-Amerindian 95.4%, Mapuche 4%, other indigenous groups 0.6%
Religion:	Roman Catholic 70%, Evangelical 15.1%, Jehovah's Witnesses 1.1%, other Christian 1%, other 4.6%, none 8.3%
Life expectancy:	78.27 years
Currency:	Chilean peso (CLP)
GDP:	US$316.9 billion (2012 est.)
GDP per capita:	US$18,200 (2012 est.)

Spindly Chile stretches 4300km — over half the continent — from the driest desert in the world (near San Pedro de Atacama) to massive glacial fields. Filling up the in-between are volcanoes, geysers, beaches, lakes, rivers, steppe and countless islands. Slenderness gives Chile the intimacy of a backyard (albeit one fenced between the Andes and the Pacific). What's on offer?

Everything. With easy infrastructure, spectacular sights and hospitable hosts, the hardest part is choosing an itinerary. Consider the sweeping desert solitude, craggy summits and the lush forests of the fjords; Rapa Nui (Easter Island) and the isolated Isla Robinson Crusoe offer extra-continental exploits. But don't forget that Chile is as much about character as it is setting. Its far-flung location fires the imagination and has been known to make poets out of barmen, dreamers out of presidents and friends out of strangers. — Lonely Planet

History and Overview

Chile is located in southwest South America. It shares a common border with Peru to the north, and Bolivia and Argentina to the east. Its west coast meets and follows the Pacific Ocean, and its southernmost point ends at the tip of the South American continent. Several islands and archipelagos are included in the country's overall area of 292,260 square miles. This narrow country's length is about 2,650 miles (4,265 kilometers) and its width is less than 110 miles (180 kilometers). Its climate ranges from the frigid, stormy sub-Antarctic rigors of Tierra del Fuego to the blistering aridity of the Atacama Desert in the north.

In between, from west to east, is a temperate land with a gamut of terrain and ecosystems starting at the seashore and culminating in one of the highest mountain ranges on Earth. In its center is the thriving, modern metropolis of the capital, Santiago. Chile is a land of spectacular scenery, inviting recreational opportunities, and vast natural resources, populated by an energetic people of various European, Asian and Amerindian ethnic groups, all of them proud to live in one of the world's most beautiful countries.

Prior to the coming of the Spanish in the 16th century, northern Chile was under Inca rule while Mapuche Indians inhabited central and southern Chile; the latter were not completely subjugated by government until the 1880s. Although Chile declared its independence in 1810, decisive victory over the Spanish was not achieved until 1818. In the War of the Pacific (1879 to 1884), Chile defeated Peru and Bolivia and won its present northern lands. Chile is now a stable democratic country whose constitution of 1833 is the second oldest in the Americas

The openly Marxist government of Salvador Allende was overthrown in 1973 by a military regime led by General Augusto Pinochet, who ruled until a freely elected president was installed in 1990. Sound economic policies, maintained consistently since the 1980s, have contributed to steady growth and have helped secure the country's commitment to democratic and representative government.

Chile has increasingly assumed regional and international leadership roles befitting its status as a stable, democratic nation and is the only Latin American country that is a member of the Organization for Economic and Economic Development (OECD).

In and around urban areas, Chile's culture is quite cosmopolitan. Santiago is a modern city by many standards, and its residents have access to all the technological wonders. The city is filled with parks and wide streets, excellent hotels and fine restaurants that offer world-class menus. During Chile's winter, from June to September, Santiago's people may wish to ski in the mountains to the east, or, throughout the year, they may visit marvelous beaches that lay an hour and a half to the west.

In the more isolated areas, the culture is dominated by a mixture of Spanish and Indian heritage. Life here is slower and centers on the land. It may be said that Chile has something to offer everyone. Indeed, many investors find that to be true in the country that has been called South America's land of opportunity.

Economy

In 1990 civilian governments took over from the military and continued to reduce government's role in the economy while shifting the emphasis of public spending toward social programs. Chile's currency and foreign reserves also are strong, as sustained foreign capital inflows, including significant direct investment, have more than offset current account deficits and public debt reduction. Its industrial growth has doubled in recent years, and its government welcomes foreign investors with unusual inducements.

Chile is a country where the future means economic opportunity. Already well known among international investors for its open trade policies, encouragement of investment, and pro-business outlook, Chile is on the rise.

For half a century, after 1900 Chile's economy was centered solely on the mining and export of copper, the government finally began to encourage industrial growth and diversification during the late 1940s. Today, Chile is one of the leading industrial countries in Latin America, and still remains one of the continent's largest mineral producers.

Chile's financial system is fully equipped with services for investors and entrepreneurs who wish to establish a business. The Central Bank of Chile has extensive powers to regulate monetary policy. The country also has a state bank, commercial and development banks, and financial services companies. Chile has a market-oriented economy characterized by a high level of foreign trade and a reputation for strong financial institutions and sound policy that have given it the strongest sovereign bond rating in South America.

Outstanding investment opportunities abound in many sectors including: manufacturing, forestry products, software design and production, fisheries, farming, mining, paper production, infrastructure expansion, and energy production.

In an environment of certainty and ample guarantees, foreign investment has made a significant contribution to economic development. *Forbes* reported: "Exports account for approximately one-third of GDP, with commodities making up some three-quarters of total exports. Copper alone provides 19% of government revenue. From 2003 through 2012, real growth averaged almost 5% per year, despite the slight contraction in 2009 that resulted from the global financial crisis."

Chile signed a free trade agreement with the U.S. in 2004. Chile has 22 trade agreements covering 60 countries including agreements with the European Union, Mercosur, China, India, South Korea, and Mexico.

Over the past seven years, foreign direct investment inflows have quadrupled to some US$15 billion in 2010, but FDI had dropped to about US$7 billion in 2009 in the face of diminished investment throughout the world. In 2012, "foreign direct investment inflows reached US$28.2 billion, an increase of 63% over the previous record set in 2011," reported in *Forbes*.

Chile deepened its longstanding commitment to trade liberalization with the signing of a free trade agreement with the U.S., which took effect on 1 January 2004. Chile claims to have more bilateral or regional trade agreements than any other country. It has 57 such agreements (not all of them full free trade agreements), including with the European Union, Mercosur, China, India, South Korea, and Mexico.

Over the past five years, foreign direct investment inflows have quadrupled to some US$17 billion in 2008. The Chilean government conducts a rule-based countercyclical fiscal policy, accumulating surpluses in sovereign wealth funds during periods of high copper prices and economic growth, and allowing deficit spending only during periods of low copper prices and growth. As of 2011, those sovereign wealth funds, kept mostly outside the country and separate from Central Bank reserves, amounted to more than US$20 billion.

The Chilean government has a countercyclical fiscal policy, accumulating billions in surpluses in sovereign wealth funds during periods of high copper prices and economic growth, and allowing deficit spending only during reverse periods.

Chile achieved growth despite the magnitude 8.8 earthquake that struck Chile in 2010, one of the top ten strongest earthquakes on record. The earthquake and subsequent tsunamis it generated caused considerable damage near the epicenter, located about 70 miles from Concepción , and about 200 miles southwest of Santiago. The Chilean Ministry of Finance estimated the total immediate losses were close to 17% of GDP.

Foreigners Capital Welcome

Some see Chile as beginning to challenge the United States as a favored entrepreneurial destination. Americans are moving to Santiago where comparisons to California include pleasant weather, beautiful landscape, friendly people, and a Silicon Valley-like tech culture. Some call it "Chilecon Valley."

The government now has a program called "Startup-Chile," which provides US$40,000 in working capital to entrepreneurs and other incentives including residence and work permits for foreign labor. For more see: http://www.startupchile.org/about/the-program/

The Foreign Investment Statute has been a major attraction for foreign capital. This law created a framework of confidence in the international economic community, so that, today, persons from over 60 countries have investments in Chile. The law offers special guarantees for investors who sign a legally binding investment contract with the government that can be changed only by mutual consent.

Companies or investors with commercial operations in Chile's remote areas are eligible for exemptions on income tax, VAT, custom duties, and similar charges. Special subsidies and fiscal bonuses may also be available.

Investors and companies with commercial activity within the forestry sector, and those that own land deemed suitable for forestry, may be eligible to benefit from specific incentives, including: a) a 75% subsidy of costs of forestry projects; b) specific properties deemed suitable for forestry are exempt from real estate taxes; or c) a 50% reduction in personal progressive income taxes on income gained from commercial forestry activities.

Residence and Citizenship

Chile historically has been a country of emigration. Since its transition to democracy in 1990, the country has slowly become more attractive to immigrants and is improving its economic stability. Most of Chile's small but growing foreign-born population consists of immigrants from other Latin American countries, especially Peru.

Citizenship is conferred in the following ways:

1. by birth: for a child born in the territory of Chile, regardless of the nationality of the parents. The exceptions are children of foreign diplomats or of transient foreigners.

2. by descent: for a child born abroad, at least one of whose parents is a citizen of Chile, provided the child establishes a residence in Chile before the age of 21.

3. by naturalization: Chilean citizenship may be acquired upon fulfillment of the following conditions:

   a) the person must have resided in the country for at least five years.

   b) the person must show proof of renunciation of previous citizenship.

Chile, as is Argentina, is also one of the Latin American countries that are given preferential treatment when applying for Spanish citizenship.

Dual citizenship is not recognized in Chile, except in the following cases: under the terms of a dual citizenship agreement Chile has with Spain; or a child born abroad to Chilean parents who obtains Spanish citizenship by country of birth may retain dual citizenship until the age of majority (21). Upon reaching the age of majority, the person must choose which citizenship to retain. Also dual citizenship is allowed for persons working or living abroad, who must acquire a foreign citizenship as a condition of remaining legally in the foreign country.

United States citizens entering Chile for business or pleasure must have a valid passport and a visa. Visas may be obtained at the port of entry upon payment of a fee. The visa is valid for multiple entries to Chile and remains valid until the expiration of the passport. U.S. citizens are admitted to Chile for up to 90 days. An extension of stay for an additional 90 days is possible, but requires payment of another fee. Visitors will be issued a Tourist Card upon entry that must be surrendered upon departure.

Contacts

Embassy of Chile
1732 Massachusetts Avenue NW
Washington, DC 20036
Tel.: (202) 785-1746
Email: embassy@embassyofchile.org
Web: http://www.chile-usa.org/

United States Embassy
2800 Avenida Andres Bello
Las Condes, Santiago, Chile
Mailing address: Casilla 27-D
Santiago, Chile
Tel.: + (56-2) 330-3000
Email: SantiagoAmcit@state.gov
Web: http://chile.usembassy.gov/

Chile maintains several agencies to assist foreign investors. ProChile acts as the Chilean Trade Commission with 35 commercial offices worldwide.

ProChile New York
866 United Nations Plaza, Suite 302
New York, NY 10017
Tel.: (212) 207-3266
Web: http://www.prochile.us/pro-chile-usa/about-prochile

Republic of Colombia

Government:	Republic; executive branch dominates
Capital City:	Bogotá
National Day:	Independence Day: 20 July (1810)
Population:	45,745,783 (July 2013 est.)
Total Area:	439,736 sq. miles / 1,138,910 sq. kilometers
Language:	Spanish
Ethnic groups:	Mestizo 58%, white 20%, mulatto 14%, black 4%, black-Amerindian 3%, Amerindian 1%
Religion:	Roman Catholic 90%, other 10%
Life expectancy:	75.02 years
Currency:	Colombian peso (COP)
GDP:	US$435.4 billion (2010 est.)
GDP per capita:	US$9,800 (2010 est.)

Colombia is back. After decades of civil conflict, Colombia is now safe to visit and travelers are discovering what they've been missing. The diversity of the country may astonish you. Modern cities with skyscrapers and nightclubs; gorgeous Caribbean beaches; Jungle walks and Amazon safaris; colonial cities, archaeological ruins, high-mountain trekking, whale watching, coffee plantations, scuba diving, surfing, the list goes on.

There is a dreamlike quality to Colombia. Here at the equator, with the sun forever overhead, the fecund earth beneath your feet, heart-stopping vistas in every direction and the warmth of the locals putting you at ease — you may find it difficult to leave.

Colombian culture, like the country's weather, varies by altitude. The essence of Colombia resides in the mountains in the alpine cities of Bogotá, Medellin and Cali, and the smaller cities of the Zona Cafetera. In the heat of the Caribbean coast, life is slower, and the culture more laid-back. The accent is the unhurried drawl of the Caribbean basin, and the infrastructure, unfortunately is still in need of some attention.

In darker days people used to say, "If only it weren't for the violence and drugs, Colombia would be paradise." Well the drugs may still be here but the violence is gone, at least for now, and it is, indeed, paradise. It is an easy country to fall in love with, and many travelers do. It could well become your favorite country in South America. — Lonely Planet

History and Overview

Colombia is located on the northern edge of South America,

bordering the Caribbean Sea, between Panama and Venezuela, and bordering the North Pacific Ocean, between Ecuador and Panama. The second most populous country in South America, it is a medium-income nation with a diverse economy. Its geography is also diverse, ranging from tropical coastal areas and rainforests to rugged mountainous terrain.

Colombia was one of the three countries that emerged from the collapse of Simon Bolivar's idealistic Gran Colombia in 1830 (others are Ecuador and Venezuela). A 40-year conflict between government forces and anti-government insurgent groups and illegal paramilitary groups both heavily funded by the drug trade escalated during the 1990s. The insurgents lacked the military or popular support necessary to overthrow the government, and violence has since decreased markedly, even though insurgents hold sway in some parts of the more remote countryside. The Colombian government has reasserted control throughout the country.

President Juan Manuel Santos Calderón first elected in 2010 and re-elected in 2014 highlighted five "locomotives" to stimulate economic growth: extractive industries; agriculture; infrastructure; housing; and innovation. Colombia is the third largest exporter of oil to the United States. Santos has held continuing peace talks with the Revolutionary Armed Forces of Colombia (FARC) in an effort to end the decade old insurgency.

Santos introduced unprecedented legislation to better distribute extractive industry royalties and compensate Colombians, who lost their land due to decades of violence. He has sought to build on improvements in domestic security and former President Uribe's pro-free market economic policies. Colombia's economy has been on a recovery trend despite the serious armed conflict. The economy continues to improve thanks to austere government budgets, focused efforts to reduce public debt levels, an export-oriented growth strategy, and an improved security situation in the country.

Because of the global financial crisis and weakening demand for Colombia's exports, the government has encouraged exporters to diversify their customer base beyond the United States and Venezuela; traditionally Colombia's largest trading partners. The Santos administration continues to pursue free trade agreements with Asian and South American partners and a trade accord with Canada went into effect in 2011.

Colombia consistently has pursued sound free market economic policies and aggressive promotion of free trade agreements. Real GDP has grown more than 4% per year since 2012 continuing a decade of strong performance. All three major ratings agencies have upgraded Colombia's government debt to investment grade. However, Colombia depends heavily on oil exports, making it vulnerable to fluctuating oil prices. In 2012, the unemployment rate of 10.3% was one of Latin America's highest.

After four years of foot-dragging by President Obama and his labor union backers, the U.S.-Colombia Free Trade Agreement (FTA) was ratified and implemented in 2012. Colombia has signed or is negotiating FTAs with a number of other countries, including Canada, Chile, Mexico, Switzerland, the EU, Venezuela, South Korea, Turkey, Japan, China, Costa Rica, Panama, and Israel.

Foreign direct investment, mainly in the oil and gas sectors, hit a new record high of US$10 billion in 2008 and reached another record high of US$16 billion in 2012. Colombia is America's largest source of imported coal. Inequality, underemployment, and narco-trafficking remain significant problems, and Colombia's infrastructure requires major improvements to sustain economic expansion.

Drugs and Displaced

Colombia is the leading world producer of coca, opium poppy, and cannabis with 83,000 hectares in coca cultivation in 2011 producing a potential of 195 metric tons of pure cocaine. As the largest producer of coca derivatives Colombia supplies cocaine to nearly all of the U.S. market and the majority of international drug markets. A major portion of narcotics proceeds are either laundered or invested in Colombia through the black market peso exchange. In 2013, the country was also a major supplier of heroin to the U.S. market.

Colombia has had major legal and illegal economic emigration and refugee flows. Large-scale labor emigration dates to the 1960s; Venezuela and the U.S. continue to be the main host countries. Colombia is the largest source of refugees in Latin America; nearly 400,000 live mainly in Venezuela and Ecuador. People have been forced to migrate because of violence by guerrillas, paramilitary groups, and Colombian security forces. Afro-Colombian and native persons disproportionately are affected.

One independent source estimated that 5.2 million people have been displaced since 1985, while the government estimates 3.6 million since 2000. These probably are undercounts because not all internally displaced persons are registered. Colombian-organized illegal narcotics, guerrilla, and paramilitary activities occur on all borders and have caused Colombians to flee into neighboring countries.

Colombia also has one of the world's highest levels of forced disappearances. About 30,000 cases have been recorded over the last 40 years, although the number is likely to be much higher, including human rights activists, trade unionists, Afro-Colombians, indigenous people, and farmers in rural conflict zones.

Residence and Citizenship

Under the law, the following hold Colombian citizenship:

1. Citizens by birth:

    a) Native-born Colombians, if the father or mother should have been natives or Colombian citizens or that, being the offspring of aliens, either of the parents was domiciled in the Republic at the time of birth;

    b) The children of a Colombian father or mother who were born abroad and then became domiciled in the Republic.

2. Citizens by naturalization:

    a) Aliens who apply for and obtain their naturalization card, in accordance with the law;

    b) Citizens by birth from Latin America and the Caribbean who are domiciled in Colombia and who, with the government's authorization and in accordance with the law and the principle of reciprocity, request that they be registered as Colombians in the municipality where they reside;

    c) Members of the indigenous (Indian) peoples who share border areas with application of the principle of reciprocity according to public treaties.

For a detailed listing of visas available for entry and for residence in Colombia, that nation's Canadian embassy provides a listing at http://colombia.visahq.ca/

U.S. citizens do not need a Colombian visa for a tourist stay of 60 days or less. Tourists entering Colombia may be asked for evidence of return or onward travel, usually in the form of a round-trip ticket. U.S. citizens who are not also Colombian citizens must present a valid U.S. passport to enter and depart. Dual-national U.S.-Colombian citizens must present a Colombian passport to enter Colombia, and both a Colombian passport and U.S. passport to exit the country and return to the United States.

Be aware that any person born in Colombia may be considered a Colombian citizen, even if never documented as such. If you are an American citizen who was born in Colombia or who otherwise may hold Colombian citizenship, you may need both a Colombian passport and a U.S. passport during your trip.

Travel Warning

Travel in Colombia can expose visitors to risk. The U.S. Secretary of State has designated three Colombian groups, the Revolutionary Armed Forces of Colombia (FARC), the National Liberation Army (ELN) and the United Self-Defense Forces of Colombia (AUC), as Foreign Terrorist Organizations. In the past, these groups have carried out kidnappings of foreigners, bombings and other attacks in and around major urban areas, including civilian targets.

For a U.S. State Department travel warning issued in October 2013, see http://travel.state.gov/content/passports/english/alertswarnings/colombia-travel-warning.html

Contacts

Embassy of Colombia
2118 Leroy Place NW
Washington, DC 20008
Tel.: (202) 387-8338
Email: emwas@colombiaemb.org
Web: http://www.colombiaemb.org

United States Embassy
Building entrance: Calle 24 Bis No. 48-50
Bogota, D.C. Colombia
Mailing address: Carrera 45 No. 24B-27

Bogota, D.C. Colombia
Tel.: + (571) 315-0811
Email: asktheembassybogota@state.gov
Web: http://bogota.usembassy.gov/

Republic of Ecuador

Government:	Republic
Capital:	Quito
National Day:	Independence Day: 10 August (1809)
Population:	15,439,429 (July 2013 est.)
Total Area:	109,483 sq. miles / 283,560 sq. kilometers
Languages:	Spanish (official), Amerindian languages (especially Quechua)
Ethnic groups:	Mestizo (mixed Amerindian-white) 65%, Amerindian 25%, Spanish and others 7%, black 3%
Religion:	Roman Catholic 95%, other 5%
Life expectancy:	76.15 years
Currency:	U.S. dollar
GDP:	US$149.5 billion (2012 est.)
GDP per capita:	US$10,200 (2012 est.)

Nowhere else on earth will you find so much natural diversity, and all the fun that accompanies it, in so tiny a place. Ecuador is the second-smallest country in South America, but its range of offerings is no less than astounding. In one day's drive, you can journey from the Amazon Basin

across glaciated Andean volcanoes, down through tropical cloud forest and into the sunset for a dinner of ceviche on the balmy Pacific coast. One day you'll pick through hand-woven wool sweaters at a chilly indigenous market in Otavalo; the next day you'll sweat all over your binoculars while spying on howler monkeys in the Amazon jungles of the Oriente.

For nature lovers, Ecuador is a dream, with exotic orchids and birds, bizarre jungle plants, strange insects, windswept paramo (Andean grasslands), dripping tropical forests and the fearless animals that hop, wobble and swim around the unique, unforgettable Galapagos Islands.

For the culture vulture, Ecuador's indigenous heritage of traditional costumes and highland markets will enchant you. As for colonial architecture, few cities top the beauty of Cuenca and Quito, both of which are UNESCO World Heritage Sites. And you won't want to miss Banos, with its enticing mix of natural beauty and jumping nightlife. — Lonely Planet

History and Overview

Ecuador is located in northwestern South America, bordering the Pacific Ocean at the Equator, between Colombia to the north and Peru to the south.

What is now Ecuador formed part of the northern Inca Empire until the Spanish conquest in 1533. Quito became a seat of Spanish colonial government in 1563 and part of the Viceroyalty of New Granada in 1717. The territories of the Viceroyalty, New Granada (Colombia), Venezuela, and Quito, gained their independence by 1819 and formed a federation known as Gran Colombia.

When Quito withdrew in 1830, the name was changed to the "Republic of the Equator." Between 1904 and 1942, Ecuador lost territories in a series of conflicts with its neighbors. A border war with Peru that flared in 1995 was resolved in 1999. Although Ecuador marked 30 years of civilian governance in 2004, the period has been marred by political instability. There have been seven presidents since 1996. Street protests in Quito contributed to the mid-term ouster of three of Ecuador's last four democratically elected presidents. In late 2008, voters approved a new constitution, Ecuador's 20th since gaining independence. General elections were held in 2013, and voters re-elected President Rafael Correa, a leftist populist in the mold of that late Hugo Chavez of Venezuela.

After a banking crisis in 2000, Congress approved structural reforms and the adoption of the U.S. dollar as the national legal tender. Dollarization stabilized the economy, and growth returned to its pre-crisis levels. However, the government more recently has reversed economic reforms that reduced Ecuador's vulnerability to petroleum price swings and financial crises, giving the central government greater access to oil windfalls and disbursing surplus retirement funds.

Ecuador has substantial petroleum resources, which accounted for 40% of the country's export earnings and one third of central government budget revenues in recent years. Ecuador has benefited from higher world petroleum prices. Fluctuations in world market prices have had a substantial domestic impact, both good and bad. In 2009, when oil prices fell, it was major jolt to Ecuador's economy and reduced government income.

In 2006, the government imposed a wind fall revenue tax on foreign oil companies, leading to the suspension of free trade negotiations with the U.S. These measures led to a drop in petroleum production in 2007. Elected in 2007, in 2008, the government of President Rafael Correa, a leftist populist, defaulted on commercial bond obligations. He also decreed a higher windfall revenue tax on private oil companies then renegotiated their contracts to overcome the debilitating effect of his tax. That and a plunge in crude oil price (Ecuador's leading export) spurred capital flight.

In late 2010, President Correa had about a 50% approval rating when an uprising by police against proposed wage cuts captured him as a hostage followed by a dramatic rescue by the military. Correa had been threatening to dissolve the national assembly before this dramatic event which strengthened his standing.

Economic policies under Correa, including possible termination of 13 bilateral investment treaties, including one with the U.S. have caused economic uncertainty and discouraged private investment. China has become Ecuador's largest foreign lender since Quito defaulted in 2008, allowing the government to maintain a high rate of social spending. Ecuador contracted with the Chinese government for more than US$9 billion in oil for cash and project loans as of 2013.

Ecuador is particularly vulnerable because it is one of only a few countries in the world — El Salvador and Panama are the next largest — that have adopted the U.S. dollar as their currencies. Because it uses U.S. dollars this poses a problem in times of major economic distress; a severe trade deficit could literally drain Ecuador of dollars, potentially causing economic collapse.

Rights Issues

An additional source of uncertainty is the economic provisions in the 2008 constitution, pending the implementing laws and regulations. This calls into question whether past guarantees still apply and whether Ecuadorians and foreigners have the same rights and obligations under the law.

The old constitution also established the principle of private property as an important development factor, and many types of requisition and seizure by the government were prohibited. In theory everyone has equal land and property ownership rights. In the past, there was no limitation on the foreign ownership of land in Ecuador, but foreign owned businesses have been expropriated by the Correa government. The future of this interesting nation that was once the Land of the Incas does not look bright.

During the year 2013, Correa got a press censorship law adopted that created Supercom, a government media regulator that has engaged in media-gagging, including fining a newspaper that published a cartoon critical of a police raid on a reporter's home. Correa, a U.S.-educated economist, has repeatedly called the media his "greatest enemy" and has filed multimillion-dollar lawsuits against those who oppose him.

In early 2014, President Correa pulled the country out the Inter-American Treaty of Reciprocal Assistance, a hemispheric agreement of mutual defense signed in 1947. The treaty, commonly known as the Rio Treaty, stipulates that an armed attack against any of the member states is to be considered an attack against all of them.

There are about 125,000 Colombian border area refugees in Ecua dor who have fled Colombia's 17,000 FARC terrorists and the 4,000-member National Liberation Army who have until recently been fighting the government of Colombia.

Residence and Citizenship

The 1998 Ecuadorian citizenship law describes the following ways to acquire citizenship:

1. by birth: to a child born within the territorial limits of Ecuador, regardless of the nationality of the mother or father

2. by descent:

   a) to a child born abroad of a native born Ecuadorian father or mother, if the child later becomes a resident of the Republic or expresses the desire to be Ecuadorian, or;

   b) to a child born abroad of a native born Ecuadorian father or mother, while either parent carried out an official appointment or was exiled for political reasons, unless he or she expresses a desire regarding the child's citizenship to the contrary.

3. by naturalization: Ecuadorian citizenship can be applied for upon fulfillment of certain conditions.

Any foreigner who has been a resident for three years may acquire an Ecuadorian passport and citizenship after application and due process. Foreign residents receive an Ecuadorian ID card; those with a resident visa may import household goods free of tariffs.

Marriage to an Ecuadorian national does not automatically confer citizenship, but it does aid in expediting the naturalization process. Congress can grant a person citizenship as a reward for important services to the country. Dual citizenship generally is not recognized, except under the terms of a special treaty between Ecuador and Spain, or when the nation of origin of the naturalized foreign person also recognizes dual nationality.

Most nationals can enter Ecuador without a visa and stay for up to 90 days. This visitor's permit is easy to extend. If you have a business in Ecuador, you can stay almost indefinitely without official residence status.

There are several ways to obtain a permanent resident visa, some requiring investing in Ecuador. That investment can be the purchase of real estate, the incorporation of a company, the purchase of local shares, or even a fixed term deposit in a local bank. The minimum investment required is only US$25,000.

An estimated one to two million Ecuadorians live abroad, mainly in Spain, the U.S. and Italy. The first major emigration of Ecuadorians (1980 to 2000) was caused by an economic crisis that drove Ecuadorians from southern provinces to New York City, where they had trade contacts. In the late 1990s, a second, nationwide wave of emigration was caused by yet another economic downturn, political instability, and a currency crisis. Spain was the destination because of its shared language and the availability of low-skilled, informal jobs. An estimated one to two million Ecuadorians live in the United States.

Ecuador has a small but growing immigrant population and is Latin America's top recipient of refugees; 98% are neighboring Colombians fleeing violence in their country. 150,000 U.S. citizens visit Ecuador annually and approximately 20,000 U.S. citizens reside there. More than 100 U.S. companies do business there.

Contacts

Embassy of Ecuador
2535 15th Street NW
Washington, DC 20009
Tel.: (202) 234-7200
Email: embassy@ecuador.org
Web: http://www.ecuador.org

United States Embassy
Ave. Avigiras E12-170 & Ave. Eloy Alfaro
Quito, Ecuador
Mailing address:

Ave. Guayacanes N52-205 & Ave. Avigiras
Quito, Ecuador
Tel.: + (593) 2-398-5000
Email: contacto.usembuio@state.gov
Web: http://ecuador.usembassy.gov/

Grenada

Government:	Parliamentary democracy, commonwealth
Capital:	Saint George's
National Day:	Independence Day: 7 February (1974)
Population:	110,152 (July 2014 est.)
Total Area:	133 sq miles, 344 sq km
Language:	English (official), French patois (Creole)
Ethnic groups:	Black 82%, mixed black-European 13%, European-East Indian 5%, and trace of Arawak/Carib Amerindian
Religion:	Roman Catholic 53%, Anglican 13.8%, other Protestant 33.2%
Life expectancy:	73.08 years
Currency:	East Caribbean dollar
GDP:	US$1.458 billion (2013 est.)
GDP per capita:	US$13,800 (2013 est.)

Isn't that the place that the U.S. invaded in the '80s? Didn't it get munched by a hurricane a few years ago? Grenada is used to bad press. But like a fighter on the ropes, it's come out swinging and has reinvented itself as the next big thing. The one big island and two small ones plonked in the sea in the southeast corner of the Caribbean are undiscovered and rarely visited.

Grenada Island is elliptically shaped and alive with a rain forested interior. Underrated beaches line the coast and sublime scuba diving is on offer just below the surface. St George's, the largest town, has one of the most picturesque waterfronts in all of the Caribbean. Stone buildings, forts from a forgotten time and houses of all colors meld into a hilly buffet of urban aesthetics. Friendly, welcoming locals go about their lives and are happy to include you in the process. Carriacou is a step back in time. With a cadence a notch or two slower than Grenada Island, this petite isle is a relaxed affair where endearing locals and an eclectic village life is added to sublime scenery. And if that sounds too busy, head over to Petit Martinique where even less happens – and the locals like it that way.

Yes, Grenada did get invaded by Uncle Sam, but that's old news. And yes, a hurricane obliterated much of the island in 2004, but they've rebuilt. Life moves on, and so has Grenada.
— Lonely Planet

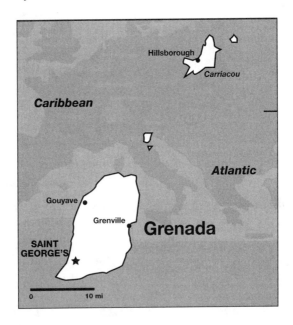

History and Overview

Grenada is an island located between the Caribbean Sea and Atlantic Ocean, north of Trinidad and Tobago. The "Spice Isle" is one of the most beautifully lush islands in the West Indies.

Carib Indians inhabited Grenada when Christopher Columbus discovered the island in 1498, but it remained un-colonized for more than a century. The French settled here in the 17th century, established sugar estates, and imported large numbers of African slaves. In 1762, Britain took the island and expanded the sugar production. In the 19th century, cacao eventually surpassed sugar as the main export crop; in the 20th century, nutmeg became the leading export.

Full independence was attained from Britain in 1974 making Grenada one of the smallest independent countries in the Western Hemisphere. Grenada was seized by a Marxist military council on October 19, 1983. Six days later President Ronald Reagan ordered an invasion by U.S. forces and a coalition of six other Caribbean nations, which captured the ringleaders and their hundreds of Cuban advisers. Free elections were reinstituted the following year and have continued since that time.

Economy

Grenada is highly dependent on international trade and finance for its development and therefore relies on tourism as its main source of foreign exchange, especially since the construction of an international airport in 1985. Hurricanes Ivan (2004) and Emily (2005) severely damaged the agricultural sector, particularly nutmeg and cocoa cultivation, which had been a key driver of economic growth. Grenada has rebounded from the devastating effects of the hurricanes but is now saddled with the debt burden from the rebuilding process.

Public debt-to-GDP is nearly 110%, leaving the government limited room to engage in public investments and social spending. Strong performances in construction and manufacturing, together with the development of tourism and an offshore financial industry, have contributed to growth in national output. Because of the island's global economic slowdown's effect on tourism and remittances, economic growth remained stagnant in 2010 to 2012 after a sizeable contraction in 2009. The island imposes no income, wealth or inheritance taxes.

In 2007, five Americans were sentenced to prison in the U.S. after defrauding over 4,000 investors out of more than US$170 million through an offshore bank known as the First International Bank of Grenada. Offering 300% interest and insured deposits, it was a classic Ponzi scheme. The bank began with a phony claim by founder Gilbert Ziegler, (also known as "Van Brink") that its assets were backed by a 10,000-carat ruby appraised at US$20 million. There were questions about involvement by Grenadian officials.

Residence and Citizenship

In 2013, the government of Grenada resurrected an existing law allowing citizenship by investment through two options: 1) authorized real estate acquisition in a designated resort development (Mount Cinnamon Hotel Beach Resort) and, 2) donation to the government Island Transformation Fund. The new inception of the old law increases the minimum real estate investment to US$500,000, plus US$250,000 in fees.

Investments of greater than US$2,000,000 can be made for villas or other commercial investments. Under this program there is a physical residence requirement. In early 2014, the law was amended to keep all applicant names confidential under the program, a move opposed by opposition parties in parliament.

A former citizenship-for-cash program was suspended after the 9/11 terror attacks in the U.S. due to fears that passports could mistakenly be sold to terrorists. During a prior three years before it was suspended in October 2001, Grenada sold passports to investors for US$40,000.

Under that program, international criminals such as Eric Resteiner, who pleaded guilty to wire and mail fraud, Viktor Kozeny, a Czech-born fraudulent financier, and Van Brink, obtained Grenadian passports. But the official Grenadian reason for suspending the program was that it posed a risk after the deadly attacks in the U.S. At that time, Grenada had also been placed on an international blacklist of countries considered uncooperative in fighting money laundering. It was removed from the blacklist in 2002.

Given this dubious history and the requirement of a two-year residence, look elsewhere if you want to buy a second passport.

Residence and Citizenship

Citizenship is governed by the Constitution (Chapter VII). Persons born in Grenada are automatically citizens. A person born outside of Grenada becomes a citizen if at the date of his/her birth either parent is a citizen of Grenada. A person who is married to a citizen is entitled to be registered as a citizen of Grenada. Dual citizenship is allowed.

Previously, the law required that a foreign national reside in Grenada for seven years before citizenship could be obtained. The 2012 law requires that after permanent residence status is obtained an applicant must reside in the island for only an additional two years before applying for citizenship. A Grenada passport allows visa-free travel to more than 100 countries including all EU and Schengen area countries.

Contacts

Embassy of Grenada
1701 New Hampshire Avenue NW
Washington, DC 20009-2501
Tel.: (202) 265-2561
Web: http://www.grenadaembassyusa.org/

The United States maintains a limited official presence in Grenada. The Ambassador and embassy officers are resident in Barbados.

United States Embassy
Wildey Business Park
Wildey, St. Michael
Barbados, West Indies
Tel.: (246) 227-4000
Email: bridgetownacs@state.gov
Web: http://barbados.usembassy.gov

Republic of Paraguay

Government:	Constitutional republic
Capital:	Asunción
National Day:	Independence Day: 14 May (1811)
Population:	6,623,252 (July 2013 est.)
Total Area:	157,047 sq. miles / 406,750 sq. kilometers
Languages:	Spanish and Guaraní (both official)
Ethnic groups:	Mestizo (mixed Spanish and Amerindian) 95%, other 5%
Religion:	Roman Catholic 89.6%, Protestant 6.2%, other Christian 1.1%, unspecified 1.9%, none 1.1%
Life expectancy:	73.97 years
Currency:	Guaraní (PYG)
GDP:	US$40.43 billion (2012 est.)
GDP per capita:	US$6,100 (2012 est.)

Paraguay is a country of fascinating contrasts. It's rustic and sophisticated. It's extremely poor and obscenely wealthy. It boasts exotic natural reserves and massive man-made dams. It is a place where horses and carts pull up by Mercedes Benz cars, artisans' workshops abut glitzy shopping centers and Jesuit ruins in rural villages near Encarnacion are just a few kilometers from sophisticated colonial towns like Asuncion.

Steamy subtropical rainforests with metallic butterflies contrast with the dry and wild frontier of Northern Paraguay & the Chaco. Here, many Mennonites have created their haven, living alongside some of the country's many indigenous groups, while the European influence is particularly strong in the laid-back towns like Filadelfia and the more chaotic capital.

While Paraguayans are more used to visits from their bordering neighbors, they are relaxed, kind and curious to anyone — share a terere (iced herbal tea) and they will impart their country's alluring secrets. The residual effects of dictators, corruption and contraband contribute to an overall sense that, for many years, much of Paraguayan life has taken place behind closed doors, as its people partake in public protests with confidence. — Lonely Planet

History and Overview

Paraguay is a small, landlocked country in central South America surrounded by Bolivia, Brazil and Argentina. The Paraguay River runs north/south through the country forming an excellent commercial trade route. Its relatively flat terrain (much of its area is a featureless plain called the Gran Chaco) lends Paraguay a reputation for uninteresting visual dullness that has discouraged potential tourists, although the land's fertility has attracted farmers from across the globe.

In the national parks, mainly located in the northern and western sections of Paraguay, large populations of native cats — jaguars, ocelots and pumas — survive, while visitors to the east of the country find a wide array of Indian lace and other handicrafts offered for sale.

Paraguay was on the edge of the Inca Empire for centuries prior to the arrival of the Spanish in 1536. Independence from Spain was declared on May 14, 1811. Unlike most of its neighbors, Paraguay's culture retains a strong coloration of the indigenous population, and the Guarani language is taught in schools and spoken among the urban elite.

The country's history is marked by numerous border wars with its neighbors with great loss of life. Military regimes and dictatorships have been a more recent facet. Since 1989, democratic elections have been held, but problems continue with periodic military coups.

This is one of the few Latin America nations that have not exploited its native Indian population. The government promotes the local Guaraní culture and language in all schools. The population is largely a mix of native Indian and European, known as Mestizo.

Economy

Landlocked Paraguay has a market economy marked by what the U.S. State Department diplomatically describes as "a large informal sector." Smuggling is a major industry. This black market, off the books economy, abounds in both re-exporting of foreign imported consumer goods (electronics, whiskeys, perfumes, cigarettes, and office equipment) to neighboring countries. It also includes thousands of service-oriented micro-enterprises and urban street vendors. A large percentage of people make a living from agriculture, many on a subsistence basis. Paraguay has one of the largest hydroelectric facilities in the world and exports most of its capacity to neighboring Brazil.

Because of the black market sector, accurate economic statistics are difficult to obtain. On a per capita basis, real income has stagnated at 1980 levels. The economy grew rapidly between 2003 and 2008 as growing world demand for commodities combined with high prices and favorable weather to support Paraguay's commodity-based export expansion. Paraguay is the sixth largest soy producer in the world. Drought hit in 2008, reducing agricultural exports and slowing the economy even before the onset of the global recession.

The economy fell 3.8% in 2009, as lower world demand and commodity prices caused exports to contract. The government reacted by starting big sending stimulus packages. Growth resumed at a 13% level in 2010, the highest in South America, but slowed to about 4% in 2011 as stimulus ended. In 2012, severe drought and outbreaks of foot-and-mouth disease led to a drop in beef and other agricultural exports and the economy contracted about 0.5%. Political uncertainty, corruption, limited progress on structural reform, and deficient infrastructure are the main obstacles to long-term growth.

Paraguay had no personal income tax until 2010 when a law took effect that taxes personal income earned within the country. Fifty percent of various forms of business and professional income, including dividends, capital gains, interest and capital gains were subject to 10% tax rate if a person's total income is greater than ten times the monthly minimum wage, which was US$373.00 monthly. Only 15% of the country's workforce is covered by the minimum wage and this formula exempts most citizens except those in upper income brackets.

Paraguay's tax burden as a percentage of GDP is among the world's lowest at about 12%, the same as Hong Kong (13%). It's nearly 30% in the U.S. and averages 35% among OECD members. This makes Paraguay a tax haven of sorts, but not one that's well known.

Along with Uruguay and Ecuador, Paraguay is one of the few Latin American countries that impose no currency controls.

Paraguay prides itself upon its independence from influence by foreign powers. Extradition demands aimed at a resident foreign national are commonly ignored if the person sought has curried favor with Paraguay's establishment.

Paraguay does not recognize tax or currency crimes and has a reputation as a haven for political and tax refugees. The prevailing attitude toward immigrants seems to be that, as long as they stay out of local politics, they are quite welcome. There are colonies of Koreans, Japanese, Germans, and of Mennonite religionists. Decent housing goes for as little as US$50,000, but luxury living is the real bargain. In Asuncion, whole neighborhoods resemble Palm Springs, California. A drive through the Villa Mora section will reveal huge mansions with swimming pools, tennis courts and staff quarters.

There is a lawless region at the convergence of the borders of Argentina, Brazil and Paraguay that is the admitted site of international money laundering, smuggling, arms and illegal narcotics trafficking, as well as fundraising for extremist groups.

Residence and Citizenship

Dual citizenship is recognized but only for native-born Paraguayans.

Under the law, citizenship is conferred in the following ways:

1. by birth: on a child born within the territory of Paraguay, regardless of the nationality of the parents.

2. by descent: on a child born abroad, one of whose parents is a natural-born Paraguayan and who is in the service of the Republic; or on a child born abroad, one of whose parents is a natural-born Paraguayan, if the child takes up permanent residence in Paraguay and has not accepted citizenship of the country of birth.

3. by naturalization: persons who will be considered for citizenship include:

   a) a person with ties to Paraguay and who declares intention to become a citizen;

   b) a child born abroad, one of whose parents is a native-born Paraguayan, who has complied with obligations required of their country of birth;

   c) a child born abroad to non-Paraguayan parents who are in the service of the Republic and have established residence in Paraguay, or;

   d) a person must be at least 18 years of age, have resided in Paraguay for at least three years, exhibited good conduct, and have continued gainful employment.

That short three-year residence requirement makes the country, like Uruguay, a possibility for a quicker second citizenship.

The residence process requires travel to Asuncion and submitting your residence application in person. You may be required to open a local bank account with a minimum deposit as evidence of self-support. Usual approval time is said to be four months unless you pay a local well-connected attorney.

The Paraguayan Constitution is very liberal in granting rights to foreigners. It proclaims all inhabitants have the right to develop their personal inclinations, trade and business. Nationals and foreigners are equal before the law, without discrimination. There are also no restrictions on property ownership by foreign nationals.

Documents submitted for consideration must include: 1) a passport from the country of origin, with photograph; 2) birth and marriage certificates, if applicable; 3) a certificate from an administrative, judicial authority, or employer evidencing occupation, academic degrees, diplomas, and/or guaranteed retirement income; 4) a certificate from a medical doctor or institution in Paraguay evidencing good health; and 5) a certificate from the police or judicial authorities of the country of residence evidencing no criminal record. Any documents not issued in Paraguay must be translated into Spanish and certified by a Paraguayan Consulate.

After about 30 days of processing in Paraguay, a Certificate of Residence will be issued, including a cédula or identity card. After three years of residence, a resident foreign national qualifies for naturalization. Paraguayan passport holders benefit from the 1995 Mercosur Agreement, which allows free entry to other member states, currently Argentina, Brazil, Chile, and Uruguay.

Passport Past

What we described above are the only legal routes to acquire citizenship in Paraguay. That distinction is made with good reason.

Some in the government of Paraguay may well have been the inventors of "instant passports" as an easy income source from foreign nationals seeking second passports. It is an established fact that, during recent decades, large numbers of this nation's official passports were sold illegally. As a result, many national border officials look closely at North Americans or Europeans who speak no Spanish and travel using a Paraguayan passport.

With a change in government 20 years ago, illegal "official" passports became more difficult to acquire and investigations began into "irregularities in the issuance of passports." Since the nation's passport must be renewed in person every two years at a Paraguayan Consulate, past issues are supposedly being scrutinized more carefully. Unfortunately, the same situation exists in almost all Latin American nations, with the possible exceptions of Argentina, Brazil, Uruguay and Chile.

For that reason and recent reports of passport scams in operation here and on the Internet, if you are interested in Paraguayan residence and a possible passport, I suggest you contact the following reliable attorney who knows the scene and can assist you while avoiding the local sharks:

Juan Federico Fischer, Esq.
Fischer & Schickendantz
Rincon 487, Piso 4
Montevideo 11000, Uruguay
Tel.: (+598) 2 915-7468 ext. 130
Cell: (+598) 99 925-106
Email: jfischer@fs.com.uy
Web: www.fs.com.uy

Paraguay is a country of emigration; it has not attracted large numbers of immigrants because of political instability, civil wars, years of dictatorship, and the greater appeal of neighboring countries. Paraguay first tried to encourage immigration in 1870 in an effort to rebound from the heavy death toll it suffered during the War of the Triple Alliance, but it received few European and Middle Eastern immigrants. In the 20th century, limited numbers of immigrants arrived from Lebanon, Japan, South Korea, and China, as well as Mennonites from Canada, Russia, and Mexico. Influxes of Brazilian immigrants have been arriving since the 1960s, mainly to work in agriculture. Paraguayans continue to emigrate to Argen-

tina, Brazil, Uruguay, the United States, Italy, Spain, and France.
A passport and visa are required for entry. U.S. citizens intending to travel to Paraguay must submit completed visa applications in person or by mail to the Paraguayan Embassy or one of the Consulates and pay a fee. Application forms are available from the Paraguayan Embassy or Consulate by e-mail or fax. Tourist visa applicants must present with their application a U.S. or other passport with at least six months validity from the date of the application.

Contacts

Embassy of Paraguay
2400 Massachusetts Avenue NW
Washington, DC 20008
Tel.: (202) 483-6960
Email: secretaria@embaparusa.gov.py
Web: http://www.embaparusa.gov.py

United States Embassy
1776 Avenida Mariscal Lopez
Asuncion, Paraguay
Mailing address: Casilla Postal 402 Asuncion, Paraguay
Tel.: + (595) 21-213-715
Email: paraguayusembassy@state.gov
Web: http://paraguay.usembassy.gov/

Oriental Republic of Uruguay

Government:	Constitutional republic
Capital:	Montevideo
National Day:	Independence Day: 25 August (1825)
Population:	3,324,460 (July 2013 est.)
Total Area:	68,039 sq. miles / 176,220 sq. kilometers
Languages:	Spanish, Portuñol, Brazilero (Portuguese-Spanish mix on Brazilian frontier)
Ethnic groups:	White 88%, Mestizo 8%, black 4%, Amerindian (practically nonexistent)
Religion:	Roman Catholic 47.1%, Christians 11.1%, non-denomination 23.2%, Jewish 0.3%, atheist, agnostic 17.2%, other 1.1%
Life expectancy:	76.61 years
Currency:	Uruguayan peso (UYU)
GDP:	US$54.67 billion (2012 est.)
GDP per capita:	US$17,120 (2013 est. — highest in Latin America)

Well, somebody let the cat out of the bag. Uruguay used to be South America's best-kept secret, with a handful of Argentines, Brazilians, Chileans and non–South Americans in the know popping in to enjoy the pristine beaches, the atmospheric cities, the huge steaks and the happening nightlife. Then the peso crashed in 2002, the place became a whole lot more affordable and people got curious. They came, loved it and went back home to tell their friends.

This is not to suggest that the place is being overrun. The main drawing cards, like Colonia del Sacramento, Punta del

Este and Montevideo, have long been set up for tourists, and are dealing with their newfound popularity well. Other destinations, such as Punta del Diablo and Maldonado, retain their charm but are no longer the undiscovered gems they once were. Elsewhere, in the interior (gaucho central Tacuarembó, for example) and the river towns, and particularly in the non-summer months, there's still a pretty good chance that you'll be the only gringo in town. — Lonely Planet

History and Overview

Uruguay is bordered by Argentina in the west, Brazil to the north and east and the Atlantic Ocean to the east and south. Lying low on South America's coast, Uruguay lacks most of the natural scenic extremes that might draw visitors to many of the continent's other countries.

Its highest mountain just tops 1,600 feet, and its temperate

climate sustains broad grasslands suitable for ranching. Excellent beaches along the Rio de la Plata, where it meets the Atlantic Ocean, attract a wealthy crowd fleeing urban congestion in nearby Buenos Aires and São Paulo to Punta del Este during the austral summer. Tourism is otherwise comparatively underdeveloped, although high-end tourism from Europe and the U.S. has seen a significant increase in recent years in areas such as Jose Ignacio, 20 miles east of Punta del Este.

In spite of Spanish and Portuguese claims based on early exploration and trade, immigration from all over Europe during the 19th century reached massive proportions. By 1880, European migrants — Spanish, British, Germans, and Italians — made up 40% of the population.

Uruguay is known as Latin America's least corrupt country (along with Chile), and has one of the highest standards of living in Latin America. Banks and currency dealers selling gold and foreign currency were once commonplace in Montevideo, the country's capital and Uruguay remains an open economy, with no exchange controls or foreign currency limitations. In fact, 80% of bank deposits in Uruguay are held in U.S. dollars or euros.

Although the emigration of professionals and skilled workers damaged the nation's reputation in recent times, the country, nevertheless remains a regional financial and logistics center. Uruguay's tax-free free trade zones attract regional and global headquarters of major multinationals.

Once a foreign national becomes assimilated into the large expatriate community of Punta del Este, Uruguay's answer to Newport, Rhode Island, life can be quite pleasant. Bridge nights and cocktail parties are part of the routine. Many people of wealth make their home here. Elsewhere in the country, Uruguay's infrastructure is fair, and declines in quality in proportion with distance from the south coast. Montevideo, the capital, is an attractive, modern city — among the safest in the world.

Uruguay may be small in area, but it's certainly big-hearted where attractions are concerned. It boasts one of South America's most interesting capitals, Montevideo, charming colonial towns, a hilly interior — true gaucho (cowboy) country — and a cluster of internationally renowned beach resorts, such as Punta del Este.

Uruguay is considered among the countries with the best climate conditions along with Ecuador and Malta, thanks to temperate weather throughout the year, moderate rainfall and little risk of natural disasters. It is in a temperate zone with uniform weather. Average temperatures for the mid-winter month of July range from 48F to 54F, while the midsummer month of January varies from 72F to 79F.

There are many interesting, safe, and solid investment options including farmland. Uruguay is a country of 3.3 million people and 12 million cattle (3.5 cows per person) and there is a lot of very fertile land. Main crops include soybeans, wheat, corn, and sorghum. Uruguay's soil quality, climate, and infrastructure have placed it as a global player and today the country is the 6th global exporter of soybeans, 5th in dairy products, and 4th in rice. Uruguay breeds mainly Hereford and Angus cattle, 90% of it on natural pastures, and the country accounts for 5% of all global beef exports. Uruguay is the only country in the world with 100% traceability of its cattle, from birth to slaughter. The country has a high sanitary status, which grants it access to the top global markets. Uruguay exports meat to 150 countries.

Investing in productive agricultural land is an appealing idea. Maybe you like the idea of retiring to a small finca of your own or maybe you have no interest whatever in becoming a farmer.

Your options would be to invest in land, then lease it out to someone to farm for you or hire farm management. Going this route, you'd make a regular but probably modest return. Engage someone to manage your farmland for you, and you would be positioned to benefit from rising crop values. In 2013, ownership of farmland by foreign governments was outlawed, as is the case in the U.S. Australia, New Zealand, Brazil and many other countries.

How would you organize this in Uruguay? Juan Federico Fischer (see "Contacts" below) can help, connecting you with the right people in the country both to buy right and then to maximize your yields over time.

Political stability has been outstanding in recent decades, and Uruguay's position at the center of the Mercosur regional trade bloc has begun to show signs of stimulating economic growth. Uruguay restructured its external debt in 2003 without asking creditors to accept a reduction on the principal. Economic growth for Uruguay resumed, and averaged 8% annually during the period 2004 to 2008.

Politics

After a brief period of military dominance of government early in the 1870s, unlike most of Latin America, Uruguay enjoyed a century of democratic government interrupted for a decade starting in the mid-1970s. Since the return to democracy in 1984, all three major political parties have alternated in power.

In 2004, the left-of-center Frente Amplio Coalition won national elections that effectively ended 170 years of political control previously alternately held by the Colorado and Blanco parties. Uruguay's political and labor conditions are among the freest and most democratic all the Americas.

Those who think the country or government is dominated by "socialist values" do not know the reality of modern Uruguay.

Yes, the aged (78) president, José Alberto "Pepe" Mujica Cordano, is a professed socialist and in his youth, decades ago, he even was imprisoned for alleged terrorism. A former anti-government guerrilla fighter he was arrested in 1972 and was shot by the police six times. After a military coup in 1973, he was transferred to a military prison where he served 14 years. During the 1970s, this included being confined to the bottom of a well for more than two years. Freed in 1985 he joined the Broad Front coalition of left-wing parties, and was Minister of Livestock, Agriculture, and Fisheries from 2005 to 2008 and a Senator afterward.

As the candidate of the Broad Front, Mujica won the 2009 presidential election and was re-elected to a second term in 2013, along with a centrist parliament that supports capitalism, free-market and free-trade policies. Based on my own conservative and libertarian political philosophy and on four visits to Uruguay in the last two years, I can say that Uruguay's is a less socialist government than the current Obama administration, and far more open and clean.

Mujica has been described as "the world's 'poorest' president" due to his austere lifestyle and the fact that he donates around 90% of his US$12,000 monthly salary to charities that benefit poor people and small entrepreneurs.

The Economist 2013 Country of the Year: "...the accomplishments that most deserve commendation, we think, are path-breaking reforms that do not merely improve a single nation but, if emulated, might benefit the world. Gay marriage is one such border-crossing policy, which has increased the global sum of human happiness at no financial cost. Several countries have implemented it in 2013 — including Uruguay, which also, uniquely, passed a law to legalize and regulate the production, sale and consumption of cannabis. This is a change so obviously sensible, squeezing out the crooks and allowing the authorities to concentrate on graver crimes, that no other country has made it. If others followed suit, and other narcotics were included, the damage such drugs wreak on the world would be drastically reduced." *The Economist*, Dec. 21, 2013.

Economy

The World Factbook reports: "Uruguay has a free-market economy characterized by an export-oriented agricultural sector, a well educated work force, and high levels of social spending. Following financial difficulties in the late 1990s and early 2000s, economic growth for Uruguay averaged 8% annually during the period 2004 to 2008. The 2008 to 2009 global financial crises put a brake on Uruguay's vigorous growth, which decelerated to 2.6% in 2009."

Nevertheless, Uruguay was one of the few the countries that managed to avoid a recession and keep positive growth rates, mainly through higher public expenditure and investment. The country has a 6.1% five-year compound annual growth of GDP. It growth reached 8.9% in 2010 but fell to about 3.5% in 2012, rebounding to over 4.1% in 2013, the result of a renewed slowdown in the global economy and in Uruguay's main trade partners and in the Common Market of the South (Mercosur) counterparts, Argentina and Brazil.

Scoring 72 points out of a possible 100 in the 2012 edition of Transparency International's Corruption Perception Index, Uruguay and Chile tied for first as the least corrupt countries in the Latin America and Caribbean region and 20th globally among 176 countries. (The U.S. was in 19th place with a score of 73.)

Taxes

But for those foreigners who seek a truly safe tax, financial or even residential haven — Uruguay is much more than just a pretty face.

Residence for tax purposes is defined as anyone with 183 days or more of physical presence in the country in any given tax year which corresponds with the calendar year in Uruguay. Credit is given for any tax paid in a foreign jurisdiction, whether or not there is a double tax treaty in force with that country.

In 2010, Uruguay changed its tax laws so that now tax interest on deposits and dividends that Uruguayan citizens hold abroad are taxed, but foreign residents living in Uruguay are not taxed. The law specifically states that foreigners who relocate to Uruguay do not face any extra taxes.

The following taxes are levied:

a) on assets: citizens (not foreign residents) will face a small tax on offshore deposits, securities and loans. The rate is 0.07% to 0.5%. This tax, known as "IP", is being phased out in annual steps and will end in 2017. It will not affect anyone obtaining citizenship after 2017.

b) on income: Three types of income generated outside of Uruguay will be taxed: interest on deposits, interest from loans to a foreign company and dividends. The rate will be a flat 12%.

However, if a person already pays income tax abroad on any of these three types of income, they will not have to pay additional taxes in Uruguay, thus avoiding double taxation (see below). This applies to both residents and citizens. Any other type of income generated abroad, other than the three named above, is excluded from taxes. Salary, capital gains on sale of shares or property, pensions, lease income, or any other type of offshore income are all untaxed. New residents are granted tax-free holiday for their first five years.

Financial Privacy

Uruguay is well-known for a very strict bank secrecy law; it is a criminal offence to reveal information about any bank account or any individual's personal financial activities. This privacy policy, together with Uruguay's history of stability, accounts for Uruguay's large financial sector. Bank deposits of non-residents far exceed those of residents.

Financial privacy in Uruguay is protected by one of the world's tightest bank secrecy statutes (Law #15,322, adopted in 1982). Under this law, banks cannot share information with any party, including the government of Uruguay or any foreign entities or governments, except in cases involving issues of alimony and child support, alleged crimes or local tax fraud.

Uruguay does comply with Article 26 of the Organization for Economic and Community Development's (OECD) model standards for tax information exchange requests. That is, banks may exchange information upon preliminary proof of foreign tax evasion or tax fraud. Uruguay limits such exchanges to countries with which it has signed tax information exchange agreements (TIEAs).

TIEAs were signed in 2013 with the United Kingdom, Canada, and Uruguay, as of January 2013 had 24 TIEAs in place, 13 of which include double taxation provisions. Most TIEAs lack parliamentary ratification. TIEAs with Ecuador, Finland, France, Germany, Hungary, Liechtenstein, Mexico, Portugal, Spain and Switzerland, Finland, India, Malta, Romania Australia, Brazil, Denmark, Faroe Islands, Greenland, Iceland, The Netherlands, Norway, Sweden and South Korea are pending parliamentary ratification. At this writing, it does not yet have a TIEA with the United States.

Residence and Citizenship

In recent years residence applications have tripled. The immigration department, with this increased inflow of applications, has stated three things it wishes to avoid: 1) People from lower income countries that come with fraudulent "proofs" of income. 2) People with gaps in their police record information. 3) People who obtain residence to later "buy" an illegal Uruguayan passport.

Immigration officials now require:

1. Better documentation of proof of ability for self-support which may be required to be updated periodically to ensure proof income has not changed during the application process. For most U.S. or European applicants this I not a problem since the income requirement is only US$1,500 monthly.

2. That if a person spends three months in Mexico (for example) between leaving their home country and coming to Uruguay, a Mexican police record must be produced.

3. That applicants for residence established a bone fide address and spend time in the country.

Unfortunately, these tougher verification requirements and the increased numbers have slowed the application process. That does not affect applicants who, from the moment they apply, are legal "temporary residents" and are issued a temporary cédula, the national ID card.

Uruguay has no immigration quota and it does not discretionally reject applications. Those who meet the basic requirements (see below) are approved for residence as a matter of official policy.

Acquiring Uruguayan citizenship is a relatively straightforward process. It starts by filing a residence application. Citizenship can be granted in final form, on average, within three to five years from the residence application date. Citizenship is obtained after three years (for couples or families) or five years (for single persons).

During the year application for residence is made immediate residence is easy to obtain with three key proof requirements: 1) a birth certificate (authenticated and stamped by the Uruguayan Consulate in the country of birth); 2) a home and any intermediate country clean police record, and; 3) proof that one can support oneself financially during the year of the residence process (known as the "income requirement").

As proof that one has a clean police record, the applicant must present a police certificate from the country of origin and from those countries where one actually resided within the past five years. In the case of U.S. citizens, the U.S. record required is a statement from the local Interpol office.

The income requirement is fulfilled by proving that the applicant has an annual income of an estimated US$18,000 or more. For example that can be a pension, a mutual fund, real estate or lease income from assets in or outside Uruguay, dividends of any nature, or certified salary sources. Uruguay's immigration authorities scrutinize this income requirement closely, so proof must leave no doubt of the authenticity and permanent or semi-permanent nature of the income source.

It's important to note that for a grant of residence, Uruguay does not require that a foreigner to own property or have investments in the country, but simply owning property does not eliminate the income requirement as described above.

To acquire residence, one must enter Uruguay as a tourist and then file a formal request at the Immigration Authority ("DNM"). Once a foreign person applies for residence, they can stay in Uruguay indefinitely. They also can request a national identification card, which allows travel without a passport to neighboring Argentina, Brazil, Chile and Paraguay, a real convenience because the high volume of traffic among these nations.

Five years after filing for residence (three years in the case of families), the foreign resident can apply for citizenship. At this point, one must have established Uruguayan residence, have had a permanent connection with the country and not have been absent for more than six straight months during the three–five year period.

Uruguay allows dual or multiple citizenships.

Deal for Retirees

A special law (#16,340) expedites a special travel document for foreign retirees with an annual official government pension of US$18,000 or more. In addition to the pension, the applicant must also own real property in Uruguay valued at US$100,000 or more.

The document granted under Law 16,340 to foreigners resident in the country appears the same as the one issued to any citizen, but in fact, it is only a "travel document," not a passport, that states on page number seven (where "Observations" may be listed) that "this passport was granted to a Uruguayan Permanent Resident with (country) nationality." The blank is filled in with the individual's actual national citizenship.

This law is not intended to expedite citizenship. Citizenship is obtained after three years for couples or families or five years (for single people) as stated above.

Under the 1995 Mercosur agreement, a Uruguayan passport carrier is entitled to free travel access to other South American countries that are party to the pact. Citizenship comes with a Uruguayan passport that allows visa-free travel to all of Latin America and several European countries. Current member states are Argentina, Brazil, Paraguay, Uruguay and Venezuela.

The immigration law states that residence is granted to those "who show intent to reside in Uruguay." The government in 2010 tightened considerably its requirement that foreigners applying for residence and/or citizenship actually spend time in the country while their application is pending.

Applicants must have an established address in Uruguay (rented or owned) and must show significant time of actual residence in country. This does allow applicants to come and go, or spend several months outside of the country during the application process.

As a result, those who apply for residence before moving to Uruguay will have their applications delayed until they meet these real presence requirements. The application will not be rejected, but it will be delayed until actual residence is established. However, immigration officials could require an updated clean criminal record.

After permanent resident status is granted, there is no longer any requirement to reside in the country. Residence status is maintained so long as the applicant does not stay out of the country for more than three years. If a permanent resident later seeks citizenship, minimal continued presence in the country is a requirement.

Contacts

Embassy of Uruguay
1913 I (Eye) Street NW
Washington, DC 20006
Tel.: (202) 331-1313
Email: uruwashi@uruwashi.org
Web: http://www.uruwashi.org/
Consulates located in Chicago, Miami, Los Angeles, New York, San Juan, and Puerto Rico.

United States Embassy
Lauro Muller 1776
Montevideo 11200, Uruguay
Mailing address: UNIT 4500, APO AA 3403
Tel.: + (598-2) 1770-2000
Emergency: + (598-2) 1770-2311
Email: MontevideoACS@state.gov
Web: http://montevideo.usembassy.gov

Recommended Consultant for Residence/Citizenship/Investment:

Juan Federico Fischer, Esq.
Fischer & Schickendantz
Rincon 487, Piso 4
Montevideo 11000, Uruguay
Tel.: (+598) 2 915-7468 ext. 130
Cell: (+598) 99 925-106
Email: jfischer@fs.com.uy
Web: www.fs.com.uy

Bolivarian Republic of Venezuela

Government:	Federal republic
Capital:	Caracas
National Day:	Independence Day: 5 July (1811)
Population:	28,459,085 (July 2013 est.)
Total Area:	352,144 sq. miles / 912,050 sq. kilometers
Languages:	Spanish (official), numerous indigenous dialects
Ethnic groups:	Spanish, Italian, Portuguese, Arab, German, African, indigenous
Religion:	Roman Catholic 96%, Protestant 2%, other 2%
Life expectancy:	74.23 years
Currency:	Bolivar (VEB)
GDP:	US$397.9 billion (2012 est.)
GDP per capita:	US$13,500 (2012 est.)

While other South American countries are romanticized for the tango, Machu Picchu or Carnival, Venezuela's international reputation swirls around oil, the brash politics that remain of the far left late President Hugo Chávez and the occasional international beauty pageant winner. However, there is so much more to Venezuela than these typical headlining issues.

As a matter of fact, Venezuela is a country of staggering variety and remains a land that is greatly under-visited by international travelers. The country claims Andean peaks; the longest stretch of Caribbean coastline to be found in any single nation; tranquil offshore islands set amid turquoise seas; wetlands teeming with caimans, capybaras, piranhas and anacondas; the steamy Amazon; and rolling savanna punctuated by flat-topped mountains called tepuis. The world's highest waterfall, Angel Falls (Salto Ángel), plummets 979m from the top of a tepui in Parque Nacional Canaima.

Those interested in culture can revel in the pulsating salsa clubs of the nation's capital, Caracas, explore various regional festivals, look for arts and crafts in the bucolic towns of the interior, or check out some of the world's best up-and-coming baseball players hit a few innings in a local stadium. —Lonely Planet

History and Overview

Venezuela is located in northern South America, bordering the Caribbean Sea and the North Atlantic Ocean, between Colombia and Guyana.

Venezuela was one of three countries that emerged from the collapse of Gran Colombia in 1830 (the others were Ecuador and New Granada, which became Colombia). For most of the first half

of the 20th century, Venezuela was ruled by generally benevolent
military strongmen, who promoted the oil industry and allowed
for some social reforms. Democratically elected governments had
held power since 1959.

The radical leftist Hugo Chávez, president from 1999 until
his death in 2013, promoted a strident anti-American policy of
"democratic socialism," which he claimed would alleviate social
ills. His policies attacked globalization and undermined regional
stability, weakened democratic institutions, polarized politics and
politicized the military. He made clear Fidel Castro was his hero
and model.

His hand-picked successor, Nicolás Maduro Moros, narrowly
elected in a questionable 2013 election, has done his best to follow
in his predecessor's repressive footsteps. In 2014, major anti-government street riots in Caracas and other cities led by students and
the fed-up middle class were met by police force and the arrest of
opposition leaders. By May, more than 50 people had been killed
during demonstrations and hundreds were arrested.

Economy

Chávez imposed Castro-style nationalization of foreign-owned
and domestic petroleum, steel, cement, telecommunications, electric power industries, banks, food processing and distribution companies. Venezuela's inflation rate hit 56% in 2013, toilet paper is
now an item that locals hoard and capital controls are so debilitating that companies are threatening to close their businesses.

The currency repeatedly has been devalued. In early 2014, the
official exchange rate was US$1.00 to 11.4 bolivars. On the black
market, it was 84 bolivars. Foreign investors fled in large numbers.
The government has implemented rigid foreign exchange controls
including a fixed official rate of exchange. Foreign exchange trans-

actions must take place through exchange houses or commercial banks at the official rate.

Chávez used his personally crafted laws to confiscate and nationalize most major industries and banks and to seize private property at will. As a result, inflation has soaring and the economy is a shambles suffering food shortages, a housing crisis, and a continuing electricity crisis.

The people of Venezuela continue to suffer from a housing crisis, high inflation, an electricity crisis, blackouts and rolling food and goods shortages, all the inevitable result of the doctrinaire hard left government's policies.

Venezuela is highly dependent on oil revenues, which account for 95% of export earnings, about 45% of federal budget revenues, and around 12% of GDP. It continues to be an important source of crude oil for the U.S. market.

Violent crime is a serious problem. The capital city of Caracas has been cited as having the highest per capita homicide rate in the world. Kidnappings, assaults and robberies occur throughout the country.

Citizenship and Residence

Since 1999, when the late Hugo Chávez came to power, more than a million predominantly middle and upper-class Venezuelans have left the country. The brain drain was caused by a repressive political system, restricted economic opportunities, steep inflation, a high crime rate, and massive corruption. The 2014 estimate of undocumented Venezuelans in the U.S. was as high as 160,000.

Thousands of oil engineers emigrated to Canada, Colombia, and the United States following Chávez's firing of over 20,000 employees of the state-owned petroleum company during a 2002 to 2003 oil strike. Thousands of Venezuelans of European descents have returned to their ancestral homelands. The country does attract immigrants from South America and southern Europe because of its lenient migration policy and free education and health care. Venezuela also has accommodated more than 200,000 Colombian refugees.

A valid passport and a visa or tourist card are required for entry. Tourist cards are issued on flights from the U.S. to Venezuela for persons staying less than ninety days. Persons traveling for reasons other than tourism should consult the Venezuelan Embassy or nearest consulate about visa requirements for their specific travel purpose.

There is no "permanent" resident status. Other than diplomats and visiting officials, foreigners can be tourists, transient (transeúntes) and residents. Residents have "residence" status (residencia), which has to be renewed every five years. Residence can only be granted by the Foreigner Status Directorate (ONIDEX), a branch of the Ministry of the Interior and Justice.

A foreigner has to apply before ONIDEX. This requires presenting one of various categories of transient visas and providing identity and other documentation showing the person has resided a minimum of two years in Venezuela.

U.S. citizens residing here should be careful to obtain legitimate Venezuelan documentation appropriate to their status. There have been numerous cases of U.S. citizens who employed intermediaries and received what they believed to be valid Venezuelan resident visas and work permits. They were subsequently arrested and charged with possessing fraudulent documentation.

Foreigners living in Venezuela as a transient or as a resident (but not as a tourist) are issued cédula or national identity card. Cards issued to Venezuelans carry a number preceded by the letter V, while cards issued to foreigners carry a number preceded by the letter E (for extranjero or foreigner). Foreigners with transient status have the word "transeúntes" written below the number on the card.

Citizenship

While other applicable provisions exist, immigration laws primarily are governed by the 2004 "Law on Foreign Nationals and Migration."

Citizenship is conferred in the following ways:

1. by birth: on a child born within the territory of Venezuela regardless of the nationality of the parents;

2. by descent: on a child born abroad, one of whose parents is a citizen of Venezuela, under the following conditions:

   a) before the child reaches the age of 18, the parents must establish residence in Venezuela; and

   b) before the age of 25, the person must declare an intention to accept Venezuelan nationality.

3. by naturalization: citizenship may be acquired upon fulfillment of the following conditions:

   a) a person has lived continuously in the country for at least five years. (Citizens of Spain and Latin America need less than five years residence.)

   b) the following may be naturalized whenever they declare their intentions: a foreign woman who marries a Venezuelan national; or a foreign minor child, natural or adopted, of a recently naturalized Venezuelan, provided the child resides in the country and makes a declaration of intent before reaching the age of 25.

Dual citizenship has not been recognized in the past, except during the period when a minor child is under the age of 25, at which time Venezuelan citizenship ceases if the foreign nationality is maintained. Although dual citizenship was expressly prohibited in the previous constitution, the latest Chavezista constitution refers to that subject in vague terms. This has been interpreted by some as favorable toward dual citizenship.

A valid passport and a visa or tourist card are required. Tourist cards are issued on flights from the U.S. to Venezuela for persons staying less than 90 days. Venezuelan immigration authorities may require that U.S. passports have at least six months validity remaining from the date of arrival in Venezuela. Some U.S. citizens have been turned back to the United States for having less than six months validity. U.S. citizens generally can expect official harassment.

Passports should also be in good condition, as some U.S. citizens have been delayed or detained overnight for having otherwise valid passports in poor condition. Venezuelan immigration authorities may require that American citizens with dual American-Venezuelan nationality to enter and exit Venezuela with a valid Venezuelan passport.

Contacts

Embassy of Venezuela
1099 30th Street NW
Washington, DC 20007
Tel.: (202) 342-2214
Email: prensa@embavenez-us.org
Web: http://venezuela-us.org/

United States Embassy
Calle F & Calle Suapure

Colinas de Valle Arriba
Caracas 1080, Venezuela
Tel.: + (58) 212-975-6411
Emergency after hours: + (58) 212-907-8400
Email: ACSVenezuela@state.gov
Web: http://caracas.usembassy.gov

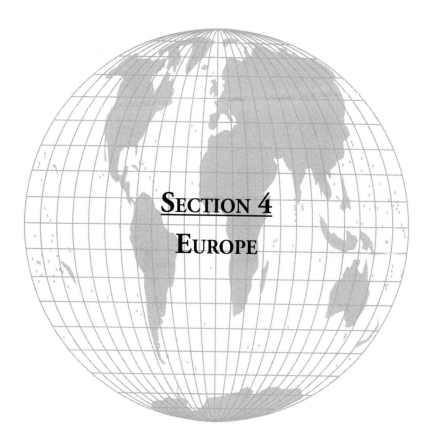

SECTION 4

EUROPE

PREFACE

Throughout its history, the European Continent or parts thereof have been united, often by force and conquest, as witness the Roman, Byzantine, Frankish, Holy Roman, Ottoman and the First French, empires, as well as Nazi Germany and the Third Reich.

In the post-World War II period, there were many calls for continental unity, typified by Winston Churchill's 1946 demand for a "United States of Europe." From 1958 to 1971 various formal European economic, trade, customs and atomic energy cooperative "communities" were formed. In 1951 France, Italy, the Benelux countries (Belgium, Netherlands and Luxembourg), together with what was then West Germany, signed the Treaty of Paris creating European Coal and Steel Community. Thus they came to be known as the founding members of what eventually would become the European Union (EU). In 1973 Denmark, Ireland and the United Kingdom (with Gibraltar) joined, followed in the 1980s by Greece, Spain and Portugal.

On May 1, 2004, the 15 nations of the EU — at that time — grew with the addition of 10 Eastern European nations, several from what was once called the "Soviet Bloc." Since then, several more have joined the EU for a 2014 total of 28 member states. A number of other European states will join the EU in future years. The Republic of Macedonia and Turkey now are officially candidate countries. The remaining candidate states, all in the Balkans, are Albania, Bosnia and Herzegovina, Montenegro, and Serbia. The combined population of the current enlarged EU now exceeds 450 million.

Immigration

During the 1990s, hundreds of thousands of people, including refugees from what was once Yugoslavia, sought a different European haven other than that of their nation of origin. Countries that bore the brunt of this inward migration included Austria, France, Italy, Switzerland and Germany.

The French and the British have restricted immigration to a minimum and the "immigrant-refugee" issue has been hotly contested in national elections in Denmark, the Netherlands, France, Sweden and other EU nations. In 2014, with EU migration restrictions finally removed from Bulgaria and Romania, the issue was raised yet again when the U.K. Conservative-Liberal coalition government Prime Minister, David Cameron, proposed to exclude from British welfare rolls migrants from both countries.

Based on total numbers alone, Germany was easily the favorite destination for immigrant refugees. It took in over four million foreigners, followed by Switzerland, the Netherlands, and France.

There is a continuing problem with stateless persons in the EU. One solution for these refugees is to be officially declared just that — stateless. Under a 1954 U.N. convention, those recognized as such get a special passport, permission to stay and work in the country where they are located and a fast track to citizenship. The U.N. High Commissioner for Refugees said that in 2012, for example, governments in France counted 217,865 refugees and asylum seekers; in Germany, 589,737; in Switzerland, 50,747; and even in the United States, 262,023 fit this definition.

Under normal circumstances EU states naturalize approximately 700,000 people every year, a number that exceeds the combined population of the smallest states, Malta and Luxembourg.

The Schengen Treaty

Countries that have signed and apply the 1985 Schengen Treaty do not impose passport controls between each other on roads, rails or at airports unless exceptional circumstances apply. Customs controls are unaffected by the Schengen Treaty. The 1985 treaty takes its name from the town in Luxembourg where it first was signed by Germany, France and the Benelux states.

The Schengen Area is comprised of 26 of the 28 European Union countries, (Ireland and the United Kingdom opted out), plus four-member countries of the European Free Trade Association, non-EU members Iceland, Liechtenstein, Norway and Switzerland. The Schengen Area also includes three European micro-states, Monaco, San Marino and Vatican City that maintain open or semi-open borders with other Schengen member countries.

Citizens of these countries enjoy the freedom to travel and work in all these countries without a visa, although individual nations may restrict the rights of citizens of newer EU member states to work in other countries.

According to My Bulgaria: Forums: "The remaining four EU member states, Bulgaria, Croatia, Cyprus and Romania, are obliged to eventually join the Schengen Area. However before fully implementing the Schengen rules, each state must have its preparedness assessed in four areas: air borders, visas, police cooperation, and personal data protection."

Most European countries still require all persons to carry or at least possess an identity card or passport. In theory, this means movement without document checks or border guards. However, most European governments have cut the immigration inflow and refuse to cede total power to the EU over which immigrants and refugees each country will accept. Another restrictive device has been to require "residence permits" for EU citizens who seek to move from one to another EU nation. The outer borders of the Schengen area countries are ringed with guards and sensors. Data on asylum seekers, including fingerprints, are logged in a computer data base in the French city of Strasbourg to which all EU countries have access.

At this writing Bulgaria and its neighbor, Romania, both EU members, which have spent more than 1 billion euros, (US$1.375 billion), developing high-tech border operations, are hoping to join the EU Schengen visa-free travel zone. They also hope to take over guarding some of the EU's outer (eastern) borders.

European Disunity

Today, there is a new conservatism at work in Europe.

Since its founding the European Union administrative structure, headquartered in Brussels, has been an object of derision and opposition by both the political right and left. Criticized as a remote and costly bureaucracy, EU policies on free immigration and the austerity demanded during the continuing Eurozone crisis that began in 2008 were attacked.

In May 2014, elections for the supranational European Parliament were held, the first EU-wide vote since June 2009. Although in the interim the euro crisis affected most EU member states, the hardest-hit economies were those in southern Europe: Greece, Cyprus, Italy, Spain, Portugal, but also Ireland. Harsh cuts in government spending to re-finance debt turned many people against the EU and its leaders, along with a resurgent nationalism in many countries.

In the 2014, parliamentary elections the center-right European People's Party won the most seats, but no majority. In Denmark, France, and Great Britain rightist groups opposed to the EU won huge, unprecedented victories and elsewhere, anti-EU populist parties won many seats. About a quarter of all seats went to anti-immigration parties skeptical of EU policies, or other protest parties. There was no doubt that the election was an anti-establishment victory that called into question the future of the united Europe the founders of the EU had envisioned.

Even before 2014, as Europe suffered a continuing economic recession, fear of more immigration from Africa and growing nationalistic fervor among member countries, much more attention was paid to these issues. In 2011, the Netherlands and Finland vetoed the entry of fellow EU members Bulgaria and Romania into the free-travel Schengen zone. They objected on the grounds of the two country's internal corruption and organized criminal activity.

Suzanne Daley and Stephen Castle of *The Hindu* reported, "Geography is another factor in the lack of enthusiasm for letting Bulgaria and Romania into the Schengen free travel zone. The two countries are paying a price for being close to Greece, which has done a poor job of controlling the flow of immigrants and illicit goods such as stolen cars and smuggled cigarettes. In recent years, officials have estimated the influx of immigrants to Greece to be around 80,000 a year."

The European Union's bid to limit members' unilateral border controls within the passport-free zone has been opposed by France, Germany and Spain. In 2011, those countries rejected a proposal by the European Commission to assert more control over how member states can implement internal border controls inside the Schengen Zone. They warned the EU's head office in Brussels not to meddle in how they manage their borders, insisting it is a question of state sovereignty. Italy, Denmark and France all have taken action to roll back visa-free travel.

Since 1995, the Schengen agreement has given residents of EU members the freedom to travel between the countries without having to produce passports. But growing tensions due to waves of immigrants coming into the bloc has tested the limits of those freedoms.

Thousands of North African refugees spilling into Italy in the wake of the 2011 "Arab Spring" revolutions and other upheavals and others from the Middle East prompted national leaders to seek a new mechanism that would allow re-imposition of border controls to bolster security. Amid a growing anti-immigrant sentiment in Europe, countries are reasserting the right to declare migration-related emergencies in order to re-impose border controls.

About one million people enter the European Union legally each year, mostly to join family members or by dodging police long enough to become eligible for amnesties that let them stay. That's about the same annual number that is admitted to the U.S. and Canada combined. Another 200,000 or so come to Western Europe as asylum seekers. By some estimates, as many as six million people may be living in European countries illegally. Compared to 20 million unemployed across the EU, those numbers have caused increasingly popular opposition to free immigration.

So much so, that both Belgium and Luxembourg have opted out of the Schengen Agreement and reintroduced border controls for citizens of other EU nations. The move, designed to cope with an influx of illegal immigrants, undermines the dream of a passport-free European Union. In 2009, non-EU member, Switzerland, joined the Schengen Agreement, but with the restriction that they only accept foreigners as residents on an individual, case-by-case basis.

Eventually, the EU goal is to allow free immigration in and out of its collective borders, but individual EU countries are refusing to go along with what they consider a much too liberal immigration policy, especially in the view of continuing high unemployment figures.

Supranational Citizenship

Greta Gilbertson of Fordham University notes that what she

calls "supranational rights" have developed over the past half-century in Europe as characterized by EU citizenship. British Commonwealth citizenship is an example of an earlier, imperial supranational membership or citizenship system that predates modern regional and political associations such as the EU.

EU citizenship embodies the idea of a common citizenship across all EU member states that could eventually serve as the basis for a unified European political identity. EU citizenship transforms the notion and practices associated with state sovereignty, a key principle underlying traditional citizenship. Freedom of movement, the most widely known right of EU citizenship, restrains the ability of states to exclude foreigners, thereby to some degree weakening national sovereignty.

Although some have hailed EU citizenship as a new, post-national form of state membership, it still remains subordinate to national citizenship. It is linked to the citizenship of an EU member state, and each state still controls who can receive their citizenship.

It should be added that with precarious huge sovereign debts still weighing down EU member states such as Greece, Ireland, Spain, Portugal, Cyprus and Italy, the continued existence of the European Union itself and it currency, the euro, has been called into question.

The Euro

On January 1, 2014, Latvia became the 18th country to adopt the euro. While most of the EU's 28 member countries are obligated eventually to end their national monetary units for Europe's single currency, skepticism among European citizens about the euro is strong.

Lithuania is scheduled to adopt the euro in 2015. Like Latvia, its neighbor and fellow former Soviet republic, it wants to link itself to the West and move further away from Russia. In Eastern Europe, several countries have failed to take required steps for euro membership. The Czech Republic, Hungary and Poland have all pushed back their starting dates for euro zone membership until near the end of the decade because of low public support.

According to The New York Times, smaller nations, including Romania and Croatia, which joined the EU last year, are unlikely to adopt the euro until about 2020, mainly because their economies cannot meet the requirement of a national budget deficit of 3% of gross domestic product and keeping debt to 60% of annual gross domestic product.

Denmark may be one of the next to join the euro. Although the euro was defeated in a referendum in 2000, a new vote will be held during parliamentary elections in December 2015. Sweden has also not taken the steps required to join, and has shown no signs of doing so.

While EU member states are required to adopt the euro, citizens can still block euro membership in a national referendum. Part of the reluctance among euro-skeptics is the fear of losing sovereignty and of being liable for supporting other countries should any new debt crisis break out. Estonia, which joined the euro in 2011, was soon after called upon to help bail out Cyprus when a banking crisis hit there.

In Britain, which has no intention of adopting the euro, Prime Minister David Cameron has distanced his government even more from the European Union recently, and has repeatedly pointed to the crisis and the haphazard response of euro zone leaders as proof that the currency bloc is a flawed project. He promised a national vote on exiting the European Union should he win the next elections in 2015.

The euro's economic troubles have damaged the currency bloc's image and highlighted structural flaws that need correction. Experts predict resistance will decline once the euro zone shows some tangible signs of recovery after a five-year recession. In early 2014, growth reappeared in some hard-hit economies. Ireland ended an international bailout in 2013 and Spain declined euro zone support for its banks.

One of the lessons learned from the crisis is that countries need to get their economic houses in order before joining the euro, to avoid the disasters that happened in countries like Greece, Cyprus and Spain. Latvia is a good example of country that did just. Smaller countries can benefit from euro membership allowing businesses to execute transactions in a single currency, lowering borrowing costs and improving exports.

In 2013, the EU moved toward establishing a banking union, although that is opposed in many quarters as too much power being given to Brussels, a common concern in Eastern European countries scheduled to join the euro club.

In spite of all it troubles, it seems the euro, however imperfect, is here to stay.

Principality of Andorra

Government:	Parliamentary democracy with chiefs of state in a co-principality; the two princes are the President of France and the Catholic Bishop of Seo de Urgel, Spain, with local "co-princes" as their representatives.
Capital:	Andorra la Vella
National Day:	Our Lady of Meritxell Day: 8 September (1278)
Population:	85,293 (July 2013 est.)
Total Area:	181 sq. miles / 468 sq. kilometers
Languages:	Catalan (official), French, Castilian, Portuguese
Ethnic groups:	Spanish 43%, Andorran 33%, Portuguese 11%, French 7%, other 6%
Religion:	Roman Catholic (predominant)
Life expectancy:	82.58 years
Currency:	Euro (EUR)
GDP:	US$3.163 billion (2012 est.)
GDP per capita:	US$37,200 (2011 est.)

All but lost between France and Spain, like the fairy tale pea in the mattresses, the pocket-sized princedom principality of Andorra comprises just a handful of mountainous landscapes and meandering rivers — but the skiing is the best in the Pyrenees. Andorra la Vella, its capital and only town, is a fuming traffic jam bordered by palaces of consumerism; Andorra has over 2000 shops, more than one for every 40 inhabitants. Shake yourself from Andorra la Vella's tawdry embrace, take one of only three secondary roads in the state and discover some of the most dramatic scenery in all of the Pyrenees.

In the last five years, its sky resorts have invested over €50 million in mountain cafes and restaurants, chairlifts and gondolas, car parks and snow-making machines. And once the snows have melted, summer activities are to be had in Ordino and around. There's great walking in abundance, ranging from easy strolls to demanding day hikes in the higher, more remote reaches of the principality.

A warning though: this may not be the case a few years from now. Greed and uncontrolled development risk spoiling those side valleys. Already the pounding of jackhammers drowns out the winter thrum of ski lifts and threatens the silence of summer. — Lonely Planet

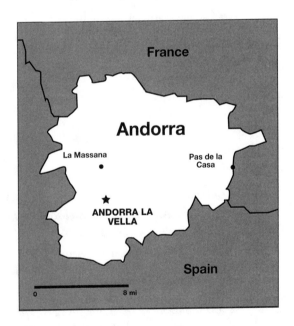

History and Overview

It lies right in the center of the continent, down in a secret valley in one of the most stunning mountain ranges in Europe. It's a secluded medieval principality not governed by any European bureaucracy. For the few in the know, this picturesque valley in the Pyrenees between France and Spain, almost forgotten by the rest of the world, offers affordable crime-free, but no longer tax-free European living.

The big secret is you don't even need a residence permit to live here, you can just move in!

Andorra is an accident of geography. The mountaintop principality is hours away from the nearest airport in Barcelona. Andorra's inhabitants speak Catalan at home, although French, Castilian and English are widely spoken in the principality's capital, Andorra la Vella, and in resort areas.

Tax Haven No More

Andorra is no longer the blissful tax haven it once was. In fact it is no longer a tax haven at all.

In 2011, a new government introduced a 10% tax for non-residents on local-sourced income; so much for foreign investment. This tax is being extended to resident individuals who have incomes of 30,000 euros (US$42,000) or more per year. Since 84% of Andorrans earn less than that each year, this was a popular soak-the-rich measure.

Until 2007 there was no capital gains tax, but a 15% CGT is now imposed on a sliding scale in what was said to be an attempt to slow real property inflation. The tax is reduced by 1% for each year of ownership when property is sold. Employees now pay national insurance contributions and there are municipal property taxes. There are customs duties on some imported goods and a number of sales taxes on various classes of goods and services, typically at single digit rates, although higher on alcohol, tobacco and cars. To bring in new revenue and diversify future sources of economic growth, in 2012 the government approved a new foreign investment law opening investment to foreign capital.

A parliamentary democracy since March 1993, Andorra retains as its heads of state a co-principality; the two princes are the President of France and Roman Catholic Bishop of Seo de Urgel, Spain, who are represented locally by officials called veguers.

Andorra is governed by a legislative Council General whose electors are the 16,000 plus native-born citizens with Andorran parents. This electorate constitutes less than one-sixth of the total Andorran population. The total population includes 30,000 Spanish, with sizeable communities of Portuguese, French and English speakers. In the 2011 election, a turnout of 74.12% constituted only 15,510 voters.

Andorra's young democracy is in the process of redefining its political party system. Three out of the five parties that dominated the political scene in recent years have dissolved.

A friend of mine, a long-time U.S. expat resident of Andorra, says that the Social Democrats won many votes in 2009 by proposing the first ever 10% income tax. The SD was voted out of power in April 2011 but the new, supposedly "conservative" Liberal Party government continued to implement the "new economic model" of the socialists including the income tax.

My friend observes that all these taxes condemn Andorra to implode because "…two real attractions for foreigners, no income tax and banking secrecy, have been eliminated. What remains is a very ugly place to live with a proposed low initial tax rate that may not be low enough to attract a very appealing class of new residents."

As we might deduce for a country covering an area less than half the size of New York City, available tracts for newcomers are few, and foreigners (defined as non-Andorrans or those resident in the country less than 20 years) are restricted to a single property, either an apartment or a plot of land, improved or not, covering no more than 1,000 square meters (0.25 acre). Thus, although average realty prices in Andorra are somewhat lower than the European norm, a residence in one of the more attractive villages or resorts could cost more than a similar dwelling in the center of Paris.

Andorra's main legislative body is the 28-member General Council (parliament). The sindic (president), the subsindic and the members of the Council are elected in the general elections to be held every four years. In the 2009 elections, the Council tied 14-14 leading to the ouster of the conservative government. One of the issues was the demand for less secrecy in the country's banking laws.

Bank Secrecy No More

Andorra used to offer strict banking secrecy guaranteed by law. That is no longer true. Local banks in advertising and promotions continue to mislead non-resident customers about secrecy in order to retain their current deposits as long as possible, taking about "numbered accounts" that no longer denote secrecy. After all, every account has a number.

Under pressure from the Organization for Economic Cooperation and Development (OECD), France and Spain, Andorra has adopted a broad definition of the crime of "money laundering." That includes having an account here that has not been declared to the tax authorities of the country where the account owner lives and is taxed. If an official foreign tax authority, such as the U.S. IRS, tells the Andorran government that one of its nationals is suspected of foreign tax evasion in Andorra, banking secrecy is automatically suspended. The local Andorran judge orders the Anti-money Laundering Police Unit to demand information about the person from all the five banks in Andorra on all present and past accounts held in the banks or in money management or investment vehicles. That information is turned over to the foreign tax authorities before the suspect is ever tried, much less convicted.

The then French President Sarkozy fired the first shot in 2009 when, as Co-Prince of Andorra, he told Andorra it could no longer make a living from fiscal fraud. The Andorran Socialist Party that governed then wanted to be exemplary in stamping out Andorra's welcome of foreign depositors who were taking advantage of banking secrecy. They succeeded.

Banking and other financial institutions contributes substantially to the economy. Andorra's comparative advantage as a tax haven eroded when the borders of neighboring France and Spain opened their markets for foreign pension providers; its bank secrecy laws have been relaxed under pressure from the EU and OECD.

Locals quietly admit that, as deposits fled, the country has been financially bleeding to death. They predict that sooner or later most of the banks will disappear. No country with a population of 85,000 needs five banks. The banks here made all their profits from the business of nonresident clients, the vast majority being Spaniards. Now the bank secrecy is gone and the foreigners are closing their accounts.

Interestingly, Andorra's two major banks, Andorra Credit Bank and Andbanc (Andorra) have offices in Panama and other leading offshore financial centers. It appears that while these banks were founded in Andorra, they look elsewhere for clients and funds.

Andorra is a member of the EU Customs Union and is treated as an EU member for trade in manufactured goods (no tariffs) and as a non-EU member for agricultural products. Andorra uses the euro as its currency and is effectively subject to the monetary policy of the European Central Bank. Slower growth in Spain and France has dimmed Andorra's economic prospects.

Tourism, the mainstay of Andorra's tiny economy, accounts for more than 80% of GDP. An estimated 11.6 million tourist visit annually, attracted by Andorra's duty free status and by its summer and winter resorts. Since 2010, a drop in tourism contributed to a contraction in GDP and a sharp deterioration of public finances, prompting the government to begin implementing several austerity measures to reduce the budget deficit, including levying a special corporate tax.

Spain is Andorra's leading trading partner accounting for 45% of the Principality's entire foreign trade. The two leading drivers of its economic activity are tourism and the financial sector.

Andorra lived for centuries on smuggling contraband and only recently made it illegal. In those bygone days Andorrans lived by selling stuff to non-residents at lower prices than in Spain. Now there is little to buy here that is any cheaper than in Spain. In addition, local observers say that greed and dishonesty has prompted many shopkeepers to sell faulty goods or cheap copies, knowing that the customer cannot get his money back without spending far more on a local lawyer to sue in a legal system that will take years, if not decades, to try the complaint and that will cost far more in legal fees than the money returned.

Passive Residence

Anyone may take up residence in Andorra without formalities, but the granting of "passive residence" permits, the first step on the road to permanent installation, is subject to a quota of 200 permits annually. After 20 years of "passive" residence, an individual can become a "privileged resident," a status allowing commercial activity on behalf of one trading company, but not conferring the right to vote. Under current law, any person in residence more than 25 years may acquire Andorran nationality after renouncing his/her previous nationality.

Under Andorra's old constitution, what were called "passive residence permits" was handed out by designated personal representatives of the Spanish and French co-princes. Andorrans, with no control over this process, resented the permits given arbitrarily to politicians' friends and cronies. After the 1992 constitution, the Council General blocked permits by refusing to pass on applications to the co-princes' representatives until a stricter immigration law was adopted. A tougher law on passive residence permits became final in 1995, and beginning again in 1997, permits again were issued.

Residence, under Andorran law, is defined as a person's permanent principal residence. A residence in Andorra does not alter an individual's domicile of origin for the purposes of home nation inheritance or estate taxes.

Due to the high ratio of foreigners to Andorrans in the Principality, the government uses selective methods of admitting new residents. Residence permits, called residencias, are available to applicants, retired or otherwise, who have an address in the Principality and who genuinely wish to reside in Andorra and become an active member of the community.

The applicants must prove private income sufficient that he/she need not seek local employment. Once the applicant is accepted, a residencia is issued for a period of one year, renewable after the first year for a period of 3 years. Applying for a residencia is a lengthy procedure and must be conducted in the official language, Catalan. Applications for residencias are handled by the Immigration Department of the Police. (Tel.: + (376) 826-222).

Those granted a passive residence in Andorra have the right to protection under the law, certain benefits from the health and social security system, the right to a driver's license and to own and register vehicles with resident plates. Residence does not confer the right to vote, either in local or national elections, nor does it allow local commercial activity, such as owning or running a business.

An individual who is not a resident is considered a tourist. But there is no legal limit on the period of stay and tourists are permitted to rent or purchase a property for personal use for as long as they wish. Thus, it is easy to live in Andorra perpetual traveler-style even without an official residence permit. In addition, there are ways to benefit from Andorran tax advantages, depending on the tax laws in your home nation or place of legal domicile. Questions on taxes should be directed to an attorney or the financial services firm Servissim, (see below for contact details.)

There are two categories of residence permits, both difficult to obtain: 1) active residence: those that give the holder the right to work in Andorra; and; 2) passive residence that does not allow work.

Residence permits are issued for periods of four years and are renewable. A holder of a permit should spend at least six months annually in Andorra and have documented proof of that fact. Failure to meet this requirement can result in revocation of the permit. The total annual maximum quota for issuance of passive, non-work permits (passive residence permits) is now 200. The earlier each year one applies, the better the chance of obtaining one. Applications are considered without regard to nationality, race or religion, but the person must be at least 18 years of age.

Applicants must also show that they and their family have "sufficient economic means" to reside in the Principality of Andorra without any professional or work activity on their part throughout the period of his/her passive residence. How much cash or assets constitute "sufficient economic means?"

An applicant must be able to demonstrate income of US$24,000 per annum. A couple must be able to demonstrate combined income of US$38,000. There is an additional income requirement if children are included on the application. Proof of annual income is sometimes waived if the applicant's net worth, as declared in a required confidential financial statement, is at the very high end. Obviously, the more wealth declared, the better the chance for a permit.

An applicant for passive residence must be able to prove he/she has in force public or private health insurance to cover illness, incapacity and old age for him/her and those in his/her charge for the duration of passive residence. Private insurance purchased from an Andorran insurer is more likely to be acceptable; the usual route since insurance can only be procured after a residence permit is granted.

The applicant must be able to show documentary evidence that he/she is the owner or tenant of a house or apartment, or that he/she has initiated the process of acquiring or renting a dwelling within the Principality, which process must be concluded within a period of one-year from the date of application. He or /she must be able to prove neither he/she, nor those in his/her, charge have any previous penal criminal convictions. Some countries, including the U.K., do not issue such certificates, but a reference from a professional person of standing, such as a solicitor or attorney, usually is sufficient.

Each applicant must supply a non-interest bearing deposit of US$24,000 for the principal applicant and US$6,000 for each additional applicant (spouse/child) to the Institute National de Finances, the financial control office. Deposits are returned in full at the end of residence. In addition, a new resident must pay an annual fee to cover the benefits he/she and the family receive from residence in the Principality.

Residence and Citizenship

After 20 years of residence, whether passive or working, an individual can become a privileged resident. (There is a pending proposal to reduce this to 10 years.) This stepped up status allows activity in commercial matters on behalf of a maximum of one trading company, but does not confer the right to vote.

Under current law, any person in residence more than 20 years may acquire Andorran nationality after renouncing his/her previous nationality. Dual nationality is not recognized. Children born in Andorra of resident foreign parents may opt for Andorran nationality when they become 18, if they and their parents are still officially residents in Andorra. These applicants also must renounce any previous nationality.

Restrictive residence laws, adopted in 1995, produced something unusual in Andorra; a national political debate involving residents and organizations that represent the major nationality groups on one side, and the politicians on the other. Opponents see the law as pushing many residents to leave and keeping others out. They cited Andorra's then sluggish summer property market, blaming the slump on the new residence laws.

Local politicians, not used to public criticism, were unsettled by the protests, and revisions in the law produced the present annual quota of 200 available residence permits.

Contacts

Embassy of Andorra
2 United Nations Plaza, 27th Floor
New York, NY 10017
Tel.: (212) 750-8064/8065
Fax: (212) 750-6630
Email: contact@andorraun.org
Web: http://www.govern.ad/

The Andorran Permanent Representative to the United Nations is accredited as Andorra's ambassador to the United States. A U.S. passport is required to visit Andorra, but a visa is not required for tourist or business stays for up to 90 days. For further information concerning entry requirements for Andorra, U.S. travelers should contact:

Embassy of Spain
2375 Pennsylvania Avenue NW
Washington, DC 20037
Tel.: + (202) 452-0100 + 202 728 23 40
Email: emb.washington@maec.es
Web: http://www.spanish-embassy.com/washington.html

The U.S. Ambassador to Spain is also accredited as ambassador to Andorra. U.S. Consulate General officials based in Barcelona are responsible for the conduct of relations with Andorra.

United States Embassy
Serrano 75, 28006, Madrid, Spain
Tel.: + (34) 91-587-2200. Fax: + (34) 91-587-2303
Email: amemb@embusa.es

U.S. Consulate General
Paseo Reina Elisenda de Montcada 23
08034 Barcelona, Spain
Tel.: + (34) 93-280-2227, Fax: + (34) 93-205-5206
Email: amemb@embusa.es
Web: http://madrid.usembassy.gov/

Servissim SA.
Head office (Private Client services /property sales / rentals)
Principality of Andorra
Tel.: + (376) 737-900 Fax: + (376) 737-904
Email: headoffice@servissim.ad
Web: http://www.servissim.ad/

Andorran Tourism Board
Email: info@andorra.be
Web: http://visitandorra.com/en/home/

Republic of Austria

Government:	Republic
Capital:	Vienna
National Day:	26 October (1955)
Population:	8,221,646 (July 2013 est.)
Total Area:	32,382 sq. miles / 83,870 sq. kilometers
Languages:	German (official nationwide) 88.6%, Turkish 2.3%, Serbian 2.2%, Croatian (official in Burgenland) 1.6%, other (includes Slovene, official in Carinthia, and Hungarian, official in Burgenland) 5.3%
Ethnic groups:	Austrians 91.1%, former Yugoslavs 4% (includes Croatians, Slovenes, Serbs, and Bosniaks), other or unspecified 2.4%, Turks 1.6%, German 0.9%
Religion:	Roman Catholic 73.6%, none 12%, Protestant 4.7%, Muslim 4.2%, other 3.5%, unspecified 2%
Life expectancy:	80.04 years
Currency:	Euro (EUR)
GDP:	US$398.6 billion (2012 est.)
GDP per capita:	US$43,100 (2012 est.)

Vienna's jewel-box palaces and Mozart melodies, sparkling Alps and problems like Maria naturally still have their place in Austria's heart. But venture further for experiences that defy expectations: from slinging on a backpack to stride through the Tennengebirge's lunar landscape to slurping cider with grizzled farmers in Mostviertel orchards, from catapulting down the jawdropping Harakiri in Mayrhofen to bathing in Salzkammergut's tingly lakes.

Visit historic spa towns like Bad Ischl or discover cities such as Linz, where a newfound street cred is adding a twist to Austria's tale. So cast aside the well-thumbed picture-book, as the real story is even more enchanting ... Austria flaunts its heritage in exuberant fashion. Vienna's bombastic Habsburg palaces and Salzburg's baroque splendor are worthy but dig deeper and you'll unearth Stone Age settlements, Roman archaeological sites at Carnuntum and medieval festivals. In the country where Mozart composed and Strauss taught the world to twirl, you won't need to search hard for culture – it waltzes right up to you. — Lonely Planet

History and Overview

Landlocked Austria is located in Central Europe, north of Italy and Slovenia, with five other countries forming its national borders. It is largely mountainous, with 40% under forest cover. The

Danube, Central Europe's major river, flows through the nation, which celebrated the first millennium of its founding in 1996.

Austria is located at the crossroads of Europe. Vienna, located on the Danube River, is the entry to the Great Plains of Central Europe, and the Brenner Pass links Italy and Germany through the Alps. Because of its strategic location, from its earliest history, Austria has been a thoroughfare, a battleground, and an outpost.

Humans have lived in Austria for at least 25,000 years. The Romans conquered present-day Austria and by 10 A.D. had divided it into provinces. In the fifth century, Roman fortifications collapsed and barbarian tribes from Germany overran Austria. For the next 700 years, Austria was governed by a succession of European, Hungarian, and Saxon rulers.

Vienna was once the seat of the Habsburg dynasty and of the powerful Austro-Hungarian Empire that ruled much of Europe. The city retains much of the legendary elegance and charm it possessed as the capital of Central Europe and the magnet that drew in and harbored artists, composers, chefs, decorators, intellectuals, and literary geniuses for many centuries. Vienna will forever be associated with the names of Mozart, Hayden, Beethoven, Schubert, Freud, and dozens of other leaders in all creative fields. It was also the home of a young unemployed veteran of the First World War, Adolf Hitler.

Outstanding museums and universities, splendid architecture, world-class orchestras and opera companies, beautiful parks around the former palaces, fine restaurants, and fabled pastry shops draw visitors and expatriates to the banks of the "Beautiful Blue Danube." The rest of the country is not without its charm and attractions, with the annual Mozart festival in the composer's birth city of Salzburg, historic churches and monasteries in the countryside or in or near many of the major cities, and renowned winter sports resorts in the mountains.

After the German-led Central Powers' defeat in World War I, Austria's geographic area shrank to a minor republic. In 1938, it became part of Nazi Germany in an ill-fated Anschluss (annexation). At the end of World War II, Austria was occupied by the four victorious Allied powers. In a 1955 state treaty, Austria was declared a "permanently neutral" country as a condition of Soviet military withdrawal from part of the occupied nation.

There was a major public debate over whether the nation could remain aloof from European security structures, but, in 1995, Austria joined the EU after a large majority voted in favor. The 1955 treaty ended the occupation, recognized Austria's independence, and forbade unification with Germany.

The Soviet Union's collapse in 1991 and Austria's entry into the European Union in 1995 have altered the meaning of this neutrality. A prosperous, democratic country, Austria entered the EU Economic and Monetary Union in 1999. As a committed neutral, Austria has not joined the defensive military alliance of the North Atlantic Treaty Organization (NATO).

What makes Austria particularly interesting in the context of dual nationality and second passports is its post-war history as a major processing center for the resettlement of refugees, especially those who fled Communism's takeover of Eastern Europe and, more recently, the Balkan wars.

The United Nations long has had a bureaucracy of "relocation experts" headquartered in Vienna providing temporary housing for stateless people. Austria offers its sympathy, life support and even an "Austrian Refugee Passport." Austria also expects refugees to be temporary visitors, soon to move on to other destinations. As of 2011, U.N. figures showed 68,656 refugees and asylum seekers lived in Austria.

In recent years, the influx of refugees has been so great that curbing immigration has become a major issue in national elections, leading to the defeat of the long-time Socialist-Christian Democrat coalition government.

Economy

Austria ranks among the 10 wealthiest countries in the world on a per-capita basis. The Austrian economy has benefited greatly in the past from strong commercial relations, especially in the banking and insurance sectors, with central, eastern, and southeastern Europe, but these sectors have been vulnerable to recent international financial instabilities, and some of Austria's largest banks required government support. Austria, with its well-developed market economy, skilled labor force, and high standard of living, is closely tied to other EU economies, especially Germany's. This country's economy features a large service sector, a sound industrial sector, and a small, but highly developed agricultural sector.

In 1973 when President Nixon removed the U.S. from what remained of the international gold standard no longer permitting foreign central banks to exchange their dollars for gold, Austria decided to tie both its exchange rate and monetary policy to the German deutschmark. The policy was highly successful: from 1971 to 2002, until the adoption of the euro, the deutschmark's value stood virtually unchanged against the Austrian schilling in Vienna's foreign exchange markets. The resulting wage and price stability contributed to the international competitiveness of Austria.

The global economic downturn that began in 2008 to 2009, followed several years of solid demand for Austrian exports and record employment growth. During the recession, investment suffered and the Austrian government's economic stabilization measures drove up the budget deficit. Stabilization measures, stimulus spending, and an income tax reform pushed the budget deficit to

4.5% of GDP in 2010 and over 3.0% in 2013, from only about 0.9% in 2008.

The international financial crisis caused difficulties for Austria's largest banks facing losses because of extensive operations in central, eastern, and southeastern Europe. The government provided bank bailouts including in some instances, nationalization, to stabilize the banking system. Austria's fiscal position compares favorably with other euro-zone countries, but it faces external risks, such as Austrian banks' continued exposure to Central and Eastern Europe as well as political and economic uncertainties caused by the wider European sovereign debt crisis.

Even after the global economic outlook improves, Austria will need to continue restructuring, emphasize knowledge-based sectors of the economy, and encourage greater labor flexibility and labor participation to offset growing unemployment and Austria's aging population and low fertility rate.

Since World War II, two parties usually have dominated Austrian political life: the conservative Austrian People's Party (ÖVP) and the center-left Social Democratic Party of Austria (SPÖ). Despite the philosophical differences between the two, these parties historically have worked together in a "Grand Coalition." That coalition persists in the form of a ruling government by the two major parties, but divisions have grown due to an aging population, an influx of illegal immigrants, and the global economic downturn.

In late September 2013, Austria's more conservative Freedom Party gained over one-fifth of the votes in a national general election and the ruling two-party centrist coalition got its worst-ever low vote. The swing came amid a Europe-wide surge in support for conservative parties. The Coalition retain its majority in parliament, but many saw the conservative vote as marking a rightward shift in the political mentality of Europeans.

Bank Secrecy

Strategically located on the Eastern European border between former Cold War blocs, East and West, the Austrian Republic used to be a bastion of banking privacy.

From 1945 to the Soviet collapse in 1991, Russia and the U.S. remained locked in confrontation, but this convenient banking haven was used as a financial go-between by both West and East Bloc governments. When Austrian national banking laws were officially codified in 1979, the well-established tradition of bank secrecy was already two centuries old. During this time, Austrian bank secrecy and privacy produced two major types of so-called "anonymous accounts." These accounts usually required no account holder identification, no mailing address and no personal references. Just deposit funds and use the account as you pleased, all anonymously. These have long since been abolished under OECD and EU pressures.

Until September 1, 2009, Austria held firm on its traditionally strict financial privacy and bank secrecy laws. But on that date, the parliament approved a law to ease banking secrecy as the last EU country then still on the Organization for Economic Co-operation and Development's (OECD) "gray list" of tax havens. It was a political challenge to assemble a two-thirds majority necessary to weaken the law, but Austria's leaders persuaded legislators of the importance of getting off the OECD's phony anti-tax haven list.

Under the old law, Austrian authorities would only release account data to foreign authorities if a criminal proceeding was underway in the requesting country against a named individual. Foreign authorities had to convince an Austrian court to order the data to be released.

This simple and common sense system has been replaced with a network of tax information exchange agreements under which Austria will release information on financial accounts held by a foreign investor upon request of foreign tax authorities. The request may be in regard to any tax inquiry, civil, criminal, or administrative. However, the inquiry must name a specific person. Austria insists that it has no obligation to allow wholesale "fishing expeditions." It is expected that Austria will sign a FATCA agreement with the U.S. eventually.

In spite of an OECD demand that each country sign at least 12 tax information exchange agreements (TIEAs) with other nations, Austria has signed TIEAs only with Gibraltar, Andorra, Monaco and Saint Vincent and the Grenadines, all in 2009, with Jersey in 2012 and none since. A foreign government must prove "foreseeable relevance" as well as request specific information on a specified account. The requesting country must prove that it has exhausted all local and domestic means of obtaining the information before applying to the Austrian authorities. Account holders are given notice of any requests and can appeal any decisions concerning the account. In practice this means there is no automatic exchange of information.

My Sovereign Society colleague, Mark Nestmann, who lived in Vienna for three years, offers this first hand observation:

"Austria offers major advantages including a stable economy, safe banks and, for foreign investors, virtually no taxes. Austria is also a popular expatriate haven. If you have sufficient wealth to support yourself, it is one of the world's top havens for residence — although unfortunately it is difficult to obtain a residence permit. Austria welcomes foreigners but it doesn't promote itself as an investment or residential haven, so you'll have to take the first step if you are interested in investing or living here."

In 2013, Austria resisted agreeing to automatic exchange of banking information between EU countries. Chancellor Werner Faymann opposed automatic exchange without a showing of due cause. The finance minister, Maria Fekter, showed no signs of backing down. "We will fight for bank secrecy," Ms. Fekter said.

As mentioned above, Austria ranks among the 10 richest countries in the world. Its capital gold reserves rank third in the western world. Its political and economic stability is reflected in its currency's performance prior to the adoption of the euro. The Austrian schilling appreciated against the U.S. dollar by 150% in the last 20 years but since has been replaced by the euro.

Residence and Immigration

Austria is also a desirable place to live. Mercer's, a human resources consultancy, rates Austria's historic capital of Vienna as the most desirable city in the world in which to live.

Because of its diminutive size, Austria does not accept many new resident aliens. Indeed, limiting immigration has become a major political issue, giving rise to the conservative Freedom Party that opposes further immigration. In response to an influx of immigrants from Eastern Europe, Turkey, and Africa, Austria enacted legislation in 2005 significantly restricting immigration. The country admits only about 8,000 immigrants annually, with the majority being foreigners married to Austrian nationals. In practice, it is difficult for non-EU nationals to obtain legal residence in Austria without an expensive and time-consuming application process.

An Austrian passport is one of the world's most desirable travel documents. It not only permits you to live or work in any of the 28 EU member countries without obtaining a visa, but also allows visa-free travel to more countries than almost any other travel document. It also permits you to visit countries that you would not otherwise be able to visit, at least not officially, with a U.S. passport such as Cuba.

A child born to Austrian parents is an Austrian citizen. If the parents are married at the time of birth, Austrian citizenship of either the mother or the father is sufficient, so long as the child was born after January 9, 1983. For children born prior to that date, the father must have been an Austrian citizen. Children born to an Austrian mother married to a non-Austrian father do not qualify. If the parents are not married, however, a father cannot pass on Austrian citizenship, whereas a mother can. Should the parents happen to marry at some time after the birth, citizenship is automatically granted to the child retroactively. If the child is over 14 at that time, however, his or her consent is needed.

It is possible to apply for Austrian citizenship by naturalization after 10 years of continuous residence. Additional requirements include: 1) knowledge of the German language "having due regard to the alien's personal circumstances"; 2) renunciation of foreign citizenship (under the law of the applicant's home country) unless this is impractical. This requirement can be waived in exceptional cases. Austrian law substantially restricts dual citizenship, but exceptions are made.

There are two other ways for a non-EU citizen to qualify for permanent residence in Austria:

1. Private Means. You may qualify if you have a pension or proof of sufficient means to support yourself without working. You must file your application in person. The process takes approximately six months if all documents are in order and you meet all other legal requirements. If you can't show proof of at least a high-school diploma, you must speak German well enough to carry on a simple conversation when you apply.

   This residence permit must be renewed annually. After five years of continuous legal residence, an application an unlimited permit may allow one to stay permanently. To get this unlimited permit, you must speak German well enough to communicate effectively in everyday situations.

2. Key Manager. A faster way to acquire residence is to become a "key manager" of an Austrian company. This permit obligates you to work at the employing company that employs for the duration of the permit, usually one year. The application process is similar to the private means procedure, but the person must also fulfill key manager requirements requiring specialized knowledge, experience and a university degree in the field of specialization. They must also possess unique work skills that are vitally important for the employer (or for the region of Austria where you'll be employed) that are unavailable from any Austrian person who is currently unemployed.

It's also possible to obtain citizenship in exchange for making a significant contribution to the Republic. Only a handful of persons gain citizenship in this manner each year, compared to the approximately 30,000 annually that become citizens by naturalization.

Special Citizenship Program

Investors of at least US$2 million in approved projects in Austria may be considered for citizenship under a law seeking to attract extraordinary contributions to the nation.

Although Austria does not have an economic citizenship program per se, statutory law does allow the granting of citizenship to a foreign person if he or she is judged to contribute in some extraordinary way, including economic, to the interests of Austria. However, this is a very difficult way to acquire citizenship and may require a year to process at a minimum.

Applicants are approved on a case-by-case basis and must be willing to invest or make a charitable contribution of at least US$2 million in an approved project in Austria. Investment proposals are submitted to the Office of Economic Development.

Those that provide export stimulation or local employment

receive preference. Representation by a knowledgeable Austrian lawyer is essential, and is likely to cost considerably more than US$50,000. Fees of €250,000 (US$325,000) or more apply, depending on the case and the number of persons in an application, as each case is handled on an individual basis. The Nestmann Group and Henley & Partners can provide details on these possibilities.

The following documentation is required for an Austrian residence application:

Document:	For:
Personal information form	Each person, including children
Birth certificate (certified copy)	Each person, including children
Marriage certificate (certified copy)	Married couples
Divorce certificate (certified copy)	Divorced persons
Certificate of no criminal record (original)	Each person (18 years and over)
Proof of apartment rental in Austria	Main applicant
Proof of health & accident insurance	Each person, including children
Copy of passport or ID document	Each person, including children
Four (4) color passport photos	Each person, including children
Power of attorney	Each person (18 years and over)

The main applicant must also submit an original bank reference proving assets of US$20,000 for each person. If documents are not in German, they must be accompanied with a certified translation in German.

Consider the foreigner who uses Austria as their second residence, but not as the "center of their vital interests," (a phrase from Austrian tax law). The person goes skiing for three or four weeks each year in Austria. Their legal domicile (the place where they live most of the time and to which they eventually intend to return) is in another country.

Unlike the United States, unless you actually reside in Austria, you pay tax only on your local income in Austria. All other income not earned in Austria is taxable in the country where they live, their domicile. Their exact tax status and obligations will be determined under the terms of a double taxation treaty that may exist between Austria and their country of domicile. It's definitely a good deal worth considering.

There is no requirement that you remain in Austria once you obtain a passport. You could live in Switzerland, which provides wealthy immigrants the opportunity to negotiate an annual payment of a flat tax. Or you could live in a zero-tax jurisdiction such as Panama or The Bahamas.

Another benefit of an Austrian passport is the country's traditional neutrality. Austrians have a long history as mediators due to the country's location in the center of Europe. The country enjoys good relations with Russia, China, Cuba, Iran, and Middle Eastern countries. You'll find that an Austrian passport is welcome almost anywhere, and, in a "terrorist" situation, less likely to raise political antagonism than, for instance, a U.S. or U.K. passport. Finally, with an Austrian passport, you'll be eligible to purchase real estate in Austria and throughout the EU, with fewer restrictions than would otherwise apply.

The biggest disadvantage of Austrian citizenship is that, in most cases, you must give up any previous citizenship, generally within two years of obtaining your Austrian passport.

A U.S. passport is required for entry into Austria. A visa is not required for business or tourist stays up to 90 days.

Contacts

Embassy of Austria

3524 International Court NW
Washington, DC 20008
Tel.: (202) 895-6700
Fax: (202) 895-6750
Email: austroinfo@austria.org
Web: http://www.austria.org/

United States Embassy

Boltzmanngasse 16 1090
Vienna, Austria
Tel.: + (43-1) 313-390
Fax: + (43-1) 310-0682
Email: embassy@usembassy.at
Web: http://austria.usembassy.gov/

Consular Section

Parkring 12a 1010
Vienna, Austria
Visa Information/ Appointment Hotline: + (43-0900) 510-300
Fax: + (43-1) 512-5835
Email: ConsulateVienna@state.gov
Web: http://vienna.usembassy.gov

Recommended Residence & Citizenship Consultants:

The Nestmann Group

Dr. Gabriela Kleeber, Esq.

Hertha Firnbergstrasse 9/311, 1100 Vienna, Austria
Tel.: + (43) 1 587 57 95 60
Email: drkleeber@nestmann.com
Web: http://www.nestmann.com/

Henley & Partners AG
Klosbachstrasse 110
8024 Zurich, Switzerland
Tel.: +41 44 266 22 22
Vienna Tel.: +43 1 532 0 777 77
Email: vienna@henleyglobal.com
Web: https://www.henleyglobal.com/countries/austria/

Kingdom of Belgium

Government:	Federal parliamentary democracy under a constitutional monarchy
Capital:	Brussels
National Day:	21 July (1831) ascension to the Throne of King Leopold I
Population:	10,444,268 (July 2013 est.)
Total Area:	30,528 sq km 203,861 sq mil
Languages:	Dutch (official) 60%, French (official) 40%, German (official) less than 1%, legally bilingual (Dutch and French)
Ethnic groups:	Fleming 58%, Walloon 31%, mixed or other 11%
Religion:	Roman Catholic 75%, other (includes Protestant) 25%
Life expectancy:	79.78 years
Currency:	Euro (EUR)
GDP:	US$427.2 billion (2012 est.)
GDP per capita:	US$38,500 (2012 est.)

At long last, Belgium, it seems, has come of age. This little country recently celebrated its 175th anniversary of independence and, following several years of big, bold moves to shake off a mousy image, life is now on a pretty even keel. Sure, there are ups (tennis greats) and downs (don't mention the national debt), but most Belgians are more than happy with their spot in the world, and wouldn't change it. For a hearty dose of the medieval architecture and atmosphere in time-capsule condition, Bruges is a lovely spot, despite the fact that hordes of tourists would agree. Brussels and Antwerp are both dynamic cities, or scale down the pace a touch in Ghent, once a medieval city to rival Paris and today one of the swingingest towns in Belgium. — Lonely Planet

History and Overview

Located in Western Europe, bordering the North Sea, between France and the Netherlands, Belgium became independent from the Netherlands in 1830. It was militarily overrun and occupied by Germany during both World Wars I and II.

Although Belgium is a parliamentary democracy, it is also a hereditary constitutional monarchy with the king as head of state. King Albert II ascended to the throne in 1993 reigning until 2013. On 21 July 2013, he abdicated the throne for health reasons and was succeeded by his son, Prince Philippe, Duke of Brabant. In doing so, he was the second Belgian king to abdicate following his father, King Leopold III, who abdicated in 1951. Under a recent constitutional reform, the throne is accessible to male and female members of the royal family.

The unitary Belgium of 1830 gave birth to a current, more complex structure on three levels: the upper level comprises the federal state, the Communities and the Regions; the middle level is occupied by the Provinces; and the lower level is that of the Communes. Accordingly, Belgium is made up of three "communities," (the Flemish, the French and the German speaking Communities) three Regions (the Flemish Region, the Brussels-Capital Region and the Walloon Region), 10 provinces and 589 communes.

Tensions between the Dutch-speaking Flemings of the north and the French-speaking Walloons of the south have led in recent years to constitutional amendments granting these regions formal recognition and autonomy. This ethnic division also has caused political stalemate following closely divided elections. In 2007 after a close parliamentary election, there was widespread talk of a possible breakup of the kingdom split into Flanders and Wallonia. Coalition talks went on for most of a year before a new prime minister was chosen.

Other challenges facing Belgium, like many Western European countries, include an ageing population, affordability of social security, integration of migrant workers, the issue of asylum seekers and sustainable development.

Politics and Economy

The only thing many Americans might know about Belgium is that it is the birthplace of Agatha Christie's best-selling, PBS television detective, Hercule Poirot. However, Belgium has been called the crossroads of Western Europe — and for good reason.

Most west European capitals are within 1,000 km (625 miles) of the capital city of Brussels, which serves as the official headquarters of both the European Union and North Atlantic Treaty Organization (NATO). As a result, about 3,800 diplomats are accredited in Brussels, second only to New York City, home of the United Nations.

With an area the size of the American State of Maryland and a population similar to the State of Michigan, Belgium prospered in the past half century as a modern, technologically advanced European state and member of NATO and the EU.

This modern, private-enterprise economy has capitalized on its central geographic location, highly-developed transport network, and diversified industrial and commercial base. Industry is concentrated mainly in the populous Flemish area in the north. With few natural resources, Belgium must import substantial quantities of raw materials and export a large volume of manufactures, making its economy unusually dependent on the state of world markets.

About three-quarters of Belgian trade is with other EU countries, and it has benefited most from its proximity to Germany. Despite a relative recent improvement in Belgium's budget deficit, public debt hovers around 100% of GDP, a factor that has contributed to investor perceptions that the country is increasingly vulnerable to spillover from the euro-zone crisis. Belgian banks were severely affected by the international financial crisis in 2008 with three major banks receiving capital bailouts from the government, and the nationalization of the Belgian retail arm of a Franco-Belgian bank. An ageing population and rising social expenditures are mid- to long-term challenges to public finances.

Residence

Belgium's liberal immigration laws make it uncommonly easy for entrepreneurs, self-employed individuals and investors, who are not EU citizens, to acquire immediate resident status. Citizenship can follow in as little as three years. After three of proven physical residence, there is an official procedure by which one can declare themselves as a citizen. The government is bound by law to accept that declaration unless there is an official statement giving a valid reason for denying citizenship. A person can also retain their existing passport since Belgium recognizes dual nationality.

The Belgian tax system is very favorable for individuals and executives, holding companies within international structures and individuals of independent means. That also makes Belgium an attractive location for relocation of other EU citizens for reasons of personal tax planning. Belgium imposes no capital gains tax, and as a result is attracting an increasing number of wealthy tax exiles.

Upon arrival in Belgium, a foreigner must report to the local authorities in the municipality where they are resident. For stays in Belgium for more than three months documentary proof may consist of documents such as marriage certificate, birth certificate, proof of divorce, etc., notarized and translated if necessary, and must be submitted to the municipal authority in your place of residence in Belgium at the time you register.

Citizens of other countries who wish to live in Belgium for more than three months are required to apply to the Belgian consulate in their home countries for a visa, submitting their work permit, a certificate of good conduct covering the last five years and a medical certificate, along with any other documents specified by the Belgian authorities.

The biggest drawback is that you must learn French, although no one expects perfect speakers. One must also demonstrate some degree of personal integration in Belgium. But if you learn some French, rent an apartment, and appear to be settling down in Belgium, you'll probably qualify for a Belgian passport, especially if you're willing to live there most of the time.

Citizenship

Belgian citizenship is based upon the Code of Belgian Nationality of 1984 and 1992 and is acquired in the following ways:

1. by birth: birth within the territory of Belgium does not automatically confer citizenship.

2. by descent: to a child born in Belgium, at least one of whose parents is a citizen of Belgium. This same rule applies for an adopted child. If a child is born abroad, at least one of whose parents was a native-born citizen of Belgium; parents have up to five years to register the child to obtain citizenship.

3. children of immigrants: citizenship may be granted when:

   a) the child is born in Belgium to non-citizens who were also born in Belgium;

   b) the child is born to non-citizens who have lived in Belgium at least 10 years before the birth of the child and who have filed a citizenship claim for the child;

   c) a child born in Belgium, who has resided there continuously since birth, may make a declaration of Belgian nationality between the ages of 18 and 30.

4. by naturalization: Belgian citizenship may be acquired upon fulfillment of the following two conditions: a person is at least 18 years of age and has resided in the country for at least 3 years, as described above.

Applications are submitted to the registrar in the Belgian municipality where the applicant is a resident. They are forwarded to the Chamber of Representatives for decision. The Belgian passport allows visa-free travel to 171 countries.

Travel Requirement, Visas

U.S. citizens do not require a visa to visit Belgium for 90 days or less.

If a visa is needed when you visit Belgium it is advisable to apply at least three weeks prior to your departure date. In some cases, the Ministry of Interior Affairs may need more time to process a visa application. A picture and fingerprints will be taken of visa applicants at the Embassy of Belgium in various countries. These biometric data are sent electronically to Belgian border control for verification at entry in Belgium or other Schengen area countries. (For more about the Schengen Area, see page 453.)

Visa requirements for visits to Belgium of up to 90 days are shown for each country on the Foreign Affairs, website at http://diplomatie.belgium.be/en/services/travel_to_belgium/visa_for_belgium/

For visits of more than 90 days, a visa is required for non-EU citizens.

Although a visa is not required, visitors may be subject to border control and asked to prove the purpose of the trip and sufficient financial means if not an EU citizen. Proof can take the form of one or more of the following documents: proof of hotel reservation, return ticket or proof of adequate means of subsistence such as cash, checks or credit cards accepted in Belgium or an original copy of a pledge of financial support.

Contacts

Embassy of Belgium
3330 Garfield Street NW
Washington, DC 20008
Tel.: (202) 333-6900
Web: http://www.diplobel.us

Consulates General: Atlanta, Los Angeles, and New York.

United States Embassy
Regentlaan, 27 Boulevard du Regent
B-1000 Brussels
Mail address: PSC 82, Box 002, APO AE 09710
Tel.: + (32-2) 811-4000
Email: usvisabrussels@state.gov
Web: http://belgium.usembassy.gov/

Recommended Immigration Consultant:

Henley & Partners BVBA
Lange Klarenstraat 22
2000 Antwerp, Belgium
Tel.: +32 328 843 43
Email: belgium@henleyglobal.com
Web: www.henleyglobal.com/belgium

The BRP Belgium Residence Program® (BRP) is a service provided by Henley & Partners for non-EU citizens who are interested in obtaining a residence permit.

Republic of Bosnia Herzegovina

Government: Republic
Capital: Sarajevo
National Day: Statehood Day: 25 November (1943)
Population: 3,875,723 (July 2013 est.)
Total Area: 19.70 sq. miles, 51,197 sq kilometers
Languages: Bosnian, Croatian , Serbian (all 3 official)
Ethnic groups: Bosniak 48%, Serb 37.1%, Croat 14.3%, other
                     0.6% (2000)
Religion: Muslim 40%, Orthodox 31%, Roman Catholic
                     15%, other 14%
Life expectancy: 76.12 years
Currency: Konvertibilna marka (BAM)
GDP: US$31.57 billion (2012 est.)
GDP per capita: US$8,100 (2012 est.)

Once known for tragic reasons, Bosnia and Herzegovina now features in travel plans as people realize what this country has to offer: age-old cultures, stunning mountain landscapes, access to the great outdoors and a sense of adventure. This most easterly point of the West and the most westerly point of the East bears the imprint of two great empires. Five hundred years of domination, first by the Turks and then briefly by the Austria-Hungarians, have inexorably influenced the culture and architecture of this land.

In Sarajevo, minarets, onion-shaped domes and campaniles jostle for the sky in a town where Muslims, Jews, Orthodox Christians and Catholics once lived in harmony. Alluring Baščaršija is a jumble of cobbled laneways spanning centuries of activity. Here workshops for ancient crafts are mixed in with cafés, souvenir shops, and trendy bars. There's also plenty to lure visitors away from the capital. Mostar's Old Bridge has been rebuilt and daring young men now plunge from its heights to amuse the tourists. Small Jajce delights with its medieval citadel and waterfall while Međugorje attracts thousands to its Virgin Mary apparition site.

Most likely it'll be in adventure sports where Bosnia and Hercegovina will make its name. Already its major rivers are rafted and kayaked and its mountains are skied, climbed and hiked over, and as more out-of-the-way areas are made safe this country could easily become the year-round adventure center of Eastern Europe. — Lonely Planet

Background and History

The Kingdom of Bosnia evolved in the 14th century and was

absorbed into the Ottoman Empire that ruled from the mid-15th to the late 19th centuries. The Ottomans brought Islam to the region, and altered much of the culture and society. This was followed by control by the Austro-Hungarian Empire that lasted until World War I. That war was sparked by the assassination of the heir to the Austro-Hungarian throne, Archduke Francis Ferdinand and his wife, Sophie, in Sarajevo on June 28, 1914 by a Serbian nationalist terrorist. In the interwar period, Bosnia was part of the Kingdom of Serbs, Croats and Slovenes and after World War II, the country was granted full republic status with a newly formed Yugoslav Federation.

Bosnia and Herzegovina's declaration of sovereignty in 1991 was followed by a declaration of independence from the former Yugoslavia on 3 March 1992 after a referendum boycotted by ethnic Serbs. The Bosnian Serbs supported by neighboring Serbia and Montenegro, responded with armed resistance aimed at partitioning the republic along ethnic lines and joining Serb-held areas to form a "Greater Serbia."

In 1994, Bosniaks and Croats reduced the number of warring factions from three to two by signing an agreement creating a joint Bosniak/Croat Federation of Bosnia and Herzegovina. On November 21, 1995, in Dayton, Ohio, the warring parties initialed a U.S. sponsored peace agreement that ended three years of ethnic civil strife. The Dayton Accords retained Bosnia and Herzegovina's international boundaries and created a multi-ethnic and democratic government.

Also recognized was a second tier of government composed of two internal entities roughly equal in size: the Bosniak/Bosnian Croat Federation of Bosnia and Herzegovina and the Bosnian Serbia Republic. These two are responsible for most government functions. The Chairmanship of the Presidency rotates every eight months among three Presidency members (Bosniak, Serb, Croat), each elected for a four-year term. The three members of the Presidency are directly elected by federation votes for the Bosniak and Croat, and the Serb Republic for the Serbs. The Parliamentary Assembly is the lawmaking body and consists of the House of Peoples and the House of Representatives each split three equal ways in membership.

An original NATO-led international peacekeeping force of 60,000 troops assembled in 1995 was succeeded by a smaller, NATO-led Stabilization Force. In 2004, EU peacekeeping troops took over and now deploy about 600 troops as police.

This bifurcated government served to institutionalize ethnic hostilities and largely failed to deliver promised services. In early 2014, demonstrators set fire to government buildings in violent protests that continued for days in the capital Sarajevo and the northern town of Tuzla. The protesters were unhappy about economic and political progress where about 40% were unemployed. The unrest was the worst since the end of the Bosnian war. Observers said the complex administrative framework of the dual government and political divisions had led to political stagnation and vulnerability to corruption.

Economy

Bosnia has a transitional economy with limited market reforms relying heavily on the export of metals as well as on remittances from abroad and foreign aid. A highly decentralized government hinders economic policy coordination and reform, while excessive bureaucracy and a segmented market discourage foreign investment.

The ethnic warfare caused production to plummet by 80% from 1992 to 1995 and unemployment to soar. Since 2009, GDP has stagnated and foreign banks from Austria and Italy now control most of the banking sector.

The Konvertibilna marka (convertible mark or BAM), the national currency since 1998, is pegged to the euro, and confidence in the currency and the banking sector has increased. Bosnia's private sector is growing, but foreign investment has dropped. Government spending, at roughly 50% of GDP, remains high because of multiple government offices at the state and municipal level. Privatization of state enterprises has been slow, particularly in the Federation, where political division between ethnically-based political parties makes agreement on economic policy more difficult. High unemployment remains the most serious macroeconomic problem.

A large share of economic activity occurs in the black market. Bosnia and Herzegovina is a member of the U.N. and became a full member of the Central European Free Trade Agreement in 2007. The country's top economic priorities are integration into the EU, a stronger fiscal system, public administration reform, World Trade Organization (WTO) membership and economic growth by fostering a dynamic, competitive private sector. In 2011, the International Monetary Fund (IMF) aid was suspended after a parliamentary deadlock left Bosnia without a state-level government for over a year.

Residence and Citizenship

The majority of people granted citizenship in Bosnia and Herzegovina in recent years originated from neighboring Serbia and Croatia, many obtaining this status on the basis of a Dual Citizenship Agreement between Bosnia and Herzegovina and Serbia. According to the Ministry of Human Rights and Refugees dating from 2008, the total number of Bosnia and Herzegovina persons who live outside the country is about 1,350,000, about 26% of the total population.

Details of visas for entry into the country can be found at: http://www.sps.gov.ba/index.php?option=com_content&id=50& Itemid=14&lang=en

Since the 1995 Dayton agreement, citizenship of Bosnia and Herzegovina and of each of the three internal entities is recognized in law without discrimination. All citizens of either entity are citizens of Bosnia and Herzegovina.

All persons who were citizens immediately prior to the entry into force of the 1992 constitution are citizens of Bosnia and Herzegovina. Citizens may hold the citizenship of another state, provided that there is a bilateral agreement with that state. Each entity may issue passports of Bosnia and Herzegovina to its citizens.

Because of the complex nature of the laws specific questions should be addressed to the embassy.

Contacts

Embassy of Bosnia Herzegovina
2109 E Street NW
Washington, DC 20037
Tel.: + (202) 337-1500
Email: info@bhembassy.org
Web: http://www.bhembassy.org/

United States Embassy
1 Robert C. Frasure Street
71000 Sarajevo, Bosnia Herzegovina
Tel.: +387 33 704-000
Email: bhopa@state.gov
Web: http://sarajevo.usembassy.gov/index.html

Republic of Bulgaria

Government:	Parliamentary democracy
Capital:	Sofia
National Day:	Liberation Day: 3 March (1878)
Population:	6,981,642 (July 2013 est.)
Total Area:	42,823 sq. miles / 110,910 sq. kilometers
Languages:	Bulgarian 84.5%, Turkish 9.6%, Roma 4.1%, other 1.8%
Ethnic groups:	Bulgarian 83.9%, Turk 9.4%, Roma 4.7%, other 2% Macedonian, (Armenian, Tatar, Circassian)
Religion:	Bulgarian Orthodox 82.6%, Muslim 12.2%, other Christian 1.2%,
Life expectancy:	74.08 years
Currency:	Lev (BGL)
GDP:	US$105.5 billion (2012 est.)
GDP per capita:	US$14,500 (2012 est.)

Five centuries subjugated to Ottoman rule and, more recently, four decades locked very firmly behind the Iron Curtain turned Bulgaria into a distant, enigmatic country in the eyes of much of the rest of the world. Images of cheap wine downed at student house parties, budget ski holidays and umbrella-wielding Cold War assassins were once among the popular stereotypes, but Bulgaria today is a vastly different country from what it was even 10 years ago.

Getting around the country is easy, with cheap and efficient public transport to ferry you between the cities and into the remoter, rural corners, where the traditional, slow pace of life continues much as it has done for centuries. Here, you'll come across multi-colored monasteries, filled with fabulous icons and watched over by bushy-bearded priests, and impossibly pretty timber-framed villages with smoke curling lazily over the stone-tiled roofs and donkeys complaining in the distance, where head-scarfed old ladies and their curious grandchildren still stare in wonderment at the arrival of outsiders.

The cities, too, are often overlooked highlights, from dynamic, cosmopolitan Sofia with its lovely parks, sociable alfresco bars and fascinating museums, to the National Revival architectural treasures and Roman remains of Plovdiv, and the youthful maritime cockiness of Varna. —Lonely Planet

History and Overview

Bulgaria is situated in southeastern Europe on the eastern Balkan Peninsula bordering the Black Sea, between Romania and Turkey. The terrain is varied containing large mountainous areas, fertile valleys, plains, and a coastline along the Black Sea.

The history of Bulgaria has been determined by its location between Asia and Europe, by its proximity to powerful states competing for land and influence at the junction of trade routes and strategic military positions, and by the strong national territorial drive of various Bulgarian states.

Before the Christian era, Greece and Rome conquered the region and left substantial imprints on the culture of the people. The Bulgars, a Central Asian Turkic tribe, merged with the local Slavic inhabitants in the late 7th century to form the first Bulgarian state. In succeeding centuries, Bulgaria struggled with the Byzantine Empire to assert its place in the Balkans, but by the end of the 14th century, the country was overrun by the Ottoman Turks. Northern Bulgaria attained autonomy in 1878 and all of Bulgaria became independent from the Ottoman Empire in 1908.

Having fought on the losing side in both World Wars, Bulgaria fell within the Soviet sphere of influence and became a People's Republic in 1946. Communist domination ended in 1990, when Bulgaria held its first multi-party election since World War II and began the contentious process of moving toward political democracy and a market economy, while combating inflation, unemployment, corruption, and crime. Reforms and democratization kept Bulgaria on a path toward integration into the EU. The country joined NATO in 2004 and the EU in 2007.

On the January 1, 2014, nine European Union states, including Germany, France, the Netherlands and Britain, lifted labor restrictions that excluded Bulgarians and Romanians. But even before then many skilled and unskilled laborers found work in those and other EU countries.

The numbers explain why Bulgarians and their Romanian neighbors want to be elsewhere.

The wealthiest one-fifth of people in Bulgaria and Romania (an EU member since 2007), have a lower median income than the poorest one-fifth of society in Britain, France, Germany or other wealthy EU states, according to income data obtained from Eurostat, the EU statistics office. The cost of living is much lower in Sofia, but higher pay beckons elsewhere. Bulgaria's unemployment has increased sharply. After bottoming a low of 6% at the end of 2008, it rose to 13.2% at the end of 2013. GDP contracted by 5.5% in 2009, stagnated in 2010, grew 1.7% in 2011 and 1% in 2012.

Politics and Economy

Bulgaria is a constitutional republic. Extensive legislative changes were made to harmonize Bulgarian laws with EU legislation and encourage development and growth of a market economy.

Bulgaria, a formerly Communist-controlled country, has experienced economic stability and strong growth since a major economic downturn in the 1990s led to the fall of the then socialist government. As a result, the government became committed to economic reform and responsible fiscal planning.

Minerals, including coal, copper, and zinc, play an important role in industry. Low inflation and steady progress on structural reforms improved the business environment. Bulgaria has averaged 4% growth since 2000 and has begun to attract significant amounts of foreign direct investment.

The global downturn sharply reduced domestic demand, exports, capital inflows, and industrial production. GDP contracted by approximately 5% in 2009, and stagnated in 2010, despite a significant recovery in exports. The economy is growing modestly in 2011. Corruption in the public administration, a weak judiciary, and the presence of organized crime remain significant challenges. In addition, Bulgaria has a large impoverished minority of Roma, also known as "Gypsies."

In 2014, Bulgarians expressed great frustrations with a succession of governments, corruption and the country's inability to escape from its Soviet roots. It remains Europe's poorest nation. Bulgaria's output, per capita, is last among the 28 EU states, according to the International Monetary Fund. Wages are among the lowest on the continent prompting long and bitter strikes as the old problems of bureaucratic incompetence and organized-crime remain. In 2013, daily street demonstrations followed when the Socialist-led government attempted to appoint a wealthy media mogul as security minister.

Until recently foreign investment had created a construction boom, not just around the larger beach and mountain tourist resorts, but in the cities, too. More tourists were discovering this country and foreigners were investing in property. Now that has slowed and the Bulgarian population is declining faster than almost anywhere else in Europe. Environmental damage caused by overdevelopment has been a cause for public alarm and several organizations campaigning to bring issues to world attention.

However much they complain, though, Bulgarians are a patriotic, if modest, bunch; when they ask you, as they often will, if you like their country, they genuinely care that you leave with good impressions.

Citizenship

Bulgarian law recognizes four methods of obtaining citizenship:

1. by descent: a person who has at least one Bulgarian citizen as a parent is considered a Bulgarian citizen of origin.

2. by birth: a person born in the Republic of Bulgaria, or on a Bulgarian boat or airplane, is considered as a citizen by birth, unless they acquire another nationality of origin.

3. by naturalization: foreigners for whom Bulgaria has been their place of usual residence for more than five years can acquire Bulgarian citizenship via naturalization. A person with a foreign nationality, an unknown nationality or no nationality, but who is married to a Bulgarian citizen, can acquire Bulgarian citizenship without waiting the five-year minimum requirement. Children under the age of 14 can acquire Bulgarian citizenship if their parents have acquired it.

4. by re-instatement: a person who had their Bulgarian citizenship revoked, have renounced it or who have had their naturalization annulled, can reapply for citizenship, but this provision is rarely exercised.

The law allows ethnic Bulgarians to be granted citizenship with a simplified process on a priority basis.

Residence and Visas

Visas are issued by Bulgarian embassies and consulates, not at the airports or the land and sea passport control points in Bulgaria. A visa is issued only to holders of passports or travel documents that are valid for Bulgaria for at least three months after the end of the intended stay and that contain a blank page for affixing of visa stamps. All children entering Bulgaria must have their own passport. Upon entry into Bulgaria, foreigners should declare in writing the purpose of their stay and the address at which they will reside on a registration form. Citizens of the EU member-states and the citizens of the countries in the Economic European Area are exempt from registering.

A U.S. passport is required for U.S. citizens who are not also dual Bulgarian nationals. U.S. citizens who enter the country without a Bulgarian visa are authorized to stay for no more than a total of 90 days within a six-month period. This law is strictly enforced.

An application to extend one's stay beyond the original 90 days can be filed for urgent or humanitarian reasons, but must be submitted to police authorities no later than five days prior to the end of the original 90-day period. Travelers who have been in the country for 90 days, and then leave, will not be able to reenter Bulgaria before the six-month period expires.

Long-term visas or "D" type visas can be obtained from the Bulgarian Consular service. This visa is for foreign nationals who intend to apply for a long-term or permanent residence in Bulgaria; processing takes up to 30 days. Foreign nationals can obtain long-term or permanent residence in Bulgaria on several grounds. Investors with a business that employs more than 10 Bulgarians and retired people with pensions are among this group.

Citizenship for Sale

In 2013, Bulgaria joined the several countries that grant permanent residence and eventual citizenship to qualified foreign investors.

In an attempt to boost that country's ailing economy, foreigners are required to invest BGN 500,000 Bulgarian levs (US$352,000) and create 10 jobs in "high-priority investment projects" in industry, infrastructure, transport or tourism BGN 600,000 (US$322,000) will qualify you, as will an investment of one million levs (US$703,000) in public companies or joint ventures or by depositing that amount a Bulgarian bank for a period of five years. Information is available from the Embassy of Bulgaria, Washington, D.C.

In 2014, the integrity of Bulgarian investor visa programs was called into serious questions when an undercover investigation by the London Daily Telegraph exposed what appeared to be illegal activities selling access to the EU for a minimum of US$250,000, plus US$50,000 for middle men.

Reporters posing as representatives of an "Indian businessman" were told that a Bulgarian passport could be obtained "legally" without the need to live or work in Bulgaria as the law requires. If an applicant deposited sufficient funds, they were told they need only visit the country for two days to obtain all the rights of EU citizens. Even someone with a criminal record who had been turned down for a British passport could qualify for Bulgarian citizenship.

Contacts

Embassy of Republic of Bulgaria
1621 22nd Street NW
Washington, DC 20008
Tel.: (202) 387-0174 / 299-0273 / 483-1386
Fax: (202) 234-7973
Email: office@bulgaria-embassy.org and consulate@bulgaria-embassy.org
Web: http://www.bulgaria-embassy.org

United States Embassy
16 Kozyak Street Sofia, Bulgaria
Tel.: + (359-2) 937-5100
Fax: + (359-2) 937-5122
Email: acs_sofia@state.gov
Web: http://bulgaria.usembassy.gov

Republic of Croatia

Government:	Presidential/parliamentary democracy
Capital:	Zagreb
National Day:	Independence Day: 8 October (1991)
Population:	4,475,611 (July 2013 est.)
Total Area:	21,831 sq. miles / 56,542 sq. kilometers
Languages:	Croatian 96.1%, other and undesignated 2.9% (including Italian, Hungarian, Czech, Slovak, and German), Serbian 1%
Ethnic groups:	Croat 89.6%, other 5.9% (Bosniak, Hungarian, Slovene, Czech, Roma), Serb 4.5%
Religion:	Roman Catholic 87.8%, none 5.2%, Orthodox 4.4%, Muslim 1.3%, other unspecified 0.9%, other Christian 0.4%
Life expectancy:	75.79 years
Currency:	Kuna (HRK)
GDP:	US$79.69 billion (2012 est.)
GDP per capita:	US$18,100 (2012 est.)

Despite the hype, Croatia's pleasures are more timeless than trendy. Along its 1104 mile coastline, a glistening sea winds around rocky coves, lapping at pine-fringed beaches. Istrian ports bustle with fishermen while children dive into the sparkling water. In Dalmatia, cities throb with nightlife amid ancient Roman ruins.

Yachts glide up the coast, movie stars discreetly arrange to buy one of Croatia's 1185 islands and no Mediterranean cruise is complete without a stop in Dubrovnik. The interior landscape is as beguiling, even though less visited. Soak in a thermal spa at

Istarske Toplice in Istria. Hike through pristine forests watered by mountain streams in the west. Let the waterfalls of Plitvice moisten your face. And then there's the culture. The country that endured Roman, Venetian, Italian and Austro-Hungarian rule has a unique and slightly schizoid identity.

You'll find a strong central European flavor in the baroque architecture of Zagreb, and Italian devotion to the good life percolates up from the coast, permeating Croatian food and style. During holidays and festivals the country's Slavic soul emerges, as colorfully costumed dancers whirl about to traditional folk melodies.

Croatians retain a strong attachment to the land and traditions that nourished the dream of independence for so long. Even as a tide of speculators and developers wash ashore, there is a real commitment to preserving the extraordinary beauty of the coast. Whether the country can hold out against the lure of easy money is an excruciating test of its character. But, so far the signs are promising. — Lonely Planet

History and Overview

Croatia is located in southeastern Europe, bordering the Adriatic Sea at the crossroads of the Mediterranean, Central Europe and the Balkans. It has an odd shape that resembles a crescent or a horseshoe, which accounts for its several neighbors: Slovenia, Hungary, Serbia, Bosnia and Herzegovina, Montenegro, and Italy across the Adriatic.

The Croats are believed to be a purely Slavic people who migrated from Ukraine and settled in present day Croatia during the 6th century. After a period of self-rule, Croatians agreed to the Pacta Conventa in 1091, submitting themselves to Hungarian authority.

By the mid-1400s, concerns over Ottoman expansion led the Croatian Assembly to invite the Habsburgs, under Archduke Ferdinand in Vienna, to assume control over Croatia. Habsburg rule proved successful in thwarting the Ottomans, and by the 18th century, much of Croatia was free of Turkish control. The lands that today comprise Croatia were part of the Austro-Hungarian Empire until the close of World War I. In 1918, the Croats, Serbs and Slovenes formed a kingdom known, after 1929, as Yugoslavia.

Following World War II, Yugoslavia became a federal independent Communist state under the strong hand of the dictator Marshal Josef Broz Tito. Although Croatia declared its independence from Yugoslavia in 1991, it took four years of sporadic, but often bitter, fighting before occupying Serb armies were mostly cleared from Croatian lands. Under UN supervision, the last Serb-held enclave in eastern Slavonia was returned to Croatia in 1998. Tensions continue between Serbia and Croatia over the alleged mistreatment of Serbian minorities within Croatia.

In 2009, Croatia joined NATO; it is a candidate for eventual EU accession. On July 1, 2013 Croatia joined the EU, following a decade long application process. Croatia will be a member of the European Exchange Rate Mechanism until it meets the criteria for joining the Economic and Monetary Union and adopts the euro as its currency. Croatia's high foreign debt, strained state budget, and over-reliance on tourism revenue could hinder immediate economic progress.

In a 2013 referendum in Croatia, 66% of its population supported a constitutional ban on gay marriage. There are efforts to ban the use of Cyrillic, the traditional Slavic script used in Russia and several Eastern European countries. The Croatian government says it will refuse to abide by a vote for a ban on Cyrillic and opposes the negative vote against same-sex marriage. Some accuse the far right in Croatia of "fascism" but it seems that events here demonstrate a larger EU problem as traditional nationalist pressures and democratic tensions collide.

Politics and Economy

Croatia is a presidential/parliamentary constitutional democracy. Since the adoption of the 1990 constitution, Croatia has been a democratic republic. The president is the head of state, directly elected to a five-year term and limited to a maximum of two terms. In addition to being the commander in chief of the armed forces, the president appoints the prime minister with the consent of parliament. The Croatian Parliament (Sabor) is a unicameral legislative body elected by popular vote to serve four-year terms.

Before the dissolution of Yugoslavia, the Republic of Croatia, after Slovenia, was the most prosperous and industrialized area with a per capita output perhaps one-third above the Yugoslav average. Growth, while impressive at about 3% to 4% for the last several years, has been stimulated, in part, through high fiscal deficits and rapid credit growth. Croatia is expected to return to growth in 2014. In 2013, Croatia's economy regressed for the fifth consecutive year.

More than 90% of the local banking industry is owned by parent banks from Italy, Austria, France and Hungary. In Croatia, more than 42% of housing loans and 47% of car loans are tied to the Swiss currency, a major concern. Nevertheless, difficult problems still remain, including a stubbornly high unemployment rate, a growing trade deficit and uneven regional development. The state retains a large role in the economy, as privatization efforts often meet stiff public and political resistance. While macroeconomic stabilization has largely been achieved, structural reforms lag because of deep resistance on the part of the public and lack of strong support from politicians.

The EU accession process should accelerate fiscal and structural reform. While long term growth prospects for the economy remain strong, Croatia will face significant pressure as a result of the global financial crisis. Croatia's high foreign debt, anemic export sector, strained state budget, and over-reliance on tourism revenue will result in higher risk to economic stability over the medium term.

Taxes

Croatia combines beautiful scenery, first-class amenities, low prices, and a convenient location within a two-hour flight from virtually any point in Europe. It also allows unique tax advantages for persons who receive certain types of foreign income or a foreign pension.

Croatian residents are generally taxed on their worldwide income. However, there are important exemptions that make Croatia attractive for tax-advantaged residence. With proper planning, dividends, interest payments, pensions received from abroad, capital gains from trading securities and other financial assets, and capital gains from long-term holdings in real estate can all be received tax-free for foreign residents of the country. Croatia also offers important tax advantages to yacht owners.

Foreign nationals who wish to stay longer than three months in Croatia must obtain a residence permit. To obtain one, it is sufficient to have a yacht moored in a Croatian marina or to rent or own an apartment. An application for residence involves submitting various government forms and identification documents, including proof of sufficient funds, and requires a visit to Croatia followed by six to eight weeks processing time. The residence permit is valid for a maximum of one year and can be renewed easily.

Residence

A foreigner can become a resident for tax purposes in Croatia in one of two ways: 1) physical presence or; 2) available residential accommodation. You meet the physical presence test if you stay for at least 183 days under circumstances that indicate your visit is not temporary. You meet the available accommodation test if you have a residence in Croatia at your exclusive and continuous disposal for at least 183 days under circumstances that indicate you intend to keep and use it.

Your length of stay is not important, nor does it matter if the residence is owned or rented. Such "deemed residence" is very attractive for foreigners who wish to maintain legal residence in Croatia without having to be physically present for a minimum period.

Prices of Croatian real estate have been increasing at an average rate of 20% per annum in recent years. However, in top locations, prices have risen much more quickly. Real estate prices in many parts of the Dalmatian coast have doubled. There is a high demand for luxury real estate on the Adriatic coast, yet only a limited supply.

Foreign persons can purchase real estate in Croatia with approval of the Ministry of Foreign Affairs, which may require up to six months. However, the restrictions can legally be avoided if a Croatian company buys the property, and it can be owned and controlled by a foreign person. Using a company for this purpose also avoids capital gains tax and the 5% transfer tax on the subsequent sale of the property.

In view of future EU membership, Croatia is already adjusting its laws and regulations to comply with EU standards. For example, the current restrictions on foreign real estate ownership will be abolished in just two years from now, a fact that will no doubt make Croatia even more attractive for foreigners in the future.

Citizenship

Since the law on Croatian citizenship came into effect in 1991, 1.15 million people have been granted Croatian citizenship. Most of the applications came from the territory of the former Yugoslavia, approximately to 800,000 people from Bosnia-Herzegovina, 93,000 from Serbia and Montenegro, 18,000 from Slovenia, and 14,000 from Macedonia.

The law on Croatian citizenship defines a Croatian citizen as every person who acquired Croatian citizenship according to the regulations applicable on the day the law took effect. This included individuals who held citizenship of the Socialist Republic of Croatia within the former Socialist Federal Republic of Yugoslavia.

For those who did not acquire citizenship automatically, the law sets out a procedure for members of the "Croatian people," who are eligible for citizenship as long as they submit a written statement that they consider themselves Croatian citizens. Others must go through a lengthy process of naturalization and fulfill stringent requirements established for naturalization.

These include possession of a registered place of residence for a period of not less than five years in Croatia before the filing of the petition; proficiency in the Croatian language and Latin script; and that he or she accepts the Croatian culture. Those born within the territory of the Republic of Croatia are exempted from some requirements.

Croatian law provides for citizenship based on ancestry. Persons of Croatian descent ("emigrants") may be naturalized as Croatian citizens without the usual residence and language requirements. Proof of Croatian-born parents or grandparents is required, along with appropriate supporting documentation. In addition, a foreign citizen who is married to a person of Croatian descent who has acquired Croatian citizenship, according to these provisions, can also acquire Croatian citizenship without residence and language requirements.

Children can acquire Croatian citizenship by naturalization only after both parents have acquired citizenship by naturalization.

Travel Requirements

A passport is required for travel to Croatia. A visa is not required for U.S. passport holders for tourist or business trips of fewer than 90 days within a six-month period. All foreign citizens must register with the local police within 24 hours of arrival and inform the office about any change in their address. Registration of foreign visitors staying in hotels or accommodations rented through an accommodation company is done automatically by the hotelier or accommodation company. Failure to register is a misdemeanor offense; some Americans have been fined as a result of their failure to register.

U.S. citizens already in Croatia who wish to remain in Croatia for more than 90 days must obtain a temporary residence permit from the local police having jurisdiction over their place of residence in Croatia. With their residence application, applicants will need to provide a copy of their birth certificate, and a police report authenticated for use abroad from their state of residence in the U.S. or from the country where they permanently reside.

Contacts

Embassy of the Republic of Croatia

2343 Massachusetts Avenue NW
Washington, DC 20008
Tel.: (202) 588-5899
Fax: (202) 588-8936
Email: public@croatiaemb.org
Web: http://www.croatiaemb.org
Consulates in New York, Chicago, and Los Angeles.

United States Embassy

2 Thomas Jefferson Street
10010 Zagreb, Croatia
Tel.: + (385) 1-661-2200
Consular services: + (385) 1-661-2300
Web: http://zagreb.usembassy.gov

Recommended Immigration Consultant:

Henley & Partners

Mihovilova Sirina 3
21000 Split
Tel.: +385 21 321 027
Fax: +385 21 321 028

Czech Republic

Government:	Parliamentary democracy
Capital:	Prague (Praha)
National Day:	Czech Founding Day: 28 October (1918)
Population:	10,162,921 (July 2013 est.)
Total Area:	30,450 sq. miles / 78,866 sq. kilometers
Language:	Czech 94.9%, Slovak 2%, other 2.3%, unidentified 0.8%
Ethnic groups:	Czech 90.4%, other 4%, Moravian 3.7%, Slovak 1.9%
Religion:	Roman Catholic 26.8%, Protestant 2.1%, other 3.3%, unspecified 8.8%, unaffiliated 59%
Life expectancy:	77.56 years
Currency:	Czech koruna (CZK)
GDP:	US$291.7 billion (2012 est.)
GDP per capita:	US$27,600 (2012 est.)

For a country that's only been around since 1993, the Czech Republic does a fine job of showcasing an exciting history. Here, the past becomes real. Castles and chateaux abound, illuminating the stories of powerful families and individuals whose influence was felt well beyond the nation's current borders. Unravel the history of Bohemia and Moravia, the two ancient lands that now make up the modern Czech Republic and you're unearthing the history of Europe itself.

And when you've had your fill of the past, return to Prague, one of the world's most beautiful and cultured cities, and one of the most exciting with a dynamic music and arts scene. Down the world's best beer in the brewery towns of Plzeň and Česke

*Budějovice, and discover the laidback scenes in Česky Krumlov
and Telč. Everywhere you go, you'll meet a forthright people,
proud of their heritage, but now confidently taking their place
in a modern, united Europe. — Lonely Planet*

History and Overview

The Czech Republic is a landlocked country in Central Europe
surrounded by Poland, Germany and Slovakia. Once part of the
Holy Roman Empire, and later the Austro-Hungarian Empire,
Czechoslovakia became an independent nation in 1918 at the end
of World War I. Independence ended with the Nazi German military takeover in 1939.

The medieval Kingdom of Bohemia was absorbed into the
Habsburg Empire at the height of its splendor, and the country's
nobility continued to lavish cultural and architectural marvels on
it throughout the Austro-Hungarian period. Prague, the capital, is

known as one of the most beautiful cities in Europe, with a vibrant and innovative cultural life. The country offers palaces, churches, museums, orchestras, fine dining, world-famous beer and wine, and a relaxed but edgy lifestyle to the visitor or expatriate.

After World War II, Czechoslovakia fell under the forced Soviet sphere of influence. In 1968, an invasion by Warsaw Pact troops snuffed out anti-Communist demonstrations. With the collapse of the Soviet Union in 1991, Czechoslovakia regained its freedom in Václav Havel's "velvet revolution. It is, perhaps, not a coincidence, that the Czechs bestowed the country's presidency upon a well-known playwright, Václav Havel, as soon as they threw off the Soviet yoke.

On January 1, 1993, the country peacefully split in a "velvet divorce" into its two traditional ethnic components, the Czech Republic, comprising Bohemia and Moravia, and the new country of Slovakia. The Czech Republic joined NATO in 1999 and the European Union in 2004.

The Czech Republic, largely by aspiring to become a NATO and EU member, has moved toward integration in world markets. Nevertheless, the government has had a difficult time convincing the public that membership in NATO is crucial to Czech security. At the same time, support for eventual EU membership continues. Coupled with the country's economic difficulties, Prague's political scene, troubled for the past few years, looks to remain so for the near future.

Economy

Of the former Communist countries in Central and Eastern Europe, the Czech Republic has one of the most developed and industrialized economies. Its strong industrial tradition dates to the 19th century, when Bohemia and Moravia were the industrial heartland of the Austro-Hungarian Empire. The Czech Republic has a well-educated population and a well-developed infrastructure. The country's strategic location in Europe, low-cost structure and skilled work force have attracted strong inflows of foreign direct investment, rapidly modernizing its industrial base and increasing productivity.

The principal industries are motor vehicles, machine building, iron and steel production, metalworking, chemicals, electronics, transportation equipment, textiles, glass, brewing, china, ceramics, and pharmaceuticals. The main agricultural products are sugar beets, fodder roots, potatoes, wheat, and hops. As a small, open economy in the heart of Europe, economic growth is strongly influenced by demand for Czech exports and the flow of foreign direct investment.

With all its problems, the Czech Republic is probably the most westernized. The transition to a free-market economy seems to have progressed more smoothly than other countries. Privatization and restitution of communist confiscated property is nearing completion. The country has adopted an income flat tax of from 17% to 19% to apply both to companies and to individuals.

The Czech Republic is one of the most prosperous of the post-Communist states of Central and Eastern Europe. Maintaining an open investment climate has been a key element of the Czech Republic's transition from a communist, centrally planned economy to a functioning market economy. As a member of the EU, with an advantageous location in the center of Europe, a relatively low cost structure, and a well-qualified labor force, the Czech Republic is an attractive destination for foreign investment. Despite the global financial crisis, the conservative Czech financial system has remained relatively healthy.

When Western Europe and Germany fell into recession in 2008, demand for Czech goods plunged, leading to double digit drops in industrial production and exports. As a result, real GDP fell but has slowly recovered with positive growth. The auto industry remains the largest single industry and, together with its suppliers, accounts for as much as 20% of Czech manufacturing. The Czech Republic produced more than a million cars for the first time in 2010, over 80% of them exported.

Foreign and domestic businesses voice concerns about corruption, especially in public procurement. Other long-term challenges include dealing with a rapidly aging population, funding an unsustainable pension and health care system, and diversifying away from manufacturing and toward a more high-tech, services-based, knowledge economy.

Czech politics have been in turmoil in recent years. There have been four different prime ministers during 2012 and 2013 and street demonstrations have been common protesting corruption and incompetence.

The former ruling parties suffered heavily in the October 2013 elections because of their austerity policies that cut living standards. In early 2014, a three-party coalition was formed by the Social Democrats, the billionaire Andrej Babis' party "Action for Dissatisfied Citizens," and the conservative Christian Democrats. Observers doubt that this government will be capable of solving the long-standing political crisis. Industry and business lobbies expect the new coalition to implement a long-planned assault upon low wages and social conditions, which has been delayed by factionalism and continuous regime changes.

Residence and Citizenship

In principle, any child born to a Czech citizen is a Czech citizen at birth, whether the child is born in the Czech Republic or elsewhere. Where only the father is Czech, and the parents are unmarried, proof of paternity is required.

Children born in the Czech Republic to non-Czech parents do not acquire Czech citizenship unless the parents are stateless and at least one parent is a permanent resident of the Czech Republic.

During the Communist regime (1948 to 1989), hundreds of thousands of Czechoslovakian citizens emigrated to Western Europe and were punished by having their citizenship revoked. Since the Velvet Revolution in 1989, many emigrants have had citizenship reinstated under a 2004 law.

Persons who have enjoyed at least five years permanent residence and have resided in the Czech Republic for most of that time can apply for naturalization. They must be of good character and prove proficiency in the Czech language.

Over 26,000 foreigners have been granted Czech citizenship since 2001, more than two-fifths of whom have come from the neighboring Slovakia, followed by 2,400 Ukrainians.

The Czech Republic grants "economic citizenship." Entrepreneurs setting up their businesses in the country are eligible for permanent residence, which may lead to naturalization after five years.

Naturalization can be applied for after five years of formal residence. During that period, a permanent resident enjoys most rights of full Czech citizens, including the right to purchase real property. Czech passports are valid for five years and allow visa-free travel to most EU countries as well as Switzerland, excluding France and the U.S. Any foreign national willing to establish a new business or is self-employed will be welcomed by the Czech government.

A valid U.S. passport is required for entry into the Czech Republic. Visas are not required for U.S. citizens for tourist, short study or business visits of up to 90 days. Visas are required for longer stays and for any gainful activity. Americans living in or visiting the Czech Republic are encouraged to register at the Consular Section of the U.S. Embassy in the Czech Republic and obtain updated information on travel and security within the Czech Republic.

Contacts

Embassy of the Czech Republic
3900 Spring of Freedom Street NW
Washington, DC 20008
Tel.: (202) 274-9100
Fax: (202) 966-8540
Email: washington@embassy.mzv.cz
Web: http://www.mzv.cz/washington

United States Embassy
Trziste 15, 11801 Praha 1 (Prague), Czech Republic
Tel.: + (420) 257-022-000
Email: consprague@state.gov
Web: http://prague.usembassy.gov

Recommended Immigration Consultant:

Henley & Partners
Na Príkope 22, Slovanský dum
110 00 Praha 1
Tel.: +420 221 451 50

Kingdom of Denmark

Government:	Constitutional Monarchy
Capital:	Copenhagen
National Day:	June 5
Population:	5,556,452 (July 2013 est.)
Total Area:	43,094 sq km
Languages:	Danish, Faroese, Greenlandic (Inuit dialect), German (minority)
Ethnic groups:	Scandinavian, Inuit, Faroese, German, Turkish, Iranian, Somali
Religion:	Evangelical Lutheran (official) 95%, other Christian (includes Protestant and Roman Catholic) 3%, Muslim 2%
Life Expectancy:	78.94 years
Currency:	Danish kroner (DKK)
GDP:	US$213.6 billion (2012 est.)
GDP per capita:	US$38,300 (2012 est.)

The Danes are, overwhelmingly, a happy bunch. In fact, if you believe those contentment surveys that come out every couple of years, Denmark is one of the happiest nations on earth with some of the best quality of life. Along winding cobbled streets Danes shop and dine at some of the most exciting places in Europe. Even standards in a workaday Danish café are generally very high.

Beyond the capital and the bigger cities, Denmark offers a mix of lively towns such as Ribe and Odense plus rural countryside, medieval churches, Renaissance castles and tidy 18th-century villages. Neolithic dolmen, preserved 2000-year-

old 'bog people', and impressive Viking ruins are just some of
the remnants of the nation's long and fascinating history.

Centuries on from the Viking era, Denmark remains very
much a maritime nation, bordered by the Baltic and the North
Sea. No place in the country is more than an hour's drive from
its lovely seashore, much of which is lined with splendid white-
sand beaches.

This first-rate destination seems like good value, and you get
the fairy tales thrown in for free: the Danish royal family is genuinely loved and respected by the vast majority of its citizens, not
least handsome Prince Frederik, his beautiful Australian-born
princess-bride, Mary, and their young family. — Lonely Planet

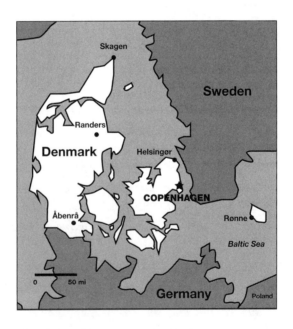

History and Overview

Once the seat of Viking raiders and later a major north European power Denmark has evolved into a modern, prosperous nation and participant in the political and economic integration of Europe. It joined NATO in 1949 and the EEC (now the EU) in 1973. However, the country has opted out of certain elements of the European Union's Maastricht Treaty, including the European Economic and Monetary Union (EMU), European defense cooperation, and issues concerning certain justice and home affairs.

Located in Northern Europe, little Denmark (26,777 square miles, of which 410 square miles are water), borders on the Baltic Sea and the North Sea, on a peninsula north of Germany (Jutland) and also includes several major islands (Sjaelland, Fyn, and Bornholm). It also includes the non-contiguous Faroe Islands and Greenland.

There appears to be nothing rotten in the state of Denmark. For the second straight year, in 2013 Denmark was named the happiest country, according to a survey of 156 nations called the World Happiness Report. Based on Gallup data collected from 2010 to 2012, the survey covered measures such as life expectancy, social support, freedom to make life choices, and perceptions of corruption and generosity.

Economy

This thoroughly modern market economy features a high-tech agricultural sector, state-of-the-art industry with world-leading firms in pharmaceuticals, maritime shipping and renewable energy, and a high dependence on foreign trade. Denmark is a member of the EU; Danish legislation and regulations conform to EU standards on almost all issues.

Danes enjoy among the highest standards of living in the world and the economy is characterized by extensive government welfare measures and an equitable distribution of income. Literacy is

100%; education is free, and about half of all Danish students who graduate from secondary school continue on to higher education. Denmark is a net exporter of food and energy and enjoys a comfortable balance of payments surplus, but depends on imports of raw materials for the manufacturing sector. Within the EU, Denmark is among the strongest supporters of trade liberalization.

After a long consumption-driven upswing, Denmark's economy began slowing in 2007 with the end of a housing boom. The global financial crisis intensified this slowdown through increased borrowing costs and lower export demand, consumer confidence, and investment. The global financial crises cut Danish GDP starting in 2008. Historically low levels of unemployment rose sharply with the recession exceeding 6%.

Denmark made a modest recovery in part because of increased government spending. An impending decline in the ratio of workers to retirees is a major long-term issue. Denmark maintained a healthy budget surplus for many years up to 2008, but the budget balance swung into deficit during 2009 to 2010. Nonetheless, Denmark's fiscal position remains among the strongest in the EU.

Despite previously meeting the criteria to join the European Economic and Monetary Union (EMU), so far Denmark has decided not to accept the euro, although the Danish krone remains pegged to the euro.

Taxes

Demark is not a low tax country if you reside here or operate a business in Denmark; however it has legislation in place that makes it a favorable center for holding companies used by international business.

Because of tax rules and the Kingdom's many international double taxation treaties, many businesses benefit from the fact that you can escape taxation on dividend income by having a Danish holding company. Such companies potentially can receive dividend payments and capital gains from its foreign subsidiaries without any Danish tax being imposed, provided that certain criteria are met.

In 2012, a coalition of major parties produced an income tax reform that benefits those employed by increasing the earned income credit, while many with middle and upper incomes benefit from having the top tax bracket increased by US$10,700 to US$860,400 by 2022.

Immigration Debate

Denmark has some of the tightest immigration regulations in the EU. Even so, it has about 320,000 "nonwestern" immigrants and their descendants constituting 5.9% of the population, most of them either Muslim or black or both. A 2011 government report claimed that this immigrant group cost the country annually US$2.8 billion in welfare and housing, while those from "western" countries contributed to the Danish economy. In 2005, when a Danish newspaper published cartoons satirizing the Prophet Muhammad, Muslims rioted and attacked violently Danes and Danish embassies in many countries.

Immigration and a declining birth rate for ethnic Danes has sparked passionate debate about the effects on a country with a history that is homogenous and mono-cultural. A center-right coalition government with its main ally in parliament, the conservative Danish People's Party, adopted curbs on immigration but narrowly lost a majority in national elections in 2011.

The Prime Minister, Helle Thorning-Schmidt, became a worldwide household name in December 2013 when a photograph of her taking a smartphone "selfie" with U.S. President Barack Obama and British Prime Minister David Cameron at Nelson Mandela's memorial service in South Africa went viral worldwide.

Thorning-Schmidt, 46, is not a new face on the world scene, despite her relative anonymity, as she was elected Denmark's first female prime minister in 2011, just six years after becoming the first woman to lead the country's Social Democratic Party. Prior to that, she served in the European parliament from 1999 to 2004.

Danish laws that govern immigration now have a strict point system allocated according to factors such as age, qualifications and Danish language ability. Demark also has introduced a "anti-ghetto strategy" aimed at preventing immigrants in public housing concentrating in large numbers. The children of immigrants deemed unable to speak proper Danish are required to attend special classes.

These laws also have targeted people using marriage as a means of gaining access to Denmark. In order to marry a foreigner; 1) both the Danish and the foreign partner need to be at least 24 years old; 2) the Danish partner needs to post a bond of collateral US$11,600; 3) the foreign partner has to pass a language and knowledge test, and; 4) both must demonstrate a combined attachment to Denmark greater than to any other country. This has reduced the number of asylum seekers by two-thirds since 2006.

Residence

Denmark is part of the Nordic passport-free zone that includes Norway, Sweden, Finland and Iceland, citizens of which can freely enter Denmark and reside in the country as long as they wish. As an EU member state, Denmark is a Schengen agreement country and citizens living in Schengen countries can travel freely between the countries without any form of border control.

Non-EU member Swiss nationals and others that live in the European Economic Area EA can obtain a special registration card from the Danish government. As an interim measure, special rules apply to citizens from certain EU countries who seek paid work in Denmark.

Permanent residence is not granted unless the applicant meets numerous criteria that are listed at http://www.nyidanmark.dk/en-us/coming_to_dk/permanent-residence-permit/permanent-residence-permit.htm

Those from outside Europe visiting as a tourist, on business or with Danish family members may need a visa. At www.newtodenmark.dk/visa there is a list of the countries whose citizens require a visa before traveling to Denmark. A visa is valid for up to three months but does not permit work.

A detailed description of Danish immigration laws and rules is at: http://www.nyidanmark.dk/en-us/authorities/the_ministry/the_organisation/the_immigration_department.htm

Citizenship

Danish nationality can be acquired in one of the following ways:

1. automatically at birth;

2. automatically if the parents marry after the child's birth;

3. automatically if a person is adopted as a child under 12 years of age;

4. by declaration for nationals of another Nordic country;

5. by naturalization by statute.

Under section 1 of the Nationality Act, a child automatically acquires Danish nationality at birth if the parents are married and either the father or the mother is a Danish national without regard to where in the world the child is born.

If the child's parents are not married at the birth, the child automatically acquires Danish nationally if born to a Danish mother. If the mother is a foreigner and the father is a Danish national, the child will only acquire Danish nationality if born in Denmark. If the child is born abroad, the child has to apply for Danish nationality by naturalization.

A special procedure applies to Nordic nationals from Finland, Iceland, Norway and Sweden. In certain situations, nationals of other Nordic counties may become Danish nationals by submitting a declaration to a regional Danish state administration office.

Contacts

Embassy of Denmark
3200 Whitehaven Street NW
Washington, DC 20008
Tel.: +1 (202) 234-4300
Email: wasamb@um.dk
Web: http://usa.um.dk/

United States Embassy
Dag Hammarskjolds Alle 24,
2100 Copenhagen O, Denmark
Tel.: +45 33-41-71-00
Emergency Tel.: + 45 33-41 7400.
Email: copenhagenirc@state.gov
Web: http://denmark.usembassy.gov/

Republic of Estonia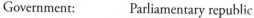

Government:	Parliamentary republic
Capital:	Tallinn
National Day:	Independence Day: 24 February (1918)
Population:	1,266,375 (July 2013 est.)
Total Area:	17,462 sq. miles / 45,226 sq. kilometers
Languages:	Estonian (official) 67.3%, Russian 29.7%, other 2.3%
Ethnic groups:	Estonian 67.9%, Russian 25.6%, other 2.2%, Ukrainian 2.1%, Belorussian 1.3%, Finn 0.9%
Religion:	Evangelical Lutheran 13.6%, Orthodox 12.8%, unaffiliated 34.1%, other and unspecified 32%, none 6.1%, other Christian 1.4%
Life expectancy:	73.82 years
Currency:	Euro
GDP:	US$29.57 billion (2012 est.)
GDP per capita:	US$22,100 (2012 est.)

Although the smallest of the Baltic countries, Estonia (Eesti) makes its presence felt in the region with its lovely seaside towns, quaint country villages and verdant forests and marshlands, all of which set the scene for discovering many cultural and natural gems.

Yet Estonia is also known for magnificent castles, pristine islands and a cosmopolitan capital amid medieval splendor. It's no wonder Estonia is no longer Europe's best-kept secret. Tallinn, Estonia's crown jewel boasts cobbled streets and rejuvenated 14th-century dwellings. Dozens of cafés and restaurants make for an atmospheric retreat after exploring

*historic churches and scenic ruins, galleries and boutiques.
By night, stylish lounges and youthful nightclubs offer a
glimpse of the city's sexier side. Some visitors have a hard
time escaping Tallinn's undeniable allure, but outside the
capital, the bucolic landscape hides numerous attractions.
South of Estonia's cosmopolitan spiritual center, Tartu, is
the hilltop town of Otepää with its laidback atmosphere
and lovely ski trails.*

*Handsome beach towns, spa resorts and medieval ruins lie
scattered about the western shores of the country. Further west
lies Estonia's biggest island, Saaremaa where iconic windmills,
19th-century lighthouses, unspoiled beaches and yet more medieval ruins transport visitors to another time. This all makes
a nice prelude to a sauna, one of the national pastimes. —
Lonely Planet*

History and Overview

Estonia's struggles for independence during the 20th century were, in large part, a reaction to nearly 700 years of foreign rule. Before 1200, the Estonians lived largely as free peasants loosely organized into parishes, which, in turn, were grouped into counties. In the early 1200s, the Estonians and the Latvians came under assault from German crusaders seeking to impose Christianity on them. Although the Estonians' resistance to the Teutonic Knights lasted some 20 years, the lack of a centralized political organization as well as inferior weaponry eventually brought down the Estonians in 1227.

After centuries of Danish, Swedish, German, and Russian rule, Estonia attained independence in 1918. Forcibly incorporated into the USSR in 1940, it regained its freedom in 1991, with the collapse of the Soviet Union. Since the last Russian troops left in 1994, Estonia has been free to promote economic and political ties with Western Europe. It joined both NATO and the EU.

Economy

Estonia, as a new member of the World Trade Organization and the EU, transitioned effectively to a modern market economy with strong ties to the West, including the pegging of its currency to the euro. The economy benefitted from strong electronics and telecommunications sectors and is greatly influenced by developments in Finland, Sweden and Germany — three major trading partners.

In 1994, Estonia became the first country in Europe to introduce a so-called "flat tax," replacing three tax rates on personal income, and another on corporate profits, with one uniform rate of 26%. The Economist commented: "Simplicity itself. At the stroke of a pen, this tiny Baltic nation transformed itself from backwater to bellwether, emulated by its neighbors and envied by conservatives in America who long to flatten their own country's taxes." Experts attribute subsequent growth in large part to the flat tax, which was adopted soon afterward by neighboring Latvia and Lithuania.

Rapid growth, however, has made it difficult to keep inflation and large current-account deficits from soaring, putting downward pressure on the country's currency. The government has not given up on joining the euro, but has repeatedly postponed its euro adoption target. Mirroring the rest of Europe and the U.S., Estonia's economy slowed and fell into recession in mid-2008, primarily as a result of an investment and consumption slump following the bursting of the real estate market bubble.

Tallinn's priority has been to sustain high growth rates — on average 8% per year from 2003 to 2007. Estonia's economy fell into recession in 2008 with GDP contracting 14.3% in 2009, as a result of an investment and consumption slump following the bursting of the real estate market bubble and a decrease in export demand as result of economic slowdown in the rest of Europe. Estonia rebounded nearly 8% in 2011 and the Estonian economy now has one of the higher GDP growth rates in a recessionary Europe at 3.9%. Estonia adopted the euro on January 1, 2011.

Estonia has developed into a strong international actor, through its membership in the EU and NATO; it is a capable advocate and promoter of stability and democracy in the former Soviet Union and beyond. Estonian troops have been in Afghanistan since 2002 and Iraq since 2003. It participates in the NATO training mission in Iraq. Estonia also provides peacekeepers for international missions in Bosnia, Kosovo, and Lebanon and contributes to EU battle groups and NATO Response Force rotations. It supports democratic developments in key countries of the former Soviet Union and beyond by providing training to government and law enforcement officials as well as nongovernmental organizations. It has valuable experience to offer new democracies from its own recent history, and it works hard to promote democracy, freedom, and stability worldwide.

Residence and Citizenship

Any alien who wishes to acquire Estonian citizenship by naturalization can submit an application if he or she had settled in Estonia before July 1, 1990, and resides permanently in Estonia when the application is submitted, or has stayed permanently in Estonia on the basis of a long-term residence permit for at least five years prior to the date of submission.

If one of those preconditions is fulfilled, an alien must: be at least 15 years of age; have knowledge of Estonian language needed in daily life; have knowledge of the constitution and the Citizenship Act; have a permanent legal income which ensures his or her own subsistence and that of his or her dependents; be loyal to the Estonian state; and take an oath: "In applying for Estonian citizenship, I swear to be loyal to the constitutional order of Estonia." One must also pass an exam on the constitution and the Citizenship Act and on knowledge of the Estonian language. Exams are given by the National Examination and Qualification Center at Sakala 21, Tallinn.

The following persons are exempted from the examination: adults who are legally incapacitated; persons with severe or serious physical disabilities; or persons with a moderate visual disorder, hearing or speech disability. In the latter cases, a certificate of medical assessment proving the disability from a doctor must be submitted. A person with basic, secondary or higher education in Estonian is exempt from the language exam.

The full text of the citizenship law may be viewed at http://www. uta.edu/cpsees/estoncit.htm. The law governing resident aliens living and working in Estonia is viewable at http://www.uta.edu/cp-sees/estonali.htm.

Foreign Investor Residence

A foreign person may apply for a residence permit for business in Estonia, if the person owns shares in a company in Estonia or acts as a sole proprietor of a business located there, and: a) the person has invested in Estonia a capital sum of at least €65,000 (US$88,500) under his/her control in the case of a company; or b) the person has invested in Estonia a capital sum of at least €16,000 (US$22,000) under his/her control in the case of a sole proprietor. The equity capital of a company subordinated liability and registered fixed assets value may be considered as investment. An official application may be made online in person at https://www.politsei.ee/en/teenused/residence-permit/tahtajaline-elamisluba/ettevotluseks/

Contacts

Embassy of Estonia
2131 Massachusetts Avenue NW
Washington, DC 20008
Tel.: (202) 588-0101
Fax: (202) 588-0108
Email: Embassy.Washington@mfa.ee
Web: http://www.estemb.org/

Estonian Consulate
600 3rd Avenue, 26th Floor
New York, NY 10016
Tel.: (212) 883-0636
Fax: (212) 883-0648

United States Embassy
Kentmanni 20

Tallinn, Estonia
Tel.: + (372) 66-88-100
Email: USASaatkond@state.gov
Web: http://estonia.usembassy.gov/

France

Government:	Republic
Capital:	Paris
National Day:	Fete de la Federation: 14 July (1790)
Population:	65,951,611 (July 2013 est.)
Total Area:	211,210 sq. miles / 547,030 sq. kilometers
Languages:	French 100%, rapidly declining regional dialects and languages: Provencal, Breton, Alsatian, Corsican, Catalan, Basque, Flemish
Ethnic groups:	Celtic and Latin with Teutonic, Slavic, North African, Indochinese, Basque minorities
Religion:	Roman Catholic 83%-88%, Muslim 5-10%, unaffiliated 4%, Protestant 2%, Jewish 1%
Life expectancy.	81.56 years
Currency:	Euro (EUR)
GDP:	US$2.291 trillion (2012 est.)
GDP per capita:	US$36,100 (2012 est.)

Good, bad or ugly, everyone has something to say about France and the French: chic, smart, sexy, rude, racist, bureaucratic, bitchy as hell, pavements studded with dog poo, baguettes that dry out by lunchtime and a penchant for torching cars is some of the chitchat on the street.

Spice up the cauldron with the odd urban riot, political scandal and a 35-hour working week and the international media is all ears too.

This is, after all, that fabled land of good food and wine, of royal chateaux and perfectly restored farmhouses, of landmarks known the world over and hidden landscapes few really know. Savor art and romance in the shining capital on the River Seine. See glorious pasts blaze forth at Versailles. Travel south for Roman civilization and the sparkling blue Med; indulge your jet-set fantasies in balmy Nice and St-Tropez. Ski the Alps. Sense the subtle infusion of language, music and mythology in Brittany brought by 5th-century Celtic invaders.

Smell ignominy on the beaches of Normandy and battle-fields of Verdun and the Somme. And know that this is but the tip of that gargantuan iceberg the French call culture. Yes, this is that timeless land whose people have a natural joie de vivre and savoir-faire and have had for centuries. — Lonely Planet

History and Overview

What is known as Metropolitan France is located in Western Europe, bordering the Bay of Biscay and English Channel, between

Belgium and Spain, southeast of the U.K.; bordering the Mediterranean Sea, between Italy and Spain.

France has several overseas colonies: 1) French Guiana: in northern South America, bordering the Atlantic Ocean, between Brazil and Suriname; 2) Guadeloupe: Caribbean, islands between the Caribbean Sea and the North Atlantic Ocean, southeast of Puerto Rico; 3) Martinique: Caribbean, island between the Caribbean Sea and North Atlantic Ocean, north of Trinidad and Tobago; 4) Reunion: Southern Africa, island in the Indian Ocean, east of Madagascar. In addition it maintains close ties with several independent African countries that were French colonies.

Although ultimately a victor in World Wars I and II, France lost many citizens, much wealth, its extensive global empire, and its rank as one of the world's dominant nation states. The Vichy collaboration with the Nazi occupiers also tarnished national honor and history. Since then, the nation has struggled to construct a strong presidential democracy that avoids the parliamentary instability that characterized France in the early 20th century. Its reconciliation and cooperation with Germany, now its largest trading partner, has been a key to the economic integration of Europe.

With at least 79 million foreign tourists per year, France is the most visited country in the world and maintains the third-largest income in the world from tourism.

France's reputation for style and elegance are well deserved, at least in Paris, and the rest of the country's regions retain many of the local culinary and cultural traditions that made traveling here so rewarding in years past. However, mass culture and consumerism have made visible inroads into France's former charms, while high prices (even without regard to euro fluctuations) and heavy taxation have eliminated most of the "bargains" once associated with travel and life in France.

Economy

Most impartial observers would admit that France is in many ways a socialist basket case. Constant budget deficits, a huge national debt, very high unemployment, especially among the young, onerous and expensive labor rules and high taxes have combined to weaken a once proud nation. After three recessions in five years, France's economic weaknesses are hard to ignore. Growth flat-lined in the third quarter of 2013, unemployment hit 10.9%, up from 7.8% in 2010, and the balance of payments current account, which was consistently in surplus before the crisis, is persistently in deficit.

Under the more conservative Nicolas Sarkozy (23rd President, 2007 to 2012), and his predecessor, Jacques Chirac, an attempt was made to address these problems, but with little success. With a parliamentary majority of their Union for a Popular Movement, Sarkozy, and Chirac before him, tried to transform France from an economy with extensive government ownership and intervention to one that relied more on free market mechanisms. They privatized many large companies, banks, and insurers, and allowed private investment in such leading firms as Air France, France Telecom, Renault, and Thales. Sarkozy was defeated for re-election in 2012 by Socialist François Hollande, who by 2014 had become the most unpopular French president in modern history.

Hit by the world recession, France's real GDP contracted staring in 2009 but recovered somewhat, while the unemployment rate increased from 7.4% in 2008 to 9.5% in 2010. In 2013, it reached the highest in 15 years at 10.4%. The government's aggressive spending, stimulus and investment measures in response to the economic crisis caused a major deterioration of France's public finances. The government budget deficit rose every year while France's public debt rose from 68% of GDP to almost 100% of GDP in 2013. In 2014, France's public debt was projected to reach nearly two trillion euros, despite President François Hollande's plans to cut spending and raise taxes.

Taxes

France's tax burden remains one of the highest in Europe — at nearly 50% of GDP.

It was a royal French finance minister who gave the essential government view toward raising tax revenues. "The art of taxation," Jean-Baptiste Colbert (1619 to 1683), the comptroller general of finances, told Louis XIV before that king's spending got really out of hand, "is to pluck from the goose the most feathers with the least hissing."

In France, the hissing is very loud. According to *Forbes* magazine's annual "tax misery index" the highest (worst) rating goes to France. A US$50,000-a-year manager costs a French company 143% of that amount pre-tax (and 89% on an after-tax basis), after calculating the employer's share of social security and other taxes.

More than 8,000 French households' tax bills topped 100% of their income in 2012. That exceptionally high taxation was due to a one-time tax on 2011 incomes for households with assets of more than US$1.67 million. The Socialist government's attempt in 2013 to introduce a 75% wealth tax on income over US$1,375,000 initially was struck down by the French Constitutional Council as "unfair" because it applied to individuals rather than households. In late 2013, the 75% was imposed as a source withholding tax on the same high income group.

That partially may explain why 500,000 French citizens now live in the lower tax U.K., and 60,000 French engineers call California's Silicon Valley home today. Unless one has a truly compelling reason to work or locate a business in France, the taxes alone should give major pause. In France, a successful US$200,000-a-year executive or entrepreneur gets to keep just US$97,050 after the state has taken its cut.

Residence and Citizenship

The obvious question is why anyone would want to become a resident or citizen of France in its present condition unless they have a very compelling reason.

France has traditionally been a country with a fairly open border policy, but there have been recent efforts, as reflected in a July 2006 law, to restrict the immigration of unskilled workers and persons who would become a burden on the French State. French nationality requirements via marriage are now more difficult. Considerable discretionary power has been given to the French Consulates in their decisions to grant or deny visas.

Non-EU nationals may receive permanent residence, and eventually naturalization, in France. The criteria for residence status are stiff and the procedures time-consuming and often frustrating. Naturalization is available after five years residence.

Foreign nationals wishing to establish residence in France use different procedures depending on their national origin. The three general groups are: 1) nationals from France's fellow EU countries; 2) those from countries with which France has immigration or visa-free travel agreements, such as the United States; and, 3) persons from all other countries.

The EU requires all member-states to allow free international movement of EU persons, including the right to freely engage in commercial business. While the official French policy agrees with this EU principle; they argue that this cannot surmount the French right to live in safety. The French have set up a system of police, judicial and customs, which they say compensates for the removal of border controls between member-states. Immigration has been a very touchy issue in France for two decades, mainly because of the large influx of Muslim, black and other racial groups from the former French colonies in Africa and elsewhere.

France requires other EU nationals wishing to do business within its borders to apply to regional police headquarters (Préfecture de Police) for a residence card (carte de séjour). The applicant must show what business is intended and provide copies of contracts, leases, and corporate documents for a new French company or a business registration certificate for a foreign company opening a French branch.

In the second entry-seeking group are those from countries that have mutual agreements allowing up to three months of visa-free travel in France. These include the non-EU countries of Andorra, Canada, Iceland, Japan, Monaco, Norway, San Marino, South Korea, Switzerland, the Vatican, and the United States. These agreements also allow citizens of each nation to take up residence, temporary or permanent, within France, but they must go through immigration procedures for approval of their status and prove they have sufficient economic means for support.

Citizens from all other countries must first obtain a visa to enter France, without regard to the purpose of the visit, even as a tourist. Proof of intent to return to the applicant's home nation is required. Strong ties to one's home country, such as presence there of close family members, income, assets, and professional status are examined.

Obtaining full citizenship is relatively easy after five years residence, but has drawbacks. Foreign citizens, who are considered to have acquired French citizenship, may be subject to compulsory military service and other aspects of French law while in France. An excellent summary of French immigration law can be found at http://www.frenchlaw.com/Immigration_Visas.htm

Employment

French immigration procedure is tedious, bureaucratic, prolonged, and, often, fruitless. The law views potential resident aliens in terms of "employment," "independent professions" or "commercial activities." Without very specialized skills that French employers are actively seeking, Americans or others will find it very difficult to find legal salaried employment in France. Many young foreigners there are forced to work in the black economy: waiting tables, bartending, washing dishes.

Unless you've been a legal resident in France for at least the past three years, and have acquired a carte de resident, you'll find a well-paid job with legal status difficult to obtain. A prospective employer must obtain authorization to hire a foreigner from the Ministry of Labor. It is unlikely this will be given if there are French citizens who could do the same job.

Except in cases of unique executive level and management jobs, statistical unemployment in the geographic region or the type of job sought precludes approval. Professional positions, medical, legal, accounting, engineering, and architecture require French or equivalent academic and professional qualifications for admission. In less professional positions, such as writers, artists, composers, consultants, and teachers, a simplified, speedier examination process is used. The performing arts are unionized and considered to be employment.

In each case, the prospective employer must initiate the application process. Applications for specific events or for a limited number of engagements are approved quickly, but long-term contracts are less likely to be approved. For foreign nationals seeking permission to buy and sell goods or render services, a special merchant's card is issued in addition to a residence card. That includes commercial agents and company executives. Anyone other than managers of major international companies is likely to have a difficult time obtaining residence and business permission in France. In each case, proof of financial means and a business plan are required.

A passport is required for entry to France. A visa is not required for tourist/business stays up to 90 days. Americans living in or visiting France are encouraged to register at the Consular Section of the U.S. Embassy in Paris or the nearest Consulate and to obtain updated information on travel and security within France.

Contacts

Embassy of France
4101 Reservoir Road NW
Washington, DC 20007
Tel.: (202) 944-6000
Email: info@ambafrance-us.org
Web: http://www.info-france-usa.org/

French General Consulate
4101 Reservoir Road NW
Washington, DC 20007
Tel.: (202) 944-6195; Visa information: (202) 944-6200
Email: info@consulfrance-washington.org
Web: http://www.consulfrance-washington.org

United States Embassy
2 Avenue Gabriel
75382 Paris Cedex 08, France
Physical Address (GPS & Google maps):
2 Avenue Gabriel 75008 Paris France
Tel.: + (33) 1-4312-2222
Web: http://france.usembassy.gov

Federal Republic of Germany

Government:	Federal republic
Capital:	Berlin
National Day:	Unity Day: 3 October (1990)
Population:	81,147,265 (July 2013 est.)
Total Area:	137,847 sq. miles / 357,021 sq. kilometers
Languages:	German, English widely spoken
Ethnic groups:	German 91.5%, Turkish 2.4%, other 6.1% (Serbo-Croatian, Italian, Russian, Greek, Polish, Spanish)
Religion:	Protestant 34%, Roman Catholic 34%, unaffiliated or other 28.3%, Muslim 3.7%
Life expectancy:	80.32 years
Currency:	Euro (EUR)
GDP:	US$3.25 trillion (2012 est.)
GDP per capita:	US$39,700 (2012 est.)

Beer or wine? That sums up the German conundrum. One is at the heart of a pilsner-swilling culture that draws keg loads of visitors annually, is the very reason for one of the world's great parties (Oktoberfest) and is consumed with pleasure across the land. The other is exported worldwide, is responsible for gorgeous vine-covered valleys and is enjoyed everywhere, often from cute little green-stemmed glasses.

And the questions about Germany continue. Berlin or Munich? East or west? BMW or Mercedes? In fact, the answers are simple: both. Why decide? The beauty of Germany is that rather than choosing, you can revel in the contrasts (except maybe with the car question...). Exploring this country and all its facets can keep visitors happy for weeks. Berlin, edgy and vibrant, is a grand capital in a constant state of reinvention.

At the other end, Munich perches atop Bavaria, the center of national traditions. Half-timbered villages can't help but bring smiles as you wander their cobblestoned and castle-shadowed lanes. Cities of all sizes boast some of Europe's best clubs, as you'd expect from the home of techno. Enjoying the outdoors, from skiing Alpine peaks to hiking carefully preserved forests, is essential. And compare the ancient traditions of the east, as beautiful Dresden adjusts to the 21st century, with Cologne, where decades of prosperity burnish its grand heritage. — Lonely Planet

History and Overview

As Europe's largest economy and second most populous nation (after Russia), Germany is a key member of the continent's economic, political, and defense organizations. European power struggles immersed Germany in two devastating World Wars in the 20th century and left the country occupied by the victorious Allied powers of the U.S., U.K., France, and the Soviet Union in 1945.

With the advent of the Cold War, two German states were formed in 1949: the western Federal Republic of Germany (FRG) and the eastern German Democratic Republic (GDR). The democratic FRG embedded itself in key Western economic and security organizations, the EC, which became the EU, and NATO, while the communist GDR was on the front line of the Soviet-led Warsaw Pact. The decline of the USSR and the end of the Cold War finally allowed for German unification in 1990. Since then, Germany has expended considerable funds to bring Eastern productivity and wages up to Western standards.

Modern German history is characterized by the immigration of massive numbers of foreign nationals, many of them refugees, but also many as recruited workers. Germany easily has been the favorite destination of European immigrants, but also the target of those from Africa, Asia and Eastern Europe, especially Turkey. The nation took in over four million foreigners by the end of the decade in 2000. In 2013, there still were over 550,000 refugees, stateless persons or asylum seekers resident in Germany. Germany also has an established policy of admitting ethnic Germans from other countries. In the years after World War II, many thousands of German-speaking persons immigrated from Russia, Poland, Ukraine, and elsewhere.

One reason for the refugee influx was the former policy of supplying all needy arrivals with housing, medical attention and relocation financial assistance as well as a temporary passport. However, with high unemployment in the 1990s, a wave of internal political protest against free immigration developed. Particular resentment has been directed against Turks and some other ethnic minorities.

Germany enjoys the world's third most powerful economy, but its capitalist market system has been dragged down by artificially high wages, costly welfare and unemployment benefits. Taxes, both on personal and corporate income, are extremely high and the tax system has been characterized as one of the worst in the world.

In recent years the German government has caused great animosity in neighboring Switzerland and Liechtenstein, accusing both of harboring German tax evaders alleged to be hiding massive funds under cover of bank secrecy laws. Germany has led the attack on financial privacy laws in other nations and against tax havens, even going so far as to pay a million dollar bribe to a convicted thief in order to obtain a list of clients in a Liechtenstein bank.

In 2011, after years of negotiations and verbal warfare, neighboring Switzerland signed a deal with German tax authorities requiring Swiss banks to make an advance payment of US$2.5 billion in back taxes to Berlin based on undeclared German accounts at Swiss banks. Under the terms of the deal, the Swiss will pay taxes in the future but will not release the names of German banking clients, thus preserving the historic principle of Swiss bank secrecy — or whatever remains of that once Swiss sacred ideal of financial privacy. In 2013, the full amount to be paid to Germany by the Swiss approached US$5 billion.

The German nation continues to wrestle with the economic and political integration of eastern Germany, an adjustment that may take decades to fully complete. Economic Minister Ludwig Earhart's astonishing rebuilding of war-ravaged western Germany in the Federal Republic's "Economic Miracle" of the 1950s and '60s was not paralleled in the eastern regions under Soviet domination. The contrast between the two sectors remains striking nearly three decades after reunification. Continued drabness and an air of desperation in the former East German Democratic Republic can still shock those familiar only with the brash consumerism (with a touch of glitz) of the West. The modernization and integration of the eastern German economy, where unemployment exceeds 30% in some municipalities, continues to be a costly long-term process, with annual transfers from west to east amounting to roughly US$80 billion.

A government subsidized, reduced working hours scheme, helps to explain the relatively modest increase in unemployment during the 2008 to 2009 recession, the deepest since World War II, and its decrease to 7.4% in 2010. GDP contracted 4.7% in 2009 but grew by 3.6% in 2010. In its annual projection for 2011, the Federal Government expected the upswing to continue, with GDP forecast to grow in 2011 at a real rate of 2.3%. The recovery was attributable primarily to rebounding manufacturing orders and exports, increasingly outside the euro zone.

Domestic demand has become a more significant driver of Germany's economic expansion. Stimulus and stabilization efforts initiated in 2008 and 2009 and tax cuts introduced in Chancellor Angela Merkel's second term increased Germany's budget deficit to 3.3% in 2010. In 2012, Germany reached a budget surplus of 0.1%. A constitutional amendment approved in 2009 limits the federal government to structural deficits of no more than 0.35% of GDP per annum as of 2016.

Angela Merkel is a centrist politician who has been the Chancellor of Germany since 2005 and the leader of the Christian Democratic Union (CDU) since 2000. She is the first woman to hold either office. She was re-elected in 2013 but failing a majority in the Bundestag, the CDU was forced to form a grand coalition with the leftist Social Democrats.

Residence

Germany encourages entrepreneur or business immigration with offers of loans, tax concessions and subsidies for new businesses that will provide jobs or stimulate the local economy. Particular preference is given to investors who create jobs in the former East Germany. Artists, creative persons, the self-employed, and those who will not compete for local jobs may be able to obtain residence permits and identity cards that have the added benefit of being valid for travel throughout the EU.

Naturalization for full citizenship may be applied for after six to eight years of residence. This time period can be reduced in special cases. These include descendants of refugees from Germany or other countries due to Nazi persecution or invasion, and ethnic Germans and their descendants who were persecuted on political, racial and religious grounds between January 30, 1933, and May 8, 1945. The naturalization process may require as much as one year.

If granted citizenship, Jews are entitled to the same government benefits guaranteed to other Germans. German citizenship is granted under a law that allows Jews who fled Hitler, as well as their children and grandchildren, to become naturalized Germans. For many people, that means receiving a European Union passport that can pave the way for living and working in all of Europe.

The German law, which dates from the 1950s, applies to Jews who were stripped of German citizenship during the Nazi era and their descendants. It can also apply to non-Jews driven from Hitler's Germany for political reasons. Most of those taking advantage of the law are from regions of the former Soviet Union, but there are also applicants from the United States, Canada and Australia. More than 4,000 Israelis also received German citizenship in 2007, a 50% increase over 2006. According to the German government, there are now some 200,000 Jews living in Germany, up from 25,000 before the 1989 collapse of the Berlin Wall.

Citizenship

German citizenship can be obtained in the following ways:

1. by birth to a German parent. Laws regarding citizenship have been changed several times over the last decades. Whether or not a person has acquired German citizenship may therefore depend on the person's date of birth;

   a) If you were born before January 1, 1975: If your parents were married at the time of your birth, you acquired German citizenship if your father was German; you did not acquire German citizenship if only your mother was German (unless you would otherwise have been stateless). If your parents were not married at the time of your birth, you acquired German citizenship if your mother was German; you did not acquire German citizenship if only your father was German.

   b) If you were born on or after January 1, 1975: If your parents were married at the time of your birth, you acquired German citizenship if at least one parent was German. If your parents were not married at the time of your birth, you acquired German citizenship if your mother was German; you did not acquire German citizenship if only your father was German. However, a person born out of wedlock on or after July 1, 1993, can acquire German citizenship if only the father is German and if the father acknowledges paternity.

2. by birth in Germany if you were born after December 31, 1999, to foreign parents in Germany. One of the parents must have been a legal resident in Germany for at least eight years at the time of your birth. In addition, at least one parent must have an unlimited residence permit (*unbefristete Aufenthaltser-laubnis*) or a residence entitlement (*Aufenthaltsberechtigung*) at

the time of your birth. If you obtain another citizenship by birth, you have to give up one or the other citizenship between the ages of 18 and 23.

3. by adoption: If you were adopted by at least one German citizen on or after January 1, 1977, you are considered to be a German citizen. If the adoption happened outside Germany, it must meet certain requirements.

4. by naturalization: Naturalization of people with permanent residence outside Germany is rare. Applicants have to meet numerous requirements; typically, one must renounce your present citizenship(s) in order to become a German citizen; fluency in the German language is another precondition.

A German law of 1913 forbids dual citizenship, but more recent rules make some exceptions. It is thought that the current coalition government may repeal this prohibition, thus easing immigration.

Germany modified their immigration law in 2013, including changes to visa processing and new options for foreign employees with vocational training. In addition, an electronic database (Visa-Warndatei) containing information on immigration violations and criminal activity was created.

A passport is required for entry into Germany. A visa is not required for tourist/business stays up to 90 days within the Schengen group of countries, which includes Germany.

Contacts
Embassy of Germany
2300 M Street NW
Washington, DC 20037
Tel.: (202) 298-4000
Web: http://www.germany.info\

Online contact form: https://www.germany.info/Vertretung/usa/en/Kontakt.html

United States Embassy
Pariser Platz 2
10117 Berlin, Germany
Mail address: Clayallee 170 14191
Berlin, Germany
Tel.: + (49) 30-238-5174
Emergencies after hours: + (49) 30-8305-0
Web: http://germany.usembassy.gov/

Gibraltar

Government:	Overseas territory of the U.K.
Capital:	Gibraltar
National Day:	10 September (1967)
Population:	29,111 (July 2013 est.)
Total Area:	2.5 sq. miles / 6.5 sq. kilometers
Languages:	English (official), Spanish, Italian, Portuguese
Ethnic groups:	Spanish, Italian, English, Maltese, Portuguese, German, North Africans
Religion:	Roman Catholic 78.1%, Church of England 7%, Muslim 4%, other Christian 3.2%, Jewish 2.1%, Hindu 1.8%, other 0.9%
Life expectancy:	78.98 years
Currency:	Gibraltar pound (GIP)
GDP:	US$2.270 billion (2013 est.)
GDP per capita:	US$63,327 (2013 est.)

Looming like some great ship off southern Spain, Gibraltar is a fascinating compound of curiosities. Despite Bobbies on the beat, red post boxes and other reminders of 1960s England, Gibraltar is actually a cultural cocktail with Genoese, Spanish, North African and other elements which have made it fantastically prosperous. Naturally, the main sight is the awesome Rock; a vast limestone ridge that rises to 1,400 feet, with sheer cliffs on its northern and eastern sides. For the ancient Greeks and Romans this was one of the two Pillars of Hercules, split from the other, Jebel Musa in Morocco, in the course of Hercules' arduous Twelve Labors.

The two great rocks marked the edge of the ancient world.

Gibraltar's location and highly defensible nature have attract-ed the covetous gaze of military strategists ever since. Gibral-tarians (77% of the population) speak both English and Span-ish and, often, a curious mix of the two. Signs are in English. Gibraltar's terrific agenda for visitors includes exploring its natural world, its military installations and its quirky town.
— *Lonely Planet*

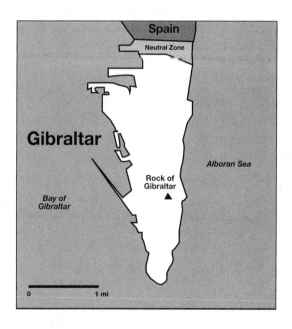

History and Overview

Gibraltar is an Overseas Territory of the United Kingdom locat-ed near the southernmost tip of the Iberian Peninsula, overlooking the Strait of Gibraltar that links the North Atlantic Ocean and Mediterranean Sea. The territory shares a land border with the province of Cadiz in Andalusia, Spain to the north.

In ancient times, people believed that they were safe from falling off the western edge of the supposedly flat world if they remained east of Gibraltar. A self-governing British colony, situated just south of Spain, Gibraltar is at the confluence of the Atlantic Ocean and the Mediterranean Sea. With about 80,000 ships passing through the Straits of Gibraltar every year, its strategic waters are some of the busiest in the world.

Strategically important, Gibraltar was ceded to Great Britain by Spain in the 1713 Treaty of Utrecht. The British garrison was formally declared a colony in 1830. In referenda held in 1967 and 2005, Gibraltarians voted overwhelmingly to remain a British dependency.

Although a 2006 constitution states that the U.K. government will not allow the people of Gibraltar to pass under the sovereignty of another state (Spain) against their freely and democratically expressed wishes, a series of talks have been held by the U.K. and Spain, since 1997, trying to settle sovereignty issues.

In response to these talks, in a 2002 Gibraltar referendum, a majority of citizens voted overwhelmingly against any sharing of sovereignty with Spain. Since the referendum, tripartite talks have been held with Spain, the U.K. and Gibraltar, and a three-way agreement was signed. Nevertheless 2013 saw a new conservative Spanish government threaten to blockade access to The Rock unless the U.K. negotiated over the issue of sovereignty, which London refused to do.

Gibraltar has historically been an important base for the British armed forces and is the site of a British naval base. It is probably most famous for the geological formation, the Rock of Gibraltar. The name of the territory is derived from the original Arabic name Jabal Ṭāriq, meaning "mountain of Tariq" or from Gibr Al-Ṭāriq, meaning "rock of Tariq."

The famous Rock of Gibraltar covers almost 1.5 acres of land and is home to over 140 caves, more than 200 Barbary Macaques (the placid apes who have lived on the rock for over 200 years), and myriad other species of wildlife. Its strategic location and history have made it an international symbol of solidity and strength, and it frequently features its strategic value increased in 1869 with the opening of the Suez Canal, since it controlled the important sea route between the U.K. and its colonies in India and Australia. During World War II, the civilian residents of Gibraltar were evacuated, and the Rock was turned into a military fortress.

Gibraltar has an elected 18-member unicameral parliament with the chief minister as the head of government. There is a well-developed judiciary and executive branch under a British common law system. Queen Elizabeth II appoints a ceremonial Governor General.

Offshore Financial Center

Gibraltar has an extensive service-based economy, dominated by offshore banking and financial services and tourism. Financial services and persons involved in the industry are regulated by the Financial Services Commission, which operates in a similar manner to the United Kingdom Financial Services Authority. Many British and international banks have operations here. Recently, a number of large volume bookmakers and online gaming operators have relocated to Gibraltar to benefit from operating in a well-regulated jurisdiction with a favorable low tax regime.

Gibraltar is the base for many international business corporations. Almost 100,000 companies have been registered to date by the Gibraltar Registrar of Companies, most of them offshore companies that are either tax-exempt or non-resident.

Gibraltar has a corporate tax regime that provides for a low 10% corporate tax. There are no capital gains taxes, inheritance tax, gift, wealth taxes or a value-added tax (VAT).

Under pressure from London, Gibraltar adopted OECD rules on the sharing on tax information as well as negotiated tax information exchange treaties (TIEAs) with other nations. In 2011, it had 18 TIEAs with other countries, including the U.K., Germany, France and the United States.

Self-sufficient Gibraltar benefits from an extensive shipping trade, offshore banking and its position as an international financial center. The British military presence has been sharply reduced and now contributes only about 7% to the local economy, compared with 60% in 1984.

The financial sector, tourism (almost five million visitors a year), shipping services fees, and duties on consumer goods also generate revenue, totaling 30% of GDP. Telecommunications accounts for another 10%. In recent years, Gibraltar has seen major structural change from a public to a private sector economy, but changes in government spending still have a major impact on the level of employment.

In 2008, Gibraltar won a significant victory when the EU's highest court ruled that the Rock had "from a constitutional point of view, a political and administrative status separate from that of the central government of the United Kingdom." In effect, this affirmed the right of Gibraltar to set its own tax policies independent of the U.K., allowing its continuation as a tax haven.

Residence and Citizenship

An application for residence is made under the Immigration Control Ordinance, which permits the governor to issue the necessary permit to any person who, in his opinion, is of good character, in circumstances where he considers that it is in the interests of Gibraltar to issue such a permit.

The Immigration Control Ordinance provides the basic requirements which must be satisfied for the issue of such a permit. Government guidelines highlight factors which are relevant in considering applications for residence as follows:

1. purchase of a property sufficient in size to accommodate the applicant and all his family for residential purposes;

2. applicant must establish that he is in good health; and

3. applicant must establish that he has adequate financial resources to maintain himself and his family without recourse to public funds.

The major factor in the determination of such an application is the purchase of a property. The property must be situated in Gibraltar, and while the granting of the residence permit does not depend on the value of the property purchased, traditionally, the government looks more favorably on applicants who purchase luxury property rather than a purchaser of low-cost housing.

The procedure for application for the citizenship is the same as in the U.K. — you can apply for the citizenship after five years of residence in the territory. Gibraltar recognizes the right to dual citizenship. Citizens of Gibraltar also may apply for registration as a British citizen under Section 5 of the 1981 Act. This is an entitlement and cannot be refused. Persons who have previously renounced British citizenship are also eligible. Persons born in a British Overseas Territory after May 21, 2002, automatically acquire British citizenship (even if they do not acquire territorial citizenship, so long as one parent is a British citizen, settled in the U.K., or settled in an Overseas Territory. There are various procedural means by which the U.K. citizenship can be formally claimed.

In 2013, changes to the Gibraltar Immigration Act eased visas for Moroccans at a time of negotiations between the EU and Morocco for a Comprehensive Free Trade Agreement with the U.K.

with the goal of closer economic integration between Morocco and the EU single market.

Category 2 Status

Gibraltar is also a leading tax haven for wealthy individuals from many nations. It is also home to many international corporations and high net worth "tax exiles" as well as international stock brokerages with access to European markets.

Gibraltar affords individuals whose net worth exceeds GIP2,000,000 (US$3.285 million) a special "Category 2" status. That limits the individual's tax liability to their first GIP80,000 (US$132,000) of assessable income. With the payment of an application fee of US$1,000 and with two letters of reference, one from your banker, the approved HNWIs receive a permanent residence certificate. British citizens resident in Gibraltar enjoy an income tax cap of about GIP30,000 (US$50,000) per annum, less if they have no Gibraltar source income. There are no capital gains, inheritance, wealth or sales taxes in Gibraltar. Assessable income includes all local income under the Gibraltar Income Tax Act 2010 but excludes income accrued from abroad, or income received from a trust.

In addition to a minimum net worth to qualify, residence time requirements are enforced, as is private medical insurance, an established home and a ban on engaging in a trade, business or employment within Gibraltar. There are exceptions to the latter rule if work is incidental to an offshore business or as a director of a Gibraltar exempt company or a director of a company that transacts no trade or business in Gibraltar.

The Category 2 status is popular among retirees but is also available to individuals based in Gibraltar who are shareholders of companies whose activities are carried out outside Gibraltar.

An individual who within the period of five years preceding his application for a Category 2 certificate, has been in Gibraltar for a period greater than 183 days in any one year or 90 days in any three of those five years, or has been in trade, business or employment in Gibraltar prior to his/her proposed application is not eligible for Category 2 status.

The Finance Center Director will issue a certificate if the individual meets the criteria and is of substantial financial standing, of good character and that the issuance will not be harm Gibraltar's reputation as a finance centre.

Contacts

Government of Gibraltar
Web: https://www.gibraltar.gov.gi/
Contacts: https://www.gibraltar.gov.gi/contact-us

Gibraltar Tourist Board
Web: http://www.visitgibraltar.gi/

Gibraltar Finance Center
Web: https://www.gibraltar.gov.gi/finance-centre

Gibraltar Information Bureau
1156 15th Street NW
Washington, DC 20008
Tel.: (202) 452-1108
Web: http://www.gibraltar.gov.uk/

Affairs for Gibraltar, a British Overseas Territory, are handled through the U.S. Embassy in London.

United States Embassy
24 Grosvenor Square London
W1A 1AE United Kingdom
Physical Address (GPS & Google map)s:

Physical Address (GPS & Google map)s:
24 Grosvenor Square
London, W1A 2LQ United Kingdom
Tel.: + (44) 207-499-9000
Email contact form: http://london.usembassy.gov/cons_new/
acs/scs/scs_contact_accordion.html
Web: http://london.usembassy.gov/

Greece (Hellenic Republic)

Government:	Parliamentary republic
Capital:	Athens
National Day:	Independence Day: 25 March (1821)
Population:	10,772,967 (July 2013 est.)
Total Area:	50,942 sq. miles / 131,940 sq. kilometers
Languages:	Greek 99% (official), English, French, ethnic groups, other 7%
Religion:	Greek Orthodox 98%, Muslim 1.3%, other 0.7%
Life expectancy:	80.18 years
Currency:	Euro (EUR)
GDP:	US$281.4 billion (2012 est.)
GDP per capita:	US$24,900 (2012 est.)

Greece offers a myriad of experiences, landscapes and activities. It is the pulsing nightclubs of Mykonos and the ancient beauty of Delos; the grandeur of Delphi and the earthiness of Ioannina; the rugged hillsides of Crete and the lush wildflowers of spring. It is the blinding light of the Mykonos sun, the melancholy throb of Thessaloniki's rembetika (blues songs), the tang of home-made tzatziki, and the gossip in the kafeneia (coffee shops). It is the Parthenon, solitary and pristine lording it over the hazy sprawl of Athens.

Greece is a country with a hallowed past and an at-times turbulent present. Appreciation of the achievements of its classical past has tended to overshadow its development as a free nation since the War of Independence from the Ottomans in 1821. Many foreign Hellenists imbued with a romantic ideal

of the Greece of Pericles and the Parthenon blithely are igno-
rant that Greece today is a vibrant modern European country.

It is equally a land where the languages of recent migrant
communities from the Balkans, Africa and Asia — not to
mention the English and German of EU migrants and retirees
— contribute to Greece's status as one of Europe's more recent
multicultural societies. — Lonely Planet

History and Overview

Greece occupies the southernmost area of the Balkan Peninsula in southeast Europe. It borders Albania, Macedonia and Bulgaria on the north; and Turkey, its largest neighbor, to the east. Over 20% of the nation consists of islands in the Mediterranean, Aegean and Ionian Seas. Visitors from all over Europe flock to the Aegean islands for their warm, Mediterranean climate, abundant sunshine on the beaches, and picturesque villages perched on craggy hillsides.

Greece was the seat of the earliest known European civilization, the Minoan that flourished on the island of Crete from 2300 B.C. to 1400 B.C. By the 2nd century A.D., Greece was part of the Roman Empire, later part of the Byzantine Empire with its capital in Constantinople.

Architectural and archeological remnants of Greece's Classical and medieval past constitute another major drawing point for visitors from abroad. In ensuing centuries, Greece was controlled by the Turks of the Ottoman Empire.

Despite ongoing hostility toward Turkey, vestiges of Turkish rule linger in Greece's cuisine and the thick, sweet coffee preferred throughout the country. The monarchy established in 1828 lasted intermittently until 1973, when Greece was declared a republic. Today, Greece is a member of the European Union, thus, its citizenship allows free access to all of Europe.

Country in Crisis

Greece had a capitalist economy with a large public sector accounting for about 40% of GDP. Until recently tourism provided 15% of GDP, but that has fallen. Immigrants make up nearly one-fifth of the work force, mainly in agricultural and unskilled jobs, but unemployment has skyrocketed to 25%.

A failing Greece has received major EU aid, equal to about 3.3% of annual GDP. The Greek economy grew by nearly 4% per year from 2003 through 2007, partly due to infrastructure spending related to the 2004 Athens Olympic Games, and in part to an increased availability of credit, which sustained record levels of consumer spending.

When the world recession hit in 2009 the economy went into recession, tightening credit, but the Athens government failed to address a ballooning budget deficit. From 2009 to 2012 the economy contracted by nearly 20% and annual deficits reached 15% of GDP.

Deteriorating public finances, inaccurate and misreported statistics, and lack of any real reform plus repeated reports of official corruption prompted major credit rating agencies to downgrade Greece's international debt rating. The country faced a major financial crisis. Under intense pressure from the EU, especially Germany, and international lenders, the government tried to cut government spending, decrease tax evasion, overhaul health-care and pension systems, and reform out da ted labor and product market rules.

This was met with widespread unrest and strikes from government workers and the country's powerful labor unions as well as the general public. In 2010, a leading credit agency assigned Greek debt its lowest possible credit rating; the International Monetary Fund and EU governments gave Greece emergency short- and medium-term loans worth US$147 billion because without help the country was unable to make debt repayments to creditors.

In exchange for the largest bailout ever assembled, the government announced more spending cuts and tax increases totaling US$40 billion over three years, added to tough austerity measures already taken. European leaders and the IMF in 2011 provided Athens a second bailout package of US$169 billion. There was a legislative election in 2012 after which none of the leaders of the top three parties were able to form a government.

This second deal hit Greece's creditors who had to write off a large portion of their Greek government bond holdings. Greece promised an additional US$7.8 billion in austerity measures during 2013 to 2015.

All these moves and massive austerity cuts expanded Greece's economic recession and depressed tax revenues. Many investors doubt that Greece can sustain fiscal efforts in the face of a bleak economic outlook, public discontent, and severe political instability including repeated street riots and destruction of private and business properties as a protest. The Greek situation had a direct damaging impact banks in Cyprus that were heavily invested in Greek loans.

Residence and Citizenship

Thirty years ago, thousands of Greeks were leaving the country in search of a better life in foreign countries, including Germany, the U.S., Canada, Australia, and South Africa. Millions of Greeks became emigrants and Greek communities sprang up all over the world. Now that exodus is being repeated.

Before the 2009 recession Greece had a massive influx of foreign immigrants, legal and illegal, forcing Greek authorities to deal with the immigration issue. In the meantime, Greece became a full member of the EU and the standard of living rose, thus attracting immigrants from other EU member countries. Now that is all reversed.

The question in 2014 is why anyone would want to acquire Greek residence or citizenship?

Greek citizenship can be obtained in two major ways:

1. Those who can prove they have a parent or a grandparent who was born in Greece, or who obtained Greek nationality by birth, can claim Greek citizenship if they can produce documents proving the Greek citizenship of their ancestor.

2. A foreign-born child of Greek citizen parents is automatically eligible for Greek citizenship. A foreign born child with a Greek father and a foreign mother also qualifies. In order to

claim Greek citizenship of a foreign-born child, a certified birth certificate must be registered with the Greek Embassy nearest the place of birth. This should be accompanied by the parents' marriage certificate and the father's birth certificate, if possible.

Greek citizenship is acquired upon the birth of a child in Greece in the event that the child does not acquire another foreign citizenship by birth or citizenship is unknown at time of birth.

Greek law supports dual citizenship and if an applicant wants to keep his/her present nationality that is allowed. Those without Greek ancestors must be at least 18 years of age and legally must have lived in Greece for 10 of the last 12 years to be considered for citizenship. The adult applicant must not have been convicted of any of several crimes, including drug trafficking, money laundering, international economic crimes, crimes committed with the use of modern technology, monetary crimes, crimes against adolescents, smuggling, or any crime with a sentence of a year or more in prison.

If an applicant has no other nationality or qualifies as a refugee, the law requires only five years of residence in Greece during the last 12 years. A non-Greek applicant must have sufficient knowledge of the language, of Hellenic history and of Hellenic civilization in general.

A person who has, or had, Greek parents or grandparents who fled the nation during the Greek Civil War in the late 1940s, is entitled to return to Greece and claim Greek nationality. This process requires from two to six months, but personal presence in Greece is needed only during the last two weeks before completion.

A male foreign national who lives in Greece for more than five years can apply for naturalization with proof of guaranteed employment for a further three years. A foreign wife is eligible for citizenship only after 10 years continuous residence with her husband in Greece. During this period, she is allowed no more than three months a year away from the country.

In rare, special instances, it is possible for foreigners to be granted Greek citizenship on the recommendation of the Greek Ministry of the Interior. Greece recognizes dual nationality, but those holding a second citizenship may be subject to Greek laws, which impose special obligations such as compulsory Greek military service and other aspects of Greek law while in Greece. Many younger Greeks seek foreign citizenship in order to avoid obligatory military service.

For a pdf copy of the Greek citizenship code, see: http://athens.usembassy.gov/uploads/7z/Z4/7zZ4A6EyE4dMjph5dNx-Few/citizenship_code.pdf

A U.S. passport is required, but no visa is needed for tourist or business stays of up to 90 days.

Contacts

Embassy of Greece
2217 Massachusetts Avenue NW
Washington, DC 20008
Tel.: (202) 939-1300
Email: gremb.was@mfa.gr
Web: http://www.greekembassy.org/

United States Embassy
91 Vasilisis Sophias Avenue
10160 Athens, Greece
The Embassy is adjacent to the Megaro Mousikis (Music Hall) near the "Megaro Mousiki" blue line Metro stop.
Tel.: + (0030) 210-720-2419, 2415, 2420, 2408

Email: AthensAmEmb@state.gov
For after-hour emergencies: + (0030) 210-729-4301 or + (0030) 210-729-4444
Web: http://athens.usembassy.gov

Republic of Hungary

Government:	Parliamentary democracy
Capital:	Budapest
National Day:	Saint Stephen's Day: 20 August
Population:	9,939,470 (July 2013 est.)
Total Area:	35,919 sq. miles / 93,030 sq. kilometers
Languages:	Hungarian 93.6%, other or unspecified 6.4%
Ethnic groups:	Hungarian 92.3%, other or unknown 5.8%, Roma 1.9%
Religion:	Roman Catholic 51.9%, Calvinist 15.9%, other 11%, Lutheran 3%, Greek Catholic 2.6%, other Christian 1%
Life expectancy:	75.24 years
Currency:	Forint (HUF)
GDP:	US$198.8 billion (2012 est.)
GDP per capita:	US$20,000 (2012 est.)

There is no place like Hungary. Situated in the very heart of Europe, this kidney-shaped country can claim a unique place in the continent's soul. Doubters need only listen to the music of Franz Liszt and Béla Bartók, view the romantic Danube River as it dramatically splits Budapest in two or taste the nation's unique (and paprika-infused) cuisine to be convinced.

Hungary's impact on Europe's history and development has been far greater than its present size and population would suggest. Hungarians, who call themselves Magyars, speak a language and form a culture unlike any other in the region — a distinction that has been both a source of pride and an obstacle for more than 1100 years.

Hungary is the best place to enter both Central and Eastern Europe. While some of its neighbors may have more dramatic scenery or older and more important monuments, Hungary abounds in things to see and do and those with special interests — fishing, horse riding, botany, bird-watching, cycling, thermal spas, and Jewish culture — will find a treasure-trove here. Under the old Communist regime, most of the government's focus and money went to Budapest. As a result, foreign visitors rarely ventured beyond this splendid city on the Danube River, except on a day trip to the Danube Bend or to Lake Balaton.

The '90s were not a stellar time for the re-born republic. Its economic development was in limbo and serious economic problems affected all aspects of daily life. Thankfully, those days are past and many now view Hungary, with its intelligent, hard-working populace, and rich and vibrant culture, as the star performer and most interesting destination of the new Europe. — Lonely Planet

History and Overview

Located in Central Europe northwest of Romania, the country borders Austria, Croatia, Romania, Serbia, Slovakia, Slovenia, and

Ukraine. A landlocked nation, Hungary enjoys a strategic location astride main land routes between Western Europe and the Balkan Peninsula as well as between Ukraine and Mediterranean basin. The north-south flowing Danube and Tisza Rivers divide the country into three large regions.

Hungary was part of the polyglot Austro-Hungarian Empire, which collapsed during World War I. The country fell under Communist rule following World War II. In 1956, a revolt and an attempt to withdraw from the Warsaw Pact were met with a massive Russian military when the U.S. government failed to assist revolutionaries. Several thousands were subsequently admitted to the U.S. as refugees. Under the Communist leadership of János Kádár in 1968, Hungary began liberalizing its economy, introducing so-called "Goulash Communism."

Conservative Viktor Orbán has been prime minister since 2010 with his Fidesz-KNDP party winning a majority in 2014 for a third five-year term. He held the same post from 1998 to 2002. He is controversial. He has been accused, often by EU officials, of being too nationalistic, of suppressing media freedom, politicizing the judiciary and the central bank, and even of stirring up ethnic tensions. His 2014 election victory may increase the concentration of his power that has been troubling to more than just his opposition. An ultranationalist, anti-Semitic party also made large gains in the parliament.

Orbán has doubts about the EU and I share those doubts. A few years ago, I flew 5,700 miles, starting the day in Bucharest, Romania, arriving in Miami, Florida 14 hours later. I had been traveling in Eastern Europe with a Sovereign Society investment and real estate tour in Croatia, Austria, the Czech Republic, Hungary and Romania.

We were there to introduce Sovereign Society tour participants to real estate investments and other profitable possibilities in Eastern European nations that now embrace the free-market principles of the West.

In Romania and Hungary, I met people who seriously questioned their nation's membership in the European Union. For decades after World War II, until the fall of Communism, their nations labored under stultifying central economic control from Moscow. The result was massive poverty and suffering. Naturally, they had misgivings about ceding economic and tax authority to distant politicians in Brussels.

The folks I conversed with saw their future in economic freedom, not in substituting new foreign EU controls for old ones that not only were ineffective, but kept them in a Dark Age.

Economy

Hungary held its first multi-party elections in 1990 and initiated a free-market economy. It joined NATO in 1999 and the EU in 2004. Hungary has made the transition from a centrally planned to a market economy, with a per capita income about 60% of the EU-25 average. Hungary continues to demonstrate strong economic growth and acceded to the EU in 2004. The private sector accounts for over 80% of GDP. Foreign ownership of, and investment in, Hungarian firms are widespread, with cumulative foreign direct investment totaling more than US$34 billion between 1990 and 2003.

Hungary has a single-chamber parliament or national assembly whose 386 members are elected by voters every four years. In April 2010, the conservative Fidesz Party won 263 seats, more than the 258 needed for the two-thirds majority in parliament, ousting the Socialists after eight years, and elevating Viktor Orbán as the country's prime minister. He formed the first non-coalition government with a two-thirds mandate in Hungary's 20-year post-communist history. His party won new elections in 2012 for a five-year term.

Opposition activists and civil rights groups say Orbán and Fidesz have passed laws eroding the democratic system of checks and balances by increasing political control over the judiciary, the central bank, religious groups and the media.

Equally controversial are Orbán's economic policies. Hungary has run up billions of euros worth of foreign currency debt, equivalent to 78% of its annual economic output. The country's debt is the highest in Central and Eastern Europe, according to Moody's Investors Service.

Before Orbán took office, in late 2008, Hungary's inability to service its short-term debt brought on by the global financial crisis, led Budapest to obtain an IMF/EU/World Bank-arranged financial assistance package worth over US$25 billion.

In 2010, Orbán's new government implemented changes including cutting business and personal income taxes, but imposed crisis taxes on financial institutions, energy and telecom companies, and retailers. The IMF/EU bail-out program lapsed at the end of 2010 and was replaced by Post Program Monitoring and consultations on overall economic and fiscal processes.

The economy began to recover in 2010 with a big boost from exports, especially to Germany, and achieved growth of 1.4% in 2011. In late 2011, the government turned to the IMF and the EU to obtain a new loan for foreign currency debt and bond obligations in 2012 and beyond. Future loans depend on Hungary meeting EU and IMF requirements for ensuring the independence of monetary, judicial, and data privacy institutions.

The EU requested that the government outline measures to sustainably reduce the budget deficit to fewer than 3% of GDP. Unemployment remains high. Ongoing economic weakness in Western Europe has further constrained growth in 2012 and 2013.

The private sector accounts for more than 80% of GDP. Foreign ownership of and investment in Hungarian firms are widespread, with cumulative foreign direct investment worth more than US$70 billion. The government's austerity measures, imposed since 2006, have reduced the budget deficit from over 9% of GDP in 2006 to 3.2% in 2010, with a target of less than 3% in 2011.

The global economic downturn, declining exports, and low domestic consumption and fixed asset accumulation, dampened by government austerity measures, resulted in an economic contraction of 6.3% in 2009. In 2010, the new government implemented a number of changes including cutting business and personal income taxes, but imposed "crisis taxes" on financial institutions, energy and telecom companies, and retailers.

Residence and Citizenship

Hungarian 1993 nationality law is based on the principles of jus sanguinis. Hungarian citizenship is acquired mainly on the basis of a Hungarian parent, or by naturalization.

Children born in Hungary to foreign parents do not generally acquire citizenship. Hungarian citizenship is inherited by birth, thus, children of Hungarian citizens are generally also Hungarian citizens. Children born before 1957 could inherit the Hungarian citizenship only from their Hungarian father, but since then, a Hungarian mother also can pass it to her child.

Since the assessment qualifications for the citizenship of a given person might be very complicated due to the historical changes of national borders and status in Central Europe, this work is done exclusively by the Citizenship Department of the Ministry of the Interior in Budapest, to which the Hungarian Embassy or the Consulate-General send the documentation submitted by the applicant.

A person may be naturalized as a Hungarian citizen on the basis of the following requirements: a) eight years continuous residence in Hungary; b) a stable livelihood; c) good character and; d) passing a test in basic constitutional studies.

The residence requirement is reduced to three years for: a) spouses of Hungarian citizens who have been married for three years (or who are widows or widowers); b) parents of Hungarian citizen minor children; c) persons adopted by Hungarian citizens or; d) recognized refugees.

A one-year residence requirement applies to those of Hungarian ancestry. If the person is a former Hungarian citizen, an application for naturalization may be made immediately upon establishing residence in Hungary.

A five-year residence requirement applies to a person who is: a) born in Hungary; b) established residence in Hungary before age 18 and; c) stateless.

A passport is required for entry. A visa is not required for tourist stays of up to 90 days. American citizen tourists may remain in Hungary for up to 90 days during any six-month period from the date of first entry. If you plan to reside or study in Hungary for a period of more than 90 days, a visa must be obtained from the Embassy.

Residence and Citizenship for Sale

The heavily indebted government of Hungary offers wealthy foreigners the chance to purchase what amounts to temporary citizenship if they agree to invest at least €250,000 (US$330,000) in the country's economy.

The potential investors and future "citizens" will have to buy special government bonds as the price for this preferential immigration treatment. Once they acquire a Hungarian passport the newly minted citizen will be able to live and work in not only Hungary, but in all the other 27 of states of the EU.

In 2012, the Hungarian Parliament amended the nation's immigration law by creating a new "investment citizenship." The change streamlined the application for a permanent residence permit in return for purchase of government residence bonds. It mirrored similar immigration programs in Bulgaria, Austria, Canada and Cyprus.

According to the Bisztrai Law Firm in Budapest, the special government residence bonds have a five-year maturity with renewal for five years. The purchase of the bonds does not guarantee Hungarian citizenship, only permanent residence. This status however allows a foreigner to travel freely within the Schengen zone countries for up to 90 days every six months. A permanent resident enjoys the right to work in Hungary, as well as the right to health service and participation in the education system.

After six months the foreigner may apply for a permanent residence permit that can lead to citizenship. The government offers an interest rate for the bonds that is 50% lower than other government bonds but the requirement of three years continuous residence prior to residence application is waived. Unlike other countries offering investment citizenship, Hungary does not require purchase of real estate, only a permanent residence address in Hungary such as a rented apartment.

Contact: Dr. Gábor Bisztrai Attorney at law
Language: Hungarian, English, German
Email: gabor.bisztrai@bisztrai.com
Cell: +36 303 723 813
Capital Square, Váci út 76, HU-1133 Budapest

A Second Blood Route

Your great-great-great-grandparents could hand you citizenship in Hungary, and, with it, the legal freedom to live and do business in any of the 27 countries of the European Union.

Another new Hungarian nationality law took effect in 2011 that confers citizenship on any person who was formerly a Hungarian citizen or, more importantly, anyone who is a descendant of a person who was a Hungarian citizen before 1920. The law does not require that the applicant live in Hungary, but they must show they can speak Hungarian.

In the first six months after the law took effect, more than 120,000 applications were filed and 20,000 people were granted citizenship, mostly from neighboring countries Romania, Serbia and Ukraine.

There are about 10 million Hungarian citizens living today, and you may be eligible to join them. Significant groups of people with Hungarian ancestry live across the world, over 1.6 million of them in the United States, others in Germany, the United Kingdom, Brazil, Argentina, Chile, Canada and Australia.

U.S. Census records show that from 1890 to 1920, over 18.2 million immigrants from Europe came to America. In the first decade of that period, 14.5% of those folks were from Hungary, in the second decade it was 24.4% and from 1910 to 1920, 18.2%. By 1920, 3.1% of all the U.S. urban population was Hungarian.

Those numbers mean that, today, many Americans may be eligible for Hungarian citizenship — if they will take the time to research and find proof of their ancestors' origins.

The 2011 Hungarian Citizenship law allows a simplified naturalization for those able to prove knowledge of the Hungarian language and evidence of Hungarian ancestry such as the birth certificate of a Hungarian parent or grandparent. But, as non-residents, they will not be entitled to vote in Hungarian elections. Dual citizenship is permitted. The Office of Immigration and Nationality handles applications. For general information on residence and citizenship visit the web site of the Hungarian Embassy in Washington, D.C.

Contacts

Embassy of the Republic of Hungary
3910 Shoemaker Street NW
Washington, DC 20008
Tel.: (202) 362-6730
Email: informacio.was@kum.hu
Web: http://washington.kormany.hu/

United States Embassy
Szabadsag ter 12
H-1054 Budapest, Hungary
Tel.: + (36-1) 475-4400
Emergency after-hours: + (36-1) 475-4703/4924
Email: infousa@usembassy.hu
Web: http://budapest.usembassy.gov/

Republic of Ireland

Government:	Republic, parliamentary democracy
Capital:	Dublin
National Day:	Saint Patrick's Day: 17 March
Population:	4,832,765 (July 2014 est.)
Total Area:	27,135 sq. miles / 70,280 sq. kilometers
Languages:	English (official), Irish/Gaelic (official)
Ethnic groups:	Irish 87.4%, other white 7.5%, Asian 1.3%, black 1.1%, mixed 1.1%, unspecified 1.6%
Religion:	Roman Catholic 87.4%, Church of Ireland 2.9%, other Christian 1.9%, other 2.1%, unspecified 1.5%, none 4.2%
Life expectancy:	80.56 years
Currency:	Euro (EUR)
GDP:	US$190.4 billion (2013 est.)
GDP per capita:	US$41,300 (2013 est.)

A small country with a big reputation, helped along by a timeless, age-caressed landscape and a fascinating, friendly people, whose lyrical nature is expressed in the warmth of their welcome.

Yes, it exists. Along the peninsulas of the southwest, the brooding loneliness of Connemara and the dramatic wildness of County Donegal. You'll also find it in the lake lands of Counties Leitrim and Roscommon and the undulating hills of the sunny southeast ('sunny' of course being a relative term). Ireland has modernized dramatically, but some things never change. Brave the raging Atlantic on a crossing to Skellig Michael or spend a summer's evening in the yard of a thatched-cottage pub and you'll experience an Ireland that has changed little in generations, and is likely the Ireland you most came to see.

Tread carefully for you tread on history. Ireland's history presents itself everywhere: from the breathtaking monuments of prehistoric Ireland at Brú na Bóinne to the fabulous ruins of Ireland's rich monastic past at Glendalough and Clonmacnoise. More recent history is visible in the Titanic museum in Cobh to the forbidding Kilmainham Gaol in Dublin. And there's history so young that it's still considered the present, best experienced on a black-taxi tour of West Belfast or an examination of Derry's astonishingly colorful political murals.

Throughout your travels you will be overwhelmed by the cultural choices on offer — a play by one of the theatrical greats in Dublin, a traditional music 'session' in a west-Ireland pub or a rock gig in a Limerick saloon. The Irish summer is awash with festivals celebrating everything from flowers in bloom to high literature.

(Taw fall-cha row-at) — 'You're very welcome'. Or, more famously, céad míle fáilte — a hundred thousand welcomes. Irish friendliness is a tired cliché, an over-simplification of a character that is infinitely complex, but there's no denying that the Irish are warm and welcoming, if a little reserved at first. Wherever you meet them — the shop, the bar, the bank queue — there's a good chance a conversation will begin, pleasantries exchanged and, should you be a stranger in town, the offer of a helping hand extended. But, lest you think this is merely an act of unfettered altruism, rest assured that the comfort they seek is actually their own, for the Irish cannot be at ease in the company of those who aren't. A hundred thousand welcomes. It seems excessive, but in Ireland, excess is encouraged, so long as it's practiced in moderation.

There's an unvarnished informality about Ireland that I cherish, based on an implied assumption that life is a tangled, confusing struggle that all of us — irrespective of where we hail from, what our politics are and how we worship — have to negotiate to the best of our abilities. We're all in this together, come hell or high water, so we may as well be civil and share a moment when we can. — Lonely Planet

History and Overview

The Republic of Ireland lies in the Atlantic Ocean, separated from the United Kingdom by the Irish Sea to the east and bounded on the northeast by Northern Ireland.

Celtic tribes arrived on the island between 600 and 150 B.C. Invasions by Norsemen that began in the late 8th century were finally ended when King Brian Boru defeated the Danes in 1014. English invasions began in the late 12th century and set off more than seven centuries of Anglo-Irish struggle marked by fierce rebellions and harsh repressions. A failed 1916 Easter Monday Rebellion touched off several years of guerrilla warfare that in 1921 resulted in independence from the U.K. for 26 counties in the southern and western part of the island; six northern (Ulster) counties remained part of the U.K.

In 1949, Ireland withdrew from the British Commonwealth; it joined the European Community in 1973. Irish governments have sought the peaceful unification of Ireland and have cooperated with Britain against terrorist groups. A peace settlement for Northern Ireland is gradually being implemented despite some difficulties. In 2006, the Irish and British governments developed and began to implement the St. Andrews Agreement, building on the Good Friday Agreement approved in 1998. In 2010, the most recent phase of the peace process was implemented with the Hillsborough Castle Agreement, which paved the way for the devolution of justice and policing powers to the province.

Ireland is a member of the European Union. As a result, Irish citizens can live and work without visas or permits in all EU countries. Tens of thousands of well-educated Irish youths have fanned out all over Europe in technical and professional jobs and were a much sought-after group of skilled workers until the global recession engulfed the EU in 2008 when the Irish economy collapsed.

The vast numbers of Irish emigrants of the past two centuries who scattered around the English-speaking world (and, indeed, many other regions as well, as the number of Irish names found among Latin Americans attests), carried with them a nostalgia for the "Emerald Isle" that translates into widespread observance of St. Patrick's Day and celebration of cultural figures from Yeats, Synge and Joyce to U2 and Bono.

This has resulted in floods of tourists each year visiting the Republic. In Ireland, one can still find rustic charm and picturesque relics of the Celtic and Anglo-Irish past in unspoiled natural settings, alongside a vibrant, cosmopolitan lifestyle and cultural scene in urban centers, especially Dublin. The country is English-speaking, although Irish (Gaelic) is a second official language.

Economy

Ireland is a common law nation with legal and commercial practice much like that of the U.K. The currency is the euro. It has excellent, modern telecommunications systems and the corporate tax breaks offered in the Dublin Free Zone have drawn multinational commercial operations from all over the world — and protests of "unfair tax competition" from high tax EU countries and some U.S. politicians.

During the 1990s in Ireland, a period dubbed the "Celtic Tiger" because of a sharp economic upturn that so resembled the tiger economies of Asia, the Irish government instituted a number of incentives for investment, and introduced a low rate of corporation tax (12.5% contrasted with 39.5% in the United States). Government-backed investment incentives, a low rate of corporation tax and a highly educated, young, flexible workforce, all combined to make Ireland the desired location for over 1,100 overseas companies to base their European operations. During this period, almost half a million new jobs were created in Ireland, a phenomenon which changed the outlook of its people and the profile of its society and economy, radically, and for the better.

GDP growth averaged 6% in 1995to 2007, but economic activity dropped sharply after the world financial crisis began in 2008. That year Ireland entered into a recession for the first time in more than a decade, with the subsequent collapse of its domestic property market and construction industry. Property prices rose more rapidly in Ireland in the decade up to 2007 than in any other developed economy. Since that 2007 peak, average house prices have fallen 47%. In the wake of the collapse of the construction sector and the downturn in consumer spending and business investment, the export sector, dominated by foreign multinationals, has become an even more important component of Ireland's economy. Agriculture, once the most important sector, is now dwarfed by industry and services.

In 2009, in continued efforts to stabilize the banking sector, the Irish Government established the National Asset Management Agency (NAMA) to acquire problem commercial property and development loans from Irish banks. Faced with sharply reduced revenues and a burgeoning budget deficit, the Irish Government introduced the first in a series of draconian budgets in 2009. In addition to across-the-board cuts in spending, the 2009 budget included wage reductions for all public servants. However, these measures were not sufficient to stabilize Ireland's public finances. In 2010, the budget deficit reached 32.4% of GDP — the world's largest deficit, as a percentage of GDP — because of additional government support for the country's deeply troubled banking sector.

In 2010, the former Cowen government agreed to a $92 billion loan package from the EU and IMF to help Dublin recapitalize Ireland's fragile banking sector and avoid defaulting on its sovereign debt. Since entering office in 2011, the current Kenny government has intensified austerity measures to try to meet the deficit targets under Ireland's EU-IMF program. Ireland has gradually grown since 2011, but managed to reduce the budget deficit to 7.2% of GDP in 2013. In late 2013, Ireland formally exited its EU-IMF bailout program, benefiting from its strict adherence to deficit-reduction targets and success in refinancing a large amount of banking-related debt.

Economic Investment Residence-Citizenship Program

The severe Irish economic crisis produced opportunities for those who desire both investment possibilities and also the prospect of immediate residence and eventual citizenship in Ireland.

For a period of about 10 years until the mid-1990s, Ireland offered one of the most popular economic citizenship programs, at least among people of great wealth. (It required a five-year, unsecured investment of over US$1.7 million.) Although this attractive instant citizenship program imposed some restrictions, its virtue was the unfettered access that an Irish passport gave to all other EU countries, plus visa-free travel to over 150 countries, including the entire British Commonwealth. It was ended because of irregularities in passport approvals and alleged corruption.

In 2012, the Irish parliament, in hopes of boosting the sagging economy, authorized new special residence visas for foreign individuals willing to invest in the country. This investment can eventually lead to full citizenship, and Irish citizenship opens the door to full personal and commercial access to the entire EU.

Under the program, potential investor immigrants have these choices, (all numbers are required minimums):

- Make a one-time payment of €500,000 (US$690,000) to a public project benefiting the arts, sports, health or education.

- Make a €2 million (US$2.76 million) investment in a low interest immigrant investor bond. The investment is to be held for a minimum of five years. The bond cannot be traded but must be held to maturity.

- Invest €1 million (US$1,376,000) in venture capital funding in an Irish business for a minimum of three years.

- Make a €1 million mixed investment in 50% property and 50% government securities. Special consideration may be given to those purchasing property owned by the National Asset Management Agency (NAMA). In such cases, a single €1m investment in property may be sufficient. NAMA is stuck with real estate from bailed-out Irish banks and financial institutions.

There is also a "Start-up Entrepreneur Program" foreigners with entrepreneurial ability, who wish to start a business in an innovation area of the economy with funding of at least €75,000 (US$104,000). They will be given a two-year residence period for the purposes of developing the business. No initial job creation targets will be set, because it is recognized that such businesses take time to establish.

The plan looks for high-growth start-ups and is not intended for retail, personal services, catering or other businesses of that nature. The department's existing immigration "Business Permission Scheme" is available for this sort of enterprise. Investors will be able to bring family members into Ireland on the resident visa. Successful applicants will be granted residence permission for two years — renewable thereafter, provided the business is still operational and the applicant is earning a living without being a burden on the country. There will be no requirement to employ people for the first two years, but the business is required to be profitable at the two-year renewal stage.

Information is available at the Ministry of Justice webpage at http://www.inis.gov.ie/ New Programmes for Investors. Emails can be directed to investmentandstartup@justice.ie

Dealing with this agency has not been easy.

I recommend you consult with a recommended specialist in Irish real estate. Contact: Executive Director, Elysium House, Ballytruckle Road, Waterford, Ireland.

"We are all Irish today." That is a ritual saying American politicians repeat each Saint Patrick's Day identifying with the nearly 40 million citizens of the United States, nearly 12% of the total, who trace their ancestry to Ireland.

Indeed, many millions of Irish have emigrated to the U.S. beginning well before America's Revolutionary War against Great Britain. In 1776 eight Irish Americans signed the U.S. Declaration of Independence, and 22 American presidents, from Andrew Jackson to Barack Obama (who knew?) were at least partly of Irish ancestry,

Ireland values its foreign sons and daughters and to maintain their ties Irish law goes well beyond what Abraham Lincoln eloquently once referred to in another context as "bonds of affection" and "mystic chords of memory."

As consequence of those laws an Irish passport is one of the most sought-after travel documents in the world. Remarkably, with a population of only 4.8 million, Ireland has millions of current official passports in worldwide circulation.

When asked about the number of Irish passports in circulation in 2006, the Minister for Foreign Affairs told the Irish Parliament that he could not give an exact number but from 1996 to 2005 about 4,650,000 passports were issued. Since adult passports expire in 10 years and children in three years, it suggests that the number of Irish passports in circulation is at least four million.

In part, this large number of passport holders stems from the principle of Irish nationality law that views blood lines as determining a birthright to citizenship — even without ever having lived in the country, the so-called doctrine of jus sanguinis.

Citizenship is governed by the Irish Nationality and Citizenship Acts of 1956 and 1986. These laws confer Irish nationality: 1) by reason of one's birth in Ireland; 2) by Irish parentage or ancestry, and; 3) by marriage to an Irish citizen.

Automatic citizenship by reason of birth in Ireland was limited in 2004 by a constitutional amendment that restricts that right to a child with at least one Irish citizen as a parent. This reflected demands for limits on the many foreign immigrants who came to Ireland specifically to get welfare and other services for their born or unborn children. Birth no longer confers citizenship automatically; the citizenship and residence history of both parents and all grandparents is then taken into account.

If you were born outside of Ireland and either your mother or father (or both) was an Irish citizen at the time of your birth, then you are entitled to Irish citizenship.

Automatic citizenship by birth in Ireland was limited in 2004 by a constitutional amendment that limits the right to a child with at least one Irish citizen as a parent. This reflects demands for limits on the many foreign immigrants who came to Ireland specifically to get welfare and other services for their born or unborn children.

Until 1986, a citizen of any nation who had at least one grandparent of Irish descent was entitled to receive full Irish citizen status and the coveted passport that goes with it. A 1986 amendment changed mere blood lines to a requirement that at least one parent or grandparent actually must have been born in Ireland. An applicant must prove this claim of Irish descent by submitting an ancestor's official marriage and birth certificates.

There are two circumstances under which a great-grandchild is eligible to apply for Irish citizenship by descent:

1. if the parent (the grandchild of the Irish born person) registered before the great-grandchild was born, or;

2. if the parent (the grandchild of the Irish born person) regis-

tered before June, 30 1986 and the great-grandchild was born after July 17, 1956.

The Irish Consulate in New York explains that the parent would need to be registered in the "Foreign Birth Register" which is held at the Consulate, a listing of Irish citizens born abroad entitled to citizenship because their births officially were "registered."

Aside from joining the country of your ancestors, there is a very practical use of an Irish passport. It entitles the holder to live, work and travel freely in any of the 28 countries in the European Union of which Ireland is a member state. You don't need a work permit and after you work in an EU country for a certain length of time, you are entitled to unemployment compensation, health care and pension rights.

Other EU countries that issue passports based on ancestry are Hungary, Italy, Spain, Poland, Lithuania, Luxembourg and Greece.

Marriage to an Irish citizen does entitle the foreign spouse to Irish citizenship. To claim citizenship by marriage you must: 1) be married for at least three years; 2) had one year of "continuous residence" in Ireland immediately before your application; and, 3) have been living in Ireland for at least two of the four years before the one year of continuous residence.

The most difficult route to citizenship is through permanent residence in Ireland for a continuous five years, after which you may be entitled to naturalization if you are over 18 years old and have no criminal record.

With three photographs, proper proof of Irish ancestry, and proof of legal residence in the country where you make application, a 10-year, renewable Irish passport will be issued in due course bearing the stamp of Ireland and the European Community.

Finding proof of Irish ancestry can be a problem since many

church and court records were destroyed in "The Troubles," the long running, sometimes violent Irish independence struggle against the British.

Irish Consulates and Embassies are adept at verifying affidavits and genealogical research. Numerous Irish genealogical sources can be found on the Internet.

Obviously, Ireland permits dual citizenship, as does the U.S. It does not require an oath of exclusive allegiance, nor does it notify the country of origin of its new passport holders. Contact the nearest Irish Consulate or Embassy for application forms and assistance.

The authoritative Genealogical Supplement is published by a company called Inside Ireland. This book is available to subscribers of the Inside Ireland Quarterly Review available from Inside Ireland, P.O. Box 1886, Dublin 16 Ireland. Email: info@insideireland.com Web: http://www.insideireland.com/home.htm

Even without Irish ancestry, it is also possible to obtain Irish citizenship and a passport after a five-year period of residence. Irish residence is not generally sought because of the nation's high income taxes. Perhaps, reflecting the poetic Irish soul, the one exception to confiscatory income taxes is made for royalty income paid to artists, writers and composers.

A foreign-born person who marries a person of Irish birth or descent may become an Irish citizen after three years of marriage by formally declaring acceptance of Irish citizenship. The marriage must continue at the time of application and grant of citizenship. A married applicant must file a notarized form at an Irish Consulate or Embassy within 30 days of its execution. Once Irish citizenship is established, an application for an official passport can be filed.

Taxation

Irish residents domiciled in Ireland are subject to taxation on all their worldwide income. Non-resident Irish citizens who live abroad are exempted from taxation. Current official practice is to allow new citizens to declare formally that they do not intend to live in Ireland and are, therefore, not domiciled. They then are obligated to pay income tax only on income actually remitted to Ireland. This practice makes Ireland an attractive tax venue for naturalized citizens.

A large number of Irish residents have abused these tax rules by obtaining offshore bank accounts, many in the Isle of Man. They then claimed non-residence while actually maintaining an Irish home. Irish revenue officials have cracked down on this practice, imposing fines and penalties.

A passport is necessary for travel into Ireland. A visa is not required for tourist or business stays of up to 90 days.

Contacts

Embassy of Ireland
2234 Massachusetts Avenue NW
Washington, DC 20008
Tel.: (202) 462-3939
Email: https://www.dfa.ie/irish-embassy/usa/contact-us/
Web: http://www.embassyofireland.org

United States Embassy
42 Elgin Road, Ballsbridge
Dublin 4, Ireland
Tel.: + (353) 1-668-8777 or after hours: + (353) 1-668-9612
Email: acsdublin@state.gov
Web: http://dublin.usembassy.gov

Republic of Italy

Government:	Republic
Capital:	Rome
National Day:	Republic Day: 2 June (1946)
Population:	61,482,297 (July 2013 est.)
Total Area:	116,306 sq. miles / 301,230 sq. kilometers
Languages:	Italian (official), German, French, Slovene
Ethnic groups:	Italian (small groups of German, French, and Slovene-Italians in the north and Albanian-Italians and Greek-Italians in the south)
Religion:	Roman Catholic 90%, other 10%
Life Expectancy:	81.95 years
Currency:	Euro (EUR)
GDP:	US$1.863 trillion (2012 est.)
GDP per capita:	US$30,600 (2012 est.)

The Belpaese (Beautiful Country) is one of the single greatest repositories of sensorial pleasures on earth. From art to food, from stunning and varied countryside to flamboyant fashion, Italy has it all. This is the country that brought us Slow Food, devoted to the promotion of fresh products and fine traditional, cooking. What started as a local protest against fast food has become a worldwide movement.

With 44 sites, Italy has more UNESCO World Heritage sites than any other country on earth. Its great cittàd'arte (cities of art), like Rome, Venice and Florence, have been attracting visitors for centuries, and with good reason. Milan, the country's financial hub, has created one of Europe's biggest and most modern trade fairs and is planning a major residential development, the CityLife complex, in the heart of the city.

Venice is possibly the city that has, in appearance, changed least down the decades but it has recently opened a sleek new bridge over the Grand Canal and a spectacular contemporary art space at the Punta della Dogana. But as much as all of this, a trip to Italy is about lapping up the lifestyle. I's about idling over a coffee at a street side cafe or lingering over a long lunch in the hot Mediterranean sun. — Lonely Planet

History and Overview

Before the birth of Christ, Italy was a major world influence in a previous well-known incarnation as the Roman Empire. Rome-based influence continued during the spread of Christianity. Arab, German and Viking influences in the Middle Ages contributed to rounding out the Italian national character.

Italy became a nation-state in 1861 when the regional states of the peninsula, along with Sardinia and Sicily, were united under King Victor Emmanuel II. Parliamentary government came to a close in the 1920s when Benito Mussolini (El Duce) established his Fascist dictatorship. His alliance with Nazi Germany led to Italy's defeat in World War II. A democratic republic replaced the monarchy in 1946 and economic revival followed.

Italy was a charter member of NATO and the European Economic Community (EEC). It has been at the forefront of European economic and political unification, joining the Economic and Monetary Union in 1999. Persistent problems include illegal immigration, organized crime, corruption, high unemployment, sluggish economic growth, huge deficits and sovereign debt and the low incomes and technical standards of southern Italy compared with the prosperous north.

Long a favored and relatively inexpensive tourist destination, Italy still offers attractive cultural, gastronomic and recreational experiences, although (as in much of Western Europe) bargain prices are few and far between. A large expatriate population continues to form substantial colonies in Rome, Milan and Venice; on the Riviera; in the Alpine Lake District; along the Amalfi coast; and on the islands off the Bay of Naples.

Economy

Italy has a diversified industrial economy, divided into a developed industrial north, dominated by private companies, and a less-developed, highly subsidized, agricultural south, where unemployment is high. The Italian economy is driven by the manufacture of high-quality consumer goods produced by small and medium-sized enterprises, many of them family-owned.

Italy also has a sizable black market underground economy,

which by some estimates accounts for as much as 17% of GDP. These activities are most common within the agriculture, construction, and service sectors. Italy is the third-largest economy in the euro-zone, but its exceptionally high public debt and political instability have raised continuing doubts in financial markets. Public debt increased steadily since 2007, topping 126% of GDP in 2012. In 2012, Italy's GDP was 7% below its 2007 pre-crisis level with negative growth at -2.3% and unemployment at nearly 11%, with youth unemployment around 35%. In late 2013, unemployment hit a new record high of 12.7%.

Investor concerns about the euro-zone crisis caused huge borrowing costs on sovereign government debt. Successive governments have adopted austerity measures to reduce the budget deficit including higher value-added taxes, pension reforms, and cuts in public jobs. Other major problems include labor market inefficiencies and widespread tax evasion. Italy was said to be exiting recession in 2014 and growth was projected to rise through 2014 to 2015 but only by one or two percent of GDP. Italian politics have become a little less volatile with the exit from the national stage of former Prime Minister Silvio Berlusconi, held to account by several court rulings and banned from public office as a result.

Residence and Citizenship

Once a foreigner is present in Italy, registering as a resident or domiciliary requires only a visit to the local, neighborhood police station. Registration is renewable at three month intervals, but local police will give six and 12-month permits once a foreign person is established and known in the community.

Italian citizenship is based on the principle of jus sanguinis (ancestor blood right) which gives a child citizenship born of an Italian father or mother is Italian; however, the mother must have been born on or after January 1, 1948, as set by a ruling by the Constitutional Court. Italian citizenship is governed by Law No. 91 of December 5, 1992, which emphasizes individual desire to gain citizenship. The law acknowledges the right to dual citizenship.

Citizenship is acquired automatically in the following ways:

1. by having an Italian parent(s);

2. by being born in Italy, including cases in which the parents are unknown, stateless or do not transmit their own citizenship to their child according to the law of the country to which they belong, as well as to children found abandoned in Italy for whom it is impossible to determine citizenship;

3. through paternal or maternal recognition while the child is a minor; in cases in which the child recognized is no longer a minor, he/she is obliged to elect to become a citizen within one year of recognition;

4. by adoption, both when a foreign minor is adopted by an Italian citizen and is confirmed by Italian Judicial Authorities, or in the case of adoption granted abroad and confirmed by the Juvenile Court and registered in the Civil Registry. If the adoptee is no longer a minor, he/she can become a naturalized Italian citizen after five years of legal residence in Italy.

Citizenship can also be acquired by naturalization:

1. by filing a declaration of desire to become a citizen, if the foreigner is of Italian descent (with Italian parents or grandparents) he/she can obtain citizenship in any of the following cases: a) by serving in the Italian armed forces; b) by becoming an employee of the Italian State, in Italy or abroad; c) by residing legally in Italy for at least two years after reaching legal age.

If the foreigner was born in Italian territory, he/she can obtain citizenship by residing legally and uninterruptedly in Italy from birth up to legal age of majority which is 18.

2. by marriage to an Italian citizen, requirements include: a) legal residence in Italy for at least 6 months after marriage or three years of matrimony if residing abroad; b) valid marriage certificate; c) absence of criminal record; d) absence of impediments associated with national security.

Applications for citizenship are to be addressed to the Ministry of the Interior and presented to the Prefecture in the Province of residence, if residing in Italy, or the diplomatic-consular authorities if residing abroad.

3. Naturalization requirements include: a) 5 years of legal residence; b)sufficient income; c) absence of criminal record; d) renunciation of original citizenship (where foreseen).

The number of years can be reduced to: a) 3 years of legal residence for descendants by birth of former Italian citizens, including parents or grandparents, and for foreigners born in Italian national territory; b) 4 years of legal residence for citizens of European Union member states; c) 5 years of legal residence for displaced persons or refugees, as well as for legal-age foreigners adopted by Italian citizens; d) no period of residence is required for foreigners who have served the State for a period of at least 5 years, even abroad.

Application for naturalization must be addressed to the President of the Republic and presented to the Prefecture in the Province of residence.

Citizenship by Ancestor

In 1992, Italy radically changed its immigration and passport policies, recognizing the principle of dual nationality. Now, regardless of where they are (or were) born, offspring of Italian nationals automatically are recognized as Italian citizens as explained above. The change was retroactive meaning Italian nationals who lost citizenship in the past by acquiring a different nationality could be reinstated. These broad rules apply to Italian citizenship for children and grandchildren as well.

The 1992 law allowed a one-time-only, two-year grace period during which those eligible could file a declaration of intent to regain citizenship. Since 1994, three years of legal residence in Italy is required for reinstatement. Even foreign citizens born in Italy, as well as those who hold Italian nationality, may be subject to compulsory military service and other laws imposing other obligations while they are within Italy.

The 1992 immigration law favors the family paternal line. The children and grandchildren of former Italian nationals can qualify for citizenship on the basis of any of the following: 1) a father who was an Italian citizen at the time of a child's birth; 2) a mother who was an Italian citizen at the time of a child's birth after January 1, 1948; 3) the father was not born in Italy, but the paternal grandfather was an Italian citizen at the time of birth; or 4) the mother was not born in Italy, but for those born after January 1, 1948, the maternal grandfather was an Italian citizen at the time of the mother's birth.

Refugees

Because of the easing of Italy's strict citizenship laws, approximately 331,000 immigrants were eligible to become Italian citizens after 1992. Italy, home to 2.5 million legal immigrants, now has the strictest citizenship legislation in Europe. In 2011, the U.N. reported 61,327 refugee or stateless persons living in Italy.

It should be noted that Italy is notorious for confusion about their immigration and visa policies and how they are administered. Some reports claim that on average it takes 15 years for an immigrant to become Italian.

In 2011, Italy's government declared a "humanitarian emergency" after thousands of asylum-seekers sailed across the Mediterranean, overwhelming authorities on the remote Italian island of Lampedusa. The majority of the asylum seekers came from nearby Tunisia, in the wake of the North African country's revolution. Later in 2011, Italy was again hit by a wave of refugees as a result of the revolution in Libya. Since the "Arab Spring" revolutions began immigration charities estimate between 17,000 and 20,000 migrants have died at sea trying to reach Europe over the past 20 years, crossing on rickety fishing boats or rubber dinghies. Italian officials have called for assistance from the European Union to deal with the sharp recent increase in refugee arrivals, calling it "a European tragedy."

Tourists

As a member of the 27 nation EU, the Italian passport is valid for visa-free travel within the EU. Italy, alone in the EU, requires an annual validation tax stamp to keep its passport current during its five-year life. Tourist visas are easy to obtain and renewable indefinitely for those who can show adequate means of financial support.

Despite high unemployment, a foreign national with a definite job offering should have little trouble getting a work permit with the employer's assistance. Foreign persons intent upon opening a new business or investing are given red carpet treatment. A valid passport is required for entry into Italy.

Italian authorities may deny entry to travelers who attempt to enter without a valid passport. A visa is not required for tourist stays up to 90 days. However, for all other purposes, such as work, study, etc., a visa is required and must be obtained from the Italian Embassy or Consulate before entering Italy.

Under Italian law, tourists are required to register with a local police station and obtain a permesso di soggiorno (permit of stay) within eight working days of their arrival, regardless of the intended length of stay. Visitors may be required to show police that they have sufficient means of financial support. Credit cards, ATM cards, travelers' checks, prepaid hotel/vacation vouchers, etc., may be evidence of sufficient means. Additional information may be obtained from the Italian Government Tourist Board via the Internet at http://www.italiantourism.com or U.S. Tel.: (212) 245-5618.

Contacts

Embassy of Italy

3000 Whitehaven Street NW
Washington, DC 20008
Tel.: (202) 612-4400
Web: http://www.ambwashingtondc.esteri.it/ambasciata_washington

Social media website: http://www.twiplomacy.it/usa/

United States Embassy

via Vittorio Veneto 121
00187 Roma, Italy
Tel.: + (39) 06-46741
Email: uscitizensrome@state.gov
Web: http://italy.usembassy.gov

U.S. Consulate General Milan

via Principe Amedeo 2/10
20121 MILANO

Tel.: ɪ (39) 02-290351
Web: http://milan.usconsulate.gov

Consulate General Florence
Lungarno Vespucci 38
50123 Firenze
Tel.: + (39) 055-266-951
Web: http://florence.usconsulate.gov

Republic of Latvia

Government:	Parliamentary democracy
Capital:	Rīga
National Day:	Independence Day: 21 August (1991) (from the Soviet Union)
Population:	2,178,443 (July 2013 est.)
Total Area:	24,938 sq. miles / 64,589 sq. kilometers
Languages:	Latvian (official) 58.2%, Russian 37.5%, Lithuanian 4.3%
Ethnic groups:	Latvian 59.3%, Russian 27.8%, Belarusian 3.6%, Ukrainian 2.5%, Polish 2.4%, Lithuanian 1.3%, other 3.1%
Religion:	Lutheran 19.6%, Orthodox 15.3%, other Christian 1%, other 0.4%, unspecified 63.7%
Life expectancy:	73.19 years
Currency:	Euro (as of January 1, 2014)
GDP:	US$37.88 billion (2012 est.)
GDP per capita:	US$18,600 (2012 est.)

If you're yearning to hit Europe's untrodden jackpot, cash in your chips in Latvia (Latvija). Still undiscovered by the tourism masses, this sizzling Baltic sexpot is poised to become the continent's next A-list star. A country in transition, Hell-bent on shedding its stalwart old-Soviet image, the Latvia of today is vibrant, enigmatic and altogether mesmerizing. Refreshingly unpretentious, Latvia manages to tantalize even the most jaded traveler. Many arrive expecting little and leave overwhelmed, certain they've uncovered long-buried treasure.

Bustling Rīga, with its pumping nightlife, cobbled streets and marvelous art-nouveau architecture is one of Eastern Europe's most fun cities. Away from the capital, the pace slows. Historic villages, miles from anywhere, sit frozen in time. Despite growing popularity, Latvia is still one of those places where you can embrace the unbeaten path and become an intrepid adventurer exploring virgin terrain.

From crumbling castles in Sigulda, to Jūrmala and its alluring resorts on the edge of the ice-blue Baltic Sea, it's very easy to just get away. Summer is an especially magical time — twilight comes near midnight and by 4:00am it's light again. After long, dark winters, Latvians seem determined to soak up as much light as possible and the whole country exudes a frenetic, turbocharged energy. Beer gardens pop up in even the smallest villages and revelers slug pints well into the night. It's hard to believe this tiny, vivacious nation shed its Russian stranglehold less than two decades ago because, despite years of intense suffering under Soviet and Nazi occupations, Latvia has a serenity and charm rarely found elsewhere in Europe. This is Latvia's moment. Visit before everyone else does. — Lonely Planet

History and Overview

Latvia lies on the eastern shores of the Baltic Sea on the level northwestern part of the rising East European platform. Its territory is slightly larger than the U.S. state of West Virginia.

Latvia was originally settled by the ancient people known as Balts. In the 9th century the Balts came under the overlordship of the Varangians, or Vikings, but a more lasting dominance was established over them by their German-speaking neighbors' to the west, who Christianized Latvia in the 12th and 13th centuries. Following the Russian Revolution of 1917, Latvia declared its independence on November 18, 1918, and, after a confused period of fighting, the new nation was recognized by Soviet Russia and Germany in 1920.

After a brief period of independence between the two World Wars, Latvia was annexed by the USSR in 1940. It reestablished its independence in 1991 following the breakup of the Soviet Union. Although the last Russian troops left in 1994, the status of the Russian minority (some 30% of the population) remains of concern to Moscow.

Economy

Latvia joined the World Trade Organization in 1999, and both NATO and the EU in the spring of 2004. Latvia's transitional economy recovered from the 1998 Russian financial crisis, largely due to the government's budget stringency, gradual reorientation of exports toward EU countries, and lessening Latvia's trade dependency on Russia.

The majority of companies, banks and real estate have been privatized, although the state still holds sizable stakes in a few large enterprises. But there's a growing perception that many of Latvia's banks facilitate illicit activity could damage the country's vibrant financial sector.

Latvia currently applies a flat tax of 15% on corporate income and flat tax of 22% on personal income which will fall to 20% from January 1, 2015. In 1994, Estonia became the first country in Europe to introduce a so-called "flat tax", replacing three tax rates on personal income, and another on corporate profits, with one uniform rate of 26%. Latvia and Lithuania promptly followed its example. In 2001, Russia too moved to a flat tax on personal income.

Latvia qualified to join the euro group by adopting a tough austerity program that shrank its economy at one point by 20%. Since then, the economy has rebounded, growing 4.5% through the third quarter of 20% from its peak, while unemployment fell to 11.3%, still high, though down from a high of 20% in 2010.

Latvia's economy experienced GDP growth of more than 10% per year during 2006 to 2007; but entered a recession as a result of unsustainable current account deficit and large debt exposure amid the softening world economy. The IMF, EU, and other donors provided assistance to Latvia as part of a package to defend the currency's peg to the euro and reduce public spending by about 5% of GDP. The majority of companies, banks, and real estate have been privatized, although the state still holds sizable stakes in a few large enterprises.

Nearly 10 years after joining the EU, Latvia adopted the euro as its currency on January 1, 2014. Observers saw this as another move out of the shadow of its large neighbor Russia. Latvia and its Baltic neighbors are pursuing further economic integration with the West as other former Soviet republics, such as Ukraine, struggle with their identity under pressure from Moscow. Latvia's pursuit of close ties to the West has been a consistent foreign-policy priority since it regained independence in 1991.

Russia demands better Latvian treatment of ethnic Russians in Latvia; there are continuing disputes over the boundary Lithuania including the maritime boundary due to concerns over oil exploration rights. As a member state that forms part of the EU's external border, Latvia has implemented the strict Schengen border rules with Russia.

Residence and Citizenship

Latvia regained its independence from the Soviet Union in 1991. During the Russian occupation, Latvians were deported from the country and thousands of Russians were shipped in by the Communist government in Moscow in an attempt to "Russify" the Baltic state.

In 2006, Latvia adopted stricter laws for granting citizenship, refusing it to those failing a Latvian language test three times. Some 450,000 ethnic Russians, Belarusians and Ukrainians currently live in Latvia. Many of them were born in the country, but are denied citizenship unless they pass a Latvian language test and take an oath of loyalty to the state. The group, which represents almost 20% of the country's population, cannot vote, hold most public posts and requires a visa to visit other EU countries, except for Estonia, Lithuania and Denmark. The 2006 rules were designed to make the naturalization process more difficult.

In 2012, it was estimated that 280,759 refugees and displaced stateless persons were living in Latvia. Persons who were Latvian citizens prior to the 1940 Soviet occupation and their descendants were recognized as Latvian citizens when the country's independence was restored in 1991; citizens of the former Soviet Union residing in Latvia who have neither Latvian nor other citizenship are considered non-citizens (officially there is no statelessness in Latvia) and are entitled to non-citizen passports.

Children born after Latvian independence to stateless parents are entitled to Latvian citizenship upon their parents' request; non-citizens cannot vote or hold certain government jobs and are exempt from military service but can travel visa-free in the EU under the Schengen accord; non-citizens can obtain naturalization if they have been permanent residents of Latvia for at least five years, pass tests in Latvian language and history, and know the words of the Latvian national anthem.

Residence by Investment

Latvia has established a residence through investment program that requires purchase of real estate of any type with a minimum value of €145,000 (US$197,000) or more. This grants a residence status valid for five years, renewable as long as the property is retained. There is no requirement to live in Latvia or spend a minimum amount of time in the country. The wider and useful benefit is that this status also grants full rights to live, work, and do business in all 28 EU member states.

Latvian citizenship can be acquired by naturalization after five years residence; based on a special contribution to the nation; or by recognition of aliens (non-citizens) and stateless persons born after August 21, 1991, as Latvian citizens.

Citizenship can also be acquired by a child if at the moment of his/her birth:

1. both of his/her parents are Latvian citizens;

2. one of his/her parents is a Latvian citizen, and the other one is an alien (non-citizen) or a stateless person, or;

3. one of his/her parents is a Latvian citizen, and the other one is a citizen of another country, and both of the parents agree the child will be a Latvian citizen.

Possessing Latvian citizenship means having the right to live, study, work, vote, and buy real estate with no limitations in the territory of Latvia. It also allows one to travel without a visa to most European destinations, as well as many other countries. Latvian citizenship further allows one to study and work legally in Europe, under the favorable conditions enjoyed by the citizens of the EU.

Dual citizenship is prohibited in Latvia, which means that you must give up your other citizenship before you acquire Latvian citizenship. For information on citizenship and residence, see http://www.am.gov.lv/en/service/ If you plan to be in Latvia over 90 days in a six-month period, or want to do business, work or stay in Latvia as a self-employed worker, you will need a residence permit.

Contacts

Embassy of Latvia
2306 Massachusetts Avenue NW
Washington, DC 20008
Tel.: (202) 328-2840
Email: embassy.usa@mfa.gov.lv
Web: http://www.latvia-usa.org

United States Embassy
1 Samnera Velsa St. (former Remtes)
Riga LV-1510, Latvia
The U.S. Embassy is located across from the shopping mall SPICE between Kalnciema and Lielirbes street. Entrance to the Consular Section is on Velsa street.
Tel.: + (371) 6710-7000
Email: Askconsular@usriga.lv
Web: http://riga.usembassy.gov

Principality of Liechtenstein

Government:	Constitutional monarchy
Capital:	Vaduz
National Day:	Assumption Day: 15 August
Population:	37,009 (July 2013 est.)
Total Area:	62 sq. miles / 160 sq. kilometers
Languages:	German (official), Alemannic dialect
Ethnic groups:	Liechtensteiner 65.6%, other 34.4%
Religion:	Roman Catholic 76.2%, other 6.2%, unknown 10.6%, Protestant 7%
Life expectancy:	81.59 years
Currency:	Swiss franc (CHF)
GDP:	US$4.5 billion (2013 est.)
GDP per capita:	US$124,485 (2013 est.)

It's true; Liechtenstein makes a fabulous wine-and-cheese-hour trivia subject. Did you know it was the sixth smallest country? It's still governed by an iron-willed monarch who lives in a Gothic castle on a hill. Yes, it really is the world's largest producer of dentures. But if you're visiting this pocket-sized principality solely for the cocktail-party bragging rights, keep the operation covert. This theme-park micro-nation takes its independence seriously and would shudder at the thought of being considered for novelty value alone. Liechtenstein would rather be remembered for its stunning natural beauty.

Measuring just 15.5 miles in length and 3.7 miles in width, the country is barely larger than Manhattan. And though it might not look like much on a map, up close it's filled with numerous hiking and cycling trails offering spectacular views of craggy cliffs, quaint villages, friendly locals and lush green forests. — *Lonely Planet*

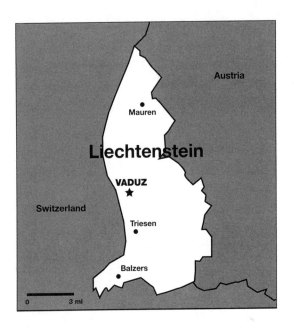

History and Overview

The Principality of Liechtenstein, located in Central Europe, between Austria and Switzerland, was established within the Holy Roman Empire in 1719; it became a sovereign state in 1806. Until the end of World War I, it was closely tied to Austria, but the economic devastation caused by that conflict forced Liechtenstein to enter into a customs and monetary union with Switzerland. Since World War II (in which Liechtenstein remained neutral), the country's low taxes have spurred outstanding economic growth.

Tiny Liechtenstein, not quite as large as the city of Washington, D.C., lies on the east bank of the Rhine River south of Lake Constance between Austria and Switzerland. It consists of low valley land and Alpine peaks. Liechtensteiners are descended from the Alemanni tribe that migrated into the region sometime after 500 A.D. German is still spoken here, although English and other languages are widely used in business. The principality had 37,009 in 2013 inhabitants, of which 34% were foreigners, mainly Swiss, Austrians and Germans.

The Liechtenstein Family of Austria acquired the fiefs of Vaduz and Schellenberg in 1699 and 1713, respectively, and gained the status of an independent principality of the Holy Roman Empire in 1719 under the name Liechtenstein The French, under Napoleon, occupied the country for a few years, but Liechtenstein regained its independence in 1815 within the new German Confederation. In 1868, after the Confederation dissolved, Liechtenstein disbanded its army of 80 men and declared its permanent neutrality, which was respected during both world wars. In 1919, Liechtenstein entrusted its external relations to neutral Switzerland.

After World War II, Liechtenstein became increasingly important as a financial center, and the country became more prosperous. In 1989, Prince Hans-Adam II succeeded his father to the throne and, in 1996, settled a long-running dispute with Russia over the Liechtenstein family's archives, which had been confiscated during the Soviet occupation of Vienna in 1945 and later moved to Moscow. In 1978, Liechtenstein became a member of the Council of Europe and then joined the U.N. in 1990, the European Free Trade Association (EFTA) in 1991 and both the European Economic Area (EEA) and World Trade Organization (WTO) in 1995.

Offshore Financial Center

With asset protection laws dating as far back as the 1920s, a host of excellent, even unique legal entities designed for wealth preservation, the Principality of Liechtenstein has much to offer.

Strict bank secrecy guaranteed by law was weakened by a 2009 government decision to abide by OECD rules governing tax information exchange, but only on an individual case basis and with a showing of probable cause of foreign tax evasion. This policy change occurred after Liechtenstein came under international pressure, particularly from Germany, to improve transparency in its banking and tax systems.

Liechtenstein was the first tax haven to announce it would comply with Article 26 of the OECD model tax information exchange treaty, previously anathema in Vaduz. As in Switzerland, this means banks will provide information in matters of foreign tax evasion when ordered to do so by the government, but, it was claimed, under limited conditions and only by applying the terms of tax information exchange treaties in individual cases.

That sounded comforting to some degree, but in 2011 the principality's government concluded a "ground breaking agreement" with the tax collectors of the United Kingdom. Under this extremely liberal deal, U.K. residents with Liechtenstein bank accounts would have their details shared with the British government to make sure they paid the right U.K. taxes.

This new tax information exchange agreement enables the U.K. and Liechtenstein to "swap information" on all accounts to ensure the right tax was paid in each country with minimal penalties, a guarantee of no prosecution in non-criminal cases and an exemption from the threat of "naming and shaming." To sweeten the deal the tax disclosure program allows penalties on unpaid tax to be capped at 10% of tax evaded over the last 10 years, a potentially huge savings, providing the taxpayer was fully open with the U.K. tax collectors.

In late 2013, it was reported that negotiations were underway with the U.S. Treasury Department concerning an agreement on applying the Foreign Account Tax Compliance Act (FATCA), but as of early 2014 no deal had been signed.

Liechtenstein devised the U.K. disclosure deal as a "creative and innovative solution" to the international outcry sparked by the evasion scandal following the 2007 theft of thousands of names from LGT Bank's trust business, stolen goods which were purchased by the tax hungry German government. (The German secret police agency, the Federal Intelligence Service (BND), (equivalent of the U.S. Central Intelligence Agency), paid an illegal €5 million (US$7.3 mil) bribe to a disgruntled employee of LGT, Heinrich Kieber, a former employee of LGT Bank.

As further evidence of how far the principality has come in weakening its once absolute bank secrecy laws, by 2013 it had signed tax information exchange agreements (TIEAs) with more than 25 countries including the aforementioned U.K. and with the United States, France, Canada and Germany.

In the not-so-distant past, one had to be a philatelist to know that Liechtenstein even existed. In those days, the nation's major export was exquisitely produced postage stamps (still available and highly prized by collectors). Until the 1960s, the principality existed mainly on income from tourism, postage stamp sales and the export of false teeth.

In the last 65 years, its lack of taxes, maximum financial privacy and highly professional financial services propelled Liechtenstein to top rank among the world's wealthiest nations. This historic Rhine Valley country, surrounded by beautiful Alpine peaks, has grown into a major world offshore financial center, achieving per capita income levels higher than Germany, France, the United Kingdom, and the United States.

Although only 14% of workers are in the financial sector, financial services account for 30% of the gross national product, with industry and manufacturing trade (4%), general services (25%) and agriculture and households (5%). Forty-six percent of the work force is employed in the industrial sector and 40% of employees work in other service activities, such as trade, hotels and restaurants, transport and public administration. About 12,000 workers commute daily from Austria and Switzerland. GDP grew during the 1990s, sometimes as much as 10% annually, but in recent years growth has diminished even as unemployment has stayed low.

Despite its small size and limited natural resources, Liechtenstein has developed into a prosperous, highly industrialized, free-enterprise economy with a vital financial service sector, and living standards on par with its large European neighbors. The Liechtenstein economy is widely diversified with a large number of small businesses.

Liechtenstein adopted in 2011 imposed a flat annual tax of 12.5% on the net earnings, including earnings from interest, of family foundations, trusts and corporations. This first-ever tax has resulted in the re-domiciling of a number of Liechtenstein trusts, foundations and companies that moved to Panama and other financial centers where no tax is imposed.

Low business taxes — the maximum tax rate is 20% — and easy incorporation rules have induced many holding or so-called "letter box" companies to establish nominal offices in Liechtenstein, providing 30% of state revenues. The country participates in a customs union with Switzerland and uses the Swiss franc as its official national currency. It imports more than 90% of its energy requirements.

Liechtenstein has been a member of the European Economic Area (an organization serving as a bridge between the European Free Trade Association (EFTA) and the EU) since 1995.

The government is working to harmonize its economic policies with those of an integrated Europe. Liechtenstein is within the Schengen travel area, which allows passport-free travel across 26 European countries.

Residence and Citizenship

The Law on the Acquisition and Loss of Liechtenstein Citizenship of January 1934 (Citizenship Act, LGBl. 1960 No. 23) is based on the fundamental principle of descent (jus sanguinis): children of married and unmarried parents acquire Liechtenstein citizenship at birth, if at least one parent (father or mother) is a Liechtenstein citizen at that time. A foreign adoptive child acquires Liechtenstein citizenship by adoption, if the adoption by a Liechtenstein adoptive father or adoptive mother takes places before the age of 10.

Upon application, citizenship may be acquired through marriage, if essentially the following conditions are jointly met: renunciation of previous citizenship, proof of 12 years of residence in Liechtenstein (years of marriage count double), and proof of three years of marriage.

Foreigners may also acquire Liechtenstein citizenship through "simplified acquisition" or "conferral." Simplified acquisition of citizenship (§5a of the Act) may be claimed by a foreigner if essentially the following conditions are jointly met: renunciation of previous citizenship, proof of 30 years of residence in Liechtenstein (years below the age of 20 count double), proof of continuous physical residence in Liechtenstein for the last five years prior to the application, and no criminal convictions.

Liechtenstein citizenship may be conferred (§6 of the Act) if the following conditions are jointly met: legal capacity, age of majority, power of judgment of the applicant, five years of continuous residence in Liechtenstein immediately prior to the application, and assurance of acceptance into a municipality. The conferral of Liechtenstein citizenship is discretionary, unlike the other means of acquisition, to which a legal entitlement exists if the conditions are met.

The authorities evaluate applications in the context of whether naturalization would be appropriate in view of state and public interests. The acquisition of Liechtenstein citizenship can be denied if criminal proceedings are pending against the applicant, a legally binding sentence of imprisonment has been passed, or other grounds indicate that the applicant poses a threat to public peace, security and order (§5 of the Act).

The legal provisions on the acquisition of a Liechtenstein passport are contained in the Citizenship Documents Act (CDA, LGBl. 1986 No. 27, articles 15 to 27). In principle, every Liechtenstein citizen is entitled to claim a passport, if no grounds for denial exist. These grounds are enumerated in Article 23 of the CDA and essentially encompass certain situations arising under administrative or private law. Once issued, a passport may be revoked if the holder is being prosecuted for a crime or is sentenced (Article 24 of the CDA). In addition, the passport must also be revoked if the holder's presence abroad gravely interferes with the interests and reputation of the country or if the internal or external security of the country would be endangered (Article 25(h) of the CDA).

Contacts

Embassy of Liechtenstein
2900 K Street NW, Suite 602-B
Washington, DC 20007
Tel.: (202) 331-0590
Web: http://www.liechtensteinusa.org/

Contact webpage: http://www.liechtensteinusa.org/index. php?page=contact

The U.S. has no Embassy in Liechtenstein; the U.S. Ambassador to Switzerland is accredited to Liechtenstein.

United States Embassy
Sulgeneckstrasse 19
CH-3007 Bern, Switzerland
Tel.: + (031) 357-7011
Email: bernacs@state.gov
Web: http://bern.usembassy.gov

U.S. Consular Agency Zurich
Dufourstrasse 101 3rd Floor
Zurich, Switzerland
Mailing Address: Dufourstrasse 101
CH-8008 Zurich, Switzerland
Tel.: + (043) 499-2960
Email: Zurich-CA@state.gov

Consular Agency Geneva
rue Versonnex 7
CH-1207 Geneva, Switzerland
Mailing Address: c/o U.S. Mission
11, rte. de Pregny
1292 Chambésy/GE
Email: Geneva-CA@state.gov

Recommended Attorney & Trust Company:

First Advisory Group
Aeulestrasse 74, Vaduz 9490, Liechtenstein
Tel.: + 423 236 30 00
Contact webpage: https://www.firstadvisorygroup.com/en-us/ kontakt.aspx

Web: http://www.firstadvisory.li
Offices in Zurich, Geneva, Singapore, Hong Kong and Panama.

Republic of Lithuania

Government:	Parliamentary democracy
Capital:	Vilnius
National Day:	Independence Day: 16 February (1918)
Population:	3,515,858 (July 2013 est.)
Total Area:	25,174 sq. miles / 65,200 sq. kilometers
Languages:	Lithuanian (official) 82%, Russian 8%, Polish 5.6%, other 4.4%
Ethnic groups:	Lithuanian 84%, Polish 6.1%, Russian 4.9%, Belarusian 1.1%, other or unspecified 3.9%
Religion:	Roman Catholic 79%, none 9.5%, other 5.5%, Russian Orthodox 4.1%, Protestant 1.9%
Life expectancy:	75.77 years
Currency:	Litas (LTL)
GDP:	US$64.31 billion (2012 est.)
GDP per capita:	US$21,400 (2012 est.)

Rebellious, quirky and vibrant, Lithuania (Lietuva) is Europe's best kept secret. Shoved successively between Russian pillar and Nazi post, tenacious little Lithuania stunned the world when it played David and Goliath with the might of the Soviet Union — and won its independence just over a decade ago. Today, the nation that vanished from the maps of Europe is back with a vengeance: it's part of the EU, was the first of the 28 EU players to give the European Constitution a stamp of approval and is a fully fledged and fighting partner of NATO, home no less to four F-16 military alliance jet fighters used to police Baltic skies.

This is a country with a colorful history, once boasting an empire stretching from the Baltic to the Black Sea. Its new pagan roots fuse with Catholic fervor, the Polish inheritance that sets it apart from its Baltic brothers, to create a land where Catholics and Orthodox mingle happily in the forest to pick wild berries and mushrooms from nature's altar. Its capital, Vilnius, is an incredibly small place with astonishing contrasts; eerie shadowy courtyards, eccentric artist community, awesome arts and beautiful baroque. Its natural treasures forests, lakes, the magical Curonian Spit in Western Lithuania — shimmer, while its oddities — the Hill of Crosses and a Soviet sculpture park — add a flavor found nowhere else. — Lonely Planet

History and Overview

Lithuania is located in Eastern Europe, bordering the Baltic Sea, between Latvia and Russia. Lithuanians belong to the Baltic group of nations. Their ancestors moved to the Baltic region in about

3000 B.C. from beyond the Volga region of central Russia. In Roman times, they traded amber with Rome and around A.D. 900 to 1000 split into different language groups, namely, Lithuanians, Prussians, Latvians, and others. The Prussians were conquered by the Teutonic Knights and, ironically, the name "Prussia" was taken over by the conquerors who destroyed or assimilated Prussia's original inhabitants. Other groups also died out or were assimilated by their neighbors. Only the Lithuanians and the Latvians survived the ravages of history.

Independent between the two World Wars, Lithuania was an nexed by Soviet Russia in 1940. On March 11, 1990, Lithuania became the first of the Soviet republics to declare its independence, but Moscow did not recognize this proclamation until September 1991, following an abortive coup in Moscow. The last Russian troops withdrew in 1993.

Economy

Lithuania subsequently restructured its economy for integration into Western European institutions; it joined both NATO and the EU in 2004. Despite this Lithuania's trade with its Central and Eastern European neighbors and Russia in particular, accounts for a major share of total trade. Foreign investment and business support have helped in the transition from the old Communist planned economy to a free market economy. In 2004, Lithuania instituted a flat tax of 33% and saw its economy grow by 8% in a single year, over double that of the world's industrialized economies. The growth was driven by exports and domestic demand. In the wake of the world recession GDP plunged nearly 15% in 2009. The three former Soviet Baltic republics were among the hardest hit by the 2008 to 2009 financial crisis.

The government's efforts to attract foreign investment, to develop export markets, and to pursue broad economic reforms has been key to Lithuania's quick recovery from a deep recession, making Lithuania one of the fastest growing economies in the EU. Despite government efforts, unemployment at 13.2% in 2012 remained high.

Residence and Citizenship

Lithuanian law automatically grants citizenship to persons born within the country's current borders. Citizenship may also be granted by naturalization. That requires a residence period, an examination in the Lithuanian language, a demonstration of familiarity with the constitution, proof of means of support, and an oath of loyalty. A right of return clause was included in the 1991 constitution for persons who left Lithuania after its occupation by the Soviet Union in 1940 and their descendants.

During World War II and afterward, many Lithuanian citizens emigrated because of its occupation by Germany and the Soviet Union until it regained its independence in 1990. Although basically a single citizenship country, in 2003 it adopted legislation that allowed former citizens of Lithuania who held its citizenship before June 15, 1940, their children, grandchildren and great-grandchildren, to acquire Lithuanian citizenship. People who acquire Lithuanian citizenship also become European Union citizens since Lithuania is a member of the EU.

The Constitutional Court of Lithuania ruled unconstitutional a provision of the 2003 Citizenship Law that provided that a foreign person willing to acquire Lithuanian citizenship did not have to renounce his or her foreign citizenship. This ruling ended the possibility of dual citizenship under the law. The court said that those acquiring Lithuanian citizenship by naturalization must renounce their foreign citizenship and prove this fact to immigration authorities.

Undoubtedly this decision has prompted some who would otherwise be eligible for citizenship to decide against applying on the basis of ancestry. The Lithuanian Seimas (parliament) in 2010 passed a law liberalizing the dual citizenship prohibition. President Dalia Grybauskaitė vetoed it, stating that: "According to the Constitution, dual citizenship is a rare exception, not a common case."

Currently, the law allows dual citizenship only for;

1. those Lithuanians who left Lithuania before March 11 1990, the Restoration of Independence (from Russia);

2. those who acquired it by birth or through marriage; and

3. exceptional cases provided by law that meet certain dual citizenship criteria. The president has the power to confer citizenship "in cases when public interest is concerned or for glorifying the name of Lithuania."

In other cases Lithuania law allows people who were citizens of Lithuania before June 15, 1940, and three generations of their descendants, to regain Lithuanian citizenship.

Under the 2003 law, the following persons are considered to be citizens of the Republic of Lithuania:

1. persons who held citizenship of Lithuania prior to June 15, 1940, their children, grandchildren and great-grandchildren (provided that the persons, their children, grandchildren, or great-grandchildren did not repatriate);

2. persons who permanently resided in the present-day territory of Lithuania from January 9, 1919 to June 15, 1940, as well as their children, grandchildren and great-grandchildren, provided that on the day of coming into force of the Law on Citizenship they were and at the present time permanently reside in the territory of Lithuania and are not citizens of any other state;

3. persons of Lithuanian descent if they are not citizens of any other state. A person whose parents or grandparents or one of the parents or grandparents is or was Lithuanian and the person considers himself Lithuanian shall be considered as being a person of Lithuanian descent;

4. persons who acquired citizenship of the Republic of Lithuania prior to November 4, 1991, under the Law on Citizenship adopted on November 3, 1989; and

5. other persons who have acquired citizenship of Lithuania under the Law on Citizenship adopted on December 5, 1991.

Economic Citizenship

Although Lithuania does not have a specific "citizenship by investment program" as such, its law provides for the possibility of granting citizenship by naturalization to people who have achieved outstanding results for the country in the fields of science, economics, arts, culture, and sport or who have invested a large sum of money in Lithuania which benefited the economy and created jobs in the country. There is no specific amount of money that must be invested, so success depends upon the economic result and the number of jobs created. The normal requirements, including the renunciation of the applicant's existing citizenship, are not applied in such cases.

Contacts

Embassy of Lithuania
2622 Sixteenth Street NW
Washington, DC 20009-4202
Tel.: (202) 234-5860
Email: info@itembassyus.org
Web: http://www.ltembassyus.org
Tourism: http://www.lithuania.travel/

United States Embassy
Akmenų g. 6, Vilnius, Lithuania LT-03106
Tel.: + (370-5) 266-5500
Email: WebEmailVilnius@state.gov
Consular email: consec@state.gov
Web: http://vilnius.usembassy.gov

Grand-Duchy of Luxembourg

Government:	Constitutional monarchy
Capital:	Luxembourg
National Day:	Birthday of Grand Duchess Charlotte: 23 June
Population:	514,862 (July 2013 est.)
Total Area:	998 sq. miles / 2,586 sq. kilometers
Languages:	Luxembourgish (national language), German and French (administrative languages)
Ethnic groups:	Luxembourger 63.1%, Portuguese 13.3%, French 4.5%, Italian 4.3%, German 2.3%, other EU 7.3%, other 5.2%
Religion:	Roman Catholic 87%, Protestants, Jews, and Muslims 13%
Life expectancy:	79.88 years
Currency:	Euro (EUR)
GDP:	US$41.86 billion (2012 est.)
GDP per capita:	US$78,000 (2012 est.)

Luxembourg is fairy-tale stuff complete with the happy ending. The story of this land's tumultuous history beguiles with its counts and dynasties, wars and victories, fortresses and promontories. Only the dragon is missing. It's no surprise that Luxembourgers are a proud people whose national motto, "Mir welle bleiwe wat mir sin." (We want to remain what we are), sums up their independent spirit. The population of 469,000 is predominantly rural-based — the only centers of any size are the capital, Luxembourg City, followed by Esch-sur-Alzette.

Though too small for its full name to fit on most European maps, pintsized Luxembourg (1607 sq mi) is wonderfully diverse. Lush highlands and valleys in the northern Ardennes merge effortlessly with the Mullerthal's ancient forested landscape to the east, where the vibrant town of Echternach makes an enjoyable base. The impossibly picturesque and ridiculously romantic (not to mention tourist-flooded) Vianden is just a short trip north from Luxembourg City; in the southeast snakes the Moselle Valley with its steep vineyards and riverside hamlets. In between all this are rolling farmlands dotted with pristine, pastel-toned houses and medieval hilltop castles. European Capital of Culture in 2007, Luxembourg's moment in the spotlight has arrived. — Lonely Planet

History and Overview

Luxembourg is located in Western Europe, between France and Germany. Founded in 963 the pie-shaped country shares borders with Germany to the east, Belgium to the west and France to the south. Luxembourg is also a part of the Benelux group along with Belgium and the Netherlands. Since 1922, Luxembourg had a fully integrated monetary and economic union with its larger neighbor, Belgium. Today both use the euro.

After 400 years of domination by various European nations, Luxembourg was granted the status of Grand Duchy by the Congress of Vienna on June 9, 1815. Although locals consider 1835 (Treaty of London) to be its year of independence, it was not granted political autonomy until 1839 under King William I of the Netherlands, who also was the Grand Duke of Luxembourg. In 1867, Luxembourg was recognized as fully independent and guaranteed perpetual neutrality, but it lost more than half of its territory to Belgium in 1839.

Overrun by Germany in both World Wars, it ended its neutrality in 1948 when it entered into the Benelux Customs Union and became a charter member of the North Atlantic Treaty Organization (NATO) in 1949. It is also one of the six original members of the European Union. In 1957, Luxembourg became one of the six founding countries of the European Economic Community (later to become the European Union) and joined the euro currency area.

Economy

The grand duchy is a major international banking and business center. This small, stable, high-income economy benefits from its proximity to France, Belgium, and Germany. It has historically featured solid growth, low inflation, and low unemployment. The industrial sector, initially dominated by steel, has become increasingly diversified to include chemicals, rubber, and other products.

Although the nation's international banking activity dates back to the late 19th century, Luxembourg began to hit its stride as an offshore haven about 30 years ago. This resulted from forces over which Luxembourg had no control. The lucky causes included: 1) the growth of foreign investment in selected European Common Market nations during the mid-1960s; 2) the imposition by the U.S. Congress of an damaging interest equalization tax in the 1980s that drove American corporations to borrow abroad; 3) German capital flow restrictions and mandatory lending ratios; 4) the 35% Swiss withholding tax on bank accounts and other interest; 5) currency exchange controls in France; and 6) stiff bank account reporting rules in nearby Holland.

To avoid these unwelcome circumstances, astute Western Europeans and Americans began searching for a safe place to invest their money. They also needed a convenient place to conduct global business with maximum freedom and lower taxes. Centrally located in, Europe Luxembourg and its banks offered a perfect solution.

But keep in mind that Luxembourg is not a tax haven. It is an offshore investment and banking center. The effective corporate tax rate is over 30%. Personal income taxes can range up to 38%. Holding companies do escape most taxes and have had a special status under the law since 1929.

About 60% of all Luxembourg bank activity is now denominated in euros. Another one-third is in U.S. dollars. Roughly, 21,000 people are employed directly or indirectly in the Duchy's more than 150 banks, and nearly 28% of the GDP flows from banking and financial business. German banks, in particular, operate here to escape domestic withholding taxes on interest and dividend loan limitations on corporate customers and they account for over 50% of all banking business. They also use the nation to deal in gold as Luxembourg imposes no VAT.

The financial sector now accounts for 27% of GDP. Most banks are foreign-owned and have extensive foreign dealings, but Luxembourg has lost some of its advantages as a favorable tax location because of OECD and EU pressures.

Although Luxembourg, like all EU members, suffered from the 2007 to 2010 global economic slump after strong expansion from 2004 to 2007, the economy contracted 3.7% in 2009, but rebounded 3.2% in 2010 but less than 1% in 2102. The country continues to enjoy an extraordinarily high standard of living — GDP per capita ranks third in the world, after Liechtenstein and Qatar, and is the highest in the EU. Turmoil in the world financial markets and lower global demand prompted the government to inject capital into the banking sector and adopt stimulus measures to boost the economy.

The World Factbook states: "Even during the financial crisis and recovery, Luxembourg retained the highest current account surplus as a share of GDP in the euro zone, mainly because of strength in financial services. Public debt remains among the lowest of the region although it has more than doubled since 2007 as percentage of GDP. Luxembourg's economy, while stabile, grew slowly in 2012 to 2013 due to ongoing weak growth in the euro area. Authorities have strengthened supervision of domestic banks because of their exposure to the activities of foreign banks."

In 2013, Luxembourg authorized the creation of private foundations aimed at entrepreneurs, wealthy families, and high-net-worth individuals. It adds to a range of wealth management instruments already in force, such as the private wealth management vehicle (société de gestion de patrimoine familial) and the family office.

Luxembourg has had a fairly strict bank secrecy law that was made less strict by the 2009 announcement of the government that it would abide by OECD rules governing tax information exchange, but on an individual case basis and with a showing of probable cause of foreign tax evasion. This policy change occurred after the grand duchy came under international pressure from the G-20 nations to improve transparency in its banking and tax systems. The government has decided to abolish strict bank secrecy by 2015 and to introduce an automatic exchange of information with third party countries.

In 2014, Luxembourg and the United States signed an agreement for automatic exchange of FATCA data between the two countries no later than September 2015. A description of that agreement can be found at http://www.irs.gov/Businesses/Corporations/International-Data-Exchange

Residence and Citizenship

Luxembourg is a unique case in the EU, not only because it is by far the smallest country, but also because of the unusual context in which immigration policy is formulated.

Thirty-seven percent of Luxembourg's residents are non-nationals, and when combined with the high number of daily trans-border commuting workers, the percentage of foreigners gathered in Luxembourg's territory reaches almost 50%. In the national labor market only 38% of the total work force is Luxembourg nationals. In the past 20 years, the foreign population of Luxembourg increased by around 70%, while the nation's native population expanded only 3%.

However, the severe hostility toward foreigners often evident in some EU countries is almost non-existent in Luxembourg. Furthermore, right-wing parties have never played a significant role in Luxembourg's political life. The political and societal atmosphere is relatively calm, and the positive attitude toward immigrants is reflected in the fact that Luxembourg nationals widely accept the idea of dual citizenship, which is currently being debated as a possible means of promoting integration. In this tiny state, therefore, there exists an unusual oasis of conflict-free co-existence, of multi-culturalism, and of non-discrimination.

Luxembourg citizenship is governed in part by the Law of January 1, 1987. This Law is based on the principle of descent (jus sanguinis). Birth within the territory of Luxembourg does not automatically confer citizenship. A child whose father or mother is a citizen of Luxembourg, regardless of the child's country of birth, is a citizen. A child born out of wedlock to a foreign mother and Luxembourg father is considered a citizen of Luxembourg if paternity is legally established.

Citizenship can be acquired in a number of ways. The most common are by descent, birth, marriage, extension of award, and business. Tourist, student and work visas are also available.

Under the Law of October 23, 2008, Luxembourgian citizenship takes into account the societal changes of the last 50 years and seeks to integrate foreigners residing in Luxembourg. Naturalization may be granted to an applicant when the following conditions are met. The person must:

1. be at least 18 years of age;

2. be able to prove that he has been legally residing in Luxembourg for the seven years preceding his application;

3. be able to show that he is integrated into Luxembourgian society, notably by a sufficient knowledge of at least one of the languages spoken in Luxembourg and by having attended the required civic instruction courses; and

4. have no criminal record.

An option is reserved for various categories of foreigners who have special ties with the country (birth within the territory, adoption or marriage to a Luxembourg national). In such cases, citizenship is granted by official declaration, subject to the approval of the Minister of Justice.

In 2009, Luxembourg adopted the principle of dual (or multiple) citizenship. The law now allows citizenship for persons who were Luxembourgers and lost their citizenship because they acquired a foreign citizenship, for persons whose lineal ancestors were Luxembourgers on January 1, 1900, for Luxembourgers who wish to acquire a foreign citizenship without losing their Luxembourg citizenship, and for foreign persons who wish to acquire Luxembourg citizenship without losing their present foreign citizenship. Many Belgian nationals have now acquired dual Luxembourg citizenship as a result.

Contacts

Embassy of the Grand-Duchy of Luxembourg
2200 Massachusetts Avenue NW
Washington, DC 20008
Tel.: (202) 265-4171
Email: washington.info@mae.etat.lu
Web: http://www.luxembourg-usa.org/

United States Embassy
22 Boulevard Emmanuel Servais
L-2535 Luxembourg
Grand-Duchy of Luxembourg
Tel.: + (352) 46-0123
Email: Luxembourgconsular@state.gov
Web: http://luxembourg.usembassy.gov

Recommended Immigration Consultant:

Henley & Partners
31, rue de Strasbourg
L-2561 Luxembourg
Tel.: +352 26 99 77 1

Republic of Malta

Government:	Republic
Capital:	Valletta
National Day:	21 September 1964 (from U.K.)
Population:	411,277 (July 2013 est.)
Total Area:	122 sq. miles / 316 sq. kilometers
Languages:	Maltese (official) 90.2%, English (official) 6%, multilingual 3%, other 0.8%
Ethnic groups:	Maltese (descendants of ancient Carthaginians and Phoenicians, with strong elements of Italian and other Mediterranean stock)
Religion:	Roman Catholic 98%, other 2%
Life expectancy:	79.98 years
Currency:	Euro (EUR)
GDP:	US$11.19 billion (2012 est.)
GDP per capita:	US$26,900 (2012 est.)

From its North African and Arabic influences (listen carefully to the local language) to the Sicilian-inspired cuisine, Malta is a microcosm of the Mediterranean. Few European countries have such concentrated history, architecture and, yes, beaches in so tiny an area. There's been an eclectic mix of influences and a roll-call of rulers over the centuries, but be in no doubt: Malta is not just a notional outpost of Italy or a relic of colonial Britain. This island nation (all 122 sq mi of it, comprising the islands of Malta, Gozo and Comino) has a quirky character all of its own. From prehistoric temples, to the baroque architecture of Valletta, feasts of rabbit to festas of noisy fireworks, rattling buses to colorful fishing boats, this nation has loads of unique charm. — Lonely Planet

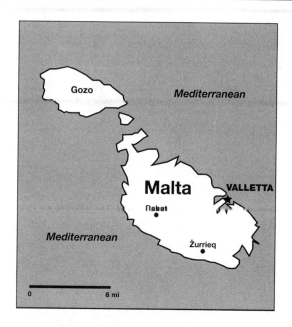

History and Overview

South of Europe is Malta, a group of islands in the central Mediterranean Sea, south of the island of Sicily and well-positioned as a cultural and political stepping stone between Europe and North Africa.

About 95% of the islanders are natives, descendants of the ancient Carthaginians and Phoenicians. The islands contain vestiges of millennia of human settlement, including some of the oldest Stone Age megalithic structures in the world. All of the subsequent cultures that flourished on the islands have left monuments, including Crusader castles and churches from the Middle Ages and ornate churches and public buildings of the Renaissance and Baroque periods. As a popular winter vacation destination, Malta has a large number of golf courses, horse ranches and resort areas. Eco-tourists are drawn to the country's rugged landscapes and Mediterranean Sea life.

In 1530, Malta was ceded to the governance of the Knights of Malta by the Holy Roman Emperor, Charles V. They built fortifications in the harbor of Valletta, so well that, in 1565, a Turkish siege was repelled largely due to excellent defenses that still are in existence today. In 1798, Napoleon invaded Malta and expelled the Knights. At the Congress of Vienna, in 1815, Britain was given possession of Malta.

With the 1869 opening of the Suez Canal, Malta became an important strategic British base. During World War II, Malta was bombed heavily by the German Luftwaffe, since it was a valuable Allied convoy port. In 1947, Malta was granted self-government and, in 1964, it became independent.

Malta is an ancient nation, but one with a thoroughly modern outlook. In recent years, the Maltese government has actively courted foreign capital with an attractive program of incentives aimed at investors and entrepreneurs. It includes generous tax incentives and inducements such as soft loans, training grants and customized facilities at subsidized costs.

This pro-business policy seeks to build on Malta's many existing strengths: favorable trade relations with countries around the world; a strategic location on world shipping lanes; a high quality, productive, English-speaking workforce, an excellent climate and quality of life; and modern health care and educational systems.

Economy

In the last decade, Malta's economy has averaged an annual growth rate of over 7%. The nation has maintained a surplus balance of payments, stable currency and low inflation (less than 1%) — all impressive numbers. These reflect the overall strength and diversity of the Maltese economy.

Traditionally, agriculture was important, but the economy has undergone significant change. Manufacturing, especially high-tech industries, now accounts for over a quarter of Malta's GDP.

About 26% of the labor force works in services, 22% in manufacturing, 37% in government, and 2% in agriculture. Major industries now include textiles, machinery, food and beverages, and high-tech products, especially electronics.

Tourism is also a growing and increasingly important sector. Key sectors that provide exceptional investment opportunities include trade, tourism, manufacturing, maintenance services, and international financial services.

The Maltese government has enacted legislation to increase the islands' role as a leader in international finance services. It has intentionally moved away from the old "tax haven" model and refashioned itself as an international business center. The government provides a variety of tax and financial incentives to banks, insurance companies, fund management firms, trading companies, trusts, and investment companies. These laws have been amended to confirm to the anti-tax haven requirements of the EU that Malta joined in 2004.

Malta's financial services industry has grown in recent years and in 2008 to 2009, it escaped significant damage from the international financial crisis, largely because the sector is centered on the indigenous real estate market and is not highly leveraged. Locally, the restricted damage from the financial crisis has been attributed to the stability of the Maltese banking system and to its prudent risk-management practices.

The global economic downturn and high electricity and water prices hurt Malta's real economy, which is dependent on foreign trade, manufacturing — especially electronics and pharmaceuticals — and tourism, but growth bounced back as the global economy recovered in 2010. Following a 1.2% contraction in 2009, GDP grew 2% in 2010. In early 2011, the EU ended excessive deficit procedures against Malta, after Malta had taken measures to correct an excessive deficit in 2010 and appeared likely to reach its deficit target of 2.8% of GDP in 2011.

Two unique factors have helped Malta's economy; online Internet gambling and generic pharmaceuticals. At a time when the United States and the U.K. both cracked down on online gaming, Malta welcomed the industry to its shores. Gaming companies are sanctioned by the Maltese government and courts. Leading online gaming companies have relocated to Malta, which has helped produce local jobs and bolster the already mature banking system. The generic pharmaceutical industry has taken advantage of Malta's liberal patent laws that protect companies that do research and testing of generic drugs before a patent expires.

Malta has an excellent infrastructure, with telecommunications, postal services, banking, and hospitals and health services all of high quality. Malta also offers a quick connection to Europe: Air Malta operates 35 routes within Europe and the Mediterranean region, and most major European airlines operate flights to Malta. There is a regular sea link with Italy.

Residence

These sunny Mediterranean islands cater to expatriates looking for a second or retirement home. Foreign nationals are eligible for Maltese citizenship after living there five years, but they are welcomed immediately as residents. Maltese residence is of three types: 1) visitors staying less than three months are counted as non-residents; 2) those remaining more than three months are temporary residents; and 3) permanent residents are granted a permit entitling them to live on the islands. Malta is one of the most attractive locations in Europe for tax advantaged private residence. For non-Maltese persons, there is the possibility of acquiring permanent residence status through an attractive and efficient program. Persons of all nationalities are eligible to apply for residence permits without discrimination.

A permanent residence permit entitles its holder to reside permanently in Malta with the freedom to come and go. Malta is a member of the European Union and of the Schengen Area agreement allowing residents of Malta to travel within that area without obtaining a visa. A permanent resident enjoys a privileged tax status, while at the same time benefiting from Malta's wide network of double taxation treaties. A further advantage of this status is that as long as the resident abides by the rules, they need not spend any particular time physically residing in Malta.

There are two routes to a Maltese residence permit for non-EU persons. One is the customary work/marriage/small investor/self-employment path practiced by many countries. It involves at least five years of continuous Maltese residence via annual permits, which in turn results in qualification for a five-year, renewable long-term residence permit. Obtaining a long-term permit requires scoring at least 75% in a course on "the social, economic, cultural and demographic history and environment of Malta."

The other route to residence for non-EU persons is through Malta's Global Residence Programme (GRP), in 2012. The GRP is based on the purchase or rental of residential property. The requirement varies from a US$301,000 purchase price (for properties on the island of Gozo and in southern Malta) to US$376,000 elsewhere, or from US$12,000 to US$13,000 annual rent.

Under the Global Residence Program, residents enjoy privileged tax status, and benefit from Malta's wide network of double taxation treaties — although, under certain treaties, limitations of treaty benefits apply. Such treaties protect an entity or individual from paying two separate taxes on the same property for the same purpose and during the same time period. And if you're not yet retired and still earning an income, the GRP gives you a flat 15% tax rate — subject to a minimum US$20,500 tax.

To obtain a residence permit under the Global Residence Programme (GRP), candidates must: 1) not be a Maltese, European Economic Area or Swiss national; 2) not benefit from any other special Maltese tax status; 3) hold a qualifying property, as described above; 4) have stable and regular income sufficient to maintain a household without recourse to the social assistance system in Malta; 5) have a valid passport or other travel document; 6) have health-insurance coverage for the entire EU area for each member of the household; 7) be fluent in either Maltese or English; 8) be a fit and proper person.

A passport is required for entry into Malta. A visa is not required for U.S. citizens for stays of up to 90 days (an extension must be applied for prior to end of 90-day period or expiration of original visa while in Malta).

Citizenship

Malta acquired independence from British rule in 1964. The Constitution, Chapter III establishes that persons born in Malta before the September 21, 1964, one of whose parents was also born in Malta, automatically became citizens of Malta on the September 21, 1964 (jus soli/jus sanguinis). It established further that persons born in Malta after independence acquired Maltese citizenship by mere birth in Malta (jus soli).

Any foreigner naturalized as a Maltese citizen is allowed to hold dual citizenship. The law also grants the same rights to the foreign husband of a citizen of Malta as those already enjoyed by the foreign wife of a citizen of Malta and ensures that foreigners married to citizens of Malta will continue to enjoy residential and employment privileges on the death of the (Maltese) spouse. Any person may apply for naturalization as a citizen of Malta after having resided there for at least five years.

Maltese welcomed special reforms to the citizenship law which allow second generation Maltese born abroad to become citizens of the island. Amendments in 2007 to the Maltese Citizenship Act for the first time allowed the obtaining of Maltese citizenship by registration and proof of lineage.

The applicant must provide documentary evidence showing direct descent from an ancestor or a parent who was born in Malta. Documents required include birth, marriage and death certificates. The registration procedure can occur at any Maltese Embassy, High Commission, Consulate, or at the Department for Citizenship and Expatriate Affairs in Malta. Physical residence in Malta is not required to qualify.

Maltese Individual Investor Program

Until 2013 Malta's approach to immigration was contradictory. On one hand, the country encouraged foreigners to take up residence via generous low tax laws. On the other, for ordinary not-so-wealthy people, it made the path to citizenship challenging.

Part of the problem was that the Maltese minister for Home Affairs and National Security had absolute discretion to give citizenship by naturalization. It was neither guaranteed nor a mere formality. The minister needed to be convinced that applicants were of a "good character" or "suitable citizens." Some commentators estimated that 20 years of residence was a good rule of thumb before citizenship was feasible.

A major change in immigration law was proposed in 2013 with the Maltese Individual Investor Program (IIP). After some delays in early 2014, in part because of concerns expressed by the European Union, the IIP became law.

To participate in the IIP, applicants must pay fees (see below) and qualify under a "strict" due-diligence system, combining several different background verification procedures with a risk-weighted assessment of whether the applicant is suitable to be admitted as a citizen under the program.

Successful applicants must make a contribution of US$890,000 to a National Development Fund (for social projects), plus US$34,000 each for spouse and minor children, and US$68,400 each for dependent children 18 to 25 years or dependent parents above 55. For a family of four, the cost per person will be around US$253,000.

Regardless of the applicant's eventual success or failure, the Maltese government will also charge due diligence fees of US$10,300 for the main applicant; US$6,800 each for spouses, adult children and parents; and US$4,100 each for minor children; as well as passport fees and bank charges of US$685 and US$275 per person.

Finally, applicants will pay a professional service fee to Henley & Partners, an international firm appointed by the Maltese government to manage the application process.

To ward off domestic criticisms that it was "selling citizenship" — and to weed out bad apples — the Maltese government stressed that "the due diligence to be applied to those applying for Maltese citizenship will be subjected to complete X-ray of applicants' and relatives' lives and the source of their riches."

IIP candidates must have clean criminal records. They must also produce a medical certificate confirming that they and their dependents aren't suffering from any contagious diseases and are in good health. Once an applicant has undergone Henley & Partners' initial due diligence process, a new government agency, Identity Malta, will subject applicants and their families to background checks. In some cases, a request for a personal interview may occur.

Opponents of the IIP program charge this constitutes a conflict of interest since Henley is the company that profits from IIP sales and also does the checks on applicants.

From there, Identity Malta will then produce a report on each individual with a recommendation detailing the rationale for approving or declining the application.

It's clear that the Maltese IIP is aimed at the top of the citizenship-by-investment market. The fee structure and cost of compliance put the minimum cost of IIP citizenship at over $1 million. But as originally proposed (see below) the benefits were extraordinary: fast-track Maltese and therefore EU citizenship, without a prior residence requirement, with a relatively short application process, and low non-resident tax rates.

Major Change

In early 2014, a defensive Maltese Prime Minister Joseph Muscat announced agreement had been reached with EU officials based on a major change in the pending law.

Whereas IIP foreign participants originally were not to be required to even reside in Malta, now they will be required to have at least 12 months of proven prior physical residence before a grant of IIP citizenship. This calls into question the original legislation's promise of secrecy of the names of foreigners who apply.

Shortly after this seemly strict residence requirement was imposed, an official of Henley & Partners essentially told an interviewer that it is meaningless: "It depends on each particular case. One cannot say generally how many days someone needs to be present. What can be said is that there are some necessary visits to Malta."

The surrender to the EU came after the European Commission said it was considering whether it could veto the Maltese IIP based on EU treaty law. The European parliament had voted to censure Malta. There is a real question whether the EU has a veto power over a country's citizenship laws.

Many other EU countries also sell residence leading to citizenship in return for investments including Austria, Belgium, Cyprus, Portugal, Poland, Hungary, Bulgaria and Romania.

The larger threat to the IIP remains in continued political opposition within Malta. No doubt all this controversy and the last minute changes will not improve IIP sales. Nevertheless, in the first 90 days of IIP operation over 100 individuals made financial commitments to the program which totaled over €100 million in foreign direct investment for Malta.

Comparison

For some time, only three countries have offered relatively fast economic citizenship such as Malta's: Austria, the Commonwealth of Dominica and Saint Kitts and Nevis. Those countries effectively offer passports for sale, since cash payments to their governments are one way to obtain them.

Within the EU, Austria, Cyprus, and Bulgaria also offer citizenship-by-investment. Compared to those programs, Malta's clearly comes out on top. Austria's program requires a US$2,750,000 donation to an Austrian "public cause," or business investment of at least US$10 million; it is notoriously difficult to qualify. And although Austria allows dual citizenship, it is on a case-by-case basis.

Cyprus' program is also expensive — requiring an investment of around US$4 million — and the country is tarred by its serious financial problems. Bulgaria offers passports at just over US$400,000, but even though it is part of the EU, it is outside the euro zone, and more importantly, its passport-holders are not yet eligible for unrestricted travel and resettlement in the rest of the EU.

At the other end of the market, Saint Kitts and Nevis' cash-for-citizenship program is currently at least US$250,000. This program is fine if your goal is a second passport, but it doesn't give you EU access.

Compared to these programs, the very expensive Maltese IIP might be the most respectable, easiest to navigate, and will offer a dual-citizenship-friendly program in the world.

Taxes

There's an interesting quirk of Maltese residence tax rules. It is possible to become a Maltese citizen and continue to be regarded as domiciled in their country of origin for tax purposes.

Maltese tax authorities define "domicile" as the country where you were born, where you were married, where your will and other important legal documents are registered, in other words, where you're "from" and might one day return. IIP participants who obtain Maltese citizenship and who can demonstrate that their "domicile" is elsewhere — not a problem if you maintain links to your other home — will pay a flat tax rate of 15% on Maltese and offshore income, but nothing on offshore investment income or capital transfers. In other words, they will be treated the same as permanent residents for the purposes of taxation.

Malta levies three types of direct taxes — private income, corporate income and estate taxes — but the government tries to keep rates low for well-heeled foreigners and corporations. There are no property taxes. Interest and royalty income on local investments are entirely exempt from tax, as are capital gains on collective investment arrangements and securities (as long as the underlying asset is not Maltese real estate).

Some aspects of Maltese tax law flirt with "tax haven" territory. Foreign companies receive tax discounts of up to 85% on profits remitted to Maltese subsidiaries. And under some circumstances, individuals who are considered not domiciled in Malta — even if they live there — only pay a 15% tax on income earned in Malta as well as foreign income remitted to Malta.

More recently, the Maltese government has intentionally refashioned the country as an "international business center." The islands conform to EU and international anti-tax haven requirements, so living in Malta is no longer seen as a red flag to the global tax authorities.

Contacts

Embassy of Malta
2017 Connecticut Avenue NW
Washington, DC 20008
Tel.: (202) 462-3611
Email: maltaembassy.washington@gov.mt
Web: http://www.foreign.gov.mt/pages/main.asp?sec=17

United States Embassy
Ta' Qali National Park
Attard, ATD 4000
Tel.: + (356) 2561-4000
Email: usembmalta@state.gov
Email for visa, consular inquiries: consularmalta@state.gov
Web: http://malta.usembassy.gov
Mailing address: P.O. Box 535
Valletta, Malta, CMR 01

Henley & Partners
Aragon House, Dragonara Road
St. Julian's STJ 3140 MALTA
Tel.: +356 2138 7400
Email: malta@henleyglobal.com
Web: https://www.henleyglobal.com/countries/malta/citizenship-by-investment/

Principality of Monaco

Government:	Constitutional monarchy
Capital:	Monaco
National Day:	Prince of Monaco Holiday: 19 November
Population:	30,500 (July 2013 est.)
Total Area:	0.75 sq. mile / 2 sq. kilometers, about three times the size of The Mall in Washington, DC
Languages:	French (official), English, Italian, Monegasque
Ethnic groups:	French 47%, other 21%, Monegasque 16%, Italian 16%
Religion:	Roman Catholic 90%, other 10%
Life expectancy:	89.63 years
Currency:	Euro (EUR)
GDP:	US$5.748 billion (2011 est.) Monaco does not publish national income figures; estimates are approximate
GDP per capita:	US$70,600 (2011 est.)

After scaling Monaco's steep terraced steps, shiny escalators and gleaming marble corridors tunneling through the rocks to a series of free public lifts running up and down the hillside (not to mention navigating the 3D road system encircling its towering high rises!), you could be forgiven for thinking you are inside a life-size MC Escher illustration of an illusionary maze.

Squeezed into a little more than three quarters of a square mile, making it the world's second smallest country, after the Vatican, this pint-sized principality is a sovereign state, with its own red-and-white flag, national holiday (19 November), country telephone code and traditional Monegasque dialect.

French is the official language, although many street signs, especially in the old Monaco Ville quarter, are in French and Monegasque, and children of all 107 nationalities that form Monaco's population are required to study the language at school. Neither is Monaco part of the EU, but because of its close ties with France, it participates in the EU customs territory, and there are no border formalities crossing to and from France.

Monaco's manicured streets presided over by palaces and its lush fountained parks are eminently safe thanks to a prolific police presence backed up by plain-clothed patrollers and omnipresent CCTV cameras. Monaco is most famed for its glamorous Monte Carlo casino, Formula One cars roaring through the streets during its glamorous Grand Prix, and the scintillating lives of its glamorous royal family, the Grimaldis. — Lonely Planet

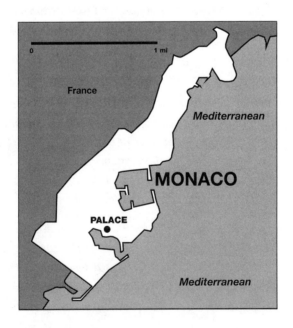

History and Overview

Founded in 1215 as a colony of Genoa, Italy, Monaco has been ruled by the House of Grimaldi since 1297, except when under French rule (1789 to 1814). Designated as a protectorate of Sardinia (1815 to 1860) by the Treaty of Vienna Monaco's sovereignty was recognized by the Franco-Monegasque Treaty of 1861. The Prince of Monaco was an absolute ruler until a constitution was promulgated in 1911. In 1918, a treaty was signed providing for limited French protection over Monaco. The treaty, formally noted in the Treaty of Versailles, established that Monegasque policy would be aligned with French political, military and economic interests.

A new constitution, in 1962, abolished capital punishment, provided for female suffrage, and established a Supreme Court to guarantee fundamental liberties. In 1993, Monaco became a member of the United Nations. It joined the Council of Europe in 2004. Three months after the death of his father, Prince Rainier III, on April 6, Prince Albert II formally acceded to the throne on July 12, 2005.

This unique and ancient principality is not for everyone. If you want to make this your permanent home, it helps to have a lot more than a modest amount of money, plus an assured income for life. Moreover, it doesn't hurt to know Prince Albert and the royal family. Monaco, in general, is for individuals who have already made their money, people who want to practice the art of living well while others mind the store for them, people who want to spend time on the Riviera. If tax avoidance is the only goal, there are other cheaper places.

Many residents are just wealthy people who have decided to retire in Monaco. They are drawn to the pleasant atmosphere, Mediterranean climate and leisure. Monaco has all the facilities that wealthy people consider necessary: country clubs, health clubs, and golf and tennis clubs.

Indeed, Monaco may have a population of only about 30,000, and an area of only three-quarters of a square mile (less than New York City's Central Park), but it has all the services and cultural activities of a city the size of San Francisco.

Monaco's prices are expensive, but no worse than London, Paris or Geneva. These days, there are as many Italian restaurants as there are French ones. Most shops and supermarkets accept euros just as readily as Swiss francs. The European common currency, in this respect, has long been established in the principality.

Monaco is a high-profile place. The world remembers Grace Kelly, the Hollywood film star, who married Prince Rainier in 1956. The international spotlight followed her until she died in a tragic auto accident in 1982. During his long rule that ended with his death in 2005, the late Prince Rainier worked hard to expand the economic and professional scope of the country. Few recent monarchs can claim credit for extending their dominions by a fifth without conquest. But, by land filling the sea, the Prince managed to expand his tiny principality by 23% in the 50 years since he succeeded his grandfather. This land expansion mirrored Prince Rainier's determination to make this a dynamic modern mini-state.

It has also been at the heart of a remarkable economic development based around trading, tourism and financial services in a tax friendly environment. On its small area and population, Monaco manages to generate, annually, over €11 billion (US$14 billion) worth of business. The state has an annual budget of €1 billion, carries no debts and possesses unpublished liquid reserves of at least €2.5 billion (US$3.2 billion).

Economy and Taxes

The Principality is no longer just a frivolous playground for the rich. In the past, the government was funded primarily through casino gambling proceeds. It is now a modern economy participating at a global level in a diverse range of sectors.

Undeniably, there are tax benefits to be gained from a move to Monaco. The authorities do not like the principality to be known as the tax haven that it is. It's a low-tax area, rather than a no-tax area, but still a haven. Since 1869, there have been no income taxes for Monegasque nationals and resident foreigners, one of the main attractions for high net worth individuals. There are no direct, withholding, or capital gains taxes for foreign nationals, except for the French, who, because of a bilateral tax treaty with Paris, cannot escape the clutches of the French tax system. There are first-time residential registration taxes, but no real estate taxes. It does charge a nearly 20% value-added tax, collects stamp duties, and companies face a 33% tax on profits unless they can show that three-quarters of profits are generated within the principality. Monaco's economic prospects remain uncertain tied to future euro-zone growth. Weak economic growth also has hurt public finances with a budget deficit of 1.3% of GDP in 2012.

Monaco, located on the Mediterranean coast, has an economy primarily geared toward finance, commerce and tourism. Low taxes have drawn many foreign companies to Monaco; the companies' production accounts for around 50% of the annual government income. The enterprises pay a 33.33% tax only if more than 25% of their revenue is generated abroad. Ever since Monaco's famed casino opened in 1856, the tourism industry has been booming. It currently accounts for close to 25% of annual revenue. Customs, postal services, telecommunications, and banking in Monaco are governed by an economic and customs union with France. The official currency is the euro. In 2011, estimates placed the national product at US$5.748 billion and the per capita income at US$70,600.

There are corporate and banking advantages, too. Confidentiality is good, as far as business records go, and the same can be said for the banking services. The Bank of France is responsible for the Monegasque banking system and carries out regular inspections. Since 1993, there has been an anti-money laundering law. The banking services in Monaco are not as comprehensive as they could be and attempts are being made to loosen the banking secrecy rules. Prosecutors in Nice, France, have expressed grave concerns about financial infiltration by the so-called "Red Mafia," the rich and ruthless Russian crime syndicates.

Under pressure from major nations, Monaco has, adopted OECD rules on the sharing on tax information as well as negotiated tax information exchange treaties (TIEAs) with other nations. In 2011, it had 21 TIEAs with other countries, Germany, Liechtenstein, the Netherlands, and the United States. It shares tax information with France under an existing treaty.

Some people may find Monaco's police presence a little severe. The Principality has the lowest crime rate of any highly urbanized area in the world. This physical security is, of course, one of its great advantages.

Can we make any predictions about Monaco?

It's not going to become a ghost town. It is stable and any major changes are unlikely to come from inside. In 1997, the Principality celebrated its 700th anniversary under the rule of the Grimaldi family. Prince Albert, now in charge, definitely is more liberal than his father in many ways. (He has admitted to fathering at least one, and possibly two illegitimate children and has made noise about cleaning up Monaco's reputation for alleged money laundering and tax evasion.) Both he and his siblings, in their youth, had wild personal reputations with the details of their private lives constantly appearing in the gossip columns of the European press. Things on that front have been quiet recently.

In July 2011, Prince Albert, 53, and Princess Charlene, 33, the former Charlene Wittstock of South Africa, were married in an elaborate wedding costing a reported US$70 million. A French newspaper claimed that a few days before the wedding, Charlene, was stopped at the Nice airport with a one-way ticket home to South Africa following claims that her husband-to-be had fathered an illegitimate child during their relationship. The paper alleged that a series of phone calls between the police and Palace officials followed before Charlene's passport was confiscated.

Residence and Citizenship

The main criteria for residence in Monaco are financial; high personal net worth and the ability to pay up to US$20,000 in professional fees, plus the added cost of buying some of Europe's most expensive real estate. The Principality borders the Mediterranean Sea on the southern coast of France, near the border with Italy, and currently has some 30,000 residents. Only 6,000 hold a Monegasque passport; all others are expat workers and rich tax exiles. The country did away with all forms of personal income tax in 1870 and, for decades, solely lived off casino revenues.

The following persons receive Monegasque nationality:

1. any person born in Monaco or abroad of a Monegasque father;

2. any person born in Monaco or abroad of a mother born Monegasque who still has this nationality at the time of the birth and of an unknown father;

3. any person born of a Monégasque mother of whom one of the ancestors in the same line was born Monegasque;

4. any person born of a mother who acquired Monegasque nationality by declaration following simple adoption;

5. any person born within Monaco of unknown parents.

For naturalization the person who wishes to acquire Monegasque nationality must prove:

1. that receiving Monegasque nationality will cause him/her to lose his/her previous nationality;

2. that naturalization will definitely relieve any obligation to perform military service abroad;

3. that he/she has resided 10 years in the Principality after reaching the age of 18; this residence must be unbroken and in effect at the moment the request for naturalization is made and not be mere residence at an earlier period. The Prince can waive this requirement.

Citizenship may also be acquired by adoption or marriage.

Any foreigner whom the Prince considers worthy of this favor may be exempt from the requirement of 10 years' residence. For a full description of Monegasque citizenship laws, see http://www.monaco-consulate.com/index.php/useful-links/monegasque-citizenship/

It is actually much easier to obtain a residence permit here than many might suppose. A clean record, solid bank references and a net worth of US$500,000 should do it. Fees for establishing residence are likely to cost in the range of US$10,000 to US$20,000.

The Principality has offered financial and fiscal concessions to foreign nationals for decades. These have been restricted in a Convention with France in 1963 and, more recently, by agreements with France after pressure from the EU. If you're on the move already, stability may not be an important issue. However, you might be looking for a base and would do well to consider Monaco. The lifestyle is attractive, but is not everybody's cup of tea. If you are contemplating a move purely for financial or fiscal reasons, you might, depending on your specific requirements, do better elsewhere.

Once there, keep a low profile. Foreign nationals who are resident are afraid to make any public criticisms of the country because if the authorities consider you a trouble maker, they can issue a 24-hour notice of expulsion. There's no one to appeal to and you'll be out the door.

A passport is required for entry into Monaco. A visa is not required for tourist/business stays up to 90 days in Monaco.

Contacts

Embassy of Monaco
3400 International Drive NW, Suite 2K - 100
Washington, DC 20008-3006
Visitors' entrance: 4000 Connecticut Avenue NW
Washington, DC 20008
Tel.: (202) 234-1530
Email: info@monacodc.org
Web: http://www.monaco-usa.org

U.S. diplomatic representation to Monaco is handled by the U.S. Embassy in Paris.

United States Embassy
2 Avenue Gabriel
75382 Paris Cedex 8, France
Tel.: + (33) 1-4312-2222
Web: http://france.usembassy.gov/
From the U.S. and Canada, dial 011-33-8-10-26-46-26

U.S. Consulate General at Marseille
12 Place Varian Fry
13086 Marseille, France
Tel.: + (33) 4-9154-9200
Web: http://france.usembassy.gov/marseille/

Recommended Immigration Consultant:

Henley & Partners AG
Klosbachstrasse 110
8024 Zurich, Switzerland
Tel.: +41 44 266 22 22
Web: www.henleyglobal.com/monaco

Republic of Montenegro

Government:	Republic
Capital:	Podgorica
National Day:	National Day: 13 July
Population:	653,474 (July 2013 est.)
Total Area:	5,332.84 sq. miles / 13,812 sq. kilometers
Languages:	Serbian 63.6%, Montenegrin (official) 22%, Bosnian 5.5%, Albanian 5.3%, unspecified 3.7%
Ethnic groups:	Montenegrin 43%, Serbian 32%, other (Muslims, Croats, Roma) 12%, Bosniak 8%, Albanian 5%
Religion:	Orthodox 74.2%, Muslim 17.7%, Catholic 3.5%, other 0.6%, unspecified 3%, atheist 1%
Life expectancy:	76.6 years
Currency:	Euro (EUR)
GDP:	US$4.157 billion (2012 est.)
GDP per capita:	US$11,600 (2012 est.)

Montenegro is coming out from its Yugoslav shadow and beginning to be admired for the beauty it is. No longer should visitors think they will fall off the edge of the world if they journey east beyond Dubrovnik. Croatia's sapphire blue Adriatic Sea does continue. However, here it's backed by a craggy, grey mountain range leaving just enough room for a ribbon of coastal towns on a sweep of sandy beaches and small coves running down to the Albanian border.

Historic walled towns like Stari Bar, Budva, Kotor and Herceg Novi are perfect for exploring, and anywhere along the coast you can find private rooms in a laze-away seaside town. The interior is a setting of dramatic mountains tufted with pine forests, dotted with lakes and scored by giddy-deep canyons. The highest region, the Durmitor National Park, is a favorite for winter skiing and summer hiking in a pristine mountain scape while below in Tara's deep canyon, intrepid rafters challenge its tumbling rapids. So much for a small country and the world's newest nation. — *Lonely Planet*

History and Overview

Europe's newest (2006) independent nation is located in southeastern Europe, between the Adriatic Sea and its former partner, Serbia.

The use of the name Montenegro began in the 15th century when the CrnojevićDynasty began to rule the Serbian principality of Zeta; over subsequent centuries, it was able to maintain its independence from the Ottoman Empire. From the 16th to 19th centuries, Montenegro became atheocratic state ruled by a series of bishop princes; in 1852, it was transformed into a secular principality.

After World War I in 1918 it lost its independence and became part of the Kingdom of Yugoslavia. At the conclusion of World War II, it became a constituent republic of the Socialist Federal Republic of Yugoslavia. When the latter dissolved in 1992, Montenegro federated with Serbia, first as the Federal Republic of Yugoslavia and, after 2003, in a looser union of Serbia and Montenegro.

In a 2006 independence referendum the vote for severing ties with Serbia exceeded the required 55% threshold, allowing Montenegro to formally declare its independence on June 3, 2006.

The Republic of Montenegro severed its economy from Yugoslav federal control and from Serbia during the Milosevic era and maintained its own central bank, using the euro instead of the Yugoslav dinar as official currency, collecting customs tariffs, and managing its own budget.

The dissolution of the loose political union between Serbia and Montenegro, in 2006, led to separate membership in several international institutions, such as the United Nations, IMF, World Bank, and the European Bank for Reconstruction and Development. Montenegro is pursuing its own membership in the World Trade Organization as well as negotiating agreements with the European Union in anticipation of eventual membership.

In 2010, the European Council granted EU candidate country status to Montenegro after negotiations to join began the EC in 2012, having met the conditions that called for steps to fight corruption and organized crime.

The World Factbook states: "Severe unemployment remains a key political and economic problem for this entire region. Montenegro has privatized its large aluminum complex, the dominant industry, as well as most of its financial sector, and has begun to attract direct foreign investment in the tourism sector." The global financial crisis has had a significant negative impact on the economy, due to the ongoing credit crunch, a decline in the real estate sector, and a fall in aluminum exports. In 2012, real GDP growth slipped to 0.5%, reflecting the general downturn in Europe.

Residence and Citizenship

Montenegro has large non-Montenegrin communities, most notably ethnic Serbs and Albanians.

Since the 2006 end of the union of Serbia and Montenegro, the issue of citizenship has created a controversy in both successor-countries. In 2007, neighboring Serbia's parliament amended its citizenship law to enable ethnic Serbs living outside the country to obtain citizenship.

Montenegrin citizens who at the time of independence were not registered as resident in Serbia, can receive Serbian citizenship through a simplified procedure that applies to all ethnic Serb citizens located in the successor-states of the former Socialist Federal Republic of Yugoslavia.

In 2011, under pressure from the EU Montenegro adopted revised citizenship legislation making it easier for naturalization for citizens of the former Yugoslav republics.

Under this law, citizens of one of the republics of the former Yugoslavia who registered and kept current their residence in Montenegro from at least five years prior to independence on June 3, 2006, are eligible for citizenship, if they fulfil financial conditions and have security clearance. Applicants are also required to deliver to the Ministry of Interior a written statement accepting the rights and duties of Montenegrin citizenship, along with a request for citizenship.

This naturalization law is among the most restrictive in the Balkans, but it means that applicants no longer will be required to end their original citizenship. Many people from other former Yugoslav republics were unable to provide proof of ending other citizenship, or wanted to keep their primary citizenship. In principle, the most recent amendment is also a step toward tolerating dual citizenship. At present, formal renunciation is not required and naturalized persons can use both passports.

Under a 1999 law governing immigration citizenship is acquired:

1. by descent (jus sanguinis) from one or more Montenegro citizen parents;

2. by birth within the territory of Montenegro;

3. by naturalization, or;

4. under the terms of international agreements.

A foreign citizen can acquire citizenship if they are 18 years old and have resided in Montenegro for at least 10 years prior to applying for citizenship. A foreign citizen who marries a citizen of Montenegro can acquire citizenship after residing not less than five years continuously prior to applying for citizenship. Children under 18 can be included in their parent's naturalization, but those 14 years old or older must give their consent. The Internal Affairs Ministry decides on applications for naturalization of Montenegrin citizenship.

Citizens of the U.S. and EU nations do not need a visa for visits of 30 days or less. See http://www.visit-montenegro.com/tourism-visas.htm

Citizenship for Sale

Until 2010, only two countries in the world offered citizenship for sale; Saint Kitts and Nevis and the Commonwealth of Dominica, both small eastern Caribbean island nations located in what was known as the British West Indies. (I describe both in Part Two of this book).

Europe's newest independent nation, Montenegro, has what euphemistically is known as "economic citizenship" — but as of this writing this program remains on hold. The program was announced in 2010 but suspended indefinitely shortly thereafter. Four years later it remains in legal limbo.

That may be because while the law was in operation, wealthy mobile phone mogul and ex-Thai prime minister, Thaksin Shinawatra, received Montenegrin citizenship. Several other internationally notorious personages were also rumored as applicants. It appears the program was suspended due to pressure from the European Union, although nothing official was made public. This dormant program remains legally authorized under Article 12 of the Citizenship Act.

Saint Kitts and Nevis, the Commonwealth of Dominica, and Austria have similar citizenship programs. Lithuania and Slovakia have citizenship programs where the residence requirement may be waived for approved investors. Since 2010 Bulgaria, Romania and others have joined the "economic citizenship for sale" bandwagon. The United States has a Green Card through Investment program which grants investors permanent residence, as does Canada.

While it lasted, foreigners were offered citizenship in return for investing in the country €500,000 (US$680,000) if they proved to be known businesspeople of good reputation. Under this suspended program, the applicant either must invest €1.5 million (US$2.3

million) in real estate from an approved real estate developer, or invest €300,000 (US$400,000) in approved real as well as making a €200,000 (US$272,000) non-refundable contribution to the Treasury of Montenegro.

A Montenegrin passport does allow visa-free travel to more than 85 countries and territories worldwide.

Contacts

Embassy of the Republic of Montenegro
1610 New Hampshire Avenue NW
Washington, DC 20009
Tel.: (202) 234-6108
Email or website unavailable.

United States Embassy
Dzona Dzeksona 2, 81000 Podgorica, Montenegro
Tel.: + (382) 020- 410-500
Email: PodgoricaPROT@state.gov
Web: http://podgorica.usembassy.gov/

Immigrant and non-immigrant visa applications are handled by the Consular Section of the U.S. Embassy in Belgrade, Yugoslavia.
Email: Consularbelgrd@state.gov
Web: http://belgrade.usembassy.gov/consular/visas.html.

The Netherlands

Government:	Constitutional monarchy
Capital:	Amsterdam
National Day:	King's Day: April 27th
Population:	16,805,037 (July 2013 est.)
Total Area:	16,033 sq. miles / 41,526 sq. kilometers
Languages:	Dutch and Frisian (both official)
Ethnic groups:	Dutch 80.7%, EU 5%, Indonesian 2.4%, Turkish 2.2%, Surinamese 2%, Moroccan 2%, Caribbean 0.8%, other 4.8%
Religion:	Roman Catholic 30%, Dutch Reformed 11%, Calvinist 6%, other Protestant 3%, Muslim 5.8%, other 2.2%, none 42%
Life Expectancy:	81.01 years
Currency:	Euro (EUR)
GDP:	US$695.8 billion (2012 est.)
GDP per capita:	US$41,500 (2012 est.)

There aren't many countries with so much land below sea level. There aren't many, if any, countries this flat. There aren't many countries with so much reclaimed land. There aren't many countries this densely populated, and yet so liberal. There aren't many countries with so much water and wind, or so many boats, sails, bikes, birds, dykes, polders, windmills, flowers, fish, bridges, cafes, cheese, and tall people. And there certainly aren't many countries who can claim such a vibrant color (vivid orange in this case) as their own. Simply put, there is no place like the Netherlands.

Start with the Dutch cities. Who hasn't heard of Amster-

dam, the capital of culture, coffee shops and canals? Its mesmerizing beauty is hard to overestimate, and yet a surfeit of stunning metropole are only hours, or even minutes, away by train. Haarlem, Groningen City, Rotterdam, Utrecht City, Den Haag, Leiden, Delft, Maastricht; the list seems endless, a mind-boggling concept considering the size of this small nation.

Outside the cities, the Netherlands once again borders on over-achievement. Its bucolic splendor of national parks and sheep-patrolled polders is perfectly complimented by shimmering lakes, sandy coastlines, and a chain of windswept islands. Best of all, it can all be seen from the comfort of a bicycle seat. As we've already said, there's no place like the Netherlands.

But don't take our word for it; come join the Dutch in their gezellig ways; you won't be disappointed. — Lonely Planet

History and Overview

The Kingdom of the Netherlands, or Holland as it is also known, is the largest of the Low Countries in the northwest corner of Europe. Almost 30% of the land is below sea level, protected by an elaborate series of earthen dykes and mechanical dams erected to prevent the reclaimed land from being flooded by the sea.

There are also several Dutch overseas territories in the Caribbean, an autonomous region. In 2010, the former "Netherlands Antilles" was dissolved and the three smallest islands, Bonaire, Sint Eustatius, and Saba, became special municipalities within the Netherlands administrative structure. The larger islands of Sint Maarten and Curacao joined the Netherlands and Aruba as constituent countries forming the Kingdom of the Netherlands.

The Dutch continue to confound attempts to categorize their culture, an easy-going blend of generous social liberalism and meticulous regularity, neatness, and moral probity, the last three possibly owing to the constant need to work together to keep the sea out of the country.

In recent years, a growing Muslim population influx from Morocco, but also from former Dutch colonial possessions, such as Indonesia, has caused considerable friction and political controversy. There is a huge backlash against them for not integrating into the Dutch society. The assassination by Muslim extremists of both a conservative political leader and a well-known writer has created major opposition to open immigration and admission of refugees.

Even so, when it comes to personal conduct, almost anything goes in Holland, as long as it does not impinge on others' rights. Excellent cheeses, tasty beer, herrings, Indonesian banquets, pea soup, and copious gin are Dutch staples still readily available to tourists and residents alike, as are fresh produce and cut flowers produced on an industrial scale.

Economy

The prosperous and open Dutch economy is based on private enterprise with a large measure of government involvement. The Netherlands is the fifth largest economy in the euro zone and the third largest exporter in the region. Industrial activity features food processing, petroleum refining and metalworking. The highly mechanized agricultural sector employs only 4% of the labor force, but provides large surpluses for export and the domestic food processing industry. As a result, the Netherlands ranks third worldwide in value of agricultural exports, behind the U.S. and France.

Sharp cuts in subsidy and social security spending since the 1980s helped the Dutch achieve sustained economic growth combined with falling unemployment and moderate inflation. The country has been one of the leading European nations for attracting foreign direct investment and is one of the four largest investors in the U.S. The pace of job growth reached 10-year highs in 2007. After 26 years of uninterrupted economic growth, the Netherlands' economy, which is highly open and dependent on foreign trade and financial services, was hard-hit by the global economic crisis. Dutch GDP contracted while exports declined nearly 25% due to a sharply reduced world demand. Finally, in 2013 to 2014, the GDP returned to slim growth levels.

The Dutch financial sector also suffered, due in part to the high exposure of some Dutch banks to U.S. mortgage-backed securities. In response to turmoil in financial markets, the government nationalized two banks and injected billions of dollars into a third, to prevent further systemic risk. The government also sought to boost the domestic economy by accelerating infrastructure programs, offering corporate tax breaks for employers to retain workers, and expanding export credit facilities.

The stimulus programs and bank bailouts, however, resulted in a government budget deficits starting in 2009 that contrasted sharply with surpluses in prior of years. With unemployment weighing on private-sector consumption, the government of Prime Minister Mark Rutte came under pressure to keep the budget deficit in check while promoting economic recovery. In 2012, tax revenues dropped nearly 9%, GDP contracted, and the budget deficit worsened. The unemployment rate remained relatively low at 6.8%.

Citizenship and Residence

Dutch immigration procedure involves two entities, 1) the municipality (de gemeente) where an applicant lives, and; 2) the Immigration and Naturalization Service (IND).

The first serves as the investigator for an applicant in a procedure that takes about 90 days; then it transmits its findings to the IND that can require up to a year before a final decision.

In the Netherlands, citizenship is granted automatically to third-generation immigrants, and to second-generation immigrants whose parents have lived there for five years, have integrated into society, and speak Dutch.

Any foreign national who lives in the Netherlands for continuous five years, even illegally, and who masters some ability with the Dutch language, is a likely candidate for citizenship. Five years continuous residence or "factual abode" in the Netherlands and/or the Dutch Antilles, immediately before applying, is required. Factual abode used to be broadly interpreted to include those who have lived there illegally without residence permits, but now the IND applies it to mean five years of continuous legal residence.

Various demonstrable personal ties with the Dutch can lower or even waive residence requirements. The requirement is reduced to two additional years for those who, earlier in life, lived in the Netherlands and/or the Dutch Antilles for at least eight years and then returned. For persons formally adopted by a Dutch national, or for the foreign spouse of a Dutch national, residence requirements are is waived.

The Dutch Nationality Act requires that spouses be screened for criminal records, but a foreign spouse of either sex is entitled to a "specially privileged naturalization procedure," meaning waiver of any residence requirement after three years of marriage. Dutch law recognizes same-sex relationships, so after a five-year non-heterosexual relationship, a non-Dutch partner can apply for naturalization.

Naturalization

The Netherlands, always in the vanguard of social policy change, requires a five-year legal residence before naturalization for foreign persons who have an extra-marital relationship of at least five years duration with a Dutch national. This was increased from three years in 2012. The affair is evidence that the foreigner is "socially integrated" into Dutch society. The IND test for integration is now much stricter and subjective.

In all Dutch naturalization cases, past "good conduct" is necessary or citizenship can and will be denied. Good conduct is measured by whether there is a "serious suspicion that the alien in question constitutes a danger to public order, good morals, public health or the security of the Kingdom." Included in prohibited categories are convicted drug dealers, those convicted of serious felonies and spies on behalf of foreign countries. Those who espouse extreme political views are not necessarily excluded.

By Birth

Dutch nationality also can be derived from a Dutch parent.

Article 3, paragraph 1 of the Netherlands Nationality Act states: "Any person whose father or mother is a Netherlands national at the time of his/her birth, as well as the person whose

Netherlands parent was deceased at the time of his/her birth, is a Netherlands national."

While birth in the Netherlands to foreign citizen parents does not confer Dutch citizenship, a unique "third generation rule" is contained in Article 3, paragraph 3: "Any person born in the Netherlands or in the Netherlands Antilles whose father or mother was resident there at the time of birth, while the relevant parent's mother [the child's grandmother] was resident there at the time of that parent's birth, is a Netherlands national."

Dutch law also allows a limited version of the jus soli rule.

A person who is born in the Netherlands of foreign citizen parents and lives there continuously thereafter may elect to acquire Dutch citizenship prior to reaching the age of 25.

With a Dutch passport, you have visa-free access to more than 120 countries including Canada, Mexico, and the USA. You can also live or work anywhere in the 27 EU countries and unless you choose to live in the Netherlands, you won't be subject to Dutch taxes when you live elsewhere. For U.S. citizens or long-term residence considering expatriation, a Dutch passport provides a first-class alternative travel document that can be used virtually anywhere in the world.

Immigration Politics

After elections in 2007, a new centrist Liberal-Labor coalition government announced amnesty for thousands of illegal immigrants who had arrived before 2001 and allowed them to stay. The move eased tough immigration laws approved by the former center-right administration. The immigration issue had gripped Dutch politics since the murders of two prominent campaigners against Muslim extremism, independent politician Pim Fortuyn and film-maker Theo van Gogh.

The Labor Party half of the Netherlands' centrist coalition is led by the Liberal prime minister, Mark Rutte. Both parties are threatened by anti-immigration rivals: the Liberals have lost voters to the conservative Freedom Party of Geert Wilders, while Labor has lost even more support to the far-left Socialists.

As the immigration issue heated the government changed the citizenship rules as of January 1, 2011 and fluency in Dutch was made a condition of naturalization. Applicants from Dutch territories (where Papiamento is the spoken language in Aruba, Bonaire, and Curacao), must also demonstrate fluency in that language.

The stricter rules resulted from a political backlash against the continued influx of Islamic immigrants, most recently from Morocco. It also was aimed at Latino immigrants, especially those from Colombia and the Dominican Republic who originally acquired residence in the Dutch Caribbean islands and became Dutch citizens.

Many of these Dutch Latinos used their EU residence to move to Spain and the Spanish government complained to the Dutch government about these migrants.

Dual nationality is a continuing issue in the Netherlands. The number of Dutch nationals with dual citizenship rose from 400,000 over 10 years to one million in 2009, almost half of them Moroccans or Turks. This increase was caused in part by lack of official coordination within the Netherlands. Today, a prohibition against dual nationality is much more strictly enforced.

While the Dutch government formally discourages dual citizenship, municipalities, which are authorized to determine their own birth and citizenship registration policies, actively maintain a dual nationality policy. People who legally cannot reject their original nationality, who marry a Dutch national, or who would be disadvantaged by losing their first nationality are allowed to retain both.

If you're a citizen from one of the countries in the EU, the European Economic Area or Switzerland, you don't need a visa to visit, live, work or study in the Netherlands — however long you stay. For stays longer than three months, you are expected to register with the Immigration and Naturalization Service (IND) and get a registration certificate, which is valid indefinitely. A residence certificate is not required by law but it's useful to have one as banks, utility companies, government agencies and employers ask for them. You don't need a work permit, either.

Dutch Caribbean Islands

The Dutch Caribbean Islands (formerly known as the Netherlands Antilles) is one of the best-kept secrets in the world of offshore residence and second passports. Not many Americans know that the Kingdom of the Netherlands (a.k.a. Holland) long had a six-island Dutch colonial possession in the eastern Caribbean off the northern coast of Latin America. These semi-independent tropical islands are still an autonomous part of the Kingdom of the Netherlands with the motherland way off in Europe.

The Dutch Caribbean islands are in two groups; (ABC) Aruba, Bonaire, and Curacao, off the Venezuelan coast, and (SSS) Saint Eustatius, Saba and Saint Maarten, located southeast of the U.S. Virgin Islands and Puerto Rico. While still associated with the Netherlands, the former Netherlands Antilles as a confederation was dissolved as a unified political entity in 2008.

Each one of these islands has its own character: from bustling St. Maarten to sleepy Saba. On some of the islands, Dutch is widely spoken. On others, English as well as a regional language called "Papiamento" that mixes English, Spanish and Dutch is more common.

Dutch Treat for Americans

As a place that U.S. citizens can gain quick official residence, these islands are unique; upon arrival Americans are eligible for six months temporary residence under the terms of a 1956 "Treaty of Friendship, Commerce and Navigation between the Kingdom of the Netherlands and the United States of America" (DAFT).

Under this treaty U.S. citizens can apply for a Dutch residence permit for self-employment in the Netherlands. Applicants can also sponsor their spouse and minor children for residence. New business opportunities are available under the treaty, with the exception of the practice of law and medicine. The minimum required business investment for a self-employed individual is US$6,000 euros. It's also possible to open a branch of an existing U.S. company or buy a share of an existing Dutch business.

The first DAFT residence permit is issued for a period of two years. The minimum required business investment must be maintained throughout the entire period. There is no requirement to learn the Dutch language with a DAFT permit, although the language test (inburgering) is needed to apply for permanent residence or citizenship.

Some treaty provisions no longer apply to the Netherlands itself but still do apply to the Dutch Caribbean islands. In 2010, a Dutch court confirmed that the treaty guarantees U.S. citizens the same rights in the Netherlands Caribbean territories as those enjoyed by European Dutch citizens, including the right to stay for a continuous six months in the Caribbean territories.

This is an important first step if you are a U.S. citizen who wants to acquire Dutch citizenship and a passport. If you maintain legal residence on one of these islands, there is a possible payoff after five years of continuous presence there. You are then eligible to apply for citizenship and a passport from the Kingdom of the Netherlands, a member of the European Union, with all the EU rights that entails, including full access to the 27 EU countries. You can live or work anywhere in the EU. And a Dutch passport gives you visa-free travel to more than 120 countries, including Canada, Mexico and the United States. But remember, the IND now enforces requirements for language proficiency in Dutch or Papiamento and actual proof of five years of integration in the community.

And unless you choose to live in the Netherlands, you won't be subject to Dutch taxes; but each of the islands has their own tax system. (Americans continue to be liable for U.S. taxes without regard to where they live offshore.) Nevertheless, for U.S. citizens considering expatriation, once you clear the legal hurdles, a Dutch passport provides a first class alternative travel document that can be used anywhere in the world.

Residence Permits

Dutch Caribbean residence for Americans for more than six months requires application for a residence permit, either in person or through a local agent. Most permits are valid for only one year and must be renewed annually.

To qualify for residence in the Dutch Caribbean islands, you must demonstrate good health, good moral character, and financial self-sufficiency. Since the residence permitting process is difficult, (most application forms are in Dutch), it is helpful to have assistance from a professional intermediary. (See below for recommended professional contact).

These Dutch islands have local autonomy and control their own immigration. For example, Aruba requires that immigrants return to their home country after only three years, unless granted a permanent residence permit. However, the Dutch government has very strong policy influence over the islands and in Bonaire, St. Eustatius, and Saba, the Dutch government does control immigration.

Dutch Citizenship

To qualify for Dutch citizenship and a passport the Kingdom Act on Netherlands Nationality requires a continuous five-year period of legal residence, either in Holland or the Dutch Caribbean islands, a record of good conduct, and "substantial integration in the community."

Domestic European Dutch politics has turned very much anti-immigrant. And the requirement for "substantial integration in the community" now is being interpreted to mean an applicant must be proficient in the Dutch language, not an easy language to learn or speak. There is also a "naturalization test" in Dutch. Given the political mood in the Netherlands, it is likely that even more restrictive immigration changes will become law.

Contacts

Royal Netherlands Embassy
4200 Linnean Avenue NW
Washington, DC 20008
Tel.: (202) 244-5300 or + 1-877-DUTCHHELP (1-877-388-2443)
Email: info@dutchhelp.com
Web: http://www.the-netherlands.org

Dutch Immigration & Naturalization Service (IND)
Web: http://english.ind.nl/
Email: https://ind.nl/EN/organisation/contact/Pages/contact-form.aspx

See also: http://www.expatica.com/nl/essentials_moving_to/essentials/Dutch-immigration-and-residency-regulations_12220.html

United States Embassy
Lange Voorhout 102

2514 EJ The Hague
Tel.: + (31) 70-310-2209
Email: ircthehague@state.gov
Web: http://thehague.usembassy.gov/

U.S. Consulate General
Museumplein 19, 1071 DJ Amsterdam, The Netherlands
Tel.: + (31) 020-575-5309
Email: USCitizenServicesAms@state.gov
Web: http://amsterdam.usconsulate.gov/american_citizen_contact.html

U.S. Consulate General Curacao
P.O. Box 158, J.B. Gorsiraweg 1
Curacao, Netherlands Antilles
Tel.: (599) 9-461-3066
Email: infocuracao@state.gov
Web: http://curacao.usconsulate.gov/

Recommended Immigration Consultant:

Henley & Partners
De Dreeftoren
Haaksbergweg 71
1101 BP Amsterdam
Tel.: +31 20 312 1212

Kingdom of Norway

Government:	Constitutional monarchy
Capital:	Oslo
National Day:	Constitution Day: 17 May (1814)
Population:	5,085,582 (July 2013 est.)
Total Area:	125,021 sq. miles / 323,802 sq. kilometers
Languages:	Bokmal Norwegian (official), Nynorsk Norwegian (official), small Sami and Finnish-speaking minorities
Ethnic groups:	Norwegian 94.4% includes Sami, other European 3.6%, other 2%
Religion:	Church of Norway 85.7%, other 8.1%, other Christian 2.4%, Muslim 1.8%, Pentecostal 1%, Roman Catholic 1%
Life expectancy:	80.44 years
Currency:	Norwegian krone (NOK)
GDP:	US$274.1 billion (2012 est.)
GDP per capita:	US$54,400 (2012 est.)

Norway is a ruggedly beautiful country of mountains, fjords and glaciers. The "Land of the Midnight Sun" has delightfully long summer days, pleasantly low-key cities, unspoiled fishing villages, and rich historic sites that include Viking ships and medieval stave churches.

Norway prizes its stunning natural wonders and retains a robust frontier character unusual in Europe. It's not all frozen tundra, either. The temperate south includes rolling farmlands, enchanted forests and sunny beaches as well as the dramatic Western Fjords.

Norway is, by any standards, one of the most beautiful countries on earth, but that beauty brings with it a responsibility that weighs heavily upon Norwegians. In the past, this was expressed in the Norwegian tradition of isolated farmsteads that colonized the most secluded corners of the country's wilderness. Increasingly, however, the irrevocable movement of Norwegians toward cities such as Bergen, Trondheim, Stavanger and Tromso has altered the relationship between Norwegians and their natural world. But one thing remains unaltered: to paraphrase that great Norwegian son, Henrik Ibsen, those who wish to understand Norwegians, must first understand Norway's magnificent but severe natural environment, for these are a people of the land, perhaps more so than any other Europeans. It's not that you'll find many Norwegians complaining about their lot. Nonetheless, you will encounter, again and again, a people wondering about their place in the world. — Lonely Planet

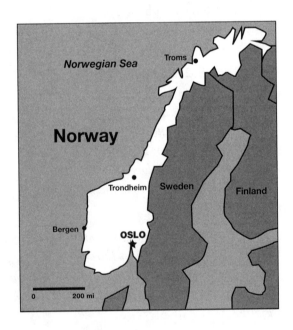

History and Overview

Norway is located in Northern Europe, bordering the North Sea and the North Atlantic Ocean, west of Sweden.

The Viking period (9th to 11th centuries) was one of national unification and expansion. The Norwegian royal line died out in 1387, and the country entered a period of union with Denmark. By 1586, Norway had become part of the Danish Kingdom. In 1814, as a result of the Napoleonic wars, Norway was separated from Denmark and combined with Sweden. The union persisted until 1905, when Sweden recognized Norwegian independence. The Norwegian government offered the throne to Danish Prince Carl in 1905.

After a plebiscite approving the establishment of a monarchy, the Parliament unanimously elected him king. He took the name of Haakon VII, after the kings of independent Norway. Although Norway remained neutral in World War I, it suffered heavy losses to its shipping. Norway proclaimed its neutrality at the outset of World War II, but was nonetheless occupied for five years by Nazi Germany (1940 to 1945).

In 1949, neutrality was abandoned and Norway became a member of NATO. Discovery of oil and gas in adjacent waters in the late 1960s boosted Norway's economic fortunes. The current focus is on containing spending on the extensive welfare system and planning for the time when petroleum reserves are depleted. In referenda held in 1972 and 1994, Norway rejected joining the EU nonetheless it contributes sizably to the EU budget.

The Norwegian economy is a prosperous bastion of welfare capitalism, featuring a combination of free-market activity and government intervention. The government controls key areas such as the vital petroleum sector (through large-scale state enterprises). The country is richly endowed with natural resources — petroleum, hydropower, fish, forests, and minerals — and is highly dependent on its oil production and international oil prices, with oil and gas accounting for one-third of exports. Only Saudi Arabia and Russia export more oil than Norway.

In anticipation of eventual declines in oil and gas production, Norway saves almost all state revenue from the petroleum sector in a sovereign wealth fund. After lackluster growth of less than 1.5% from 2002 to 2003, GDP growth picked up to 2.5 to 6.2% in 2004 to 2007, partly due to higher oil prices. Growth fell to 2.3% in 2008 as a result of the slowing world economy and the drop in oil prices.

In 2011, a right-wing extremist who opposed Islam and multiculturalism, Behring Breivik, killed 77 people in two attacks, was convicted of mass murder and terrorism. He first setting off a bomb outside government offices in Oslo and then carrying out a shooting massacre at a Labor Party youth summer camp on an island near Oslo. Sixty-nine people, mostly young people, were shot dead in the rampage on Utoya Island, and eight others died in the bombing.

These murders and their aftermath raised national concerns about immigration and strengthened the impression that Islam is a challenge to national values. This widely shared concern on both the left and right of the political spectrum, and in 2013 put the Conservative Party into office after eight years of government by Labor Party-led leftist coalitions.

Norway has long prided itself on its liberal sensibilities, but the debate about immigration and its effects on national identity and the country's social welfare system has been intense. The issue was sued by the anti-immigration Progress Party, which is now part of the new Conservative-led government. Norway's Justice Minister, a Progress Party member, slammed the former Labor government's handling of immigration policy, and vowed to tighten up the system.

Residence and Citizenship

Dual citizenship is not allowed for Norwegian citizens, except for children born of parents from two different countries, or born in a country where they automatically obtain that country's citizenship at birth.

A child acquires Norwegian nationality at birth where: (a) the mother is a Norwegian national, (b) the father is a Norwegian national and the child is born in wedlock, (c) the father is deceased, but was a Norwegian national and married to the mother of the child when he died.

Immigrants and refugees may be granted Norwegian nationality after applying to the Directorate of Immigration. As a general rule, the person applying for citizenship must:

1) be at least 18 years of age; 2) have had permanent residence in Norway for the past seven years; 3) have a record of good conduct; and 4) must not owe significant maintenance payments.

Exemptions from these requirements may be allowed to a person who has formerly been a Norwegian national, a person married to a Norwegian national, and in cases with special circumstances. For nationals of the Nordic countries, exemptions may be made to the requirement concerning the length of residence.

Contacts

Royal Embassy of Norway
2720 34th Street NW
Washington, DC 20008
Tel.: (202) 333-6000
Email: emb.washington@mfa.no

Web: http://www.norway.org/

Norwegian Directorate of Immigration:
http://www.udi.no/norwegian-directorate-of-immigration/

United States Embassy
Henrik Ibsens gate 48
0244 Oslo, Norway
Tel.: + (47) 21 30 85 40

Visas and all matters concerning entering, working in, or residing in the U.S.:

Email: oslovisa@state.go
American Citizen Services: osloamcit@state.gov
Web: http://norway.usembassy.gov/

Republic of Poland

Government:	Republic
Capital:	Warsaw
National Day:	Constitution Day: 3 May (1791)
Population:	38,383,809 (July 2013 est.)
Total Area:	120,728 sq. miles / 312,685 sq. kilometers
Languages:	Polish 97.8%, other and unspecified 2.2%
Ethnic groups:	Polish 96.7%, German 0.4%, Belarusian 0.1%, Ukrainian 0.1%
Religion:	Roman Catholic 89.8%, Eastern Orthodox 1.3%, Protestant 0.3%, other 0.3%, unspecified 8.3%
Life expectancy:	76.45 years
Currency:	Zloty (PLN)
GDP:	US$792.4 billion (2012 est.)
GDP per capita:	US$20,600 (2012 est.)

Overrun countless times by marauding aggressors, subjugated to overbearing foreign rule for centuries, and now told their beloved vodka can be made from anything, the Polish nation has endured more than most. Yet Poland, a country crushed flat so many times it has become indestructible, is shaking off the last vestiges of forced slumber and rushing with great abandon into a modern 21st century.

Despite the country's rush to embrace the future, its past cannot be ignored, particularly when it confronts you at every turn. Warsaw may be embracing New World cuisine, cafe culture and clubs that never close, but you'll still encounter peasant women selling bunches of flowers in its beautifully reconstructed Old Town. Or choose almost any major city, from Lublin to Poznań — and too many small towns — and you'll bear witness to extermination camps established by Nazi Germany, derelict Jewish cemeteries, and dark political prisons, terrible reminders from the last 70 years.

This massive land in the heart of Europe has become the epitome of a changing continent. As a member of the EU it is enjoying the rewards and experiencing the challenges of this exclusive club. Money has begun to flow into the country, repairing roads, building shopping malls and beautifying streets, but the progress is laboriously slow for some. Poland still has an unemployment rate twice as high as some of its EU compatriots, and its young, educated citizens are leaving in droves for wealthier pastures. But don't take our word for it: spend some time here and you'll discover a unique land where East meets West and helpings of joy and sorrow have been served up in equal proportions. And you'll come away with new-found admiration for this unbreakable country. — Lonely Planet

History and Overview

The Poles possess one of the richest and most venerable historical traditions of all European peoples. Convention fixes the origins of Poland as a nation near the middle of the 10th century, contemporaneous with the Carolingians, Vikings and Saracens, and a full 100 years before the Norman conquest of Britain in 1066. Throughout the subsequent centuries, the Poles managed despite great obstacles to build and maintain an unbroken cultural heritage. The same cannot be said of Polish statehood.

Its golden age occurred in the 16th century. During the following century, the strengthening of the gentry and internal disorders weakened the nation. Poland is located in Central Europe, east of Germany but in a series of agreements between 1772 and 1795, Russia, Prussia and Austria partitioned Poland among themselves. Poland regained its independence in 1918 only to be overrun by Germany and the Soviet Union in World War II. It became a Soviet satellite state following the war, but its government was comparatively tolerant and progressive.

In 1980, Labor turmoil led to the formation of the independent trade union "Solidarity" that over time became a political force and, by 1990, had swept parliamentary elections and the presidency. A "shock therapy" program during the early 1990s enabled the country to transform its economy into one of the most robust in Central Europe, but Poland still faces the lingering challenges of high unemployment, underdeveloped and dilapidated infrastructure, and a poor rural underclass. Solidarity suffered a major defeat in the 2001 parliamentary elections when it failed to elect a single deputy to the lower house of Parliament, and the new leaders of the Solidarity Trade Union subsequently pledged to reduce the Trade Union's political role.

Poland joined NATO in 1999 and the European Union in 2004. With its transformation to a democratic, market oriented country largely completed, Poland is an increasingly active member of Euro-Atlantic organizations.

Economy

Poland has pursued a policy of economic liberalization throughout the last 20 years and today stands out as a success story among transition economies. Poland's economy was the only one in the EU to avoid a recession through the 2008 to 2010 world economic down turn. Although EU membership and access to EU structural funds have provided a major boost to the economy, GDP per capita remains significantly below the EU average while unemployment continues to exceed the EU average.

Even so, much remains to be done, especially in bringing down the unemployment rate — currently the highest in the EU. The privatization of small and medium-sized, state-owned companies and a liberal law on establishing new firms has encouraged the development of the private business sector, but legal and bureaucratic obstacles alongside persistent corruption are hampering its further development.

Further progress in public finance depends mainly on reducing losses in Polish state enterprises, restraining entitlements and overhauling the tax code to incorporate the growing gray economy and farmers, most of whom pay no tax.

While the Polish economy has performed well over the past five years, growth slowed in 2012, in part due to the ongoing economic difficulties in the euro zone. The key policy challenge is to provide support to the economy through monetary easing, while maintaining the pace of structural fiscal consolidation.

Poland's economic performance could improve over the longer term if the country addresses some of the remaining deficiencies in its road and rail infrastructure and its business environment. An inefficient commercial court system, a rigid labor code, red tape, and a burdensome tax system keep the private sector from realizing its full potential.

Poland joined the EU in 2004, and surging exports to the EU contributed to Poland's strong growth in 2004, though its competitiveness could be threatened by the zloty's appreciation. GDP per capita roughly equals that of the three Baltic states. Poland benefited from nearly US$23.2 billion in EU funds. Farmers alr eady reap the rewards of membership via booming exports, higher food prices and EU agricultural subsidies.

Residence and Citizenship

Polish nationality law is based upon the principles of jus sanguinis. Children born to Polish parents usually acquire citizenship irrespective of place of birth. Persons born in Poland to foreign parents do not normally become Polish citizens. Dual citizenship is permitted but Polish law treats a dual citizen as if he or she was solely Polish.

Many of its former citizens have not returned to Poland since the end of World War II and their descendants have acquired the citizenship of the countries in which they were born. However, an individual is entitled to citizenship if his or her ancestors were Polish and did not acquire another citizenship voluntarily.

Under Polish law, a person acquires citizenship by descent from parents, when at least one parent is a Polish citizen (jus sanguinis). A child acquires Polish citizenship by birth when: 1) both parents are Polish citizens, or 2) one of the parents is a Polish citizen, and the other is of unknown citizenship or does not possess any citizenship.

A child of parents where one is a Polish citizen, while the other is a citizen of another state, acquires Polish citizenship by birth.

However, the parents may, in a declaration made within three months from the day of the birth of the child, choose for the child the citizenship of the foreign state of which one of the parents is a citizen if, according to the law of that state, the child acquires its citizenship. A child who was born or found within the territory of the Republic of Poland acquires citizenship when both parents are unknown, whose citizenship cannot be established, or who are stateless.

An alien can acquire Polish citizenship, if she/he is married for at least three years to a Polish citizen, and obtained a residence permit. Applicant needs to apply in her/his place of residence in Poland and declare intention of becoming a Polish citizen. Application needs to take place within six months from obtaining the residence permit.

Persons whose parents or grandparents were Polish citizens may be eligible to obtain Polish citizenship for themselves based on that relationship. Citizenship can generally be claimed only by descendants of Polish citizens who left Poland after the country became an independent state in 1918. Also, there can be no break in Polish citizenship between the emigrant ancestor and the descendant. Application for "Confirmation of Possession or Loss of Polish Citizenship" can be made through Polish embassies or consulates abroad.

Naturalization by the President of the Republic can occur and a foreigner may be granted citizenship at his or her request, if he or she has resided in Poland for at least five years on the basis of a permanent residence permit. In justified cases, a foreigner may be granted Polish citizenship at his or her request, even though he or she does not meet the conditions defined above.

U.S. citizens are not required to obtain a visa for visit of 90 days or less. A visa is required for a stay of longer than three months or for the purpose of taking up gainful employment. As a country that forms part of the EU's external border, Poland has implemented the strict Schengen border rules to restrict illegal immigration and trade along its eastern borders with Belarus and Ukraine.

Dual citizenship is officially prohibited in most of the countries covered by the law and is not recognized in Poland.

The Polish Card

In an unusual move in 2008, the Polish parliament adopted a long-discussed "Pole Card" (Karta Polaka) law. The document confirms Polish nationality without conferring Polish citizenship or EU rights. The law guarantees limited rights for people of Polish descent living in 15 former Soviet controlled countries, including Lithuania, Moldova, Russia and Tajikistan. The Pole Card is given to people with documented proof of Polish roots, or "a connection with Polish culture," who also display at least a "passive understanding" of the Polish language. Applications for the document are approved and issued by Polish consuls in the respective countries.

The card does not give neither the right to vote in Poland but it does confer many rights that citizens of other EU countries enjoy in other states, including the right to establish a business, to work, attend educational institutions and even health services.

Contacts

Embassy of Poland
2640 16th Street NW
Washington, DC 20009
Tel.: (202) 499-1700
Email: polemb.info@earthlink.net
Web: http://www.polandembassy.org/
Consulates general in New York, Chicago, and Los Angeles

United States Embassy
Aleje Ujazdowskie 29/31
00-540 Warsaw, Poland
Tel.: + (48) 22-504-2000
Web: http://poland.usembassy.gov/

U.S. Consulate Krakow
Ul. Stolarska 9
31-043 Krakow, Poland
Tel.: +48-12/424-5100

U.S. Agency Poznan
Ul. Paderewskiego 8
Tel.: +48-61/851-8516
Email: CAPoz@post.pl

Recommended Immigration Attorney:

Michal Wisniewski
CK and Partners Law Office
02-791 WARSZAWA STR
YJEN'SKICH 6/126 Poland
Tel.: +48 22 243 49 52
Email: polish.citizenship@cklawoffice.eu
Web: http://www.cklawoffice.eu/contact.html

Republic of Portugal

Government:	Parliamentary democracy
Capital:	Lisbon
National Day:	Portugal Day (Camoes Day): 10 June (1580)
Population:	10,799,270 (July 2013 est.)
Total Area:	35,672 sq. miles / 92,391 sq. kilometers
Languages:	Portuguese (official), Mirandese (unofficial but locally used)
Ethnic groups:	Mediterranean stock, black Africans from ex-colonies
Religion:	Roman Catholic 84.5%, other Christian 2.2%, other 0.3%, unknown 9%, none 3.9%
Life expectancy:	78.85 years
Currency:	Euro (EUR)
GDP:	US$244.3 billion (2012 est.)
GDP per capita:	US$23,000 (2012 est.)

While it's true that Portugal is no longer the Iberian Peninsula's best-kept secret, it's fairly easy to escape the crowds. Even at the busiest resorts in the Algarve, it only takes a short bus ride or a walk across countryside to reveal rarely visited places that still offer the feeling of discovery — a sentiment close to the Portuguese soul. Portugal has an old fashioned charm, with medieval castles and picture-perfect villages scattered over meandering coastlines and flower-covered hillsides. From the ancient university town of Coimbra to Lord Byron's favorite Portuguese haunt, Sintra, the country's proud history can be felt everywhere.

Sun-kissed beaches like Cascais and Sagres offer enticements of a more hedonistic sort. Indeed, the dramatic, end-of-the-

world cliffs, wild dune-covered beaches, protected coves and long, sandy islands of Portugal's coastline have long enchanted visitors and locals alike. Meanwhile, the country's capital, Lisbon, and its northern rival, Porto, are magical places for the wanderer, with riverside views, cobblestone streets and rattling trams framed by looming cathedrals. — Lonely Planet

History and Overview

Portugal is on the Atlantic coast of the Iberian Peninsula in southwestern Europe, surrounded by Spain. Its territory includes the Azores and Madeira, island groups a few hundred kilometers offshore in the Atlantic.

Portugal became part of the Roman Empire in the 2nd century B.C. and embraced Christianity by the 5th century AD. The Moorish conquest of the Peninsula in AD 716 resulted in Muslim rule until the 9th century. By the early 16th century, Portuguese explorers had extended its international empire to Africa, Asia and Brazil. For a time, Portugal was controlled by Spain. The early 17th century saw an absolute monarchy that remained for 200 years.

The Napoleonic wars unsuccessful invasion of the Iberian Peninsula, by France, caused the royal family and government to flee to Brazil. The abolition of slavery, in 1869, further weakened Portugal's overseas colonies. In 1910, Portugal officially became a republic, but the first three-quarters of the 20th century saw a succession of dictatorships. In 1974, a leftwing military coup installed broad democratic reforms.

The following year, Portugal granted independence to all of its African colonies. In 1949, Portugal became a founding member of NATO and, in 1955, a member of the U.N. It has been a member of the EU since 1986.

Portugal has been the poor relation of Western Europe with the lowest EU living and labor costs. Tourism in the southern coast Algarve region, and in Lisbon, has brought foreign wealth into the country over the last two decades.

English is widely spoken and there are large British expatriate communities. Wealthy foreigners are a major source of income and the government protects the expatriate community and its property. This trend was somewhat weakened with new real estate taxes aimed at expatriate land ownership.

Beaches and golf courses are amongst the best in the world. The finest merchandise, wines and foods are available at typically very low prices. In undiscovered areas, adequate condominium apartments start at US$25,000, while good farm houses with land sell for under US$50,000. Mansions with grounds, a pool and a sea view sell in the US$1 million range. Competent, cheap household help is available everywhere.

Travel from Portugal to most European destinations, particularly to London, is low cost. The government subsidizes air routes to the autonomous Azores and Madeira Islands in the Atlantic Ocean.

Taxes

Portugal has tried to establish itself as a tax-free retirement haven for foreigners. Portugal offers foreigners the status of a "non-habitual resident" with an income tax free holiday for ten years, including no taxes on foreign source pensions, interest and royalties — unless this income flows from a listed "tax haven" as the government defines them. Income from within the country is taxed at 20%. The country has numerous double tax treaties to protect income from being taxed in the country of origin. Capital gains, however, remain taxable in most circumstances in Portugal.

The 10-year tax holiday started in 2009, but tax authorities have been slow to grant these exemptions. With careful tax planning, this exemption will be granted and when combined with other tax structures, such as an offshore trust (not located in a "tax haven,") Portugal itself might be an attractive retirement tax haven.

Exchange controls are in effect, but they do not impact on foreign income or assets held abroad. Annual property taxes are around one month's rental value, or 1% of total real estate value. There are restrictions and taxes on real estate purchased or owned by foreigners. Residents of Portugal are taxed on their worldwide income at rates varying from 16% to 40%, but, in fact, taxes are collected only on income generated within Portugal. In the last 20 years the government has pursued a massive privatization program and now offers major incentives to foreign investors.

Economy

The economy grew by more than the EU average for much of the 1990s, but the rate of growth slowed in 2001to 2008. The economy contracted 2.5% in 2009, before growing 1.4% in 2010, but GDP fell again in 2011to 2013, as the government implemented spending cuts and tax increases to comply with conditions of a 2011 EU-IMF financial rescue package of US$106 billion. GDP per capita stands at roughly two-thirds of the EU-27 average. A poor educational system and a rigid labor market have been obstacles to greater productivity and growth. Portugal also has been increasingly overshadowed by lower-cost producers in Central Europe and Asia as a destination for foreign direct investment.

Portugal's low competitiveness, low growth prospects, and high levels of public debt have made it vulnerable to bond market turbulence. The government has implementing austerity measures, including a 5% public salary cut which went into effect and a 2% increase in the value-added tax, to reduce the budget deficit, but some investors have expressed concern about the government's ability to achieve these targets and cover its sovereign debt.

Portugal has little choice but to take tough steps. The country sought international help in 2011 after failing to convince investors it was doing enough to shore up its shaky finances. In exchange for a US$106 billion, three-year loan, Lisbon promised the EU and the IMF that it would slash its deficit and make structural changes to spur growth in key sectors. This prolonged the economic slump and drove up unemployment, already at 12%.

Along with Ireland, Greece and Spain, Portugal (PIGS) is considered one of the prime EU countries that may default on its large sovereign debt unless it receives continuing financial help.

Residence and Citizenship

Under the Portuguese Citizenship Act, the following persons are Portuguese by birth:

1. the children of a Portuguese father or a mother born on Portu-

guese territory or territory under Portuguese administration, or born abroad if the Portuguese parent there is in service of the Portuguese state;

2. the children of a Portuguese father or mother born abroad, if they declare that they want to be Portuguese or if they register the birth in a Portuguese civil register;

3. persons born on Portuguese territory as children of aliens who reside in Portugal possessing a valid residence permit for at least five years, depending on whether they are a citizen of countries with Portuguese as official language or citizen of other countries, and who are not in service of their state, if they declare that they want to be Portuguese, or;

4. persons born on Portuguese territory, when they possess no other nationality.

Even before the 2009 changes citizenship rules were quite liberal and marriage is one avenue available. Citizenship in Portugal is available to individuals six years after being granted permanent residence if they make a government approved investment of US$100,000. Spouses of Portuguese nationals who live in the country for three years continuously are eligible for naturalization.

Portugal is under pressure to conform to EU standards that allow a foreign spouse to apply for citizenship only after three years of continuous residence with no more than six months' absence from the country. Other avenues toward citizenship include family reunification.

Major Law Change

Portuguese citizenship law is complicated by the existence of several former overseas colonies. In some cases, it is possible to claim Portuguese citizenship by connection with one of these jurisdictions. The most notable of these are Goa (annexed by India in 1961), East Timor that achieved independence in 2002 and Macau, now a Special Administrative Region of the People's Republic of China.

There are more than 500,000 legally documented immigrants living in Portugal, more than 100,000 Ukrainian workers who constitute the second largest immigrant community in the country, after about 120,000 Brazilians.

Until 2009, all citizenship was based on the principle of jus sanguinis (right of blood), whereby nationality or citizenship is determined by the nationality or citizenship of one's parents.

In 2009, the government adopted the principle of jus soli (right of the soil) fir second and third generation immigrants. That gave the grandchildren of immigrants a right to citizenship if one of their parents was born in Portugal. The children of immigrants now have the same right even if neither parent was born in Portugal, as long as one of their parents has lived in the country as a legal resident for at least five years.

The 2009 law was described as a key step in fighting the social exclusion suffered by many of the 600,000 immigrants and their descendants living in the country. Until then, the offspring and grandchildren of immigrants were denied Portuguese nationality, even though born in Portugal, generally speak only Portuguese, studied in Portuguese schools and have never lived outside of the country.

This 2009 law was good news for the vast communities of Portuguese in Brazil and other countries of Latin America, especially Venezuela and Argentina, where waves of Portuguese immigration date back decades.

Portugal offers special considerations to members of its former colonies. Brazilian citizens qualify for Portuguese nationality after only three years of official residence; no visa is required to enter or take up residence in Portugal. Citizens of former Portuguese colonial enclaves in India (Goa, Daman and Diu); and parts of Asia, East Timor (a former Indonesian province), Macao in China, and Africa (Cape Verde, Guinea-Bissau, Angola, Mozambique, and Sao Tome-Principe) may also qualify for Portuguese citizenship.

The same applies to Brazil, the largest Portuguese ex-colony on the world map. However, Brazilian citizenship is not cheap. Citizenship in any one of these former colonies could provide a short-cut into the EU via Portugal. After a three-year residence period, reciprocal Brazilian citizenship is allowed with visa-free movement to and from this former colony. Brazilians are allowed to vote in Portuguese elections after registration as a resident.

The government also issues to some legal residents what is called a "Portuguese Aliens Passport." This allows for visa-free travel throughout the EU, but is only issued under exceptional circumstances, usually, to stateless refugees.

In 2013 Portugal adopted a law granting citizenship to descendants of Sephardic Jews. The Jews were persecuted in Spain and Portugal during the Inquisition which the Catholic Church and royal houses of both countries led against non-Christians in the 15th and 16th centuries.

Residence for Sale

For an approved investment in Portugal for an initial period of five years one can obtain permanent residence that can lead to citizenship after six years. There are three options:

1. a capital investment of €1 million (US$1.4 million);

2. purchase of unencumbered real valued at least €500,000 (US$685,000);

3. creation of at least 10 new jobs.

One assumes that qualified investors will have verifiable offshore income sufficient to support themselves. Investment may be in an existing business, or by establishing a new enterprise. Successful applicants must spend at least seven days a year in Portugal or any other EU country. The investor is not treated as a resident for tax purposes unless they live in the country more than 183 days in any one year.

In addition to the above program, any other foreigner applying for permanent residence must purchase or rent a home place prior to final approval of a residence permit. Problems have occurred with real estate agents who promise, and fail to secure, residence status for buyers as part of a purchase arrangement.

An applicant for a permanent residence visa must submit:

1) a written declaration stating reasons for applying and evidence of financial support; 2) a local certificate that adequate housing has been obtained; 3) documentation showing establishment of a Portuguese bank account, and a sufficient deposit, averaging a minimum of US$5,000 per applicant; 4) a certificate of good character; 5) a medical certificate of good health; 6) copies of a current passport; 7) three passport-size photos; 8) three copies of the executed official visa application Form V-3; and 9) testimonials from acquaintances in Portugal (optional).

Application processing through a Portuguese Consulate can require from six to 24 months with an average of 12 months. A successful applicant receives a residence visa and an official residence card is issued once the person arrives in Portugal. Initially, a one-year, type "A" residence card is issued, renewable annually. After five years residence, a type "B" card valid for five years is issued. After 20 years, foreign residents may apply for a type "C" card, valid for life. Although these residence cards are not valid for travel within the EU, they assure that visas can be obtained easily from EU countries.

After six years of residence, a resident can qualify for naturalization and a passport. Continuous presence in Portugal is not a requirement, but some proof of actual residence during the period may be required when applying for citizenship.

A new Portuguese citizen must swear allegiance and give a pro forma renunciation of prior nationality. After obtaining Portuguese nationality, dual nationality is permitted, in theory, by the rule "once Portuguese, always Portuguese." Foreign citizens who acquire Portuguese citizenship may be subject to certain aspects of Portuguese law, such as mandatory voting and military service. This should be checked beforehand.

Portugal's immigration bureaucracy, the Servi de Estrangeiros, is notoriously slow moving. Obtaining a residence permit can require a year and 18 months is not unusual. A well-connected local lawyer can usually speed the process.

Even without a permit, foreign residents who cause no problems are not officially bothered. Local police have a reputation for being among the friendliest in Europe. The Portuguese are non-racist and have provided a home for 100,000 African and Asian stateless people, mostly former colonials, who now call this their home.

A valid foreign passport is required for entry into Portugal. A visa is not required for tourist or business stays of up to 90 days. Portuguese law requires some non-EU foreign nationals to register with immigration officials within three days of entering Portugal.

Contacts
Embassy of Portugal
2012 Massachusetts Avenue NW
Washington, DC 20036
Tel.: (202) 350-5400

Email: info@embassyportugal-us.org
Web: http://www.embassyportugal-us.org/

Consulates General in New York, Boston, San Francisco, Newark, N.J., Providence, R.I., and New Bedford, Massachusetts.

Portuguese National Tourist Office
590 Fifth Avenue
New York, NY 10036
Tel.: (212) 354-4403

United States Embassy
Avenida das Forcas Armadas
1600-081 Lisbon, Portugal
or mail: Apartado 43033, 1601-301 Lisboa
Tel.: + (351) 21-727-3300
Email: lisbonweb@state.gov
Web: http://lisbon.usembassy.gov/

U.S. Consulate, Azores
Avenida Principe Monaco
6-2 Frente, Ponta Delgada
9500-237 Sao Miguel, Azores
Tel.: + (351) 29-628-2216
Web: http://www.usconsulateazores.pt/

Recommended Immigration Consultant:

Henley & Partners
Palacio Alagoas
Rua da Escola Politecnica No. 183
Bloco A, 1° Andar
1250-101 Lisboa
Tel.: + 351 213 970 977
Email: portugal@henleyglobal.com

Republic of Romania

Government:	Republic
Capital:	Bucharest
National Day:	Unification Day (Romania & Transylvania): 1December (1918)
Population:	21,790,479 (July 2013 est.)
Total Area:	91,699 sq. miles / 237, 500 sq. kilometers
Languages:	Romanian (official) 91%, Hungarian 6.7%, Romany (Gypsy) 1.1%, other 1.2%
Ethnic groups:	Romanian 89.5%, Hungarian 6.6%, Roma 2.5%, other 0.4%, Ukrainian 0.3%, German 0.3%, Russian 0.2%, Turkish 0.2%
Religion:	Eastern Orthodox 86.8%, Protestant 7.5%, Roman Catholic 4.7%, other (mostly Muslim) and unspecified 0.9%, none 0.1%
Life expectancy:	74.45 years
Currency:	New leu (RON)
GDP:	US$277.9 billion (2012 est.)
GDP per capita:	US$13,000 (2012 est.)

Traveling in Romania is like being somewhere between an eternal Halloween and the Led Zeppelin IV cover that features a twig-carrying farmer. Even in cities where Audis zoom across highways under video-camera speed traps, Romanian life is defined by its sweet country heart. Most anywhere, you'll spot horse-drawn buggies crossing the (often cratered) paved roads, up green mountains, past cone shaped hay stacks and herds of sheep, which bounce along as if the roads themselves are aliens to the land.

And then there's that Dracula thing. Many visitors, lured by bloodcurdling tales, make full trips out of Transylvania's castles and lovely medieval Saxon towns like Sighişoara, where the "real Dracula" (Vlad Ţepeş) first grew his teeth. But travelers limiting themselves to chasing vampires will miss so much.

The capital, Bucharest, has its critics, but the blend of grotesque Communist monuments and purposefully hidden-away cathedrals makes for fascinating exploring. Excellent hiking, biking and skiing are found all over the Transylvanian Alps (aka the Carpathian Mountains), which curl across central Romania.

Romania's neighbor Moldova, a trickier place to visit, but equally as fascinating, is no closer to EU consideration than when the Soviet Union collapsed, largely because it lives on as if this had never happened. Russian is spoken commonly here and its renegade province, Transdniestr, still supports a Communist government. Adding a few days in this Cold War time warp on a trip to Romania's vampire trails and Alp-like ski runs easily makes up one of Europe's most interesting, and least understood, destinations. Go now, before it changes. — Lonely Planet

History and Overview

Romania is located in southeastern Europe, bordering the Black Sea, between Bulgaria and Ukraine. Extending inland halfway across the Balkan Peninsula and covering a large elliptical area of 91,699 square miles, Romania occupies the greater part of the lower basin of the Danube River system and the hilly eastern regions of the middle Danube basin. It lies on either side of the mountain systems collectively known as the Carpathians, which form the natural barrier between the two Danube basins.

The principalities of Wallachia and Moldavia, for centuries under the suzerainty of the Turkish Ottoman Empire, secured their autonomy in 1856; they united in 1859 and a few years later adopted the name of Romania. The country gained recognition of its independence in 1878. It joined the Allied Powers in World War I and acquired new territories, most notably Transylvania, following the conflict. In 1940, Romania allied with the Axis powers and participated in the 1941 German invasion of the USSR. Three years later, overrun by the Soviets, Romania signed an armistice.

The post-war Soviet occupation led to the formation of a Communist "people's republic" in 1947 and the abdication of the king. The decades-long rule of the dictator Nicolae Ceauşescu, who took power in 1965, and his Securitate police state became increasingly oppressive through the 1980s. He was overthrown and executed in late 1989. Former Communists dominated the government until 1996, when they were swept from power.

Romania joined NATO in 2004 and became a member of the EU in 2007. Romania, which joined the EU on January 1, 2007, began the transition from Communism in 1989 with a largely obsolete industrial base and production unsuited to the country's needs. The country emerged in 2000 from a punishing three-year recession thanks to strong demand in EU export markets.

Domestic consumption and investment have fueled strong GDP growth in recent years, but have led to large current account imbalances. Romania's macroeconomic gains have only recently started to spur creation of a middle class and address Romania's widespread poverty. Corruption and red tape continue to handicap its business environment.

Inflation rose in 2007 to 2008, driven in part by strong consumer demand and high-wage growth, rising energy costs, a nation-wide drought affecting food prices, and a relaxation of fiscal discipline. Romania's GDP contracted markedly in the last quarter of 2008 as the country began to feel the effects of a global downturn in financial markets and trade, and GDP fell more than 7% in 2009, prompting Bucharest to seek a $26 billion emergency assistance package from the IMF, the EU, and other international lenders.

Worsening international financial markets, as well as a series of drastic austerity measures implemented to meet Romania's obligations under the IMF-led bail-out agreement contributed to a GDP contraction of 6.6% in 2009, followed by a 1.1% GDP contraction in 2010. Due to strong exports, in 2011, the economy returned to positive growth, a better than expected harvest, and weak domestic demand. In 2012, however, growth slowed to less than 1%, due to slackened export demand and an extended drought that resulted in a poor harvest.

The Financial Times reported in early 2014: "Romania's economy has on average performed better than the rest of the EU and prospects in the Balkan country look brighter than elsewhere." They said that GDP was expected to grow 2.1% in 2014 and 2.4% in 2015, with a budget deficit lower than in most EU countries. Romania's export-driven economy has a robust automotive industry and a resurging agricultural sector, which could offer thousands of new blue-collar jobs, government officials contend.

Roaming Refugees

Citizens of the 28-nation EU have the right to live and work anywhere within those countries but when Romania and Bulgaria, significantly poorer than the rest of the EU, joined in 2007, nine EU countries imposed limits on this right for their citizens.

On January 1, 2014, those nine EU states, including Germany, France, the Netherlands and Britain, lifted labor restrictions that excluded Romanians and Bulgarians. But even before then many skilled and unskilled laborers found work in those and other EU countries. The poor economic numbers explain why Romanians want to be elsewhere.

The wealthiest one-fifth of people in Romania have a lower median income than the poorest one-fifth of society in Britain, France, Germany or other wealthy EU states, according to income data obtained from Eurostat, the EU statistics office.

According to Eurostat data agency 96% of Romanian migrants to EU countries choose destinations other than the U.K. In 2013, the U.K. had 80,000 of the total 2.12 million Romanian migrants in the EU. The figure was much higher in Italy (888,000) and Spain (823,000). Germany had 160,000. The U.K. also had 26,000 of 437,000 Bulgarian migrants in the EU. However, Spain has 168,000, Germany 66,000, Greece 55,000 and Italy 46,000.

A report published by the National Institute for Economic and Social Research (NIESR) in 2013 found that the main destination choice for Bulgarian and Romanian nationals was Italy and Spain. However, in early 2014 there were no reports of masses of Romanians rushing to the U.K. or other EU countries, perhaps because of improving prospects at home.

Moldovan Immigration Issue

In 2009, EU authorities were disturbed at a Romanian immigration proposal the EU said could threaten both the standing of Romania as an EU member and regional stability. A draft citizenship law was proposed that extended the right of naturalization for citizens of the neighboring country of Moldova, one of the EU's poorest countries, whose grandparent or great grandparent was once a Romanian citizen. Under the previous law, only Moldovans with Romanian grandparents were granted citizenship. The draft also sped up the duration of processing paperwork to five months and abandoned the Romanian language test. Moldovan officials charged this was a move toward Romania, its neighbor to the east, annexing parts of Moldovan territory.

Moldova is Europe's most impoverished country and its 4.1 million people can only travel to the EU if they have a special visa. But Romania has offered passports to up to one million Moldovans, alarming both Moldova and some in the EU. Most of Moldova was part of Romania until it was annexed by the Soviet Union in 1940.

Under EU laws, Romania is entitled to give citizenship to anybody it chooses. Amid fears that up to a million impoverished migrants could enter Europe through the back door, Romanian diplomats said only 20,000 cases were pending because many Moldovans failed to complete the complex application procedures. Others claim as many as 800,000 applications may be submitted. In 2013, there were 198,839 immigrants living in Romania, of which 13,000 were refugees. Over half of the country's foreign-born residents originate from Moldova.

Residence and Citizenship

Under the law, citizenship can be granted upon application made by a foreign citizen or by a person without citizenship on the following conditions:

1. At the time of application, the person must have been born in

Romania and still reside there, or in case he/she was not born there, he/she must legally have lived in Romania for at least eight years. If married to a Romanian citizen, the person must legally have lived in Romania for at least five years. These residence requirements can be reduced by half if the applicant is a renowned international personality or if he/she has invested more than €500,000 (US$154,000) in Romania. (For more about residence and citizenship by investment, see the Romanian Foreign Ministry website at http://www.mae.ro/en/node/2054).

2. Behavior, attitude and actions must prove loyalty to the Romanian state; the individual must not support or be involved in illegal activities or against the national security; the individual must also state that he/she has never been involved in such actions in the past.

3. The person must be 18 years or older.

4. He/she must enjoy a good reputation among other citizens and have never been convicted in another country of any crime that makes them unworthy of becoming a Romanian citizen.

5. The individual must be able to speak, read and understand Romanian and have basic knowledge of Romanian history and civilization and the Romanian Constitution.

Romanian citizenship may be granted or restored to those individuals who lost their right to Romanian citizenship before December 22, 1989, or to their descendants.

U.S. and many other nationals do not need a visa for visits of 90 days or less. In each case, a passport must be valid for three months beyond the intended stay, tickets and documents for return or onward travel must be available. Extension of stay is possible upon application to Romanian immigration authorities, as is the granting of residence status.

Contacts

Embassy of Romania
1607 23rd Street NW
Washington, DC 20008
Tel.: (202) 332-4848
Fax: (202) 232-4748
Email: Consular@roembus.org
Web: http://washington.mae.ro/

Romanian Mission to the UN
573 Third Avenue
New York, NY 10016
Tel.: (212) 682-3273

Romanian National Tourist Office
573 Third Avenue
New York, NY 10016
Tel.: (212) 697-6971

Romanian Cultural Center
200 E. 38th Street
New York, NY 10016
Tel.: (212) 687-0180

Official Romanian Immigration Website:
http://ori.mai.gov.ro/home/index/en

United States Embassy
Strada Tudor Arghezi 7-9
Bucharest, Romania
Tel.: + (40) 21-200-3300
Fax: + (40) 21-200-3442
Email: csbucharest@state.gov
Web: http://bucharest.usembassy.gov/

Russian Federation

Government:	Federation
Capital:	Moscow
National Day:	Russia Day: 12 June (1990)
Population:	142,500,482 (July 2013 est.)
Total Area:	6,592,772 sq. miles / 17,075,200 sq. kilometers
Languages:	Russian, many minority languages
Ethnic groups:	Russian 79.8%, other 12.1%, Tatar 3.8%, Ukrainian 2%, Bashkir 1.2%, Chuvash 1.1%
Religion:	Russian Orthodox 15-20%, Muslim 10-15%, other Christian 2%. Estimates are of practicing worshipers; Russia has many non-practicing believers and non-believers, a legacy of over seven decades of atheistic Communist rule.
Life expectancy:	69.85 years
Currency:	Russian ruble (RUR)
GDP:	US$2.486 trillion (2012 est.)
GDP per capita:	US$17,500 (2012 est.)

Winston Churchill's "riddle wrapped in a mystery inside an enigma" remains an apt description of Russia; most outsiders have only a hazy idea of its realities. A composite of the extravagant glories of old Russia and the drab legacies of the Soviet era, it's a country that both befuddles and beguiles. This is a land of snow and deadly winters, but also of rivers that meander across meadows and a mid-summer sun that never sets. Its people, in the words of a Russian proverb, "love to suffer," yet they also love to party and can be disarmingly generous and hospitable.

For centuries, the world has wondered what to believe about Russia. The country has been reported variously as a land of unbelievable riches and indescribable poverty, cruel tyrants and great minds, generous hospitality and meddlesome bureaucracy, beautiful ballets and industrial monstrosities, pious faith and unbridled hedonism. These eternal Russian truths coexist in equally diverse landscapes of icy tundra and sun-kissed beaches, dense silver birch and fir forests and deep and mysterious lakes, snow-capped mountains and swaying grasslands — those famous steppes.

Factor in ancient fortresses, luxurious palaces, swirly spired churches and lost-in-time wooden villages and you'll begin to see why Russia is simply amazing. — Lonely Planet

History and Overview

Russia is the largest of the 15 geopolitical entities that emerged in 1991 from the collapse of the Communist Union of Soviet Socialist Republics (USSR). Covering more than 10 million square miles in Europe and Asia, Russia is the largest country in the world.

As was the case in the Soviet and tsarist eras, the center of Russia's population and economic activity is the European sector, which occupies about one-quarter of the country's territory. Vast tracts of land in Asian Russia are virtually unoccupied. Although numerous Soviet programs had attempted to populate and exploit resources in Siberia and the Arctic regions of the Russian Republic, the population of Russia's remote areas decreased in recent years.

Founded in the 12th century, the Principality of Muscovy was able to emerge from over 200 years of Mongol domination (13th to 15th centuries) and to gradually conquer and absorb surrounding principalities. In the early 17th century, a new Romanov Dynasty continued this policy of expansion across Siberia to the Pacific. Under Peter the Great (1682 to 1725) hegemony was extended to the Baltic Sea and the country was renamed the Russian Empire.

During the 19th century, more territorial acquisitions were made in Europe and Asia. Repeated devastating defeats of the Russian army in World War I led to widespread rioting in the major cities and to the overthrow, in 1917, of the imperial household headed by the last of the Romanovs, Tsar Nicholas II. On the night of July 17, 1918, the Tsar, the Tsaritsa, Alexandra, their son and his heir, Alexey, and their four daughters, Maria, Olga, Tatiana and Anastasia, were all shot and stabbed to death by Communists in Yekaterinburg. Today their recovered remains are interred in honor in the Russian Orthodox Cathedral in Saint Petersburg.

The Communists, under Vladimir Lenin, seized power and formed the Union of Soviet Socialist Republics. The brutal rule of Josef Stalin (1928 to 1953) strengthened Communist rule and Russian dominance of the USSR at a cost of tens of millions of lives. The Soviet economy and society stagnated in the following decades until General Secretary Mikhail Gorbachev (1985 to 1991) introduced glasnost (openness) and perestroika (restructuring) in an attempt to modernize Communism, but his initiatives inadvertently released political forces that, by December 1991, splintered the USSR into Russia and 14 other independent republics.

Since then, Russia has struggled unsuccessfully to build a democratic political system and market economy to replace the strict social, political and economic controls of the Communist period. While some progress has been made on the economic front there has been a centralization of power and an erosion of nascent democratic institutions under Vladimir V. Putin, former KGB agent, former and now again president, who has been a virtual dictator since 2000. Putin served as president from 2000 to 2008 but was limited by the Constitution to two consecutive terms so he became prime minister for four years and again was elected president for a six-year term in 2012.

Putin, who transformed post-Soviet Russia by re-imposing Kremlin control over most aspects of public life, announced that he could remain during two, six-year terms until 2024, giving him a potential rule comparable in length to that of Communist dictators Leonid Brezhnev or Josef Stalin. Russia's post-Soviet democratic ambitions have been thwarted in favor of a centralized authoritarian state whose legitimacy is buttressed, in part, by carefully managed national elections, Putin's genuine popularity, and the management of Russia's windfall energy wealth.

But Putin will face some serious internal economic and budgetary problems, as well as threats of internal terrorism. Putin has severely disabled a Chechen rebel movement, although repeated bombings and violence still occur throughout the North Caucasus and elsewhere in the country.

As we go to press the major question is how far Putin will push Russian territorial expansion. In the face of confused and ineffective EU and U.S. opposition, Putin engineered the forced reaccession of the Crimea as part of the Russian Federation. Similar military tactics used in the eastern Ukraine also have called into question what designees Putin has on that country, formerly part of the USSR. In spite of threats from the West and damage to the Russian economy, Putin has shown little inclination to curb his expansive plans. Some have described this as a renewal of the Cold War.

Economy

The economy had averaged 7% growth in the decade following the 1998 Russian financial crisis, resulting in a doubling of real disposable incomes and the emergence of a middle class. The Russian economy, however, was one of the hardest hit by the 2008 to 2009 global economic crisis as oil prices plummeted and the foreign credits that Russian banks and firms relied on dried up. The economic decline bottomed out and the economy began to grow again in late 2009. High oil prices buoyed Russian growth in 2011 to 2012 and helped Russia reduce the budget deficit inherited from 2008to 2009. Russia has reduced unemployment to a record low and has lowered inflation below double digit rates.

Although high oil prices and a relatively cheap ruble are important drivers of this economic rebound, since 2000, investment and consumer-driven demand have played a noticeably increasing role. Real fixed capital investments have averaged gains greater than 10% over the last five years, and real personal incomes have realized average increases over 12%.

During this time, poverty has declined steadily and the middle class has continued to expand. Russia has also improved its international financial position since the 1998 financial crisis, with its foreign debt declining from 90% of GDP to around 31%. Strong oil export earnings have allowed Russia to increase its foreign reserves. Foreign exchange reserves grew from US$12 billion in 1999 to almost US$600 billion by 2008, which include US$200 billion in two sovereign wealth funds. Oil, natural gas, metals, and timber account for more than 80% of exports, leaving the country vulnerable to swings in world prices.

Russia's manufacturing base is dilapidated and must be replaced or modernized if the country is to achieve broad based economic growth. Other problems include a weak banking system, a poor business climate that discourages both domestic and foreign investors, corruption, and widespread lack of trust in institutions. The protection of property rights is still weak and the private sector remains subject to heavy state interference.

Russia's long-term challenges include a shrinking workforce, a high level of corruption, difficulty in accessing capital for smaller, non-energy companies, and poor infrastructure in need of large investments.

Politics

Investigations of a major privately owned Russian oil company, culminating with the arrest of its CEO and the confiscation of the company by a state-owned firm, raised concerns that Putin has reinstituted Soviet style government and with a quasi-communistic state control over the economy. State control increased with a number of large acquisitions with foreign investors being forced to sell their interests to the government.

Government pressure continued to weaken freedom of expression and the independence and freedom of some media, particularly major national television networks and regional media outlets. A government decision resulted in the elimination of the last major non-state television network in 2003.

National press is also increasingly in government hands or owned by government officials, narrowing the scope of opinion available. Self-censorship is a growing press problem.

Of even greater concern, Russia has made little progress in building the rule of law and a fair judicial system, the bedrocks of a modern market economy. Poisonings and assassination of vocal anti-Putin opponents, especially journalists, support charges of a renewal of KGB-style force and control again in Russia.

Visas

The Russian government maintains a restrictive and complicated visa regime for foreign travelers who visit, transit or reside in the Russian Federation. The Russian system includes requirements of sponsorship, visas for entry and exit, migration cards, and registration. American citizens who also carry Russian passports face additional complicated regulations. Dual citizen minors who travel on their Russian passports also face special problems.

The Russian government does not recognize the standing of U.S. Consular officers to intervene in visa cases. The U.S. diplomatic mission in Russia is not able to act as a sponsor, submit visa applications, register private travelers, or request that visas or migration cards be corrected, replaced or extended. Before traveling to Russia, U.S. citizens should verify the latest requirements with the Russian Embassy or nearest consulate.

Sponsorship: Under Russian law, every foreign traveler must have a Russian-based sponsor (a hotel, tour company, relative, employer, etc.). Generally speaking, visas sponsored by Russian individuals are "guest" visas, and visas sponsored by tour agencies or hotels are "tourist" visas. Note that travelers who enter Russia on tourist visas, but who then reside with Russian individuals, may have difficulty registering their visas and migration cards and may be required by Russian authorities to depart Russia sooner than they had planned.

Police have the authority to stop people and request their documents at any time without cause. Due to the possibility of random document checks by police, U.S. citizens should carry their original passports, registered migration cards and visas with them at all times. Failure to provide proper documentation can result in detention and/or heavy fines.

Russia does not currently recognize dual citizenship. If you have ever held Russian citizenship, you must either travel to Russia using a Russian passport, or prove that you have renounced your Russian citizenship (or that your parents renounced their citizenship before you were born). This includes anyone born in Russia, or born overseas to at least one Russian parent.

For current information about visas, see the U.S. Visa Information Service for Russia, http://www.ustraveldocs.com/ru/

Citizenship

Should you be one of those rare foreign individuals who wishes to acquire Russian citizenship, my advice is to obtain a very good lawyer who knows Russian immigration law.

As the U.S. Consulate in St. Petersburg said on its website "Russian immigration and visa laws recently have been changed, and reportedly, more changes are being contemplated. The implementation of these laws has not always been transparent or predictable. In addition, Russian Immigration officials at times implement the laws and regulations governing entry and exit inconsistently, especially in remote areas."

Tough rules for acquiring Russian citizenship include; those who apply for citizenship must have lived at least five years in Russia must pass a Russian language exam and have a job. The law also rejects dual citizenship and demands that applicants reject the citizenship of other nations in order to become Russian citizens.

The law says that immigrants from former Soviet republics must follow standard rules for seeking Russian citizenship and are deprived of privileges they had enjoyed since the 1991 Soviet disintegration. The law's supporters said prior rules were too lax, encouraged illegal migration and fueled crime, while critics claimed that the legislation makes Russia's population decline worse by stalling needed immigration.

The 2009 Russian Federal Law on Citizenship was supposedly aimed at the simplification of the citizenship acquisition procedure for nationals of the former Soviet republics, if they were born in the territory of Russia when it was a part of the Soviet Union, and for their immediate relatives. The requirements of a five-year residence, knowledge of the Russian language and constitution, and proof of a legal source of income are waived for such individuals, regardless of their place of residence. The law allows foreign citizens and stateless persons who were previously citizens of the Soviet Union and were legally registered in Russia before July 1, 2002, to receive preferential treatment when applying for Russian citizenship.

Although legislative records indicate that the law supposedly was passed with the purpose of assisting those compatriots who intend to relocate to Russia, Ukrainian government observers suggest that making eight million Ukrainian individuals eligible for Russian citizenship and granting them Russian passports was a tactic designed by Russian authorities to support the annexation of Ukrainian lands in the future. A similar passport tactic was used in 2008 when, after prolonged military occupation of parts of Georgia, Russia granted citizenship to those living in the separatist provinces in the Republic of Georgia that the Russian military had occupied by force. Putin has exerted major pressure on the government of Ukraine for closer integration, causing major riots in that country during 2013 to 2014.

Travel Warning

The U.S. Department of State continues to warn of extreme risk to personal security in the North Caucasus region, including Chechnya, Dagestan, North Ossetia, Ingushetia, Karbadi-no-Balkaria (including the Elbrus area), Abkhazia, the southeast parts of the Stavropol region and Karachay-Cherkessia. Terrorism, kidnapping and military activity in these areas present a significant risk to security.

State warns that acts of terrorism, including bombings and hostage takings, continue to occur in Russia, particularly in the North Caucasus region. Between October 15 and December 30, 2013, there were three suicide bombings targeting public transportation in the city of Volgograd (600 miles from Sochi), two of which occurred within the same 24-hour period. In early January 2014, media reports emerged about the possible presence of so-called "black widow" suicide bombers in Sochi. In January 2011, an explosion occurred at Moscow's Domodedovo International Airport, killing over 35 people and injuring more than 100 others. Other bombings over the past 10 to 15 years occurred at Russian government buildings, airports, hotels, tourist sites, markets, entertainment venues, schools, and residential complexes. There have also been large-scale attacks on public transportation including subways, buses, trains, and scheduled commercial flights, within the same time period.

Contacts

Embassy of the Russian Federation
2650 Wisconsin Avenue NW
Washington, DC 20007
Tel.: (202) 298-5700
Web: http://www.russianembassy.org/

Consular Section
2641 Tunlaw Road
Washington, DC 20007
Tel.: (202) 939-8907/-8913/-8918

Russian Consulates: Houston, New York, San Francisco, and Seattle

United States Embassy
Bolshoy Deviatinsky Pereulok No. 8
Moscow 121099; Russian Federation
Tel.: + (7) 495-728-5000
Email: consulMo@state.gov
Web: http://moscow.usembassy.gov/

U.S. Consulate General
Ulitsa Furshtadskaya, 15
St. Petersburg 191028 Russia
MAIL: PSC 78, Box L, APO AE 09723
Tel.: + (7-812) 331-2600
Email: acsstpete@state.gov
Web: http://stpetersburg.usconsulate.gov/

Republic of San Marino

Government:	Independent republic
Capital:	San Marino
National Day:	Founding of the Republic: 3 September (A.D. 301)
Population:	32,448 (July 2013 est.)
Total Area:	24 sq. miles / 61 sq. kilometers
Language:	Italian
Ethnic groups:	Sammarinese, Italian
Religion:	Roman Catholic
Life expectancy:	83.12 years
Currency:	Euro (EUR)
GDP:	US$1.335 billion (2012 est.)
GDP per capita:	US$34,830 (2010 est.)

Perched on the top of a 657m lump of rock, the 37 square mile Repubblica di San Marino is Europe's third smallest state after the Vatican and Monaco. A favorite day-trip destination; in 2006, about 2.1 million visitors made the very steep climb to the historic center; it's largely given over to tourism. Hundreds of souvenir stalls line the not unattractive streets selling everything from samurai swords to San Marino stamps and locally minted coins, and restaurants do a brisk trade feeding the visiting hordes.

However, if you catch it at a quiet time (during the week, preferably in winter) the old town is pleasant enough and the views are spectacular. Several legends describe the founding of San Marino, including one about a stonecutter who was given the land on top of Monte Titano by a rich Roman woman whose son he had cured. Throughout history, it's pretty much been left to its own devices. Cesare Borgia took possession early in the 16th century, but his rule was short-lived as he died soon after. Then in 1739 one Cardinal Giulio Alberoni took over the republic, but the pope backed San Marino's independence and the cardinal was sent packing. During WWII it remained neutral and played host to 100, 000 refugees until 1944, when the Allies marched into town. — Lonely Planet

History and Overview

Landlocked San Marino is the smallest independent state in Europe dominated by the surrounding Apennines and its surrounding neighbor, Italy. The third smallest state in Europe (after the Holy See and Monaco) also claims to be the world's oldest republic.

According to tradition, it was founded by a Christian stone mason named Marino in 301 A.D. San Marino's foreign policy is aligned with that of Italy, which conducts diplomatic affairs on its behalf. Social and political trends in the republic also track closely with those of its larger neighbor.

Economy

When it comes to tiny San Marino, (its official title, "The Most Serene Republic of San Marino" is more of an endorsement than a title), is a colossus of the miniature. In its entirety, it is not much bigger than two or three American suburbs strung together.

San Marino's economy relies heavily on tourism (over 50% of GDP), the banking industry and the manufacture and export of ceramics, clothing, fabrics, furniture, paints, spirits, tiles, and wine. More than three million tourists visit San Marino each year. The manufacturing and financial sectors account for more than half of GDP. The per capita level of output and standard of living are comparable to those of the most prosperous regions of Italy which supplies much of its food. The economy benefits from foreign investment because of low corporate taxes and low taxes on interest earnings. The income tax rate is also very low, about one-third the average EU level.

San Marino does not issue public debt securities; when necessary, it finances deficits by drawing down central bank deposits. The economy has encountered five years of GDP contraction, due to weakened demand from Italy, which accounts for 90% of its export market, and financial sector contraction. Difficulties in the banking sector, the global economic downturn, and the sizeable decline in tax revenues contributed to negative GDP. The government has tried to counter the economic downturn with subsidized credit to businesses. Beginning in 2009 improvements in the financial sector began.

Another unusual source of revenue is the sale of postage stamps and coins — both are popular with collectors and together account for over 10% of government income. Statistical details of San Marino's external trade are included with those of Italy, with whom San Marino has a longstanding customs union.

Tax Haven in Decline

There are differences in taxation and regulatory structures which have afforded San Marino the status of a tax haven, as a large amount of non-resident deposits in the past have been made in the principality's banks. According to the International Monetary Fund (IMF): "San Marino has enjoyed an extended period of remarkably strong economic performance, posting real GDP growth well above the levels recorded in neighboring regions or in the euro-area, low unemployment, and declining inflation. The country has become increasingly integrated with the world economy, as evidenced by trade and tourism, the rapid increase in the share of Italian commuters in the workforce, and a rising intermediation of foreign savings by the local banks. The challenge at hand is to sustain this performance in an increasingly competitive international environment."

San Marino has tried to harmonize its fiscal laws with EU and international standards. In 2009, the OECD removed San Marino from its list of tax havens that had not fully adopted global tax standards. In 2010, San Marino signed tax information exchange agreements with most major countries. By 2013, San Marino had signed 26 tax information exchange agreements (TIEAs) including those with Canada, Germany, France, and the U.K., but not the United States or Italy as yet. It also has 18 double taxation treaties. San Marino's Government continues to work with Italy to ratify a financial information exchange agreement, seen by businesses and investors as crucial to strengthening the economic relationship between the two countries.

Under pressure from the Organization for Economic Cooperation and Development (OECD), San Marino has adopted an anti-money laundering law and amended its tax laws, weakening financial privacy standards in order to facilitate better "exchange of information in tax matters." It joined other so-called "tax havens" in pledging to apply OECD standards in allowing exchange of tax information.

Because of changes in its tax and reporting laws and the signing of a double taxation agreement, in 2014 the government of Italy removed San Marino from its "black list" of uncooperative countries were it had been since 1999.

Fitch financial ratings service has cited San Marino's high income per capita, stable political situation and strong public finances, but noted problems faced by the large banking sector, including uncertainties over the country's largest bank, the Cassa di Risparmio della Repubblica di San Marino — CRSM. Italy declared a fiscal amnesty in 2009 to 2010, which resulted in significant deposit outflows from San Marino's banks, severely shrinking their liquidity.

Residence and Citizenship

The 2000 citizenship law provides that both men and women can transmit to their children citizenship either through birth or naturalization.

In theory, the law allows 12 months for all children of San Marino citizens to attain permanent citizenship after reaching legal majority (18), however, the law phrases this right slightly differently for the children of male citizens and the children of female citizens. The children of male citizens only need to state their intent to retain citizenship, whereas the children of female citizens must state their "desire" to retain citizenship. It is not clear if this will affect the transmission of citizenship in practice.

Travelers must enter San Marino from Italy. Since there are no frontier formalities imposed, any visitor must comply with Italian passport/visa regulations. A valid foreign passport is required for entry into Italy. Italian authorities may deny entry to travelers who attempt to enter without a valid passport. A visa is not required for tourist stays up to three months. However, for all other purposes, such as work, study, etc., a visa is required and must be obtained from the Italian Embassy or Consulates before entering Italy.

Contacts

State Board of Tourism
Contrada Omagnano, 20
47890 - Rep. of San Marino
Tel.: +378 (0549) 882914
Information on politics, trade, and events at:
http://www.visitsanmarino.com/on-line/en/home.html

Honorary Consulate General
888 17th Street NW, Suite 900
Washington, DC 20006
Tel.: (202) 337-2260

Nearest U.S. Consulate General
Lungarno Amerigo Vespucci 38
50123, Firenze, Italy
Tel.: + (39) 055-226-951
Web: http://florence.usconsulate.gov/english/

For information concerning visas and entry requirements for Italy contact:

Embassy of Italy
3000 Whitehaven Street NW
Washington, DC 20008
Tel.: (202) 612-4400
Web: http://www.ambwashingtondc.esteri.it/ambasciata_wash-ington

Social media website: http://www.twiplomacy.it/usa/

Republic of Serbia

Government:	Republic
Capital:	Belgrade
National Day:	National Day: 15 February
Population:	7,243,007 (July 2013 est.)
Total Area:	29.72 sq. miles 77,474 sq kilometers
Languages:	Serbian (official) 88.1%, Hungarian 3.4%, Bosnian 1.9%, Romany 1.4%, other 3.4%, undeclared or unknown 1.8%
Ethnic groups:	Serb 83.3%, Bosniak 2%, Hungarian 3.5%, Romany 2.1%, other 5.7%, undeclared or unknown 3.4% (2011 est.)
Religion:	Serbian Orthodox 84.6%, Catholic 5%, Muslim 3.1%, Protestant 1%, other 1.9%, undeclared or unknown 4.5% (2011 est.)
Life expectancy:	74.79 years
Currency:	Serbian dinars (RSD)
GDP:	US$77.83 billion (2012 est.)
GDP per capita:	US$10,700 (2012 est.)

Serbia (Srbija) is yet to come within most tourists' comfort zone, but having got rid of Slobodan Milošević and become a democracy, the nation is now knocking on the doors of Europe, and in the meantime is a safe and welcoming place to visit. The most exciting spot is undoubtedly its capital, Belgrade, a gritty, energetic city. Cultural buffs can revel in its architecture and museums, foodies in its restaurants, while party animals will get no rest exploring its incessant nightlife.

Vojvodina's flat plains and the tranquil Fruška Gora mon-

asteries provide an effective antidote to urban chaos, while Novi Sad is home to the world-famous Exit music festival. Proud and traditional Southern Serbia is a land of lush rolling hills and wooded valleys brushing up against rugged mountains. The medieval monasteries of Manasija, Sopoćani and Studenica remain the keepers of Serbian faith and Byzantine art, while the mountains of Zlatibor and Kopaonik provide snow fun in winter and glorious hiking in summer. Mosques mix with monasteries in Novi Pazar, where life in the Turkish quarter continues much as it did a century ago when the Turks were still in power.

A few kilometers south lies Kosovo a disputed land riven by different interpretations of history. For Serbs it is the cradle of their nationhood, for Kosovo Albanians it is their future independence. The UN still recognizes Kosovo as part of Serbia until current talks decide its future. — Lonely Planet

Background and History

Serbia is located in Southeastern Europe, between Macedonia and Hungary bordering also on Bosnia and Herzegovina, Bulgaria, Croatia, Kosovo, Montenegro and Romania. Its location controls one of the major land routes from Western Europe to Turkey and the Near East.

From parts of the Hapsburg's defunct Austro-Hungarian Empire, the Kingdom of Serbs, Croats, and Slovenes was formed at the end of World War I at the Versailles peace conference in 1918; its name was changed to Yugoslavia in 1929. The Partisans, the military-political group headed by Josip "Tito" Broz, took control in 1945. Although Communist, Tito's government and his successors managed to steer a path between the Russian-dominated Warsaw Pact nations and the U.S. and the West for the next 45 years.

In 1989, Slobodan Milošević became president of Serbia in the country's first democratic elections since World War I. His ultra-nationalist calls for Serbian domination led to the violent breakup of Yugoslavia along ethnic lines. In 1991, Croatia, Slovenia, and Macedonia declared independence, followed by Bosnia in 1992. The remaining republics of Serbia and Montenegro declared a new Federal Republic of Yugoslavia in April 1992. Under Milošević Serbia led ultimately unsuccessful military campaigns forcefully to unite ethnic Serbs in neighboring republics into a "Greater Serbia" but that ended in 1995.

Milošević became president of the Federal Republic of Yugoslavia in 1997. In 1998, an Albanian insurgency in the formerly autonomous Serbian province of Kosovo provoked Serbian attacks that resulted in brutal massacres and massive expulsions of ethnic Albanians living in Kosovo. Milošević refusal to negotiate led to NATO's bombing of Serbia in 1999, to the withdrawal of Serbian military forces from Kosovo in June 1999, and to the stationing of a NATO-led force in Kosovo to provide a safe environment for ethnic communities.

In 2000 elections Milošević was replaced by a democratic government. In 2003, Yugoslavia consisted of a loose federation of Serbia and Montenegro. Widespread violence targeting ethnic Serbs in Kosovo in 2004 killed thousands and caused the international community to force negotiations on the status of Kosovo.

During the year 2006, Montenegro seceded from the federation and declared itself to be an independent nation. Serbia became the successor state to the former union of Serbia and Montenegro. And in 2008, after two years of negotiations, the U.N.-administered province of Kosovo declared itself independent of Serbia, an action Serbia refuses to recognize.

At Serbia's request, the U.N. General Assembly in 2008 obtained an advisory opinion from the International Court of Justice (ICJ) that international law did not prohibit Kosovo's unilateral declaration of independence. In 2010, Serbia agreed to an EU-drafted U.N. resolution acknowledging the ICJ decision and calling talks between Serbia and Kosovo. The EU-moderated Belgrade-Pristina dialogue began in 2011.

Economy

Serbia has an economy mostly dominated by market forces, but the state sector remains large and many institutional reforms are needed. The economy relies on manufacturing and exports, driven largely by foreign investment. International economic sanctions, civil war, and the damage to Yugoslavia's infrastructure and industry during the NATO airstrikes in 1999 left the economy only half the size it was in 1990.

In 2000, the Democratic Opposition of Serbia coalition government adopted stabilization measures, free market reforms, trade liberalization and privatization, but many large enterprises, including the power utilities, telecommunications, natural gas, the national air carrier, and others remain in state hands.

Serbia applied for EU membership, signing a Stabilization and Association Agreement with Brussels in 2008, and an Interim Trade Agreement with the EU that took effect in 2010. Needed structural economic reforms have stalled since the global financial crisis began in 2009. Major challenges include: high unemployment, high government expenditures, a need for new government borrowing; rising public and private foreign debt and attracting new foreign direct investment.

Other serious challenges include an inefficient judicial system, high levels of corruption, and an aging population. Factors favorable to Serbia's economic growth include a strategic location, a relatively inexpensive and skilled labor force, and free trade agreements with the EU, Russia, Turkey, and countries that are members of the Central European Free Trade Agreement (CEFTA).

Residence and Citizenship

With a history of numerous unions and break ups of various provinces over recent years, the citizenship laws of Serbia are complex. Serbia is a country of origin, transit and refuge to many people who have been forced to flee their original homes.

With 86,000 refugees from Croatia and Bosnia and Herzegovina, and 206,000 internally displaced persons from Kosovo, Serbia ranks first in Europe for the number of refugees and "internally displaced persons." The adoption of the 2012 law on migration management established a coordinated system for migration management and created a Commissariat for Refugees.

Applicants who wish to acquire Serbian citizenship, without renouncing their own citizenship must be over the age of 18 and able to work. Prior to submitting an application, they must sign a statement declaring that they accept Serbia as their own country.

Montenegrin citizens who were registered as residents in Serbia on June 3, 2006, when Montenegro ended its union with Serbia, are considered Serbian citizens by Serbia, provided they submit written documentation stating that they consider themselves to be Serbian citizens, together with a request for their names to be entered into the citizens register.

The Law on Serb Citizenship adopted in 1992 and amended in 1996 provides that Serb citizenship is acquired by:

1. origin (jus sanguinis);

2. birth in the territory of the Republic;

3. naturalization;

4. international agreement.

Serb citizenship by origin is acquired by a Serb child:

1. whose parents both have Serb citizenship at the time of the child's birth;

2. One of whose parents has Serb citizenship at the time of the child's birth, and the child is born on the territory of Republic;

3. One of whose parents has Serb citizenship at the time of the child's birth and the other is without citizenship or is unknown, and the child is born abroad.

A child who is born abroad and one of whose parents has Serb citizenship at the time of the child's birth acquires Serb citizenship by origin if he is registered officially as a Serb citizen before the age of 18 or if he establishes residence on the territory of Republic before the age of 18.

A child who is born or found on the territory of Republic acquires Serb citizenship if both of his parents are unknown or of unknown citizenship or are without citizenship.

A foreigner can acquire Serb citizenship by naturalization if he has submitted a request for admission into citizenship and fulfills the following requirements:

1. That he has reached the age of 18 and has not been found incompetent or is still under the lawful custody of his parents , or that he has acquired his majority at the age of 16 through emancipation;

2. That he has actually and continuously lived for at least five years on the territory of Republic before submitting the request;

3. That he knows the Serbian language and the Cyrillic alphabet;

4. That his previous behavior demonstrates that he respects the legal order and customs of Republic and that he accepts Serbian culture;

5. That he has not been denied residence in Republic;

6. That he has not been received a prison sentence longer than one year for a crime prosecuted ex officio;

7. That his acceptance into Serb citizenship does not represent a danger for public order, security, or defense of the country.

A foreigner who is married to a Serb citizen shall be admitted to Serb citizenship even if he does not meet the requirements in points 1, 2, and 3 of Article 7.

Travelers who do not need a visa to enter Serbia may stay for a maximum of 90 days within a period of 180 days. For a list of countries that do not require a visa, see the website at http://www.mfa.gov.rs/en/consular-affairs/entry-serbia/visa-requirements

It is required that persons register with the local police in the town/city where they are staying within 24 hours of arrival unless you are staying in a hotel where you will be registered automatically on checking-in. If you don't register you could be fined, detained or face a court appearance.

Contacts

Embassy of the Republic of Serbia
2134 Kalorama Road NW
Washington, DC 20008
Tel.: + 1 202 / 332-0333
Email: info@serbiaembusa.org
Web: http://www.washington.mfa.gov.rs

United States Embassy
92 Bulevar kneza Aleksandra Karadjordjevica
11040 Belgrade, Serbia
Tel.: +381 11 706-4000
Email: BelgradeACS@state.gov
Web: http://serbia.usembassy.gov/

Slovak Republic

Government:	Parliamentary democracy
Capital:	Bratislava
National Day:	Constitution Day: 1 September (1992)
Population:	5,488,339 (July 2013 est.)
Total Area:	18,859 sq. miles / 48,845 sq. kilometers
Languages:	Slovak (official) 83.9%, Hungarian 10.7%, other 2.6%, Roma 1.8%, Ukrainian 1%
Ethnic groups:	Slovak 85.8%, Hungarian 9.7%, other 1.8%, Roma 1.7%, Ruthenian/Ukrainian 1%
Religion:	Roman Catholic 68.9%, none 13%, Protestant 10.8%, Greek Catholic 4.1%, other 3.2%, none 13%
Life expectancy:	76.24 years
Currency:	Euro (EUR)
GDP:	US$130.5 billion (2012 est.)
GDP per capita:	US$24,100 (2012 est.)

Having emerged from its frumpy, communist-era chrysalis in time to welcome a horde of low-cost carrier junkies, the increasing numbers of flights and EU membership have pushed costs up in the capital of Slovakia. Outside the city and you'll find traditional villages, terrific trails and prices a fraction of those in Western Europe.

Slovakia is not about jaw-dropping sights and superlatives; it's about experiencing a place less touched by the glitz and glam of its more famous neighbors. Get outside the cities and you can still find traditional villages, strong folk traditions and tourist walking trails meandering through the hilly coun-

tryside. A plethora of fortresses and castles pay testament to a history of conquerors and domination in this small country, which became an independent nation only in 1993. Foreign influences can be seen in the 18th century rococo town buildings, Gothic churches and a few 15th-century town squares. History's evolution has created an interesting contrast in styles and the people have come through it all with their welcoming spirit intact. — Lonely Planet

History and Overview

Slovakia is located in Central Europe, south of Poland, between the Czech Republic to the west and Hungary to the east.

Slovak history has its roots in the Great Moravian Empire, founded in the early 9th century. The territory of Great Moravia included all of present western and central Slovakia, the Czech Republic, and parts of neighboring Poland, Hungary, and Germany. Saints Cyril and Methodius, known for the creation of a Cyrillic alphabet, came to Great Moravia in the early 10th century as missionaries to spread Christianity at the invitation of the king. The empire collapsed after only 80 years as a result of the political intrigues and external pressures from invading forces. Slovaks then became part of the Hungarian Kingdom, where they remained for the next 1,000 years.

The dissolution of the Austro-Hungarian Empire at the close of World War I allowed the Slovaks to join the closely related Czechs to form Czechoslovakia. Following the chaos of World War II, Czechoslovakia became a Communist nation within Soviet-ruled Eastern Europe. Soviet influence collapsed in 1989 and Czechoslovakia once more became free. The Slovaks and the Czechs agreed to separate peacefully on January 1, 1993. Slovakia joined both NATO and the EU in the spring of 2004.

Economy

Slovakia has made significant economic reforms since its separation from the Czech Republic in 1993. Reforms to the taxation, health care, pension, and social welfare systems helped Slovakia consolidate its budget and get on track to join the EU in 2004 after a period of relative stagnation in the early and mid-1990s and to adopt the euro in 2009. Major privatizations are nearly complete, the banking sector is almost entirely in foreign hands, and the government has helped facilitate a foreign investment boom with business friendly policies, liberalization and a 19% flat income tax.

Slovakia's economic growth exceeded expectations in 2001 to 2008 despite a general European slowdown. Foreign direct investment (FDI), especially in the automotive and electronic sectors, fueled much of the growth until 2008. Cheap and skilled labor, low taxes, no dividend taxes, a relatively liberal labor code, and a favorable geographical location are Slovakia's main advantages for foreign investors.

In 2009, the economy contracted 5% primarily as a result of smaller inflows of FDI and reduced demand for Slovakia's exports before rebounding in 2010to 2011, but growth slowed in 2012 due to weakening external demand. In 2012, the government of Prime Minister Robert Fico imposed tax increases on higher-earning individuals and corporations, effectively scrapping the flat tax to help meet budget deficit targets of 4.9% of GDP in 2012 and 3% of GDP in 2013.

To maintain a stable operating environment for investors, the European Bank for Reconstruction and Development advised the Slovak government to refrain from intervening in important sectors of the economy. However, Bratislava's approach to mitigating the economic slowdown has included substantial government intervention and the option to nationalize strategic companies.

Residence and Citizenship

Prior to 1993, the Slovak Republic was part of the former state of Czechoslovakia. However, since 1968 most Slovaks had held citizenship of the Slovak Republic alongside Czechoslovak citizenship. At the time (and up to 1993), Slovak citizenship was an internal distinction within Czechoslovakia.

However, at the formation of the independent Slovak Republic on January 1, 1993, this was the basis for conferral of citizenship of the Slovak Republic upon citizens of Czechoslovakia. A citizen of Czechoslovakia as of December 31, 1992 who was not a citizen of the Slovak Republic had one year from that date to apply for Slovak citizenship. This generally caused loss of Czech citizenship.

In Slovakia, normally five years stay in the territory of the Republic, as well as knowledge of the Slovak language, are required to qualify for citizenship. However, there is an exception from this rule in the case of persons with three generations of Slovak ancestry. Such persons can obtain what is called the "Slovak expatriate status." This status can be granted to applicants over 15 years of age who are not citizens of the Republic and can prove their Slovak nationality, ethnic origin and cultural and linguistic awareness. Persons who have been granted expatriate status and have received an expatriate card can then submit an application for citizenship.

A child acquires citizenship by birth only if: 1) at least one of the parents is a citizen of the Slovak Republic; 2) the child was born within the territory of the Republic, its parents being without any citizenship; or 3) the child was born within the territory of the Slovak Republic, its parents being citizens of another country, when the child does not by birth gain the citizenship of either of the parents.

Citizenship can be granted upon request to a person who is not a citizen and who has lived permanently in the territory of the Republic for at least five years and speaks the Slovak language; and who has not been convicted of an intentional crime.

Citizenship can also be granted to a person who marries a Slovak citizen; or for reasons worth special recognition, if the person has done something of great benefit for the Slovak Republic in the field of economics, science, culture, or technology. Citizenship is granted by the Ministry of Interior.

Citizenship for Sale

Slovakia is yet another ancient country that has gone modern by adopting a law offering citizenship by investment to foreigners with a price tag of a mere €1 million (US$1.4 million).

In certain cases it is possible to apply for Slovak citizenship under the Citizenship-by-Investment provisions (Art. 7 Sec. 2b) of the Slovak Citizenship Act. What are described as "serious investors" in certain cases can apply for Slovak citizenship under Article 7 Section 2b of the Slovak Citizenship Act. The procedure involves acquiring temporary residence, permanent residence, and then applying for citizenship.

Acquiring Slovak citizenship and passport, even at the price of €1 million (US$1.4 million), takes 12 to 18 months. Under the citizenship-by-investment provisions, an applicant is required to invest actively and substantially in the Slovak economy, usually in an industrial or real estate project favored by the government.

Substantial fees are charged, depending on circumstances and number of persons in an application, as each case is handled on an individual basis. Knowledge of the Slovak language is not required. Because of the substantial investment requirements, which are similar to those of Austria, this program is too expensive for most persons unless they already plan to make a substantial investment in Slovakia.

The law also allows granting residence and citizenship not only for investors but also for people of involved in the arts, science, and other professions who are judged to contribute significantly to the interests of Slovakia.

As a member state that forms part of the EU's external border, Slovakia must implement the strict Schengen border rules. Citizens of the following countries do not need a Slovak entry visa: all EU member states, plus Andorra, Argentina, Australia, Bolivia, Brazil, Brunei, Bulgaria, Canada, Chile, Costa Rica, Croatia, Guatemala, Honduras, Hong Kong, Israel, Japan, Malaysia, Mexico, Monaco, New Zealand, Nicaragua, Panama, Paraguay, Romania, Salvador, San Marino, South Korea, Switzerland, Uruguay, USA, Vatican, and Venezuela.

Citizens of other countries must apply for a visitor's visa. The maximum length of a short-term stay in the Republic must not exceed 180 days. See http://www.slovakia.org/tourism/visainfo.htm/

Contacts

Embassy of the Slovak Republic
3523 International Court NW
Washington, DC 20008
Tel.: (202) 237-1054
Email: emb.washington@mzv.sk
Web: http://www.mzv.sk/washington
See: http://www.slovak-republic.org/citizenship/

United States Embassy
Hviezoslavovo namestie 4
811 02 Bratislava, Slovakia
Mailing Address: P.O. Box 309
814 99 Bratislava, Slovakia
Tel.: + (421) 2-5443-0861 / + (421) 2-5443-3338
Email: consulbratislava@state.gov
Web: http://slovakia.usembassy.gov/

Recommended Immigration Consultant:

Henley & Partners
Dunajská 4 81108 Bratislava
Tel.: + 421 257 206 123

Republic of Slovenia

Government:	Parliamentary republic
Capital:	Ljubljana
National Day:	Independence/Statehood Day: 25 June (1991)
Population:	1,992,690 (July 2013 est.)
Total Area:	7,827 sq. miles / 20,273 sq. kilometers
Languages:	Slovenian 91.1%, Serbo-Croatian 4.5%, other 4.4%
Ethnic groups:	Slovene 83.1%, other 12%, Serb 2%, Croat 1.8%, Bosniak 1.1%
Religion:	Catholic 57.8%, other 23%, none 10.1%, unaffiliated 3.5%, Muslim 2.4%, Orthodox 2.3%, other Christian 0.9%
Life expectancy:	77.3 years
Currency:	Euro (EUR)
GDP:	US$57.22 billion (2012 est.)
GDP per capita:	US$27,800 (2012 est.)

It's a tiny country, about half the size of Switzerland, and counts just over two million people. But the only way to describe pint-sized Slovenia (Slovenija), an independent republic bordering Italy, Austria, Hungary, Croatia and the Adriatic Sea, is that it's "a mouse that roars".

Slovenia has been dubbed a lot of things since independence in 1991 — Europe in Miniature, The Sunny Side of the Alps, The Green Piece of Europe — and though they may sound like tourist brochure blurbs, they're all true.

From beaches, snow-capped mountains, hills awash in grapevines and wide plains blanketed in sunflowers, to Goth-

ic churches, baroque palaces, historic castles and art nouveau civic buildings, Slovenia offers more diversity than countries many times its size. Its incredible mixture of climates brings warm Mediterranean breezes up to the foothills of the Alps, where it can even snow in summer. With more than half of its total area covered in forest, Slovenia truly is one of the greenest countries in the world — and in recent years it has also become Europe's activities playground.

Among Slovenia's greatest assets, though, are the Slovenes themselves: welcoming, generous, multilingual, and broad minded. As far as they are concerned, they do not live emotionally, spiritually or even geographically in Eastern Europe — their home is the very heart of the continent. — Lonely Planet

History and Overview

Slovenia is located in Central Europe in the eastern Alps bordering the Adriatic Sea, between Austria and Croatia. Slovenia is today a vibrant democracy, but the roots of this democracy go back deep in Slovene history. According to the 16th century French political philosopher, Jean Bodin, Slovenes practiced the unique custom of the Installation of the Dukes of Carinthia for almost a thousand years, until the late 14th century. From as early as the 9th century, Slovenia fell under foreign rulers, including Bavarian dukes and the Republic of Venice.

The Slovene lands were part of the Austro-Hungarian Empire until the latter's dissolution at the end of World War I. In 1918, the Slovenes joined the Serbs and Croats in forming a new multinational state, named Yugoslavia in 1929. After World War II, Slovenia became a republic within Communist Yugoslavia. Dissatisfied with the exercise of power by the majority Serbs, the Slovenes succeeded in establishing their independence in 1991 after a short 10-day war.

Historical ties to Western Europe, a strong economy and a stable democracy have assisted in Slovenia's transformation to a modern state. Slovenia joined both NATO and the EU in 2004. As a member state that forms part of the EU's external border, Slovenia must implement the strict Schengen border rules to curb illegal migration and commerce through southeastern Europe while encouraging close cross-border ties with Croatia.

Since the breakup of Yugoslavia in the 1990s, Croatia and Slovenia each have claimed sovereignty over disputed areas and Slovenia has objected to Croatia's claim of an exclusive economic zone in the Adriatic Sea. In 2009, the two neighbors signed a binding international arbitration agreement to define their disputed land and maritime borders. The agreement ended Slovenia's objections to Croatia joining the EU.

Slovenia continues to impose a hard border Schengen regime with Croatia, which joined the EU in 2013 but has not yet fulfilled

Schengen requirements. As a member EU state that forms part of the EU's external border, Slovenia has implemented the strict Schengen border rules to control illegal migration and commerce through southeastern Europe while encouraging close cross-border ties with Croatia.

Economy

With its small transition economy and population of approximately two million, Slovenia is a model of economic success and stability for its neighbors in the former Yugoslavia. The country has excellent infrastructure, a well-educated workforce and an excellent central location. It enjoys a GDP per capita substantially higher than any of the other transitioning economies of Central Europe.

Slovenia adopted the euro in 2007 and has met the EU's Maastricht criteria for inflation. Despite its economic success, Slovenia faces challenges. Much of the economy remains in state hands and foreign direct investment in Slovenia is one of the lowest in the EU on a per capita basis.

Despite its economic success, foreign direct investment (FDI) in Slovenia has lagged behind the region average, and taxes remain relatively high. Furthermore, the labor market is often seen as inflexible, and industries are losing sales to more competitive firms in China, India, and elsewhere. In 2009, the world recession caused the economy to contract, through falling exports and industrial production, by more than 8%, and unemployment to rise above 9%. Although growth resumed the unemployment rate continued to rise, topping 10%.

Residence and Citizenship

Citizenship is acquired:

1. by descent (*jus sanguinis*);

2. by birth within the territory of the Republic;

3. by naturalization or;

4. in compliance with international agreements.

A child obtains citizenship by origin:

1. if the child's father and mother were citizens at the time of the child's birth;

2. if one of the parents was a citizen at the time of the child's birth and the child was born within the territory of the Republic or;

3. if one of the parents was a citizen at the time of the child's birth and the other was unknown, or of unknown citizenship, or without citizenship and the child was born in a foreign country.

In order to be naturalized as a citizen, the applicant must be at least 18 years old, have lived in Slovenia for at least 10 years (continually for five years), have adequate income to assure that they are be able to support themselves, speak and write the Slovenian language and have no criminal convictions. Slovenia does not allow dual citizenship, and if citizenship is granted the applicant must relinquish any other citizenship.

The so-called "erased" persons in Slovenia are persons that had permanent residence in Slovenia plus the citizenship of another republic of the former Yugoslavia who, after the breakup of that country in the early 1990s, failed to apply for Slovenian citizenship. There were about 200,000 such persons, 30,000 of whom were deleted from records without any rulings; they illegally but formally ceased to exist. Documents issued to them earlier in Slovenia became invalid, and they lost their residential rights. Many suddenly were interned at a center for foreigners and later deported. The government has moved to address this problem and recognize the erased as having Slovenia citizenship.

For foreign citizens, no visa is required for visits of up to 90 days.

Contacts

Embassy of Slovenia
2410 California Avenue NW
Washington, DC 20008
Tel.: (202) 386-6601
Email: vwa@gov.si
Web: http://washington.embassy.si

United States Embassy
Prešernova cesta 31
1000 Ljubljana, Slovenia
Tel.: + (386) 1-200-5500
Email: usembassyljubljana@state.gov
Web: http://slovenia.usembassy.gov/

Kingdom of Spain

Government:	Constitutional monarchy
Capital:	Madrid
National Day:	National Day: 12 October
Population:	47,370,542 (July 2013 est.)
Total Area:	194,897 sq. miles / 504,782 sq. kilometers
Languages:	Castilian Spanish (official nationally) 74%, Catalan 17%, Galician 7%, Basque 2%
Ethnic groups:	Mediterranean and Nordic
Religion:	Roman Catholic 94%, other 6%
Life expectancy:	81.37 years
Currency:	Euro (EUR)
GDP:	US$1.388 trillion (2012 est.)
GDP per capita:	US$30,100 (2012 est.)

Stretching sun-drenched and untamed to the south of the wild and majestic Pyrenees, this passionate nation works a mysterious magic. Spain is littered with hundreds of glittering beaches; flamenco bailaors (dancers) swirl in flounces of color; and toreros (bullfighters) strut their stuff in the bullrings. Summer holidaymakers gather around great pans of steaming paella (at its tasty best in Valencia) and pitchers of sangria.

Beyond these clichéd images, a vast, unexpected panorama unfolds before you. Emerald green mountains seem to slide into the wild blue Atlantic in the north. Proud, solitary castles and medieval towns are strewn across the interior. White villages glitter in inland Andalucia. Rugged mountain ranges such as the Sierra Nevada (Europe's most southerly ski resort) are draped across the country.

From its Roman relics to Muslim palaces, from baroque cathedrals and Modernista constructions, the country is a treasure chest of artistic and architectural marvels across a matchless cultural palette. More than 30 years of democracy and rapid economic development have spurred Spain's cities to bedeck themselves with sparkling new ornaments. Up and down the country, a zest for life creates an intense, hedonistic vibe in its effervescent cities. Indeed, if there is one thing Spaniards love, it is to eat, drink and be merry, whether gobbling up tapas over fine wine in Madrid and the south, or its elaborate Basque Country equivalent, pintxos, over cider in the north. — Lonely Planet

History and Overview

With its smaller neighbor, Portugal, to the west, Spain occupies the Iberian Peninsula in southwest Europe. It's the third largest European country, a few miles from North Africa, just across the

Straits of Gibraltar. External Spanish territories include the Balearic Islands off the southeast coast in the Mediterranean Sea, as well as the enclaves of Ceuta and Melilla in North Africa.

In spite of Spanish claims of sovereignty over Gibraltar, it remains under U.K. control, as it has since 1702, although active discussions about the future of "The Rock" continue with the stated British guarantee that any change must be with the approval of Gibraltar's residents. The Gibraltarians are overwhelmingly opposed to Spanish rule and have so voted.

Spain's history dates back to before 1000 B.C. In 27 B.C., Iberia came under Roman dominance until the 4th century. From then until 1212, Christians and Muslim Moors vied for control. In the latter year, Moorish influence was confined to a small area of Granada. Led by Spanish-sponsored explorers, such as Christopher Columbus, in the Middle Ages colonial interests grew rapidly.

Columbus' 1492 voyage reached the Americas and made Spain a New World power. However, by the Spanish-American War, in 1899, Spain had lost most of its colonial possessions, and the war added Cuba and the Philippines to that list.

A peaceful transition to democracy followed 40 years of his control after the death of the dictator Francisco Franco in 1975, brought the restoration of the Spanish monarchy. At the same time, Spain joined the United Nations, remaining outside NATO until 1982.

Reminders of its past inhabitants and rulers abound on Spain's soil. Throughout the countryside, local customs and cuisine reflect the heritage of Iberians, Romans, Arabs, Jews, Crusaders, and Moors. The great wealth brought from the New World by Habsburg and Bourbon monarchs adorns Madrid and its environs in the form of palaces and museums, while a resurgent Catalan culture, suppressed under the Franco regime, undergoes a vibrant cultural renaissance in Barcelona.

Spain is a constitutional monarchy and the Chief of State is Juan Carlos de Borbon y Borbon, King of Spain. The head of the government is the prime minister elected by the Congress of Deputies. The current holder is Mariano Rajoy Brey, the leader of the conservative Partido Popular (PP) or People's Party who was elected in 2011.

Economy

Growing affluence after Spain joined the EU in 1986 produced a boom of new construction throughout the country, including world-class museums and public structures as well as housing and offices. The Spanish economy grew every year from 1994 through 2008 before entering a recession in 2008 that has continued. The Spanish banking system was considered solid, thanks in part to conservative oversight by the European Central Bank, and government intervention to rescue banks on the scale seen elsewhere in Europe in 2008 was not necessary at first.

After considerable success since the mid-1990s in reducing unemployment to a 2007 low of 8%, Spain suffered a major spike in unemployment in 2008. In 2014, despite unemployment falling by 65,000 in 2013, the jobless rate in early 2014 was above 26% owing to a smaller working age population. 198,900 jobs were lost in 2013. The total number of unemployed in early 2014 was 5.9 million. The percentage has risen because the working age population has fallen by 267,900, through retirement or migration. About 260,000 people left Spain in 2013, around 40,000 of them Spanish nationals, the rest departing foreign migrants.

After almost 15 years of above average GDP growth, the Spanish economy began to slow in late 2007 and entered into a recession in 2008. GDP contracted ending a 16-year growth trend. The Bank of Spain estimated that GDP fell by 1.2% in 2013. The reversal in Spain's economic growth reflected a significant decline in construction amid an oversupply of housing and falling consumer spending, while exports actually have begun to grow.

Government efforts to boost the economy through stimulus spending, extended unemployment benefits, and loan guarantees did not prevent a sharp rise in the unemployment rate. The government budget deficit worsened from 3.8% of GDP in 2008 to 9.2% of GDP in 2010, more than three times the euro-zone limit.

Spain's large budget deficit and poor economic growth prospects have made it vulnerable to financial contagion from other highly indebted euro zone members despite the Conservative Party government's efforts to cut spending, privatize industries, and boost competitiveness through labor market reforms. Spanish banks' high exposure to the collapsed domestic construction and real estate market also poses a continued risk. The previous Socialist government oversaw a restructuring of the savings bank sector in 2010, and provided some US$15 billion in capital to various institutions.

Investors remain concerned that Madrid may need to bail out more troubled banks. The Bank of Spain, however, is seeking to boost confidence in the financial sector by pressuring banks to come clean about their losses and consolidate into stronger groups.

Spain, along with Portugal, Italy and Greece (so-called PIGS), is an EU country that may need a bailout from other wealthier EU countries, a subject of major debate within the EU.

The 2014 Conservative government continues to battle the separatist Basque Fatherland and Liberty (ETA) terrorist organization, a continuing threat, but its major focus is on measures to reverse the severe economic recession that started in mid-2008.

World Favorite

Spain is one of the most popular tourist destinations in the world and has much to offer as a location for investment, vacation or residence. There are more than 50 million visitors each year — a number greater than its total population.

Developers and speculators have reaped fortunes in real estate, property and building developments. Many have lost their shirts in recent years. Restaurants, transportation companies, brewers, hotel operators, golf and tennis clubs, and the tourist industry all prosper. Prime Spanish attractions include year-round sunshine, low prices and low rents. Spain is not as inexpensive as Portugal, but prices are below the European average. Domestic help is inexpensive, but strict Spanish employment laws provide that after a year of service, employees have a right to 30 paid days of vacation annually.

While home ownership is not required to become a permanent resident, owning may be more economically desirable than renting because real estate here is usually an excellent long-term investment if you are careful. For the rich, country club communities and private villas are protected from burglars by dogs, guards and high walls.

Residence and Citizenship

Ordinary immigrants to Spain must maintain permanent residence there 10 years before becoming eligible for naturalization.

Nationals of former Spanish colonies may have the waiting period reduced to two years if they "originate" from their country of citizenship. (See below). Persons living in Spain for six years become eligible to work there.

Citizenship is provided as follows:

1. by birth: birth within the territory of Spain does not automat-

ically confer citizenship. The exception is a child born to un-known or stateless parents.

2. by descent:

a) to a child, at least one of whose parents is a citizen of Spain, regardless of the child's country of birth, or;

b) to a child born of non-Spanish citizen parents, provided at least one of the parents was born in Spain.

3. by naturalization: Spanish citizenship may be acquired upon fulfillment of conditions which vary according to the person involved:

a) persons with no ties to Spain must reside in the country for at least 10 years;

b) persons who are former nationals of Portugal, the Philippines, or certain South American countries need only reside for two years, or;

c) persons who were born in Spain, who have married a citizen of Spain, or who were born outside of Spain of a mother or father who was originally Spanish, need only reside one year.

Spanish authorities require naturalization applicants to renounce their existing citizenship and to swear an oath of allegiance to Spain. Dual nationality is recognized only if the applicant's home nation has a dual nationality treaty with Spain. Currently, such treaties exist with Chile, Peru, Paraguay, Nicaragua, Guatemala, Bolivia, Ecuador, Costa Rica, Honduras, the Dominican Republic, Argentina, Colombia, and Venezuela. Those of Spanish-Jewish descent are also allowed to hold dual nationality.

It used to be that marriage provided the easiest means to citizenship in Spain. Under the old law, foreigners were able to apply as a spouse or ex-spouse of a Spaniard, even if the marriage had been dissolved. Now, tighter rules require a foreigner to be married to a Spaniard at the time of application and for at least one year prior.

One can still acquire Spanish citizenship by birth in Spain or in certain Spanish territories. If one parent was born in Spain, citizenship can also be claimed. A Spanish Embassy or Consulate can explain the qualifications.

Strict Residence

In the ordinary course of events, a foreign person must first be a resident in Spain for a daunting 10 years before naturalization. Certain refugees are granted citizenship after only five years of residence. Persons of Spanish-Jewish descent are also eligible for Spanish citizenship after two years of residence.

Purchasing a home is not a requirement for obtaining citizenship. And with or without citizenship, you will likely have the legal right to work, though six months of residence is usually required first. Prerequisites include the ability to speak passable Spanish and maintenance of a real presence in the country. During residence (between two and 10 years depending on your category), international travel is unrestricted. However, a "token" residence is not acceptable.

Spanish police keep close tabs on foreigners and actually visit homes and interview neighbors to confirm residence and good reputation. Authorities will expel a resident alien considered undesirable. It is relatively easy to prove residence in the country by obtaining a renta, a permanent residence income tax form. All permanent residents also have an ID card (called an NIF) that identifies them as Spanish resident taxpayers.

It is estimated that about 2% of Spain's population are immigrants from other countries, but a large number of these are from

Spain's North African enclaves that work as low paid agricultural workers in the southwest coastal area, a source of much controversy. In 2005, Spain granted an amnesty that made citizens of about 600,000 illegal immigrants as part of a package of reforms, which included tighter borders. In 2011, only 6,566 were listed by the U.N. as refugees in Spain.

The descendants of those exiled from Spain during the Spanish Civil War (1936 to 1939), and during the subsequent rule of the late General Francisco Franco, were allowed to claim Spanish citizenship under a 2008 law. This change in Spanish citizenship law covered the period July 18, 1936, to December 31, 1955, which included the Spanish Civil War from 1936 to 1939 and the first decades of Franco's rule, which ended with his death in 1975.

The act is part of the "law of historical memory," a controversial policy sponsored by the then Socialist government aimed at encouraging resolution of issues from its bloody 20th century history. Many Spaniards oppose the law as a needless stirring up of old animosities.

The 2008 law was a departure from much stricter past Spanish naturalization laws. Prior to this exception citizenship by naturalization could only be acquired with difficulty. Persons without ties to Spain had to reside in the country for at least 10 years.

Taxes

Spain taxes permanent residents on worldwide income at rates from 20% to in excess of 50%. Taxable income is established by authorities based upon the value of a home, car and lifestyle. To avoid these taxes many wealthy Spanish passport holders establish legal residence in a tax haven nation or they hide their cash in places such as neighboring Andorra.

Unlike the U.S., Spain does not tax its non-resident citizens.

Tax laws consider an individual to be a resident if they stay in the country for longer than 183 days annually, or if their main professional, business or economic activity is located in Spain. If a spouse or dependents remain resident in Spain, a head of household is also considered a resident unless you can prove residence for more than 183 days in another country. Temporary absences are included in the tax collector's calculations.

Spain has double taxation tax treaties with many non-EU countries, including the U.S. and Switzerland. Wealthy foreigners should consider Spain a fine place for leisure, but not a place to live tax-free after acquiring a passport. Spain now has OECD style tax information agreements with Portugal, San Marino, The Bahamas, Andorra, Aruba and the Netherlands Antilles.

In 2013 Spain, together with Germany, France, Italy, and the U.K., signed a multilateral automatic information exchange agreement to crack down on tax evasion. This involves the exchange of financial information between the countries, based on the model agreements negotiated by the five countries with the U.S. government to comply with the U.S. Foreign Account Tax Compliance Act (FATCA).

Visas

Despite this discouraging tax situation, a Spanish passport is an excellent guarantee of visa-free travel for many more places than a U.S. passport allows. In addition, Spain has a good relationship with its former colonies, much as the U.K. does with Commonwealth members.

EU nationals can remain in Spain for up to six months without a residence permit; non-EU nationals for three months. Requirements for obtaining a permit are: payment of a small fee; four passport photos; a residence visa from the Spanish Consulate in your home nation; proof of income or pension; the Form E-111 endorsed by Spanish health authorities, or proof of medical insurance; a certificate that you have registered with your nation's consulate in Spain; and an escritura (rental contract).

A passport is required for entry into Spain. A visa is not required for tourist or business stays up to 90 days. Individuals who enter Spain without a visa are not authorized to work. American citizens planning to study in Spain should be aware that Spanish immigration regulations require applications for student visas to be submitted 60 days before anticipated travel to Spain.

Latin American Route

A passport issued by any one of the 28 European Union member countries is a prized possession. With that document in hand, you're free to roam, live and do business in any of the EU countries, few questions asked. However, while EU member states don't grant citizenship easily, some of their former colonies do. One can apply directly for residence in one of the various 28 EU countries, but unless you qualify for either immediate citizenship or a reduced period of residence due to marriage or your ancestry, you won't become eligible to be an EU citizen for periods of from five to 10 years, depending on the country.

Few seem aware of it, but for those who qualify, the quickest "back door" route to EU citizenship is through several South American countries, long ago colonies of Spain and Portugal. A similar arrangement exists between Spain and another of its former colonies, the Philippines. In recent years, Spain has been much stricter on applicants using the "colonial route" who now must prove their personal origins in the country from which they seek to move to Spain.

Persons who were nationals of Portugal, the Philippines, or

certain South American countries need only reside for two years in Spain.

Spanish law requires most naturalization applicants to renounce their existing citizenship and to swear an oath of allegiance to Spain. Dual nationality is recognized only if the applicant's home nation has a dual nationality treaty with Spain. Currently, such treaties exist with Chile, Peru, Paraguay, Nicaragua, Guatemala, Bolivia, Ecuador, Costa Rica, Honduras, the Dominican Republic, Argentina, Colombia, and Venezuela. Those of Spanish-Jewish descent were also allowed to hold dual nationality.

Spain will grant citizenship within two years after application to persons of "Spanish blood" or descendants of Sephardic Jews. Spanish blood is normally taken for granted whenever an applicant is already a citizen of a former Spanish colony or has a Spanish surname and speaks Spanish.

In 2014, the Spanish parliament was considering a proposed bill to naturalize descendants of Sephardic Jews, which the government said was to atone for their expulsions 500 years ago during the Inquisition. Spanish Muslims also urged the government to grant citizenship to descendants of Muslims who were expelled from Spain.

An Argentine passport allows visa-free travel to 133 countries, including most of Europe and nearly all of South and Central America. It's also the first passport in South America that entitles its holder to visa-free entry into the U.S., although some post-9/11 restrictions now apply.

Argentineans also qualify for a reduced, two-year residence period in Spain when seeking Spanish nationality. A Guatemalan passport is good for travel to most countries in Europe without a visa, and dual citizenship is common in the nation. Most upper-class Guatemalans hold U.S. and Spanish passports. Spain gives special consideration to Guatemalans, who by treaty, need only two years of residence in Spain to acquire Spanish citizenship or vice-versa. Both a Honduran and a Uruguayan passport entitle holders to Spanish citizenship after two years of residence in Spain.

You should cross-check in The Passport Book these named countries to see how easy it is to acquire citizenship there as a possible stepping stone to eventual Spanish and EU citizenship. This two-step process is achievable and I know of patient, peripatetic persons who have done it.

Contacts
Embassy of Spain
2375 Pennsylvania Avenue NW
Washington, DC 20037
Tel.: (202) 452-0100
Email: embespus@mail.mae.es
Web: http://www.spainemb.org/

United States Embassy
Serrano 75, 28006 Madrid, Spain
Tel.: + (34) 91-587-2200
Email: amemb@embusa.es
Web: http://madrid.usembassy.gov/

U.S. Consulate General
Paseo Reina Elisenda de Montcada 23
08034 Barcelona, Spain
Tel.: + (34) 93-280-2227
Email: Consularbarcel@state.gov

Kingdom of Sweden

Government:	Constitutional monarchy
Capital:	Stockholm
National Day:	Flag Day: 6 June
Population:	9,647,386 (July 2013 est.)
Total Area:	173,732 sq. miles / 449,964 sq. kilometers
Languages:	Swedish, small Sami and Finnish-speaking minorities
Ethnic groups:	Swedes with Finnish and Sami minorities; foreign-born or first-generation immigrants: Finns, Yugoslavs, Danes, Norwegians, Greeks, Turks
Religion:	Lutheran 87%, other includes Roman Catholic, Orthodox, Baptist, Muslim, Jewish, Buddhist 13%
Life expectancy:	81.28 years
Currency:	Swedish krona (SEK)
GDP:	US$385.1 billion (2012 est.)
GDP per capita:	US$40,300 (2012 est.)

The midnight sun, the snowbound winters, meatballs, herring, Vikings and Volvos, ABBA and the Hives; whatever your pre-existing notions about Sweden may be, a visit to this multifaceted country is bound to both confirm and confound them. Though you're unlikely to be greeted at the shore by throngs of mead-swilling berserkers in long ships, evidence of the Vikings and their pillaging days is easy to find. A stroll through the Swedish countryside will often lead to a picnic on some ancient king's burial mound.

But Sweden's days as a warlike nation are long gone. Instead, its domestic and international policies serve as models of neutrality and consensus-building. This is, after all, the birthplace of the Nobel Peace Prize.

That's not to say all the excitement ended thousands of years ago; far from it. While tradition reigns in places like Dalarna in the Swedish heartland and the Sami territory up north, much of Sweden today buzzes with a more contemporary energy. A wave of immigration in recent years has added spark and variety to the cultural milieu. Urban centers like Stockholm, Goteborg (otherwise known as Gothenburg) and Malmo consistently churn out cultural artifacts for an international audience (think IKEA, H&M, Absolut Vodka).

The Island of Gotland, lying roughly equidistant between Sweden and Latvia, is Sweden's most richly historical area but also has a hip party vibe. In short, try the meatballs and dig the Vikings, but don't stop there; history hasn't. — *Lonely Planet*

History and Overview

Sweden is located in Northern Europe between Finland and Norway, bordering the Baltic Sea and Gulf of Bothnia.

During the 7th and 8th centuries, the Swedes were merchant seamen well-known for their far-reaching trade. In the 9th century, Nordic Vikings raided and ravaged the European continent as far as the Black and Caspian Seas. During the 11th and 12th centuries, Sweden gradually became a unified Christian kingdom that later included Finland.

Queen Margaret of Denmark united all the Nordic lands in the "Kalmar Union" in 1397. Continual tension within the countries and within the union gradually led to open conflict between the Swedes and the Danes in the 15th century. The union's final disintegration in the early 16th century brought on a long-lived rivalry between Norway and Denmark on one side and Sweden and Finland on the other.

A military power during the 17th century, Sweden has not participated in any war in almost two centuries. Armed neutrality was preserved in both World Wars. Sweden's long successful economic formula of a capitalist system interlarded with substantial welfare elements was challenged in the 1990s by high unemployment and, in 2000 to 2002, by the global economic downturn, but fiscal discipline over the past several years has allowed the country to weather economic vagaries. Indecision over the country's role in the political and economic integration of Europe delayed Sweden's entry into the EU until 1995, and blocked the introduction of the euro in 1999.

Economy

Aided by peace and neutrality for the whole of the 20th century, Sweden has achieved an enviable standard of living under a mixed system of high-tech capitalism and extensive welfare benefits. It has a modern distribution system, excellent internal and external communications, and a skilled labor force. Timber, hydropower and iron ore constitute the resource base of an economy heavily oriented toward foreign trade. Privately owned firms account for about 90% of industrial output, of which the engineering sector accounts for 50% of output and exports. Agriculture accounts for only 2% of GDP and of jobs.

The Swedish central bank (Riksbank) focuses on price stability with its inflation target of 2%. Presumably because of generous sick-leave benefits, Swedish workers report in sick more often than other Europeans. In 2003, Swedish voters rejected entry into the euro system, concerned about the impact on their democracy and sovereignty.

Until 2008, Sweden was in the midst of a sustained economic upswing, boosted by increased domestic demand and strong exports. This and robust finances allowed the center-right government in power since 2006 considerable scope to implement its reform program aimed at increasing employment, reducing welfare dependence, and streamlining the state's role in the economy.

Despite strong finances and underlying fundamentals, the Swedish economy slid into recession in 2008 as deteriorating global conditions reduced export demand and consumption. Strong exports of commodities and a return to profitability by Sweden's banking sector drove a strong rebound after 2010.

During the past 20 years, huge changes have been made to the socialist "Swedish Model." A housing bubble burst in the 1990s causing mass unemployment, falling GDP, and interest rates of 500%. It was obvious that the Swedish welfare state could no longer be afforded. Taxes were cut and public spending reduced from 67% to 49% of GDP. In 2013, the corporate tax rate was cut from 26.3% to 22%.

To finance cradle-to-the-grave welfare with less tax revenues and public spending, Sweden turned to the free market allowing private companies to compete for government funding to provide services like health care and education.

In May 2013, youth riots broke out in a suburb of Stockholm reportedly in response to the shooting and killing by police of an elderly man, allegedly a Portuguese immigrant, and then an alleged police cover-up. Several hundred rioters were involved and resulted in injuries to police officers and firemen. At least 100 vehicles were burned, as well as a garage, forcing evacuation of an apartment block, and a shopping center was vandalized. A few days later, riots spread to at least nine other towns, with many arrests. In total, 150 vehicles were set on fire, most belonging to immigrants, and total damages were estimated at US$9.5 million.

Swedish reports suggested the causes were substandard schools, racism, unemployment, failure to integrate immigrants, and social inequality. Some saw the riots as reason to question Sweden's immigration policy. Regardless of the cause, this impulsive behavior hardly presented a picture consistent with the traditional world view of a socialist welfare paradise.

Residence and Citizenship

The Citizenship Act of 2001 fully endorses dual citizenship. Anyone who acquires Swedish citizenship can keep his/her previous citizenship if the law of that country permits. Swedish citizens who acquire another citizenship can also keep their Swedish citizenship. The 2001 law also makes it easier for children and young people to become Swedish citizens.

Swedish citizenship laws are based on the principle of descent (jus sanguinis); citizenship is acquired at birth if one parent is a Swedish citizen. Another basic principle is prevention of statelessness. The Swedish Migration Board is the central government agency primarily dealing with matters concerning citizenship.

Foreign citizens who hold a residence permit and are registered as residents, in principle have the same rights and responsibilities as Swedish citizens with certain differences. Only Swedish citizens have an absolute right to live and work in Sweden and only Swedish citizens are entitled to vote in parliamentary elections. Only Swedish citizens can be elected to the Riksdag, the national parliament. Certain jobs, for example in the police force, as a professional soldier, and in some protective services, that may only be filled by Swedish citizens.

One can become a Swedish citizen by: 1) birth; 2) adoption; 3) legitimization (parent's marriage); 4) naturalization; or 5) notification (by children, young people 18 to 20 years old and residents of the Nordic countries).

U.S. citizens visiting Sweden for a period of less than 90 days normally do not need a visa. For details on Swedish citizenship, see http://www.migrationsverket.se/info/start_en.html

Contacts

Embassy of Sweden
2900 K Street NW
Washington, DC 20007
Tel.: (202) 467-2600
Email: ambassaden.washington@foreign.ministry.se
Web: http://www.swedenabroad.com/washington

United States Embassy
Dag Hammarskjolds Vag 31
115 89 Stockholm, Sweden
Tel.: + (46) 08-783-5300
Email: stkacsinfo@state.gov
Web: http://stockholm.usembassy.gov/

Swiss Confederation

Government:	Confederation, structured as a federal republic
Capital:	Bern
National Day:	Founding of the Swiss Confederation: 1 August (1291)
Population:	7,996,026 (July 2013 est.)
Total Area:	15,942 sq. miles / 41,290 sq. kilometers
Languages:	German (official) 63.7%, French (official) 19.2%, other 8.9%, Italian (official) 7.6%, Romansch (official) 0.6%
Ethnic groups:	German 65%, French 18%, Italian 10%, other 6%, Romansch 1%
Religion:	Roman Catholic 41.8%, Protestant 35.3%, none 11.1%, Muslim 4.3%, unspecified 4.3%, Orthodox 1.8%, other 1%
Life expectancy:	82.28 years
Currency:	Swiss franc (CHF)
GDP:	US$359 billion (2012 est.)
GDP per capita:	US$44,900 (2012 est.)

If you could travel through only one European country, which might you choose? Italy? France? Germany? How about a taste of three in one? That can only mean Switzerland!

Known as a summer and winter sports paradise (just look at those glistening white 4000m-plus Alpine peaks and glittering lakes), Switzerland is where people first skied for fun. Illustrious names evoke all the romance and glamorous drama of the mountain high life: Zermatt, St Moritz, Interlaken, Gstaad, the Jungfrau, Verbier and more. Cities like Geneva (the most cosmo-

*politan), Zurich (the most outrageous), Basel and Lausanne heave
with heady artistic activity and sometimes incendiary nightlife.*

*Beyond the apres-ski chic, edelweiss and Heidi lies a complex
country of cohabiting cultures. It not only has four languages
(Swiss German, French, Italian and Romansch), but the cultural variety to match. The grandeur of the finest churches,
such as the cathedrals in Lausanne and Bern, contrasts with
sparkling but lesser-known treasures like the frescoes of Mustair
or the abbey complex of St Gallen (both World Heritage sites).*

*Whether visiting the remotest Ticino villages or sampling
the finest of Valais wines you'll find Switzerland a chocolate
box bursting with unexpected flavors. — Lonely Planet*

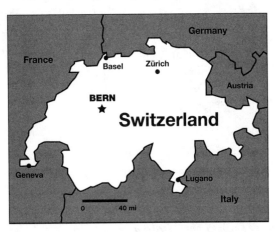

Preface: Switzerland remains The Sovereign Society's choice as
the best all-around asset and financial haven in the world.

For centuries this country has acted as banker to the world and
in that role has acquired a reputation for integrity and strict financial privacy. It is also a great place for the wealthy to reside.
Switzerland may be neutral in politics, but it's far from flavorless.
The fusion of German, French and Italian ingredients has formed

a robust national culture, and the country's alpine landscapes have enough zing to reinvigorate the most jaded traveler.

Goethe summed up Switzerland succinctly as a combination of "the colossal and the well-ordered." You can be sure that your trains and letters will be on time. The tidy, just-so precision of Swiss towns is tempered by the lofty splendor of the landscapes that surround them. There's a lot more here than just trillions of dollars (and euros).

History and Overview

For many centuries, the Swiss have maintained more or less strict neutrality toward other countries, including those with which it shares a common border — France, Germany, Liechtenstein, Austria, and Italy. Isolated in the valleys of their Alpine redoubt, the various Burgundian, Germanic and Italianate people who formed the Swiss Confederation found common cause in rebuffing imperial efforts from all sides: rejecting French, Habsburg, Lombard, and Piedmont over-lordship.

The Swiss talents for precision machinery from cuckoo clocks to hydropower generators, chemicals from explosives to pharmaceuticals, and culinary delights from fondue to chocolate, all driven by a genius for industrial organization and distribution, continue to bring the country customers from all over the world.

In 1945, after the second "war to end all wars," the Swiss people overwhelmingly rejected membership in the United Nations. Not until a narrow national vote in 2003 did they join the U.N. In national polls, Swiss voters also have rejected membership in the European Union, rightly fearing EU bureaucratic interference with Swiss privacy and banking laws. However, in 2004, Switzerland signed several bilateral accords with the EU, for example including the country in the Schengen visas area.

National ballots soundly have rejected specific proposals to ease

Swiss bank secrecy laws and recent public opinion polls support this view. Since 1992, Switzerland has been a member of both the World Bank and the International Monetary Fund.

Economy

The World Factbook states that "Switzerland is a peaceful, prosperous, and modern market economy with low unemployment, a highly skilled labor force, and a per capita GDP among the highest in the world. Switzerland's economy benefits from a highly developed service sector, led by banking and financial services, and a manufacturing industry that specializes in high-technology, knowledge-based production. Its economic and political stability, transparent legal system, exceptional infrastructure, efficient capital markets, and low corporate tax rates make Switzerland one of the world's most competitive economies."

The global financial crisis and resulting economic downturn put Switzerland in a recession in 2009, as global export demand stalled. The Swiss National Bank during this period effectively implemented a zero-interest rate policy in a bid to boost the economy and prevent appreciation of the franc.

In 2010, Bern implemented a third fiscal stimulus program, but its prized banking sector faced significant challenges. The country's largest banks, UBS and Credit Suisse, suffered major losses in 2008 to 2009 due to investments in the same sort of mortgages that almost bankrupted some major U.S. banks.

The Swiss National Bank (SNB) provided an unprecedented multi-billion franc government rescue bailout, in part with funds from the U.S. Federal Reserve. This was not repaid until 2013. The SNB implemented a zero-interest rate policy to boost the economy as well as prevent appreciation of the franc, and Switzerland's economy began to recover in 2010 with 3.0% growth.

The continuing sovereign debt crises in neighboring euro-zone countries pose a significant risk to Switzerland's financial stability because it drives up demand for the Swiss franc by investors seeking a safe-haven currency. The independent SNB has stuck to its zero-interest rate policy and conducted major market interventions to prevent further appreciation of the Swiss franc. The franc's strength has made Swiss exports less competitive and weakened the country's GDP growth.

Bank Secrecy

Switzerland's bank secrecy laws dating from 1934 long have been under attack from major welfare, high tax nations, especially Germany and France. These nations saw Switzerland as a secret haven for their citizen tax evaders.

Switzerland became the object of a full scale media and political war waged by Germany and France, the EU, the U.S. and international institutions to weaken its traditional bank secrecy laws. In 2010, the government agreed to conform to the OECD model Article 26 tax exchange agreement including tax evasion or tax fraud. Parliament passed the first five double-taxation tax information exchange agreements, including a revised tax treaty with the U.S. in 2010. In 2013, the Swiss and the U.S. signed a treaty to implement the U.S. Foreign Account Tax Compliance Act (FATCA).

At this writing, Switzerland has signed 42 double taxation agreements that include international exchange of information and 36 are in force. The Swiss government has signed historic tax agreements with Germany and the U.K. and paid billions in lump sums to resolve back tax issues with these governments. It also agreed in the future to pay taxes on Swiss bank deposits held by Germans and British without revealing names, perhaps the last vestige of once absolute Swiss bank secrecy.

In 2009, Swiss financial regulators ordered the country's largest bank, UBS, to reveal under threat of a U.S. Justice Department lawsuit, the names of 4,500 U.S. accountholders suspected of using UBS to commit tax fraud. UBS paid the U.S. government nearly US$1 billion in fines for assisting in tax evasion and SEC violations. By 2014 the U.S. Department of Justice had indicted several Credit Suisse officials and was threatening suits against that bank and several Swiss private and cantonal banks, including Julius Baer.

These events have certainly damaged Switzerland's good reputation. In spite of all these troubles, there is a widespread and valid view that Switzerland is the still place to safeguard cash and other personal assets.

It is currently estimated that Swiss banks manage at least one-third of all assets held offshore by the world's wealthy, an estimated three to four trillion U.S. dollars.

Residence and Citizenship

Once accepted for permanent residence status, Swiss citizenship may be available after 12 years.

Birth in Switzerland does not guarantee citizenship unless at least one parent is Swiss. A foreign national who marries a Swiss can obtain citizenship after a five-year residence. If it is later discovered to be a marriage of convenience, citizenship or residence is instantly revocable.

Residence permits are difficult to arrange, but not impossible. Swiss cantonal, not federal, authorities issue what can be described as a combination residence-work permit allowing work in that canton for a specific employer. ("Canton" is the local term for a state or province. There are 26 cantons with Bern as the federal capital).

Residence

Switzerland has one of Europe's highest percentages of foreigners living within its borders. Switzerland has been faced with the task of absorbing 80,000 foreigners a year, a lot for a country of eight million. Of the over eight million residents, about 20% are from other countries, 85% of them European, mainly workers from Spain, Portugal, Italy, and the former Yugoslavia.

In recent years, the resistance to more immigration and granting citizenship has grown. Many cantons now require a public referendum on admitting specific lists of applicants and many individuals have been rejected.

For a foreign national, Switzerland is not the easiest place in the world to obtain either permanent residence or full citizenship, but neither is it an impossible goal. Obtaining residence has become increasingly difficult as the Swiss, like most Western Europeans, have come to resist the migration of workers from the Mediterranean basin, Eastern Europe and Africa. In 2012 there were about 60,000 refugees or asylum seekers in Switzerland according to U.N. statistics.

In 2014, voters in a national referendum narrowly approved a proposal to curb immigration. It imposed limits on the number of foreigners allowed entry and cast doubt on the country's status as a member of the EU's Schengen accord that allows multi-national free movement and residence.

The "Stop Mass Immigration" proposal was opposed by many business and labor groups, but was approved by 50.3% of the votes and by a majority of cantons. The curb proposed by the conservative Swiss People's Party imposed quotas on all foreign nationals, including cross-border commuters and asylum seekers, restricted immigrant rights to social benefits and required preference for the Swiss in employment hiring.

One in five people living in Switzerland is a foreign national. Industry groups say foreign workers account for 45% of employees at pharmaceutical, chemical, and biotechnology companies. Some 25% of Swiss bank employees are citizens of neighboring EU countries, according to the Swiss Bankers Association.

For financially independent individuals, business investors, and entrepreneurs, it may be possible to obtain residence in Switzerland, but life here is not cheap. In early 2014, prices in Switzerland's booming housing market approached a level not seen since 1989, shortly before a recession and lower values that hurt the Swiss economy for years. The 2014 residential property values were still below the 1989 market peak.

There are generally two ways to establish official Swiss resident status:

1. **Business Investment:** Each canton makes its own rules, but all offer some form of tax breaks and/or subsidies for foreign nationals who agree to relocate a business or start a new one in Switzerland. It must create new employment and help economic development. If the business is substantial, residence permits for the foreign director/owner and his or her family are normally granted without delay. In some cantons, it is permissible to simply open your office and work on your own.

2. **Retirement:** Wealthy, financially independent foreign applicants over 55 years of age, who can show close ties to Switzerland, may also be eligible for residence. Although done on an individual basis and at the discretion of the cantonal authorities, such persons may negotiate a one-time agreement on an annual lump sum income tax payment on their worldwide income, far below usual Swiss tax rates.

Residence Permits

Annual Residence Permit: The standard one-year residence permit issued to foreigners during their first years of residence in Switzerland is known as a "B" permit. After five or 10 years, depending on existing bilateral conventions, the "B" permit holder becomes eligible for a permanent resident or "C" permit. The "B" permit allows specific employment and is renewable annually.

Permanent Residence Permit: The "C" permit gives its holder full residence status with most of the same rights as Swiss citizens enjoy, except political rights such as voting or holding office.

Seasonal Work Permit: This "A" permit is limited to nine consecutive months within a 12-month period, usually for seasonal employment in the building, hotel and tourism industries. Entry and exit dates are strictly enforced.

Border Commuter Work Permit: The "L" permit is issued only to foreign nationals who are residents near the Swiss national border and work in Switzerland.

Citizenship

After 12 years residence in Switzerland, a foreign national with permanent resident status may apply for naturalization as a Swiss citizen.

For foreign national children, any years spent in the country between the ages of 10 and 20 years count double for application purposes. Conditions for granting citizenship depend on laws and rules of the canton and community where the foreign person lives. Generally, the applicant must be acquainted with national customs, be well integrated in society and, usually, be fluent in one of the national languages.

The application process may involve an in-depth investigation, plus detailed personal questioning of Swiss neighbors. Swiss rules allow instant citizenship for "Persons of International Stature," including noted poets, authors, deposed royalty, movie stars, scientists, ex-heads of state, and religious leaders, but very rarely is citizenship granted on this unique basis.

Switzerland accepts the principle of dual nationality, but foreign citizens who also have Swiss citizenship may be subject to compulsory military service and other requirements while living in Switzerland. Switzerland has a liberal attitude toward foreign tourists, allowing visits twice a year for up to three months each time, so long as visits are separated by an adequate time period.

Taxes

Switzerland has an international reputation as a tax haven, but that is untrue. It certainly is not an automatic "no tax" nation, however, smart foreign investors can avoid many taxes by choosing certain types of investments that are exempt from Swiss taxes.

By law, Swiss banks collect a withholding tax of 35% on all interest and dividends paid by Swiss companies, banks, the government, or other sources. Foreign investors to whom this tax applies may be eligible for refunds of all or part of the tax under the terms of bilateral tax treaties between Switzerland and the person's home nation.

Since 2004 Switzerland, in agreement with the EU, enforces withholding taxes on EU nationals with Swiss accounts and interest income. Although names are not revealed, all taxes collected and remitted to the foreign nationals' home governments.

Under the terms of Article 23 of the 1996 Swiss-U.S. Tax Treaty, Switzerland now taxes U.S. citizens who are Swiss residents on all their worldwide income, but the taxpayer is eligible for a U.S. tax credit for payment of these taxes in order to avoid double taxation.

There is no Swiss withholding on payments to foreigner arising from Swiss life insurance or annuities. Nor is there a tax on dividends or interest from securities that originate outside Switzerland. For this reason, many Swiss banks offer investment funds with at least 80% of earnings in foreign investments or, even better, investments in money market funds based in Luxembourg or Ireland. (Be careful about such investments; consult a U.S. tax attorney because unless properly arranged the U.S. tax consequences can be brutal.)

Personal income taxes in Switzerland vary depending on the canton and local community in which an individual resides, works or has his/her investments. While a Swiss federal tax applies throughout Switzerland, each of the 26 cantons has its own tax system and sets its own tax rates. As a rule, individuals who are deemed resident for tax purposes in Switzerland are subject to income tax on their worldwide income regardless of its source.

Trying to figure out total Swiss taxes is not easy. Federal, cantonal and communal taxes all have complex tax rates and deductions. Federal income tax rates range from 0% to 11.5%. Cantonal and communal tax rates vary, but are generally twice as high as federal rates. Switzerland also has a network of over 70 bilateral international tax treaties.

Swiss nationals domiciled in Switzerland and foreign nationals holding "C" permanent residence permits are assessed on income and net wealth taxes based on their filing periodic tax returns. The individual taxpayer then is responsible for tax compliance and payment of income taxes when billed by the state.

Border commuters and foreign nationals living in Switzerland who do not hold a "C" permit, usually, are subject to withholding taxes levied by employers on gross taxable earned income. Progressive withholding tax rates depend on gross taxable income, marital status and the number of dependents.

Negotiable Lump Sum Tax Payments

For the very wealthy immigrant, Switzerland's cantonal tax system allows the development of a unique personalized income tax plan called lump-sum tax regime payments, called (forfait fiscal in French, Pauschalbesteuerung in German).

Foreign citizens who fulfill certain requirements may be eligible for a special tax arrangement in which Swiss taxes are levied on the basis of a person's personal expenditure and standard of living in Switzerland, rather than on worldwide income and assets.

This lump sum arrangement is available throughout the country except in the canton of Zurich. This unique lump-sum taxation effectively caps the income and net wealth tax for qualifying foreign citizens. This tax break has generated much political opposition in Switzerland and some cantons have curtailed its scope.

Switzerland is also attractive because it imposes no federal inheritance or gift taxes. Instead, the cantons levy inheritance and gift taxes which means that there are 25 different inheritance and gift tax regimes. The 26th canton of Schwyz levies neither inheritance nor gift taxes.

Campione d'Italia: Little-Known Swiss Back Door

Switzerland may be the world's most famous haven country, but there's another residential haven that's not only more exotic, but is itself an enclave geographically surrounded by Switzerland. And it's under Italian jurisdiction!

The Commune de Campione d'Italia, on the shores of beautiful Lake Lugano, is distinguished by its very uniqueness; a little plot of Italian soil, completely surrounded by Swiss territory. Home to about 2,000 people, it's located within the southern Swiss canton of Ticino, about 16 miles north of the Italian border and five miles by road from Lugano, Switzerland, a beautiful scenic drive.

With no border controls, there is complete freedom of transit. This Italian village uses Swiss banks, currency, postal service, and telephone system. Even automobile license plates are Swiss. Strangely enough, because of ancient history and treaties, the enclave legally is part of the territory of the Republic of Italy.

Campione is also a very pleasant place to live, located in the heart of one of the best Swiss tourist areas. The region boasts lakes, winter sports and the cultural activities of Milan, Italy, only one hour away by auto.

All that's needed to become an official resident is to rent or buy property here, although formal registration is required. However, living here is very expensive; US$750,000 for a very small townhouse. Foreigners may buy real estate without restrictions, unlike Switzerland. But real estate prices are well above surrounding Ticino. Condominiums range from US$5,500 to US$6,500 per square meter (US$500 to US$600/sq. ft.), and broker fees add a 3% commission.

The real estate market is very small and prices are extremely high. The same apartment across the lake in Switzerland can easily cost half of what it costs in Campione. This small market is served by a few local real estate agents, some of whom operate rather unprofessionally and some even without a license. A foreign buyer has to be very careful. If you are interested in establishing your residence in Campione and purchasing real estate there, you should be represented by a competent lawyer from the beginning.

Corporations registered in Campione have distinct advantages over Swiss companies. They use Swiss banking facilities and have a mailing address that appears to be Swiss, while escaping Switzerland's relatively high income and withholding taxes. Corporations are governed by Italian corporate law and can be formed with a minimum capitalization of about US$1,000.

Corporations can be owned and directed entirely by foreigners, a status Swiss law denies. Corporate registrations are usually handled by Italian lawyers in nearby Milan, and fees are modest. As part of Italy, EU business regulations do apply to Campione businesses, as do Italian corporate taxes.

Campione's generous tax breaks apply only to naturalized persons but it is not completely tax-free. For companies established in Campione, Italian taxes apply and are very high. The official currency is the Swiss franc, but the euro is accepted as well. All banking is done through Swiss banks, which gives its residents additional financial privacy.

A famous casino generates substantial revenue, which is among the reasons Campione residents enjoy some special tax concessions. Campione is exempt from the Italian value added tax (VAT). However, the tax advantages only apply to private persons resident in Campione, and not to companies domiciled or managed from there.

Residents of Campione do not pay the full Italian income tax. Based on a special provision in Italian law, the first CHF200,000 (US$222,300) of income is exchanged into the euro, the official currency in Italy, at a special exchange rate. This results in a lower effective income and consequently a lower tax rate is applied.

However, this only applies on the first CHF200,000 of income. Besides this special concession, the usual Italian tax laws and tax rates apply. The 2014 Italian individual income tax rate is between 23% to 43% and the corporate rate is 27.5%. As in Italy, there are no inheritance or gift taxes, and income from interest of foreign bonds paid through an Italian bank is taxed at a special, reduced rate of 12.5%. Capital gains taxes range from 12.5% to 27.5%.

Residence

To obtain a Campione residence permit, you must buy an apartment or a house. There is very rarely an opportunity to rent. Usual police clearance from the Italian authorities as well as approval by the local Campione authorities is also required. While residence permits are issued by Italian authorities, access to the territory of Campione is governed by Swiss visa regulations. This means that the passport you hold should allow you to enter Switzerland without a visa, or you will have to apply for a Swiss visa beforehand.

A passport is required for entry into Switzerland. A visa is not required for U.S. citizens for stays of up to 90 days.

Obtaining facts about Campione is much more difficult than for other tax havens because the enclave does not promote itself. There is no central office of information. Outsiders are not unwelcome, but no one readily volunteers news about this secret haven. A personal visit is mandatory for anyone seriously interested in making this their home.

For information about Campione contact:

Dr. Ernst Zimmer
Consulting International, S.R.L.
Corso Italia 2, Campione d'Italia, 6911
Tel.: + 41 91 649 5244
Email: capione@tele2.ch

Government: Amministrazione Comunale
Comune di Campione d'Italia.
Tel.: + 031 27 24 63
Web: http://www.comune.campione-d-italia.co.it/
Tourist information: http://www.campioneitalia.com/

Contacts

Embassy of Switzerland
2900 Cathedral Avenue NW
Washington, DC 20008
Tel.: (202) 745-7900
Email: was.vertretung@eda.admin.ch
Web: http://www.swissemb.org
Consulates General in Atlanta, Chicago, Los Angeles,
New York, and San Francisco.

United States Embassy
Sulgeneckstrasse 19
CH 3007 Bern, Switzerland
Tel.: + (41) 31-357-7011
Emergency: + (41) 31-357-7777
Email: bernacs@state.gov
Web: http://bern.usembassy.gov

U.S. Consular Agency
Dufourstrasse 101 3rd Floor
Zurich, Switzerland
Mailing Address:
Dufourstrasse 101
CH-8008 Zurich, Switzerland
Tel.: + (043) 499-2960
Email: Zurich-CA@state.gov

Residence & Citizenship Assistance:

Henley & Partners AG
Klosbachstrasse 110
8024 Zurich, Switzerland
Tel.: + 41 44 266 22 22
Web: http://www.henleyglobal.com/switzerland

United Kingdom and Northern Ireland

Government:	Constitutional monarchy
Capital:	London
Population:	63,395,574 (July 2013 est.)
Total Area:	94,526 sq. miles / 244,820 sq. kilometers
Languages:	English, Welsh, Scottish form of Gaelic
Ethnic groups:	White 92.1%, black 2%, Indian 1.8%, other 1.6%, Pakistani 1.3%, mixed 1.2%
Religion:	(Anglican, Roman Catholic, Presbyterian, Methodist) 71.6%, unspecified or none 23.1%, Muslim 2.7%, other 1.6%, Hindu 1%
Life expectancy:	80.29 years
Currency:	British pound sterling (GBP)
GDP:	US$2.313 trillion (2012 est.)
GDP per capita:	US$36,600 (2012 est.)

England: Throughout its long history, it's been a green and pleasant land, a sceptered isle and a nation of shopkeepers. It's stood as a beacon of democracy and a bastion of ideological freedom, as well as a crucible of empire and a cradle of class oppression. Magna Carta, the King James Bible and the welfare state were all dreamt up here, but then again, so were beer bellies, Bovril and Mr Bean. It's a nation of tea-tippling eccentrics and train spotters, of dog lovers and footy fanatics, of punk rockers, gardeners, gnome collectors, celebrity wannabees, superstar chefs, freewheeling city traders, pigeon fanciers, cricket bores and part-time Morris Dancers. To some it's Albion. To others it's Blighty. To many it's the most eccentric, extraordinary and downright incomprehensible place on earth.

Welcome to England.

To journey through England is to journey through time (interspersed with several cups of tea) — from the ancient megaliths of Stonehenge to the space-age domes of the Eden Project in Cornwall. It's also a trip to the 21st-century: Cities like London, Manchester, Leeds and Newcastle revel in their heritage and confidently face the future, with industrial buildings revitalized as waterfront galleries or trendy apartments, flanked by tempting bars, shops, restaurants and some of the finest music venues on the planet.

Northern Ireland: Crossing from the Republic into Northern Ireland you immediately notice two differences: the street signs are in miles and the roads are well maintained. Soon enough, you find that these aren't the only differences; the accent here is distinctly different, the currency is pounds sterling and you remark again about how nicely maintained the roads are. You are now (although historically not everyone would be happy about it) in the UK.

From the looming city walls of Derry to the breathtaking scenery along the Causeway Coast to Belfast's glorious Victorian architecture, Northern Ireland has always had a bevy of things to attract visitors. Unfortunately, decades of guerrilla warfare deterred tourism and it wasn't until within the past 10 years that it finally returned.

Today, Northern Ireland seems rejuvenated. Belfast is a happening place with a stellar nightlife and an excellent culinary scene while Derry appears to be coming into its own as a cool, artistic city. The stunning Causeway Coast and its namesake, the geologically anomalistic Giant's Causeway, get more and more visitors each year, while lesser known towns are finding that they have a tourist trade too.

That's not to say that the scars of the Troubles have healed, but at least people are getting along, which at this point is all that anyone can ask for. — Lonely Planet

History and Overview

Located off Western Europe, between the Atlantic Ocean and the North Sea and northwest of France, Great Britain — now known as the United Kingdom — is a highly developed constitutional monarchy comprising England, Scotland, Wales, and Northern Ireland.

Great Britain was the dominant industrial and maritime power of the 19th century. It played a leading role in developing parliamentary democracy and in advancing trade, industry, literature, and science. At its zenith, the British Empire covered approximately one-fourth of the Earth's surface, with African possessions stretching "from the Cape to Cairo," and others encompassing virtually every region in the rest of the world. Its keystone was India (including what are now Pakistan, Bangladesh and Burma).

In the first half of the 20th century, its strength was seriously depleted by two world wars. Since the end of World War II, the British Empire has been dismantled and Great Britain has rebuilt itself into a modern European nation with significant international political, cultural and economic influence. The United Kingdom still is debating its degree of integration with continental Europe. While a member of the European Union, for the time being, it is staying out of the euro currency area in favor of retention of the pound sterling.

In many ways, the United Kingdom is one of the more attractive places in the world both to live and do business. Among the many U.K. advantages are: 1) complex immigration laws offering many useful options; 2) full citizenship after only five years' residence; 3) a tax system somewhat favorable to resident foreigners; 4) competitive tax rates; 5) an attractive lifestyle; and 6) excellent transport, communications and financial services.

Economy

According to *Forbes*, "The UK, a leading trading power and financial center, is the second largest economy in Europe after Germany. Over the past two decades, the government has reduced public ownership and the growth of social welfare programs. Agriculture is intensive, highly mechanized, and efficient by European standards, producing about 60% of food needs with less than 2% of the labor force. The UK has large coal, natural gas, and oil resources, but its North Sea oil and natural gas reserves are declining and the UK is now a net importer of energy. Services, particularly banking, insurance, and business services, account by far for the largest proportion of GDP while industry continues to decline in importance."

In 1992, after emerging from recession, Britain's economy enjoyed the longest period of expansion on record and outpaced most of Western Europe. In 2008, the global financial crisis hit the economy particularly hard, mainly because of the importance of its financial sector. Sharply declining home prices, high consumer debt, and the global economic slowdown compounded Britain's economic problems, pushing the economy into recession. At that time, the Labor government adopted stimulation of the economy and tried to stabilize financial markets including bank bailouts, nationalizing parts of the banking system, temporary tax cuts, easier public sector borrowing, and massive deficit spending.

After the 2010 elections, Labor was ousted and replaced by a coalition government of Conservatives and Liberal Democrats that began a five-year austerity program aimed at reducing the debt growth. This has been only partially successful and weak consumer spending and subdued business investment still weighs on the economy.

Residence and Citizenship

British citizenship comes in many forms. The forms of nationality are British citizenship; British overseas citizenship; British overseas territories citizenship; British national (overseas); British protected person; and British subject. For explanation of each form of nationality see: http://www.ukba.homeoffice.gov.uk/britishcitizenship/

Immigration is a politically charged topic in Britain, with the coalition Conservative/Liberal government under pressure to address high unemployment. Most immigrants are either from within the EU where there is a general right to migrate, returning Britons or people entering on family or human rights grounds. British business groups are concerned that businesses will not train and invest in foreign talent if workers have no assurance of staying.

Census data shows that only 13% or one eighth of the population was born abroad. More than half of people questioned in an early 2014 poll believed that immigration has had negative consequences for the country.

The majority opinion has been that stringent curbs should be imposed on immigration in order to reduce the numbers seeking entry. Visa rules were amended several times and the British missions abroad were instructed to allow only a limited number of immigrants.

The move began with curbs imposed on students intending to study and stay in the U.K. Rules adopted set the immigration cap for non-European Economic Area (EEA) workers at 21,700, about 6,300 lower than before.

In early 2014, with EU migration restrictions finally removed from Bulgaria and Romania, the issue was raised yet again when the U.K. Prime Minister, David Cameron, proposed to exclude from British welfare rolls migrants from both countries. Facing election in 2015, Cameron was said to be trying to counter growing support for the new anti-EU and anti-immigration British National Party (BNP).

The rise of Islamic fundamentalism and terrorism has had its impact on the U.K. U.K. has a large number of Muslim immigrants, especially from Pakistan, Bangladesh and Arab countries. Fundamentalism-related organizations have been covertly supporting export of terrorism. Some U.K. born Pakistanis and Arabs were arrested and indicted for supporting terrorism and this has been cited as a major cause of imposing more immigration curbs. The London Tube terrorist bombings in 2005 and riots in London in 2011 further amplified the argument against immigrants.

Immigration to the United Kingdom of Great Britain and Northern Ireland since 1922 has been substantial, especially from Ireland and the former colonies of the British Empire, India, Bangladesh,

Pakistan, the Caribbean, South Africa, Kenya and Hong Kong, all of which come under British nationality law. Others have come as asylum seekers, seeking protection as refugees from member states, exercising one of the EU's Four Freedoms under the United Nations 1951 Refugee Convention, or from the European Union (EU).

About half the population increase from the 1991 census to the 2001 census was due to foreign-born immigration. Nearly 4.9 million people, 8.3% of the population at the time were born abroad, although the census gives no indication of their immigration status or intended length of stay.

The U.K. Border Agency was established in 2008 as a full executive agency of the Home Office working with HM Revenue and Customs, the Foreign and Commonwealth Office and the police. The agency's role is to secure U.K. borders, control migration for the benefit of its country, to protect the public from crime and terrorism and to protect the collection of tax revenues. It has multiple website pages explaining every aspect of travel to the U.K., residence and citizenship questions. For information see http://www.ukba.homeoffice.gov.uk/

In an effort to control U.K. immigration and a massive influx of foreign workers flooding the market, often to reap the benefits of a socialized society, in 2009 the U.K. Border Agency introduced the Borders, Citizenship and Immigration Bill to parliament. This legislation further restricts the residence rights of migrants and it has been reported that foreigners residing in the U.K. may face up to an additional three years before being able to attain British citizenship.

The U.K. immigration law is one of the world's most complex rivaling that of even the United States. However, the law offers foreign nationals numerous possibilities for low-tax residence, plus the option to acquire U.K. citizenship after only five years of legal residence. Some of these possibilities are:

Business-Investor: Beginning in 2012 several new categories were created for what is called "High Value Migrants" to the U. K. The Tier I "investor" is required to invest between GBP1 million (US$1.7 million) and GBP10 million (US$16.6 million). The Tier 1 "entrepreneur" must invest between GBP200,000 (US$331,000) and GBP50,000 (US$83,000). Two persons can jointly apply.

Those who qualify receive an initial three year visa which can be extended for two more years if criteria are met. Investment must be in a new or existing business, the applicant must be actively involved as a director of the business, it must create employment and there is an English language requirement. Test to determine these factors are made and proof is required.

In return the successful applicant receives immediate five year residence and potential citizenship for the applicant and their family.

In 2012, there were 1,682 entrepreneur applications and 594 investors. Because of a related business graduate student program that also allowed applicants for as little as a GBP50,000 (US$83,000) investment, the backlog rose to 9,000. The rejection rate was over 50% mainly because this was a new program suffering from unexpectedly high demand and a rightfully cautious bureaucracy. In Britain the number of investor visas rose by a quarter in the first three-quarters of 2013. Over the last five years, half of those visas went to Russian and Chinese investors.

Retirement: A person at least 60 years old with investment or rental income of not less than GBP25,000 per year may be granted residence if they can demonstrate close U.K. ties. These ties may be U.K. close relatives, previous residence, business connections, or even a strong sense of identity with the United Kingdom. While an applicant must show an income that they receive "without working," they can manage their investments, including U.K. real property investments, and they can hold non-executive directorships.

While a retiree is not allowed to work in the U.K., after four years of residence, they may apply for permanent residence and, once granted, there are no restrictions on working.

Ancestry: Commonwealth citizens with a grandparent born in the U.K. are admitted for a four-year period of employment, after which, permanent residence is usually granted. For those not Commonwealth citizens who do meet the ancestry requirement, it may be possible to acquire Commonwealth status through an economic citizenship program offered by a commonwealth nation such as Dominica or Saint Kitts and Nevis or residence program such as that offered by the Turks and Caicos Islands, a British overseas territory.

Work Permit: The U.K. employer, and not the prospective employee, may apply to obtain a work permit for an overseas employee. Stringent requirements include a minimum pay level and the employer's certification that the employee's talents are unique and unattainable locally. There are special provisions for entertainers, sports stars and models. Work permit applications are considered by the U.K. Department for Education and Employment and processing generally takes between one and two months, resulting in a permit for between six months and four years. The full work permit is usually granted to high-level executives, managers and those with technical skills not readily available in the U.K. and the European Union.

Key workers: So-called "key worker" permits are often granted to those who, while not high-level executives, have language, cultural, or culinary knowledge rare in the U.K. This category of permit is often used for hotel/restaurant managers, head chefs, highly skilled waiting staff, and senior hotel receptionists. Key worker permits will not generally be granted or extended for more than a total of three years. Thus, they do not lead to permanent residence.

Sole Company Representative: You may apply as the representative of an overseas company whose major business is offshore and has no U.K. branch, subsidiary or other agent. To qualify, one must be a present employee of an established, legitimate foreign firm, and not the majority owner of that firm. No significant investment is required and applications are usually processed quickly. Residence is granted for one year, renewable based on the continued success of the business.

Permanent Residence and Citizenship: In the above investor, business-related, or work permit categories, U.K. permanent residence is usually granted after four years. The person may then apply for U.K. citizenship after one additional year's residence.

Special Status: Under special provisions, foreign lawyers, writers, and artists of any nationality are exempt from the investment or employment creation requirements. Thus, they can more easily start a U.K. business and obtain immediate residence. Foreign lawyers and legal professionals may enter the U.K. to establish self-employment or to join other lawyers in partnership. They can only practice non-U.K. law, and must have accreditation from their local foreign Bar Association.

Those establishing a new office must prove sufficient funding. Performing artists and authors (whether of words or music) may enter the U.K. to pursue their career if they can demonstrate a successful record elsewhere during the preceding year. Such persons must present a realistic business plan and show adequate finances. Upon first arrival, they must have a valid entry visa issued by a U.K. Embassy or Consulate abroad.

There are numerous other categories allowing entry into the U.K. that work for extended periods of time; among them clergy and religious, students, young adult children of Commonwealth residents, and work trainees. A person who is recognized as a dual national is entitled to a special "Right of Abode" stamp in their foreign passport to enable travel into the U.K. without any hindrances should they wish to use their second passport.

Naturalization

A person who has been physically present in the U.K. for a year as an approved permanent resident may apply to become a naturalized U.K. citizen. The processing of an application is likely to require from 12 to 18 months. Other than those seeking naturalization after marriage, the following requirements must be met.

The applicant must be aged 18 or over and of sound mind and good character. They should have a sufficient knowledge of the English language. They should intend to live in the U.K. or work directly for the U.K. government, an international organization of which the U.K. is a member, or be employed by a company or association established in the United Kingdom.

The five-year residence period is the period ending with the date the application is received by the Home Office. The requirements are as follows: the candidate must have been in the U.K. at the beginning of the five-year period and, during that period, must not have been outside the U.K. for more than 450 days; and, in the last 12 months of the period, must not have been outside the U.K. for more than 90 days; and in the last 12 months of the five-year period, the candidate's U.K. stay must not have been subject to any time limit under the immigration laws; and, at no time, must the candidate have been in the U.K. in breach of the immigration laws.

Marriage

In order to prevent abuse of this category, the government imposes a number of conditions:

1. a visa is granted for only one year, at the end of which, if the

marriage is still intact, permanent residence will be granted. After a three-year period, the spouse may apply for U.K. nationality;

2. to prevent arranged marriages, the U.K. citizen must have actually met the non-U.K. spouse;

3. the couple must intend to live together permanently;

4. the couple must possess sufficient funds for themselves and their dependents without recourse to public funds;

5. housing for the couple and any dependents must be available; and

6. spouses seeking U.K. entry on the basis of marriage should apply for entry clearance before entering the United Kingdom. Children of the marriage under 18 years old are allowed entry and can apply at the same time as the main applicant.

In recent years, there has been considerable debate in the U.K. about adoption and enforcement of stricter political asylum laws. This has been prompted by the influx of many thousands of refugees from former British colonial areas and from Eastern Europe, many of them Muslims.

A passport is required for entry into the United Kingdom. Tourists do not need a visa for stays of up to 90 days. Those planning to stay in the United Kingdom for any purpose longer than six months must obtain a visa prior to entering.

For more information on ever aspects of U.K. residence, immigration and visas, see the website of the U.K. Border Agency at http://www.ukba.homeoffice.gov.uk/

Contacts

Embassy of the United Kingdom of Great Britain and Northern Ireland
3100 Massachusetts Avenue NW
Washington, DC 20008
Tel.: (202) 588-6500
Web: http://www.britainusa.com/

United States Embassy
24 Grosvenor Square
London W1A 1AE England
Tel.: + (44) 020-7499-9000
Web: http://london.usembassy.gov/

U.S. Consulate General
Danesfort House
223 Stranmillis Road
Belfast BT9 5GR Ireland
Tel.: + (44) 028-9038-6100

U.S. Consulate General
3 Regent Terrace
Edinburgh EH7 5BW Scotland
Tel.: + (44) 013-1556-8315

United Kingdom Immigration Consultant:

Henley & Partners UK Ltd
20 Grosvenor Place
London SW1X 7HN United Kingdom
Tel.: +44 207 823 1010
Email: london@henleyglobal.com
Web: https://www.henleyglobal.com/ Part III

SECTION 5
MIDDLE EAST AND AFRICA

Republic of Cyprus

Government:	Republic*
Capital:	Nicosia
National Day:	Independence Day: 1 October (1960); Turkish Cypriots, Independence Day: 15 November (1983)
Population:	1,155,403 (July 2013 est.)
Total Area:	3,571 sq. miles / 9,250 sq. kilometers
Languages:	Greek, Turkish and English
Ethnic groups:	Greek 77%, Turkish 18%, other 5%
Religion:	Greek Orthodox 78%, Muslim 18%, Maronite, Armenian Apostolic, and other 4%
Life expectancy:	78.17 years
Currency:	Euro (EUR)
GDP:	US$17.36 billion (2014 est.)
GDP per capita:	US$26,800 (2012 est.)

The Turkish Cypriot community (north Cyprus) refers to itself as the "Turkish Republic of Northern Cyprus" or TRNC. It is recognized only by Turkey.

Floating on the waters of the European Mediterranean, but pointing longingly towards the shores of Syria, Turkey and Lebanon, Cyprus is an odd mixture. It is a kaleidoscopic blend: its cultural influences are dominated by Western Europe, but its geographic proximity to Asia and Africa gives it more than just a hint of the East. Long coveted by mainland Greece and Turkey, this small island has its own definite and beguiling character.

Whether you know it as the "island of sin" (or fun) thanks to wild stories from Agia Napa; the country that entered the EU only as a half; or, as the tourist brochures love to point out, "the island of Aphrodite", Cyprus both confirms and confounds the stereotype. Parts of Cyprus have been overrun by keen developers who (depending on who you're talking to) have either "sold the country's soul" or "are bringing great wealth to the island".

Whatever the truth, in the tourist centers of places like Pafos, Agia Napa or Lemesos (Limasol), you might feel as if you've entered a sunny, scorching Essex suburb with lobster-red Brits letting it all hang loose with a lukewarm can of Foster's in tow. Wander through the sea of wildflowers covering the island in spring, and Cyprus will take your breath away. With good walking shoes, a swimsuit and some sunscreen in your bag, you can have a trip you'll remember for years. — Lonely Planet

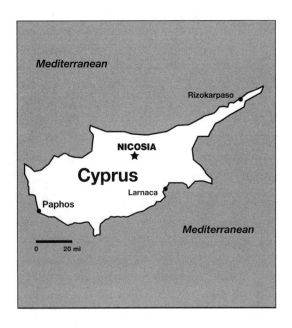

History and Overview

Cyprus is a developed island nation, south of Turkey, the third largest island in the Mediterranean Sea, after Sicily and Sardinia. Archeologists have found remains of some of the oldest Neolithic settlements on the island, which was famous in antiquity for copper mines. Indeed, its name (in Greek) is the word for copper. Ruins from virtually every period of recorded history are found on Cyprus, a crossroads of the ancient world, which is also justly famous for excellent wines and local variants on Greek and Turkish cuisine, especially seafood.

The island is politically and sharply divided into two distinct geographic areas. The government of the Republic of Cyprus is the internationally recognized authority, but it controls only the Greek Cypriot southern part of the island. The northern area operates under an autonomous Turkish Cypriot administration that governs about 37% of the land area.

A former British colony, Cyprus became independent in 1960 following years of resistance to British rule. Tensions between the Greek Cypriot majority and Turkish Cypriot minority came to a head in 1963, with violence in the capital of Nicosia.

Despite the deployment of U.N. peacekeepers in 1964, sporadic violence continued forcing most Turkish Cypriots into enclaves throughout the island. In 1974, a Greek government-sponsored attempt to seize control of Cyprus was met by military intervention from Turkey, which soon controlled more than a third of the island. In 1983, the Turkish-held area declared itself the "Turkish Republic of Northern Cyprus," but it is recognized only by Turkey.

Since 2008, the leaders of the Greek Cypriot and Turkish Cypriot communities have been negotiating under U.N. auspices aimed at reuniting the divided island. The entire island entered the EU in 2004, although the EU body of common rights and obligations applies only to the areas under direct government control, and is suspended in the areas administered by Turkish Cypriots. Individual Turkish Cypriots able to document their eligibility for Republic of Cyprus citizenship legally enjoy the same rights accorded to other citizens of EU states.

The majority of the Cypriot population is Greek, with a minority of Turks and other nationalities. Languages are Greek and Turkish, but English is widely used, especially in the legal and business communities. Technical communications are excellent, and it is a popular tourist destination. As a result of its relationship with the U.K., Cyprus is a common law country.

Economy

Once part of the Byzantine Empire, until recently Cyprus was a great place in which to make things disappear. This nation has long been a way station for international rogues and scoundrels, where officials have traditionally been willing to look the other way. Just 150 miles from Beirut, closer to the Middle East than to Europe, Cyprus has been a hub for cigarette smuggling, money laundering, arms trading, and such. The site of secret meetings between Israelis and Palestinians, it has also been a refuge for the Russian mafia importing and transporting wealth of immense size and dubious provenance.

Cyprus remains a popular low tax haven for the creation and registry of public and trading companies, which have significant advantages in the double taxation treaties network available to offshore companies. The 2014 current 12.5% corporate tax matches the other lowest rate in the EU of Ireland, well below Germany's 29.5% and France's 33.3%. (The Isle of Man, Jersey and Guernsey, all have a zero corporate rate.) Other areas of business are expensive and subject to significant disclosure requirements.

The island long has been a favored tax haven for Russian businessmen. Indeed, so much Russian money flowed through Cyprus that in 2009 the island registered as the third largest source of foreign direct investment in the Russian economy, at US$9 billion, just behind the Netherlands and the U.K. Cyprus was particularly important for the Russian investment and securities trade. The possibility that the island could default on its debts in the 2011 euro zone crisis pushed Russia into talks to rescue the Cypriot economy.

Bail-Out, Bail-In

In early 2013, the government of Cyprus was on the verge of bankruptcy but was rescued by a €10 billion (US$13.8 billion) bailout loan from EU nations worried about the collapse of the euro. In order to meet the loan terms, Cyprus and its EU creditors introduced the world to a new term — "bail-in."

The parliament approved what amounted to confiscation of vast sums from the island's personal and corporate bank accounts, much of it deposits from wealthy Russians. Because part of the money seized was converted into bank shares, one result of the bail-in was that wealthy Russians became some of the largest shareholders in the remaining Cypriot banks. The raid on deposits, known as "a haircut" in international financial circles, was described by Russian Prime Minister Dmitry Medvedev as "stealing".

A year after the bailout, Cyprus's economy was still in deep trouble and its banking sector was half its former size with one of two major banks out of business. With bank tellers, construction workers and retail employees caught in the fallout, unemployment has jumped to 17.5% from 14% a year earlier; youth unemployment is above 40%.

The remaining banks sharply curbed lending as the level of deposits shrank, and nearly half their outstanding loans were in arrears or default in early 2014. Private debt surged to around 300% of Cyprus's €17 billion (US$22 billion) economy. The government liquidated Laiki Bank, Cyprus's second-biggest financial institution, and folded its remains into the island's largest banking and financial services group, Bank of Cyprus, where the government then confiscated 60% of deposits above €100,000 (US$137,000) to recapitalize the lender.

Total deposits in Cypriot banks, which were €57 billion (US$77.3 billion) in April 2013, dropped to €47 billion (US$63.7 billion) by November. They might have fallen further and faster if the government had not tightly controlled withdrawals and foreign transfers at the height of the crisis. Controls are now moderately relaxed since everyone who could do so probably has fled. It is expected that all remaining controls will be removed by the end of 2014.

To date, controls still in effect limited the amount that could be taken out of Cyprus in one year to €3,000 (US$4,100). The maximum amount of cash withdrawn could not exceed a daily allowance of €300 (US$413) for each natural person or €500 (US$688) for each legal person in each credit institution, including an equivalent amount in foreign currency. All cash withdrawals were calculated per person against all accounts held. The cashing of checks was prohibited.

But the one rebounding business in 2014 was foreigners incorporating new companies. The registration of what are mostly shell companies created to shelter income was 1,454 in January, 2014 alone. As a result, there are now about 273,000 companies on Cyprus's corporate registry, an amazing figure in the Republic whose population is only about 839,000 in its southern area of the island. Needless to say, all those companies now do their banking anywhere else other than Cyprus.

Many businesses are taking no chances. In fact, they are opening bank accounts entirely outside of the euro zone based on the concern that, as in Cyprus, their assets could be seized to pay for banking crises that might erupt in other European countries.

Before the 2013 debt and banking crisis, the offshore regime in Cyprus already had changed as part of the island's joining the EU and as a result of agreements with the Organization for Economic Cooperation and Development (OECD). Further proposals include the exchange of tax and finance information by Cyprus as well as the signing of double tax treaties. Cyprus is a party to the 39-nation European Convention on Mutual Assistance in Criminal Matters (MLAT) including a fiscal protocol. Since 2012 Cyprus has been "actively engaged" in talks with the U.S. Treasury looking toward concluding an agreement to enforce the U.S. FATCA.

The government of Cyprus maintains its company and trust management regime, although the identities of beneficiaries are disclosed to the tax authorities when a company is registered or when a change of ownership takes place. The island also boasts one of the world's toughest anti-money laundering laws.

Retirement Tax Benefits

Until recently, Cyprus usually did not offer citizenship to foreign nationals, but for some people it might be a good place to settle or retire as residents.

Residence is straightforward if you can demonstrate an annual income of at least US$7,500 for one or US$19,000 for a family of four. Cyprus offers interesting tax benefits for a retired investor, author, musician, or inventor — from the right nation. To obtain these tax benefits, one must become resident, but need not be domiciled in Cyprus. There are also residence programs for foreign nationals willing to make substantial investment in the island's economy.

Cyprus is an attractive destination for a retired investor or anyone who receives substantial royalty income. It is relatively easy to obtain a residence permit with proof of adequate means of support. Foreigners who become residents are not allowed to engage in any local business unless granted permission. Nevertheless, they can conduct business from Cyprus anywhere else in the world. Foreign citizens the government considers to be Cypriot citizens may be subject to compulsory military service and other aspects of local law while in Cyprus.

Cyprus is a perennially popular location for international consultants and independent contractors. And its burgeoning offshore sector accounts for the greatest percentage of expatriate workers. However, it is also a popular destination for active retirees. They are attracted by the lifestyle but also by the many double taxation treaties that mean foreign retirement income usually will not be subject to withholding taxes at source, and both of these groups are positively encouraged by the Cypriot government.

Persons with modest annual income may become residents of Cyprus, but naturalization is generally not available. Certain classes of individuals with royalties or passive income are entitled to Cypriot residence if they are not domiciled there. This may be attractive to citizens of other countries whose tax relations with Cyprus provide a flat 5% tax in the country on investment income from abroad. Unfortunately, the United States and U.K. treaties with Cyprus do not make this benefit available.

Taxes

Although residence for the purposes of taxation in Cyprus is defined as "presence in the country for more than 183 days," calculation of tax liabilities is complex because the country has several different levels of taxation for various categories of citizens living there.

For tax purposes, those living in Cyprus are divided into: Cypriot residents, foreign residents working for Cypriot companies, foreign residents working for foreign companies, foreign residents working for offshore entities, non-working foreign residents, Cypriot non-residents, and foreign non-residents.

As a basic guide, with the exception of foreign nationals working for offshore entities for whom the rate of income tax is reduced by half, all groups mentioned above are liable to pay the following taxes on income arising within Cyprus; 1) income tax at a progressive rate of up to 30%; 2) capital gains tax at a rate of 20%; 3) estate duty at between 20% to 45% and; 5) real estate taxes.

Low Tax for Non-Domiciled Residents

A non-domiciled Cyprus resident pays a flat tax of 5% on investment income received from abroad and remitted to Cyprus. The first US$4,000 of remitted investment income, and all investment income that is not remitted to Cyprus, is tax-free. Royalties are treated as investment income. Foreign earned income can be remitted to Cyprus in order to reduce foreign withholding taxes under one of Cyprus many tax treaties. When that is done, any foreign withholding tax paid can be credited against any Cyprus tax owed.

That may well wipe out the 5% Cyprus tax obligation. Unfortunately, these benefits are not available under the terms of either the Cyprus-U.K. or Cyprus-U.S. tax treaties, but nationals covered by most other of the 39 Cyprus double taxation tax treaties can benefit. Cyprus has tax treaties with the United Kingdom, Denmark, Sweden, Ireland, Norway, Greece, Germany, Hungary, Italy, France, Russia, Romania, the United States, Canada, and Bulgaria.

Cyprus has ended almost all currency exchange controls, but new foreign residents were usually exempted in any case. Cyprus imposes death taxes, but the estates of non-domiciled residents are liable for taxes only on assets located in Cyprus at the time of death.

Economic Citizenship

It may fall within the status of "Would you buy a used car from this man?" — but in 2013, in the midst of the Cyprus bankruptcy and bank crisis, the Cypriot Department of Immigration decided to try and raise some quick cash by selling "economic citizenship" to gullible foreigners. Asking price was as much as €10 million (US$13.8 million) but was reduced in 2013 after the government confiscated billions of euros in Cyprus bank accounts.

Keep in mind that with a Cyprus passport, you have the right to take up residence there or in any of the 28 EU countries.

Under this plan there are several ways to qualify for citizenship by making investments. There is no requirement that you be resident in Cyprus to qualify although you must own property there.

Investment/Donation: Invest at least €2 million (US$2.7 million) in shares and/or bonds of the Cyprus State Investment Company and, donating at least €0.5 million (US$0.7 million) to the Cypriot Research and Technology Fund.

Investment: Investing at least €5 million (US$6.8 million) in: 1) property (but not undeveloped land); 2) businesses or companies; 3) bonds, securities, debentures, or; 4) investment or participation in public works. In one to three investments must be maintained for three years. Investment in shares or bonds, the value of must stay above €5million (US$6.8 million) for the entire three years.

Bank Deposits: Deposit at least €5 million (US$6.8 million) in a Cypriot bank for three years on fixed terms. You also can qualify by a portfolio of mixed investments and donations to state funds totaling at least €5 million (US$6.8 million).

Business activities: Ownership of a company that has paid taxes and other fees to the government and that employs people.

The many Russian national investors in the failed banks were none-too-pleased with their losses, which for some depositors, amounted to millions of euros. The Cyprus government came up with a plan to compensate them for their losses.

Depositors in the Bank of Cyprus or Laiki Bank who lost more than €3 million (US$4 million) due to the "bail-in" became eligible for a Cyprus certificate of citizenship and a passport. Russian nationals (and some others) who qualified for this offer became eligible to live or work not only in Cyprus, but in any other of the 27 members of the EU. And, while the Russian passport permits visa-free travel to only about 90 countries, a Cyprus passport provides similar privileges to more than 150 countries. In 2013, Cypriot President Nicos Anastasiades told a Russian business conference in Limassol that this passport deal would "mitigate to some extent, the damage" caused to Russian deposit holders. It was not reported as to whether he was smiling as he spoke.

Residence and Citizenship

Consider before you decide to take up residence in Cyprus as the island country has suffered from political instability for more than 400 years. More instability, efforts by Greece to reunify Cyprus or by Turkey to resist such efforts, could harm Cyprus passport-holders if a large number of residents leave the country seeking refuge elsewhere. That might even lead to a suspension of the automatic right Cyprus passport-holders currently have to live and work in other EU countries.

To qualify for local residence, an applicant must provide evidence of good character, show independent financial means and document income. The Cypriot Immigration Control Board also imposes minimum amounts of income that must be received by residents during a tax year. For information on residence applications, contact: Chief Immigration Officer, Migration Department, Ministry of Interior Affairs, Nicosia 1457 and Website: http:// www.mfa.gov.cy/

Foreigners allowed residence may purchase real property in Cyprus, but only after obtaining a permit. Approval to buy real property is usually a formality for a house or apartment in which you plan to live.

Citizenship is acquired by birth, by descent, by registration, or by naturalization.

1. by birth/by descent: a person born in Cyprus is a citizen of the Republic if at the time of birth any one of his parents was a citizen of the Republic or, in case at the time of birth, his parents were not alive, any one of them would, but for his or her death, have been entitled to become a citizen of the Republic.

2. by naturalization: an alien of full age and of good character may apply for citizenship by naturalization if he satisfies the Minister of the Interior that during the eight years immediately preceding the date of his application, he has resided in Cyprus for periods amounting in the aggregate to not less than five years, the last year of which must be continuous in Cyprus.

3. by registration: certain classes of persons such as spouses of deceased citizens, children born out of wedlock, Commonwealth citizens who have lived in Cyprus, and others can be granted citizenship by registration.

A foreign passport is required for entry into Cyprus. Tourist and business visas are issued at the port of entry for a stay of up to 90 days. Entry regulations apply only to the areas controlled by the government of the Republic of Cyprus. A passport is required, except for holders of: 1) passports issued by the United Nations; 2) documents issued to stateless persons and recognized refugees; or 3) citizens of the Schengen Area countries including the EU, plus Switzerland, Iceland, Liechtenstein, and Norway, who may enter Cyprus with their national identity card provided there is a photograph. The government of the Republic of Cyprus refuses admission to holders of "passports issued illegally by the secessionist entity, the so-called 'Turkish Republic of Northern Cyprus.'"

Contacts

Embassy of the Republic of Cyprus
2211 R Street NW
Washington, DC 20008
Tel.: (202) 462-5772
Email: info@cyprusembassy.net
Web: http://www.cyprusembassy.net

Cyprus Trade Center
13 East 40th Street
New York, NY 10016
Tel.: 212-213-9100
Email: ctcny@cyprustradeny.org
Web: http://www.cyprustradeny.org

Turkish Cypriots maintain an office in Washington, DC
Tel.: (202) 887-6198

United States Embassy
Metochiou & Ploutarchou Streets
2407, Engomi, Nicosia, Cyprus
Mail: P.O. Box 24536

1385 Nicosia Cyprus
Tel.: + (357) 22-393-939
Email: consularnicosia@state.gov
Web: http://nicosia.usembassy.gov

Recommended Residence & Citizenship Consultants:

Mark Nestmann LLM, President
The Nestmann Group
2303 N. 44th Street #14-1025
Phoenix, AZ 85008
Tel.: (602) 688-7552
Email: service@nestmann.com
Web: http://www.nestmann.com/

Henley and Partners
95 Archbishop Makarios III Avenue
Charitini Court, 1st Floor, Office 102
1071 Nicosia
P.O. Box 27266
1643 Nicosia - Cyprus
Tel.: + (357) 22 499 924
Email: cyprus@henleyglobal.com

Arab Republic of Egypt

Government:	Republic
Capital:	Cairo
National Day:	Revolution Day: 23 July (1952)
Population:	85,294,388 (July 2013 est.)
Total Area:	386,662 sq. miles / 1,001,450 sq. kilometers
Languages:	Arabic (official), English, French understood by educated classes
Ethnic groups:	Egyptian 98%, Berber, Nubian, Bedouin, and Beja 1%, Greek, Armenian, other European (primarily Italian and French) 1%
Religion:	Muslim (mostly Sunni) 90%, Coptic 9%, other Christian 1%
Life expectancy:	73.19 years
Currency:	Egyptian pound (EGP)
GDP:	US$534.1 billion (2012 est.)
GDP per capita:	US$6,500 (2012 est.)

The land that gave birth to the first great civilization needs little introduction.

The pyramids, the minarets, the Nile; the scope of Egypt is magnificent. Visitors are surprised to discover that those legendary pyramids are merely the tip of the archaeological iceberg. Pharaonic nations, ancient Greeks, Romans, Christians and Arab dynasties have all played their part in fashioning Egypt's embarrassment of architectural wealth.

Cairo's chaos whirrs around a medieval core that has remained unchanged since the founding days of Islam. Upriver, Luxor, the site of ancient Thebes, is lined with warrens of op-

ulent burial chambers and boasts some of the most formidable monuments in all antiquity. Further south at Aswan, even more geometrically imposing temples write a testament to the power of archaic gods and omnipotent pharaohs. It is here that the Nile is best explored by ancient sail, on a felucca (Egyptian sailing boat) at the hands of the prevailing currents and winds.

Out west, Egypt's ocean of sand stretches infinitely to the Sahara, with a handful of oases feeding solitary islands of green. Hive-like, medieval fortresses cower out here, interspersed with bubbling springs and ghostly rock formations. Meanwhile, the deep, crystal waters of the Red Sea lie brilliantly awash in coral, surrounded by an aquatic frenzy of underwater life. In the deserts of Sinai's interior, visitors can climb the mount where God had words with Moses.

Thirty years of authoritarian rule, an erratic economy and rising living costs fanned the flames of social unrest. Still, Egyptians are a resilient lot, and visitors making the journey here will find as much ancient history as they will modern hospitality. — Lonely Planet

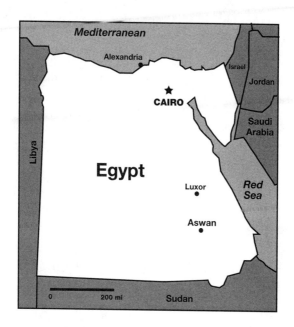

History and Overview

Egypt is located in northern Africa, bordering the Mediterranean Sea, between Libya and the Gaza Strip, and the Red Sea north of Sudan, and includes the Asian Sinai Peninsula.

The regularity and richness of the annual Nile River flood, coupled with semi-isolation provided by deserts to the east and west, allowed for the development of one of the world's great civilizations. A unified kingdom arose circa 3200 B.C., and a series of dynasties ruled in Egypt for the next three millennia. The last native dynasty fell to the Persians in 341 B.C., who in turn were replaced by the Greeks, Romans and Byzantines.

It was the Arabs who introduced Islam and the Arabic language in the 7th century and who ruled for the next six centuries. A local military caste, the Mamluks took control about 1250 and continued to govern after the conquest of Egypt by the Ottoman Turks in

1517. Following the completion of the Suez Canal in 1869, Egypt became an important world transportation hub, but also fell heavily into debt. Ostensibly to protect its investments, Britain seized control of Egypt's government in 1882, but nominal allegiance to the Ottoman Empire continued until 1914.

Partially independent from the U.K. in 1922, Egypt acquired full sovereignty following World War II. The completion of the Aswan High Dam in 1971 and the resultant Lake Nasser have altered the time-honored place of the Nile River in the agriculture and ecology of Egypt.

The Arab Spring

Following the popular overthrow of the government of Tunisia and an open revolt in neighboring Libya in 2010, Egypt witnessed the start of its own popular revolution on January 25, 2011.

Weeks of rioting and labor strikes in Cairo and elsewhere led to the resignation of President Mohamed Hosni Mubarak after 30 years in power. He was replaced by de facto military rule with generals who had backed Mubarak replacing him. Egypt's military assumed leadership until a new parliament was in place in 2012.

That same year, radical Islamist Mohammed Morsi won the presidential election, but in July 2013 the military ousted Morsi and he was replaced by an interim president. In January 2014, a new constitution was approved by referendum, replacing the one approved in 2012. The 2014 elections produced a new president in General Abdel Fattah el-Sisi who had become the de facto dictator indicating that the military would continue to control the government, if not the country.

Unrest has continued and Egyptian security services have been unable to control sporadic unrest. Most violent protests have occurred in major metropolitan areas, including Cairo and its suburbs, Alexandria, and Port Said. The U.S. State Department in

2014 warned U.S. citizens to avoid all demonstrations in Egypt, even peaceful ones that can quickly become violent. U.S. citizens were encouraged to enroll in the Smart Traveler Enrollment Program (STEP) making it easier for the U.S. Embassy to contact them in case of emergency. For current information see:

If revolutionary unrest was not enough, in recent years, Egypt has suffered a series of deadly terrorist attacks in or near tourists. Under Mubarak a heavy security presence was apparent to travelers throughout the country but that is no longer the case.

The U.K. Foreign and Commonwealth Office advises against non-essential travel to all of Egypt apart from the Red Sea resorts. For the latest security Egypt information, U.S. citizens should monitor the Department of State Internet website at: http://travel. state.gov/content/passports/english/country/egypt.html

Economy

Occupying the northeast corner of the African continent, Egypt is bisected by the highly fertile Nile valley, where most economic activity takes place. During his 30-year rule, the Mubarak government reformed the highly centralized economy. A rapidly growing population (the largest in the Arab world), limited arable land, and dependence on the Nile all continue to overtax resources and stress society. The government has struggled to meet the demands of Egypt's population through economic reform and massive investment in communications and physical infrastructure.

Despite these achievements, the government failed to raise living standards for the average Egyptian, and continued subsidies for basic necessities. The subsidies contributed to a growing budget deficit and represent a significant drain on the economy. Foreign direct investment remained low.

The January 2011 revolution disrupted all parts of the economy, causing food and other shortages and unrest. The government back-tracked on economic reforms, drastically increasing social spending to address public dissatisfaction, but political uncertainty at the same time caused economic growth to slow significantly, reducing the government's revenues. Tourism, manufacturing, and construction were among the hardest hit sectors of the economy, and economic growth is likely to remain slow during the next several years.

In recent years Egypt was one of the leading recipients of American foreign aid, totaling as much as US$2 billion in some years. Since 1948, Egypt has received over US$70 billion in U.S. aid.

In 2013, there were over 70,000 refugees in Egypt and by 2014 another 133,924 were added from civil war torn Syria.

Residence and Citizenship

Citizenship is based on the concept of legitimate descent conferred in the following ways:

1. birth within the country does not automatically confer citizenship. Citizenship by birth in the country is only granted under the following conditions:

    a.) to a child born in Egypt, out of wedlock, to an Egyptian mother, when the father is unknown or stateless, or;

    b.) to a child born in Egypt of unknown parents.

2. by descent; a child, born in wedlock, whose father is an Egyptian citizen, automatically becomes a citizen, regardless of the child's country of birth.

3. by naturalization: There is no standard law for naturalization but there follows several categories of eligible candidates:

    a.) persons born in Egypt, of a father who was born in Egypt and who is a member of a racial minority, faces no residence requirements if their language is Arabic or religion is Islam.

b.) a person, who was born in and has resided most of their life in Egypt, may opt for Egyptian nationality upon reaching the age of majority. However, a presidential decree is required.

c.) a woman who marries an Egyptian national becomes a citizen of Egypt, providing that she declares her desire to acquire her husband's nationality. Upon making the declaration, two years of marriage must follow before citizenship is granted.

d.) most other persons face a residence requirement of 10 years as well as the necessity of obtaining a presidential decree, for citizenship to be granted.

Dual citizenship is not recognized.

A foreign passport and visa are required for entry. Travelers can obtain a renewable, 30-day tourist visa on arrival at Cairo International Airport for a US$15 fee, payable in U.S. dollars. Visitors arriving overland and/or those previously experiencing difficulty with their visa status in Egypt should obtain a visa prior to arrival.

Travelers arriving from Israel at the Taba border crossing without an Egyptian visa may be granted a 14-day visa valid for travel within Sinai only. Military personnel arriving on commercial flights are not exempt from passport and visa requirements. Foreigners can acquire a work permit from the Ministry of Manpower and Training to work in Egypt, and can be authorized residence in the country. Work permits must be obtained through the employer. Foreigners are generally not allowed to change residence status from non-working to working status while in the country.

Contacts

Egyptian Embassy
3521 International Court NW
Washington, DC 20008
Tel.: (202) 895-5400
Email: Embassy@egyptembassy.net
Web: http://www.egyptembassy.net

Consulates in New York, Texas, Illinois, and California

United States Embassy
5 Tawfik Diab Street
Garden City, Cairo, Egypt
Tel.: + (20) 2-797-3300
Email: cairoircref@state.gov
Web: http://egypt.usembassy.gov/

State of Israel

Government:	Parliamentary democracy
Capital:	Jerusalem (proclaimed as official capital in 1950; most countries maintain embassies in Tel Aviv)
National Day:	Independence Day: 14 May (1948)
Population:	7,707,042 (July 2013 est.)
Total Area:	8,019 sq. miles / 20,770 sq. kilometers
Languages:	Hebrew (official), Arabic (unofficial), English commonly used
Ethnic groups:	Jewish 76.4% (of which Israel-born 67.1%, Europe/America-born 22.6%, Africa-born 5.9%, Asia-born 4.2%), non-Jewish 23.6%
Religion:	Jewish 75.6%, Muslim 16.9%, Christian 2%, Druze 1.7%, and other 3.8%
Life expectancy:	80.96 years
Currency:	Israeli shekel (ILS)
GDP:	US$219.4 billion (2010 est.)
GDP per capita:	US$29,800 (2010 est.)

Israel is one of the world's oldest travel destinations. Everyone from Moses to Mark Twain has dreamed of going there. The appearance of prophets seems to be dwindling and the Crusaders have long since hung up their swords and shields, but travelers still come in droves, almost magnetically, to this land still considered holy by countless millions.

The appeal of Israel's ancient and holy past may be obvious enough but many new arrivals are surprised to see that it's much more than a lesson in history. While Jerusalem is a dazzling amalgam of past and present, and a contested hotbed for the world's monotheistic faiths, the whole country is a tightly packed ball of everything from Mt Masada and the Negev desert to the beaches of Eilat. On a leisurely weekend you could surf, ski, sip wine, ride horses, go clubbing in Tel-Aviv or enjoy some cutting-edge theatre — and that's just the start. You can also work on a kibbutz, volunteer at a West Bank school, float in the Dead Sea, hike across the Israel National Trail.

Like the patchwork of new arrivals at Ben-Gurion airport, Israel is an amalgamation of peoples who arrived over centuries of time, each one staking their claim to the land. Territorial disputes led to violence, which in turn made for some epic accounts in the Bible; not terribly dissimilar to what is playing out on nightly TV newscasts today. But contrary to popular belief, Israel is not a war zone to be avoided, and it has such rigid security that travel is surprisingly safe.

Somewhere along the line, politics and the bitter facts of life in this uncertain land will nudge their way into your trip. And while Israelis and Palestinians love nothing more than to argue, muse and prognosticate over the latest political currents, it's best to leave your own opinions at the door. Enter the Holy Land on a clean slate and you'll never watch the nightly news the same way again. — Lonely Planet

History and Overview

The State of Israel is located at the eastern end of the Mediterranean Sea, which forms its western border. It also has common, but highly disputed, northern borders with Lebanon and Syria. It is bordered to the southwest by Egypt and to the east by Jordan. Israel occupied the West Bank, Gaza Strip, Golan Heights, and East Jerusalem as a result of the 1967 Six-Day War. By agreement with Israel, an elected Palestinian authority now exercises jurisdiction in most of Gaza and the major cities of the West Bank, but this authority is divided into internally warring factions.

The Hamas faction controls the parliament and continues to call for the destruction of Israel. Palestinian Authority police have responsibility for keeping order in those areas, and the Palestinian Authority exercises a range of civil functions in other areas of the West Bank, although it is virtually bankrupt.

The Israeli nation occupies an area in which history dates back to Biblical times, at least 4000 B.C. The ancestors of most modern Jews emigrated from the area later called Palestine in waves beginning in the 6th century B.C. and ending in the 2nd to 6th centuries A.D., leaving a small remnant behind. Modern Israel is a parliamentary democracy with a modern economy.

The first international Zionist conference, in 1899, called for an eventual Jewish state. By 1909, Jews had founded the new city of Tel Aviv in what was then Palestine. By 1914, over 60,000 Jewish immigrants had moved into an area with 450,000 Arab residents. To enlist the inhabitants' and foreign Zionists' aid in ousting the Ottoman Turks from the region (and to thwart French colonial aims as well), the British government promised land in Palestine for a "Jewish national home" via the Balfour Declaration, which the Foreign Secretary signed in 1917. After Palestine came under a British mandate in 1929, restrictions on Jewish land purchases and immigration were imposed. By 1937, it was proposed, but the Arabs later rejected, that Palestine be partitioned into Arab and Jewish states. The British attempted controls on Jewish immigration but, by then, Jews in Palestine numbered 200,000, about 30% of the total population.

After World War II, the British abandoned their Palestine mandate, and a new partition plan emerged, culminating on May 14, 1948, when the United Nations proclaimed the existence of the State of Israel. Since then, the Middle East has been wracked with wars between Arabs and Israelis, and, only in the last few years, did negotiation replace violence, but not for long. The goal of stability for these lands remains elusive, as new cycles of violence have erupted.

In 2003, President George W. Bush, working in conjunction with the EU, U.N., and Russia (the "Quartet") took the lead in laying out a roadmap to a final settlement of the conflict by 2005, based on reciprocal steps by the two parties leading to two states, Israel and a democratic Palestine.

However, progress toward a permanent status agreement was undermined by Israeli-Palestinian violence from 2003 to 2005. In the summer of 2005, Israel unilaterally disengaged from the Gaza Strip, evacuating settlers and its military while retaining control over most points of entry into the Gaza Strip.

The election of the terrorist party Hamas to head the Palestinian Legislative Council froze relations between Israel and the Palestinian Authority (PA). There was a 34-day conflict with Hezbollah based in Lebanon June-August 2006 and a 23-day conflict with Hamas in the Gaza Strip December 2008 to January 2009.

In 2007, talks resumed with PA President Mahmoud Abbas. Prime Minister Benjamin Netanyahu formed a coalition in 2009. Direct talks launched in 2010 collapsed following the expiration of Israel's 10-month partial settlement construction moratorium in the West Bank. Diplomatic initiatives to revive the negotiations through proximity talks began at the end of 2010. In 2011, PA insistence on seeking U.N. recognition of Palestine as an independent state stymied two-party negotiations as Israel felt threatened from all sides with the fall of Mubarak in Egypt and the spreading violence of the Arab Spring, especially in neighboring Syria.

Direct talks with the Palestinians launched in 2010 collapsed following the expiration of Israel's 10-month partial settlement construction moratorium in the West Bank. In 2012, Israel engaged in a seven-day conflict with Hamas in the Gaza Strip. Prime Minister Netanyahu formed a new coalition government in 2013 and sporadic direct talks with the Palestinians resumed.

Economy

Israel has become a leading center of high-technology development and manufacturing, and is, at this writing in mid 2014, the only democratic society in the Middle East area. Israel has a technologically advanced market economy with substantial government participation. It depends on imports of crude oil, grains, raw materials, and military equipment. Despite limited natural resources, Israel has intensively developed its agricultural and industrial sectors over the past 20 years. Israel imports substantial quantities of grain, but is largely self-sufficient in other agricultural products. Cut diamonds, high-technology equipment and agricultural products (fruits and vegetables) are the leading exports.

Israel usually posts sizable current account deficits, which are covered by large transfer payments from abroad and by foreign loans. Roughly half of the government's external debt is owed to the U.S., which is its major source of economic and military aid. Since 1987, the U.S. Congress has annually approved an average of US$3 billion of aid to Israel; US$1.2 billion in economic aid, and US$1.8 billion in military aid. Since the Gulf War in 1991, the U.S. has provided Israel US$2 billion annually in federal loan guarantees, which brings the total U.S. foreign aid to Israel to about US$5 billion annually.

The global financial crisis of 2008 to 2009 spurred a brief recession in Israel, but the country entered the crisis with solid fundamentals following years of prudent fiscal policy and a strong banking sector. The economy has recovered better than most advanced, comparably sized economies. Israel's economy also weathered the Arab Spring because strong trade ties outside the Middle East insulated the economy. Natural gas fields discovered off Israel's coast in 2011 improved Israel's energy security outlook. The Leviathan field is one of the world's largest offshore natural gas finds and production from the Tama field is expected to meet all of Israel's natural gas demands.

Israel has adopted money laundering laws and controls. The U.S.

Justice Department has been investigating one unnamed Israeli bank for possibly assisting U.S. citizens to illegally evade U.S. taxes.

Residence and Citizenship

An Israeli passport is highly desirable because it is widely accepted throughout the world. It is the only non-European Union passport that gains entry to all EU countries without need for a visa. The Israeli passport can provide its holder reduced residence periods when applying for foreign citizenship in Spain and Germany. Many other countries, including the U.S., permit generous quotas for immigrants from Israel.

New immigrants to Israel with substantial income from foreign source investments are given a 30-year holiday from most exchange controls. The new citizen can keep assets wherever he/she wishes and in any currency. During the first seven years of residence, a new immigrant may even be exempt from income and capital gains taxes on foreign source income.

One drawback to citizenship is that all males, ages 18 to 48, are liable to serve in the military. Women between ages 18 and 25 also must serve.

The Law of Return

Israel's official policy has been to welcome the scattered Jews of the world ("the Diaspora") to the Jewish homeland. Adopted in 1950, the "Law of Return" decrees that anyone with one Jewish grandparent has an automatic right to Israeli citizenship, even if they are not observant religious Jews. The law has long provided an automatic second passport and dual citizenship for all who qualified, many of them U.S. citizens.

Periodic outcries of dissatisfaction with the Law of Return are heard, usually from ultra-Orthodox Jews or disgruntled taxpayers, but the tense state of Israeli-Palestinian relations has a tendency to quiet these complaints since survival is more important. Those interested in exploring their rights under the law should check the current status of the Law of Return.

The Law of Return defines a "Jew" as anyone who is at least one-quarter Jewish (having one Jewish grandparent), or any convert to Judaism who does not embrace another faith. Documentary certification of a male's circumcision ceremony (briss) or other important Jewish ceremonies (e.g., bar mitzvah, Jewish wedding, and synagogue membership) can serve as supporting evidence.

According to the website of the Israel Ministry of Foreign Affairs the Law of Return (1950) grants every Jew the right to come to Israel as an oleh (a Jew immigrating to Israel) and become an Israeli citizen. For the purposes of this Law, "Jew" means a person who was born of a Jewish mother, or has converted to Judaism and is not a member of another religion.

But foreigners qualified for citizenship cannot just fly into Ben Gurion Airport, go to a government agency and pick up an Israeli passport after providing proof of qualification.

Israeli citizenship becomes effective on the day of arrival in the country or the day of receipt of an oleh's certificate, whichever is later. This means a 90-day period of residence in Israel is required before a certificate of citizenship and a passport is issued.

It is an Israeli custom for new immigrants to choose a Hebrew name. This involves a legal change of name using a simple procedure at the local office of the Ministry of Interior. Once the Hebrew name has been recorded, it is used in all official documents, including the Israeli passport.

Under the 1950 Law of Return, in theory, Jews across the world are granted Israeli citizenship 90 days after immigrating there and making proper application. In fact, the process takes much longer than 90 days after arrival and in the interim a temporary status is granted pending final approval.

Under the Law of Return, an accepted immigrant is granted a document known as a "laisser-passer," rather than an official passport during the first year of citizenship. This requires visas for most travel. Israel permits dual citizenship for those who come in under the Law of Return and does not report acquisition of citizenship to an immigrant's home country. Passports are renewable every five years.

A gentile (non-Jew) also can become a citizen at the discretion of the Ministry of Interior. The applicant must satisfy five conditions: 1) be present in Israel to apply; 2) have been in Israel three years out of the five-year period immediately preceding application; 3) be entitled to permanent resident status; 4) have settled in Israel or intend to do so; and 5) surrender former citizenship, or prove that foreign citizenship will end upon becoming an Israeli. Jews who become citizens through the Law of Return are not restricted in this way.

Israeli citizens naturalized in the United States retain their Israeli citizenship, and their children are considered Israeli citizens also. Children born in the U.S. to Israeli parents acquire both U.S. and Israeli nationality at birth.

Israeli citizens, including dual nationals, are subject to service in the armed forces. U.S.-Israeli dual nationals of military age who do not wish to serve in the military may contact the Israeli Embassy in Washington, D.C., to obtain proof of exemption or deferment before going to Israel. Otherwise, they may be conscripted into military service or subject to criminal penalties for failure to serve. Israeli citizens, including dual nationals, must enter and depart Israel on their Israeli passports. Similarly, all U.S. citizens with dual nationality must enter and depart the United States on their U.S. passports.

A foreign passport valid for six months beyond duration of stay, an onward or return ticket, and proof of sufficient funds are required for entry. A no-charge, three-month visa may be issued upon arrival and may be renewed. Travelers carrying official or diplomatic U.S. passports must obtain visas from an Israeli Embassy or consulate prior to arrival in Israel.

Anyone who has been refused entry or experienced difficulties with his/her status during a previous visit, or who has overstayed the authorized duration of a previous visit or otherwise violated the terms of their admission to Israel should consult the Israeli Embassy or nearest Israeli Consulate before attempting to return to Israel.

Anyone seeking returning resident status must obtain permission from Israeli authorities before traveling. Occasionally, the government of Israel has declined to admit individual American citizens or groups who have expressed sympathy with the Palestinian cause, sought to meet with Palestinian officials or intended to travel to the West Bank or the Gaza Strip.

The 2008 Nationality Law regulates the revocation of Israeli citizenship in cases specified by law. The main significance of the law is the transfer of the authority to revoke citizenship from the Minister of Interior to the Court of Administrative Matters upon the Minister's request. A judicial determination is required for a revocation at the termination of a three-year period from the acquisition of citizenship, in cases where the person committed an act that constitutes a "breach of loyalty to the State of Israel."

Contacts

Embassy of Israel
3514 International Drive NW
Washington, DC 20008
Tel.: (202) 364-5500

Email: info@israelemb.org
Web: http://www.israelemb.org/washington/pages/default.aspx

Consulates General in Atlanta, Boston, Chicago, Houston,
Los Angeles, Miami, New York, Philadelphia, and
San Francisco.

United States Embassy
71 HaYarkon Street
Tel Aviv 6343229, Israel
Email: AMCTelAviv@state.gov
Web: http://israel.usembassy.gov/

U.S. Consulate General
Agron Street 18
Jerusalem 9419003
Tel.: + (972) 02-622-7230
Email: UsConGenJerusalem@state.gov
Web: http://jerusalem.usconsulate.gov

Republic of Mauritius

Government:	Parliamentary democracy
Capital:	Port Louis
National Day:	Independence Day: 12 March (1968)
Population:	1,331,155 (July 2014 est.)
Total Area:	788 sq. miles / 2,040 sq. kilometers
Languages:	Creole 80.5%, Bhojpuri 12.1%, other 3.7%, French 3.4%, English (official; spoken by 1%), unspecified 0.3%
Ethnic groups:	Indo-Mauritian 68%, Creole 27%, Sino-Mauritian 3%, Franco-Mauritian 2%
Religion:	Hindu 48.5%, Roman Catholic 26.3%, Muslim 17.3%, other Christian 6.4%, other 0.6%, none 0.7%, unspecified 0.1% (2011 est.)
Life expectancy:	75.17 years
Currency:	Mauritian rupee (MUR)
GDP:	US$20.95 billion (2013 est.)
GDP per capita:	US$16,100 (2013 est.)

Mauritius is a fascinating, world-in-one-island slice of paradise. Its very name of conjures up images of tropical luxury and stupendous extravagance. While in many destinations famed for cobalt-blue seas, white sandy beaches and luxury hotels, you may eventually find yourself wishing for something to do besides sunbathing and swimming, it's often hard to know what to do next in Mauritius. The island is loaded with historic sites, cultural diversity, geographic variation and almost limitless activities to distract you from the daily grind of beach and pool. But perhaps its single biggest asset is the relaxed charm of its warm and welcoming people.

Mauritius is the most developed of the Mascarene Islands, but with a bit of effort and resourcefulness you can escape the crowds and find your own patch. The smells, noises and bustle of the mercantile capital Port Louis, Africa's wealthiest city, are never far away, while the busy garment markets in the Central Plateau towns of Quatre Bornes and Curepipe and Black River Gorges National Park's dramatic virgin forests give the lie to Mauritius being just another beach destination.

But what beaches! From the stunning sand-rimmed lagoons and popular wide public beaches to the picturesque islands off the country's coastline, there's truly something for everyone here. Add to this the joys of Chinese, Indian, French and African cuisine, the rousing beat of sega music and the infectious party spirit of the locals, and you soon understand why Mauritius really is so many people's idea of paradise on earth. — Lonely Planet

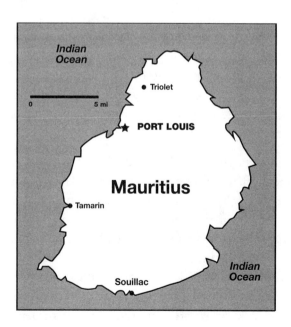

History and Overview

Mauritius, a volcanic island of lagoons and palm-fringed beaches in the Indian Ocean, has a reputation for stability and racial harmony among its mixed population of Asians, Europeans and Africans. The island has maintained one of the developing world's most successful democracies and has enjoyed years of constitutional order.

Although known to Arab and Malay sailors as early as the 10th century, Mauritius was first explored by the Portuguese in 1505; and subsequently settled by the Dutch, who named it in honor of Prince Maurits van Nassau, in the 17th century. The French assumed control in 1715 and the British captured the island in 1810, during the Napoleonic Wars. Mauritius remained a strategically important British naval base, and later an air station, playing an important role during World War II for anti-submarine and convoy operations, as well as the collection of signals intelligence. Independence was attained in 1968.

A stable democracy with regular free elections and a positive human rights record, the country has attracted considerable foreign investment and has earned one of Africa's highest per capita incomes. Recent poor weather and declining sugar prices have slowed economic growth, leading to some protests over standards of living in the Creole community.

Since independence in 1968, Mauritius has developed from a low income, agriculturally based economy to a middle-income diversified economy with growing industrial, financial and tourist sectors. For most of the period, annual growth has been in the order of 5% to 6%. This remarkable achievement has been reflected in more equitable income distribution, increased life expectancy, lowered infant mortality, and a much-improved infrastructure. Sugarcane is grown on about 90% of the cultivated land area and accounts for 25% of export earnings. The government's development strategy centers on expanding local financial institutions and building a domestic information telecommunications industry.

Economy

The country has attracted considerable foreign investment and has earned one of Africa's highest per capita incomes.

The ambitious Mauritius offshore financial sector travels the middle road. Until 1998, the offshore company and the international company (equivalent to an international business corporation, IBC) allowed zero taxation across a range of offshore activities, including banking, shipping, insurance and fund management, as well as in free-trade zones.

These companies are known as Global Business Companies, Categories 1 and 2. Mauritius long ago decided to be a "respectable" offshore financial center. Thus "tax-free" is no longer replaced by a minimum tax rate of 15% in almost all areas. Mauritius has tax treaties with 27 countries that can be combined with offshore laws to produce profitable trade and investment, especially for many thousands of wealthy Indian investors. Mauritius has become a favorite of the Indian financial elite and a prime target of the Indian government campaign trying to curb chronic tax evasion by wealthy Indians.

Mauritius has attracted more than 32,000 offshore entities, many aimed at commerce in India, South Africa, and China. India's share in total number of investments made by global companies through Mauritius has almost halved in the past two years to about 15%, while Africa now accounts for over 50%. Investment in the banking sector alone exceeds US$1 billion. Mauritius, with its strong textile sector, has been well placed to take advantage of the Africa Growth and Opportunity Act (AGOA). Mauritius' sound economic policies and prudent banking practices helped to ease effects from the global financial crisis in 2008 to 2009. The country continues to expand its trade and investment outreach around the globe.

Considered part of Africa geographically, Mauritius has friendly relations with other African states in the region, particularly South Africa, by far its largest continental trading partner. Mauritian investors are gradually entering African markets, notably Madagascar and Mozambique. Mauritius coordinates much of its foreign policy with the Southern Africa Development Community and the Organization of African Unity (OAU).

Tax Free Investing in India

More than 68% of the population is of Indian origin, commonly known as Indo-Mauritians. Mauritius sees itself as a Cayman Islands to India, allowing investors in India to cut their tax bills by channeling money that is destined there. In the period of 2000 to 2012, 38% of all foreign direct investment in India, or US$65.29 billion, traveled through this offshore center.

Under a residence taxation rule, Article 13 of the Indo-Mauritian tax treaty provides for attribution of taxation rights among the two countries for capital gains taxes. It says gains derived by a resident of a contracting State shall be taxable only in that State. This gives the residence state taxation superior rights over the source state where the gains are earned. Although the same provision is present in most of India's tax treaties, the Mauritius treaty provides a huge CGT exemption loophole because Mauritius does not tax capital gains.

Smart investors use this loophole for investing in India. They set up a subsidiary in Mauritius that is used to earn capital gains from Indian companies, usually through share acquisition. With no CGT in Mauritius, the transaction is tax exempt, resulting in what might be called "double non-taxation." Indian tax authorities derisively call it "treaty shopping."

There has, as you might imagine, been a lot of litigation over this loophole and its individual case application, but the highest court in India has approved it. That ruling acted as a huge incentive to the Indian economy and promoted both foreign investment in India, and the welfare of Mauritius corporate and legal service professionals.

In early 2014, the two governments announced agreement on changes to the India-Mauritius tax treaty aimed at preventing "treaty shopping" or abuse of tax treaties by third-country investors. These would limit treaty benefits to those who meet certain conditions related to business, residence and investment commitments. India is planning anti-avoidance tax rules that may close the loophole, but if you are interested in tax-free investing in India, check Google for attorneys in Port Louis.

Residence and Citizenship

The law makes it simple for expatriates to work and live in the country. A category of occupational permit combines work and residence permits into a single document. To apply for occupation permits, investors have to generate an annual turnover of more than US$100,000, while professionals need to have jobs with a salary of around US$1,000 per month. Self-employed individuals need to generate an annual income of US$20,000 a year. Applications for occupation permits are submitted to the board of investment (BOI) which will help the qualifying candidates to secure an occupation permit for themselves and residence permits for a spouse and dependents.

Any firm can apply through BOI for an occupation permit for a foreign employee it pays more than US$1,000 a month and a residence permit for the employee's spouse and children. An important feature of the law is that a noncitizen retiree, providing evidence that he/she will bring in at least US$40,000 annually, can also apply through BOI for a residence permit. However, he or she will have to provide a bank guarantee of US$2,000. The same rule applies to self-employed professionals. All foreigners applying for occupation or residence permits must provide health certificates issued by any accredited doctor in Mauritius.

Besides fast-track clearance, yet another advantage for immigrants to Mauritius is that the spouse of a holder of an occupation permit can take up any job paying more than US$1,000, set up a business or work as a self-employed professional earning at least US$20,000 a year, under the same provisions as investors and skilled professionals.

Finally, after three years of activity in Mauritius, consistent with the terms of entry, the foreign national, spouse and dependents can apply for permanent residence. The permanent residence permit is valid for 10 years and allows unrestricted work and residence as well as purchase of real estate.

Mauritius has what might be called a form of "economic residence." With a minimum investment of US$500,000, a foreign investor may be eligible for Permanent Residence Status and can be exempted from work and residence permits. He can also apply for PR status for his spouse and family. But for each next-of-kin or child 18 years or older a non-interest bearing minimum deposit of US$100,000 must be made with the Accountant General.

A wide range of business activities qualify under the scheme, including manufacturing, headquarters of multinational companies, hotel, tourism and related services, and financial services. Alternatively, investment of the same amount (US$500,000) in the Permanent Resident Investment Fund is also regarded as an investment in a qualifying business activity.

Citizenship is conferred:

1. by birth on a child born in the territory of Mauritius, regardless of the nationality of the parents.

2. by descent to:

   a.) a child born abroad in wedlock, whose father is a citizen of Mauritius;

   b.) a child born abroad and out of wedlock, whose mother is a citizen of Mauritius;

   c.) all citizen-children born abroad must be registered in Mauritius.

3. by registration: a foreign woman who marries a Mauritius citizen is automatically granted citizenship by registration. A foreign man who marries a Mauritius citizen can be granted citizenship on an individual case basis.

4. by naturalization, which may be granted to any alien or British Commonwealth person of majority age (18 years) who makes an application in the prescribed manner and satisfies the government that:

   a.) he is of good character;

   b.) he has an adequate knowledge of the English language or any other language current in Mauritius and of the responsibilities of a citizen of Mauritius;

   c.) he has resided in Mauritius for a continuous period of 12 months immediately preceding the date of his application; and

   d.) during the seven years immediately prior to the period of 12 months referred to above, he has resided in Mauritius for periods amounting to not less than five years.

Dual citizenship is not recognized in the law.

A valid foreign passport, onward/return ticket and proof of sufficient funds are required for entry into the country. Immigration authorities require the validity of the entrant's passport to be greater than six months upon both arrival and departure. Travelers must also provide a local address where they will stay in Mauritius. Visas are issued at the point of entry.

Contacts
Embassy of Mauritius
1709 N Street NW
Washington, DC 20036
Tel.: (202) 244-1491
Email: mauritius.embassy@verizon.net
Web: http://www.maurinet.com/embasydc.html

United States Embassy
Rogers House, 4th Floor
John F. Kennedy Avenue
Port Louis, Republic of Mauritius
Tel.: + (230) 202-4400
Email: usembass@intnet.mu
Web: http://mauritius.usembassy.gov/

Kingdom of Morocco

Government:	Constitutional monarchy
Capital:	Rabat
National Day:	Throne Day (accession of King Mohamed VI): 30 July (1999)
Population:	32,649,130 (July 2013 est.)
Total Area:	172,414 sq. miles / 446,550 sq. kilometers
Languages:	Arabic (official), Berber dialects, French
Ethnic groups:	Arab-Berber 99.1%, other 0.7%, Jewish 0.2%
Religion:	Muslim 98.7%, Christian 1.1%, Jewish 0.2%
Life expectancy:	76.31 years
Currency:	Moroccan dirham (MAD)
GDP:	US$168.9 billion (2012 est.)
GDP per capita:	US$5,200 (2012 est.)

Morocco is an exotic gateway to Africa; its mountains, desert and coast are populated by Berbers and nomads, and its ancient medina lanes lead to souqs and riads.

From Saharan dunes to the peaks of the High Atlas, Morocco could have been tailor-made for travelers. Lyrical landscapes carpet this sublime slice of North Africa like the richly colored and patterned rugs you'll lust after in local cooperatives. The mountains — not just the famous High Atlas but also the Rif and suntanned ranges leading to Saharan oases — offer simple, breathtaking pleasures: night skies glistening in the thin air; views over a fluffy cloudbank from the Tizi n'Test pass. On lower ground, there are rugged coastlines, waterfalls and caves in forested hills, and the mighty desert.

The varied terrain may inform your dreams, but it shapes the very lives of Morocco's Berbers, Arabs and Saharawis. Despite encroaching modernity, with motorways joining mosques and kasbahs as manmade features of the landscape, Moroccan people remain closely connected to the environment. The nomadic southern 'blue men' brave the desert's burning expanses in robes and turbans, with mobile phones in hand. Likewise, traditional life continues — with tweaks — in the techniques of Berber carpet makers; in date cooperatives; in medina spice trading; and in the lifestyles in ports like Essaouira and mountain hamlets.

Often exotic, sometimes overwhelming and always unexpected, these ancient centers are bursting with Maghrebi mystique and madness: the perfect complement to the serene countryside. When you hit town and join the crowds, you follow a fine tradition of nomads and traders stretching back centuries. UNESCO has bestowed World Heritage status on medinas including Fés, the world's largest living medieval Islamic city, and the carnivalesque Djemaa el-Fna in Marrakesh. — Lonely Planet

History and Overview

The Kingdom of Morocco is the most westerly of the North African countries known as the Maghreb. Strategically situated with both Atlantic and Mediterranean coastlines, but with a rugged mountainous interior, it stayed independent for centuries while developing a rich culture blended from Arab, Berber, European, and African influences.

In 788, about a century after the Arab conquest of North Africa, successive Moorish dynasties began to rule in Morocco. In the 16th century, the Sa'adi monarchy, particularly under Ahmad Al Mansur (1578 to 1603), repelled foreign invaders and inaugurated a golden age. In 1860, Spain occupied northern Morocco and ushered in a half-century of trade rivalry among European powers that saw Morocco's sovereignty steadily erode. In 1912, the French imposed a protectorate over the country. A protracted independence struggle with France ended successfully in 1956. The internationalized city of Tangier and most Spanish possessions were turned over to the new country that same year.

After the French protectorate from 1912 to 1956, Sultan Mohammed became king. He was succeeded in 1961 by his son, Hassan II, who ruled for 38 years. He played a prominent role in the search for peace in the Middle East, given the large number of Israelis of Moroccan origin, but was criticized for suppressing domestic opposition. A truth commission set up to investigate human rights violations during Hassan's reign has confirmed nearly 10,000 cases, ranging from death in detention to forced exile. After his death in 1999, Hassan was succeeded by his son, who became King Mohammed VI and was seen as a modernizer.

There has been some economic and social liberalization, but the monarch has retained sweeping powers. Gradual political reforms in the 1990s resulted in the establishment of a bicameral legislature, which first met in 1997. Under King Mohammed human rights were said to have improved. Morocco enjoys a moderately free press, but the government occasionally takes action against journalists who report on three broad subjects considered to be taboo: the monarchy, Islam, and the status of Western Sahara. It is alleged that Morocco Telecom blocked several blogging sites and often censors political websites supporting independence of Western Sahara.

Despite the continuing reforms, ultimate authority remains in the hands of the monarch. Influenced by protests elsewhere the Arab Spring in the Middle East and North Africa, thousands of Moroccans in 2011 rallied in Rabat and several other major cities to demand constitutional reform and more democracy and to protest government corruption and high food prices. Police response to most of the protests was subdued compared to the violence elsewhere in the region. King Mohammed VI agreed to establish a commission to reform the country's constitution; a popular referendum held in 2011 overwhelmingly approved the new constitution. Three years after this popular movement, opposition groups claim that the idea of "gradual reform" has been abandoned.

Morocco virtually annexed Western Sahara during the late 1970s, but final resolution on the status of the territory remains unresolved. A dispute with Spain, in 2002, over the tiny island of Perejil, revived the issue of the sovereignty of the islands of Melilla and Ceuta. The small enclaves on the Mediterranean coast are surrounded by Morocco but have been administered by Madrid for centuries.

Economy

Morocco has capitalized on its proximity to Europe and relatively low labor costs to build a diverse, open, market-oriented economy. In the 1980s Morocco was a heavily indebted country before pursuing austerity measures and pro-market reforms, overseen by the IMF. Since ascending to the throne in 1999, King Mohammed

VI has presided over a stable economy marked by steady growth, low inflation, and gradually falling unemployment.

Industrial development and infrastructure improvements, most visibly illustrated by a new port and free-trade zone near the city of Tangier, are improving competitiveness. Morocco also seeks to expand its renewable energy capacity with a goal of making renewable 40% of electricity output by 2020. Key sectors of the economy include agriculture, tourism, phosphates, textiles, apparel, and subcomponents.

Long-term challenges include preparing the economy for freer trade with the U.S. and European Union, improving education and job prospects for Morocco's youth, and raising living standards, which the government hopes to achieve by increasing tourist arrivals and boosting competitiveness in textiles.

Morocco has a Free Trade Agreement (FTA) with the U.S and has advanced status in an Association Agreement with the EU. However, poverty, illiteracy, and unemployment rates remain high. In response to these challenges, The King launched a National Initiative for Human Development, a US$2 billion program aimed at alleviating poverty and underdevelopment by expanding electricity to rural areas and replacing urban slums with public and subsidized housing, among other policies.

Morocco's long-term challenges include improving education and job prospects for young Moroccans, closing the disparity in wealth between the rich and the poor, confronting corruption, and expanding and diversifying exports beyond phosphates and low-value added products.

Residence and Citizenship

The law confers citizenship in the following ways:

1. by birth: within the territory of Morocco does not automatically confer citizenship.

2. by descent: for a child of a Moroccan father, regardless of the child's country of birth; or for a child of a Moroccan mother and an unknown or stateless father, regardless of the child's country of birth.

3. by marriage: a foreign woman who marries a Moroccan citizen can become a Moroccan citizen by declaration after two years residence and marriage.

4. by naturalization: citizenship may be acquired when a person continually has resided in the country for five years; and is of full age. Citizenship must be approved by Cabinet decree.

Dual citizenship is recognized, but permission must be granted by the government before a second citizenship is acquired. Dual citizenship by default is not recognized.

The government of Morocco considers all persons born to Moroccan fathers to be Moroccan citizens. In addition to being subject to all Moroccan laws, U.S. citizens who also possess Moroccan nationality may be subject to other laws that impose special obligations on citizens of that country.

Foreign travelers to Morocco must have a valid passport. Visas are not required for American tourists traveling to Morocco for fewer than 90 days. For visits of more than 90 days, Americans are required to apply for an extension with a valid reason for the extension of stay.

Travelers who plan to reside in Morocco must obtain a residence permit. A residence permit may be requested and obtained from immigration authorities (Service Etranger) at the central police station of the district of residence. U.S. citizens are encouraged to carry a copy of their U.S. passports with them at all times, so that, if questioned by local officials, proof of identity and U.S. citizenship is readily available.

Travel advisory: Travel to the Western Sahara region is not advised due to the presence of land mines.

Contacts

Embassy of Morocco

1601 21st Street NW
Washington, DC 20009
Tel.· (202) 462-7979
Email: ambmoroccoffice@gmail.com
Web: http://www.embassyofmorocco.us/

Consulate General

10 East 40th Street
New York, NY 10016
Tel.: (212) 758-2625
Email: info@moroccanconsulate.com
Web: http://www.moroccanconsulate.com

United States Embassy

2 Avenue de Mohamed El Fassi
Rabat, Morocco
Tel.: + (212) (537) 76-22-65
Email: Webmaster_Rabat@state.gov
Web: http://morocco.usembassy.gov/

Republic of South Africa

Government:	Republic
Capital cities:	Pretoria (Executive), Cape Town (Legislative), Bloemfontein (Judicial)
National Day:	Freedom Day: 27 April (1994)
Population:	48,601,098 (July 2013 est.)
Total Area:	471,011 sq. miles / 1,219,912 sq. kilometers
Languages:	IsiZulu 23.8%, IsiXhosa 17.6%, Afrikaans 13.3%, Sepedi 9.4%, English 8.2%, Setswana 8.2%, Sesotho 7.9%, other 7.2%, Xitsonga 4.4%
Ethnic groups:	Black African 79%, white 9.6%, colored 8.9%, Indian/Asian 2.5%
Religion:	Christian 11.1%, Pentecostal/Charismatic 8.2%, Catholic 7.1%, Methodist 6.8%, Dutch Reformed 6.7%, Anglican 3.8%, other 2.3%, Islamic 1.5%
Life expectancy:	49.48 years
Currency:	Rand (ZAR)
GDP:	US$576.1 billion (2012 est.)
GDP per capita:	US$11,300 (2012 est.)

Every country in the world displays some diversity, but South Africa, stretching from the hippos in the Limpopo River to the penguins waddling on the Cape, takes some beating. It befits its position at the southern end of the world's most epic continent, with more types of terrain than photographers can shake their zoom lens at. There's the deserted Kalahari, Namakwaland's springtime symphony of wildflowers, iconic Table Mountain and Cape Point, Kruger National Park's wildlife-stalked savannah (scene of the famous lion-buffalo-crocodile battle watched more than 40 million times on YouTube) and, running through the east of the country and into Lesotho, the Drakensberg. KwaZulu-Natal's iSimangaliso Wetland Park alone has five distinct ecosystems, attracting both zebras and dolphins.

If you're interested in another kind of wildlife, hit the nightclubs on Cape Town's jumping Long St or sample African homebrew in a township shebeen (unlicensed bar). When it's time to reflect on it all, do it over seafood on the Garden Route, curry in Durban's Indian Area, a sizzling Cape Malay dish, or a braai (barbecue) in the wilderness — accompanied by a bottle of pinotage produced by the oldest wine industry outside Europe.

Of course, it's impossible for travelers to South Africa to remain oblivious to the fact that, despite the rise of "black diamonds" (middle-class black folk), racial inequality persists here. Black and colored townships face problems such as a horrific HIV/AIDS rate and xenophobic tensions caused by economic refugees from nearby countries.

Nonetheless, South Africans are some of the most upbeat, welcoming and humorous folk you'll encounter anywhere, from farmers in the rural north who tell you to drive safely on those dirt roads, to Khayelitsha kids who wish you molo ("good morning" in Xhosa). — Lonely Planet

History and Overview

The Republic of South Africa occupies the large landmass that forms the southern tip of the African continent. It surrounds one independent state, Lesotho. Namibia, Botswana and Zimbabwe are on the north, while Mozambique and Swaziland are to the east.

At the dawn of South Africa's recorded history, about 8000 B.C., two major groups roamed the land, the pastoralist Khoi and the hunter-gatherer San. In 1488, Portuguese explorers sailed around and landed at what is now the Cape of Good Hope. In 1652, the Dutch East India Company established a fort that grew into modern Cape Town. The fort served as a supply station for ships to and from the East Indies, but soon attracted settlers. The Cape Dutch white settlers, known as Boers (farmers) were joined, in 1688, by French Protestant Huguenot refugees. Germans and other Europeans were also assimilated into the colony, and this mixed group eventually became known as Afrikaners, who saw themselves as indigenous natives to South Africa. Movement by whites into the interior resulted in fierce battles with black tribesmen, known as Bantus ("people").

The Dutch East India Company imported Malay political prisoners and slaves from their territories in the East Indies, who intermingled with the Khoi and their white owners, eventually evolving into the group known in South Africa as "colored," still predominantly based in Cape Town. Later in the 19th century, British sugar-cane planters around Durban on the east coast imported hundreds of thousands of indentured laborers from India, adding yet another ethnic population to the mix.

The British consolidated their control over the region in the early 1800s, using it as an important staging post on the ocean route to Hong Kong, Australia, New Zealand, and the Pacific. In 1820, with the government in London encouraging settlers from Britain, clashes between the Bantu and European settlers increased dramatically, as did friction between the Afrikaners and the English.

In 1830, an Afrikaner group from the Cape started what is now known as the "Great Trek," heading north and inland. Seeking to escape British domination and resisting the decreed liberation of their slaves, in 1843 they proclaimed a new independent state of the Transvaal, followed by the Orange Free State in 1854. The discovery of diamonds and gold in the Afrikaner-controlled interior led to British adventurism, which resulted in the defeat of the Afrikaners in the brutal Boer War (1899 to 1902). On May 31, 1910, the Union of South Africa was formed as a self-governing British dominion, paradoxically with an Afrikaner as Prime Minister.

Tensions between English- and Afrikaans-speaking whites continued over the course of the next half century, and were complicated by the emergence of a wealthy and powerful mining industry on the Witwatersrand, near Johannesburg. The emergence of African migrancy to serve the mines' labor needs created a complex social and territorial system that prefigured the system of racial segregation known as apartheid.

In 1948, the National Party, dominated by Afrikaners, came to power and adopted apartheid as official state policy. When Britain began to grant independence to its African colonies, the Nationalist government decided to make black African enclaves in South Africa into independent states known as Bantustans, and stripped blacks of their citizenship. This led to severe domestic and international protest.

Although gold-rich South Africa prospered economically for a time, eventually political tensions led to massive unrest. This lasted until the National Party, led by President Willem de Klerk, voluntarily relinquished power in 1994. With the election of Nelson Mandela as president representing the African National Congress (ANC), the apartheid regime was dismantled and the new South Africa became a democratic nation. In 1999, Thabo Mbeki was elected to succeed Mandela as president and was re-elected in 2004 by an even larger margin.

South Africa has struggled to address apartheid-era imbalances in decent housing, education, and health care. ANC infighting, which has grown in recent years, came to a head in 2008 when President Thabo Mbeki resigned. Jacob Zuma became president after the ANC won general elections in 2009. In 2011, major dissent emerged in the ANC political ranks as younger leaders openly attacked Zuma, who has been an incompetent and corrupt leader at a time when leadership was badly needed. The death of the revered Nelson Mandela in 2013 served to underscore the poor leadership of those who followed him in the presidency. In spite of the discontent with the ANC and Zuma, in May 2014 elections the party again won control with 62% of the votes.

Economy

South Africa first came into international economic prominence with the discovery of diamonds (1867) at Kimberly and other mineral wealth, including gold (1886) in the Johannesburg area. Mines and mining came to dominate the national economy, with cheap black labor as a major component of its success. The country is rich in other mineral resources such as platinum and coal. It has the largest deposits of chromium, manganese, vanadium, and platinum in the world and has long been the world's largest producer and exporter of diamonds and gold.

South Africa today is a middle-income, emerging market with an abundant supply of natural resources; well-developed financial, legal, communications, energy, and transport sectors and a stock exchange that is the 15th largest in the world. Even though the country possesses modern infrastructure that supports a relatively efficient distribution of goods to major urban centers throughout the region, some components retard growth. Unemployment, poverty, and inequality remain a challenge, and the economy has stagnated relative to its peers such as Brazil, India, and China. The unemployment rate in South Africa was reported at 25.7% in 2012. This counts only people looking for work; the proportion of the population excluded from formal economy is closer to 40%. Since 2007 there have been periodic electricity shortages. Other major problems are rampant crime and government corruption.

Great Possibilities

In South Africa, a person of relatively modest financial means by U.S. or European standards can live like a person of some wealth. This is especially true for foreign currency holders because of a favorable exchange rate. With the right currency in your offshore bank account, you can live in South Africa like the proverbial king.

Local prices in Rands for real estate are low but rising, but bargains still abound. Many homes traditionally have accommodation for live-in servants whose monthly wages average about US$50. Wages in general are about a tenth of those paid in the U.K. or U.S. for comparable service jobs.

A magnificent 10-room mansion on the Indian Ocean near Cape Town can be bought for US$400,000. Something similar in the U.K. would cost over a million dollars. A luxury flat at cosmopolitan Sea Point on the Atlantic Ocean, in Cape Town, goes for around US$100,000. For retirees, having a flat in South Africa is a perfect way to enjoy the glorious summers (December to April), while the Northern Hemisphere is locked in winter. Summer in subtropical Durban lasts all year round.

South Africa can be a great place to do business, although it is not without its challenges. English is widely spoken, there is a strong international orientation, good infrastructure and tele-communications, and you can drink the local water. The tourism and services sectors are booming, especially in the Cape Town area. The real need is for labor-intensive businesses that will gen-erate local employment, but the country has made little progress in this regard. Reliable electricity has also emerged as a major problem area.

The ANC government has professed its commitment to open markets, privatization and a favorable investment climate with tax incentives to stimulate new investment in labor intensive proj-ects. This is especially the case in expansion of basic infrastruc-ture services, the slow restructuring and partial privatization of state assets, continued reduction of tariffs, subsidies to promote economic efficiency, improved services to the disadvantaged, and integration into the global economy. Serious structural rigidities remain, including a complicated and relatively protectionist trade regime, some currency controls, and highly restrictive labor laws, rooted in the labor union element of the ruling ANC coalition.

Some argue that eventual economic success is guaranteed because labor is plentiful and cheap. Standing in the way, however are unresolved issues of inequality, transparency, and corruption as well as a sense of entitlement among some elements of the population. Continuing white-black earnings differentials are a sore point, but so too are the emergence of super-wealthy black families connected to the ANC.

Skilled individuals are paid wages comparable to other countries to forestall their migration. But the white "brain drain" has been significant. Nevertheless, there is optimism in the business community, largely because the transition to majority black rule occurred much more smoothly than anticipated and the society continues to have a robust internal political discourse.

The major unknown is how long the patience of the black majority will endure. After 20 years of ANC majority rule, most citizens still await "their share" and continue to be mired in poverty and deprivation. The ANC still has not made good on its pledges to "uplift" this impatient majority, and the ANC bureaucracy is just as corrupt and incompetent as the former white National Party rulers. A critical problem is the emergence of interest groups among the black elite who continue to profit from the economic arrangements that originated in the apartheid era, who have significant influence in the ANC.

South African economic policy is fiscally conservative but pragmatic, focusing on controlling inflation, maintaining a budget surplus, and using state-owned enterprises to deliver basic services to low-income areas as a means to increase job growth and household income. The country is one of the few among emerging economies to have avoided significant external public debt in recent years.

Crime

Anyone considering living or investing in South Africa must consider the country's crime rate, which is among the highest in the world. Crime is a significant threat to the welfare of South African citizens. Murder, rape, assault, and armed robbery are prevalent, especially in major cities. Crimes against immigrants from other African countries are particularly common and are rooted in open xenophobia.

Notwithstanding government anti-crime efforts, crimes such as carjacking, mugging, "smash and grab" attacks on vehicles, and other incidents are regularly reported. Crimes against property, such as vehicle hijacking, are often accompanied by violent acts, including murder. Home invasions are common, even in daytime.

In the Western Cape, police resources have been strained by continuing gang conflicts and vigilante violence in the townships near Cape Town. Some townships near major cities, most notably Durban, Johannesburg, and Cape Town, have been scenes of violent demonstrations and factional conflict. Credit card fraud, counterfeit U.S. currency, and various check-cashing scams are frequently reported.

There is still some political violence, although it has significantly decreased in most areas of South Africa since the establishment of a democratically elected government in 1994. Recently, however, there has been an uptick in violent public protest against government corruption and slow and poor service delivery.

Immigration

Since 1995, immigration requirements have tightened in an effort to stem migrations from poorer African countries to the north. South Africa admits only immigrants with special skills unavailable locally. Wages are low and real unemployment hovers around an astronomical 40%. Survival dictates that a huge part of the national economy operates in a gray market totally off the books.

Foreign investors and entrepreneurs receive special treatment. If you are willing to invest approximately US$12,000 to US$17,000, you can apply for a 12-month residence visa, renewable annually. This can lead to a permanent resident visa after three years. A three-year visa is offered to investors who bring R1,500,000 (US$182,000) into South African investments and live there off the income. After five years, one can apply for South African citizenship and a passport.

A South African passport is not one of the best, and visas are required for travel to most European countries. South African citizens do benefit from visa-free travel to many emerging market countries, however.

A major roadblock to foreign investment is currency exchange control that avoid what the government fears would be major capital flight. All foreign exchange transactions are subject to exchange control regulations governed by the South African Reserve Bank. South Africans who travel abroad are permitted a single discretionary allowance of R1 million (US$92,700) per calendar year. The emigration allowance for a whole family is only R200,000. Obviously, foreign nationals should only import as much cash as they need for their immediate purposes, lest they get caught in exchange controls. The South African government has taken steps to gradually reduce remaining foreign exchange controls, which apply only to South African residents.

A South African fortunate enough to have dual citizenship (and many white, English-speaking South Africans do hold U.K. passports) can arrange to transfer assets elsewhere. South Africans who do emigrate are allowed to receive only income earned from capital, but most of that capital must remain in South Africa. These self-defeating controls definitely discourage foreign investors, who might otherwise invest in a developing country with such great potential.

Residence and Citizenship

Residence

In granting residence status emphasis is placed on immigrants who can "make a meaningful contribution to broadening the economic base of South Africa." Applicants must prove several negative tests showing why "…he or she should be declared not to be a prohibited person or an undesirable person." See http://www. home-affairs.gov.za/index.php/permanent-res

Citizenship by naturalization depends upon prior admission for permanent residence. Minors admitted to permanent residence may be granted citizenship without satisfying these conditions upon application by a parent. In the case of permanent resident aliens married to South African citizens, the main requirement for citizenship is residence with the citizen spouse in South Africa for two years.

Permanent residence is governed by the Immigration Act of 2002 and Regulation 33 of the Immigration Regulations. A permit for permanent residence (called an "immigration permit") is available to an applicant who, among other things, is of good character; who will be a desirable inhabitant of the republic; who is not likely to harm the welfare of the republic; and who does not, and is not likely to, pursue an occupation in which there are already sufficient numbers of people available in the republic.

Other provisions allow for (but do not mandate) immediate permanent residence without conditions for destitute, aged, or infirm family members, and for spouses or dependent children of permanent residents and citizens. Normally, applicants for permanent residence apply from outside South Africa. There are exceptions for persons in possession of a temporary residence work permit;

persons who are destitute, aged, or infirm and a member of the family of a permanent resident or citizen who is able and willing to support that person; and persons who are married to or dependent children of permanent residents or citizens.

The Bill of Rights of the 1996 Constitution provides that almost all rights benefit all persons within South Africa, whether they are citizens or aliens. South Africa also recognizes the principle of dual nationality, but with some restrictions.

Citizenship

South African citizenship is granted in three primary ways:

1. By birth: Under existing statutes, citizenship by birth is limited to a child of a South African citizen, or to a child whose parents are both permanent residents. As implemented by the Department of Home Affairs, however, this rule is relaxed to a significant degree; if only one of the parents is a permanent resident, then the citizenship by birth may be claimed by the child of that parent. Children born in South Africa to temporary residents and to undocumented persons do not acquire citizenship at birth.

2. By descent: Citizenship by descent is granted to children born outside the republic who have at least one parent with South African citizenship, where notice of the birth is given to South African authorities. There is no cutoff to this transmission; thus, citizens born outside of South Africa may apparently transmit citizenship to their children born outside South Africa.

The citizenship system, therefore, is a mix of jus soli and jus sanguinis principles. Although most South Africans become citizens under jus soli rules, large numbers of persons born in South Africa do not acquire citizenship at birth. Nonetheless, it seems clear that there is comparatively greater weight placed on the jus soli principle in South Africa than in many other countries. The bar against citizenship for a large class of people born in South Africa makes the conditions for obtaining naturalization of particular importance.

3. By naturalization: For people born in South Africa to parents without permanent residence, it is only through naturalization that there is an opportunity of becoming a citizen. In order to be naturalized, a person must be over 21; be admitted for permanent residence; have been continuously resident for one year before applying for naturalization; have been ordinarily resident for at least four of the eight years preceding the application; be of good character; intend to continue to reside in the republic; be able to communicate in one of the official languages; and have knowledge of the responsibilities and privileges of South African citizenship.

Visa Requirements

Citizens of the U.S., Canada, Australia, and New Zealand need only a valid passport to stay for up to three months in South Africa. EU nationals with a valid passport can stay for up to six months. All visitors need a valid return ticket; if you try to enter South Africa without one, you may be required to deposit the equivalent of your fare home with customs (the money will be refunded to you after you have left the country). Visitors must also be able to prove that they have sufficient funds to cover their stay.

Citizens of other African and most Eastern European countries require a visa to enter South Africa, and this must be obtained before arrival. Visas are not issued at the border. If you come under this category and plan on traveling to Lesotho and Swaziland, you'll need a multi-entry visa to get back into South Africa. If you don't have one, it will be issued free of charge on return, although this can be time consuming.

South Africa has tightened its visa requirements. Only visitors for tourism or short business meetings or in-transit do not require visas. All others visitors, including academics, students on educational trips, and volunteers, may need visas; otherwise they take the chance that they will be refused admission and returned to their point of origin.

Traveler's passports must contain at least two clean (unstamped) pages whenever they enter South Africa. Otherwise, they run the risk of being turned back, even when in possession of a valid South African visa. All travelers are advised to carry a photo copy of the photo/bio information page of their passport and keep it in a location separate from their passport.

Contacts

Embassy of South Africa
3051 Massachusetts Avenue NW
Washington, DC 20008
Tel.: (202) 232-4400
Email: info@saembassry.org
Web: http://www.saembassy.org

Annex for RSA visas, passports, immigration:
4301 Connecticut Avenue NW, Suite 220
Washington, DC 20008
Tel.: (202) 274-7991
Email: consular.wa@dirco.gov.za

United States Embassy
877 Pretorius Street
Arcadia, Pretoria 0001
Republic of South Africa
Tel.: + (27-12) 431-4000
Email: embassypretoria@state.gov

Web: http://southafrica.usembassy.gov/

U.S. Consulate, Cape Town
2 Reddam Avenue, Westlake 7945, RSA
Tel.: +27 (21) 702-7300

U.S. Consulate, Durban
303 Dr. Pixley KaSeme Street, 31st Floor
Old Mutual Center Durban 4001, RSA
Tel.: +27 (31) 305-7600

U.S. Consulate, Johannesburg
1 Sandton Drive, Sandhurst, RSA (Opposite Sandton City Mall)
Tel.: +27 (11) 290-3000

Recommended Immigration Consultant:

Henley & Partners
Building 9, Fairways Office Park
Somerset West
Cape Town 7130
Tel.: +27 21 850 0596
Email: southafrica@henleyglobal.com

Republic of Turkey

Government:	Republican parliamentary democracy
Capital:	Ankara
National Day:	Republic Day: 29 October (1923)
Population:	80,694,485 (July 2013 est.)
Total Area:	301,384 sq. miles / 780,580 sq. kilometers
Languages:	Turkish (official), Kurdish, Dimli (or Zaza), Azeri, Kabardian
Ethnic groups:	Turkish 70-75%, Kurdish 18%, other minorities 7–12%
Religion:	Muslim 99.8% (mostly Sunni), other 0.2% (Christians, Jews)
Life expectancy:	73.03 years
Currency:	Turkish lira (YTL)
GDP:	US$1.109 trillion (2012 est.)
GDP per capita:	US$14,800 (2012 est.)

When you set foot in Türkiye (Turkey), you are following in the wake of some remarkable historical figures. Ottoman sultans used to luxuriate in İstanbul's Topkapı Palace, surrounded by fawning courtiers, harem members, eunuchs and riches from an empire stretching from Budapest to Baghdad. Centuries earlier, Byzantine Christians cut cave churches into Cappadocia's fairy chimneys and hid from Islamic armies in underground cities. At other points over the millennia, Romans coursed down the Curetes Way at Ephesus (Efes), medieval Armenians built Ani's churches on the Anatolian steppe, whirling dervishes gyrated with Sufi mysticism, and the mysterious Lycians left ruins on Mediterranean beaches. Turkey has hosted A-list history-book figures including Julius Caesar, who famously 'came, saw and conquered' near Amasya, and St Paul, who crisscrossed the country.

Of course, Turkey's current inhabitants are just as memorable. The extroverted Turks have the most in common — out of all of their varied neighboring countries, from Azerbaijan to Bulgaria — with their hot-blooded southern-European neighbors. They're also understandably proud of their heritage, and full of information Turkey's long history, coupled with its unique position at the meeting of Europe and Asia, has given it a profound depth of culture.

The greatest surprise for first-time visitors to Turkey, with its stereotypes of kebabs, carpets and mustachioed hustlers in the bazaar, is the sheer diversity found between its Aegean beaches and eastern mountains. In İstanbul, you can cruise — on the Bosphorus as well as through markets and nightclubs — in a Westernized metropolis offering equal parts romance and overcrowded insanity. In holiday spots such as Cappadocia and the southwestern coasts, mix trekking, horse-riding and water sports with meze-savoring on a panoramic terrace. Then there are the less-frequented eastern quarters, where honey-colored outposts overlook the plains of ancient Mesopotamia, and weather-beaten relics add lashings of lyricism to mountain ranges. It's hardly surprising Turkey has attracted so many folk over the centuries. — Lonely Planet

History and Overview

Turkey is located in both southeastern Europe and southwestern Asia (that portion of Turkey west of the Bosporus is geographically part of Europe), bordering the Black Sea, between Bulgaria and Georgia, and bordering the Aegean Sea and the Mediterranean Sea, between Greece and Syria. This transcontinental country also borders in the east on Armenia, Iran, and Iraq.

Modern Turkey was founded in 1923 from the Anatolian remnants of the defeated Ottoman Empire by national hero Mustafa Kemal, who was later honored with the title Ataturk, or "Father of the Turks." Under his authoritarian leadership, the country adopted wide-ranging social, legal, and political reforms. After a period of one-party rule, an experiment with multiparty politics led to the 1950 election victory of the opposition Democratic Party and the peaceful transfer of power. Since then, Turkish political parties have multiplied, but democracy has been fractured by periods of instability and intermittent military coups (1960, 1971, 1980, 2013 to 2014), which, in each past case, eventually resulted in a return of political power to civilians.

In 1997, the military again helped engineer the ouster of the then Islamic-oriented government. Turkey intervened militarily on Cyprus in 1974 to prevent a Greek takeover of the island and has since acted as patron state to the "Turkish Republic of Northern Cyprus," which only Turkey recognizes. (See the section on the Republic of Cyprus).

A separatist insurgency begun in 1984 by the Kurdistan Workers' Party (PKK) — now known as the People's Congress of Kurdistan or Kongra-Gel (KGK) — that has dominated the Turkish military's attention and claimed more than 30,000 lives. Turkey joined the UN in 1945, and in 1952 it became a member of NATO. In 1964, Turkey became an associate member of the European Community; over the past decade, it has undertaken many reforms to strengthen its democracy and economy, enabling it to begin accession membership talks with the European Union. The issue of Turkey's EU membership has become a major debate topic among other EU states, some of which are opposed on the grounds that the country is not really a part of Europe, others because of its Muslim majority.

Turkey is located on a major migration route with increasing numbers of illegal immigrants from the unstable East trying to cross its territory toward Europe. Turkey suffers from having to shelter a huge number of refugees from its neighbors, Iraq (15,000) and Syria (800,000+), the latter as a result of the prolonged civil war there. It already had over a million displaced persons from 1984 to 2005 because of fighting between Kurdish PKK and Turkish military, mostly in eastern and southeastern provinces.

In 2013, violent anti-government protests started when protests against development plans in central Istanbul escalated into a wider expression of continuing discontent with the authoritarian governing style of Erdoğan. Those Turks concerned over their country's secular tradition claim Prime Minister Recep Tayyip Erdoğan is using his parliamentary majority to monopolize all power and push for a gradual Islamization of the Turkish society. Erdoğan, for his part, accuses the protesters of trying to destabilize a democratically elected government.

In early 2014 cabinet resignations occurred over a corruption investigation and demands that Erdoğan quit. In office since 2003, Erdoğan's government has been the subject of a wide-ranging corruption investigation and prosecutors said they planned to charge at least 24 jailed suspects with bribery, money laundering and gold smuggling, among other misdeeds. Erdoğan's response was to push through new laws curbing prosecutions and police investigations. Nevertheless, Erdoğan and his party won a solid re-election victory in 2014.

Economy

The rapid rise of Turkey's economic and political power since 2000 has been the envy of the Middle East. Once a laggard hopelessly chasing the dream of entering the European Union, Turkey has become a regional power in its own right. The economy grew by 5% a year on average between 2002 and 2012, placing Turkey well ahead of the stagnant European economies and its politically troubled regional peers.

Turkey's dynamic economy is a complex mix of modern industry and commerce along with a traditional agriculture sector that still accounts for more than 35% of employment. It has a strong and rapidly growing private sector, yet the state still plays a major role in basic industry, banking, transport, and communication. The largest industrial sector is textiles and clothing, which accounts for one-third of industrial employment; it faces stiff competition in international markets with the end of the global quota system. However, other sectors, notably the automotive and electronics industries are rising in importance within Turkey's export mix. Real GNP growth has exceeded 6% in many years. Economic fundamentals are sound, marked by moderate economic growth and foreign direct investment. Nevertheless, the Turkish economy was faced with more negative economic indicators in 2009 as a result of the global economic slowdown.

After Turkey experienced a severe financial crisis in 2001, Ankara adopted financial and fiscal reforms as part of an IMF program. The reforms strengthened the country's economic fundamentals and ushered in an era of strong growth — averaging more than 6% annually until 2008, when global economic conditions and tighter fiscal policy caused GDP to contract. Turkey's well-regulated financial markets and banking system weathered the global financial crisis and GDP rebounded as exports returned to normal levels.

The economy, however, continues to be burdened by a high current account deficit and remains dependent on often volatile, short-term investment to finance its trade deficit. Turkey's relatively high current account deficit, uncertainty related to monetary policy-making, and political turmoil within Turkey's neighborhood leave the economy vulnerable to destabilizing shifts in investor confidence.

The foreign direct investment stood at US$112 billion in 2012, but inflows have slowed considerably due to continuing economic turmoil in Europe, the source of much of Turkey's foreign investment. Further economic and judicial reforms and prospective EU membership are expected to boost Turkey's attractiveness to foreign investors.

At the end of 2011, with the "Arab Spring" and associated revolutionary turmoil in the Levant continuing, Turkey became embroiled in international disputes with Israel with whom it had formerly been relatively friendly, the issue being Palestine refugees and statehood. An article in About.com News & Issues reported, "In a reversal of its policy of non-interference, Turkey has thrown its weight behind the Syrian rebels. This puts the Sunni Turkey increasingly at odds with the Shiite power Iran, at a time of growing Sunni-Shiite tension in the Middle East."

Residence and Citizenship

Citizenship is conferred in the following ways:

1. by birth: within the territory of Turkey does not automatically confer citizenship except in the case of a child born to unknown or stateless parents.

2. by descent: on a child, at least one of whose parents is a citizen of Turkey, regardless of the child's country of birth.

3. by marriage: a foreign woman who marries a citizen of Turkey may acquire Turkish citizenship upon making a declaration of intent.

4. by naturalization: Turkish citizenship may be acquired upon fulfillment of the following conditions:

   a.) the person has resided in Turkey for at least five years;

   b.) the person has shown intent to remain in Turkey;

   c.) the person is familiar with the Turkish language;

   d.) the person has sufficient means for self-support; and

   e.) the person has no illness threatening public health.

The following persons may be eligible for citizenship without fulfilling the residence requirement:

1. persons of Turkish descent, their spouses, and minor children;

2. a child of a person who, regardless of circumstances, has lost citizenship;

3. a spouse of a Turkish citizen and the spouse's minor children.

Dual citizenship is not recognized. In 2009, an amended Turkish Citizenship Law ended the practice of stripping citizenship from Turkish citizens who have either not fulfilled their required military service, or who have acquired passports to other countries without official approval.

The 2009 law makes changes in citizenship laws for children born to parents in Turkey who are not themselves Turkish citizens, making it easier for the children, and the parents retroactively, to obtain Turkish citizenship.

A foreign passport and visa are required for entry to Turkey. Currently, holders of all types of passports can purchase a 90-day sticker visa at the port of entry if they are traveling to Turkey as tourists. All travelers planning to stay more than three months for any purpose are required to obtain a visa from a Turkish Embassy or consulate. New arrivals who wish to work must apply for a residence/work permit or Turkish ID card within the first month of their arrival. This includes anyone who plans to stay more than three months doing research or studying in Turkey.

Contacts

Embassy of Turkey

2525 Massachusetts Avenue NW
Washington, DC 20008
Tel.: (202) 612-6700
Email: embassy.washingtondc@mfa.gov.tr
Web: http://www.washington.emb.mfa.gov.tr/Default.aspx

Turkish Consulates in Boston, Houston, Los Angeles, New York, and Chicago.

United States Embassy

110 Atatürk Blvd.
Kavaklıdere, 06100 Ankara - Turkey
Tel.: + (90-312) 455-5555
Email: webmasterankara@state.gov
Web: http://turkey.usembassy.gov

U.S. Consulates in Istanbul, Izmir, and Adana

United Arab Emirates

Government:	Federation with specified powers delegated to the UAE federal government and other powers reserved to member emirates
Capital:	Abu Dhabi
National Day:	Independence Day: 2 December (1971)
Population:	5,473,972 (July 2013 est.)
Total Area:	32,278 sq. miles / 83,600 sq. kilometers
Languages:	Arabic (official), Persian, English, Hindi, Urdu Ethnic groups: South Asian 50%, Emirati 19%, other Arab and Iranian 23%, other expatriates (includes Westerners and East Asians) 8%
Religion:	Muslim 96% (Shi'a 16%), Christian, Hindu, and other 4%
Life expectancy:	76.91 years
Currency:	Emirati dirham (AED)
GDP:	US$378.6 billion (2012 est.)
GDP per capita:	US$29,200 (2012 est.)

While the United Arab Emirates (UAE) these days appears to be little more than a stage for Dubai to strut its increasingly crazy stuff, there's far more to this fabulous little federation than Disneyesque dioramas. The UAE is a contradictory destination, an Islamic state where the DJ's turntables stop spinning just before the muezzin' morning call to prayer can be heard, and where a traditional Bedouin lifestyle and customs continue alongside a very Western version of rampant consumerism. While many visitors marvel at the fantastic (in the true sense of the word) hotel and real estate projects, the real wonder is how the savvy sheikhs manage to harmonize such disparate and seemingly opposing forces.

*For Western visitors, the UAE is a very safe Middle East
destination, with the comforts of home and a taste of the exotic. Here, you can max out those credit cards at designer clothes
shops, laze on a gorgeous beach and sip a cocktail as you plan
which fine dining restaurant to book and which international
DJ to dance to until the early morning. On a less hedonistic
stay, you can soak up the atmosphere of the heritage areas or the
magnificent mountain scenery of Hatta, haggle over souvenirs
in the souqs of Sharjah, head out to Abu Dhabi's desert sands
for a camel ride under a star-filled sky, or dive the coral-filled
waters of the Gulf (the beaches near Ras Al-Khaimah are as
unspoiled as you'll anywhere in the region). Or simply mix up
a blend of everything; after all, that's what makes the UAE
unique. — Lonely Planet*

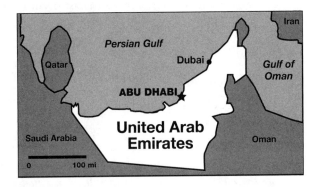

History and Overview

The "UAE" as it is called, is located in the Middle East, bordering the Gulf of Oman and the Persian Gulf, between Oman and
Saudi Arabia south of the strategic Straits of Hormuz.

The Trucial States of the Persian Gulf coast granted the United
Kingdom control of their defense and foreign affairs in 19th century treaties. In 1971, six of these states, Abu Zaby, 'Ajman, Al Fu-
jayrah, Ash Shariqah, Dubayy, and Umm al Qaywayn, merged to

form the United Arab Emirates (UAE). They were joined in 1972 by Ra's al Khaymah.

Economy

The UAE has an open economy with a high per capita income and a sizable annual trade surplus. Successful efforts at economic diversification have reduced the portion of GDP based on oil and gas output to 25%. Since the discovery of oil in the UAE more than 30 years ago, the country has undergone a major transformation from an impoverished region of small desert principalities to a modern state with a high standard of living.

The government has increased spending on job creation and infrastructure expansion and is opening up utilities to greater private sector involvement. In 2004, the UAE signed a Trade and Investment Framework Agreement with Washington and agreed to undertake negotiations toward a Free Trade Agreement with the U.S.; however, nothing has been done since. The country's Free Trade Zones, offering 100% foreign ownership and zero taxes, are attracting foreign investors.

The global financial crisis, tight international credit, and deflated asset prices constricted the economy starting in 2009. UAE authorities tried to blunt the crisis by increasing spending and boosting liquidity in the banking sector. The crisis hit Dubai hardest, since it suffered heavily depressed real estate prices. Dubai lacked sufficient cash to meet its debt obligations, prompting global concern about solvency. The UAE Central Bank and Abu Dhabi-based banks provided bailouts and Dubai received a US$10 billion loan from the emirate of Abu Dhabi. Dependence on oil, a large expatriate workforce, and growing inflation pressures are long-term challenges. The UAE's plans focus on diversification and creating more opportunities for nationals through improved education and increased private sector employment.

In recent years, the United Arab Emirates have made a conscious effort to recreate themselves as offshore financial centers.

Jebel Ali, the first free-trade zone in Dubai, in 2003, led the way as a planned offshore financial center. That was followed by another free-trade zone in the United Arab Emirates, at Ras Al Khaimah (RAK), which also launched an offshore financial facility, hoping to lure investors looking for a new tax haven. RAK created an International Companies Registry which allows foreign investors to register offshore companies without the need to establish a physical presence. Ras Al Khaimah officials hoped foreign companies would find their offshore system more appealing than the Jebel Ali offshore center, which positioned itself as a tax haven comparable to the Cayman Islands, The Bahamas or Liechtenstein. Some observers have predicted the UAE could become a world center for Islamic finance.

The UAE avoided the "Arab Spring" unrest that occurred elsewhere in the Middle East, although political activists and intellectuals signed a petition calling for greater public participation in governance that was widely circulated on the Internet. In an effort to stem potential unrest, the government announced a multi-year, US$1.6 billion infrastructure investment plan for the poorer northern emirates and aggressively pursued silencing advocates of political reform.

Residence and Citizenship

The UAE issues several types of "residence permits" with various restrictions and length of time. Usually these deal with employment and are sponsored by a UAE company. These include permits for family, relative, student and domestic help. A "Real Estate Investor Visa" is sponsored by a "Master Developer" for foreigners who purchase properties and can prove a monthly income of 10,000 AED (US$2,700).

UAE citizenship in 1971 was conferred on all persons who were legal citizens of the separate Emirates at the time of the unionization of the new country. Citizenship may be conferred in the following ways:

1. by birth: birth within the UAE territory does not automatically confer citizenship, except in the case of a child born of unknown parents.

2. by descent: citizenship applies to all persons born on or after January 1, 1972, as follows:

   a.) a child of a UAE father, regardless of the child's country of birth;

   b.) a child born out of wedlock will obtain citizenship upon being legally recognized by the father;

   c.) a child of a UAE mother and an unknown father, regardless of the child's country of birth;

   d.) children of UAE fathers automatically acquire UAE citizenship at birth and must enter the UAE on UAE passports.

3. by marriage: a foreign woman who marries a UAE citizen may obtain citizenship, provided the woman resides three years in the country after application for citizenship, has given up previous citizenship, and has obtained approval of the Ministry of the Interior. A foreign husband is not eligible for citizenship.

4. by naturalization: citizenship may be acquired by various groups of persons under the following conditions:

   a.) citizens of Qatar, Oman and Bahrain who must have resided in the UAE for three years;

b.) citizens of Arab descent who must have resided in the UAE for seven years.

A foreign passport is required for entry. For stays of less than 60 days, U.S. citizens holding valid passports may obtain visitor visas at the port of entry for no fee. For a longer stay, a traveler must obtain a visa before arrival in the UAE.

In addition, an AIDS test is required for work or residence permits; testing must be performed after arrival. A U.S. AIDS test is not accepted. Unlike other countries in the region that accept U.S. military ID cards as valid travel documents, the UAE requires U.S. military personnel to present a valid passport for entry/exit.

The UAE government does not recognize dual nationality. UAE authorities have confiscated U.S. passports of UAE/U.S. dual nationals in the past. This act does not constitute loss of U.S. citizenship, but should be reported to the U.S. Embassy in Abu Dhabi or the U.S. Consulate General in Dubai. In addition to being subject to all UAE laws, U.S. citizens who also hold UAE citizenship may also be subject to other laws that impose special obligations on citizens of the UAE.

Contacts
Embassy of the U.A.E.
3522 International Court NW
Washington, DC 20008
Tel.: (202) 243-2400
Email contact: http://www.uae-embassy.org/contact-embassy
Web: http://www.uae-embassy.org/

United States Embassy
P.O. Box 4009
Abu Dhabi, UAE
Tel.: + (971) 2-414-2200

Email: abudhabiACS@state.gov
Web: http://abudhabi.usembassy.gov/

U.S. Consul General, Dubai

Dubai World Trade Center
P.O. Box 9343, Dubai, UAE
Tel.: + (971) 4-311-6000

Commercial Office
Tel.: + (971) 4-311-6149
Web: http://dubai.usconsulate.gov/

Recommended Immigration Consultant:

Henley & Partners

Reef Tower, Suite #1301
P.O. Box 213757
Dubai, United Arab Emirates
Tel.: +971 56 172 0054
Email: dubai@henleyglobal.com

SECTION 6

ASIA AND OCEANIA

Commonwealth of Australia

Government:	Federal parliamentary democracy
Capital:	Canberra
National Day:	Australia Day: 26 January (1788)
Population:	22,262,501 (July 2013 est.)
Total Area:	2,967,909 sq. miles / 7,686,850 sq. kilometers
Languages:	English 78.5%, Chinese 2.5%, Italian 1.6%, Greek 1.3%, Arabic 1.2%, Vietnamese 1%, other 8.2%, unspecified 5.7%
Ethnic groups:	Caucasian 92%, Asian 7%, Aboriginal and other 1%
Religion:	Catholic 25.8%, Anglican 18.7%, Uniting Church 5.7%, Presbyterian and Reformed 3%, Eastern Orthodox 2.7%, other Christian 7.9%, Buddhist 2.1%, Muslim 1.7%, other 2.4%, unspecified 11.3%, none 18.7%
Life expectancy:	81.98 years
Currency:	Australian dollar (AUD)
GDP:	US$1.6 trillion (2013 est.)
GDP per capita:	US$42,000 (2012 est.)

Island, country, continent… Australia is a big'un whichever way you spin it. The essence of the place is diversity: deserts, coral reefs, tall forests, snow-cloaked mountains and multicultural melting-pot cities.

Most Australians live along the coast, and most of these folks live in cities. In fact, Australia is the 18th-most urbanized country in the world, with around 70% of Australians living in the 10 largest towns. It follows that cities here are a lot of fun!

Sydney, the sun-kissed Harbor City, is a glamorous collusion of beaches, boutiques and bars. Melbourne is all arts, alleyways and Australian Rules football. Brisbane is a subtropical town on the way up; Adelaide has festive grace and pub poise. Boomtown Perth breathes west-coast optimism; Canberra transcends political agendas. If you're looking for contrast, the tropical northern frontier town of Darwin and chilly southern sandstone city of Hobart couldn't be more different. But whichever city you're wheeling into, you'll never go wanting for a decent coffee, live bands, art-gallery openings or music festival mosh-pits.

Australia has broken the binds of its Anglo meat-and-two-veg culinary past, serving up a multicultural fusion of European techniques and fresh Pacific-rim ingredients. 'Mod Oz' (or Modern Australian) is what the locals call it. Seafood plays a starring role. And of course, beer in hand, you'll still find beef, lamb and chicken at traditional Aussie BBQs. Australian wines are world-beaters. Italian cafes have always known how to make the perfect espresso, but now there are coffee machines in pubs and petrol stations, and baristas in downtown coffee carts — you're never far from a double-shot, day or night.

There's a heckuva lot of tarmac across this wide brown land. From Margaret River to Cooktown, Jabiru to Dover, the best way to really appreciate Australia is to hit the open road. Australia's national parks and secluded corners are custom-made for down-the-dirt-road camping trips. So embrace your inner road warrior and sing it loud: "Get your motor runnin'... Head out on the highway..." — Lonely Planet

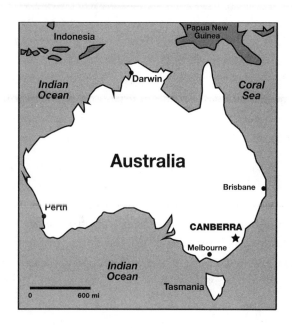

History and Overview

Australia is the sixth-largest continent in the world, situated between the Pacific Ocean to the east and the Indian Ocean to its west. The country derives its name from the Latin word australes, meaning "southern" the word once commonly used to describe the Southern Hemisphere below the equator.

Almost half of the Australian continent lies in the tropics, with much of the north coast consisting of rain forests and marshy lowlands. Off the northeastern coast, the Great Barrier Reef extends for nearly 1,300 miles southward from the tip of the Cape York Peninsula, covering an area of more than 135,000 square miles. Its 2,800 individual reefs harbor 1,500 species of fish amid 400 types of coral. Ecotourism in Australia does not stop there, however.

Australia is home to 10% of the world's biodiversity, and a great number of its flora and fauna exist nowhere else in the world. The continent contains a vast range of landforms and habitats, home to populations of animals and plants of types that are rare or non-existent in the rest of the world. Against that backdrop, most of Australia's major cities, Sydney, Melbourne, and Perth, among others, lie in the temperate zone and are recognized as among the world's most vibrant and attractive places to visit and live.

There is strong evidence that the Aborigine people were living in Australia at least 40,000 years ago. They were first sighted or partly discovered by Spanish and Dutch navigators (the first European structure on Australian soil was a gallows on the desolate west coast to hang murderous mutineers of the wrecked Dutch ship, the Batavia). The Dutch charted the coast of Tasmania in 1642. Australia's fertile east coast was explored by Captain James Cook who claimed the territory as New South Wales for King George III on August 22, 1770.

On January 26, 1788, Captain Arthur Phillip arrived at Botany Bay to establish the penal settlement which became Sydney. Self-government was introduced for the colony of New South Wales in 1850, and, in 1901, the by then six colonies federated as the Commonwealth of Australia, a self-governing Dominion of the British Crown. Unlike other countries, full independence was an evolutionary process starting with adoption of the Statute of Westminster in 1942 and only legally completed in 1986 when the U.K. parliament passes the Australia Act.

The new country took advantage of its natural resources to rapidly develop agricultural and manufacturing industries and to make a major contribution to the Allied effort in World Wars I and II. Australia has become an internationally competitive, advanced market economy due to economic reforms adopted in the 1980s and its location in one of the fastest growing regions of the world economy. Long-term concerns include de-industrialization due to "Dutch disease" and inflated utility costs, an aging population, pressure on infrastructure, and environmental issues such as floods, droughts, and bushfires. Australia is the driest inhabited continent on earth, making it particularly vulnerable to the challenges of climate change.

In 2013, Prime Minister Anthony John "Tony" Abbott and his Liberal/National Coalition were elected with 53.45% of the vote, defeating the Labor Party.

Economy

Australia has a prosperous Western-style capitalist economy with a per capita GDP at the level of dominant Western European economies. Rich in natural resources, Australia is a major exporter of agricultural products, minerals, metals, and fossil fuels. Commodities account for 57% of the value of total exports, so that a downturn in world commodity prices could have a big impact on the economy. Exports, such as iron ore and natural gas, go largely to China, Europe, North America and Latin America. The government is pushing for increased exports of manufactured goods, but competition in international markets continues to be severe.

High electricity and other input costs have recently seen the announced closure of car manufacturing in Australia by Ford, GM and Toyota. Australia suffered from the low growth and high unemployment characterizing European countries in the early 1990s, but the economy has expanded at reasonably steady rates in recent years. Canberra's emphasis on reforms is a key factor behind the economy's resilience to the Asian regional crisis (cushioned by a falling floating exchange rate) and its stronger than expected growth rates.

The Australian economy has experienced continuous growth and features low unemployment, contained inflation, very low public debt, and a strong and stable financial system (though concerns have been raised about increasing Federal and State debts as well as private mortgage borrowing in a land price boom). To date, Australia has experienced more than 22 years of continuous economic growth, averaging 3.5% a year. Demand for resources and energy from Asia and especially China has grown rapidly, creating a channel for resources investments and growth in commodity exports.

The strong Australian dollar has hurt the manufacturing sector, while the services sector is the largest part of the economy, accounting for about 70% of GDP and 75% of jobs. Australia was comparatively unaffected by the global financial crisis as the banking system remained strong and inflation was kept under control (thanks partly to cheaper imported goods which have partly offset escalation of domestic utility and other costs).

Australia has benefited from a dramatic surge in trade in recent years and from rising global commodity prices. It is a significant exporter of natural resources, energy, and food. Australia's abundant and diverse natural resources attract high levels of foreign investment and include extensive reserves of coal, iron, copper, gold, natural gas, uranium, and renewable energy sources. A series of major investments, such as the US$40 billion Gorgon Liquid Natural Gas project, will significantly expand the resources sector. The country is an open market with minimal restrictions on imports of goods and services. This open policy has increased productivity, stimulated growth, and made the economy more flexible and dynamic.

Australia plays an active role in the World Trade Organization, APEC, the G20, and other trade forums. It has bilateral free trade agreements (FTAs) with Chile, Malaysia, New Zealand, Singapore, Thailand, and the U.S., has a regional FTA with ASEAN and New Zealand, is negotiating agreements with China, India, Indonesia, Japan, and the Republic of Korea, as well as with its Pacific neighbors and the Gulf Cooperation Council countries, and is also working on the Trans-Pacific Partnership Agreement with Brunei Darussalam, Canada, Chile, Malaysia, Mexico, New Zealand, Peru, Singapore, the U.S., and Vietnam.

Residence and Citizenship

Australia was founded as a nation of immigrants — a penal colony for those who languished in 18th century British Imperial jails. After it became a Commonwealth in 1901, it actively courted new immigrants from the "Mother Country." Also in 1901, Parliament passed the Immigration Restriction Act, intended to protect local wages being undercut by cheap imported non-European labor, (such as indentured islanders working on Queensland sugar farms). The Act effectively enshrined a "White Australia" policy that persisted for most of the 20th century.

Australia's population has more than tripled since World War II, and the former "all white, all English, Scottish and Irish" flavor has been replaced by a cosmopolitan mix including six million immigrants, Italians, Greeks, Slavs, and Russian Jews. Since 1990, a growing movement to curb new immigration has taken hold, largely because of the influx of Southeast Asians seeking citizenship.

Australia's population has grown in recent years to an estimated 22.2 million in 2013, helped in part by record immigration levels. The country has experienced the largest immigration influx in decades. In 2006 to 2007, nearly 150,000 new immigrants were admitted. Along with immigration, increased birth rates helped to bolster the population.

Previous population booms in Australia were experienced after World War II and during the 1980s. Australia's official policy seeks skilled worker immigrants and investors. There are numerous immigration categories, and it pays to verify which is most appropriate for you, because immigration is possible under two or more categories. In some cases, temporary visas can be replaced by permanent migration visas.

This is also true for investors and business immigrants. Australia is also an ideal place to retire, and, to this end, Australia offers a special visa for retirees, (minimum age 55 years old).

After only four years of residence in Australia (subject to some restrictions on interim absences), it is possible to become a citizen and to obtain an Australian passport, which is an added attraction to some immigrants from countries whose passports restrict their traveling (such as India, China and Vietnam). Many international businessmen from Asia settle in Australia to obtain this very attractive passport. Visas generally have an English language requirement and may have age restrictions.

Residence

The residence requirements for people seeking citizenship who first become permanent residents are as follows:

1. lawful resident in Australia for four years immediately before applying;

2. at least 12 months as a permanent resident; and

3. may not have been absent from Australia for more than 12 months, including no more than a three-month absence in the 12 months immediately prior to applying.

If you want to immigrate to Australia, depending on the category you choose, your age, education, professional occupation and experience, and other factors are assessed against a points system. A temporary business visa is available with a business investment of as little as A$250,000 (US$244,500).

In order to be eligible for a grant of citizenship by naturalization, an applicant must:

1. be a permanent resident;

2. usually have been present in Australia as a permanent resident for four years in the previous five years, including for 12 consecutive months in the past two years;

3. be of good character;

4. have a basic knowledge of English; (people age 60 and over are exempt from having to pass a basic English test)

5. have an adequate knowledge of the responsibilities and privileges of being an Australian citizen; and

6. intend to live in, or maintain a close and continuing association with Australia.

Citizenship is conferred on a child born of at least one Australian citizen parent. Under the law, a person may be registered as a citizen by descent if the application for registration is made before the person turns 25. All applicants over the age of 16 must be of good character. You may be asked to provide additional information, including police clearance certificates, once you have submitted your application.

The 2007 Australian Citizenship Act, the most comprehensive revamp of immigration law since the Citizenship Act of 1948 tightened the rules governing who becomes a citizen. In the post-9/11 anti-terrorism era the changes were said to be partly a response to security concerns. The Australian Security Intelligence Organization now has the power to veto a person's citizenship application if they deem them to be a direct or indirect security risk.

Dual Citizenship

Australia now recognizes dual citizenship. Before 2002, a person ceased to be an Australian citizen by acquiring the citizenship or nationality of another country. The Australian Citizenship Act of 2007 allows reinstatement for former Australian citizens who were forced to end their citizenship because of laws in other nations while living or working elsewhere.

Prior to January 1, 1949, all Australians were simply British subjects and British subject status continued to be relevant for many legal purposes, such as public sector employment, until the 1990s. In June 1999, the High Court of Australia held, for the first time, that the United Kingdom was a "foreign power" for the purposes of citizenship law following the Australia Act of 1986. The 1948 Citizenship Act meant that Australians, who moved away and were naturalized elsewhere, were stripped of their original nationality. About 50,000 Australians, including at least 15,000 war brides who moved to the U.S., lost citizenship between 1948 and 2002.

Oddly, one category of expatriate Australians included about 2,000 Australian-born citizens who were forced to renounce their citizenship in order to acquire full rights as Maltese citizens. Under the 1948 Act, about 3,000 Maltese children with Australian-born parents also were not allowed Australian citizenship. With a 2007 law change, these Maltese are now allowed to re-apply for Australian citizenship.

Points System

As in neighboring New Zealand, Australia awards "points" toward residence based on education, work experience, age, and language skills.

Points are added for family members or a sponsor in Australia. With certain job skills in demand by the government (job lists available at any consulate), an immigration application can be given priority. The process takes several months, but some applications take much longer.

Formerly, citizenship and a passport were granted to desired new immigrants only one year after arrival. Now, it takes four years to obtain citizenship and a passport. That is still shorter than the world average of five years in-country residence periods, with no fees or investments required by job qualified immigrants.

Under the General Skilled Migration (GSM) program, the points-based system is designed to attract skilled foreign workers. Its requirements include English language proficiency, emphasis on skilled work experience, and a simplified GSM visa structure. A temporary work visa is granted to graduates. There are nine GSM visa subclasses that allow applicants to easily identify the visa subclass best suited to their occupation.

Marriage and Relatives

Those with family in Australia, or who marry an Australian, can more easily gain residence, but citizenship still requires two years residence. Australia, along with Denmark, the Netherlands, New Zealand, Belgium, France, Iceland, Norway, Sweden and some Canadian provinces and several American states now officially recognize same-sex relationships for migration, taxation and social security purposes but "same-sex marriage" is not recognized.

Couples must prove they have lived together for six months in order for the non-Australian partner to qualify for residence.

The following persons may qualify if their sponsor has been an Australian citizen or a permanent resident for at least two years and has the following relationship to the sponsor: spouses, fiancés, adopted children, parents, orphan relatives, special needs relatives, aged dependent relatives, remaining "isolated" relatives, and inter-dependent partners.

Business and Investor Program

For 15 years, the government has promoted an official business migration program. Prior applicants only had to show assets of A$500,000 (US$450,000), and intent to transfer the money into an Australian investment or bank account. They were initially granted permanent residence and the unlimited right to enter and leave Australia, and then, after two years of residence, Australian citizenship.

This program was a bonanza for private "immigration consultants," who were paid by the government to do screening, but this program was attacked because of the ability of would-be immigrants to circumvent currency controls.

The current scheme concentrates more on business experience than wealth. A system similar to those used in Canada and New Zealand requires applicants to score a minimum number of points, with awards based on age, existing type and size of business, assets, and English language skills.

Applications are reviewed by Department of Immigration officials, as well as by private sector consultants. Stricter monitoring procedures are in place, and a business skills visa can be canceled if its holder does not attempt to start a business within three years. Australia's immigration policy now favors people who establish permanent ties to the country rather than those who merely own capital investments there.

The stricter terms described above dramatically reduced applicants for the business migration program. During ten years of the former program, about 10,000 immigrants and 30,000 dependents were admitted to Australia.

As a result, the business migration program was substantially revised again making the "investor" citizenship more accessible. This category requires individuals to invest between A$750,000 (US$674,000) and A$2 million (US$1.8 million) in designated government securities for a minimum of three years. Successful applicants must show satisfactory business or investment skills. Recent business and management experience is essential.

Present parameters for the program require individuals to have a personal net worth greater than A$2.5 million (US$2.247 million). They must invest from A$1.5 million (US$1.348 million) to A$2 million (US$1.797 million) to be granted a four-year provisional investor's visa, leading to permanent residence and naturalization. If the investment is in a state-sponsored project, the probationary period is decreased to two years.

In the past, applications were only accepted from people situated in their home country. Now, business people can have applications processed while they are in Australia on a temporary stay. The government actively promotes the business migration program abroad and has simplified travel arrangements for this class of immigrant.

Business migration applicants do undergo a background check, which is intended to screen for major criminals. A conviction for something not considered a major crime in Australia will not necessarily be held against the applicant.

Preferred industries include non-polluting, high-tech and export-oriented enterprises. Real estate "investors" are unwelcome, since Australians think "speculators" have already pushed land prices too high. Agriculture, Australia's major industry, has suffered from historically low commodity rates caused by the erosion of traditional European markets. Any product or service that would help local farmers compete more effectively will get fast consideration and approval.

Once residence is obtained, there is a simple, straightforward path toward citizenship. Permanent residents are free to leave and return to Australia and, after four years of residence immediately before the application, can apply for citizenship. The four-year residence need not be continuous, but absences cannot be longer than one year in total and no more than 90 days in the year before applying. There is also a brief interview and submission of required proofs, including testimony to good character.

This expansion of the business migration program has definitely opened things up and the number of applicants has risen dramatically.

Business migration visa details can be found at http://www.immi.gov.au/skilled/business/

Working Holiday Visa

This visa offers an excellent way for young people to establish a temporary residence and explore various options available for permanent residence and for later citizenship.

To qualify under this program, an applicant must: 1) be 18 to 25 years old; 2) desire to travel extensively in Australia, while working to supplement holiday funds; 3) hold a valid U.K., Irish, Canadian, Dutch, or Japanese passport; 4) have a return air ticket, or money for a return fare, plus "normal maintenance" finances for the duration of the planned holiday, about US$3,000; and; 5) be childless.

The "Holiday Visa" is for young traveling types who want to supplement their funds with part-time casual work. In actual practice, the type of work or length of stay is limited only by the jobs available. The money requirement can be met with proof of a bank account balance. Once the visa is granted, no further checks are made. This visa does not qualify the holder for a passport, but it can lead to permanent residence based on in-country contact.

U.S. citizens and other eligible passport holders from more than 60 countries can apply online for visitor, business and short-term work visas. See the "Find a visa" service is at: http://www.immi.gov.au/Visas/Pages/Find-a-visa.aspx

Taxes

Individuals whose annual stay in Australia exceeds 183 days are considered residents for tax purposes, unless they prove Australia is not their home and they have no intention of establishing permanent residence in the country.

In the past workers admitted to Australia from outside the country under various skilled work visas were not required to declare their offshore income on their Australian tax forms. Work permit holders pay taxes on all income generated while working in Australia, but their foreign income is tax exempt.

Resident taxpayers are taxed on their worldwide income. Migrants (permanent residents) and visitors, who are subject to Australian taxes, must pay taxes on income derived from business activities in their country of origin or elsewhere offshore. Tax returns must be filed annually. Non-resident taxpayers are also liable for taxes on ordinary income earned in Australia, and interest and dividends from Australian bank accounts or shares in an Australian company. Offshore business activities of non-resident taxpayers are not generally subject to taxation.

At the disposal of assets, a capital gains tax is imposed. Land, buildings and other assets situated in Australia as well as shares in Australian private companies and interests of 10% or more in public companies are all taxable. These stiff rules prompt some to sell certain assets before taking up residence.

There is a temporary loophole for some approved business migrants who initially may escape designation as a resident for tax purposes. They must show intent to establish a permanent business in Australia but they need not immediately settle there. They can return to their country of origin, or travel elsewhere to honor existing business commitments.

Absences from Australia are restricted only by the requirement that the migrant makes genuine efforts to establish a business in Australia. However, if they are in Australia for less than 183 days annually, they are not subject to Australian taxation. If they eventually wish to apply for citizenship, sooner or later, they cannot avoid becoming a resident for tax purposes.

In the past, before the anti-offshore tax crackdown, tax authorities accepted to some extent the use of offshore trusts that were established before immigration. Now, offshore trusts must be reported, where an Australian resident is either deriving trust income or has contributed to the trust fund.

Unlike the U.S., Australians who evade taxes are not usually sent to jail, but an offender faces a civil fine plus penalties and interest on the amount owed. However, tax fraud (including wilful non-disclosure) and other tax-related crimes that violate Australian law are punished harshly; with offenders prosecuted, jailed and even extradited from other countries. Failure to report accurate income from interest, dividends or profits on a personal tax return may be tax evasion, but in Australia it is not usually treated as a crime.

For a tax crime to be prosecuted as such there must usually be proof of active fraud, such as submission of false and forged bills and receipts seeking to justify false deductions and losses. In recent years, Australian tax collectors have been in a much publicized hot pursuit of citizens it alleges to be engaged in offshore tax evasion. This has included police raids on private homes and offices, not only of accused taxpayers, but of their lawyers and accountants as well.

Since 2005 and the discovery of wealthy Australians who were evading taxes with offshore accounts and trusts in tax havens such as Switzerland, Liechtenstein and Jersey, the Tax Office and Federal Police have gone on an anti-offshore tax offensive, titled "Project Wickenby." Individuals' homes and offices have been raided by armed police and government tax agents, as have the offices and files of their attorneys. All this official strong arm activity has raised issues of civil liberties, such as in cases where a person has been compelled to testify against his/her spouse.

It has even gone so far as government authorities preventing a naturalized American citizen leaving the country after his mother's funeral on the basis of asserted tax claims — none other than the well-known actor (and former Australian), Paul Hogan, better known as "Crocodile Dundee." He was held for almost two months for alleged non-payment of several years of Australian income taxes, until he proved that during the period in question he was a U.S. permanent resident alien who paid U.S. taxes as U.S. law required, for which he was due credit under a U.S.-Australian double taxation treaty!

In 2012 it was announced that the government was actively engaged in negotiations with the U.S. Treasury looking toward an agreement for the enforcement of FATCA in Australia. As of early 2014, no final announcement had been made.

An Australian passport can be obtained by an Australian citizen without paying any legal fees, gratuities or under-the-table money, other than the normal fee. For intending migrants, a visit to your nearest Australian Consulate is the best plan to check possible visa categories (as these change from time to time). Pick up their brochures and job preference list. This has a do-it-yourself rating scale to figure out if you score enough points to qualify. And remember, after just four years of residence, you might qualify for a passport.

The Australian Citizenship Act does allow the government discretionary power to waive residence requirements for certain people in exceptional cases.

U.S. citizens are required to have a valid U.S. passport to enter Australia. Americans may enter with an Australian visa or, if eligible, through Electronic Travel Authority (ETA). The ETA, which replaces a visa and allows a stay of up to 90 days, is free when obtained from airlines and many travel agents in the United States.

U.S. citizens who overstay their ETA or visa, even for short periods, may be subject to detention and removal. The ETA may be obtained for a service fee at http://www.eta.immi.gov.au/. More information about the ETA and entry requirements may be obtained from the Embassy of Australia in Washington, D.C.

Further information:

http://www.immi.gov.au/Pages/Welcome.aspx

http://www.austlii.edu.au/au/legis/cth/consol_act/aca2007254/ (Australian Citizenship Act)

http://www.austlii.edu.au/au/legis/cth/consol_act/ma1958118/ (Migration Act)

Contacts
Embassy of Australia
1601 Massachusetts Avenue NW
Washington, DC 20036
Tel.: (202) 797-3000
Web: http://www.usa.embassy.gov.au

Consulates General: New York, San Francisco, Honolulu, Los Angeles, and Chicago.

United States Embassy
Moonah Place, Yarralumla
Canberra, Australian Capital Territory 2600
Tel.: + (61) 26-214-5600
Email: usrsaustralia@state.gov
Web: http://canberra.usembassy.gov/

Recommended Attorney:

Terence M. Dwyer, CTA
Ph.D. (Harvard), Dip. Law (Sydney)
Dwyer Lawyers
Suite 4, Level 2,
161 London Circuit, Canberra City ACT 2601
Tel.: + 61 (02) 6247 8184
Email: Email: info@dwyerlawyers.com.au
Web: http://www.dwyerlawyers.com.au/

People's Republic of China

Government:	Communist Party state
Capital:	Beijing
National Day:	Founding of Peoples Republic: 1 October (1949)
Population:	1,349,585,838 (July 2013 est.)
Total Area:	3,705,407 sq. miles / 9,596,960 sq. kilometers
Languages:	Standard Chinese or Mandarin (Putonghua, based on Beijing dialect), Yue (Cantonese), Wu (Shanghaiese), Minbei (Fuzhou), Minnan (Hokkien-Taiwanese), Xiang, Gan, Hakka dialects, minority languages
Ethnic groups:	Han Chinese 91.5%, Zhuang, Uygur, Hui, Yi, Tibetan, Miao, Manchu, Mongol, Buyi, Korean, and other nationalities 8.5%
Religion:	Taoist, Buddhist, Christian 3%-4%, Muslim 1%-2%. The nation is officially atheist.
Life expectancy:	74.99 years
Currency:	Renminbi, yuan (RMB)
GDP:	US$13.37 trillion (2013 est.)
GDP per capita:	US$9,800 (2013 est.)

Antique yet up-to-the-minute, familiar yet unrecognizable, outwardly urban but quintessentially rural, conservative yet path-breaking, space-age but old-fashioned, China is a land of mesmerizing and eye-opening contradictions.

China is an epic adventure. From the wide open and empty panoramas of annexed Tibet to the push and shove of Shanghai, from the volcanic dishes of Sichuān to beer by the bag in seaside Qīngdao, a journey through this colossus of a country is a mesmerizing encounter with the most populous, perhaps most culturally idiosyncratic nation on earth.

The sheer diversity of China's terrain takes you from noisy cities fizzing with energy to isolated mountain-top Ming-Dynasty villages where you can hear a pin drop. Pudong's ambitious skyline is a triumphant statement, but it couldn't be further from the worldly renunciation acted out in conquered Tibet's distant monasteries.

Curator of the world's oldest continuous civilization, China will have you bumping into history at every turn. But, it's not just a museum of imperial relics: the frisson of development that has left China's coastline glittering with some of the world's most up-to-the-minute cities propels the land on with a forward-thinking dynamism.

And it's the people — unavoidable in their immense numbers — who provide the ceaseless drama and entertainment. Loud, garrulous and quick thinking, you'll see the Chinese squeezing onto dangerous-looking buses, walking in pajamas around Shanghai or inviting each other to sit down to some of the most varied cuisine in the world. Animated by a palpable sense of pride, the Chinese are reveling in their country's ascendency. Everyone is talking about China, so why not find out what all the fuss is about? — Lonely Planet

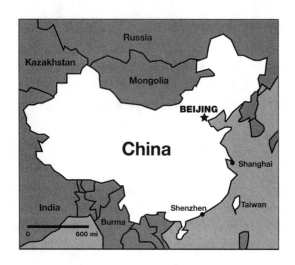

History and Overview

China is located in eastern Asia, bordering the East China Sea, Korea Bay, Yellow Sea, and South China Sea, between North Korea and Vietnam.

The history of China, as documented in ancient writings, dates back some 3,300 years. Modern archaeological studies provide evidence of still more ancient origins in a culture that flourished between 2500 and 2000 B.C. in what is now central China and the lower Huang He (Yellow River) Valley of North China. Centuries of migration, amalgamation and development brought about a distinctive system of writing, philosophy, art, and political organization that came to be recognizable as Chinese civilization. What makes the civilization unique in world history is its continuity through over 4,000 years to the present century.

For centuries, China stood as a leading civilization, outpacing the rest of the world in the arts and sciences, but in the 19th and early 20th centuries, the country was beset by civil unrest, major famines, military defeats, and foreign occupation.

After World War II, the Communists under Mao Zedong established an autocratic socialist system that, while ensuring China's sovereignty, imposed strict controls over everyday life and cost the lives of tens of millions of people. After 1978, his successor, Deng Xiaoping, and other leaders focused on market-oriented economic development and, by 2000, output had quadrupled. For much of the population, living standards have improved dramatically and the room for personal choice has expanded, yet political controls remain tight.

The People's Republic of China was established on October 1, 1949, with Beijing as its capital city. With well over 1.3 billion citizens, China is the world's most populous country and the third largest country in the world in terms of territory. China is undergoing rapid, profound economic and social change and development. Political power remains centralized in the Chinese Communist Party.

China: Past and Future

Thirty-five years ago, in 1979, I spent a week in China as part of an official delegation when I was a Member of the U.S. House of Representatives. We met with Deng Xiaoping in the Great Hall of the People in Beijing's Tiananmen Square.

The impression I came away with back then was of a backward, Third World nation, tightly controlled by the Communist Party that still governs, as it has since Mao's successful 1949 revolution. The people seemed downcast, dressed in the same drab, Mao padded jackets and cotton shoes; the hotels were old and musty; and evidence of Western commerce consisted of Coca-Cola bottles in a glass case at the backwater Beijing airport. Cars were few, and bicycles clogged the streets, coal smoke filled the air and cabbages hung from every window sill and balcony — the government distributed them in piles in the streets since it was the one of the few foods available for millions in the winter months.

The rise of China on the world stage is one of the monumental stories of our time. Yet despite its modernization, China is still ruled by an authoritarian communist regime, one that does not hesitate to use deadly violence to enforce its rule, as it has in Tibet and more recently, to put down popular uprisings that are becoming much more frequent in protest of government corruption.

After 25 years, the changes I saw in China during a return visit were astounding. Today, China is a modern nation in every respect, at least in its major cities, and I did visit Beijing, Shanghai and Hangzhou, with air and road travel in between. Today the streets are filled with fashionably dressed workers and business people, teenagers and young students wearing the latest fashions from the U.S. and Europe.

In 2014, the scene has cooled more than a little, as the global recession has had its impact. During my visit in China, redevelopment and massive construction was happening in urban areas. Literally thousands of construction sites, high rises for apartments, sometimes 50 stories high, new offices and factories, new super highways and overpasses (flyovers), and every airport was spacious and modern.

In fact, the Chinese infrastructure is in stark contrasts to the pot-holed roads and streets in the U.S. and America's congested airports, but then in China, almost everything is new — and Western business and products are everywhere — from high-fashion designer shops, to names you know.

Within a block of the St. Regis Hotel in Beijing, where we (and a week later, President George W. Bush) stayed, there were shops and eateries bearing the familiar signs of 7-Eleven, Haagen-Dazs, Sizzler Steakhouse, McDonald's, KFC, and the ubiquitous Starbuck's, plus a Tex Mex taco place.

There even was a Starbuck's inside the Forbidden City at Tiananmen Square, until a young nationalist movement convinced the government to remove this capitalist symbol. No doubt the last Emperor, Pu Yi, would be rolling in his imperial grave had he not been brainwashed by the Communists, who deposed him and reduced him to a humble gardener.

Walk down the main thoroughfare, Nanjing Road, in Shanghai, and you see not only huge Chinese department stores, but major shops selling Versace, Dolce & Gabbana, Ermenegildo Zegna — or how about a sleek new Bentley, Mercedes Benz or BMW from the shining art-deco showrooms of local Chinese auto dealers? Buicks and VWs (made in China) clog the streets, replacing the thousands of bicycles I recall from my earlier visit in 1979.

In a book that gives an excellent description of modern China (One Billion Customers by James McGregor, Wall Street Journal Books, 2005), the author says the Chinese have "nothing to believe in but making money." And it is very apparent that a minority of those 1.3 billion people are upwardly mobile from the dreary life of 1979 I witnessed.

But China is a social powder keg of haves and have-nots, with state socialism being replaced by a Chinese brand of semi-capitalism.

The question is — how long can the relatively few Communists (maybe a million or so that staff the police, military and government) keep the lid on. All this growing, glowing wealth for the many, still leaves the many more out in the cold. And once the more or less free market has been allowed to operate for a while in China when will the peoples, whose republic it is said to be, demand a voice in their own governance?

The press and media are totally controlled, official corruption occurs at every level, there have been thousands of local citizen uprisings, protesting taxes and corruption, many of them met with bullets and jail.

Would I invest in this state controlled, corrupt economy?

No. Not unless you have cash to gamble and lose and not unless you are very careful. The people of China may be free one day, perhaps sooner than many think, when this last of the imperial dynasties — the Communist dynasty — finally disappears.

Economy

China's economy during the past 30 years has changed from a centrally-planned system that was largely closed to international trade to a more market-oriented economy that has a rapidly growing private sector and is a major player in the global economy.

In 2010, China became the world's largest exporter. The country's reforms began with the phasing out of collectivized agriculture, and expanded to include the gradual liberalization of prices, fiscal decentralization, increased autonomy for state enterprises, creation of a diversified banking system, development of stock markets, rapid growth of the private sector, and opening to foreign trade and investment. In recent years, China has renewed its support for state-owned enterprises in sectors it considers important to "economic security," while explicitly looking to foster globally competitive national champions.

According to *The World Factbook*, "The restructuring of the economy and resulting efficiency gains have contributed to a more than tenfold increase in GDP since 1978. Measured on a purchasing power parity (PPP) basis that adjusts for price differences, China in 2013 stood as the second-largest economy in the world after the U.S., having surpassed Japan in 2001. The dollar values of China's agricultural and industrial output each exceed those of the U.S.; China is second to the U.S. in the value of services it produces. Still, per capita income is below the world average."

China's economic development has progressed further in coastal provinces than in the interior, and by 2014 more than 250 million migrant workers and their dependents had relocated from rural to urban areas to find work. One consequence of population control policy is that China is now one of the most rapidly aging countries in the world. In addition to the country's aging population, China also faces environmental issues, such as deterioration in the environment — notably air pollution, soil erosion, and the steady fall of the water table, especially in the North — which is another long-term problem.

The new government of President XI Jinping has signaled a greater willingness to undertake reforms that focus on China's long-term economic health, including giving the market a more decisive role in allocating resources. The government vowed to continue reforming the economy and emphasized the need to increase domestic consumption in order to make China less dependent on foreign exports for GDP growth in the future. For much of the population, living standards have improved and the room for personal choice has expanded somewhat, yet political controls remain tight. Any sign of organized opposition, individually or collectively, is met with brutal force and imprisonment.

The government of China is engaged in numerous conflicts with neighboring countries including India, Pakistan and Burma as well as concerning claims in the South China Seas. There they are in conflict with Vietnam, the Philippines and Taiwan. China and Taiwan continue their conflict over the status of Taiwan, although more peaceful travel and trade policies have developed after more than 60 years of separation.

Residence and Citizenship

In 2013, a new China immigration law came into effect, the first major overhaul of border regulations in more than two decades. The law replaced the immigration law for foreigners and another for Chinese nationals from 1986. The major thrust of the law was harsher punishments for foreigners who illegally enter, live, study or work in China. Illegal migrants are now fined 5,000 yuan to 20,000 yuan (US$800 to US$4,000) and face deportation. Employers are fined up to 100,000 yuan (US$16,000) per individual illegal employee. Some 47,100 foreigners were caught violating the immigration law in 2012.

The new law also reformed the green card system which allows foreigners to reside permanently in mainland China. By 2012, only 4,752 people had been granted the green cards that are very difficult to obtain. The permits allow foreign nationals to reside in China for a term of one to five years, depending on the terms of approval. About 594,000 foreigners live in China, according to the 2010 national census; most from South Korea, the U.S. and Japan.

Citizenship is based in The Nationality Law of the PRC and is conferred:

1. by birth: birth within the PRC territory does not automatically confer citizenship. The exception is a child born to unknown or stateless parents.

2. by descent: to a child, at least one of whose parents is a Chinese citizen, regardless of the country of birth. A child born abroad, whose parents have settled abroad and the child has acquired the nationality of the parents' new country, is not considered a citizen of the PRC.

3. by naturalization: when the applicant fulfills one of the following conditions:

    a.) A person who has close relatives living in China, a person who has settled in China, or the person has other legitimate reasons for acquiring citizenship.

    b.) Foreign nationals who once held Chinese nationality

may apply for restoration of Chinese nationality if they have legitimate reasons. Once the application is approved, the person may not retain a foreign nationality.

Dual citizenship is not recognized.

Many wealthy Chinese are acquiring second citizenship and passports now. A recent study found that 27% of Chinese with more than 100 million yuan (US$15.6 million) in assets have already migrated and 47% more are considering leaving China.

While some observers say that wealthy Chinese are leaving because the government is tightening its grip on the economy and curbing private enterprise, a survey of 36 individual Chinese millionaires who have already migrated or are thinking about it did not support this view. None reported government interference in legitimate business operations as a top reason for acquiring foreign passports.

Over 90% with foreign passports kept businesses in China and remained in the country on average eight months a year. The two main reasons wealthy Chinese took foreign passports were for education and health care reasons since having a foreign, non-PRC passport made it easier to secure travel visas to seek medical care abroad.

A valid passport and a visa are required to enter China and must be obtained from Chinese Embassies and Consulates before traveling to China. When I last visited China, using a visa service, it required a month to obtain a visa from the Chinese embassy in Washington. Americans arriving without valid passports and the appropriate Chinese visa are not permitted to enter and will be subject to a fine and immediate deportation at the traveler's expense. Chinese authorities have tightened their visa issuance policy, in some cases, requiring personal interviews of American citizens.

Foreign nationals must register their Chinese residence/hotel address with the district police departments within 24 hours of their arrival in China. If a foreign national stays in a hotel, the reception desk usually assists with this registration. Failure promptly to register will result in a maximum penalty of RMB 2,000 (US$330) as compared to the previous penalty of RMB 500 (US$84). Failure to register promptly can substantially delay and later complicate the application for resident permits.

Although a bilateral United States-China agreement provides for issuance of multiple entry visas with validity of up to one year for tourists and business visitors, Chinese Consulates often limit visas to only one entry.

Contacts

Embassy of the People's Republic of China

3505 International Place NW
Washington, DC 20008
Tel.: (202) 495-2266
Email: chinaembassy_us@fmprc.gov.cn
Web: http://www.china-embassy.org/eng/

Consulates: Chicago, Houston, Los Angeles, New York, and San Francisco.

United States Embassy

No. 55 An Jia Lou Lu Road
Beijing 100600
People's Republic of China
Tel.: + (86-10) 8531-3000
Email: AmCitBeijing@state.gov
Web: http://beijing.usembassy-china.org.cn

Recommended Attorney:

Jeffrey Y.F. Chen, Esq.
3A, Yunhai Garden Office Tower
118 Qinghai Road, Shanghai, 200041, China.
Tel.: (86) 21 52281952 F
Cell: (86) 13916089368
Email: lawyer_chen@lawyers.cn

Hong Kong

Government:	Limited democracy
Capital:	Hong Kong
National Day:	National Day (Peoples Republic of China): 1 October (1949)
Population:	7,082,316 (July 2013 est.)
Total Area:	422 sq. miles / 1,092 sq. kilometers
Languages:	Cantonese (official) 90.8%, English (official) 2.8%, Putonghua (Mandarin) 0.9%,; Chinese dialects 4.4%, other 1%
Ethnic groups:	Chinese 93.6%, Filipino 1.9%, Indonesian 1.9%, other 2.6%
Religion:	Christian 10%, eclectic mixture of local religions 90%
Life expectancy:	82.2 years
Currency:	Hong Kong dollar (HKD)
GDP:	US$325.8 billion (2010 est.)
GDP per capita:	US$45,900 (2010 est.)

On first acquaintance Hong Kong can overwhelm. Navigate its teeming, tightly packed sidewalks and you're met at every turn with neon signage, steam-filled canteens, molasses-slow traffic and Babel of chatter.

Once this first sensory wave has rolled over you, though, take a deep breath and start swimming with the current, because you'll find Hong Kong is a place to delight in. Utterly safe and fantastically well organized, it offers little moments of perfection. You may find them on a plastic stool enjoying a bargain bowl of beef brisket soup or simply gazing at the thrilling harbor vistas.

You'll find them taking afternoon tea in the cool of a five-star hotel lobby or enjoying balmy open-air beers in the party zones. Hong Kong can nudge you out of your comfort zone but usually rewards you for it, so try the stinky bean curd, sample the shredded jellyfish, brave

the hordes at the city center horse racing and join in the dawn tai chi. Escape the city limits and other experiences await — watching the sun rise from a remote mountain peak, hiking surf-beaten beaches or exploring deserted islands.

If it's pampering you're after, money can buy the ultimate luxuries in a city well used to serving its tiny, moneyed elite. Yet Hong Kong is also a city of simple pleasures. Most often it's the least pricey experiences — a $2 tram or ferry ride, a whiff of incense curling from temple rafters, savoring fishing-village sundowners and seafood — that are the stuff of priceless memories. — Lonely Planet

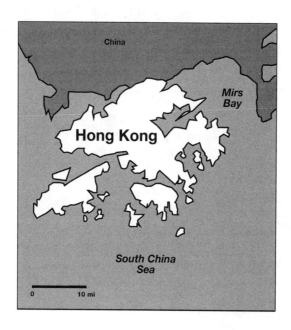

History and Overview

One of the most striking contrasts I witnessed during my last visit in 2005 to the so-called People's Republic of China occurred when we flew from there to Hong Kong.

The far greater personal freedom I felt was emphasized by the welcome we got on the bus on the way in from the gleaming new international airport. Our local guide, William, spoke of the democracy movement in Hong Kong in a way no mainland Chinese would ever be allowed to express an opinion. His freedom of expression is owed to the "one nation, two systems" arrangement under which the British ended their colonial control.

Even though Hong Kong has been a "Special Administrative Region" of China since the British handed it over in 1997, you can feel the freer atmosphere; there was none of the TV or Internet censorship I experienced in China. Instead, there was the hustle and bustle of free commerce and the flow of free people coursing through the streets at all hours. When the Honorable Martin Lee, a freely elected member of the Legislative Council, met with us, his call for full democracy for Hong Kong emphasized how nervous the Communist controllers in Beijing are about letting people have a say in their own government.

By many measures the Hong Kong economy remains one of the freest in the world, as well as a major offshore financial center with strong common law-based laws governing banking and finance, even though it is controlled, ultimately, by a Communist government in Beijing.

Occupied by Great Britain in 1841, Hong Kong was formally ceded by China the following year; various adjacent lands were added later in the 19th century. Pursuant to an agreement signed by China and the U.K. on December 19, 1984, Hong Kong became the Hong Kong Special Administrative Region (SAR) of China on July 1, 1997. In this agreement, China promised that, under its "one country, two systems" formula, China's socialist economic system will not be imposed on Hong Kong and that Hong Kong will enjoy a high degree of autonomy in all matters except foreign and defense affairs for the next 50 years.

Beijing's rule began in 1997 and has imposed many restrictions. While on balance, semi-democratic Hong Kong remains relatively free, Beijing's guaranteed political freedoms have been repeatedly delayed. Britain showed little interest in developing democracy in Hong Kong until the 1997 handover to China drew near. Then, under the "one country, two systems" framework, it negotiated what were supposed to be greater freedoms for the region and a commitment to eventual universal suffrage that Beijing has ignored.

Since 1997, mass demonstrations in Hong Kong have forced Communist mainland authorities to back down to some degree. In 2003, plans to require adoption of laws banning acts of "treason, secession, sedition and subversion" were dropped after half a million took to the streets. In 2012, Beijing proposals for compulsory "patriotic and national education" were scrapped after critics accused the government of trying to brainwash children, launching large-scale protests. Huge demonstrations against mainland control have been held annually. In 2014, new and larger demonstrations protested the murders and assaults on leading Hong Kong editors and journalist who support faster reforms, rallying for press and speech freedoms.

In 2014, native Hong Kong leaders in the city-state's important financial sector organized against trends they denounced including money laundering by mainland government officials and their families as a cover for official corruption. The anti-Beijing financial group said they feared the destruction of Hong Kong's reputation as a clean and desirable offshore financial center. They wanted a political awakening among the bankers, stockbrokers and financial traders whose livelihoods have become increasingly enmeshed in the mainland's cash and influence. Among their demands was popular election of local government officials, rather than an electoral system stacked in favor of the Communist rulers on the mainland. During 2014 Hong Kong saw some of the largest mass anti-Beijing demonstrations on the 25th anniversary of the Tiananmen Square massacre. Tens of thousands flooded streets in protest. Hong Kong citizens cast their ballots in an unofficial referendum on democratic reform in a poll that drew more than 690,000 votes online against Beijing.

China's top leaders have responded to such demands in the past by saying that importing a western-style democratic system to the region could prove catastrophic. They claimed that copying a foreign electoral system could "become a democracy trap ... and possibly bring a disastrous result." One can well guess what that threat eventually could mean.

Economy

Hong Kong has a free-market economy, highly dependent on international trade and finance; the value of goods and services trade, including the sizable share of re-exports, is about four times GDP. Hong Kong has no tariffs on imported goods.

Hong Kong's open economy exposed it to the global economic slowdown that began in 2008. Although increasing integration with China, through trade, tourism, and financial links, helped it to make an initial quick recovery, its continued reliance on foreign trade and investment leaves it vulnerable to world financial market volatility or a slowdown in the global economy.

Even before Hong Kong reverted from the United Kingdom to Chinese administration in July 1997, it had extensive trade and investment ties with China. Hong Kong has been further integrating its economy with China because China's growing openness to the world economy has made manufacturing in China much more cost effective. Hong Kong's re-export business to and from China is a major driver of growth. The mainland has long been Hong Kong's largest trading partner, accounting for nearly 49% of Hong Kong's exports trade by value.

During the past decade, as Hong Kong's manufacturing industry moved to the mainland, its service industry has grown rapidly and now accounts for more than 92% of the territory's GDP. As a result of China's easing of travel restrictions, the number of mainland tourists to the territory has surged from 4.5 million in 2001 to 34 million in 2013, outnumbering visitors from all other countries combined. Hong Kong has also established itself as the premier stock market for Chinese firms seeking to list abroad.

In 2012 mainland Chinese companies constituted about 46.6% of the firms listed on the Hong Kong Stock Exchange and accounted for 57% of the Exchange's market capitalization. The Hong Kong government adopted several temporary fiscal policy support measures in response to the crisis that it may discontinue if strong growth is sustained.

Credit expansion and tight housing supply conditions caused Hong Kong property prices to rise rapidly in 2010, and some lower-income segments of the population are increasingly unable to afford adequate housing.

Hong Kong continues to link its currency closely to the U.S. dollar, maintaining an arrangement established in 1983 that pegs: US$1.00 = 7.75000 HKD. However, the government is promoting Hong Kong as the site for Chinese renminbi (RMB) internationalization. Hong Kong residents are allowed to establish RMB-denominated savings accounts; RMB-denominated corporate and

Chinese government bonds have been issued in Hong Kong; and RMB trade settlement is allowed.

Hong Kong's financial services sector is a mainstay of the economy. It accounts for 16% of gross domestic product and provided 228,000 jobs in 2012 in a population of 7.2 million, according to the government.

Residence and Citizenship

Economic Residence: Hong Kong has in place a high dollar investor residence program aimed at attracting wealth foreigners as residents known as the "Capital Investment Entrant Scheme" (CIES). About 8,200 investors with 15,500 spouses, children and other dependents had been admitted by 2010 when the qualifications for admission were changed.

The current threshold of investment for admission is HK$10 million (US$1.28 million). Real estate has been suspended temporarily as a class of permissible investment assets counting toward the investment total, but permitted investments include an array of Hong Kong equities, bonds, debt instruments and government paper. In early 2013, applications were approved for 18,639 applications for an investment total of HK$129.82 billion (US$16.6 billion).

Initial residence term is for two years with further two-year extensions possible. After seven years a CIES resident can apply for permanent residence that gives the right to live in Hong Kong indefinitely.

Hong Kong also has a "Quality Migrant Admission Scheme" operated on a points-based system. It seeks to attract highly skilled or talented persons from the Mainland and overseas to settle in Hong Kong in order to enhance Hong Kong's economic competitiveness in the global market.

For more information see http://www.gov.hk/en/about/
abouthk/factsheets/docs/immigration.pdf

Dual U.S.-H.K. Nationality

Under the People's Republic of China nationality law, persons
who are of Chinese descent and who were born in mainland China
or Hong Kong are considered PRC citizens. However, under an
agreement between the United States and the PRC, all U.S. citizens entering Hong Kong on their U.S. passports, including such
persons as may be considered PRC nationals by the PRC authorities, are considered U.S. citizens by the Hong Kong SAR authorities for purposes of ensuring U.S. consular access and protection.

Australia reckons 30,000 people hold both Australian and
Hong Kong passports. Canada estimates that 220,000 Canadians live in Hong Kong. Britain controversially refused to make
a blanket offer of citizenship when it quit Hong Kong in 1997,
but it slipped citizenship papers to a favored few. And about 3.5
million people, mostly still living in Hong Kong, hold "British
National Overseas" passports, which provide the holder with no
right of abode in Britain.

Dual nationals, who are or previously were Hong Kong residents, and who wish to ensure U.S. consular access and protection
after the initial 90-day period of admission into Hong Kong, must
declare their U.S. nationality by presenting their U.S. passports to
the Hong Kong Immigration Department and completing an application for declaration of change of nationality. This declaration
of change of nationality will ensure U.S. consular protection and
may also result in loss of one's Chinese nationality (but not necessarily one's right of abode). Although such individuals' failure to
declare U.S. nationality may jeopardize U.S. consular protection,
such failure will not jeopardize their U.S. citizenship. Dual national residents of Hong Kong who enter Hong Kong on their Hong

Kong identity cards rather than their U.S. passports and who desire to guarantee U.S. consular protection should declare their U.S. nationality to the Hong Kong Immigration Department as soon as possible after entry.

Dual nationals contemplating onward travel to the PRC should be especially attentive to use of their U.S. passports, as the PRC authorities may require them to use the same document for entry into the PRC as they used to enter Hong Kong. The Nationality Law of the PRC does not recognize dual nationality. U.S. citizens, including such persons as may be considered Chinese nationals by the PRC authorities, who enter and depart the PRC using a U.S. passport and a valid PRC visa retain the right of U.S. consular access and protection under the U.S.-PRC Consular Convention. The ability of the U.S. Embassy or Consulates General in the PRC to provide normal consular services would be extremely limited should a dual national enter the PRC on a non-U.S. passport. Therefore, travelers should carefully consider whether or not to use a passport or travel document other than their U.S. passport.

A foreign passport with a minimum of six months validity remaining and evidence of onward/return transportation by sea/air are required. A visa is not required for tourist visits of up to 90 days by U.S. citizens. U.S. citizens who arrive in Hong Kong with an expired or damaged passport may be refused entry and returned to the United States at their own expense.

Contacts
Hong Kong Economic and Trade Offices
1. 1520 18th Street NW
Washington, DC 20036
Tel.: (202) 331-8947
Email: hketo@hketowashington.gov.hk
Web: http://www.hketowashington.gov.hk/dc/index.htm

2. 115 East 54th Street
New York, NY 10022
Tel.: (212) 752-3320
Web: http://www.hketony.gov.hk/ny/index.htm

3. 130 Montgomery Street
San Francisco, CA 94104
Tel.: (415) 835-9300
Web: http://www.hketosf.gov.hk/sf/index.htm

United States Consulate General
26 Garden Road, Hong Kong
Tel.: + (852) 2523-9011
Email: information_resource_center_hk@yahoo.com
Web: http://hongkong.usconsulate.gov/

Recommended Immigration Consultant:

Henley & Partners
3304 Office Tower
Convention Plaza
1 Harbour Road
Wanchai, Hong Kong
Tel.: + 852 3101 4100
Email: hongkong@henleyglobal.com

Republic of India

Government:	Federal republic
Capital:	New Delhi
National Day	Republic Day: 26 January (1950)
Population:	1,220,800,359 (July 2013 est.)
Total Area:	1,269,346 sq. miles / 3,287,590 sq. kilometers
Languages:	English (most important language for national, political and commercial use); Hindi (national language and primary tongue of 30% of the people); 14 other official languages
Ethnic groups:	Indo-Aryan 72%, Dravidian 25%, Mongoloid and other 3%
Religion:	Hindu 80.5%, Muslim 13.4%, Christian 2.3%, Sikh 1.9%, other 1.8%, unspecified 0.1%
Life expectancy:	67.48 years
Currency:	Indian rupee (INR)
GDP:	US$4.962 trillion (2013 est.)
GDP per capita:	US$4,000 (2013 est.)

Bamboozling. There's simply no other word that convincingly captures the enigma that is India. With its in-your-face diversity, from snow-dusted mountains to sun-washed beaches, tranquil temples to feisty festivals, lantern-lit villages to software-supremo cities, it's hardly surprising that this country has been dubbed the worlds' most multidimensional. Love it or loathe it, and most visitors see-saw between the two, India promises to jostle your entire being, and no matter where you go or what you do, it's a place you'll never forget.

Home to more than one billion people, the subcontinent

bristles with an eclectic mélange of ethnic groups, which translates into an intoxicating cultural cocktail for the traveler. For those seeking spiritual sustenance, India has oodles of sacrosanct sites and stirring philosophical epics, while history buffs will encounter gems from the past almost everywhere; from grand vestiges of the British Raj serenely peering over swarming spice bazaars, to crumbling fortresses looming high above plunging ravines.

Meanwhile, aficionados of the great outdoors can paddle in the shimmering waters of one of many balmy beaches, scout for big jungle cats on a blood-pumping wildlife safari, or simply inhale pine-scented air on a meditative forest walk.

Once you touch down on sub-continental soil, you'll quickly discover that cricket, India's sporting obsession, is one of the most spirited topics of conversation, along with the latest shenanigans in the razzle-dazzle world of Bollywood. However, it is politics — whether at the national, state or village level — that consistently dominates news headlines, with middle and upper class India also keenly keeping its finger on the pulse of international events.

On the home front, economic matters feature high on the national political agenda. With one of the world's fastest-growing economies, India has certainly made giant strides over the past decade. However, despite averaging an annual growth rate of around 9% in recent years, vast sections of the country's billion-plus population have seen little benefit from the economic boom.

Indeed, the government's ongoing challenge is to spread both the burden and bounty of India's fiscal prosperity. Not an easy task given that the gap between the haves and the have-nots is far from shrinking, and poverty is set to spiral upward if

India's population rate continues to gallop beyond that of its economic growth. — Lonely Planet

Travel Alert: India continues to experience terrorist and insurgent activities which may affect U.S. citizens directly or indirectly. Anti-Western terrorist groups, some on the U.S. government's list of foreign terrorist organizations, are active in India. Past attacks have targeted public places, including some frequented by Westerners, such as luxury and other hotels, trains, train stations, markets, cinemas, mosques, and restaurants in large urban areas. Attacks have taken place during the busy evening hours in markets and other crowded places, but could occur at any time. Beyond the threat from terrorism and insurgencies, demonstrations and general strikes, or "bandh," often cause major inconvenience and unrest. These strikes can result in the stoppage of all transportation and tourist-related services, at times for 24 hours or more. Check the U.S. State Department Travel Warnings before travel: http://travel. state.gov/content/passports/english/country/india.html

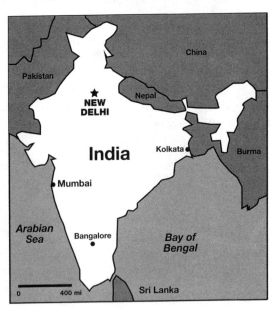

History and Overview

The Indus Valley civilization, one of the oldest in the world, dates back at least 5,000 years. Aryan tribes from the northwest infiltrated onto Indian lands about 1500 B.C. Their merger with the earlier Dravidian inhabitants created the classical Indian culture. Arab incursions starting in the8th century and Turkish in the 12th century were followed by those of European traders, beginning in the late 15th century.

By the 19th century, Britain had assumed colonial political control of virtually all Indian lands. Indian armed forces in the British army played a vital role in both World Wars. Non-violent resistance to British colonialism led by Mohandas Gandhi and Jawaharlal Nehru brought independence in 1947.

The subcontinent was divided into the secular state of India and the smaller Muslim state of Pakistan. A third war between the two countries in 1971 resulted in East Pakistan becoming the separate nation of Bangladesh. Despite impressive gains in economic investment and output, India faces pressing problems, such as the ongoing dispute with Pakistan over Kashmir, massive overpopulation, environmental degradation, extensive poverty, as well as ethnic and religious strife. Recently, the Indian-Pakistan border wars have flared anew and there have been serious Pakistani terrorist attacks within India, most notably in Mumbai (Bombay) in 2008 and again in 2011.

Kashmir remains the site of the world's largest and most militarized territorial dispute with portions under the de facto administration of China, India, and Pakistan. India and Pakistan have maintained a continuing dialogue since the 2003 cease-fire in Kashmir, and continue disputes over water sharing of the Indus River and its tributaries. A U.N. Military Observer Group in India and Pakistan has maintained a small group of peacekeepers since 1949.

India provides a home to almost three quarters of a million refugees and displaced persons including over 100,000 from Tibet, at least 540,000 from Kashmir, and another 80,000 or more from Sri Lanka, Afghanistan and Burma.

In May 2014, Narendra Modi became the 15th prime minister of India after his Hindu nationalist Bharatiya Janata Party won an absolute majority of 282 seats in the 543-seat lower house of Parliament, the first independent win by any single political party in three decades. Credited for his pro-business approach as the chief of the State of Gujarat, India's new leader raised expectations that his government will turn around India's slow economy, generate more jobs and rein in soaring prices and deeply entrenched corruption, issues that are widely believed to have assured his party's landslide election.

Economy

India is developing into an open-market economy, yet traces of its past self-sufficient policies remain. Economic liberalization, including industrial deregulation, privatization of state-owned enterprises, and reduced controls on foreign trade and investment, began in the 1990s and accelerated the country's growth, which averaged 7% annually from 1997 to 2011.

India's diverse economy encompasses traditional village farming, modern agriculture, handicrafts, a wide range of modern industries, and a multitude of services. Services are the major source of economic growth, accounting for half of India's output with less than one-quarter of its labor force.

About three-fifths of the work force is in agriculture, leading the government to articulate an economic reform program that includes developing basic infrastructure to improve the lives of the rural poor and boost economic performance.

Government controls on foreign trade and investment have been reduced in some areas, but high tariffs (averaging 20% on non-agricultural items in 2004) and limits on foreign direct investment are still in place.

Privatization of government-owned industries essentially came to a halt in 2005, and continues to generate political debate; continued social, political and economic rigidities hold back needed initiatives.

India has capitalized on its large educated English-speaking population to become a major exporter of information technol ogy services, business outsourcing services, and software workers. India's economic growth began slowing because of a decline in investment, caused by high interest rates, rising inflation, and investor pessimism about the government's commitment to further economic reforms and about the global situation.

Despite strong growth in 2006, the World Bank and other institutions worried about the combined state and federal budget deficit; government borrowing kept interest rates high. Economic deregulation attracted additional foreign capital and lower interest rates. The huge and growing population is the fundamental social, economic and environmental problem.

In 2013, India's economic growth declined to a decade low based on weak fundamentals, and India's economic leaders are now struggling to improve the country's wide fiscal and current account deficits. Improving conditions in Western countries have led investors to shift investment away from India and prompted a severe depreciation in the rupee.

Many wealthy Indians have moved assets offshore and Mauritius is one of the main tax havens they use. (See section on the Republic of Mauritius.) The government has tried to control these capital movements, with little success. The total foreign direct investment from Mauritius to India during the period 2000 to 2013 amounted to US$73.666 billion, 38% of all FDI in India in this period making Mauritius the single largest FDI source for India. Indian companies have invested over US$200 million in Mauritius since 2009.

Residence and Citizenship

Despite the variety of states, peoples and languages in India, the law recognizes only one type of Indian citizenship.

Citizenship is conferred in the following ways:

1. by birth: to a child born within India, regardless of the nationality of the parents. Though the law of India does recognize citizenship by birth within the country, unless the citizenship is actively applied for, the Indian government does not consider the child to be a citizen. The person has the right to return to India upon reaching the age of 18 and apply for Indian citizenship. Children born abroad must be registered at an Indian Consulate.

2. by descent:

   a.) to a child born of an Indian father, regardless of the child's country of birth;

   b.) to a child of an Indian mother and a foreign father, considered a citizen if the mother and child continue to live in India and the father does not give the child his country's citizenship, or;

   c.) to a child born out of wedlock to an Indian mother, regardless of the child's country of birth.

3. by naturalization:

   Indian citizenship may be acquired by persons who have resided in the country for the last five years and have renounced previous citizenship.

Since 2005, dual citizenship has been recognized, and the law allows those who lost Indian citizenship to reapply for it. The Indian government recently launched a program called "Overseas Citizens of India" or "OCI." This program often has been mischaracterized as "dual nationality" or "dual citizenship." However, a person who holds an OCI card, in reality, is granted an Indian travel and residence visa, not Indian citizenship.

Thus, an American or other citizen who obtains OCI status remains a citizen only of the United States or his home country. The OCI card is a special visa, which grants the holder the right to indefinitely remain, study or work in India, and also the right to own most types of property in India (excluding certain agricultural and plantation properties). A holder of an OCI card also need not register with local police/immigration authorities, unlike other holders of Indian visas. An OCI holder, however, does not receive an Indian passport, and has no other political rights in India, including the right to vote or eligibility for government employment.

U.S. citizens require a passport and visa to enter and exit India for any purpose. Visitors, including those on official U.S. government business, must obtain visas at an Indian Embassy or Consulate abroad prior to entering the country, as there are no provisions for visas upon arrival. Those arriving without a visa are subject to immediate deportation.

Contacts

Embassy of India
2107 Massachusetts Avenue NW
Washington, DC 20008
Tel.: (202) 939-7000
Email: indembwash@indiagov.org
Web: http://www.indianembassy.org/

Consulates in New York, Chicago, Houston, and San Francisco.

United States Embassy
Shantipath, Chanakyapuri
New Delhi 110021, India
Tel.: + (91) 11-2419-8000
Web: http://newdelhi.usembassy.gov
Email: NDwebmail@state.gov

U.S. Consulate General
5/1, Ho Chi Minh Sarani
Kolkata- 700071
Tel.: + (91) 33-3984-2400
Email: KolkataPAS@state.gov
Web: http://kolkata.usconsulate.gov/

Japan

Government:	Constitutional monarchy with parliamentary government
Capital:	Tokyo
National Day:	Birthday of Emperor Akihito: 23 December (1933)
Population:	127,253,075 (July 2013 est.)
Total Area:	145,883 sq. miles / 377,835 sq. kilometers
Language:	Japanese
Ethnic groups:	Japanese 98.5%, Koreans 0.5%, Chinese 0.4%, other 0.6%
Religion:	Shintoism 83.9%, Buddhism 71.4%, Christianity 2%, other 7.8%
Life expectancy:	84.18 years
Currency:	Yen (JPY)
GDP:	US$4.729 trillion (2013 est.)
GDP per capita:	US$37,100 (2013 est.)

Japan is a world apart — a cultural Galápagos where a unique civilization blossomed, and today thrives in delicious contrasts of traditional and modern. The Japanese spirit is strong, warm and incredibly welcoming.

Standing at the far-eastern end of the Silk Road and drawing influences from the entire continent, the Japanese have spent millennia taking in and refining the cultural bounties of Asia to produce something distinctly Japanese. From the splendor of a Kyoto geisha dance to the spare beauty of a Zen rock garden, Japan has the power to enthrall even the most jaded traveler. And traditional culture is only half the story: emerg-

ing from Tokyo's Shibuya Station and soaking up the energy, lights and sound of the city is like stepping out of a time capsule into a future world.

Since the Jesuits first visited Japan in the 17th century, travelers to Japan have found themselves entranced by a culture that is by turns beautiful, unfathomable and downright odd. Staying in a ryokan (traditional Japanese inn) is utterly different from staying in a hotel. Sitting in a robe on tatami (woven floor matting) eating raw fish and mountain vegetables is probably not how you dine back home. And getting naked with a bunch of strangers to soak in an onsen (hot spring) might seem strange at first, but try it and you'll find it's relaxing.

The wonders of Japan's natural world are a well-kept secret. The hiking in the Japan Alps and Hokkaidō is world class, and with an extensive hut system you can do multiday hikes with nothing more than a knapsack on your back. Down south, the coral reefs of Okinawa will have you wondering if you've somehow been transported to Thailand. And you never have to travel far in Japan to get out into nature: in cities like Kyoto, a few minutes of travel will get you into forested mountains.
— Lonely Planet

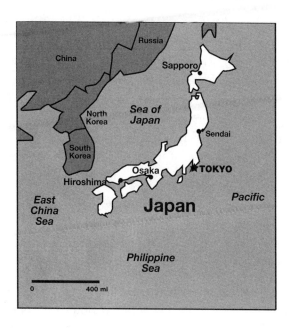

History and Overview

Japan, located in eastern Asia, is an island chain between the North Pacific Ocean and the Sea of Japan, east of the Korean Peninsula.

In 1603, a Tokugawa shogunate (military dictatorship) ushered in a long period of isolation from foreign influence in order to secure its power. For 250 years, this policy enabled Japan to enjoy stability and a flowering of its indigenous culture. Following the Treaty of Kanagawa with the U.S. in 1854, Japan opened its ports and began to intensively modernize and industrialize.

During the late 19th and early 20th centuries, Japan became a regional power that was militarily able to defeat the forces of both China and Russia. It occupied Korea, Formosa (Taiwan) and southern Sakhalin Island. In 1931 to 1932, Japanese troops occupied Manchuria and in 1937, it launched a full-scale military and naval invasion of China.

Japan attacked U.S. forces at Pearl Harbor, Hawaii on December 7, 1941, triggering America's entry into World War II, and it soon occupied much of East and Southeast Asia. The atomic bombings of the cities of Hiroshima and Nagasaki in Japan were conducted by the U.S. Army Air Force during the final stages of World War II in August 1945 after Japan failed to respond to a demand for unconditional surrender. It is estimated that over 200,000 people died as result of these raids. On August 15, just a few days after the bombing Japan announced its surrender to the Allies.

After its defeat in 1945, Japan recovered to become an economic power and an ally of the U.S. after several years of American occupation and military control under the direction of the late U.S. Army General Douglas McArthur.

While the emperor retains his throne as a symbol of national unity, actual power rests in networks of powerful politicians, bureaucrats and business executives and in the National Diet, the bicameral legislature.

Economy

After World War II, government-industry cooperation, a strong work ethic, mastery of high technology, and small defense spending (1% of GDP) helped Japan develop a technologically advanced economy. Two notable aspects of the post-war economy were the close monopoly-like interlocking structures of manufacturers, suppliers, and distributors, known as keiretsu, and the guarantee of lifetime employment for a large portion of the urban labor force. Both features are now eroding under the dual pressures of global competition and domestic demographic change.

Japan's industrial sector is heavily dependent on imported raw materials and fuels. A small agricultural sector is highly subsidized and protected, with crop yields among the highest in the world.

While self-sufficient in rice production, Japan imports about 60% of its food on a caloric basis. For three decades, overall real economic growth had been spectacular — a 10% average in the 1960s, a 5% average in the 1970s, and a 4% average in the 1980s.

The economy experienced a major slowdown starting in the 1990s following three decades of unprecedented growth, but Japan still remains a major economic power, both in Asia and globally as it is the fourth largest economy in the world after the U.S., China and India. The Japanese financial sector was not heavily exposed to sub-prime mortgages or their derivative instruments and weathered the initial effect of the global credit crunch, but a sharp downturn in business investment and global demand for Japan's exports in late 2008 pushed Japan further into a recession. Japan's huge government debt, which totals 170% of GDP, and the aging of the population are two major long-running problems. Debate continues on the role of and effects of reform in restructuring the economy.

In March 2011, Japan's strongest-ever earthquake, and an accompanying tsunami, devastated the northeast part of Honshu island, killing thousands and damaging several nuclear power plants. The catastrophe hobbled the country's economy and its energy infrastructure, and severely strained its capacity to deal with the humanitarian disaster. The economy contracted in 2011 as a massive 9.0 magnitude earthquake and the ensuing tsunami disrupted manufacturing. The economy has largely recovered since the disaster. Estimates of the direct costs of the damage, rebuilding homes and factories, range from US$235 billion to US$310 billion.

Citizenship and Residence

Japanese citizenship is conferred as follows:

1. by birth: within the territory of Japan does not automatically

confer citizenship. Only in the case of a child whose parents are unknown or stateless is the child considered a citizen.

2. by descent:

    a.) on a child whose father is a citizen of Japan, regard less of the child's country of birth. This law also applies if the father dies before the birth of the child, or;

    b.) on a child born to a Japanese mother and unknown or stateless father.

3. by naturalization: citizenship is available after five years continuous residence in Japan for those 20 years or older, with a good personal record and financial means.

A new citizen must renounce any former citizenship. Under the Nationality Law of 2008, Law No. 88, Japanese nationality is granted to a child whose father recognizes paternity after birth, whether or not the parents later marry. The Law states that a child can obtain Japanese nationality if the mother or father is a Japanese national at the time of the child's birth (Law No. 147 of 1950).

Current law requires a Japanese father to acknowledge the child while it's in the womb. A child born out of wedlock to a Japanese father and a foreign mother cannot obtain Japanese nationality by birth, unless the father legally recognizes the child before the birth. If the father recognizes a child after the birth, the father is not considered legally the father at the time of the birth. Article 3 provides that, if the parents marry before the child reaches 20 years old, Japanese nationality is given to the child.

A 2008 amendment to the country's nationality law may allow thousands of mixed-race children to become citizens. The change applies only to out-of-wedlock children of Japanese fathers and non-Japanese mothers. Under the new law, children will be able to claim citizenship for up to 20 years after their birth. As many as

20,000 children living in Japan may be eligible for citizenship after the change.

Dual nationality is not generally recognized. However, if a child is born abroad to Japanese parents, the child can acquire dual nationality if citizenship is acquired in the country of birth. A person with dual nationality must choose one nationality by the age of 22. If one does not choose Japanese nationality within this period, the Minister of Justice can require one to make a choice. Failure to comply with this requirement within one month of the 22nd birthday will result in loss of Japanese citizenship.

Visas

A valid passport and an onward/return ticket are required for entry. Passports must be valid for the intended period of stay in Japan. A visa is not required for tourist/business stays up to 90 days. Americans cannot work on a 90-day visa-free entry. As a general rule, visa-free entry status may not be changed to any other visa status without departing and then re-entering Japan with the appropriate visa such as a spouse, work or study visa.

U.S. citizens entering or transiting Japan should ensure that their passports and visas are up to date before leaving the United States. Many Asian countries deny entry to travelers whose passports are valid for less than six months. U.S. citizens must carry their U.S. passports or Japanese alien registration cards with them at all times, so that, if questioned by local officials, the U.S. citizen can establish proof of identity and citizenship. Under Japanese law, the police may stop any person on the street at any time and demand ID. If a foreigner does not have either a passport or valid Japanese Alien Registration Card, they are subject to arrest. Such random stops for ID are becoming increasingly more common, especially in areas frequented by foreigners.

Contacts

Embassy of Japan
2520 Massachusetts Avenue NW
Washington, DC 20008
Tel.: (202) 238-6700
Email: jicc@ws.mofa.go.jp
Web: http://www.us.emb-japan.go.jp/english/html/

United States Embassy
1-10-5 Akasaka
Minato-ku, Tokyo 107-8420, Japan
Tel.: + (81) 03-3224-5000
Web: http://tokyo.usembassy.gov

Malaysia

Government:	Constitutional monarchy
Capital:	Kuala Lumpur
National Day:	Independence Day/Malaysia Day: 31 August (1957)
Population:	29,628,392 (July 2013 est.)
Total Area:	127,317 sq. miles / 329,750 sq. kilometers
Languages:	Bahasa Melayu (official), English, Chinese, Tamil, Telugu, Malayalam, Panjabi, Thai
Ethnic groups:	Malay 50.4%, Chinese 23.7%, indigenous 11%, Indian 7.1%
Religion:	Muslim, Buddhist, Daoist, Hindu, Christian, Sikh
Life expectancy:	74.28 years
Currency:	Ringgit (MYR)
GDP:	US$525 billion (2013 est.)
GDP per capita:	US$17,500 (2013 est.)

Malaysia is really like two countries in one cleaved in half by the South China Sea. The peninsula is a multicultural buffet of Malay, Chinese and Indian flavors while Borneo hosts a wild jungle smorgasbord of orangutans, granite peaks and remote tribes. Within and throughout these two very different regions are an impressive variety of microcosms ranging from the space-age high-rises of Kuala Lumpur to the smiling long-house villages of Sarawak and the calm, powdery beaches of the Perhentian Islands.

And did we mention the food? Malaysia (particularly along the peninsula west coast) has one of the best assortments of deli-

cious cuisines in the world. Start with Chinese–Malay 'Nonya' fare, move on to Indian banana leaf curries, Chinese buffets, spicy Malay food stalls and even some impressive Western food.

Yet despite all the pockets of ethnicities, religions, landscapes and the sometimes-great distances between them, the beauty of Malaysia lies in the fusion of it all, into a country that is one of the safest, most stable and easiest to manage in Southeast Asia. — Lonely Planet

History and Overview

Malaysia has grown under many different influences. It has been ruled by the Portuguese, Dutch and British, over a period of five centuries. During the late 18th and 19th centuries, Great Britain established colonies and protectorates in the area of current Malaysia; these were occupied by Japan from 1942 to 1945. In 1948, the British-ruled territories on the Malay Peninsula formed the Federation of Malaya, which became independent in 1957. It is a member of the Commonwealth nations.

Malaysia was formed in 1963 when the former British colonies of Singapore and the East Malaysian states of Sabah and Sarawak on the northern coast of Borneo joined the Federation. The first several years of the country's history were marred by Indonesian efforts to control Malaysia, Philippine claims to Sabah, and Singapore's secession from the Federation in 1965.

During the 22-year term of Prime Minister Mahathir bin Mohamad (1981 to 2003), Malaysia was successful in diversifying its economy from dependence on exports of raw materials, to expansion in manufacturing, services and tourism. His leadership converted the nation's plantation-based economy into an "Asian Tiger."

Current Prime Minister Mohamed Najib bin Abdul Razak, in office since 2009, has continued these pro-business policies. The western half of Malaysia is bustling and commercial, with urban centers sprinkled throughout the lush, green, tropical vegetation of the country. Much of its development in the west of the country is driven by the entrepreneurial energy of its Chinese community. In the east, Malays constitute the majority, and people make their living from agriculture, fishing and cottage industries. Life in the east is quieter, and more laid back, and this is where you're most likely to really experience the traditional Malay culture.

Most visitors to Malaysia stick to the Peninsula, but both Penang, an island that retains a distinctly colonial English image, and Langkawi, a scenic honeymoon haven, are easily accessible by sea and air, and are well worth a visit.

The society in this country is truly multicultural, with Malays, Chinese and Indians living side by side. Festivals abound throughout the year, to mark the Malay, Chinese and Indian holidays, as well as those of the indigenous Orang Asli, and the tribes of Sabah and Sarawak on Borneo.

One Party State

Nominally headed by paramount ruler, commonly referred to as the king, and a bicameral Parliament consisting of a non-elected upper house and an elected lower house; all Peninsular Malaysian states have hereditary rulers, commonly referred to as sultans, except Melaka (Malacca) and Pulau Pinang (Penang); those two states, along with Sabah and Sarawak in East Malaysia have governors appointed by government. Powers of state governments are limited by federal constitution; under terms of federation, Sabah and Sarawak retain certain constitutional prerogatives including the right to maintain their own immigration controls.

In 2014, the mysterious disappearance of Malaysia Airlines Flight MH370 with 239 people aboard exposed to the world the near dictatorial and less than competent actions of its government. Malaysia's governing elite has clung to power without interruption since independence from Britain almost six decades ago through a combination of tight control of information, intimidation of the opposition and, until recently, robust economic growth.

This arbitrary political culture began in 1969, following bloody rioting between Malays and the large ethnic Chinese minority. The government granted numerous privileges to Malays, in effect ensuring them of perpetual power. This quota system enabled the ruling party, which has held office for 60 years, to do pretty much as it pleases, including extensive corruption and criminal persecution of opponents. 2014 is an election year and the aftermath of Flight MH370 may bring change.

While the 2002 "Declaration on the Conduct of Parties in the South China Sea" has eased tensions over the Spratly Islands in the South China Sea, it is not the legally binding "code of conduct" sought by some parties; Malaysia was not party to the 2005 joint accord among the national oil companies of China, the Philippines, and Vietnam on conducting marine seismic activities in the Spratly Islands. Those islands have become a point of tension with China that claims them to within their jurisdiction.

Economy

Malaysia, a middle-income country, transformed itself from 1971 through the late 1990s from a producer of raw materials into an emerging multi-sector economy. Growth was almost exclusively driven by exports — particularly of electronics.

As an oil and gas exporter, Malaysia has profited from higher world energy prices, although the cost of government subsidies for domestic gasoline and diesel fuel has risen and offset some of the benefit. Exports, particularly of electronics, oil and gas, palm oil and rubber, are a significant driver of the economy.

Under the current Prime Minister Najib, Malaysia is attempting to achieve high-income status by 2020 and to move farther up the value-added production chain by attracting investments in Islamic finance, high-technology industries, biotechnology, and services. Najib's Economic Transformation Program is a series of projects and policy measures intended to accelerate the country's economic growth, but its success is questionable.

Bank Negara Malaysia, the central bank, maintains large foreign exchange reserves, and a well-developed regulatory regime that has limited Malaysia's exposure to riskier financial instruments and the global financial crisis.

Malaysia unpegged the ringgit from the U.S. dollar in 2005, but so far there has been little movement in the exchange rate. Healthy foreign exchange reserves, low inflation and a small external debt are all strengths that make it unlikely that Malaysia will experience a financial crisis over the near term. The economy remains dependent on continued growth in the U.S., China and Japan, leading export destinations and key sources of foreign investment.

Corporate Tax Haven

In the mid-1980s Malaysian leaders, with British controlled

Hong Kong about to be handed over to the Communist Chinese, decided to establish their own international offshore financial center, (what used to be called a "tax haven). They located it on Labuan, a small island off the coast of Borneo and formally launched it in 1990.

Labuan offered then and now low-tax/no-tax corporate structures and provides a modern banking system. There are two categories of companies, trading and non-trading.

A Labuan "trading" company is an operating business that sells products or services to customers. A Labuan "non-trading" company is a traditional holding company that owns assets or other companies that earns dividends, rents, and royalties. Its offshore income is tax-free and there is no withholding, capital gains, or dividend tax.

For trading companies that operate a business, there is an option to either pay 3% of their profits, or simply pay a flat tax of 20,000 Malaysian ringgits, (US$6,000). Since Malaysia has double taxation treaties with many countries, foreigners whose business qualify under a tax treaty can operate a Labuan company and pay the low Malaysian tax instead of higher taxes in their home country.

Residence and Citizenship

More than two million people have been granted Malaysian citizenship since 1957. There is a complex set of rules defining citizenship eligibility revolving around the date of Independence Malaysia Day, September 16, 1963, and the actual date of birth.

A person can become a citizen either by registration or naturalization. Malaysia does not allow dual citizenship. Those applying for citizenship by registration must have an "an adequate knowledge of the Malay language" and have resided in the country for

10 of the past 12 years, including the 12 months immediately preceding the application. Permanent residence is granted by individual states.

Malaysia has a special law to attract retirees known as the "My Second Home Program." It is available for those below 50 years of age with assets worth a minimum of RM500,000 and offshore income of RM10,000 per month.

Applicants aged 50 and above must show proof of RM350,000 (US$107,000) in liquid assets and off shore income of RM10,000 (US$3,000 per month). Those who purchase property worth at least RM1 million (US$305,000) may qualify for a lower fixed deposit amount. Those below 50 years can qualify by opening a fixed deposit account of RM300,000 (US$91,000).

American and other foreign citizens are required to have a passport valid for at least six months to enter Malaysia, but Americans do not need to obtain a visa in advance for a pleasure or business trip if their stay in Malaysia is 90 days or less.

Upon, or prior to, entry into Malaysia, visitors will be given a Malaysian Disembarkation Card to complete and present to Malaysian immigration upon arrival. Immigration officials will then issue a social visit pass (visa) in their passport. In some cases a visa may be issued for travel within the country between the western and eastern parts.

Malaysia does not recognize or permit dual nationality. If Malaysian authorities learn that an American citizen is also a citizen of Malaysia, they may require that the dual national either renounce United States citizenship immediately or forfeit Malaysian citizenship. Dual American/Malaysian citizens should consider this issue seriously before traveling to Malaysia.

Contacts

Embassy of Malaysia
3516 International Court NW
Washington, DC 20008
Tel.: (202) 572-9700
Email: malwashdc@kln.gov.my
Web: http://www.kln.gov.my/perwakilan/washington

United States Embassy
376 Jalan Tun Razak
50400 Kuala Lumpur, Malaysia
Tel.: + (60) 3-2168-5000
Email: klacs@state.gov
Web: http://malaysia.usembassy.gov/

New Zealand

Government:	Parliamentary democracy
Capital:	Wellington
National Day:	Waitangi Day (Treaty of Waitangi established British sovereignty over New Zealand): 6 February (1840)
Population:	4,401,916 (July 2014 est.)
Total Area:	103,738 sq. miles / 268,680 sq. kilometers
Languages:	English and Maori (both official)
Ethnic groups:	European 56.8%, Asian 8%, Maori 7.4%, Pacific islander 4.6%, mixed 9.7%, other 13.5%
Religion:	Anglican 13.8%, Roman Catholic 12.6%, Presbyterian, Congregational, and Reformed 10%, Christian (no denomination specified) 4.6%, Methodist 3%, Pentecostal 2%, Baptist 1.4%, other Christian 3.8%, Maori Christian 1.6%, Hindu 1.6%, Buddhist 1.3%, other religions 2.2%, none 32.2%, unidentified 9.9%
Life expectancy:	80.93 years
Currency:	New Zealand dollar (NZD)
GDP:	US$136 billion (2013 est.)
GDP per capita:	US$30,400 (2013 est.)

Plucked straight from a film set or a coffee-table book of picture-perfect scenery, New Zealand is jaw-droppingly gorgeous. 'Wow!' will escape from your lips at least once a day.

Forget New Orleans… New Zealand can rightly claim the 'Big Easy' crown for the sheer ease of travel here. It isn't a place where you encounter many on-the-road frustrations: buses and trains run on time; roads are in good nick; ATMs proliferate;

pickpockets, scam merchants and bedbug-ridden hostels are few and far between; and the food is unlikely to send you running for the nearest public toilets (which are usually clean and stocked with the requisite paper). And there are no snakes, and only one poisonous spider — the rare katipo — sightings of which are considered lucky. This decent nation is a place where you can relax and enjoy (rather than endure) your holiday.

There are just 4.4 million New Zealanders, scattered across about 270,534 sq km: bigger than the UK with one-fourteenth the population. Filling in the gaps are the sublime forests, mountains, lakes, beaches and fiords that have made NZ one of the best hiking (locals call it 'tramping') destinations on the planet

If you're even remotely interested in rugby, you'll have heard of the all-conquering All Blacks, NZ's national team, who would never have become world-beaters without their awesome Maori players. But this is just one example of how Maori culture impresses itself on contemporary Kiwi life: across NZ you can hear Maori language, watch Maori TV, see mainstreet marae (meeting houses), join in a hangi (Maori feast) or catch a cultural performance with traditional Maori song, dance and usually a blood-curdling haka (war dance). And don't let us stop you from considering ta moko, traditional Maori tattooing (often applied to the face). — Lonely Planet

History and Overview

New Zealand is a group of islands in Oceania in the Pacific Ocean, southeast of Australia. The nation also includes affiliated jurisdictions of the Cook Islands and Niue, both autonomous countries, and several other small island groups.

New Zealand's two main islands are mountainous, with several dormant volcanoes on and around the North Island. The craggy South Island draws adventure tourists from all over the globe for climbing, skiing and white water rafting, as well as admirers of the land's breathtaking beauty, made familiar to moviegoers globally in the highly successful "Lord of the Rings" films. Eco-tourists, too, congregate in New Zealand, where millions of years of isolation from other landmasses have allowed a remnant population of animal and plant species with unique characteristics to develop from earlier forms, many extinct elsewhere.

Dutch East Indian Company explorers sighted South Island in 1642 and, in 1769 Captain John Cook became the first European to land and survey the area. European settlers began arriving in 1790. In 1840, Britain claimed rights to the area, and, in 1907, New Zealand became a Dominion under the British Crown.

Historically, the islands received migrants from the Polynesian Pacific as early as 800 A.D., the ancestors of the present-day native Maori. In 1840, their chieftains entered into a compact with Britain, the Treaty of Waitangi, in which they ceded sovereignty to HRM Queen Victoria while retaining territorial rights.

In that same year, the British began the first organized colonial settlement. A series of land wars between 1843 and 1872 ended with the defeat of the native peoples. The British colony of New Zealand became an independent dominion in 1907 and supported the U.K. militarily in both world wars. New Zealand's full participation in a number of defense alliances lapsed by the 1980s. In recent years, the government has sought to address longstanding Maori grievances.

Economy

The government has accomplished major economic restructuring, moving an agrarian economy dependent on British market access toward a more industrialized, free-market economy that can compete globally. This dynamic growth has boosted real incomes, broadened the capabilities of the industrial sector and reduced inflationary pressures. Inflation remains among the lowest in the industrial world. Per capita GDP has moved to levels of major European economies. New Zealand's heavy dependence on trade leaves its growth prospects vulnerable to economic performance in Asia.

New Zealand has not always been so prosperous. After years of having the highest tax rates in the world, the government verged on bankruptcy. Massive overspending on welfare state schemes, plus low world commodity prices triggered a fiscal crisis. No one starved, but inflation, unemployment, and large-scale emigration were common.

As a result, major changes were implemented, labor unions curbed, inflation was reduced to less than 1%, and property prices leveled off. The government tried to attract new foreign investments, entrepreneurs and talent by reducing confiscatory income taxes, making them lower than any European country and roughly equal to those in the U.S.

New Zealand law makes intentional income tax avoidance without other proper justification illegal. As in the United States, worldwide income is taxed and various events within the nation, such as owning a second home there, may bring a foreign person within the NZ tax laws. There are no capital gains or estate taxes.

The conservative National Party has governed in coalition since 2011 with elections in 2014.

Residence and Citizenship

New Zealand's British Nationality and New Zealand Citizenship Act of 1948 created the status of New Zealand citizenship. Prior to that time people born in New Zealand legally were considered as British subjects.

Under the law, citizenship is conferred:

1. by birth: of a child born in the territory of New Zealand, regardless of the nationality of the parents. The only exception is a child born to foreign diplomats while they are posted to New Zealand, unless one parent is a New Zealand citizen.

2. by descent: to a child who at the time of birth has one parent that is a New Zealand citizen other than by descent (such as

by birth in New Zealand or through a Grant of Citizenship). Application for official recognition of this status must be made before the person attains the age of 22.

3. by registration: citizenship may be granted to persons in the following categories:

   a.) a foreign national who marries a citizen of New Zealand and intends to establish residence in the country, or;

   b.) a child born abroad, at least one of whose parents is a citizen by descent.

4. by naturalization: citizenship may be acquired by a foreign person at least 18 years old who has been resident in-country for at least five years, is of good character, knows the language and customs, and intends to permanently settle in the country.

Any child born in New Zealand after January 1, 2006, can only be a New Zealand citizen by birth, if at least one parent is a New Zealand citizen or permanent resident.

Immigration

Immigration is a highly contentious issue and has provoked fierce debate from time to time in New Zealand. The 2009 Immigration Act replaced the 1987 Act and enhanced border security and reformed the immigration services. Key aspects of the Act include use of biometrics, a new refugee and protection system, a single independent appeals tribunal and a universal visa system.

New Zealand has one of the highest populations of foreign born citizens. In 2005, almost 20% of its people were born overseas, one of the highest percentages of any country in the world. There are a wide variety of ethnicities, with people from over 120 countries represented.

In 2007, New Zealand lowered its projected immigration targets in response to inflation worries, causing talk that the country might see a population drop in the future. Currently, New Zealand has a population of almost 4.4 million. Before the global recession began in 2008, the government had an annual target of about 50,000 new immigrants, but New Zealand experienced a small exodus as people left for better job opportunities in Australia.

It is worth noting that a New Zealand passport is one of the most accepted worldwide with visa-free access to most countries. In addition, New Zealand passport holders have free entry into Australia as if they are Australian citizens.

Points System

New Zealand has a points system, much like that used in Canada and Australia, except that persons 60 years and older generally are not admitted. The four categories used are: 1) general, 2) family, 3) humanitarian, and; 4) business investment.

1. General category: aimed at young persons and awards points for employability; education; work experience; age, with ages 25-29 scoring highest; and settlement factors, including assets, sponsorship or an offer of skilled employment. Processing requires only six to eight weeks.

2. Family category: family reunion: this includes parents, children, brothers, and sisters; or partnership with a New Zealand citizen or resident is recognized and includes a legally married husband or wife, or a de facto or same-sex partner.

3. Residence is also granted for "humanitarian" reasons involving serious physical or emotional harm to the applicant or a resident of New Zealand.

4. New Zealand's Business Investor's Policy aims to increase the

nation's human capital, enterprise, and innovation in foreign trade. The applicant must show his/her capital was lawfully earned and resulted from personal business or professional skills. In addition to qualifying under a points system, a minimum investment of NZ$1 million (US$856,000) is required, conferring one point upon the potential immigrant. Additional points are awarded for larger investments, up to 11 points for an investment of NZ$6 million (US$5.1 million).

To enter New Zealand one must be in good health and of good character, and have a passport that is valid for at least three months past the date you are to leave.

After five years of residence, a person is eligible for naturalization. Foreign travel during these five years is unrestricted. Annually, about 500 approved applications are in this category. For details, see http://www.immigration.govt.nz/

Contacts

Embassy of New Zealand
37 Observatory Circle NW
Washington, DC 20008
Tel.: (202) 328-4800
Email: wshinfo@mfat.govt.nz
Web: http://www.nzembassy.com/usa

Consulate General
2425 Olympic Blvd, Suite 600E
Santa Monica, CA 90404
Tel.: (310) 566-6555
Email: contact@nzcgla.com

Consulate General
295 Madison Avenue — 41st Floor
New York, NY 10017-6702

Tel.: (212) 832-4038

New Zealand Tourism Board
Suite 300, 501 Santa Monica Blvd
Santa Monica, CA 90401-2443
Tel.: (310) 395-7480
Web: http://www.tourismnewzealand.com

United States Embassy
29 Fitzherbert Terrace Thorndon
Wellington, New Zealand
Tel.: + (64) 4-462-6000
Web: http://newzealand.usembassy.gov

U.S. Consulate General
3rd Floor, Citibank Building
23 Customs Street East
Auckland, New Zealand
Tel.: + (64) 9-303-2724

Recommend Attorney:

David A Tanzer & Assoc., PC.
Email: Datlegal@aol.com
Web: http://www.DavidTanzer.com
Auckland, New Zealand:
Tel.: (64) 9-353-1328
Brisbane, Australia:
Tel.: (61) 7-3319-6999
Vail, Colorado USA:
Tel.: (970) 476-6100

Republic of the Philippines

Government:	Republic
Capital:	Manila
National Day:	Independence Day (from Spain): 12 June (1898)
Population:	107,668,231 (July 2014 est.)
Total Area:	115,831 sq. miles / 300,000 sq. kilometers
Languages:	Filipino and English (both official); eight other major dialects
Ethnic groups:	Tagalog 28.1%, Cebuano 13.1%, Ilocano 9%, Bisaya/Binisaya 7.6%, Hiligaynon Ilonggo 7.5%, Bikol 6%, Waray 3.4%
Religion:	Roman Catholic 80.9%, Muslim 5%, other Christian 4.5%, Evangelical 2.8%, Iglesia ni Kristo 2.3%, Aglipayan 2%, other 1.8%
Life expectancy:	72.48 years
Currency:	Philippine peso (PHP)
GDP:	US$351.4 billion (2010 est.)
GDP per capita:	US$3,500 (2010 est.)

The second-largest archipelago in the world, with over 7000 tropical islands, the Philippines is one of the great treasures of Southeast Asia. Often overlooked by travelers because of its location on the "wrong" side of the South China Sea, the Philippines rewards those who go the extra distance to reach it. And because it's off the beaten path, the Philippines is a great place to escape the hordes who descend on other parts of Southeast Asia.

The Philippines is a land apart from mainland Southeast Asia — not only geographically but also spiritually and cul-

turally. The country's overwhelming Catholicism, the result of 350 years of Spanish rule, is its most obvious enigma. Vestiges of the Spanish era include exuberant town fiestas (festivals) like Kalibo's Ati-Atihan, unique Spanish-Filipino colonial architecture, and exquisite, centuries-old stone churches lording over bustling town plazas. Malls, fast-food chains and widespread spoken English betray the influence of Spain's colonial successor, the Americans. Yet despite these outside influences, the country remains very much its own unique entity.

First and foremost, the Philippines is a place of natural wonders — a string of coral-fringed islands strewn across a vast expanse of the western Pacific. Below sea level, the Philippines boasts some of the world's best diving and snorkeling. Above sea level, it has a fantastic landscape with wonders enough to stagger even the most jaded traveler.

Of course, any traveler who has been here will tell you that it's the people and their culture that makes the Philippines unique. Long poised at the center of Southeast Asian trade, colonized by a succession of world powers, the Philippines is a vivid tapestry that reflects its varied cultural inheritance.

And despite the poverty that afflicts much of the nation, the Filipinos themselves are among the most ebullient and easygoing people anywhere. The Philippines truly qualifies as one of the last great frontiers in Southeast Asian travel. Cross whichever ocean you need to and see for yourself. — Lonely Planet

Travel Alert: The U.S. Department of State warns U.S. citizens of the risks of travel to the Philippines, in particular to the Sulu Archipelago and the island of Mindanao. This reflects continuing threats in those areas due to terrorist and insurgent activities. U.S. citizens should continue to defer non-essential travel to the Sulu Archipelago, due to the high threat of kidnapping of international travelers and violence linked to insurgency and terrorism there and should continue to exercise extreme caution if traveling to the island of Mindanao in the southern Philippines. See: http://travel.state.gov/content/passports/english/alertswarnings/philippines-travel-warning.html

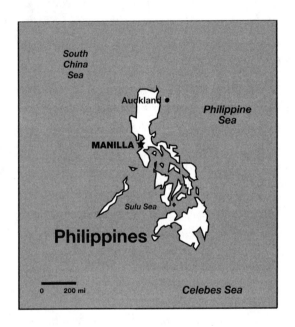

History and Overview

Located in southeastern Asia, this 7,000 island archipelago is between the Philippine Sea and the South China Sea, east of Vietnam. The major island groupings are Luzon in the north, the Visayas in the center and Mindanao in the south.

The Philippine Islands became a Spanish colony during the 16th century but were ceded to the United States in 1898 following the Spanish-American War. In 1935, the Philippines became a self-governing commonwealth under American control with a non-voting delegate in the U.S. House of Representatives. Manuel

Quezon was elected President and worked to prepare the country for independence after a planned 10-year transition.

In 1942, the islands were attacked and occupied by the Japanese during World War II. U.S. forces and Filipinos fought together during 1944 to 1945 to regain control. On July 4, 1946, the Philippines attained independence from the U.S. The 20-year rule of Ferdinand Marcos ended in 1986, when a widespread popular rebellion forced him into exile and installed Corazon Aquino as president.

In the ensuing years, presidents have been elected, impeached and defeated amidst constant turmoil, including street riots and attempted coups. All the while, the Philippine government, such as it has been, has faced threats from armed Communist insurgencies and from Muslim separatists in the south. Benigno Aquino III was elected to a six-year term as president in 2010.

The Philippine government faces threats from three terrorist groups on the U.S. government's Foreign Terrorist Organization list, but has scored some major successes in capturing or killing key wanted terrorists.

Manila has waged a decades-long struggle against ethnic Moro insurgencies in the southern Philippines, which led to a peace accord with the Moro National Liberation Front and ongoing peace talks with the Moro Islamic Liberation Front. The decades-long Maoist-inspired New People's Army insurgency also operates through much of the country. The Philippines also face increased tension with China over disputed territorial and maritime claims in the South China Sea.

The country also has been afflicted by natural disasters including typhoon Bopha (December 2012), the Bohol earthquake (October 2013), and typhoon Haiyan (November 2013).

Economy

The Philippines was less severely affected by the Asian financial crisis of 1998 than its neighbors, aided in part by its high level of annual remittances from thousands of overseas workers spread around the world. GDP growth accelerated reflecting the continued resilience of the service sector, and improved exports and agricultural output.

Experts say it will take a higher, sustained growth for any appreciable progress in the alleviation of poverty, given the Philippines' high annual population growth rate and unequal distribution of income. The country also faces higher oil prices, higher interest rates on its dollar borrowings and higher inflation. Fiscal constraints limit Manila's ability to finance infrastructure and social spending.

Large budget deficits have produced a high debt level, and this has forced Manila to spend a large portion of the national budget on debt service. The current account balance had recorded consecutive surpluses since 2003; international reserves are at record highs; the banking system is stable; and the stock market was Asia's second best-performer in 2012. Efforts to improve tax administration and expenditure management have helped ease the Philippines' tight fiscal situation and reduce high debt levels. The Philippines has received several credit rating upgrades on its sovereign debt, and has had little difficulty tapping domestic and international markets to finance its deficits.

Long-term challenges include reforming governance and the judicial system, building infrastructure, improving regulatory predictability, and the ease of doing business, attracting higher levels of local and foreign investments. The Philippine Constitution and the other laws continue to restrict foreign ownership in important activities/sectors such as land ownership and public utilities.

Special Resident Retiree Visa

Over 27,000 foreign retirees from 107 countries live in the Philippines under the Special Resident Retiree's Visa program (SRRV) administered by the Philippine Retirement Authority.

Foreign retirees can retire and live in the Philippines for as long as they want. They can come in and out of the country exempt from the airport travel tax, and from the need for a Study Permit or Student's Visa for their dependent-children who pursue education in the Philippines. PRA retirees can use foreign issued health insurance cards in Philippine hospitals and clinics accredited by selected health insurance companies. They are also eligible for a one-time tax free importation of household goods and personal effects.

A Principal Retiree must be at least 35 years old to qualify. Foreign retirees can choose from four options:

1. SRRV Smile – for active / healthy principal retirees 35 years old and older above who maintain a deposit of US$20,000 in a PRA designated bank;

2. SRRV Classic – for active / healthy principal retirees who use a visa deposit of US$10,000 or US$20,000 (50 years old +) or US$50,000 (35 to 49 years old) to purchase condominium units or for long term lease of a house and lot;

3. SRRV Courtesy – for former Filipinos (35 years old +), and foreign nationals (50 years old +) who served in the Philippines as diplomats, ambassadors, or officers/staff of international organizations. The visa deposit is US$1,500.

4. SRRV Human Touch – for ailing principal retirees, (35 years old +), who have medical/clinical needs and services. Under this option, the retiree only needs to have a visa deposit of US$10,000, a monthly pension of at least US$1,500 and a Health Insurance Policy. For more http://www.pra.gov.ph/

Residence and Citizenship

American citizens made up the bulk of former Filipinos who reacquired their original nationality under the country's dual citizenship law, the "Citizenship Retention and Reacquisition Act of 2003" adopted by the Philippine Congress.

Through 2009, more than 43,000 former Filipinos had reacquired their Philippine citizenship. The government has used the repatriation law to encourage former Filipinos now living overseas to return to the land of their birth, buy properties and invest in businesses in the country.

Birth within the territory of the Philippines does not automatically confer citizenship. Citizenship is conferred in the following ways:

1. by descent on a child, at least one of whose parents is a citizen of the Philippines, regardless of the child's country of birth.

2. by naturalization: Filipino citizenship may be acquired upon fulfillment of the following conditions:

    a.) the applicant has resided in the Philippines for at least 10 years;

    b.) the person provides proof of livelihood and permanent residence; and

    c.) the person shows familiarity with the customs and language of the Philippines.

Under the 2003 Act dual citizenship is only recognized in the following cases:

1. A child born abroad to Filipino parents who acquires the citizenship of the country of birth. He or she is not obliged to choose a preferred citizenship until they reach the age of majority, 21.

2. When a Filipino citizen marries a foreign national and acquires the citizenship of their spouse, he or she becomes an unofficial dual citizen. However, in all cases, the Filipino citizenship takes legal precedence.

3. The 2003 Act declared that all Philippine citizens who became citizens of another country shall be deemed not to have lost their Philippine citizenship. Anyone who was born to Filipino parents, in the Philippines or elsewhere in the world can enjoy dual citizenship.

U.S citizens may enter the Philippines without a visa upon presentation of their U.S. passport, valid for at least six months after the date of entry and a return ticket to the United States or an onward ticket to another country. Upon arrival, immigration authorities will annotate your passport with an entry visa valid for 21 days. If you plan to stay longer than 21 days, you must apply for an extension at the Philippine Bureau of Immigration and Deportation's main office at Magallanes Drive, Intramuros, Manila, or any provincial office.

In 2014, foreigners and returning overseas Filipinos used the new and simplified Arrival and Departure Cards, issued by the Bureau of Immigration at the country's entry and exit points, particularly at Manila's Ninoy Aquino International Airport (NAIA). See http://www.immigration.gov.ph

Before leaving the country, long-term foreign residents must obtain an emigration clearance certificate that is issued to departing foreigner nationals to prove that they have no derogatory records in the country or any accountability with other government agencies.

Contacts
Republic of the Philippines Embassy
1600 Massachusetts Avenue NW

Washington, DC 20036
Tel.: (202) 467-9300
Web: http://www.philippineembassy-usa.org/

Consulates General: New York, Chicago, San Francisco, Los Angeles, Honolulu, Agana, and Guam.

United States Embassy
1201 Roxas Boulevard 1000
Manila, the Philippines
Tel.: + (632) 301-2000
Web: http://manila.usembassy.gov

Republic of Singapore

Government:	Parliamentary republic
Capital:	Singapore City
National Day:	National Day: 9 August (1965)
Population:	5,567,301 (July 2014 est.)
Total Area:	268 sq. miles / 693 sq. kilometers
Languages:	Mandarin 35%, English 23%, Malay 14.1%, Hokkien 11.4%, Cantonese 5.7%, Teochew 4.9%, Tamil 3.2%, other Chinese dialects 1.8%, other 0.9%
Ethnic groups:	Chinese 76.8%, Malay 13.9%, Indian 7.9%, other 1.4%
Religion:	Buddhist 42.5%, Muslim 14.9%, none 14.8%, other Christian 9.8%, Taoist 8.5%, Catholic 4.8%, Hindu 4%, other 0.7%
Life expectancy:	84.38 years
Currency:	Singapore dollar (SGD)
GDP:	US$339 billion (2013 est.)
GDP per capita:	US$62,400 (2013 est.)

It's popular to dismiss Singapore as a kind of Asia Lite — blandly efficient and safe, a boringly tasteless, disciplinarian and unadventurous place where citizens are robbed of their cherished freedom to spit on the street and chew gum. Utter nonsense.

Singapore is in fact one of the most enjoyable cities in Southeast Asia. As you zoom in from one of the world's best airports along the lushly tree-shaded expressway or on the zippy MRT train line, you'll quickly realize this is no traffic-snarled

Bangkok. And as you stroll through the fashion emporiums of Orchard Rd, poke around antique shops in Chinatown or take a walk around one of the dozens of beautiful city parks, you'll know the city bears no comparison to crime- and poverty-ridden Manila or Jakarta.

Few cities in Southeast Asia can boast Singapore's fascinating ethnic brew. Where else in the world can you dip into the cultures of China, India and Muslim Malaysia all in one day, against a backdrop of ultra-modern Western commerce? Not only has Singapore's history of migration left a rich cultural and architectural legacy that makes wandering the streets an absorbing delight, it has created one of the world's great eating capitals.

If there's one thing more stylish than the bars and restaurants, it's the boutiques that have made Singapore a byword in Asia for extravagant shopping. Away from the Gucci and Louis Vuitton onslaught of Orchard Road, however, there are bargains to be found on everything from clothes to electronics — and a range of art and antique shops that few Asian cities can match.

It's a fascinating place and a remarkable achievement. No-one is denying that Singaporeans have had to sacrifice some level of freedom in their island's rise from racially divided, resource-starved port town. But you get the feeling that if Western development aid had ever matched Singapore's strides in poverty reduction, education, infrastructure and health care, they'd be patting themselves on the back and saying that political freedom was a small sacrifice to make.

Besides, it's not all strait-laced conformity. You don't have to look far to find echoes of the islands colorful, rakish past, or evidence of a thriving and creatively unfettered artistic com-

munity. Singapore's soul is alive and well and it is unique. — *Lonely Planet*

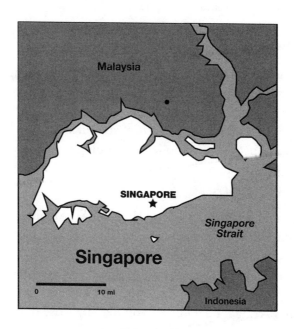

History and Overview

The Republic of Singapore has the distinction of being a small island, a state and a city all in one. Located just a few miles north of the equator, it has Malaysia and Indonesia as close neighbors. The climate is equatorial, hot and very humid with rainfall of over 90 inches annually.

Singapore was a British colony until independence in 1965. Lee Kuan Yew became its autocratic leader and served until 1990, when his son replaced him in his official capacities. He built a one-party state that still does not tolerate dissent or opposition of any kind. There are no jury trials and civil matters, such as alleged libel or slander, can escalate into criminal issues with serious consequences, especially for political opponents. Draconian laws keep crime (and freedom) to a minimum, but the enforced stability attracts massive foreign investment. Moreover, the streets are very clean, since spitting or littering can land you in jail.

Singapore has an open economy with strong service and manufacturing sectors as well as excellent international trading links. Rising labor costs and appreciation of the Singapore dollar against its neighbors' currencies are threats to competitiveness. The government's strategy includes cutting costs, increasing productivity, improving infrastructure, and encouraging higher value-added industries. In applied technology, per capita output, investment, and labor discipline, Singapore has key attributes of a developed country.

The common language is English. Most Singaporeans are Asian, with commerce dominated by ethnic Chinese. Malays make up less than 15%, with Indians, Thais, Vietnamese, Laotians, and a very small number of Europeans. Europeans hold most management positions and are generally well regarded. In Singapore, state regulation has created a paradise if you like high-rise buildings, crass materialism, and minimal personal freedom.

Singapore is not a tax haven. It supports welfare state programs of free schools, low-fee universities, childcare, socialized medicine, and subsidized housing. Tax rates are slightly below those of the United States. Income over S$400,000 (US$315,000) is taxed at 33%. New exporters can usually get a 15-year tax holiday. Under a territorial tax system, income from offshore sources is tax-exempt. Only income earned in Singapore is taxed. Non-residents are taxed on Singapore net income after expenses, at 15% for employment income and 20% for directors' and consultant fees.

Real estate is taxed at 15% of the annual rental value. The maximum estate tax is 10% with an exemption of S$500,000 to S$1 million, depending upon the nature of the assets. Import duties are very low, except on motor vehicles, which bear a 125% duty. Generally, Singapore is a shopper's paradise. Restaurants and hotel services are of very high standard and charge about half of European prices. Prices in nearby Thailand are half of the Singapore rates. Some rate Singapore along with cities like San Francisco and Sydney for quality of life and economic opportunity.

Economy

An article in *International Man* reports, "Singapore ranks at the top of every list for good governance and market freedoms, and so it has become a magnet for significant sums of Southeast Asian money looking for a home in the stable Singapore dollar.

All of that is helping Singapore attract business. It is the gateway to Southeast Asia for conventions, tourists and money. Scads of immigrants chasing employment opportunities, incoming businesses and their employees, hordes of tourists who come here for the shopping, and gamblers ready to dump cash into newly legalized casinos are pouring in. Casinos have helped propel Singapore's economy at torrid, double-digit rates this year.

Every month, Singapore sets a new tourist record, with some months seeing more than a million tourists arrive, the equivalent of 20% of the permanent population."

Singapore is one of the rising offshore financial havens of the world. Singapore has grown into a premier investment and business haven, comparable with Hong Kong, London, New York or Tokyo. While Hong Kong sees itself as a financial gateway to expanding China, Singapore is the gateway to all of Southeast Asia.

I visited there a few years ago for a trust law conference and saw how local trust and other laws have been fully updated on a par with leading offshore trust creation centers, such as Bermuda, Jersey or Panama.

Today, Singapore is a modernized, western city. When I was there for the first time, I discovered what veteran Asian travelers already knew — Singapore long ago traded its ancient Oriental image for towers of concrete, glass and high-tech industry. And the rickshaws have been replaced by more Ferraris, Rolls-Royces and Mercedes than you can shake a stick at.

Since my visit six years ago, Singapore has strengthened its banking secrecy laws patterned after those in Switzerland. However, under pressure from major nations, as have all offshore financial centers, the government now adheres to the OECD Article 26 standards governing the exchange of tax information among nations. Singapore has signed 12 tax information exchange agreements (TIEAs) with other countries. Singapore also has double taxation agreements (DTA) with more than 50 countries which it uses for information exchange.

Singapore actively recruits wealthy business persons as residents. For those active in offshore finance, this is a match made in financial heaven because the island city-state has become Asia's newest private banking hub by luring the super-wealthy away from places such as Hong Kong and Switzerland.

Singapore's strengthened bank secrecy laws, even with its OECD compromise, are one enticement but the government also is allowing foreigners, especially Europeans, who meet its wealth requirements, to buy land and become permanent residents. The goal is to attract private wealth from across Asia, as well as riches that Europeans and other Westerners are moving out of Switzerland and EU nations to avoid new tax and reporting laws there.

Many Swiss banks, such as Bank Julius Baer, have beefed up their operations in Singapore to capitalize on the new business opportunities. The number of private banks operating in Singapore has nearly doubled, to 35, in the past 10 years, officials say.

Authorities reported that total assets for all domestic banks in Singapore totaled US$786 billion in January 2014. Singapore's financial sector in 2014 was six times larger than its economy, with local and foreign banks holding assets worth S$2.1 trillion (US$1.7 trillion). Financial services grew 163% between 2008 and 2012. After construction, financial services have been the second most important driver of Singapore's economic growth in recent years. *Forbes* magazine in early 2014 alleged that Singapore was caught up in major real estate and credit bubble and warned about its economic future.

The Singapore government runs two large sovereign wealth funds that manage and invest its foreign reserves: Government of Singapore Investment Corporation, or GIC, and Temasek Holdings, which have US$285 billion and US$173.3 billion in assets under management respectively, mostly invested in Asian equities.

Entrepreneurs

Singapore offers a foreign investors' citizenship program called the "Scheme for Entrepreneurs." It was designed mainly for wealthy residents of Hong Kong who wished to secure a place for themselves and their families in a similar bustling economic environment before Communist China's takeover in 1997.

The program begins with a commitment to invest a minimum of S$1 million, about US$650,000. At least 50% of the amount must be in industrial, commercial or residential property. Prior government approval before a purchase of property is advised. These funds can be deposited with the government treasury at interest, but must be invested within two years, for a minimum period of five years. An acceptable condo can be had for US$300,000 and an equal amount might be invested in a local business, and then capitalized with a loan.

Foreign nationals with investment residence status are eligible to apply for naturalization after two years. There is no requirement that the entire time be spent in Singapore, but a home must be maintained. Singapore does not recognize dual nationality. This means that there is an oath of allegiance and a requirement to surrender any passport from another nation before receiving the Singapore passport. The surrendered passport can be reissued with no notice to Singapore.

Dual nationality also means that the government strictly enforces universal national service for all male citizens and permanent residents until the age of 21. Travel abroad of males may require Singapore government approval as they approach national service age and may be restricted. The Ministry of Defense can advise about national service obligations.

Those with desired skills or in certain professions need not make an investment to gain permanent resident status. After five years as a resident, they can apply for citizenship. Children born in Singapore are automatically citizens.

A valid passport is required for entry. U.S. citizens do not need a visa if their visit is for business or pleasure, and their stay is for 90 days or less. Travelers to the region should note that Singapore and some neighboring countries, particularly Indonesia, do not allow Americans to enter with fewer than six months of validity remaining on their passport under any circumstances.

Contacts

Embassy of the Republic of Singapore
3501 International Place NW
Washington, DC 20008
Tel.: (202) 537-3100
Email: singemb_was@sgmfa.gov.sg

Web: http://www.mfa.gov.sg/washington

United States Embassy
27 Napier Road
Singapore 258508
Tel.: + (65) 6476-9100
Email: singaporeacs@state.gov
Web: http://singapore.usembassy.gov/

Recommended Immigration Consultant:

Henley & Partners
50 Raffles Place
Singapore Land Tower, Level 30
Singapore 048623
Tel.: +65 6438 7117
Email: singapore@henleyglobal.com

Taiwan (Republic of China)

Government:	Multi-party democracy
Capital:	Taipei
National Day	Republic Day (Chinese Revolution): 10 October (1911)
Population:	23,359,928 (July 2014 est.)
Total Area:	13,892 sq. miles / 35,980 sq. kilometers
Languages:	Mandarin Chinese (official), Taiwanese (Min), Hakka dialects
Ethnic groups:	Taiwanese (including Hakka) 84%, mainland Chinese 14%, Aborigine 2%
Religion:	Mixture of Buddhist, Confucian, Taoist 93%, Christian 4.5%
Life expectancy:	79.84 years
Currency:	Taiwan dollar (TWD)
GDP:	US$926.4 billion (2013 est.)
GDP per capita:	US$39,600 (2013 est.)

Ilha Formosa — Beautiful Island; this is what a group of Portuguese sailors, said to have been the first Westerners to lay eyes on the island, uttered upon seeing Taiwan for the first time. We imagine they must have been pretty enamored. While not every Westerner has the same love-at first-sight reaction to Taiwan, our Portuguese seafaring friends were just the first of many.

True, Taiwan hasn't yet made it to the top of everybody's "to visit" list, but we think this is partially a result of people not quite knowing what Taiwan has to offer. But within the borders of this small, sweet-potato shaped island barely the size of many American states lies a world of contrasts and a mélange of cultural influences you're not likely to find anywhere else on the planet.

In the first decade of the 21st century, Taiwan is increasingly drawing travelers of all stripes: from spiritual seekers looking to experience the island's religious heritage to gourmands in search of the perfect night-market — meal to computer geeks scanning the horizon for the latest high-tech gadgets. Taiwan offers visitors a hypermodern skin, an ancient Chinese skeleton and an aboriginal soul. And more than that, Taiwan has some of the world's warmest people, affable to a fault and so filled with ren-qing wei (which, roughly translated, means "personal affection") that few who come to Taiwan a stranger leave that way.

Much has changed in the centuries since the Portuguese first saw Taiwan. Still, we think if the same group of sailors came back in the present day, they'd call it Ilha Formosa all over again. — Lonely Planet

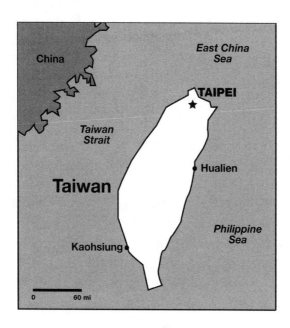

History and Overview

Located in eastern Asia, these islands border the East China Sea, Philippine Sea, South China Sea, and Taiwan Strait, north of the Philippines, off the southeastern coast of mainland China.

In 1895, military defeat forced China to cede Taiwan to Japan. Taiwan reverted to Chinese control after World War II. Following the Communist victory on the mainland in 1949, two million Nationalists fled to Taiwan and established a government using the 1946 constitution drawn up for all of China. Over the next five decades, the ruling authorities gradually democratized and incorporated the native population within the governing structure. In 2000, Taiwan underwent its first peaceful transfer of power from the Nationalist to the Democratic Progressive Party.

Throughout this period, the island prospered and became one of East Asia's economic "Tigers."

The dominant political issues continue to be the relationship between Taiwan and China, specifically, the question of eventual unification, as well as domestic political and economic reform. The United States government has gone from a policy of strong support of the Nationalist government on Taiwan after World War II, to a near neutral policy that caters to mainland China's demand for eventual reunification.

In 2012, Taiwan Central Bank signed a memorandum of understanding on cross-Strait currency settlement with its Chinese counterpart. This allowed for the direct settlement of Chinese RMB and the New Taiwan dollar across the Strait, which could help develop Taiwan into a local RMB hub. Closer economic links with the mainland bring greater opportunities for the Taiwan economy, but also poses new challenges as the island becomes more economically dependent on China while political differences remain unresolved.

At the rate events are going, it appears economic reunification by bilateral trade with the mainland may occur well before a political solution. In 2014 mass protest demonstrations led by young people against pending economic agreements with Beijing disrupted Taiwan's parliament and government buildings were occupied for days.

Economy

Taiwan has a dynamic capitalist economy with gradually decreasing guidance of investment and foreign trade by government authorities. In keeping with this trend, some large, government-owned banks and industrial firms are being privatized. Exports have provided the primary impetus for industrialization.

The trade surplus is substantial, and foreign reserves are the world's third largest. Agriculture contributes less than 2% to GDP, down from 32% in 1952. Taiwan is a major investor throughout South-East Asia. China has overtaken the U.S. to become Taiwan's largest export market and Taiwan's third-largest source of imports after Japan and the U.S. Taiwan has benefited from cross-Strait economic integration and a sharp increase in world demand to achieve substantial growth in its export sector. The service sector, which accounts for 69% of Taiwan's GDP, has continued to expand, while unemployment and inflation rates have declined.

The island runs a large trade surplus, and its foreign reserves are among the world's largest. Recently opened cross Strait travel, transportation, and tourism links are likely to increase Taiwan and China's economic interdependence.

China has overtaken the U.S. to become Taiwan's largest export market and its second-largest source of imports, after Japan. China is also the island's number one destination for foreign direct investment. Growth fell below 2% in 2008 because of the global economic slowdown.

Residence and Citizenship

The Nationality Law of the Republic of China governs citizenship, which is based primarily on descent from the father (jus sanguinis). Birth within the territory of Taiwan does not automatically confer citizenship except in the case of a child of unknown parentage.

Citizenship by descent is conferred on:

1. a child whose father is, at the time of that child's birth, a Taiwanese national, even if the father died before birth;

2. a child whose father is unknown or stateless but whose mother is a Taiwanese national, or;

3. a child born out of wedlock to a foreign woman and Taiwanese national father who has been legitimatized (recognized) by the father.

Citizenship is granted to a person who is the foreign wife of a Taiwanese national, except when the law of her own country requires that she retain her original citizenship.

Citizenship by naturalization can be acquired upon fulfillment of the following conditions: 1) a person has resided in the territory for at least five years; 2) has reached the age of 20 years, 3) is of good character, 4) and has sufficient property or skill to make an independent living.

The spouse and non-majority age children of a naturalized citizen acquire the Taiwanese citizenship unless it is contrary to the law of the spouse's, or children's original country. Dual citizenship is not recognized.

U.S. passport holders are allowed to enter Taiwan without a visa for up to 30 days (no extensions allowed) if their passport is valid for at least six months from the date of entry and the traveler has a confirmed return or onward air ticket. Travelers must have already met any additional visa requirements for the next destination, if applicable. If the passport is valid for less than six months from the date of entry into Taiwan, travelers may apply for a landing visa that allows a stay of no more than 30 days.

Contacts

Taipei Economic & Cultural Representative Office
4201 Wisconsin Avenue NW
Washington, DC 20016
Tel.: (202) 895-1800
Email: tecroinfodc@tecro.us
Web: http://www.roc-taiwan.org/us/mp.asp?mp=12

American Institute in Taiwan
No.7, Ln. 134, Sec. 3, Xinyi Road
Da-an Dist., Taipei City 106-59, Taiwan
Tel.: +886 (02) 2162-2000
Email: aitamcit@mail.ait.org.tw
Web: http://www.ait.org.tw/en/home.html

Kingdom of Thailand

Government:	Constitutional monarchy
Capital:	Bangkok
National Day:	Birthday of King Phumiphon: 5 December (1927)
Population:	67,741,401 (July 2014 est.)
Total Area:	198,456 sq. miles / 514,000 sq. kilometers
Languages:	Thai, English (second language of the elite)
Ethnic groups:	Thai 75%, Chinese 14%, other 11%
Religion:	Buddhist 94.6%, Muslim 4.6%, Christian 0.7%, other 0.1%
Life expectancy:	74.18 years
Currency:	Baht (THB)
GDP:	US$674.3 billion (2013 est.)
GDP per capita:	US$9,900 (2013 est.)

Friendly and fun-loving, exotic and tropical, cultured and historic, Thailand beams with a lustrous hue from its gaudy temples and golden beaches to the ever-comforting Thai smile.

Thailand's beaches are mythical: tall palms angle over pearlescent sand, coral gardens flourish in the shallow seas and beach parties are liberally lubricated with alcohol and fun. With a long coastline (well, actually, two coastlines) and jungle-topped islands anchored in azure waters, Thailand is a tropical getaway for the hedonist and the hermit, the prince and the pauper. And in between the kissing cousins of sea and sky are dramatic limestone mountains standing sentinel.

The celestial world is a close confidant in this Buddhist nation, where religious devotion is a colorful and ubiqui-

tous spectacle. Gleaming temples and golden Buddhas frame both the rural and modern landscape with exuberance. Ancient banyan trees are ceremoniously wrapped in sacred cloth to honor the resident spirits; fortune-bringing shrines decorate humble noodle houses as well as monumental malls, while garland-festooned dashboards ward off traffic accidents. The Thai's ongoing dialogue with the divine anchors the day-to-day chaos to a solid base of tranquility.

No matter what draws you to the country first, a Thai meal will keep you hooked. Adored around the world, Thai cuisine expresses fundamental aspects of Thai culture: it is generous and warm, outgoing and nuanced, refreshing and relaxed. And it is much more delicious in its native setting. Each Thai dish relies on fresh and local ingredients – from pungent lemongrass and searing chilies to plump seafood and crispy fried chicken. With a tropical abundance, a varied national menu is built around the four fundamental flavors: spicy, sweet, salty and sour. And then there are the regional differences, which propel travelers on an eating tour of Bangkok noodle shacks, seafood pavilions in Phuket, Burmese market stalls in Mae Hong Son, and luscious tropical fruit everywhere. — Lonely Planet

Travel Alert: The U.S. Department of State warns U.S. citizens of the potential risks of travel to Thailand, particularly Bangkok, due to ongoing political and social unrest. Demonstrations, primarily in the greater Bangkok area and occasionally elsewhere continue, and there have been regular incidents of violence. U.S. citizens are advised to avoid all protests, demonstrations, and large gatherings.

History and Overview

The Kingdom of Thailand, formerly known as Siam, is part of the Indochinese Peninsula in Southeast Asia. The nation borders the Andaman Sea and the Gulf of Thailand, southeast of Burma. The Mekong River forms the border with Laos.

The only country in Southeast Asia to maintain its independence during the European colonial expansion of the 17th through 19th centuries, Thailand is richly endowed with architectural and artistic monuments of its Buddhist heritage. Terrain ranging from idyllic beaches to mountain rain forests and a warm, tropical climate provide recreational and adventure opportunities. A wide variety of tribal lifestyles may be observed among Thailand's many ethnic groups.

Thais think differently from Occidentals. Their culture, religion and morality are quintessentially Oriental. Thais are proud and patriotic and revere their king. The government is a constitutional monarchy, but the army wields major power. The Buddhist religion is a major influence on national life and on individuals.

Economy

With a well-developed infrastructure, a free-enterprise economy and pro-investment policies, Thailand fully recovered from the 1997 to 1998 Asian financial crises. In 2004, a major tsunami took 8,500 lives in Thailand and caused massive destruction of property in the southern provinces of Krabi, Phangnga and Phuket.

With a well-developed infrastructure, a free-enterprise economy, and generally pro-investment policies, Thailand was one of East Asia's best performers from 2002 to 2004, averaging more than 6% annual real GDP growth. However, overall economic growth has fallen sharply — averaging 4.9% from 2005 to 2007 as persistent political crisis stalled infrastructure mega-projects, eroded investor and consumer confidence, and damaged the country's international image. That crisis continues to the time of this writing, with Thailand's political and social future very much in doubt.

Exports were the key economic driver as foreign investment and consumer demand stalled. Export growth from 2005 to 2008 averaged 17.5% annually. Business uncertainty escalated, however, following the 2006 coup when the military-installed government imposed capital controls and considered far-reaching changes to foreign investment rules and other business legislation. Although controversial capital controls have since been lifted and business rules largely remain unchanged, investor sentiment has not recovered. The 2008 global financial crisis further darkened Thailand's economic horizon. Continued political uncertainty will hamper resumption of infrastructure mega-projects.

Politics

For almost a decade beginning in 2006 mob or military rule has seemed to be the only two choices in Thai politics.

A military coup in 2006 ousted then-Prime Minister Thaksin Chinnawat. In 2007, elections saw the pro-Thaksin People's Power Party (PPP) emerge at the head of a coalition government that took office in 2008 with majority support from rural areas.

The anti-Thaksin People's Alliance for Democracy, mainly based in urban Bangkok, began street demonstrations against the new rural backed government, eventually occupying the prime minister's office and Bangkok's two international airports. Thaksin supporters under the banner of the United Front for Democracy Against Dictatorship (UDD) won elections in 2009. Following a 2010 court verdict confiscating half of Thaksin's frozen assets, the UDD staged large protests and occupied downtown Bangkok. Clashes between security forces and armed protesters resulted in 92 deaths and an estimated US$1.5 billion in arson-related property losses.

The protests exposed major cleavages in the Thai body politic between urban Bangkok and the countryside that continue to this day. A 2011 general election saw Thaksin-backed parties win control. In 2014, scheduled elections were held but again massive street demonstrations disrupted the process and the courts ruled a new election must be held. In May 2014 the courts ousted Prime Minister Yingluck Shinawatra and some of her cabinet in what foreign observers called a "judicial coup d'état" based on questionably charges.

All this was too much for the Thai military. In late May Thailand's military junta, headed by Gen. Prayuth Chan-ocha, overthrew the elected government and announced that it would stay in power "indefinitely." The military coup was endorsed by King Bhumibol Adulyadej, the monarch for nearly seven decades who has semi-divine status in the country. The military promised that it would create a "genuine democracy" but gave no time frame for doing so.

Best to stay away until the people of Thailand decide where they are going.

Residence and Citizenship

There are a few non-Asian residents who are white (known locally as "farangs"), making up less than 1% of the population. Until recently, Thailand was under-populated and willing to absorb all immigrants. Mass migrations, due to nearby revolutions, caused the population of Thailand to triple during the past 40 years. Today, immigration is restricted. Residence permits and naturalized citizenship are limited.

The major reason for a foreign national to acquire Thai residence and/or citizenship is to make the nation your home and center of activity. This is especially true if you are a non-Asian. A Thai passport is useful for Asian travel, but a westerner with a Thai passport will be asked more questions than an Asian. Most European countries will demand a visa and residents can't leave Thailand without an official tax clearance for each trip.

It's not easy for a foreign national to gain residence in Thailand (it restricts immigration to 100 new permanent residents for each country of origin), but there are several categories under which one may qualify. Two of these are loosely described as "business" and "investor." No specific amount is demanded, but the government will want an organizational chart showing all job positions, including the total number of non-Thai aliens. Retirees also receive special treatment, but Thai laws give no description of the exact requirements.

Other categories for admission are government officials, missionaries, evangelists, and "experts or advisors."

For investors, a B10 million (US$323,500) investment for at least three years ensures permanent residence. Applicants are charged B7,600 (US$245) each for processing and B191,400 for issuance of a residence permit book, plus B95,700 (US$3,128) for a spouse and each dependent under 20. The investment may be in a company, condominiums, bonds from the Ministry of Finance, or a fixed bank deposit. Applications should be submitted to the Immigration Bureau, Sathorn Road, Soi Suan Plu, Thailand. The process takes 45 to 60 days for approval.

Residence Permit

Requirements for permanent residence are as follows: The applicant must:

1. enter in a non-immigrant status and stay for a period not less than three years. Travel abroad is allowed, but the holder must return prior to the visa expiration date. Before leaving, an intention to return must be filed with the immigration office;

2. show proof of adequate assets and income, preferably with employment in a managerial or executive position. Proof of investment must be kept showing foreign amounts transferred into the Bank of Thailand;

3. invest in a Thai company or partnership shown by registration and trade certificates issued by the Commercial Ministry;

4. submit evidence of corporate tax and personal tax payments for three years; and

5. accompany the application with a B2,000 (US$65) fee. When approval is granted, another B5,000 (US$162) fee must be paid.

(Note: restrictions placed on foreign ownership may vary or even negate the above-stated requirements.)

Thailand grants only 100 permanent residence permits annually. This quota is waived for investors of more than B10 million and also waived in special cases.

Citizenship

Birth within Thailand does not automatically confer citizenship. The law confers citizenship:

1. by birth:

   a.) on a person born of a father or mother of Thai nationality, whether within or outside the Kingdom, or;

   b.) on a person born within the Kingdom, except a person of alien parents if, at the time of birth, the father was not married to the mother, unless the mother was given leniency for temporary residence or had been permitted to stay temporarily in the Kingdom, unless she had entered the Kingdom without permission.

2. by descent:

   a.) on a child born in wedlock, either of whose parents is a citizen of Thailand, regardless of the child's country of birth, or;

   b.) on a child born out of wedlock, whose mother is a citizen of Thailand and whose father is unknown or stateless, regardless of the child's country of birth.

3. by naturalization: Before applying for Thai citizenship, a foreign person must have the following qualifications: no criminal record; regular employment; have been domiciled in the Kingdom for a consecutive period of not less than five years; and have knowledge of the Thai language.

Dual citizenship is not recognized except in two instances:

1. A child born abroad to Thai parents who obtains the citizenship of the foreign country of birth may retain dual citizenship until reaching the age of majority (18). At that point, the person must choose which citizenship to retain.

2. A Thai woman who marries a foreign national and acquires her husband's citizenship has technically lost her Thai citizenship. Should the marriage end in death or divorce, the Thai national woman could regain her Thai citizenship.

U.S. citizen tourists staying for less than 30 days do not require a visa, but must possess a passport and may be asked to show an onward/return ticket. For longer stays, obtain a visa in advance. A passenger service charge must be paid in Thai baht when departing the country from any of Thailand's international airports. When a traveler enters the country, Thai Immigration stamps the date on which the traveler's authorized stay in Thailand will expire in his or her passport. Any traveler remaining in Thailand beyond this date without an official extension will be assessed an immediate cash fine when departing Thailand.

Contacts

Royal Thai Embassy
1024 Wisconsin Avenue NW
Washington, DC 20007
Tel.: (202) 944-3600
Web: http://www.thaiembdc.org/

United States Embassy
120/22 Wireless Road
Bangkok 10330, Thailand
Tel.: + (66) 2-205-4000
Email: visasbkk@state.gov
Web: http://bangkok.usembassy.gov/

U.S. Consulate General
387 Witchayanond Road
Chiang Mai 50300, Thailand
Tel.: + (66) 5-325-2629
Email: acsbkk@state.gov

Socialist Republic of Vietnam

Government:	Communist state
Capital:	Hanoi
National Day:	Independence Day: 2 September (1945)
Population:	93,421,835 (July 2014 est.)
Total Area:	127,244 sq. miles / 329,560 sq. kilometers
Languages:	Vietnamese (official), English, French, Chinese, and Khmer, mountain area languages (Mon-Khmer and Malayo-Polynesian)
Ethnic groups:	Kinh (Viet) 85.7%, Tay 1.9%, Thai 1.8%, Muong 1.5%, Khmer 1.5%, Mong 1.2%, Nung 1.1%, others 5.3%
Religion:	None 80.8%, Buddhist 9.3%, Catholic 6.7%, Hoa Hao 1.5%, Cao Dai 1.1%, Protestant 0.5%, Muslim 0.1%
Life expectancy:	72.91 years
Currency:	Dong (VND)
GDP:	US$358.9 billion (2013 est.)
GDP per capita:	US$4,000 (2013 est.)

Blessed with a ravishing coastline, emerald-green mountains, breathtaking national parks, dynamic cities, outstanding cultural interest and one of the world's best cuisines, Vietnam has it all.

Vietnam is a nation going places. Fast. Its people are energetic, direct, sharp in commerce and resilient by nature. This is an outrageously fun country to explore, the locals love a laugh (and a drink) and you'll have plenty of opportunities to socialize with them and hear their tales. The American War is over, and yet its impact endures — you'll find reminders of that cataclysmic conflict everywhere you travel. That said, the country was never broken and emerged with its pride intact. Poor in parts but never squalid, Vietnam is developing at an astonishing pace. For travelers, there are issues to consider (including minor scams), but little real danger – on the whole it's a safe, wonderfully rewarding and incredibly varied country to explore.

This is a country of myriad influences and reference points. In the south, Indian and Hindu culture had a lasting influence in the Cham temples and spicy regional cuisine, spiked with chilli and tempered with coconut. Head north and Chinese connections are far more apparent. Between these two competing cultures, you'll find a quintessential Vietnam in the central provinces: the graceful historic old port of Hoi An, and the royal tombs, pagodas and imperial cuisine of Hue.

Oh, and there's more, far more. Factor in an enduring French colonial legacy, which is evident in Hanoi's graceful boulevards, in Ho Chi Minh City's stately museums and in the crispy baguettes and coffee culture you'll find on every street corner. Add the American interlude, more than 50 hill tribes, and of course the proud (battle-tested and victorious) ruling Communist Party ideology and you've got Vietnam: heady, intoxicating and unique. — Lonely Planet

History and Overview

Vietnam is located in southeastern Asia, bordering the Gulf of Thailand, Gulf of Tonkin, and South China Sea, bordered by China, Laos, and Cambodia.

The conquest of Vietnam by France began in 1858 and was completed by 1884. It became part of colonial French Indochina in 1887. Vietnam declared independence after World War II, but France continued to rule until its 1954 defeat by Communist forces under Ho Chi Minh.

Under the Geneva Accords of 1954, Vietnam was divided into the Communist North and anti-Communist South. U.S. economic and military aid to South Vietnam grew through the 1960s in an attempt to bolster the government, but U.S. armed forces were withdrawn following a cease-fire agreement in 1973. Two years later, North Vietnamese forces overran the South reuniting the country under Communist rule.

Despite the return of peace, for over a decade the country experienced little economic growth because of communist leadership policies, the persecution and mass exodus of individuals — many of them successful South Vietnamese merchants — and growing international isolation.

However, since the enactment of Vietnam's "doi moi" (renovation) policy in 1986, Communist authorities have increased economic liberalization and enacted structural reforms needed to modernize the economy and to produce more competitive, export-driven industries.

The country continues to experience protests from various groups, such as the Protestant Montagnard ethnic minority population of the Central Highlands and the Hoa Hao Buddhists in southern Vietnam over religious persecution. Montagnard grievances also include the loss of land to Vietnamese settlers.

The Communist leaders maintain control on political expression and have resisted outside calls to improve human rights. The country continues to experience small-scale protests from various groups, the vast majority connected to land-use issues, calls for increased political space and the lack of equitable mechanisms for resolving disputes.

Economy

Vietnam is a densely populated, developing country that in the last 30 years has had to recover from the ravages of war, the loss of financial support from the old Soviet Bloc, and the rigidities of a Communist centrally planned economy.

Substantial progress was achieved from 1986 to 1997 in moving forward from an extremely low level of development and significantly reducing poverty. Growth averaged around 9% per year from 1993 to 1997. The 1997 Asian financial crisis highlighted the problems in the Vietnamese economy and temporarily allowed opponents of reform to slow progress toward a market-oriented economy. GDP growth averaged 6.8% per year from 1997 to 2004 even against the background of the Asian financial crisis and a global recession, and growth hit 8% in 2005.

Since 2001, Vietnamese authorities have reaffirmed their commitment to economic liberalization and international integration. Vietnam's membership in the ASEAN Free Trade Area (AFTA) and entry into force of the U.S.-Vietnam Bilateral Trade Agreement, in 2001, have led to even more rapid changes in Vietnam's trade and economic regime. Vietnam became an official negotiating partner in the Trans-Pacific Partnership trade agreement in 2010.

Since the U.S.-Vietnam Bilateral Trade Agreement was approved, there has been greatly increased trade between the U.S. and Vietnam, combined with large-scale U.S. investment in Vietnam. Agriculture's share of economic output has continued to shrink from about 25% in 2000 to less than 20% in 2013. Deep poverty has declined significantly and is now smaller than that of China, India, and the Philippines.

Vietnam is working to create jobs to meet the challenge of a labor force that is growing by more than 1.5 million people every year. The global financial crisis constrained Vietnam's ability to create jobs and further reduce poverty.

Vietnam's managed currency, the dong, continues to face downward pressure due to a persistent trade imbalance, and, since 2008, the government devalued it by 20% through a series of small devaluations.

The government's strong growth-oriented economic policies have caused it to struggle to control one of the region's highest inflation rates. Vietnam's economy also faces challenges from falling foreign exchange reserves, an undercapitalized banking sector, and high borrowing costs. Although Vietnam unveiled a broad, "three pillar" economic reform program in 2012, proposing the restructuring of public investment, state-owned enterprises, and the banking sector, little progress has been made. Vietnam's economy continues to face challenges from an under-capitalized banking sector. Non-performing loans weigh heavily on banks and businesses.

Residence and Citizenship

Birth within Vietnam does not automatically confer citizenship except when a child is born in Vietnam to parents who are stateless and have permanent residence in Vietnam, or when a child is found abandoned within Vietnam. Other methods include:

1. Citizenship by descent is conferred on:

   a.) a child, both of whose parents are citizens of Vietnam, regardless of the child's country of birth;

   b.) a child, one of whose parents is a citizen of Vietnam and the other is stateless, regardless of the child's country of birth, or;

   c.) a child, one of whose parents is a citizen of Vietnam and the other is a foreign national, if the child was born in Vietnam or the parents had permanent residence in Vietnam at the time of birth.

2. by naturalization: citizenship may be obtained upon fulfillment of the following conditions: a person is at least 18 years of age; knows the Vietnamese language; and has lived in Vietnam at least five years. Dual citizenship is not recognized.

A valid passport and Vietnamese visa are required for entry into Vietnam. A visa must be obtained from a Vietnamese Embassy or Consulate before traveling to Vietnam; entry visas are not available upon arrival. Americans arriving without an appropriate visa will not be permitted to enter and be subject to immediate deportation. Vietnamese visas are usually valid for only one entry. Persons planning to leave Vietnam and re-enter from another country should be sure to obtain a visa allowing multiple entries.

Contacts

Vietnam Embassy
1233 20th Street NW, #400
Washington, DC 20036
Tel.: (202) 861-0737
Email: info@vietnamembassy.us
Web: www.vietnamembassy-usa.org/

United States Embassy
7 Lang Ha Street
Ba Dinh District
Hanoi, Vietnam
Tel.: + (84) 4-772-1500
Web: http://hanoi.usembassy.gov/

U.S. Consulate General
4 Le Duan Boulevard
District 1, Ho Chi Minh City, Vietnam
Tel.: + (84) 8-822-9433
Web: http://hochiminh.usconsulate.gov/